CASSINO:
THE HOLLOW VICTORY

John Ellis

CASSINO
THE HOLLOW VICTORY

The Battle for Rome
January–June 1944

I am tired and sick of war. Its glory is all moonshine. It is only those who have neither fired a shot, nor heard the shrieks and groans of the wounded, who cry aloud for blood, more vengeance, more desolation. War is hell.

General W. T. Sherman,
Michigan Military Academy, 1879

McGraw-Hill Book Company

New York • St. Louis • San Francisco
Hamburg • Toronto • Mexico

1 2 3 4 5 6 7 8 9 DOC DOC 8 7 6 5 4

ISBN 0-07-019427-0

LIBRARY OF CONGRESS CATALOGING IN PUBLICATION DATA
Ellis, John, 1945-
    Cassino, the hollow victory.
    Bibliography: p.
    Includes index.
    1. Cassino (Italy), Battle of, 1944. I. Title.
D763.I82C263 1984   940.54'21   84-850
ISBN 0-07-019427-0

To the Memory of my Mother

BEATRICE IRIS ELLIS
(1922–82)

whose courage in the face of certain
death cannot have been surpassed on
any battlefield.

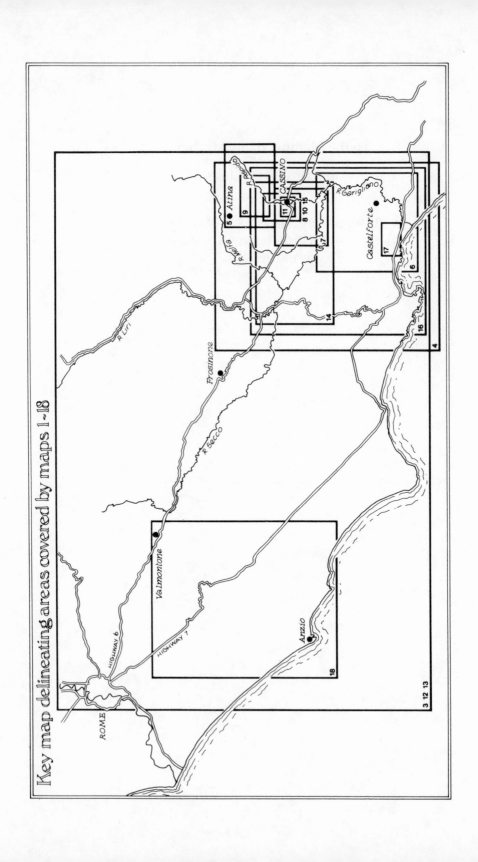

Key map delineating areas covered by maps 1~18

Contents

PART ONE   ROADS TO ROME
(A Historical Background)

PART TWO   THE FIRST BATTLE
(12 January– 9 February 1944)

PART THREE   THE SECOND BATTLE
(15–18 February 1944)

Maps

Photographs

Photographs have been reproduced with the kind permission of:

The Imperial War Museum: 1, 5, 7, 9, 10, 17, 19, 22, 26, 30, 31, 32, 36, 37, 38, 39, 40, 41, 43, 44, 45, 46, 47.
The Polish Institute & Sikorski Museum: 4, 6, 16, 18, 29, 42.
The Robert Hunt Library: 2, 19.
The Bundesarchiv, Koblenz: 8, 11, 12, 13, 14, 15, 23, 24, 25, 27, 28, 33, 34, 35.

Panoramic View of the Cassino Massif ~ seen from Monte Trocchio

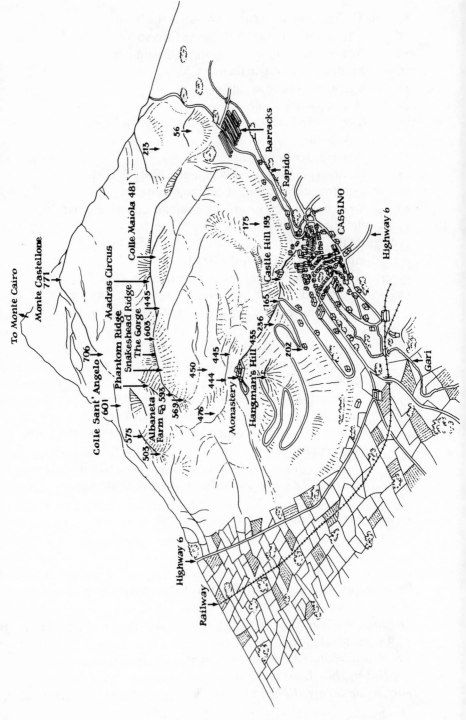

To Monte Cairo

Monte Castellone
771

Colle Sant' Angelo
601

Madras Circus

Phantom Ridge
706

Snakeshead Ridge

The Gorge
605

Colle Maiola 481

445

575

503

Albaneta
Farm 533

569

476

444

450

445

Monastery

Hangman's Hill 455

236

202

213

56

175

165

Castle Hill 195

Rapido

Barracks

CASSINO

Highway 6

Gari

Highway 6

Railway

Preface

When Saint Benedict decided to found a monastery in Italy in 524 AD, he had more on his mind than just finding the peace necessary for the wholehearted glorification of God. Christianity at this time was very much on the defensive against the assaults of succeeding waves of barbarians and the leader of any monastic brotherhood had to keep military considerations very much in mind. At Cassino, though it had once been the site of a temple to Apollo and the setting for the nameless orgies of the Emperor Tiberius, Benedict found what he was looking for. The town was dwarfed by an almost sheer peak which rose 1600 feet behind it. Its top could only be reached with extreme difficulty and it afforded perfect observation in all directions for miles around. On this summit Benedict and the brothers began to build.

Yet Benedict perhaps chose too well, for the very inaccessibility of the Monastery lulled succeeding generations of monks into a false sense of security. Marauding bands of Lombards (581) first, then Saracens (883) and finally Normans (1030), destroyed the Monastery. After the last depredation the next three hundred years was peaceful until God himself decided to test the brothers' resolve: the Monastery was completely devastated in an earthquake. The monks stoically set to work yet again and after the last rebuilding they had created a daunting fortress, surrounded by fifteen-feet-high walls, ten feet thick at their base, and approachable only via a five-mile-long hairpin track.

Apart from an incursion by French Revolutionary freebooters in 1799 and 'nationalization' by the new Italian government in 1868, the Monastery of Monte Cassino then remained inviolate – until 1944. In this year its military significance once again became paramount. The Allied Fifth and Eighth Armies had invaded Italy in the preceding September and were clawing their way towards Rome. The Germans had resolved not to give up this symbolic Axis capital without a fight. Their whole Italian strategy now hinged upon the selection of suitable defensive lines behind which to deploy most effectively their overstretched but still determined divisions. Monte Cassino, dominating as it did the most obvious route to Rome, the old Via Casilina or Highway Six as it was now known, was an obvious linch-pin of such a line, being easily linked with the Aurunci Mountains to the south, reaching almost to the coast, and with the Cairo massif and the Simbruini Mountains to the north.

So the Germans set to work and in January 1944 the Allied advance was pulled up short in front of a formidable *Stellung*, dubbed the Gustav

Line. For the next *six months* they battered their heads against it in an agonizing series of battles that were distinguished equally by the sufferings of the ordinary soldiers and the ineptitude, on the Allied side at least, of their commanders.

The sufferings of these fighting troops, mainly 'the Poor Bloody Infantry', cannot be overstated. Only such abattoirs as Verdun and Stalingrad, Passchendaele and Iwo Jima, can justly be compared. Four major assaults were launched against the fearsome defences that barred the way to Rome. Thousands died in these assaults and, in each interval, thousands more endured terrible privations as they shivered in their slit trenches and dugouts awaiting the order for the next attack, the next anguished scramble to prise the Germans off Monte This or Point That, the next suicidal dash into the murderous maze of pillboxes, wire and minefields that had once been some sleepy mountain village. So much for 'sunny Italy'. Many Germans, indeed, were adamant that the fighting in Italy in winter 1944 was far worse than anything they had encountered on the Russian Front. So much, too, for 'a war of movement'.

As will emerge from all that follows, comparison with the charnel houses of the Western Front, between 1914 and 1918, is in no way misplaced. The battles for Cassino should be borne in mind by anyone who might think that World War Two was any sort of soft option for the men at the sharp end. For the PBI *plus ça change plus c'est la même chose*.

The senior Allied commanders did little to alleviate these hardships. Though most were very conscious of the sufferings of those in the front lines, there was nothing they could do about the appalling weather, or the chronic supply shortages, or the intractable terrain all along the Gustav Line which made it extremely difficult to get reliefs, hot food, winter clothing, etc., up to the front. Although they all were aware of the terrible casualties – in particular those who had fought in the First World War were determined to avoid the bloody frontal assaults that had characterized Haig's and Foch's conception of the set-piece offensive – almost all the Allied generals made a poor showing, displaying a conspicuous lack of either tactical or strategic flair.

Often enough they could not even agree between themselves as to what should be done. The whole Italian campaign was badly vitiated from the start by profound American and British disagreements about the value of full-scale Mediterranean operations. Though the British point of view eventually prevailed, and Tunisia, Sicily and Italy were successively invaded in force, most Americans continued to believe that they had been duped by the devious Limeys.

In Italy itself relations were if anything more strained. The senior British and American commanders, Generals Sir Harold Alexander and

Mark Clark, did not work well together, the latter's attitude to his nominal superior being coloured by a virtual contempt for the British Army and all its works. The Cassino campaign, indeed, was a sorry example of coalition warfare. For not only was Clark led on at least one occasion to ignore Alexander's clear wishes, but each of them seemed to have little regard for the other nationalities that were fighting under the Allied banner. Certainly, these national contingents were often sent into action in a somewhat cavalier fashion. New Zealanders and Indians were broken in tactically hopeless, head-on assaults against Monte Cassino; Poles likewise in another bloody attack that was devoid of any real strategic rationale. Hundreds of Canadians also perished in front of the barbed wire and machine guns on the Hitler Line, during an attack that was as shoddily orchestrated as it was careless of the losses in men and equipment. Thousands of Frenchmen, too, died around Cassino. Though they can point to this battle honour as a token of their own military expertise, their attacks always being brilliantly conceived and executed by General Alphonse Juin, they remain justifiably bitter about the low esteem in which they were held by the 'Anglo-Saxon' High Command and about the way in which almost all of Juin's strategic suggestions, invariably pertinent and clear-sighted, were completely ignored.

In the end, of course, Cassino and Rome did finally fall, but these were at best hollow victories. For in the last full-scale battle, in May, though Alexander had at last massed the major part of his forces for a full-scale Army Group offensive, much of his planning was ill-conceived. In the attack by which he set the greatest store seven divisions were pushed up the bottleneck along Highway Six and only succeeded in getting embroiled in horrendous traffic jams. The progressive atrophy of their advance enabled the opposing German Army to undertake a measured withdrawal, their task made easier yet by Alexander's failure to attack along their open flank and so block the most obvious routes of retreat.

So the Germans escaped to fight again on yet another mountain line further north where the whole thing had to start over again, and drag out over yet another agonizing winter. A hollow victory indeed. Perhaps not for Alexander who shortly afterwards received his Field Marshal's baton, but assuredly so for the hundreds of thousands who had already clung for so long to their icy slit trenches and dugouts and for the tens of thousands who had already bled and died. And especially hollow for certain of the Allied contingents. For the French Expeditionary Corps and Juin, whose advice to bypass Cassino was consistently ignored, whose favoured axis of attack, which *would* have cut off the Germans' escape routes, was rejected, and whose pre-eminent role in the final rupture of the Gustav

Line has never been properly acknowledged, even in France. Hollow, too, for the Polish Corps, under General Wladyslaw Anders, who displayed epic heroism in an attack which should have never taken place and who fought on behalf of a vision of a free Poland that had in reality already passed into the Stalinist maw.

Hollow too, perhaps, even for those Germans who fought with such tenacity and in the end extricated themselves so brilliantly during the final battle. For they were fighting for a country that had already been virtually written off by Hitler and in a war that was already lost. Many, too, were fighting on behalf of a régime with which they had no sympathy at all, none more so than General Frido von Senger und Etterlin, along with Juin by far the ablest of the commanders in Italy. His achievements encapsulate the tragic irony of the German Army in World War Two, whose military excellence demanded professional admiration and whose cause could only evoke disgust. For von Senger und Etterlin, the man who defended Monte Cassino monastery and so helped ensure its destruction, not only despised Hitler and the Nazi state but was also a Rhodes Scholar and a lay Benedictine brother. But such is the logic of war and in the last analysis, as at Cassino, there are no victors. And even those who would plead the justice and rectitude of their cause are perhaps best answered by the sardonic rictus of the highest skull on Golgotha.

During the production of this book I have travelled, talked and read widely. A full listing of the various archival holdings and secondary works consulted will be found in the Sources and Bibliography but such a terse listing does scant justice to the splendid efforts of the many individuals who have helped me on my way. I am especially grateful to the directors and staffs of the various national archives I have consulted, in each of which advice and assistance was unfailingly helpful and efficient. I would like to record my particular thanks to George Wagner and Ed Coffee of the Modern Military Section of the US National Archives; Morris Izlar of the Modern Military Field Branch, Washington National Records Center at Suitland; Ted Ballard in the Center for Military History at the US Department of Defense. M. Pascal Santo and Mme Monique Bascop of the Fonds des Petites Unités, Service Historique de l'Armée de Terre at Vincennes.

John Clarke of the Cassino Veterans' Association in Manchester has also been consistently helpful and generous with the loan of books, letters and membership lists. My most sincere thanks as well to those members who gave of their time to speak to me and lent me highly treasured mementos. Messrs J. Raywood, J. Beach, F. Jones, R.S. Grose, C. Barlow, T. Hoyle and D. Clare were of particular assistance in this respect. My thanks also to those other Cassino veterans, notably Sir Denis Forman, 'Johnny' Kerr, Mr R. Goodhall and Mr R. Greatorex, who were kind enough to relate their experiences to me.

My knowledge of the available foreign sources was considerably enhanced by the distinguished historians Alistair Horne and Raleigh Trevelyan, both of whom were kind enough to reply in detail to letters of mine attempting to tap their enormous funds of knowledge. Polish sources were particularly intractable and in this regard I am greatly indebted to Colonel H. Baranski and Mr W. Pierog who were tireless in offering leads for further research and the memories of their own personal experiences. None of this, however, would have borne much fruit without the invaluable assistance of Ms Malgorzata Kmita-Dawson who undertook to isolate and translate particularly pertinent passages from the Polish texts.

With this book above all I have been most fortunate with regard to those who have seen it into print. My thanks, as ever, to my literary agent, John Parker, who believed in it, to Piers Burnett and André Deutsch who commissioned it, and to Dieter Pevsner and Sara Menguc who showed remarkable forbearance when they must have wondered whether a manuscript would ever appear. Then, however, Sara Menguc's problems really began and it would be impossible to exaggerate her contribution to this book in almost every regard. The quality of the narrative, the maps, the illustrations have all been greatly enhanced by her tireless efforts. With editors of this calibre the creative process does not end at the typewriter. And my most sincere thanks to three people who also did much to give the narrative such clarity as it has: to Harry Bawden on whom fell the unsung burden of splicing my infinitives and restoring order to typographical chaos; to Steve Cox and Ken Turpie whose intelligence and scrupulousness were equal even to the remorseless drumbeat of the galley; and to Sue Lawes who drew the maps with a skill that is self-evident and with a tolerance for last-minute alterations that was positively Jobian.

Finally, and most importantly of all, I would like to thank my friends, without whom the business of writing would lead ineluctably to the padded cell. Nick Sekunda and Steve Ridgeway offered invaluable bibliographical aid, whilst Hugh Dent, Andy Callan, Phil Eades, Aiden Roe, Ian Marrow, Barry Munslow, Dave Affleck, Ian Anderson, Gerry Hennessy and Mike Beames stoically kept the beer flowing when they might have preferred to hear a little less about the Battle of Cassino.

John Ellis
Manchester 1983

PART ONE

ROADS TO ROME
A Historical Background

Before we embark on major operations on the mainland of Europe we must have a master plan and know how we propose to develop these operations. I have not been told of any master plan and I must therefore assume that there was none.

General B.L. Montgomery,
5 September 1943

I
'A Dispersion Debauch'
The Allies and the Mediterranean, 1941–43

It's jolly to look at the map
And finish the foe in a day.
It's not easy to get at the chap;
These neutrals are so in the way.
But if you say 'What would you do
To fill the aggressor with gloom?'
Well, we might drop a bomb on Baku
Or what about bombs on Batum?

A.P. Herbert, 1940

With the benefit of hindsight the Allied campaigns in the Mediterranean can easily seem all of a piece – the long drive from Egypt, through Libya, Tunisia and Sicily, to the gates of Rome as a deliberate and considered re-enactment of Belisarius' epic march over fifteen hundred years before.* In so far as one is speaking of a genuinely Allied policy, however, nothing could be further from the truth. From the very inception of close British and American co-operation, Mediterranean operations were always a bone of contention and their overall direction was beset by bitter disagreement, grudging compromise, petulant threats and, on one side at least, a deeply-held suspicion, which still persists, of having been had.

To understand why this should have been so one must go back to America's entry into the war, in December 1941, and to their and

---

* Belisarius, the ablest of the Byzantine Emperor Justinian's generals, was despatched, in 533 AD, to recapture Rome from the Goths. He retook the city in 535, after marching through Tunisia, where he twice defeated the Vandals, Sicily and southern central Italy. The city was retaken by the Lombards in 568 and thereafter ceased to be an important military objective. Subsequent campaigning in Italy was almost all conducted to the north of Rome, where there was some degree of economic prosperity, and the Eternal City was only threatened when there seemed a need to court or caution a Pope or to pacify one's soldiery with the prospect of plunder.

In this respect it is worth noting that even in 1944 the only approaches to Rome from the south were the same two Roman roads between which Belisarius had had to choose. One was the Via Appia, which followed the western coast through Gaeta and the Pontine Marshes, and the other the Via Latina, which wound beneath the massive bulk of Monte Cassino before threading its way up the Liri Valley between the Abruzzi Mountains, on the right, and the successive ranges of the Aurunci, the Lepini and the Alban Mountains, on the left.

Britain's differing perceptions of the massive strategic task ahead. American experience of warfare on this scale was very much of a *tabula rasa*. They had only once before raised substantial forces to fight outside their own country and thus had very few preconceived notions about the 'correct' way to fight a war against a major European power bloc. Moreover, after the disasters at Pearl Harbor and in the Philippines, all but a fraction of their forces were concentrated in America itself, most of them in the process of induction and training. On one level, therefore, the Americans saw their initial strategic decisions as being very straightforward.

One simply looked at a map of the world, picked the most direct routes to the heart of Germany and Japan, and then drew up the plans to despatch as many troops as possible, as soon as possible, along these routes. These decisions were, in fact, quickly made. With regard to the defeat of Germany, one of the earliest cogent statements of American thinking was a staff paper drawn up by one Major-General Dwight Eisenhower, in February 1942. This document was passed on to the planning staff and the ideas in it incorporated into a more authoritative memorandum, written on 25 March, by General George Marshall, the United States Army Chief of Staff. The basic thrust of the memorandum was that an invasion of North-West Europe should be mounted from England, as quickly as possible, by both American and British troops. According to Marshall:

> The element of time is of the utmost importance. . . . We must begin a sustained offensive before Russia can be defeated and before Vichy France, Spain, Sweden, Portugal and Turkey are drawn into the ranks of the enemy. Our proposal . . . provides for an attack, by combined forces of approximately 5800 combat airplanes and 48 divisions, against Western Europe as soon as the necessary means can be accumulated in England – estimated at 1 April 1943, provided decision is made *now* and men, material and shipping are conserved for this purpose.[1]

But the Americans did not envisage merely waiting passively in England until these means had been accumulated. Some sort of military foray, they felt, should be made as soon as humanly possible and the memorandum went on to stress the necessity of establishing a 'preliminary active front [in northern France] this coming summer – for training, demonstration, deception and destruction'; and, moreover, 'if the imminence of Russian collapse requires desperate action', this front could be expanded to form the basis of 'a sacrifice attack [which] could be made immediately'.[2]

On 4 April, Marshall and Harry Hopkins, President Roosevelt's special adviser and confidant, left Washington for London to press this plan upon Churchill and the British Chiefs of Staff. Both the President's representatives were quite happy in their own minds that what they were advocating, quite simply to take the shortest route in the shortest time, was the only real strategic option open to the Allies. The British, however, were far from convinced and felt growing misgivings about the overall soundness of American thinking. Air Marshal Sir John Slessor, then Assistant Chief of the Air Staff, wrote afterwards that 'the American attitude to the problem seemed to us somewhat over-simplified, a bit too much in black and white – there was Hitler on the Continent, right? Well, then, go for him bald-headed and as soon as possible, by the shortest and most direct route.'[3]

But the attitude of the British planners was not based on mere condescension, and two reasons for their suspicion stand out. First was the simple fact that the British had been involved in numerous previous European wars. They felt that their experiences in these conflicts had above all taught that one could not approach military problems like a bull at a gate, but should always stress pragmatism and flexibility as the keynotes of strategic planning. To commit oneself from the beginning to specific jumping-off points, specific beachheads, specific dates, purely on the basis of a cursory glance at the map and a brief analysis of theoretical logistical requirements, was to invite disaster. All kinds of nebulous variables had to be taken into account. Who could say what the condition of the enemy would be on a certain date? His successes or failures on other fronts could well mean that one's own arbitrary invasion date would come too late to capitalize on a temporary setback, or before the enemy had been over-stretched elsewhere. Who, anyway, could say that immediate head-on confrontation with one's major opponent was the best way to bring him down? Was it not possible that attacks on his allies might at least be a vital preliminary to final victory?

Historical experience also determined Britain's second, more concrete objection to the American proposals. For the former, the Mediterranean had long been an area of prime concern, particularly since the opening of the Suez Canal and the much shorter route to India. Over the centuries the British had fought Spaniards, Frenchmen, Russians and Turks to safeguard their free passage of the Mediterranean and it was still very much at the centre of their thoughts in early 1942. But this was not simply an unthinking historical reflex, nor even, as many Americans thought, a desire by Churchill to avenge the failure of Britain's last major Mediterranean foray, the Gallipoli invasion of 1915. It was rather that, in 1942, unlike the Americans, the British had substantial numbers of troops actually fighting overseas and that the bulk of these men were in the Middle East, protecting Egypt and the gateway to India from the combined Axis divisions. When Hopkins and Marshall arrived in London the North African issue hung in the balance and British thoughts, at the highest level, were haunted by the prospect of total defeat in this their only active theatre. The American memorandum, therefore, with its bravura advocacy of a commitment to major operations in northern France in the near future, was not at all welcome, and in certain quarters was regarded as completely irrelevant to the demands of the immediate military situation.

Shortly after their arrival the two Americans dined at Downing Street and after dinner Hopkins was left in little doubt as to the attitude of Sir Alan Brooke, the Chairman of the Chiefs of Staff Committee, who, Hopkins wrote, '. . . got into [the main business] . . . enough to indicate that he had a great many misgivings about our proposal'.[4] Nevertheless, subsequent meetings did seem to indicate that the British had decided to accept the main points of the memorandum and the Americans left London with the firm conviction that an *early* cross-Channel invasion was now a top joint priority. In private, however, the British were far from convinced. In a paper to the War Cabinet, Churchill made it clear that he had particularly little faith in any kind of preliminary invasion to be carried out in 1942: '[While] preparations should proceed on the basis that we should make a resolute effort to capture a bridgehead on the Continent in the late summer, we are *not committed* to carry out such an operation this year.'[5] In fact, such reservations were not limited to Churchill alone and undoubtedly went further than merely questioning the feasibility of the preliminary 1942 operation. General Hastings Ismay, Chief of Staff to the Minister of Defence, felt that in seeming to accept the American proposals the British had been less than honest and that 'it would have obviated future misunderstandings if the British had expressed their views more frankly.'[6]

Certainly, once the American party had left, the British lost no time in agreeing among themselves that cross-Channel operations in 1942 were out of the question. On 8 May a meeting of the Chiefs of Staff and their force commanders decided that such a venture, 'with the resources available, is not a sound military operation'.[7] Churchill fully agreed and, according to the minutes of a War Cabinet meeting on the 24th, said that 'in view of the authoritative arguments put forward . . . he was not prepared to give way to the popular clamour for the opening of a second front in Europe in these circumstances.'[8]

In June an Anglo-American conference was held in Washington and here the latter began to get wind of the real feelings of the British policy-makers. Lord Louis Mountbatten, the Chief of Combined Operations, was a key figure here when he was deputed to explain British reservations in a tête-à-tête with Roosevelt. According to General Albert Wedemeyer, a senior member of the US General Staff, and a vigorous proponent of an early second front: 'Lord Louis was closeted with Roosevelt for five hours . . . . Now we had an extremely articulate Britisher endeavouring to raise bogies about the hazards of a cross-Channel operation.' Mountbatten's persuasiveness certainly had its effect and according to Wedemeyer 'Churchill's animus against . . . [a cross-Channel operation in 1942], as conveyed by the subtle Mountbatten, had its reportedly corrosive effect on Roosevelt's certainties about the *whole principle* of concentration on the invasion of northern Europe.'[9] In the event, an uneasy compromise was hammered out at the conference proper. On the one hand, the Americans agreed that 'a plan for immediate landings should be adopted "only in the case of necessity or of exceptionally favourable opportunity".'[10] On the other, the British declared themselves ready to advocate an immediate build-up of forces in their country with a view to a major amphibious assault in 1943.

Many Americans remained unconvinced about British sincerity and their doubts were not simply a response to their ally's 'negative' attitude towards a speedy invasion of northern Europe. For another strand of British thinking had already become apparent, one that threatened to involve American forces in a theatre in which most of their commanders had little strategic interest. Ever since the Americans threw in their lot with Britain, in fact, Churchill had been trying to find a way of enlisting their aid in the Mediterranean. At one of his earliest meetings with Roosevelt, the Arcadia Conference in Washington in December 1941, he had recommended the invasion and occupation of French North Africa, averring that at that stage even a blow against Vichy France, one of Germany's more desultory allies, was better than leaping into the unknown across the Channel. Roosevelt had shown himself sympathetic and by the end of the Arcadia Conference 'the President set great store on organizing a "Super-Gymnast"* – a combined United States-British expedition to North Africa. A tentative timetable had been worked out for putting 90,000 United States and 90,000 British troops . . . into North Africa.'[11]

* Operation GYMNAST was an Allied plan for projected amphibious landings in French North Africa.

Roosevelt's military chiefs, however, never favoured such an operation, looking on the Mediterranean as a traditional British obsession which had no real relevance to the most effective pursuit of the war against Germany. Once they had formulated their own ideas about how best to carry on this war they became even more suspicious about any North African landings and for a time at least simply tried to ignore the President's stated wishes. At the London Conference, in April 1942, they had presented their memorandum without any reference to the Arcadia decisions about Operation GYMNAST and Henry Stimson, the American Secretary of War, spoke of it privately as 'the wildest kind of dispersion debauch'. But for the moment Churchill had kept his peace and though he still very much favoured a North African expedition he made no mention of it during his meetings with Marshall and Hopkins.

It did come up, however, at the Washington Conference in June. On the 20th, Churchill sent a note to Roosevelt asking: 'Ought we not to be preparing within the general structure of . . . [the cross-Channel planning] some other operation by which we may gain positions of advantage, and also directly or indirectly to take some of the weight off Russia? It is in this setting and on this background that the French North-West Africa operation should be studied.'[12] Sir Alan Brooke was an even more ardent advocate of large-scale joint Mediterranean operations and a note in his diary on 21 June indicated his preference for these over any kind of cross-Channel attack. At a meeting with Roosevelt, Marshall, Hopkins and others they discussed 'the Middle East position and accepted offer of American Armoured Division for Middle East. This may lead to a USA front in Middle East at expense of the European front.'[13] Luckily, no American ever saw this entry and the final compromise that was reached at Washington did seem to indicate a reasonably definite British commitment to cross-Channel operations. Nevertheless, the more perspicacious American participants must have noted that the British had at least managed to keep some Mediterranean options open. Not only had they obtained a whole US armoured division to help the Eighth Army but they had also managed to append to the Conference resolutions an American promise to look in detail at the possibility of staging GYMNAST, as envisaged at the Arcadia meeting, in 1942.

The store the British set by this addendum became increasingly apparent and once again the Americans began to fear that the Mediterranean, rather than north-west Europe, was still very much the favoured British theatre. On 10 July, Stimson wrote: 'The British War Cabinet are weakening and going back on [the cross-Channel operation in 1943] . . . and are seeking to revive GYMNAST. . . . This would be simply another way of diverting our strength into a channel in which we cannot effectively use it, namely the Middle East. I found Marshall very stirred up and emphatic over it. He is naturally very tired of these constant decisions which do not stay made.'[14] Marshall's irritation was not lessened by a telegram from Churchill to Roosevelt in which the former stated quite bluntly: 'I am sure that GYMNAST is by far the best chance for effective relief to the Russian front in 1942. . . . Here is the true second front of 1942. . . . The Cabinet and Defence Committee . . . all agree. Here is the safest and most fruitful stroke that can be delivered this autumn.'[15]

By now Marshall and the American planners were so upset at the prospect of any American involvement in the Mediterranean that they resurrected the idea of a 1942 cross-Channel assault and tried to ride roughshod over Britain's strictly military objections – objections the Americans had seemed to accept at the end of the Washington Conference. On 8 July the Operations Staff of the US War Department said that a commitment to undertake emergency operations in Europe in 1942 should not be delayed longer than 1 August. On the 10th Marshall wrote to Roosevelt suggesting crude blackmail: 'I believe that we must now put the proposition up to the British on a definite basis and leave the decision up to them. It must be made at once. My object is to force the British into the acceptance of a concentrated effort against Germany, and if this proves impossible, to turn immediately to the Pacific with strong forces and drive for a decision against Japan.'[16] But Roosevelt took strong exception to this memo, particularly the petulant threat to take their bat home and concentrate on the Pacific campaign. He realized that only a face-to-face meeting with the British offered any hope of effective compromise and ordered Marshall and Hopkins to set off for London.

In fact, Roosevelt had already realized what shape the compromise must probably take and his brief to Marshall was at all costs to agree on *some* kind of joint operation in 1942, even if this should be GYMNAST. The War Department, however, was not prepared to give up so easily and the draft instructions they drew up for their negotiating team omitted any mention at all of GYMNAST and concentrated exclusively upon an attack in northern Europe in 1942. Roosevelt quickly rejected the draft and added an explicit instruction that if an early cross-Channel assault 'is finally and definitely out of the question I want you to consider the world situation as it exists at that time and determine upon another place for US troops to fight in 1942.'[17]

But Marshall was still determined upon showdown rather than compromise. He arrived in London on 18 July and on the 22nd presented a paper demanding that a landing be made in northern France before the end of summer. On the very day that the Americans had landed, the British Chiefs of Staff had once again concurred that 'GYMNAST was the only feasible proposition and identified it as the right wing of our Second Front, which must be extended to embrace Algiers and Oran as well as Casablanca.'[18] Marshall's proposal, therefore, was rejected outright and he reported back to the President that deadlock had been reached. Roosevelt testily reminded his delegation of the instruction to reach some sort of compromise at all costs and instructed them to accept the GYMNAST option. Marshall reluctantly followed these instructions, on 24 July, yet even at this late hour he attempted a personal sleight of hand. GYMNAST was accepted by the Americans as the major operation for 1942 but this acceptance was made conditional upon the situation on the Russian front on 15 September. The War Cabinet reluctantly accepted this proviso but as soon as Roosevelt heard of it he cabled London with the unequivocal instruction that GYMNAST, or TORCH as Churchill had redubbed it, should be launched no later than 30 October, whatever happened elsewhere.

But Marshall was still not finished and on 30 July, now back in Washington, he made one last effort to undermine the President's decision. Flying in the face of the spirit and the letter of the resolutions just signed in London, he tried to claim that no definite decision had in fact been taken and that a 1942 cross-Channel effort was still a real possibility. Roosevelt came down hard on this specious reasoning and made an announcement in which 'the President stated very definitely that he, as Commander-in-Chief, had made the decision that TORCH would be undertaken at the earliest possible date. He considered that this operation was now our principal objective and the assembly of the means to carry it out would take precedence over other operations, as for instance [the build-up for a cross-Channel assault].'[19]

The major decision had now been taken and the Americans were to participate fully in Mediterranean operations. But a large section of their military establishment, at senior and junior levels, was profoundly disappointed, not simply because they disagreed on broad strategic grounds, but because they also felt that the British had somehow deceived them, in particular by playing upon Roosevelt to coax him into overruling his own military advisers. Allied co-operation in the Mediterranean did not, therefore, begin on a very happy note and for at least the next twelve months planning was undertaken in an atmosphere of profound distrust; the Americans always suspicious of being lured further and further into what they regarded as a back alley, and the British perennially anxious lest the Americans should abruptly decide to pull the plugs. TORCH at least now seemed safe but many British politicians and military leaders, notably Sir Alan Brooke, were keen that North Africa should be only the springboard for much more ambitious operations. The most favoured target was Italy, with either Sicily or Sardinia as an intermediate jumping-off point. Sicily had been mentioned as a possible British objective as early as October 1941, though this was simply one of a dozen plans floated at the time in the hope of drawing at least a few German divisions away from the Eastern Front. It was soon dropped but within a few months, as the British intensified their efforts to draw the Americans into TORCH, they began to drop broad hints about future options in the Mediterranean. On 20 July Churchill noted that if Auchinleck were to break through Rommel's lines 'ACROBAT [projected advance into Tripolitania] might then again come into view, with possibilities of action against Sicily and Italy. . .'[20]

Once the Americans had actually sanctioned TORCH the British came more and more into the open on the subject of further Mediterranean exploitation. In September Churchill again mentioned Sicily and Italy as possible targets and on 9 November he told the Chiefs of Staff that 'the effort for the campaign of 1943 should clearly be a strong pinning down of the enemy in northern France . . . by continuous preparations to invade, and a decisive attack on Italy.'[21] With regard to the latter point, Churchill was simply preaching to the converted, Brooke in particular being most eager to commit the Allies to large-scale Mediterranean operations. Brooke, in fact, did not really go along with Churchill's dual analysis of the tasks for 1943, and one American later heard him express 'himself to the effect that it was not the role of the Western Allies to exert their power on land in Europe – that our power should be utilized in the air and on the sea and that the Russians should do the land fighting.'[22] Such an extreme analysis was based more on hope than reality but certainly Brooke at this time was most anxious to avoid any immediate commitment to a cross-Channel assault. At a meeting of the Chiefs of Staff and Churchill, on 3 December, he stated quite bluntly that 'any talk of reopening a Western Front was anathema, and his original policy remained inflexible: to begin with the conquest of North Africa [and to] follow this up by putting Italy out of the war.'[23]

Brooke's theories were equally anathematized by the Americans. Throughout the second half of 1942, in fact, their attitude to TORCH was so dilatory that it seemed increasingly remarkable that they had ever been talked round in the first place. Throughout August and September Brooke railed against 'Marshall's deep-seated conviction that nothing could be achieved by the British policy of reopening the Mediterranean and tightening the ring around the Axis from the South. . .'[24] On 18 August, General MacReady, with the British Mission in Washington, observed that, 'although everyone here is at least paying lip-service to TORCH, my impression is that they are not in it heart and soul and at the moment there is quite a tendency to say how difficult various parts of the business are.'[25] In October even the Allied commander for this operation, Dwight Eisenhower, said that 'he personally had always considered the TORCH operation to be unsound strategically. . .'[26]

The North African landings did eventually take place on 8 November but the fair degree of success they achieved did little to cheer many senior Americans, who remained steadfastly opposed to any post-Tunisian exploitation. On 25 November Marshall told the President and the Joint Chiefs of Staff that after Tunisia he 'felt that the occupation of Sicily, Sardinia and Crete would be necessary [if the Mediterranean were to be cleared for sea-traffic] and he [doubted] whether or not the large . . . forces required for such a project could be justified, in view of the results to be expected.'[27] In December Marshall seemed more cheered by the positive results in Tunisia, but this was largely because he began to envisage the possibility of speedily winding up the whole campaign and concentrating once more on the main business of the cross-Channel assault. According to one British observer he was 'getting more and more convinced that . . . as soon as North Africa is cleared of Axis forces, we [should] start pouring American forces into England instead of sending them to Africa for the exploitation of TORCH.'[28]

The beginning of the new year, therefore, seemed to offer little hope to the British that they would be able to bend their ally to their way of thinking. Yet, remarkable though it still seems, at the next two full-scale Anglo-American conferences, at Casablanca in January 1943, and Washington in May, they managed to extract explicit approval for an invasion of Sicily, code-named HUSKY, and to at least keep the door open for a further assault against the mainland of Italy. The American accept–ance of the HUSKY plan has never been fully explained. During the greater part of the Casablanca meetings they refused to budge from their normal position, maintaining that all operations in Europe should be completely subordinated to the speedy mounting of a cross-Channel offensive. Brooke was equally adamant on behalf of his own favoured strategy. On 16 January he asserted: 'Since we cannot go into the Continent until Germany weakens, we should try to make the Germans disperse their forces as much as possible. This can be accomplished by attacking Germany's allies, Italy in particular.'[29] This statement seemed almost

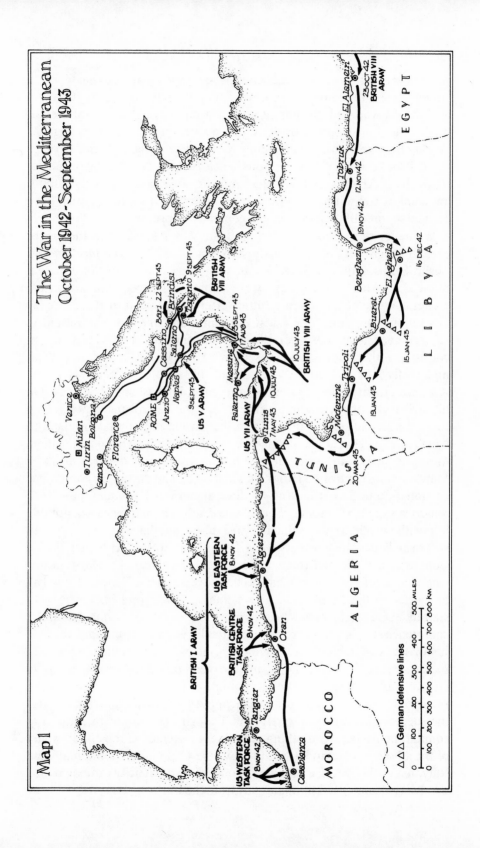

Map 1

The War in the Mediterranean
October 1942 – September 1943

MOROCCO

US WESTERN TASK FORCE
8 NOV 42
Casablanca

Tangier

BRITISH I ARMY
US CENTRE TASK FORCE
8 NOV 42
Oran

US EASTERN TASK FORCE
8 NOV 42
Algiers

ALGERIA

△△△ German defensive lines

0   100   200   300   400   500 MILES
0 100 200 300 400 500 600 700 800 KM

Venice
Milan
Turin
Genoa
Florence
Bologna
ROME
Anzio 9 SEPT 45
Naples
US V ARMY
Cassino
Salerno 9 SEPT 45
Bari 22 SEPT 45
Brindisi
Taranto 9 SEPT 45
BRITISH VIII ARMY

Messina 3 SEPT 45
Nossaina
Palermo 22 JULY 43
US VII ARMY
10 JULY 43
10 JULY 43
17 AUG 43
BRITISH VIII ARMY

Tunis 7 MAY 43
20 MAR 43
Mareth 19 JAN 43
TUNISIA

Tripoli
Buerat
15 JAN 43
El Agheila
16 DEC 42
Benghazi
Tobruk 12 NOV 42
19 NOV 42

LIBYA

EGYPT

El Alamein 23 OCT 42
BRITISH VIII ARMY

calculated to infuriate the Americans, who had never agreed that German strength was a fundamental determinant of the date of the cross-Channel assault and who had absolutely no intention of becoming embroiled in further Mediterranean operations, particularly ones that seemed to go far beyond Brooke's earlier calls simply to clear the sea-lanes there. Perhaps it was Brooke's sheer presumption that carried the day, for the proposals to which the Americans did finally agree, i.e. an invasion of Sicily without any kind of commitment to further Mediterranean ventures, must have seemed to some of their delegates a genuine compromise.

Whatever the reason, the British team was astonished at this major breakthrough. Sir John Kennedy spoke of a 'sudden *volte-face*' and Sir Leslie Hollis, Military Secretary to the War Cabinet, of 'an apparent miracle'.[30] Many Americans were more disgusted than surprised. General Wedemeyer wrote a bitter letter to the head of the US Army Operations Division: ' "We lost our shirts and are now committed to subterranean umbilicus operation in mid-summer." I was referring, of course, to the phrase often used by the Prime Minister, the "soft underbelly" of Europe.'[31] This kind of sentiment permeated the American team at the 'Trident' Conference, in Washington in May. On his arrival Brooke wrote in his diary: '. . . the Americans are taking up the attitude that we led them down the garden path by taking them to North Africa. That at Casablanca we again misled them by inducing them to attack Sicily. And now they do not intend to be led astray again.'[32] Marshall soon confirmed Brooke's worst fears, and during the conference he stated quite flatly that 'the Mediterranean was a vacuum into which America's great military might could be drawn off until there was nothing left with which to deal the decisive blow on the Continent.'[33] Not surprisingly deadlock was soon reached. Hollis noted: 'At the end of the Conference, it seemed that little had been resolved . . . Marshall was wholly in favour of a cross-Channel invasion . . . while Brooke pinned all his hopes on the Mediterranean scheme. . . . We were back where we started.'[34] General Ismay was even more forthright, observing that at this conference 'the arguments . . . occasionally got so acrimonious that the junior staffs were bidden to leave the principals to continue the battle in secret session.'[35] Yet once again the very depth of feeling acted to Britain's advantage, and the 'compromise' that was hammered out in reality left the door open for further moves in the Mediterranean after the successful completion of HUSKY. Though the Americans refused to commit themselves to anything definite they seemed in the end to weary of the whole debate and agreed to a vague formulation about mainland Italy that authorized Eisenhower to plan the whole Sicily campaign 'in a way best calculated to eliminate Italy from the war'.

This, in fact, was a crucial concession for it meant that the American Chiefs of Staff were leaving the ultimate decisions about post-HUSKY exploitation to the men on the spot. These had made such reputations as they had in the Mediterranean context and were much more likely, therefore, to favour continued operations in their own theatre. British and American planners on Eisenhower's staff had been working together for many months now and national prejudices had been, to some extent at least, subordinated to a common belief in the primacy of their own 'back yard'. Churchill was not slow to grasp this point and as soon as ultimate responsibility was passed to Eisenhower, he flew off to Algiers to meet him, 'determined to obtain before leaving Africa the decision to invade Italy should Sicily be taken'.[36] He was not as successful as he would have wished and, as Eisenhower wrote, had to be content with 'an agreement which, in effect, left exploitation of the Sicilian operation to my judgement – but expected me to take advantage of any favourable opportunity to rush into Italy. . .'[37]

Churchill's enthusiasm left its mark, however, and over the next weeks Eisenhower made a series of decisions that all increasingly committed his forces to further operations in the Mediterranean. On 12 June he authorized the Mediterranean Air Forces to bomb the Rome marshalling yards. On the 30th he suggested that, in the event of success in Sicily, it might be worthwhile to push the Germans out of Sardinia or even to make some limited expedition on to the toe of Italy. Once the invasion of Sicily had begun, on 9 July, and was seen to be successfully under way, he and his staff became bolder still. On the 17th they held a planning conference at which it was decided that 'the mainland of Italy is the best area for exploitation with a view to achieving our object of forcing Italy out of the war and containing the maximum German forces.'[38] On the 18th, in the words of Eisenhower's Naval Aide:

. . . Ike . . . drafted a recommendation to the Combined Chiefs of Staff that as soon as we take Messina we proceed across the Strait to the toe of Italy. The gist of his recommendation is that we carry the war to the mainland and the attack on the toe and ball would be accomplished by other landings and perhaps an attack on Naples.[39]

The latter ancillary landing had been mooted for some weeks, largely on the inspiration of Churchill, who felt that the Italian peninsula offered ideal opportunities for probing amphibious assaults that would threaten Axis communications and keep the defenders perpetually off balance. For a while Marshall, too, was a reasonably enthusiastic advocate and on

16 July, at Trident, he spoke on behalf of some such venture to the Combined Chiefs of Staff. Churchill immediately saw this as full-blooded support for the British Mediterranean strategy but was quickly told by Stimson that Marshall was merely thinking in terms of a limited, one-off operation that would mark the last gasp of the Mediterranean campaign. This was also made clear a few days later when

> the British Chiefs of Staff urged their American colleagues to plan the direct attack on Naples [the Salerno landings, code-named AVALANCHE] on the assumption that extra shipping and aircraft carriers would be available. The Americans took a different view. While agreeing to the attack they adhered to their original decision that no reinforcements from America should be sent to General Eisenhower for this or any other purpose.[40]

Clearly, Anglo-American co-operation still left a lot to be desired and respective conceptions of the future of the Mediterranean campaign remained as far apart as ever. Nevertheless, the British had been given the lever they required in that the basic decisions about a possible Italian campaign had been left to the local commander and he finally had been prevailed upon to take at least certain preparatory steps. Eisenhower's decision was a bitter blow to his superiors but, as even the staunchly partisan editor of Brooke's papers was prepared to concede, they accepted defeat with honour:

> Though he had always been opposed to Britain's concentric strategy, the American Chief of the Army Staff had given his word that, if the Sicilian campaign ended quickly enough to allow further operations . . . an attack should be made on Italy. He was a man of the strictest honour and on [the 21st] he and his colleagues gave their consent.[41]

What remains to be seen is whether 'honour' was sufficient reason for ignoring one's strongest military instincts.

2

Sicily to Cassino

The Allies and the Italian Campaign, July–December 1943

If you take a flat map
and move wooden blocks upon it strategically,
The thing looks well, the blocks behave as they should.
The science of war is moving live men like blocks.
And getting the blocks into place at a fixed moment.
But it takes time to mould your men into blocks
And flat maps turn into country where creeks and gullies
Hamper your wooden squares. . .
It is all so clear in the maps, so clear in the mind,
But the orders are slow, the men in the blocks are slow
To move, when they start they take too long on the way –
The General loses his stars and the block-men die
In unstrategic defiance of martial law
Because still being used to just being men, not block-parts.

Stephen Vincent Benét, John Brown's Body, *1928*

One of Churchill's least prophetic remarks was made

> at a meeting of the [British] Chiefs of Staff in the middle of July [1943
> when he] . . . was reported to have said, 'It is true, I suppose, that
> the Americans consider that we have led them up the garden path
> in the Mediterranean – but what a beautiful path it has proved to
> be. They have picked peaches here, nectarines there. How grateful
> they should be!'[1]

His remarks were not wholly baseless, in that the Americans did most
definitely feel that they had been led up the garden path. Furthermore,
one might well argue that early stages of the campaign had been
reasonably balmy. Even so, the successful conclusion of the Tunisian
campaign and the large bag of German prisoners could not hide the fact
that the whole operation had taken a great deal longer than anticipated,
and had spotlighted Allied inadequacies in combat as well as the
remarkable resilience of the Germans when fighting a defensive,
positional battle. But the fruits of further progress up this path were far
from succulent and the story of the Italian campaign up to the beginning
of the Battle of Cassino, in January 1944, was one of constant frustration,

the result both of the intractable terrain and of the almost complete lack of vigorous strategic direction at the highest levels.

Even in July 1943 there was still no coherent Allied policy as to exactly what post-HUSKY operations were supposed to achieve. Honourable as Marshall's approval of such operations might have been it was in no way based upon a clear set of objectives and a well thought-out timetable. There was not even any agreement as to where the Allies were aiming for. In a paper written in May 1943, Churchill had spoken of the capture of Rome as 'an evident step', thus forcing the Germans back 'to maintain a new front along the Po',[2] but no formal directives had been issued to the theatre commanders by the time of the Sicily invasion. At the 'Quadrant' Conference in Quebec, in August 1943, the Allies belatedly tried to thrash out the precise objectives of the campaign they had already set in motion. Just before the Conference began, Roosevelt and his Chiefs of Staff agreed that these should be limited, and according to Stimson 'the President . . . was more clear and definite than I have ever seen him since we have been in this war, and he took the policy that the American Staff have been fighting for fully. He was for going no further into Italy than Rome and then [only] for the purpose of establishing air bases.'[3] The Joint Chiefs welcomed this unexpected support with open arms and immediately sent off a paper to their British counterparts that primly noted: 'We must not jeopardize our sound overall strategy simply to exploit local successes in a generally accepted secondary theatre, the Mediterranean, where logistical and terrain difficulties preclude decisive and final operations designed to reach the heart of Germany.'[4] At Quebec, Marshall was even more adamant that further Italian ventures should be as low-key as possible and his meeting with Brooke, on the 15th, 'was . . . most painful and we settled nothing. I entirely failed to get Marshall to realize the relation between cross-Channel and Italian operations . . . The only real argument he produced was a threat . . . that if we pressed our point, the build-up in England [for the cross-Channel invasion] would be reduced to that of a small corps and the whole war reorientated towards Japan.'[5]

Fortunately for the British, however, the sudden withdrawal of the Germans from Sicily and, more important still, the first peace overtures from the Italians, who seemed ready to surrender unconditionally, caused the Americans to unbend somewhat. As usual, nothing precise was agreed upon but once again the Americans did agree to a vague formula that at least allowed the possibility of a self-sufficient Mediterranean theatre, and they agreed that in certain eventualities resources other than those agreed on at 'Trident' might be reallocated to this theatre.

But American approval was still at best qualified. Always fearful that the British saw the Mediterranean as an *alternative* to a cross-Channel invasion, the Americans had drawn up rigid timetables, agreed to at 'Trident', governing the withdrawal of landing craft, etc., from the Mediterranean. However, even before 'Trident', the local commanders had agreed that, should a move to the Italian mainland be sanctioned, it should be a two-pronged offensive: Montgomery's Eighth Army crossing the Straits of Messina into the heel and toe of Italy and Mark Clark's newly constituted Fifth Army attempting an amphibious landing near Naples, at Salerno. The latter assault was authorized by Clark on 26 July, though it soon became clear to the planners that the growing shortage of landing craft meant that the operation could not possibly be undertaken until early September. Then came the news of imminent Italian collapse which led Clark's staff to hope that the Americans would relax their stipulations about the concentration of resources for the invasion of north-west Europe. But Marshall resolutely refused to alter these schedules one jot and, as Brooke put it, 'he admits that our objective must be to eliminate Italy . . . yet is always afraid of facing the consequences of doing so . . .'[6]

Such continued disagreements got the Italian campaign off to a poor start. Even the relatively successful clearance of Sicily ended on a sour note when the absence of clear strategical directives seemed to render the Allies incapable of finishing off their opponents as they had done in Tunisia. The Axis forces were able to extricate themselves from the Allied pincers and from 11 August onwards they ferried as many as 8000 men a day across the Straits. By the time Patton occupied Messina, late on the 16th, they had managed to evacuate the total German force of 40,000 men as well as 62,000 Italians and a substantial number of tanks and guns. It seems clear that if the local commanders had had a clear brief about post-HUSKY operations, as well as the necessary landing craft, they could easily have sanctioned some sort of pre-emptive landing in Calabria which would have sealed off the German disembarkation points. Indeed, this is what Field-Marshal Albert Kesselring, the German theatre commander, expected the Allies to do and he remained amazed at the relative ease with which he had been allowed to pluck his forces from beneath their pursuers' very noses. As a later commentator has noted: 'That the chance was not taken reflects, above all, upon the politicians who had allowed the campaign to begin with no clear decision about what was to follow. The tactical requirements of HUSKY were thus, in one vital respect, sacrificed to uncertainty about the scope of future Mediterranean strategy.'[7]

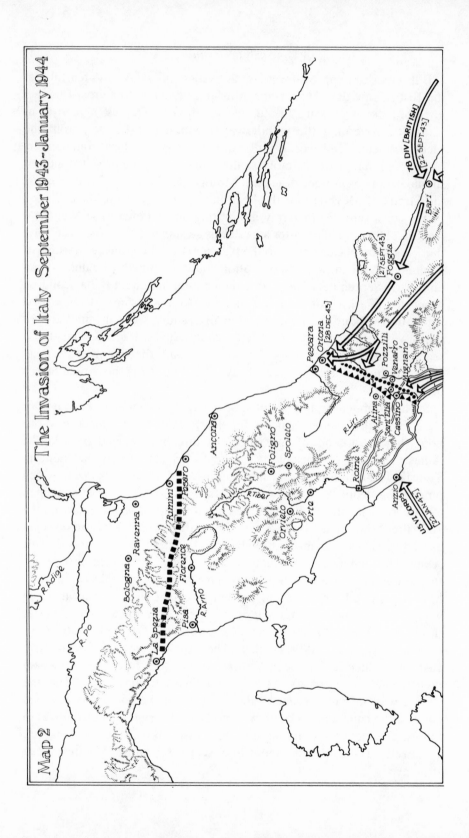

Map 2

The Invasion of Italy September 1943 - January 1944

78 DIV (BRITISH)
[22 SEPT 43]
Bari
[27 SEPT 43]
Foggia
Pescara
Ortona
[28 DEC 43]
Pozzilli
Venafro
Isernia
Atina
Sant'Elia
Cassino
R.Liri
Rome
Anzio
[22 JAN 43]
US II CORPS
Spoleto
Foligno
Ancona
R.Tiber
Orvieto
Otto
Pesaro
Rimini
Florence
Pisa
R.Arno
La Spezia
Ravenna
Bologna
R.Po
R.Adige

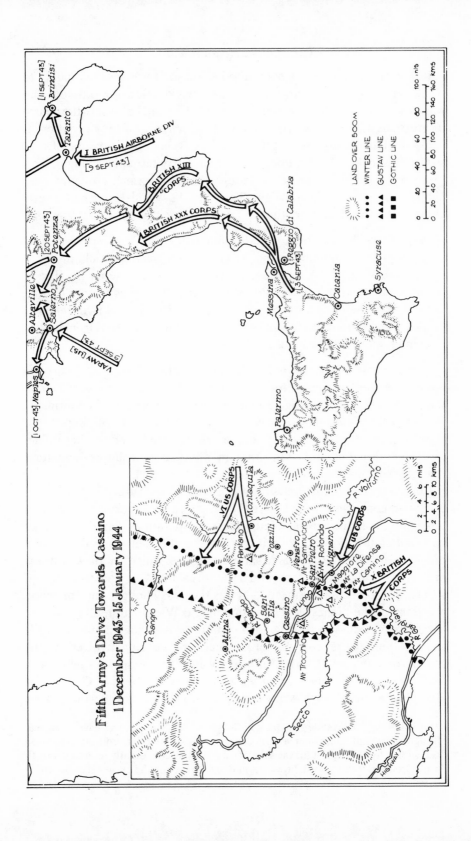

Fifth Army's Drive Towards Cassino
1 December 1943 ~ 15 January 1944

[11 SEPT 43] Brindisi
Taranto
I BRITISH AIRBORNE DIV
[9 SEPT 43]

BRITISH XIII CORPS

BRITISH XXX CORPS

Reggio di Calabria
[3 SEPT 43]
Messina
Catania
Syracuse
Palermo

[1 OCT 43] Naples
[20 SEPT 45] Potenza
Salerno
Alavilla
V ARMY (US) [9 SEPT 43]

LAND OVER 500M
WINTER LINE
GUSTAV LINE
GOTHIC LINE

0   20 40 60 80 100 mls
0 20 40 60 80 100 120 140 160 kms

VI US CORPS
Montaquila
Mt Fantano
Pozzilli
Venafro
Mt Sammucro
San Pietro
Mignano
Mt Maggiore
Mt La Difesa
Mt Camino
R Volturno
II US CORPS
X BRITISH CORPS
R Garigliano
R Sangro
Alina
R Rapido
Sant' Elia
Cassino
Mt Lungo
Mt Rotondo
Mt Trocchio
HIGHWAY 6
R Secco
HIGHWAY 7

0 2 4 6 mls
0 2 4 6 8 10 kms

It is worth noting at this point another reason for the Allied failure to block German withdrawal, for it gave early evidence of a problem that was to have serious repercussions during the Cassino battles. In the course of the Sicily fighting the Air Force had claimed that if the need arose it could singlehandedly prevent the Germans evacuating across the Straits, strafing their ships by day and bombing the ferry terminals at night. This they signally failed to do, even though the last German crossings were almost all made in broad daylight. The official naval historian had several severe criticisms to make of the Air Force, noting among other things that

> At no stage did the three Allied Commanders-in-Chief represent to the Supreme Commander that an emergency, such as would justify the diversion of all available air-strength, had arisen. . . . The enemy later expressed his astonishment that the Allies had not used their overwhelming air superiority to greater effect . . . Even when the enemy's intention was plain, the action taken suffered from lack of inter-service co-ordination.[8]

But lack of co-ordination was not the only problem. Even had there been a much heavier concentration of aircraft it would have remained to be seen just how much damage they could have inflicted on the Germans. For, as will be seen in later chapters, though the value of aircraft in a tactical ground support role was much vaunted during the Italian campaign, its actual impact in either an interdiction or simple demolition role was sadly inadequate.

But even after the occupation was complete the future of the Italian campaign continued to be blighted by the lack of a thorough-going and far-sighted commitment to Mediterranean operations. Hard as Brooke and Churchill had pleaded their case, neither of them offered any clear directives on how the campaign should progress, whilst senior Americans preferred to sulk in their tents and try to forget that they had ever allowed themselves to become embroiled in this theatre. Though much planning was done at the highest level in London and Washington, all eyes were increasingly focussed on the forthcoming cross-Channel invasion. Of course, there were also numerous planners directly involved in the Mediterranean itself. Clark's Fifth Army and Montgomery's Eighth both had sizeable staffs. Their activities were under the aegis of General Sir Harold Alexander's 15th Army Group,* a HQ well endowed with analysts

---

* Until May 1943, Alexander had been in charge of 18th Army Group in North Africa. His new command underwent several confusing changes of name during the period dealt with in this book, but for the sake of clarity I shall consistently refer to it as 15th Army Group. For the record, however, and to help explain the provenance of certain

and planners. Alexander was also Eisenhower's deputy commander in the Mediterranean and the latter, too, had a full complement of staff officers eager to formulate plans to best co-ordinate the activities of the various land, air and naval forces. But, if their military and political masters could do no better than commit them one nudge at a time to strategic operations in Italy, it was obviously almost impossible for the theatre planners to work on anything but a short-term, *ad hoc* basis. There were more than enough imponderables anyway. How resolute were the Italians in breaking the Axis? What exactly would Hitler do about it? Would the American *idée fixe* about the cross-Channel invasion leave sufficient landing craft and combat troops in the Mediterranean? What effect would the dubious Italian climate have on air operations, a vital adjunct to any large-scale offensive against the Germans and their well-proven defensive techniques?

The drawbacks of such off-the-cuff planning became all too apparent with regard to the Salerno landings, for which the staffs had only six weeks to prepare. More pernicious still was the American refusal to put any real muscle behind their grudging agreement to invade mainland Italy and to allow Eisenhower to retain an adequate number of landing craft. Alexander very soon began to have serious reservations about Clark's forthcoming amphibious effort, feeling that neither the initial assault nor the subsequent build-up could be made in sufficient strength. On 30 August he confided in a small group of British and American visitors:

> The operation, he told us, was a dangerous gamble, because such inadequate forces had been allocated to it. The Germans already had some 19 divisions in Italy, built up since the month of Mussolini's overthrow [on 25 July]. The Italians had 16 divisions who might jump either way. But Alexander said he would have only from 3–5 Anglo-American divisions for our initial landings, to a maximum build-up of 8 divisions over the following two weeks.[9]

Nor was his pessimism misplaced. Though the landings, on 9 September, did gain a small beachhead, the Germans very swiftly concentrated their available forces and sealed it off. Subsequent heavy counter-attacks came within an ace of throwing the Allies back into the sea and at one stage only massed gunfire from the offshore armada prevented the Germans from concentrating for another, probably decisive assault.

of the source references, the following were the changes: on 11 January 1944 it was renamed HQ Allied Armies in Italy; on 18 January this became HQ Central Mediterranean Forces; on 10 March it reverted to HQAAI.

Certainly the troops themselves had not expected such fierce resistance and morale slumped dangerously. A British observer at Salerno, on 14 September, saw the reactions of American troops to a rumour that a German breakthrough was imminent. Senior officers began to distribute carbines before themselves taking off into the blue yonder:

> Outright panic now started and spread among the American troops left behind. In the belief that our positions had been infiltrated by German infantry they began to shoot each other . . . Official history will in due time set to work to dress up this part of the action . . . with what dignity it can. What we saw was ineptitude and cowardice spreading down from the command and this resulted in chaos. [10]*

Even before this, Alexander had deemed the situation so grave as to demand a personal visit. On the 13th he told Churchill, 'I consider the situation critical.' On the 14th he wrote, 'I am not satisfied with the position . . . I have instructed Eighth Army to push ahead with all speed.' On the 16th he reported with somewhat more equanimity though he still felt that the Allies were in a very vulnerable position. A major reason for this, he felt, stemmed from the inadequacy of the original assault and the lack of fresh reserves. Thus 'our present weakness is due to the fact that . . . our troops are tired [and] there is very little depth anywhere. We have temporarily lost the initiative.' [11]

In the event the beachhead perimeter did just hold and on 16 September Generaloberst Heinrich von Vietinghoff, the commander of the German Tenth Army, asked Kesselring for permission to withdraw from Salerno, this being granted next day. Moreover, the Allies on the beachhead could congratulate themselves on having survived through their own efforts. Montgomery's Eighth Army, it will be remembered, had crossed the Straits of Messina a couple of weeks earlier and it had been hoped that his troops would push back the few Germans in front of them with little difficulty and, if necessary, quickly link up with the Salerno forces. In fact, the two armies never joined up until the crisis had passed, Montgomery's progress through Calabria being much slower than anyone had foreseen.

The whole incident rankled greatly with Clark and brought to the fore a strong antagonism to the British that was seriously to jeopardize genuine Allied co-operation during the drive towards Rome. After the

---

* Nor was the Allied record entirely one-sided. Salerno was not a happy chapter in the history of the 6th Grenadier Guards or the 8th Royal Fusiliers, as is evidenced in H. Pond, *Salerno*, White Lion Books, 1974, p. 109.

war Montgomery was to acknowledge freely that his men, in this instance, could hardly be cast as gallant rescuers: 'I have never thought we had much real influence on the Salerno problem; I reckon General Clark had it well in hand before we arrived. . . . Fifth Army did their own trick without our help – willing as we were.'¹² But Clark did not feel that this was the attitude at the time. According to him 'the news broadcasts and press reports (all British) continued to state that Eighth Army was rushing to save and then had saved Fifth Army from destruction. Nothing is farther from the truth. . . . Fifth Army . . . won its own battle. On about the 16th of September or so Clark received a message from Montgomery saying how glad he was his forces had joined up with Fifth Army. Clark flashed back a reply, "Received your message. I have felt nothing." '¹³ When the two actually met, however, Clark kept his feelings to himself and

> took him to his van. Clark then went on to say to Monty that Monty had had a lot more experience than he had in battle and knew a lot more about it. Monty ate this crap up and began saying to Clark [that] you want to watch this and that and then indicated he thought Clark would do all right. Clark was enjoying building the old boy up. Then before he left Monty said, 'By the way, do you know Alex?' 'Why I've met him,' Clark replied. 'Well I say to you that he may order you to carry out some crazy plan. If he does, just tell him to go to hell.' Clark replied, 'I'll tell you about it if he does and you can tell him to go to hell.'¹⁴

Lighthearted though the banter might have seemed, Clark's anti-British prejudices were obviously a very real factor in his relationships with his allies, whilst Montgomery's patronizing attitude to their joint commander could hardly have done much to enhance Clark's respect for Alexander.* Certainly, as we shall see, the time was to come when Clark would effectively tell him to 'go to hell' and ignore his quite explicit directive.

But it is also important at this point to see a little more clearly than Clark and appreciate why Montgomery was not able to render assistance.

---

* Being patronizing was certainly one of Montgomery's longer suits. Clark's antipathy to the British would hardly have been lessened by the following assessment of him, less than two months later. In a letter to Brooke, Montgomery referred to a forthcoming Eighth Army offensive which would 'hit the Boche a crack that will be heard all over Italy. . . . I fear, however, the Fifth Army is absolutely whacked. . . . My own observation leads me to the conclusion that Clark would be only too delighted to be given quiet advice as to how to fight his Army. I think he is a very decent chap and most co-operative; if he received good and clear guidance he would do very well.' (Quoted in Bryant, (see note 13), vol. 2, p. 99.)

Certainly the terrain did not help, the British having to cover '300 miles in 17 days, in good delaying country against an enemy whose use of demolition caused us bridging problems of the first magnitude. The hairpin bends on the roads were such that any distance on the map was [doubled and more] on the ground.'[15] But even this was not the most important factor, and once again we have to return to the pernicious effects of the lack of a coherent Allied strategy, even after the decision to invade Italy had been taken. Thus, though the idea of a two-pronged offensive looked very well on paper, hardly any effort was made to work out complementary timetables so that one prong could support the other, either in the event of an emergency or if there seemed a chance of encircling at least part of the enemy forces in southern Italy. Fifth and Eighth Armies' objectives were decided upon in isolation and, as Montgomery put it:

> No attempt was made to co-ordinate my operations with those of the Fifth Army . . . [Indeed] it was not visualised that the Eighth Army would go further than the Catanzaro neck, a distance of about 60 miles from Reggio. . . . The following is an extract from my diary written [on 5 September] . . . 'Before we embark on major operations on the mainland of Europe we must have a master plan and know how we propose to develop these operations. I have not been told of any master plan and I must therefore assume that there was none.'[16]

That this assumption was correct is further borne out by the fact that Alexander was not given a clear directive from Eisenhower to capture Rome until 25 September. Even this order seems to have been the subject of some doubt, for on 8 November Eisenhower felt it necessary to issue another one, which 'reaffirmed the objectives given on 25th September – the capture of Rome and the maintenance, subsequently, of maximum pressure on the enemy. The directive recognized that the enemy "intends to resist our occupation of southern Italy to a greater degree than hitherto contemplated." '[17]

The need to reiterate this order was also a reflection of growing pessimism in the Allied camp about the prospects for the Italian campaign. Even before the Salerno landings Eisenhower had informed the Combined Chiefs of Staff that the Allies in Italy were 'likely to face bitter fighting. A firm hold on Naples might be all they could get. Beyond Naples, the . . . troops would undoubtedly have to attack "slowly and painfully" up the peninsula. A rapid drive to the Alps . . . was "a delightful thought . . . but not to be counted upon with any certainty." '[18]

After the landings, Alexander was even less sanguine about the fighting that lay ahead. On 18 October, Arthur Tedder, Eisenhower's air chief,

> learned from 'Mary' Coningham that Alexander had for some two or three days been expressing his disquiet. The Germans now had more than twenty divisions in Italy, with a total of more than twenty-six in sight. Alexander was unlikely even to have this strength in 1944. . . . [He was] fighting in terrain favourable to the defensive without the means of getting round the flank [and] Alexander said that he saw no reason why we should ever get to Rome.[19]

Various factors fuelled this growing despondency. One has already been dealt with; namely the persistent uncertainty about exactly what were the aims of the Italian campaign, an uncertainty that had already led to one glorious opportunity missed and one near-disaster. Another was the nature of Italy itself; both the terrain, which slowed progress almost to a snail's pace, and the climate, which imposed the severest strains on the weary fighting soldiers. The crucial factor, however, was the attitude of the Germans, who swiftly realized how the Allies' difficulties might be turned to their own advantage. Hitler, in fact, had long felt that if the Allies succeeded in driving the Axis forces out of North Africa they would at some stage attempt a major seaborne operation in the Mediterranean, against either the Italian or the Balkan peninsulas. Early in 1943 he decided to defend the whole of this region and a skeleton army headquarters, under Erwin Rommel, was set up in Munich to co-ordinate planning for the defence of Italy. However, fears about the reliability of the Italian Army, as well as an awareness of the increasing number of German divisions being sucked into the Eastern Front, made both Rommel and Hitler dubious about their chances of occupying and defending the whole of Italy, and plans drawn up in July 1943 only envisaged a solid defence in the Apennines, well north of Rome. In August a contingency plan was drawn up to cover the possibility of Italian defection and again this plan, code-named ACHSE, was almost entirely concerned with operations north of Rome.

Thus, even before the Italians had formally surrendered on 3 September, German divisions began to move into northern Italy, with or without the consent of local Italian commanders, and in August alone, five infantry and two panzer divisions were sent across the frontier. In the same month Tenth Army was activated in central Italy, in the Gaeta-Naples-Salerno region, though it comprised only five divisions, with possible recourse to two others stationed near Rome. Hitler was well aware how thinly it was spread and he made it clear to Vietinghoff that as 'Italian defection was only a matter of time . . . the most important task was a safe withdrawal of the army to the north. . . . [It] was to withdraw first to the Rome area and from there to the northern Appenines.'[20]

By now both Vietinghoff and Kesselring were becoming conscious of the concentration of Allied shipping in the western Mediterranean and the latter, in particular, insistently warned of a major assault in the Naples-Salerno region, with the probable aim of taking the Foggia airfields and possibly Rome. Nevertheless, Kesselring was not unduly alarmed, having for some time been in favour of defending Italy as far south as possible. Early in August he had sent a memo to Hitler and the OKW stating that it was 'certain that the Italian leadership and armed forces want to co-operate with us' and therefore urging the despatch of 'reinforcements of German troops in southern Italy'.[21] So convinced was Kesselring that this was the only proper course that when the OKW spurned his advice he offered his resignation. Hitler refused to accept it, however, and issued another order that in the event of a landing in the south only mobile divisions were to put up any resistance, and that only in the form of a fighting withdrawal. Above all, even in the event of passive or active Italian resistance, Kesselring was to ensure that the army escaped well to the north with all of its formations relatively intact. This concept was reaffirmed on 30 August when an updated version of ACHSE was issued.

But Kesselring's protestations had not been without their effect, particularly in the light of the evident military difficulties that faced the Allies. In Sicily, as we have seen, the Germans were able to evacuate the majority of their forces without too much difficulty, and at Salerno, having concentrated their rather sparse units with exemplary speed, they came, somewhat to their own surprise, within an ace of driving the Allies back into the sea. Hitler followed these developments with the keenest interest and gradually began to reconsider his original strategy, one that after all ran quite contrary to his instinctive notions about the nature of military success. Indeed, in the light of his orders to the armies in Tunisia, at Stalingrad and elsewhere, one is only surprised that Hitler was ever so ready to consider simply giving up so much of a country to an invader. Field-Marshal Manstein, for example, made great play in his memoirs of the contradictions that bedevilled the German high command, contrasting the 'realism' of the commanders in the field with Hitler's 'conception of strategy and grand tactics . . . which arose from the personal characteristics and opinions . . . of a dictator who believed in the power of his will not only to nail down his armies wherever they might be but even to hold the enemy at bay.'[22]

Having found a theatre commander who would pander to these predilections, Hitler was not slow in letting them reassert themselves. His original plan for defending only northern Italy had envisaged handing over command of the entire theatre to Rommel, but on 12 September Hitler deferred this decision and informed Kesselring that for the time being he should retain autonomous control in central Italy, being only answerable to Hitler and the OKW. On the 15th Kesselring informed the OKW that he expected the Allies to pause after capturing the Foggia airfields and he put forward a suggestion, which was approved by the OKW, that some sort of stand should be made in central Italy, to at least delay the Allies before the onset of winter. This notion was incorporated into Vietinghoff's new orders at the end of the Salerno battle. Although his withdrawal from the immediate battlefield was sanctioned, on the 16th, he was ordered to retreat as slowly as possible, and then only to the Rivers Bifurno and Volturno, where he was to make at least a temporary stand on the outposts of the so-called Winter Line.

On 6 October Kesselring submitted a memorandum to the OKW in which he once again argued against withdrawal to the Grosseto–Perugia–Ancona line, in the north. Instead he suggested a prolonged stand south of Rome, with troops slowly falling back from the Winter Line, anchoring themselves on the yet more formidable Gustav Line, running along the Rivers Garigliano and Gari, through Monte Cassino and into the Cairo massif. Hitler was clearly already sympathetic to this idea because on 1 October he had allotted Kesselring extra Todt Organization personnel and substantial amounts of building equipment to improve this same *Stellung*. In fact, by the time Kesselring's recommendation had arrived, Hitler and the OKW had already reached the same decision and on 4 October Hitler issued the crucial order that a prolonged stand was to be made south of Rome. A few lingering doubts must have remained in his mind and for the next month Hitler declined to choose between Kesselring and Rommel as supreme commander in Italy. But these doubts were gradually dispelled and on 6 November the job was given to Kesselring* in an order which stated quite emphatically that the present German positions 'will mark the end of withdrawals'.

As we now know, the 'Ultra' organization had almost total access to all German coded messages, at virtually every level. As a result this whole

---

* Rommel left Italy for good on 21 November, to take charge of improving the Atlantic Wall defences in northern France. His willingness to evacuate most of Italy had not pleased Hitler, however, and for the time being he was given no tactical command in the event of an actual Allied invasion.

debate was carried on *en clair* and senior Allied commanders were made immediately aware of each decision. The following telegram from Churchill to Roosevelt, sent on 10 October, makes a clear reference to 'evidence' that can only have come from 'Ultra':

> The German intention to reinforce immediately the south of Italy and to fight a battle before Rome is what Eisenhower rightly calls a 'drastic change within the last forty-eight hours'. We have trusted this kind of evidence and I therefore agree that we must now look forward to very heavy fighting before Rome is reached instead of merely pushing back rearguards.[23]

The German decision only served to make the local commanders yet more pessimistic about the chances of ever reaching Rome. The onset of winter complicated their task even further and by December the Allied push had slowed so much that Churchill despatched Brooke to Italy to report on the situation. His visit did little to cheer him. On the 14th he wrote in his diary:

> Monty . . . does not feel that Clark is running the Fifth Army right nor that Alex is gripping the show sufficiently. He . . . asked me how much importance we attached to an early capture of Rome, as he saw little hope of capturing it before March.
>   To my mind it is quite clear that there is no real plan for the capture of Rome. . . . Frankly I am rather depressed from what I have seen and heard today.[24]

Nor did his subsequent visit to Fifth Army headquarters do much to alleviate his gloom. On 16 December 'we dined with Clark in his mess. I had a long talk with him about the offensive on his front and do not feel very cheered up as to the prospects of the future from what I heard from him. He seems to be planning nothing but penny packet attacks.'[25]

Yet one can hardly blame the local commanders for their singular lack of panache. The political direction of the campaign to date had hardly encouraged them to plan well ahead or to think in terms of large-scale concerted offensives, whilst the German decision to make a stand south of Rome was the last straw for those who had already spent weary months battering their way through some of the most inimical terrain in Europe.

For Italy is a country where much of the terrain offers an endless series of obstacles to an advancing force. Below the northern plains one finds simply one great mountain range, the only low ground being the narrow coastal strips and the river valleys which fan out from the central spine like spindly fishbones. Each of these river courses offered a superb defensive position, the Germans usually flooding the attacker's side of the river, building deep dugouts and machine gun posts on the far bank and siting their artillery and observers in the mountains behind. After their narrow shave at Salerno, the Allies spent the rest of 1943 banging their heads against a whole series of such positions. Clark's Fifth Army went up the western side of the country and had to force its way across the Volturno. Montgomery's Eighth Army followed the Adriatic coast and successively had to make assault crossings of the Bifurno, the Trigno, the Sangro and the Moro. Even when there were no rivers, life was little easier. Once across the Volturno, Fifth Army ran up against the Winter Line, anchored on Monte Camino, Monte La Difensa and Monte Maggiore, all of which had to be stormed and painstakingly cleared of the enemy. Occasionally the troops had to attack small towns and, even with heavy artillery and bombers, these could prove remarkably hard nuts to crack.

This type of combat placed enormous strains on the fighting soldiers. Casualties were frighteningly high. By the end of 1943 Fifth Army had suffered nearly 40,000 battle losses and the American component alone had lost 50,000 men sick. The figures for some individual battalions are even more grotesque. Between 9 September and 31 October the 5th Sherwood Foresters sustained 560 battle casualties, the 9th Royal Fusiliers 572, and the 5th Hampshires 448. Almost all these casualties were from amongst the riflemen, of whom there were less than 400 in a battalion. Eighth Army suffered just as badly. In the street-fighting in Ortona, for example, a brigade of the 1st Canadian Division suffered 1372 casualties, or one quarter of all Canadian deaths in Italy.

Moreover, the ordinary soldier's troubles were far from over even when he was not actually going forward under fire. In fact, in terms of false expectations, Italy was undoubtedly the most unpleasant surprise to troops who served there. Wet, cold and raw, it was the very antithesis of the 'sunny' Italy of the tourist handbills. The first winter there was appalling and as the Allied offensive ground to a halt the troops were left terribly exposed to the full blast of its drenching rain, snow and freezing temperatures.

As the Allies inched nearer to the Gustav Line, and the hoped-for breakthrough to Rome, conditions remained implacably grim. In the Winter Line an American Corps commander wrote: 'It has rained for two days, and is due to rain for two more say the meteorologists. In addition, it is cold as hell . . . I don't see how our men stand what they do.'[26] On Monte Camino, Flanders veterans of 1917 might have felt themselves in a timewarp. Lieutenant D. Helme (3rd Coldstream Guards) wrote:

> After the first couple of days we had to stretch groundsheets and gas-
> capes to catch rainwater for drinking. No chance of shaving, as any
> cut would have become infected; but I had a good wash in a shell
> hole. Men's hands and feet were rather swollen after the rain and
> exposure. . . . Had only one blanket each . . . and had to sleep two
> or three together to keep warm.[27]*

Above all, perhaps, the fighting on the mountains of the Winter Line
offered a terrible foretaste of the conditions that were to dominate the
front-line soldiers' lives for the next six months. Alan Moorehead, one
of the best Allied war correspondents, was closely involved in the British
attack on Monte Camino and the following impressions offer a vivid
prelude to the story to come, highlighting as they do the ghastly day-to-
day conditions of Italian mountain warfare and the appalling physical and
mental strains that they imposed on men:

> And then there were the . . . infantry in their camouflaged water-
> proof gas-capes, the rain streaming off their steel helmets, their
> hands gone blue with cold. They climbed numbly, contemplating
> each step, each few yards in front of them, since no-one there could
> comprehend the whole battle or the worse discomforts that were to
> be added. Each man found it enough to contain himself, to keep
> himself alive and moving. . . .
>   At the top of the exposed slopes . . . the men lay in slit trenches

---

* Not that such conditions should have come as a surprise to the more erudite of the
Allied soldiers. In 1503 French and Spanish armies had found themselves drawn up
along the Garigliano, along which the Gustav Line now ran. The campaign had started
late and by the time the Spanish commander had entrenched his forces, both sides
were beset by the full rigours of winter. Ceaseless rain and snow pelted the shivering
soldiers, caused the river to flood, making an assault crossing virtually impossible,
rendered gunpowder unusable and prevented any movement by cavalry, transport or
artillery. The rival armies remained immobilized for three months, the ordinary
soldiers suffering terrible privations from the remorseless conditions. One historian
wrote: 'The situation . . . was indeed deplorable. Those who occupied the lower level
were up to their knees in mud and water; for the extensive rains, and the inundation
of the Garigliano, had converted the whole country into a mere quagmire . . . The
only way in which the men could secure themselves was by covering the earth as far
as possible with boughs and bundles of twigs . . . Those on the higher ground were
scarcely in better plight. The driving storms of sleet and rain, which had continued
for several weeks without intermission, found their way into every crevice of the flimsy
tents and crazy hovels, thatched only with branches of trees, which afforded a
temporary shelter to the troops.' (W.H. Prescott, *History of the Reign of Ferdinand
and Isabella*, Richard Bentley, 1853, vol.3, p.127.)

and these were half-filled with water. There comes a time when the mind will react no more to cold and danger. Those who had been exposed up there for two days and nights slept waist deep in water. In utter weariness they lost all sense of time and place and even perhaps the sense of hope. Only the sense of pain remained, of constantly reiterated pain that invaded sleep and waited for the end of sleep to increase. For these soldiers the risk of war had passed out of consciousness and was replaced by the misery and discomfort of war, which in the end is worse than anything.[28]

This utter weariness was the real reason for the Allied failures that so disappointed Brooke. It was easy for him to dismiss Clark's 'penny packet' attacks and Alexander's failure to formulate any 'real plan' for the capture of Rome. It was even easier for Churchill, in response, to fulminate that 'there is no doubt that the stagnation of the whole campaign . . . is becoming scandalous. The C.I.G.S.'s visit confirmed my worst forebodings.'[29] Yet whose fault was this? The hands of the local commanders had largely been tied by their superiors. Because the Americans had been so reluctant to go into Italy at all, Churchill and Brooke had been far too willing to accept *ad hoc* compromises that allowed little chance of comprehensive forward planning and that never permitted an adequate commitment of fighting troops or material resources. Attacks had to be made in penny packets because there simply were not enough men and guns, and plans were bound to seem somewhat fanciful both because of this same shortage and because they always had to be drawn up too hastily.

Nor were the ground forces given maximum support from the one arm in which they had total preponderance, the Air Forces. Between October and December 1943 the strength of Luftflotte II, the major Luftwaffe formation in Italy, fell from 430 to 370 aircraft of all types. By the latter date Mediterranean Allied Air Force, incorporating Mediterranean Strategic, Tactical and Coastal Air Forces, could deploy around 4000. But this vast force proved to be more of a liability to Alexander than an asset. On the one hand it was absorbing a vast amount of shipping and supplies – the maintenance requirements of the 315,000 men and their planes were nearly as great as those of either Fifth or Eighth Army – and on the other, since the capture of the Foggia airfields in early October, the bulk of strategic bombing activity was directed against Germany. Some bombers did undertake raids against Italian railway facilities, to try to disrupt the German supply network, but these were only of limited usefulness, a point to which we shall return in more detail with regard to the Fourth

Battle. Of course the Allies also had a considerable number of tactical aircraft, mainly employed as fighter-bombers, but their operations were hamstrung by a factor that had been largely overlooked by the planners – the appalling winter weather which kept all aircraft grounded for days at a time and which badly affected visibility even when they did get airborne.

Thus the ground forces were very much on their own and they too felt the effects of the planners' blasé underestimation of the rigours of the Italian climate and terrain. Neither Brooke nor Churchill, in particular, had given adequate attention either to the serious restrictions on movement imposed by mountains, rivers and shrewd German demolitions or to the awful sufferings of the fighting soldiers, constantly exposed to the numbing wind, rain and snow. Even at the end of the Sicilian campaign a soldier of 51 (Highland) Division had written a bitter farewell which concluded:

'Then fare weel, ye banks o' Sicily,
Fare ye weel, ye valley an' shaw.
There's nae Jock will mourn the kyles o' ye.
Puir bliddy bastards are weary.'[30]

How much poorer, bloodier and wearier they were to become as the battalions, inadequate in number and all increasingly under strength, toiled towards the gates of Rome. Peaches and nectarines there were none.

Yet Alexander, Clark and Montgomery did try to make the best of what they had. Alexander's plans, through no fault of his own, might look somewhat unrealistic but he did at least try to fulfil Eisenhower's directive to take Rome. As early as November he drew up a plan that envisaged a combined push, right through both the Winter and Gustav Lines, by Eighth and Fifth Armies; the former driving to the high ground north of Pescara prior to turning south-west towards Avezzano and Rome, and the latter smashing their way through the Liri Valley at least as far as Frosinone. This plan also included provision for a one-division amphibious assault, at Anzio, just south of Rome. This operation was to be launched some time in December, when it could most easily make a dash inland and link up with the advancing Fifth Army. Yet even as Alexander was writing this order his troops were beginning to run out of steam. Eighth Army had found the Winter Line alone a tough enough nut to crack and by the end of December, after the Sangro crossing and the bloodbath at Ortona, Montgomery's battalions were so debilitated that they were deemed incapable of any further concerted offensive in the near future.

Fifth Army, as we have seen, had found the Winter Line an equally formidable proposition. Their *point d'appui* had been the Mignano Gap, overlooked on the south by the Camino massif* and Monte Lungo, and on the north by the twin peaks of Monte Rotondo and Monte Sammucro. The first attacks against the southern bastion, in early November, were mounted in insufficient strength and both the British assault against Monte Camino itself and the American against Monte la Difensa had to be abandoned in mid-November. Clark asked for time to regroup and in the interim he and his staff laboured to draw up a plan that not only looked to breaching the Winter Line but also went at least some of the way to fulfilling Alexander's much more ambitious directive. Two sets of operational orders were mooted and scrapped before the final version was issued on 24 November. The offensive actually began on 1 December and envisaged three phases. Phases I and II combined another assault against the Mignano Gap with a drive along the Colli–Atina road to secure at least some of the hill-mass north and north-west of Monte Cassino. Phase III envisaged these attacks rolling right forward into the Liri Valley; Monte Cassino being nipped out by converging attacks from the south and north-west and exploitation up the Liri Valley being entrusted to 1st US Armoured Division.

Once again, however, the tenacity of the German defenders had been sadly underrated. Phases I and II were successfully completed but as each objective fell the troops showed increasing signs of war-weariness as their casualties mounted on the bare, rain-swept mountains. Monte Camino was not taken until 11 December, and though Monte Sammucro had been taken two days earlier, strong German counter-attacks were not finally beaten back until the 14th. Between these two strongpoints was the village of San Pietro and it was not until the 17th that the Americans cleared the last pockets of resistance there. Some progress was also made to the north where VI US Corps, thanks in large part to the exploits of 2nd Moroccan Division, the first French formation to come into the line, on 8 December, managed to advance some two and a half miles along the Atina and Sant' Elia roads. However, both they and the troops who had hammered their way through the Mignano Gap were still a long way from closing the pincers that were to nip out the garrison in Cassino and the

---

* Incorporating, from south to north, Monte Camino, Monte la Difensa, Monte Ramatanea and Monte Maggiore.

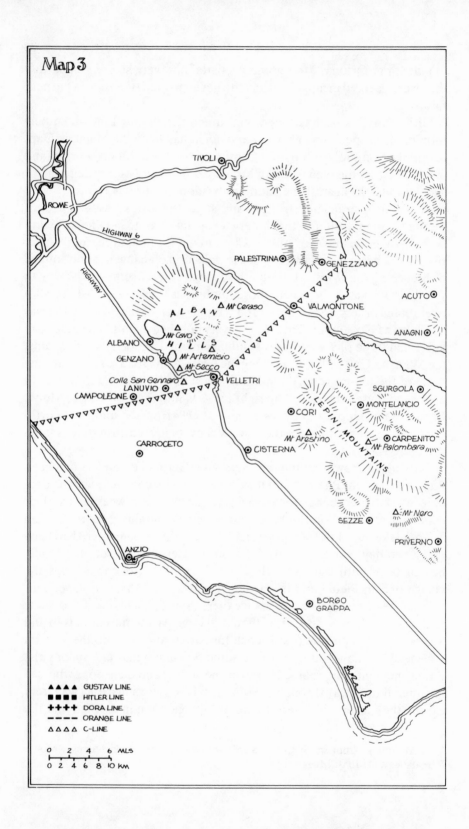

Map 3

TIVOLI

ROME

HIGHWAY 6

PALESTRINA   GENEZZANO

ACUTO

ALBAN   △ Mt Ceraso
                          VALMONTONE
HIGHWAY 7
                                              ANAGNI
            △ Mt Cavo
ALBANO   HILLS
GENZANO   △ Mt Artemisio
                  △ Mt Secco   SGURGOLA
Colle San Gennaro △   VELLETRI
LANUVIO   MONTELANCIO
CAMPOLEONE   CORI
                                    LEPINI MOUNTAINS
                                    △ Mt Arestino
CARROCETO   △ CARPENITO
                        CISTERNA   △ Mt Palombara

                              SEZZE   △ Mt Nero

ANZIO   PRIVERNO

                      BORGO
                      GRAPPA

▲▲▲▲ GUSTAV LINE
■■■■ HITLER LINE
++++ DORA LINE
---- ORANGE LINE
△△△△ C-LINE

0   2   4   6 MLS
0 2 4 6 8 10 KM

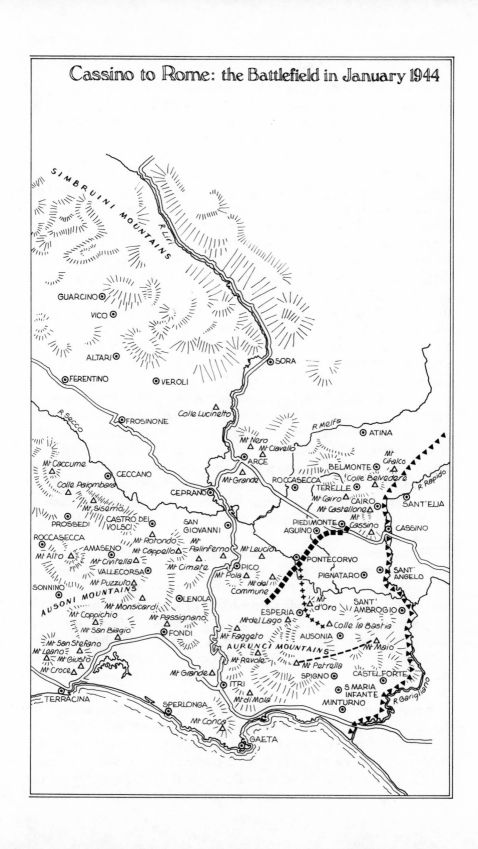

Cassino to Rome: the Battlefield in January 1944

SIMBRUINI MOUNTAINS

R. Liri

GUARCINO

VICO

ALTARI

FERENTINO

VEROLI

SORA

Colle Lucinetto

R. Secco

FROSINONE

Mt Nero

Mt Clavello

ATINA

R. Melfa

Mt Caccume

CECCANO

ARCE

BELMONTE

Mt Cifalco

R. Rapido

Colle Paiombara

Mt Grande

ROCCASECCA

Colle Belvedere

TERELLE

SANT'ELIA

CEPRANO

Mt Sisemo

PROSSEDI

CASTRO DEI VOLSCI

SAN GIOVANNI

PIEDIMONTE

Mt Cairo

CAIRO

Mt Castellone

Mt Cassino

CASSINO

ROCCASECCA

Mt Alto

AMASENO

Mt Rotondo

Mt Cappello

Mt Palinferno

Mt Leucio

AQUINO

Mt Civitella

VALLECORSA

Mt Cimate

PICO

PONTECORVO

SANT' ANGELO

SONNINO

Mt Puzzuto

Mt Pola

Mt dal Commune

PIGNATARO

AUSONI MOUNTAINS

LENOLA

Mt d'Oro

SANT' AMBROGIO

Mt Monsicardi

ESPERIA

Colle la Bastia

Mt Coppichio

Mt Passignano

Mt del Lago

Mt Faggeto

AUSONIA

Mt San Biagio

FONDI

AURUNCI MOUNTAINS

Mt Maio

Mt San Stefano

Mt Ravole

Mt Petrella

CASTELFORTE

Mt Losna

Mt Giusto

SPIGNO

Mt Croce

ITRI

Mt Grande

Mt di Mola

S MARIA INFANTE

MINTURNO

R. Garigliano

TERRACINA

SPERLONGA

Mt Conca

GAETA

massif behind. It soon became clear to Clark that Phase III, the opening up of the Liri Valley, was not going to be rolled forward by the simple momentum of earlier attacks, but would have to be an autonomous operation, prior to which the troops must be given time to rest and regroup.

Alexander tacitly acknowledged the necessity of such a respite by issuing, on 2 January, another separate order for a drive up the Liri Valley. Fifth Army planners set to work at once and though some of their troops were still involved in the final stages of Phase II, only fully completed with the capture of Monte Trocchio on the 15th, most of their attention was now directed towards a concerted assault across the Garigliano and Rapido Rivers. Their plans were translated into orders on 10 January. The French Expeditionary Corps, now strengthened by the arrival of 3rd Algerian Division, between 3 and 19 January, was to set the ball rolling in the north with a continuation of VI US Corps' drive towards Atina and Sant' Elia. This attack was to begin on 12 January. On the 17th, X British Corps was to attack in the south, across the lower reaches of the Garigliano, and II US Corps was to follow this up the next day with an attack across the Rapido, opposite Sant' Angelo. The victims of these attacks were, respectively, 5 Mountain Division, 94 Infantry Division and 15 Panzer Grenadier Division. Cassino, and the massif behind, was held by 44 Infantry Division but, as in his November plan, Clark hoped to so trouble the other three divisions by the thrusts to north and south and up the Liri Valley that a frontal assault against Cassino would be unnecessary, its defenders' communications along Highway Six becoming too vulnerable to allow them any other option but to pull back from the Gustav Line.

This vulnerability was to be emphasized by an ancillary strike into the rear of the Gustav Line and provision was still made for the amphibious landing at Anzio, already alluded to. This had now been upgraded to a two-division effort, involving 1 British and 3 US Infantry Divisions under the command of Major-General John P. Lucas' VI Corps HQ. The disappointing progress of Fifth Army through the Winter Line had earlier put this idea very much on a back-burner and at one stage it had seemed that the rigid American timetables concerning the withdrawal of landing craft for the invasion of France would not allow the landing to be launched at the optimum moment. But Churchill had become very committed to the idea during a convalescence in Marrakesh and he so badgered Roosevelt and the American Chiefs of Staff that they agreed to postpone the deadline for the withdrawal of the landing craft, as well as to leave enough to permit the doubling of the original strike force. Operation

SHINGLE, as it was christened, was now timed for 22 January, by which time there should be every hope of speedily linking up with the main force inland as the Germans, looking anxiously to their lines of communication, began to fall back.

This concept was made explicit by Alexander and in a grandiloquently titled order of the 12th, 'The Battle for Rome', he stressed the importance of not allowing the enemy

> any respite in which to reorganize or take up new positions. The momentum of our advance must be maintained at all costs to the limit of our resources. The enemy will be compelled to react to the threat to his communications and rear, and advantage must be taken of this to break through his main defences, and to ensure that the two forces operating under . . . Fifth Army join hands at the earliest possible moment.[31]

By now, certainly, German units were beginning to pull back from the Winter Line and, in an order of 11 January, OKW conceded that 'in the event of attacks by far superior enemy forces a step-by-step withdrawal to the Gustav position will be carried out.'[32] But if Alexander and Clark hoped that this withdrawal indicated German weakness or that a new assault would be able to catch their forces on the hop, before they had properly settled into this new *Stellung*, they were to be sadly disappointed. The Germans were past masters of this kind of fighting withdrawal and the Gustav Line itself, as will be seen, was no mere chinagraph pencil line on Hitler's maps but a truly formidable example of German military engineering.

PART TWO

THE FIRST BATTLE
(12 January–9 February 1944)

Within the next few days the 'Battle for Rome' will begin. It will be decisive for the defence of Central Italy and for the fate of 10th Army. . . . All officers and men . . . must be penetrated by a fanatical will to end this battle victoriously, and never to relax until the last enemy soldier has been destroyed. . . . The battle must be fought in a spirit of holy hatred for an enemy who is conducting a pitiless war of extermination against the German people. . . . The fight must be hard and merciless, not only against the enemy, but against all officers and units who fail in this decisive hour.

Adolf Hitler, January 1944

3
'The Battle of the Last 100 Metres'
The French Drive to the Gustav Line, 11–24 January 1944

To take risks is a matter of honour.

Captain Bernard Brézet, 1943

When the first French troops went into the line, in December 1943, there were few of their Fifth Army colleagues who expected great things from them. In their eyes the French had shown their true colours during the débâcle of 1940, whilst the pusillanimous attitude of the authorities in French North Africa, after the Armistice, had done little to enhance French prestige. To be sure, some troops and civilian officials had rallied to de Gaulle's Free French – notably 7000 of the Dunkirk evacuees, Catroux in Indo-China, Marchand in Chad and Leclerc in the Cameroons. But the absolute passivity of the authorities in Morocco, Algeria and Tunisia, apparently more than satisfied with the German promise not to station occupation forces in any of the territories, seemed to augur badly for any hopes of concerted resistance in the French colonies.

The unfolding of the North African campaign did little to renew Allied confidence. A hodge-podge of Senegalese, Foreign Legion and Marine units fought well in Libya and Eritrea, and Koenig's stand at Bir Hacheim, in early 1942, remains one of the enduring epics of the Second World War. Nevertheless, most of the Armée d'Afrique was still reluctant to renounce what they saw as their binding oath to the French Army and nation, now represented by Pétain and the Vichy running dogs. Syria actually had to be invaded by a Free French–British force, and even after its conquest only a little over 6000 of the incumbent Vichy Army, less than 20 per cent, agreed to go over to de Gaulle.

Allied leaders thus entertained little hope of any spontaneous uprising in the French territories in Rommel's rear, and in July 1942 initiated detailed planning for an Anglo-American invasion of Morocco and Algeria. Even as this was launched, in November, the attitude of the local French forces remained ambiguous. Certain junior generals, notably Mast and Béthouart, were known to be vigorously pro-Allied but their seniors were much more hesitant. Juin himself, then the commander-in-chief in North Africa, still had enormous reservations about flouting his oath of loyalty; Generals Barré and Koeltz would only follow his lead,

41

Noguès had got cold feet, and Vice-Admirals Fenard and Estéva were creatures of Darlan, the head of all Vichy armed forces. The Allies' problems did not end there, for they soon discovered that de Gaulle and his Free French would provide no rallying-point in this part of the Empire, where even officers who favoured the Allies regarded him as little short of a traitor who had shrugged off his patriotic duty in the cause of personal ambition. Just before the landings Roosevelt confided to Churchill that he was 'very apprehensive in regard to the adverse effect that any introduction of de Gaulle into the "Torch" situation would have on our . . . efforts to attach a large part of the French North African forces to our expedition. Therefore I consider it inadvisable for you to give de Gaulle any information in regard to "Torch" until subsequent to a successful landing.'[1] The Allies had thus thought it wise to avail themselves of another figurehead, General Giraud, a widely respected commander who had escaped from German captivity in April 1942. Unfortunately, no sooner had this doughty warrior been unveiled than it became awfully apparent that his influence on local commanders was absolutely nil. A major reason for this was simple bad luck for the Allies, in that on the very day the invasion was launched it was discovered that Darlan had just flown to Algiers and his presence there acted as a further disincentive to those officers who were agonizing about the validity of their oath of loyalty.

    All this boded ill for the three task forces coming ashore at Casablanca, Oran and Algiers. An attempted *putsch* in the former, by Béthouart, came to nothing and everywhere, notably in Oran, the Allies faced some sort of armed opposition. The presence of Darlan, however, was soon to prove a blessing in disguise. For if *he* could be prevailed upon to throw his lot in with the Allies, however cynical his motives, his authority might well be sufficient to bring over almost all of the French officers. Juin immediately set to work and by the afternoon of D-Day – Darlan having received particularly vague instructions from Pétain as to how to respond to the invasion – he had wrested from him permission to negotiate a ceasefire in the Algiers area. But getting this ceasefire extended to other areas proved yet more difficult. Darlan refused to see General Giraud and his relations with the senior American mediator, Mark Clark, swiftly went from bad to worse. Even when he did eventually agree to an extension of the ceasefire he resolutely refused to commit his forces to co-operating with the Allies – an urgent necessity in view of the sudden German decision to pour reinforcements into Tunisia. Further progress was also hampered by the fact that many local commanders now insisted that any agreement be ratified by General Noguès, newly named by Pétain as his senior representative in North Africa. Luckily Noguès proved reasonably amenable and on 13 November he and Darlan agreed to take over administration with Giraud and Juin as the leading commanders. Most important of all, they pledged their forces to help in the liberation of Tunisia and, eventually, of metropolitan France.

The almost farcical character of these extended negotiations did little to endear the Armée d'Afrique to the Allies. Nor were their reservations about its military value noticeably dissipated in the following months. Certainly there were some encouraging signs. Even before the TORCH landings the French had not been completely idle and in the first months after the Armistice Noguès had been instrumental in creating an unofficial force of some 70,000 reservists, on top of the 120,000 men allowed by the Germans, and in establishing secret arms dumps containing 60,000 rifles and machine guns, as well as almost 200 artillery pieces. Immediately after the agreement of 13 November the French authorities proclaimed a general call-up, going back as far as the class of 1919, by which they mustered a total European force of 176,000 men. To this could be added 13,000 soldiers from Corsica, as well as 20,000 escapees from mainland France. These latter were in large part Alsatians and Savoyards, the survivors of a hazardous overland journey through Spain which another 40,000 of their compatriots failed to complete. Fifteen thousand Free Frenchmen also joined the Armée d'Afrique in April 1943, and the rest of its burgeoning manpower was supplied by 233,000 native Moroccans, Algerians and Tunisians.* In late November, Clark and Darlan agreed that these forces were to be split into fourteen divisions which were to be organized on American lines and entirely equipped by them. All this took time, but in the interim quite a number

* It is worth noting, therefore, that the divisions of the Armée d'Afrique were somewhat different from the Indian and West African divisions employed by the British in that a much higher proportion of their men were Europeans. The figure for the Army as a whole was just under 50 per cent. It has also been pointed out that over 16 per cent of the total European population of North Africa served with the colours, as opposed to only 1.6 per cent of the indigenous population. The racial breakdown in two typical units is given below:

Unit	Officers		NCOs		ORs	
	European	Other	European	Other	European	Other
2 DIM	562	0	1522	293	4494	7024
5 Bataillon de Marche	25	0	60	35	238	620

of poorly equipped French troops went immediately into the line in Tunisia and fought with some distinction. They were given the task of holding a group of ridges south of the main British advance and more than once gave important service in helping to repel strong German thrusts in this area.

Yet many of the Allied commanders remained far from convinced that the French forces could ever constitute a reliable component of the forthcoming invasion of Europe. Even though they had made the best of their very inadequate equipment during the Tunisian campaign, it remained difficult for many English and American officers to override their first impressions of the Frenchmen's obsolescent armaments and tatterdemalion appearance. Nor were they at all convinced that the French could make full use of their new equipment or adapt to the 'modern' methods of mechanized warfare. For the process of Americanization went far from smoothly, as de Gaulle observed:

Our African troops, accustomed to living under improvised conditions, regarded the accumulation of so many men and supplies, in depots, supply centres, convoys and workshops as a waste of manpower. This divergence of view produced frequent and, occasionally, vehement disputes between the Allied general staff and our own. Furthermore, among the French, it gave rise to disappointment at having to disband crack regiments and having to make them into auxiliary forces.[2]

Nor were these continued reservations only at the military level. The agreement with Darlan had served its purpose at the time but it did nothing to facilitate a rapprochement between the Armée d'Afrique and the Free French. De Gaulle had sent representatives to Algiers, in December 1942, whilst the Free French military forces, marching with the Eighth Army hard on Rommel's heels, were daily getting nearer to Tunisia. But the recognition of Darlan had only served to drive a deeper wedge between de Gaulle and the new leaders in North Africa. The latter felt that they were somehow the real heirs of 'legal' French government and this only hardened their antipathy towards what they regarded as the apostasy of de Gaulle and his followers. He, on the other hand, could only see the new government as a gang of ex-collaborators, not fit to spearhead any attempt to liberate France itself. The Allies, who were not helped by Roosevelt's deep suspicions of de Gaulle, proved incapable of bringing the two sides together. In December Giraud refused an offer of Free French military co-operation and, though a Joint Committee of National Liberation was established in June 1943, de Gaulle refused to have any truck with suggestions that Giraud might be a logical choice as French commander-in-chief.

The deep divisions between the 'Africans' and the Free French became particularly apparent as the latter's fighting troops finally arrived in Tunisia. On 8 June, some four weeks after the German surrender, their presence in Tunisia 'was deemed "undesirable" and they received the order to quit the territory they held by right of conquest and to return into the Tripolitanian desert, near Zuara. . . . Officially the order came from the Americans. In reality, even in the desert bivouacs of Libya, it was known perfectly well that the "marriage" between Giraud and de Gaulle was in no way a love match.'[3] This order was rescinded towards the end of August but even then the Giraudistes continued to be pettily obstructive. The 1st Free French Division, as it was now known, had been equipped by the British and various attempts were made to change it to the American TO&E which was now the French standard. Giraud, however, refused repeated requests for its re-equipment, yet when he was asked to nominate the first French divisions to be sent to Italy he insisted on including the 1st Free French, knowing full well that this would be impossible. When Alexander had to insist that only Americanized divisions could be slotted into the Allied supply chain, Giraud immediately nominated a Senegalese division in its place. As Harold Macmillan, Churchill's personal representative in North Africa, noted: 'This was a foolish affair, very damaging to French morale. It looked like a childish and peevish attack upon de Gaulle's veteran troops.'[4]

None of this internecine conflict did much to endear the French to the Allies or to make them particularly optimistic about their cohesiveness in prolonged combat. Though the re-equipment of the French divisions went ahead and Juin was formally commissioned, in September, to form a French Expeditionary Corps to fight in Italy, there were few Allied planners who saw its divisions as anything more than useful reserves for the temporary relief of exhausted veteran formations, or as glorified garrison troops in static parts of the line. An AFHQ planner remembered the continued distrust about their fighting abilities. According to the notes of a later interview, Brigadier K.W.D. Strong, the G2 at AFHQ, 'and others . . . were agreeably surprised by the good French performance in Italy – they were better than he had thought they would be. As far as French leaders were concerned, Strong said the Allied officers at AFHQ never trusted them or thought they could rely on what the French said.'[5]

These strong reservations about the integrity of the French leaders were a further reason for trying to commit their troops as piecemeal reserves, and so avoid the creation of a unified French corps or army that might insist on having its own voice in the Allied military councils or, worse still, vote with its bayonets regarding the post-war organization of France. Such feelings were still paramount in April 1944, when the French in Italy had already scored several notable military successes. It was suggested then that a second French Corps HQ and staff be sent to Italy to help administer a force that had grown to four divisions. Alexander's reaction was brusque. 'Introduction into Italy of a second French Corps HQ will almost certainly lead to a request for constitution of a French Army in Italy, which cannot be accepted.'[6]

In fact, Juin had already had considerable difficulties in persuading Alexander to let his original two-division force fight as a unified formation. In this he was successful, but only after vigorous protests about individual units being put into the line to bolster other Allied formations. As late as 17 November 1943 he wrote:

> As circumstances might demand the immediate employment of the [2 Moroccan] Division before the establishment of my Corps HQ, I can permit, if absolutely necessary, that it be put at the disposal of a US Army Corps during the time required for my Corps HQ to begin functioning properly. But I could not subscribe to its *employment as dispersed Combat Teams*. This is not simply a question of the prestige of the French High Command . . . but also one of efficiency . . . [as] units of the same nationality only function well under their own . . . divisional command, where they were formed and trained.[7]

But Juin's motives were not quite as professionally disinterested as he tried to imply. He was much more to the point in a letter to Giraud, on 29 November, when he described his labours to set up his own rear echelons and lines of communication:

> In my opinion, this question of rear echelons is fundamental because the American High Command, which is itself busy with its own back-up troops, would very much like to have us organize such things for ourselves. It is by this path, moreover, that we will little by little attain our goal, which is the creation of a small French Army of Italy with its own autonomous services.[8]

The key phrase here is 'little by little' and it is this circumspection, rather than the modesty or self-effacement ascribed to Juin by other historians, that explained his willingness to temporarily forgo his rank of full general and the Army command that would have been his rightful due. As he explained to Giraud in the same letter:

I have the feeling that we will only make our mark here by showing tact and discretion. The Americans are not people one can hustle. . . . They like us a lot, but they are also imbued with their sense of omnipotence and with a touchiness that you could hardly imagine. . . . The French always seem a little excitable to them and it is important for me to first gain their confidence, particularly before the fighting begins . . . and once I have this confidence our position will improve of its own accord. . . . Similarly, because it is necessary to be discreet and wait for the right moment, I have decided, until receipt of orders to the contrary, to retain the name 'French Expeditionary Corps' for the French troops who have disembarked in Italy. It would look ill, I am convinced, for me to appear at this time before General Clark with the title of Army Commander. This matter will sort itself out in due time, when they have seen what we can do and when the tool placed in my hands has shown itself to be a proper Army.[9]

But let it not be thought for a moment that French motives were merely cynical. We have already seen Juin speak of the 'prestige of the French High Command' and he might well also have mentioned *national* prestige, for there is no doubt that the greater part of the French Expeditionary Corps was animated by a fierce desire to wipe out all memories of the humiliation in 1940 and to re-establish the proud reputation of French arms. Not surprisingly, such sentiments were particularly strong amongst the European element* and one of the *évadés d'Espagne* wrote just before he went off to war:

I leave with the same feeling of duty as in 1939 . . . full of serenity and perfectly at peace with myself. . . . The present drama demands that one take sides; that is what I am doing, with all the risks that it entails. To take risks is a matter of honour. There are moments when, whatever the cost, one must follow the path down which one is called by the deepest of feelings. . . . That is what I am doing.[10]

Another, a captain in the 2nd Moroccan Division, spoke for thousands of his compatriots languishing in North Africa as they awaited a definite order for embarkation to Italy. After one particularly tedious day he

* Though almost all the native troops actually fought with just as much fervour as their European comrades-in-arms. Moreover, despite isolated racist incidents, front-line relationships between the two groups were extremely good. See, for example, R.Merle, *Ben Bella*, Michael Joseph, 1967, pp.52-4 and 61-3.

scribbled in his notebook: 'More than the malaria which is eating away at our strength, boredom is destroying our spirits, enervated by this interminable waiting. There are even rumours that the disagreements with the Allies are keeping us out of combat, the sole end of all our thoughts, the only hope capable of reinvigorating our hearts.'[11]

The French soon showed that this was not just empty bluster, but that such sentiments provided a mainspring for the most energetic and effective performance in combat. First in the line was the 2nd Moroccan Division which, attached to VI US Corps, took up positions in the Monte Marrone–Monte Pantano sector, straddling the Colli–Atina road. They relieved 34 US Division and in front of Monte Pantano found over 400 American corpses, the ghastly detritus of an earlier assault on this position.* The whole division, in fact, was just about at the end of its tether and the newcomers, oblivious to Allied doubts as to their own abilities, were themselves fairly scathing about the situation that the Americans had allowed to develop. Sergeant Ben Bella (5th Moroccan Regiment) wrote:

> German . . . patrols were operating all over no man's land, throwing grenades and shouting insults at us, and playing on our nerves. We soon realized, as the insults were all in English, that the Germans thought the Americans were still there. The Americans had hardly sent out any patrols and had not even been able to tell us where the enemy outposts were located.[12]

The Moroccans were soon given a chance to prove whether they could do any better. To the surprise of many observers they succeeded brilliantly, 8th Regiment taking Monte San Michele on 15 December and 5th Regiment storming up Monte Pantano on the following day. Taken aback by the ferocity of the French assaults, the Germans relieved 305th Division with the 5th Mountain Division, a formation they hoped would be more at home in such bleak, icy terrain. The ploy was not entirely successful and the Germans were pushed back again during a renewed attack towards San Biagio. This began on 24 December and by the 28th the Moroccans had gained a strong foothold on the Mainarde massif. The next day they attacked further south, aiming at the so-called *Jumelles*, which guarded the approaches to Monna Casale. After initial successes, however, the assaulting battalions were obliged to withdraw and the

* The dead included all three battalion commanders of 168th Regiment.

French suspended their offensive to give time to regroup and absorb replacements.

For casualties had been heavy. In the preceding three weeks the division had sustained 923 casualties, over 200 of them being killed. Yet it had not been in vain. The speed with which they had taken an objective that had for so long defied the Americans, and the determination with which they had pressed on yet further, had impressed friend and foe alike. Juin's staff were more than justified in reporting to Giraud, on the 26th, that

> The infantry, in particular . . . are now self-confident. Vigorous, flexible, already well used to the enemy's artillery and mortars, they constitute a first-class tool in the hands of their commanders. After the first hard fighting, they very quickly took a grip on themselves. . . . The worth of the cadres is well known. They behaved admirably, as was expected. The young French officers and NCOs conducted themselves perfectly, inspiring by example and paying a heavy price for it.[13]

The Germans seemed to agree. In the first days, as the battalions of 5 Mountain Division were rushed into the line almost as soon as they stepped off the troop trains, they came close to being completely overwhelmed. The division had arrived from the Eastern Front, yet found the conditions in Italy even more severe. Their corps commander wrote:

> . . . it became evident that all divisions brought from other theatres of war were at first unable to cope with the twofold strain caused by the freezing cold in high mountains, to which they were unaccustomed, and the massed drum-fire employed by the enemy [artillery] in major battles. Although it was not as cold as in Russia, the constant changes in the weather, alternating between rain, snows, frost and storms, were equally hard on their system . . . [Their] first field post cards contained remarks indicating that they 'would rather return to Russia on all fours'.[14]

Nevertheless, General Ringel soon took hold of his troops and determined to obey to the letter a strict OKW injunction not to give up any further ground until 25 January at the earliest.

Thus, when the French, now strengthened by the arrival of 3 Algerian Division, prepared to play their part in Clark's revamped Phase III offensive, their first attacks were not against the Gustav Line proper. In this sector the Gustav position was anchored on a line running northwards across Colle Belvedere, Monte Carella, Monte San Croce to Monte

ATINA

5 Mt Div

2 Moroccan Div
[11 JAN]

ARCE

HIGHWAY 6

BELMONTE
Mt Cifalco

3 Algerian Div
[11 JAN]

Mt Grande

Colle Belvedere

TERELLE

131

CEPRANO

SANT'ELIA

191

R. Sacco

Mt Cairo

CAIRO

134

R. Rapido

SAN GIOVANNI

R. Liri

PIEDIMONTE

132

AQUINO

Mt Cassino

CASSINO

211

104
PG

36 US Div [20 JAN]

PICO

PONTECORVO

PIGNATARO

[To be followed by
34 US Division +
1 US Armoured
Division]

Mt Pola

Mt del
Commune

LENOLA

Mt d'Oro

R. Ausente

SANT'
AMBROGIO

ESPERIA

129
PG

British 46
Division
[19 JAN]

Mt Lago

Colle la
Bastia

FONDI

Mt Faggeto

AUSONIA

Mt Maio

R. Garigliano

HIGHWAY 7

Mt Revole

Mt Faito

276

British 56 Division
[18 JAN]

Mt
Grande

Mt Calvo

Mt Petrella

SPIGNO

Mt Rotondo

CASTELFORTE

ITRI

Mt di
Mola

S MARIA
INFANTE

274

British 5 Division
[18 JAN]

267

Colle
San Martino

MINTURNO

[18 JAN]

SPERLONGA

Mt Conca

GAETA

▲▲▲▲ GUSTAV LINE
■■■■ HITLER LINE
++++ DORA LINE
- - - - ORANGE LINE

131   German Troops in the
      line in early January –
      number refers to Regt.

      Projected Allied attacks
      according to General Clark's
      Operations Instruction of
      10 January

0   2   4   6 MLS
0 2 4 6 8 10 KMS

Marrone, but at the beginning of the French offensive the Germans were well forward of these peaks, holding an outer ring of defences based upon Costa San Pietro, Monna Casale, Monna Aquafondata and the village of Aquafondata itself. For the Germans reckoned that the deeper the buffer zone between their front and their vulnerable flank at Atina, the more chance they had of reducing the momentum of French attacks before they threatened a breakthrough that might turn the whole Gustav Line.

Nor were their fears about this sector ill-founded. Juin, too, was keenly aware that a strong assault towards Atina could well lead to a decisive breakthrough, with troops fanning out beyond it and fatally threatening German communications along Highways Six and Seven. Even as his offensive opened he was looking well beyond the forward German positions, beyond even the Gustav Line itself, to a vigorous thrust along the Monte Carella–Monte Rotolo–Monte Bianco axis and so to Atina itself. General Clark was not entirely unaware of the possibilities of such a manoeuvre but in Juin's eyes he seemed strangely reluctant to commit sufficient men and resources. Juin, in fact, was rather dismissive of the whole direction of the Italian campaign, feeling that little effort was being made to properly co-ordinate the efforts of the various Corps, or even of the two Armies. His views rather echoed those of Brooke and Churchill, already cited, though Juin did have the good sense to realize that the shortage of fighting troops seriously limited Alexander's strategic options. During Christmas he had written to Giraud pointing out that the Allies needed upwards of another ten divisions to back up a really effective offensive involving the whole Army Group. Without these divisions

> only short-range attacks are possible, a succession of little nudges which get us hardly anywhere and in fact pin down few enemy troops. Eighth Army's operations, despite all the fuss that is made of them, will not be any more decisive than those of Fifth Army. The road which leads to Rome is long and bristles with thorns. In Europe one must wage war with Armies and Army Groups and not just with Divisions and Corps.[15]

For just these reasons Juin was rather dismissive of the whole 12 January directive, feeling that the attacks envisaged were too localized and that no real thought had been given to the possibility of destabilizing the whole Gustav Line with a series of simultaneous attacks and feints.[16] He was above all dubious about the possibility of a breakthrough into the Liri Valley. Though he applauded the absence of any frontal assault on Cassino town or the mountain behind, he still could not agree that there was any real chance of punching through the centre of the German defences until there had been decisive breakthroughs, fully exploited, on one or the other of the flanks.

According to Clark, it will be recalled, the decisive punch in the centre was to be delivered by 1st US Armoured Division and here again Juin was far from convinced. When he arrived in Italy, in October, one of his first trips had taken him along the Salerno–Naples road, where

> along the whole length of the road . . . we ran into the 7th British Armoured Division in close column, incapable of leaving the road and deploying in a terrain completely given over to mountains. I immediately concluded . . . that the widespread mechanization of the British and American forces constituted a serious obstacle to any swift progress up the Italian peninsula.[17]

Juin's troops, however – and this was why he favoured a decisive breakthrough on his own flank rather than by X Corps on the Garigliano – were not tied to the roads in the same way. Even though their divisions were equipped according to American practice, the French had very few tanks and had from the very beginning tried to amass as many mules as possible and so make themselves much less dependent on motor transport. Even more important, such previous military experience as the troops had, had been acquired in North Africa during the interminable mountain warfare against the dissident Kabyle tribesmen. Thus the prevailing military doctrine of the Armée d'Afrique stressed such factors as mobility on foot, infiltration, and small-unit autonomy, all invaluable attributes in the kind of rugged terrain through which the French were to advance. This doctrine was clearly stated in the divisional orders issued prior to the first attacks. General Joseph de Monsabert, the commander of the 3rd Algerian Division, spoke of the overriding need to

> feel out the front and respond to any weakening of enemy resistance, as soon as it is detected. . . . In this period there must be no rigid timetable for anyone; everything will be decided in response to how the attack progresses. . . . [We must] exploit as vigorously as possible. . . . Each regiment should have strong forces . . . [for just such] exploitation which will act resolutely without bothering about communications with their neighbours.[18]

The French jumped off on the night of 11/12 January. Though their intended axis of exploitation was a fairly narrow one, across Monte Carella, Monte Rotolo and Monte Bianco and then towards Villa Latina

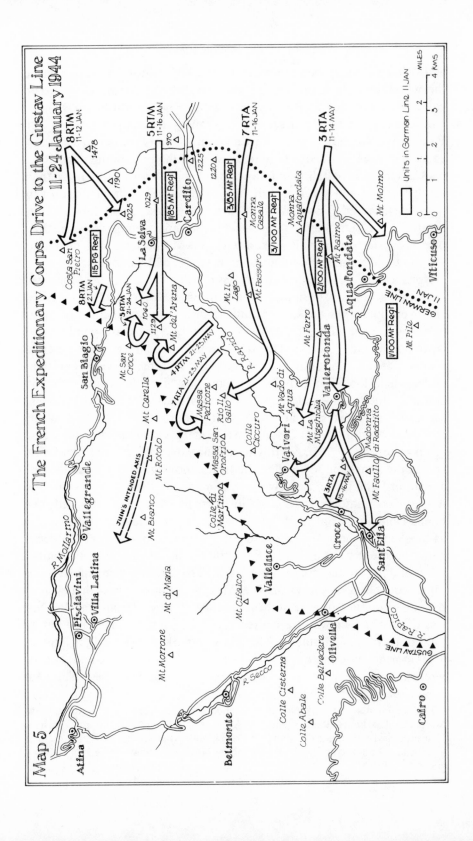

Map 5

The French Expeditionary Corps Drive to the Gustav Line
11-24 January 1944

8 RTM
11-12 JAN

5 RTM
11-16 JAN

7 RTA
11-16 JAN

3 RTA
11-14 MAY

JUIN'S INTENDED AXIS

Units in German Line, 11 JAN

MILES

KMS

115 PG Regt

185 Mt Regt

3/65 Mt Regt

5/100 Mt Regt

2/100 Mt Regt

1/100 Mt Regt

8 RTM
21 JAN

5 RTM
21-24 JAN

4 RTM 21-25 MAY

7 RTA 21-25 MAY

3 RTA
15-16 MAY

GERMAN LINE
11 JAN

GUSTAV LINE

Atina

Piscavini

Villa Latina

Vallegrande

San Biagio

R. Melfa

Mt. Morrone

Mt. di Maria

Mt. Bianco

Mt. Rotolo

Mt. San Croce

Mt. Corella

Costa San Pietro

1478

1190

1025

1029

La Selva

1040

1225

1220

970

Cardito

Monna Casale

Monna Aquafondata

Mt. Molmo

Mt. dell'Arena

1129

Mt. Il Lago

Mt. Passero

Mt. Raimo

Aquafondata

Mt. Ferro

Mt. Vado di Aqua

Vallerotonda

Mt. La Mesghiola

Valvori

Massa Pelicore

Rio Il Gallo

Colle Ciacuro

Massa San Onofrio

Colle di Martimo

R. Rapido

Madonna di Raoditto

Mt. Faullo

Croce

Sant'Elia

Mt. Cifalco

Valleluce

Belmonte

R. Secco

Colle Cisterna

Colle Abale

Colle Belvedere

Olivella

R. Rapido

Cairo

and Atina, the initial assault was made on a fairly wide front, to unbalance the whole defensive line and so make it difficult for the Germans to concentrate around the chosen *point d'appui*. The 2nd Moroccan Division was allotted the northern sector, its primary targets being Costa San Pietro and two pairs of peaks further south: Points 1025/1029 and 1225/1220. All three Moroccan regiments were in the line, though each held back at least one battalion to follow up any initial breakthrough. To their south was the newly arrived 3rd Algerian Division, though one of its regiments, the 4th Tunisian Tirailleurs, was not yet ready for offensive action.* The Division's targets were Monna Casale, where their operations were integrally linked with the Moroccan attack on Points 1225/1220, Monna Aquafondata and the village of Aquafondata.

None of the regiments had an easy task. Those of the Moroccan Division had already been much tried during the Monte Pantano attacks, and even during the subsequent lull conditions in the line had been far from easy. A captain on the Divisional Staff told war correspondents: 'It is not possible to understand the operations which I am going to describe if one does not constantly bear in mind the extremely trying conditions under which the Tirailleurs had to fight . . . throughout the winter, in glutinous mud, rain and snow.'[19] The last was a particular problem, especially as most French troops were poorly equipped against the elements. A report by Juin's staff, on 6 January, noted that 'the storm rose again yesterday. . . . Snow crowns the summits; the rain and violent wind add to the problems of keeping the traffic moving. The units in the line are suffering in this extremely harsh climate and their kit is ill-suited to it. . . . 600 reinforcements have just disembarked at Naples with one blanket and no special kit.'[20] Such neglect caused casualties just as severe as those in the most savage rounds of fighting. In one typical Moroccan battalion there were 93 cases of frostbite and trench-foot in December 1943 and 89 in the following month. The drain on manpower this represented becomes particularly evident when one realizes that even by the end of January only 12 of these cases had returned from hospital. Nor was it just the men who were affected. During a relief made just before the offensive, one Battalion War Diary remarked: 'The cold is intense. The mortar base-plates of the [incumbent] battalion could not be wrenched out of the frozen ground. We exchanged our base-plates for

---

* The Regiments that took part in the January battles were the 4th, 5th and 8th Moroccan Tirailleurs, the 3rd and 7th Algerian Tirailleurs and the 4th Tunisian. Henceforward I shall use the standard French abbreviations and designate them as 4,5,8 RTM; 3 and 7 RTA, and 4 RTT. Battalions will be designated (e.g.) 1/8, 2/8 and 3/8 RTM.

theirs. It was the same with the groundsheets covering the slit-trenches. We had to exchange them all.'[21] In some battalions the situation became critical. Just after the opening of the January offensive the commander of 1/4 RTT sent a hastily pencilled report to his regimental headquarters complaining that 'the battalion has now spent a total of 37 days in the line: 25 days in the front line, 6 days in transit, either marching or on alert, 6 days . . . in reserve. This state of affairs threatens to [illegible] the men's morale.'[22] Regarding the state of the Division as a whole its historian vividly recalled 'the terrible sufferings from the cold . . . Faces ravaged by pain. Tirailleurs whose feet could no longer support them and who moved around by dragging themselves on their hands and knees to tell the platoon commander that they could no longer keep their stationary vigil amidst . . . the freezing rain. . . . There is not a single survivor of the campaign in Italy who does not remember, as a nightmare, the horrendous winter in the Abruzzi.'[23]

As usual in the Italian campaign the terrain, too, presented seemingly insuperable difficulties. A report prepared by the 2nd Moroccan Division highlighted the overriding influence of the lunatic jumble of peaks, crevasses and knife-edge ridges that made up the battlefield. Every tactical plan was dictated by

a topography that was even more irregular on the ground than was shown on the map; the predominance of clay which meant mud and damp in all the fox-holes dug by man or nature; jagged rocks everywhere . . . hardly any tracks, and those hard to negotiate being under constant enemy mortar fire and mined everywhere. . . . The infantryman became an expert mountaineer, though when he had to take cover the rocks did not guarantee full protection, particularly when the explosion of the enemy shells also sent splinters of rock flying in all directions. It was no longer even a question of small-unit combat, but rather of one man against another in a terrain in which one could spend hours on end without having any clear idea of what was happening only ten yards from the forward positions.[24]

Nevertheless, the offensive went well in the early stages. The assaulting troops jumped off late at night, on the 11th, and, carrying only their individual ammunition, six grenades and one day's American 'K' rations all stuffed into a small haversack, they moved remarkably quickly along the gullies and ravines leading to their objectives. To the north the lower slopes of Costa San Pietro were swiftly seized by 8 RTM and were firmly held despite numerous determined counter-attacks by 115 Panzer

Grenadier Regiment (PGR), on the 12th and 13th. Those on the 13th were particularly fierce and the battalion then holding the ground gained, 3/8 RTM, lost three-quarters of its officers and had each of its companies reduced to forty men or less. Similar breakthroughs were achieved to the south. The twin summits of Points 1025/1029 and 1225/1220 all fell in the early hours of the 12th and the assaulting regiments quickly pushed forward towards the River Rapido, on the other side of which were their primary targets, Monte San Croce and Monte Carella, two of the linch-pins of the Gustav Line proper.

Points 1225/1220 had been attacked by 4 RTM and one of its senior officers was keen to show how fitted his Moroccan tribesmen were for this sort of warfare. They were particularly adept at surprise night attacks, so much so in fact that the author wondered whether the standard preparatory artillery barrage was not at best a mixed blessing. For

> the Moroccan loves the night and the mountains. Rocks, thickets and sheer crevasses, all obscured in the treacherous darkness, are his best allies and over a thousand years his eyes have become accustomed to not losing their way in the gloom. He knows when to creep forward and when to wait. He knows also that there is no more fearsome weapon than that ancestral dagger which his forefathers have plunged into sentries' backs since time immemorial. Why, therefore, wake the Germans before the striking of the hour of *Baroud*? The Germans are brave, but a brave man asleep is like a woman.[25]

In the event, the Moroccans followed the barrage so closely that a considerable degree of surprise was achieved. Here and there companies were held up in front of a solidly built blockhouse but the bulk of the troops 'pushed on into the night. They were now no longer men, they were there to kill. Grenades exploded in the dugouts and screams came from within; elsewhere the Germans rushed out into the snow, some still in stockinged feet. Half-dressed, they dashed towards their weapon-pits through bursts of machine gun fire which forced them to throw themselves flat. Some put up a half-hearted resistance but this was soon broken by the relentless tide of hellish giants that surged all around them.'[26]

One of the most important objectives in the outer German defensive line was Monna Casale, a key bulwark in the massif that lay between the French and the Rapido. Its capture was entrusted to the untried Algerian Division, 7 RTA being the particular regiment selected by General de Monsabert. Not that being untried in combat meant that the Algerians were any less weary than their Moroccan comrades-in-arms. For three days before the attack they had been engaged in moving up stores and munitions to their start line and the acute shortage of mules had meant that much of this equipment had to be carried up on the backs of the men themselves. On the very eve of the attack

all the men not absolutely necessary to secure our defences were thus employed throughout the day . . . even though they had to attack with the next dawn. It seemed as if our Tirailleurs had extended the limits of human resistance. Throughout the day boxes of light and heavy machine gun ammunition, grenades, 81mm shells, 60mm shells, anti-tank grenades, all packed in heavy and awkward bundles of boxes, were slowly carried up, back-breaking work that lacerated hands already raw and tender from the cold. The men poured with sweat despite the temperature. . . . It was without doubt the most arduous phase of the whole battle. . .[27]

It was this same battalion that was to spearhead the Algerian assault against Monna Casale, though their initial objective was an intermediate pair of peaks, the so-called *Jumelles*, that guarded the approaches. An officer in an adjoining battalion described the forbidding landscape that faced the Algerians. 'The tightly packed waves of the grey rocky ridges, their bare crests sparsely covered with reddish-brown scrub, and the dark shadows of the numerous ravines all served to leave a poor impression on the tourist. As for a combatant, he immediately experienced a feeling of unease as he faced this hostile mass, made yet more inhospitable by the climate, which rose up like a mysterious barrier.'[28] The attacking troops could only try and shrug off such feelings of foreboding. The preliminary barrage was a help in this respect, as Monna Casale was 'literally set alight by the explosions of the shells. The noise was infernal . . .'[29] Initial progress was good and by 07.45 on the 12th both of the *Jumelles* had been taken.

Not without casualties, however, particularly amongst the officers. The War Diary of 3/7 RTA gave vent to a complaint that was to be a common feature of French post-combat analyses: 'The . . . young officers . . . led their units forward magnificently. . . . In our North African units the mettle of the Tirailleur depends entirely on his officers. He follows them blindly. The officers thus have to lead by example, to inspire the men. Each leader is destined for the sacrificial altar.'[30] Such selflessness was soon to be needed in its fullest measure. Within minutes of the *Jumelles* being captured their defenders, 3/85 Mountain Regiment, counter-attacked and swept the Algerians off both crests. They established new positions only fifty yards from the summit but concerted pressure seemed certain to drive them back to their start line. Part of a reserve company was called forward by the battalion commander, who said brusquely to the Sergeant-Major:

> 'Mayeux, you can see the peak 10th Company are on. Get going.'
> 'Very well, *mon capitaine*.'
> These were his last words. . . . Without giving any orders he ran towards the objective. His whole platoon followed him. Leadership by example. Heroism stimulating heroism . . . It was a stirring sight, the glittering bayonets climbing towards the 10th as they fell back. The two waves, flux and counterflux, ran one towards the other, met, coalesced . . . and now it was a single wave, running towards the Boche, carrying all before it. Mayeux was the first to the summit. He fell, struck in the face by an exploding grenade.[31]

But the positions were still not secure. At 08.15 the Germans brought down a fearsome barrage on the crests of the *Jumelles*, causing terrible casualties amongst the forward companies. 'Aspirant Mouget was seriously wounded in the legs. A sergeant, whose head had been sliced open, ran by screaming, tearing at his brains with his hands, and fell dead on top of Mouget, increasing the latter's agony.'[32] The companies had no option but to fall back. Immediately the battalion commander came forward and moved amongst them, supervising the distribution of fresh ammunition and trying to restore their flagging morale. For they would have to try again. Sheer willpower would have to make up for the derisory lack of effectives and of any realistic chance of success. A captain gave terse orders to a dazed *sous-lieutenant*:

> 'Piau, the Jumelles. Quickly.'
> 'But, *mon capitaine*, I've neither men nor weapons.'
> 'No matter. Move.'
> 'But I haven't even any bullets in my revolver.'
> 'No matter. Go. Go whatever'
> And *sous-lieutenant* Piau, alone and unarmed, set off to attack the objective.[33]

The Tirailleurs watched incredulously. Two or three emerged from the rocks and began to follow. Other small groups began to rise slowly, only needing someone to actually tell them to go forward. The commander of one company got forty of his men together and said simply: 'You have no officers left. But the 10th Company doesn't need them. Go, take this peak for me.' And they went. Soon the remnants of the whole battalion were surging forward up the rocky slopes. 'The battalion was no longer in the land of the living. The battalion was exalted . . . The spirit of heroism had borne it away. I do not know what drug made them the slaves of a sense of duty carried to the point of self-sacrifice. The battalion was now as unflinching as a block of steel. Their spirits were completely fused together. It was capable of collective madness. It was sublime.'[34] By 12.30 both *Jumelles* were securely held.

The Germans were now in some disarray and the whole Regiment pressed forward to take Monna Casale itself. But the task was still far from easy and once again 3/7 RTA were in the thick of the fighting. A captain described the attack launched in the afternoon of the 12th and not completely carried through until early on the following day. It was

> a battle of grenades, an unequal battle, in which the enemy occupying the heights threw or rolled down grenades on to the Tirailleurs. The latter had to crawl up the slopes . . . to reach a position where they could reach the enemy with their grenades. . . . The Germans . . . had to be attacked each time with bayonets and grenades. If he was overwhelmed he counter-attacked at once. The summit was taken and retaken four times. Each time bayonets and grenades were decisive. . . . More than a thousand grenades were thrown by the two assaulting companies.[35]

With the fall of Monna Casale the French Expeditionary Corps had seized all its initial objectives and effectively overrun the German holding line east of the Rapido. On 15 January, the War Diary of XIV Panzer Corps noted: 'The sector of the 5th Mountain Division continued to be the focal point of battle. . . . Enemy troops, driven back repeatedly, finally succeeded in penetrating at numerous points. In view of the overwhelming enemy pressure it became necessary to order withdrawal to the Gustav Line.'[36] And so the Division, as well as the reinforcement from 115 PG Regiment, began to fall back, soon having to abandon any hope of making an intermediate stand on the Rapido. As a French staff report noted on 15 January: 'The German XIV Panzer Corps, no longer having any immediate reserves to call upon, has been forced to throw into the battle battalions taken from formations fighting [on other parts of the front], in order to counter the French threat on their northern flank. . . . The enemy does not seem capable of re-establishing his front on the line of the Rapido, or of putting up serious resistance there.'[37] After the war, von Senger und Etterlin made it clear just what a critical stage of the battle this had been for the Germans. Although 'the division occupied the [Gustav] positions in an orderly fashion, and brought the attack to a halt at this point, I must confess . . . that on more than one occasion the success of these operations seemed to hang by a thread.'[38]

For over the next four days the French followed hard on the Germans' heels. The Moroccan Division crossed the Rapido and took Points 1040 and 1129 as well as Colle d'Arena. 7 RTA pushed along the line of peaks Monte Passero–Monte Vade d'Aquo–Rio Il Gallo, whilst to the south 3 RTA, having taken Monna Aquafondata and Aquafondata village, pushed through Vallerotonda and then fanned out to seize a line running between Valvori and Sant' Elia. Juin was well satisfied with progress thus far and an operational order of the 17th showed that he was still confident of thrusting forward on his original axis 'to break the centre of the enemy position, towards Monte Bianco, and then without delay to exploit towards San Giuseppe, on the one hand, and Villa Latina and Atina on the other.'[39]

But he could not ignore the fact that his two divisions had already suffered serious casualties and that a major attack on the Gustav Line, mounted before the retreating Germans had time to consolidate, should ideally be spearheaded with fresh reserves. But the Corps had none and General Clark remained unconvinced that Juin's chosen axis merited the redeployment of any Fifth Army divisions. In his memoirs Juin remained critical of this lack of vision:

> With an extra division, it would perhaps have been possible, on the evening of 15 January, to push deeper towards Atina, a vital hinge on which we could develop a broad flanking movement above Cairo and Cassino before descending again into the Liri Valley. But both my divisions were in the line, and somewhat exhausted, and behind them I had nothing left. The plan drawn up by the Anglo-Saxon high command was at fault in that it lacked any logical and clearly defined conception of manoeuvre involving the whole army.[40]

But Juin was determined to try and push forward, no matter how meagre his resources. After four days' regrouping the attack on the Gustav Line opened on the 21st. The Algerian push was again spearheaded by 7 RTA, aiming this time at Monte Carella. To their right were two Moroccan regiments, 5 RTM on the extreme right, driving towards Monte San Croce, and 4 RTM in the centre, trying to rupture the defences between these two bastions. The Algerians made good initial progress as they closed right up to the Gustav Line but the actual assault on Monte Carella, on the 23rd, failed. The regimental commander forwarded a report on the fighting:

The fighting in this sector became extremely confused because of the use of smoke shells and the zero visibility. The battalion mortars were unable to do anything to help the forward company. . . . When the battalion got close to the crest (about 100 yards) heavy small arms fire was unleashed on the leading elements. . . . This fire came from very well protected pillboxes crowning the line of the crest. Our men were by then so close to the enemy that it proved impossible to bring down artillery fire on the crest. Any movement on our part was impossible because of very heavy machine gun fire.[41]

The Algerians were pulled back to their start line during the night and the attack was temporarily abandoned.

Both 4 and 5 RTM also made good progress right up to the Gustav Line. Colle d'Arena and Points 1040 and 1129 had all fallen by late on the 21st, but both Regiments' endeavours to break the line itself failed. 4 RTM were repulsed on the 23rd and their sister Regiment spent four agonizing days in fruitless attacks against Monte San Croce. One Moroccan soldier remembered it as 'a remarkably tough battle at a height of over 5000 feet, the same position changing hands several times. The enemy line . . . [and ours] were so close together that we could hardly distinguish between the Germans and our men.'[42] To make matters worse, just as on Monte Carella, the whole position was swathed in mist and smoke.

A Moroccan divisional report remarked that 'the enemy fought bitterly for San Croce with the strength of about one battalion.'[43] This, in fact, was 3/8 PGR, which had only just come into the line, and the fighting was just as dour for them as it was for the attackers. An Oberleutnant who was taken prisoner said that he 'had never seen the likes of the [Allied] artillery' and that the ensuing casualties were causing 'a manpower crisis which could not be kept secret. Almost everywhere now units were practically at half strength.'[44] A Gefreiter captured on the 21st, who had previously fought in Norway, Greece and Russia, told his interrogator that never had he had to 'endure such violent artillery fire as that on the 21st on San Croce. He spent several hours in his slit trench without being able to move.' His captors were also able to read his diary, whose fragmentary entries were the most convincing proof of the desperate German situation:

12 January. Constantly on alert. Morale is dropping.
17 January. Climb into positions on Monte San Croce.
18 January. Heavy losses.
20 January. Tonight will be decisive – the assault section will not return, wiped out 500 yards from our positions.

21 January. 04.00. Terrific artillery fire. Huddled in my slit trench, unable to leave it. 14.00. Am a prisoner.

22 January. Treated well, am at my nerves' end.[45]

Yet the Germans were far from ready to break. On the evening of the 23rd an order was handed out to the troops on San Croce, and most other strongpoints along the Gustav Line, which said: 'The Führer orders that the Gustav position be held at all costs, bearing in mind that a completely successful defence will have political repercussions. The Führer expects every yard of ground to be bitterly defended.'[46] Such exhortations were not without their effect on the troops. Even those who set no great store by Hitler himself generally had a tremendous pride in their own and their unit's capacity to endure, a pride which could steel them for the most obdurate resistance. Staff officers of the Moroccan Division scanned the POW interrogation reports with great interest, yet at the height of the San Croce battle they were forced to conclude:

> This fighting has caused heavy losses in 8 PGR. Artillery and mortar bombardments have decimated its companies. The 11th Company, after four days of combat, is reduced to a dozen men. Four Prussian officers, two of them company commanders, have been taken prisoner. Whether the sons of good families or soldiers risen from the ranks, they all show the same faith in German victory. They are too deeply convinced of the incontrovertible superiority of the German soldier to seriously admit the possibility of defeat. Their demeanour varies according to temperament and education, but the certainty is always the same: the German infantryman will prevail, because the German race must prevail.[47]

On the 25th the War Diary of the Moroccan Division sadly admitted: 'On the advice of the commander of 2nd Division and of 5 RTM the idea of retaking San Croce has been abandoned. . . "the game being not worth the candle".'[48]

Both French divisions had now ground to a halt and the French high command was obliged to admit that the assault on the Gustav Line would have to be temporarily abandoned. For not only were the French exhausted, and their opponents proving far more resilient than anyone had expected, but, in some respects at least, the German position had actually improved since the beginning of the offensive. Like the rest of the Cassino front, the French sector was the responsibility of General von Senger und Etterlin, and once he had ascertained the axis of the French attacks he concentrated a large proportion of his artillery just where it could provide the greatest all-round protection:

From the still intact forward line of 5 Mountain Division on Monte Cifalco, I could ... get a view of the arc of the enemy's penetration. ... As ... [Monte Cifalco] was the front and an excellent vantage point ... I concentrated all the artillery there that was covering the arc of penetration as far as Cassino. The eventual defensive success can be ascribed among other factors to this operational use of artillery.[49]

But Monte Cifalco was more than a convenient vantage-point or fire base. It was also a tremendous psychological weapon for the Germans in that their opponents *knew* that all their movements could be watched and bombarded at will, whilst they themselves could do little about it. The historian of the Algerian Division described it as 'a kind of personal enemy ... a sort of Argus whose innumerable eyes each convoy or battery commander felt were fixed on him, a bird of prey ready to swoop, with a massed mortar barrage, upon any badly camouflaged assemblage.'[50] In the end the problem becomes one not just of tactical but also of moral advantage, considerations that will come very much to the fore when we discuss the German positions on the Cassino massif and the vexed question of the bombing of the Monastery.

For the moment, then, the French had shot their bolt and the Gustav Line remained relatively intact. Yet they had already won one very important battle and from now on only an inveterate Francophobe could claim that their troops were not of the finest stamp. Few such remained. In late January the German newspaper for the Italian theatre, *Süd Front*, felt 'obliged to grant that the French troops have versatile commanders ... and are willing to get to grips and to press forward when we attempt to break contact. ... [We must also acknowledge] the dash and ... the offensive spirit of the Algerian and Moroccan divisions of the CEF.'[51] The British and Americans had attached various liaison officers to the French units during the January offensive and one of them, Colonel Robert T. Shaw, with 7 RTA, noted of one attack: 'I had the occasion to move forward with the advancing troops: there were no stragglers; nor were any weapons or equipment abandoned. I was able to see numerous dead Germans; many showed the signs of bayonet wounds; some had their skulls caved in. morale excellent: very few prisoners have been taken.'[52]

Yet the French did not simply rest on their laurels. Even during the hardest fighting, commanders at all levels were analysing their own and German methods, eagerly trying to formulate the most effective way of breaking down such stubborn defences. Reports flew thick and fast and those of two battalion commanders are well worth citing, both as relative newcomers' descriptions of the realities of 'mechanized' warfare and as a foretaste of the superb tactical flexibility that the French were to display during the May battles. With regard to the latter, the commander of 1/3 RTA laid particular emphasis upon the need to be prepared at any moment to make the transition from frontal attack to a speedy and deep exploitation of any breakthrough:

> It seems that there is one thing very difficult to sense. The moment, that is, when audacity ought to take complete precedence over prudence . . . However, this is a crucial question, for from that precise moment speed should be the only tactical consideration.
> . . . Any hesitation, any delay, any lack of audacity, simply allows the enemy to pull back at the least cost and perhaps restore the situation.
> One must have an intense intellectual awareness of the progress of the fighting. Neither tiredness, shortage of ammunition nor casualties, no matter how heavy, should allow any deviation whatever from this idea of speed.[53]

The commander of 2/8 RTM concerned himself more with the attack itself and the qualities an infantryman would be called upon to show at the decisive moment. His remarks should be borne in mind throughout the rest of this book, as an incisive summary of the essential nature of the infantryman's war, a war that had changed so little over the centuries:

> . . . as far as infantry fighting is concerned, I am more than ever convinced that *the standard infantry action consists in a body of attackers seeking hand-to-hand combat.* Bear in mind that all advances in armament over the centuries have only aimed at one thing: to fire from as far away as possible to avoid this hand-to-hand combat which men fear. The job of the infantry is to break through the enemy lines; to do that they must get in among these lines. In an attack, no matter how powerful the artillery and the heavy weapons, there comes the moment when the infantryman gets close to the enemy lines, all support ceases, and he must mount the charge that is his last argument, his sole *raison d'être.* Such is the infantryman's war . . . [and] the object of his training should be to prepare him for what one might call 'the battle of the last hundred metres'.

To British and American ears, in particular, much of this might have seemed to have a rather mystical ring, redolent of a suicidal affirmation of *human* capabilities that paid scant attention to the realities of modern technology. Such a judgement would have been unfair, for the writer, Commandant Delort, had had plenty of combat experience himself. It was simply that this experience had forced him to realize that a battle that hinges on the retention or seizure of an area of ground must, in the last analysis, depend upon the willingness of the attacker to occupy it physically. In no way, however, did Delort see his troops as supermen or *berserkers* who could triumph in combat by a pure act of will. A little later in his report he ridiculed those newspaper correspondents who so lauded the French infantrymen that they seemed invincible and invulnerable: 'By trying to ennoble the fighting man they more often ridicule him. I say to you that it is ordinary men who do the fighting and it is all on a human scale. Our troops are excellent . . . but beware of being needlessly disillusioned. In battle there is fear, there are the wounded who cry out . . . and . . . it is always the infantryman whose job is the hardest and sometimes the least understood.'[54]

4
'Dig or Die'
x British Corps on the Garigliano,
17 January–9 February 1944

. . . it would appear doubtful if the enemy can hold the
organized defensive line through Cassino against a co-
ordinated Army attack . . . [and he will] withdraw from his
defensive position once he has appreciated the magnitude of
that operation.

Fifth Army HQ, 16 January

The enemy remains firm . . . [and] our troops have now been
fighting for seven days and are tired. No further advance can
be expected on the Corps front for some days unless the enemy
withdraws.

x Corps HQ, 24 January

According to Clark's plan of 10 January, the French Expeditionary Corps
offensive was not the only shot in the Allied locker. The Fifth Army
commander had called for attacks on both flanks of the Gustav Line and
accordingly, late on 17 January, British x Corps launched a three-division
assault across the Garigliano and Gari Rivers. However, even before
these attacks began, it was apparent that the British plan differed in one
very important respect from Clark's. For the latter, the efforts of both the
French and x Corps were only secondary attacks, albeit on a fairly large
scale, meant to support operations in the Liri Valley where II US Corps
was to make the decisive thrust. The French, as we have seen, were to
provide support by drawing German units away from the central sector
and this was also part of the rationale of the British offensive, in which
a part of their forces was to try and unbalance the Germans by a vigorous
exploitation up the Ausente Valley towards San Giorgio a Liri. But that
was not the primary task. This was to lend direct support to the American
effort in the Liri Valley and, in the words of Clark's Operation
Instruction, to 'force a crossing of the Liri . . . in the general vicinity of
San Ambrogio . . . exploit to the west . . . [and] maintain contact with
II Corps.'[1] However, the actual allocation of divisions for these two
operations was left up to the x Corps commander, General Richard
McCreery, and he chose to use two, the 5th and the 56th, to carve out
the Garigliano bridgehead and only the lone 46 Division to attempt the

much more difficult task of gaining a foothold on the edge of the Liri Valley. This switch of emphasis was to have important repercussions when II Corps actually did attack.

Clearly, McCreery had far less faith than Clark in the possibilities of a decisive breakthrough into the Liri Valley and so committed only the minimum number of troops commensurate with the Army Orders. But this was not mere wilfulness on his part. He had to accord one of his two tasks a much lower priority simply because he did not have enough men to perform both of them adequately. We have already had cause to note the effect of inadequate reserves on Juin's operations and, at the very beginning of the January offensive, General A.F. Harding, Alexander's Chief of Staff, was convinced that Clark did not have enough men to attain all his objectives. As for X Corps, Clark himself admitted that 'the British divisions in the Fifth Army were tired from months, and even years, of constant fighting, but . . . few replacements were available, owing to their loss of officers and men.'[2] In fact, so acute was the shortage of men that even after keeping the Liri Valley assault force to the barest minimum, McCreery could hold back only one Commando Brigade as a freely disposable reserve.

But this was not the only problem facing the British. Except for the swampy fringes of the Garigliano itself, the area to be attacked was typically mountainous terrain, with few roads or even tracks leading into the seemingly endless rings of peaks that overlooked the river. In such terrain motor transport was virtually useless and only mules provided an acceptable alternative. Unfortunately, after five months of mountain fighting, the whole of X Corps possessed barely one thousand mules, hardly enough to supply the ordinary infantrymen let alone the mortars, machine guns and forward artillery. Throughout the offensive mules had to be replaced by human porters and the paucity of Pioneer Corps men inevitably meant that the already overstretched fighting battalions had to use their own men to keep the supplies flowing forward.

Not that the Germans were ever content to rely simply upon terrain as nature intended it. As the whole German front was now behind the Gustav Line, and as the British were to be the first to make any real dent in it, this is an appropriate place in which to examine its defences in a little detail. Construction had begun in autumn 1943, under the supervision of Pioneer General Bessell, and in October extra Todt Organization personnel had been drafted in to ensure the highest standards of workmanship. In November Hitler began to take great personal interest in these defences. Concerned that the positions in central Italy should be as strong as possible he not only authorized the construction of a whole series of fall-back, or switch positions, behind the Gustav Line proper, but he also speeded up the flow of materials into the main *Stellung*. Prominent among these latter were a hundred steel shelters, to provide the inner skin of large dugouts, and seventy-six armoured pillboxes. These, weighing three tons each, had their own towing platforms and once in position were dug into the ground to shelter a two-man heavy machine gun crew. Known officially as casemates, they were usually referred to by the German soldiers as 'armoured crabs'.

Large quantities of concrete were also utilized, mostly to build pillboxes, some large enough to contain sleeping accommodation for twenty or thirty men, others just big enough to squeeze in a light machine gun and a charcoal brazier. Many of these pillboxes were connected one with the other by subterranean passages and most also had exits that led directly into the infantry fire-trenches. Whenever possible existing buildings were made an integral part of the defensive line. In many farmsteads and villages small inner rooms were built into the ground floors of the buildings and these were walled and roofed with heavy logs and thick layers of crushed stone. Even direct hits with large-calibre artillery shells often failed to knock out such positions. The surrounding hills provided the Germans with superb observation posts from which they could direct the fire of the mortars, sited on the reverse slopes, and of the artillery massed somewhat further back.

The actual approaches to the main defence line, which in the Garigliano sector were sited 1000 yards beyond the west bank, were little less than a death trap. Mines were everywhere, at least 24,000 of them. Many were the vicious S-42 anti-personnel or Schümine. Only about ten pounds pressure was needed to detonate it, the most common result being the blowing off or mangling of a man's foot. Common, too, was the 's' mine which threw a small charge into the air, at about groin height, before it exploded with an inevitably ghastly effect. Most of the smaller mines were housed in wooden casings which made it almost impossible to locate them with ordinary detectors. Barbed wire was also laid in lavish abundance and should any attackers succeed in penetrating these obstacles the whole area was also covered by numerous machine guns, precisely sited to ensure interlocking fields of fire, especially around the most likely avenues of approach.

But the Germans did not passively put their trust in concrete, steel, bullets and shells. Far from simply staying crouched in his dugout or pillbox, the German infantryman was expected at all times to try and gain the initiative by constant probing and harassment of the attacking troops. A German divisional order of the period observed that 'the mission of the fusiliers is above all to send out reconnaissance parties and patrols to ensure the safety of the heavy weapons, to take part in close-quarters fighting, and to conduct counter-attacks.'[3] It was the latter that were the very linch-pin of German defensive tactics, as the French had already discovered to their cost. One battalion commander's report had this to say about the method and rationale of such attacks:

> Counter-attacks are *the classic method* by which the Germans defend a position. A unit mounting an attack on its objective or having just occupied it is generally the object of a local counter-attack, carried out by few men but those being very well led by one or two keen officers or warrant officers. They know the ground perfectly and are well aware how effective can be this kind of short, sharp attack on partially exhausted troops who think they have definitely secured the objective . . . [Too often] the position, occupied a few minutes before, is retaken by the Germans who scrupulously avoid pursuing our men so as not to get caught by the artillery on our fire base. And the peak, once again apparently void of defenders, is occupied by a few snipers, automatic weapons and the bodies of our men which we have had to abandon.[4]

All in all, General McCreery had little reason to feel very optimistic about the forthcoming battle. His men were under-strength and weary, faced with the grim prospect of an assault river crossing and an advance against some of the strongest German defences yet encountered. The men manning these defences, 94 Division, were well up to strength, had had a long period of rest out of the line, and were as experienced as any unit in the techniques of flexible positional defence. But Clark dearly wanted a decisive breakthrough on the Cassino front to compensate for the endless frustrations of the previous months. His concern had obviously communicated itself to his staff and a report prepared by Fifth Army G-2,* on 16 January, seems to have owed a lot more to wishful thinking than to a balanced assessment of the magnitude of the task ahead. Many at X Corps headquarters were less than convinced when they read that

* At Army, Corps and Divisional level most staffs were organized in the same way. Below is a comparative listing of the major subdivisions and their basic responsibilities:

	AMERICAN	FRENCH	BRITISH	GERMAN
Personnel	G–1	1^e Bureau	AA & QMG	IIa/IIb
Intelligence	G–2	2^e Bureau	G I	Ic
Operations & Planning	G–3	3^e Bureau	G OPS	Ia
Logistics	G–4	4^e Bureau	DAQMG	Ib

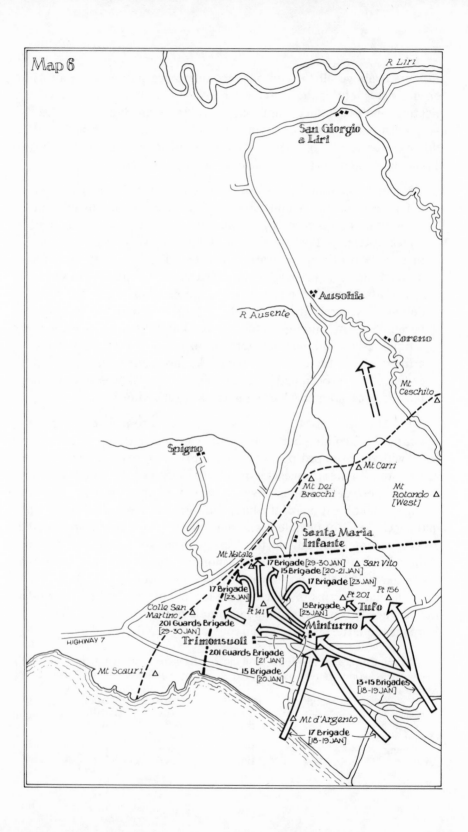

Map 6

R Liri

San Giorgio
a Liri

Ausonia

R Ausente

Coreno

Mt
Ceschito

Spigno

Mt Carri

Mt Dei
Bracchi

Mt
Rotondo
[WEST]

Santa María
Infante

Mt Natale

17 Brigade [29-30 JAN]   San Vito

15 Brigade [20-21 JAN]

17 Brigade [23 JAN]   Pt 156

17 Brigade
[23 JAN]

Pt 141   13 Brigade   Pt 201   Tufo
         [23 JAN]

Colle San
Martino   Minturno

201 Guards Brigade
[29-30 JAN]

HIGHWAY 7

Trimonsuoli

201 Guards Brigade
[21 JAN]

15 Brigade
[20 JAN]

Mt Scauri

13 + 15 Brigades
[18-19 JAN]

Mt d'Argento

17 Brigade
[18-19 JAN]

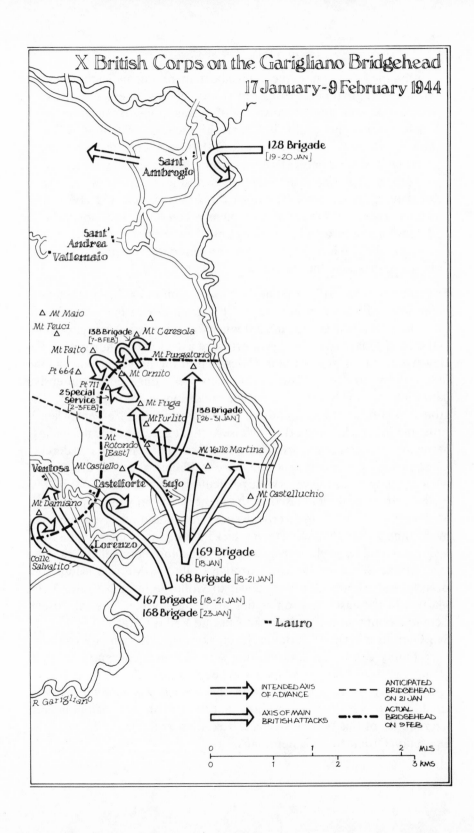

X British Corps on the Garigliano Bridgehead
17 January - 9 February 1944

128 Brigade
[19-20 JAN]

Sant'
Ambrogio

Sant'
Andrea
Vallemaio

△ Mt Maio
Mt Feuci
△
138 Brigade   △ Mt Ceresola
[7-8 FEB]
Mt Faito   △ Mt Purgatorio
△
Pt 664 △   △ Mt Ornito
Pt 711
2 Special
Service   △ Mt Fuga
[2-3 FEB]   △
                MtPurlito   138 Brigade
                             [26-31 JAN]
                Mt
                Rotondo △   Mt Valle Martina
                [East]
Ventosa   Mt Castiello △
              Castelforte   △
                          Sujo   △ Mt Castelluchio
Mt Damiano
△
                              169 Brigade
                              [18 JAN]
Lorenzo
                              168 Brigade [18-21 JAN]
Colle
Salvatito △
              167 Brigade [18-21 JAN]
              168 Brigade [23 JAN]
                                  ∴ Lauro

R Garigliano

⇢ INTENDED AXIS OF ADVANCE	- - - ANTICIPATED BRIDGEHEAD ON 21 JAN
⇨ AXIS OF MAIN BRITISH ATTACKS	-·-·- ACTUAL BRIDGEHEAD ON 9 FEB

0   1   2   MLS
0   1   2   3 KMS

Within the last few days there have been increasing indications that
enemy strength on the Fifth Army front is ebbing, due to casualties,
exhaustion, and possibly lowering of morale. One of the causes of
this condition, no doubt, has been the recent, continuous Allied
attacks. From this it can be deduced that he has no fresh reserves
and very few tired ones. His entire strength will probably be needed
to defend his organized defensive positions. In view of the
weakening of enemy strength on the front as indicated above it
would appear doubtful if the enemy can hold the organized
defensive line through Cassino against a co-ordinated Army attack
. . . [and he will have] to withdraw from his defensive position once
he has appreciated the magnitude of that operation. [5]

The men of the rifle battalions would doubtless have contented
themselves with a weary 'Oh yeah?' For even before the attack began
conditions along the Garigliano left much to be desired. A few gay blades
in the Scots Guards did manage to organize a duck shoot shortly after the
New Year, but most front-line troops shared the nerve-racking routine
followed by 10 Royal Berkshires, who were engaged in 'intensive
patrolling . . . for ten days. . . . The conditions were unpleasant. The
ground was often flooded and the mud was shin-deep, except when it
froze and ice cracked underfoot. Noise at night became a second enemy,
betraying and threatening friend and foe alike – loose shutters on derelict
houses banging suddenly, and the more insidious rasping of the wind in
the wires supporting the vines were particularly frightening.'[6]

The mental strain increased as the night of the crossing approached.
McCreery's aims in the main crossing area were ambitious. He hoped that
by the time II Corps launched their attack into the Liri Valley, on the 20th,
X Corps would be well on the way to establishing a bridgehead running
from Monte Scauri in the west, through Colle San Martino, Monte dei
Bracchi and Monte Ceschito, down to Colle Siola and Monte Valle
Martina in the east. As soon as this bridgehead was secure the British
were to mount a strong push up the Ausente Valley towards Ausonia and
San Giorgio a Liri. At battalion level, however, the primary concerns
were purely day-to-day and the first sets of orders concentrated upon
getting the troops across the river and keeping them there. Their laconic
style offers a striking contrast with the French post-combat analyses
already cited, yet they clearly show that the British, too, had pondered
the realities of this type of warfare. Take, for example, Point 22 of the
Operation Orders for 2 Cameronians:

Warn all ranks
a) No-one except a stretcher-bearer or a wounded man helps a wounded man out of action. . .
c) Silence is vital. Noise will cost lives. No coughs. Tools and equipment padded. No light. No smoking.
d) German tactics are to evacuate position and then put in immediate counter-attack with grenades and tommy guns.
e) It is fatal to halt when mortared. Once you are in among his troops he will stop mortaring.
f) Dig or die.[7]

The crossings began late on the 17th and by the next morning all first-wave units had got across. Casualties had been heavy, however, particularly in 5 Division, to the east, whose 13 and 17 Brigades were spearheading the attack. The latter was on the left, the extreme flank being guarded by 2 Royal Scots Fusiliers, who had a particularly grim time of it. They were to take Monte d'Argento, a large mound near the seashore from which the Germans could enfilade a considerable stretch of the Garigliano. Two companies of Fusiliers were to land from the sea in DUKWs and capture it, after which the other two were to pass through and drive on Minturno. The first stage went badly awry and was not without its farcical elements. One company's DUKW was ineluctably drawn out to sea and eventually floated alongside a cruiser. They were about to hail her to ask directions when a submarine suddenly popped up immediately to port:

Uncertain of its nationality the Fusiliers manned their PIAT and were about to sink it when a head popped out of the conning tower and shouted:
'Who the hell are you?'
'Royal Scots Fusiliers,' was the prompt and somewhat relieved reply.
'Never heard of you,' was the even prompter rejoinder as the hatch closed and the submarine submerged.[8]

Humour was noticeably absent for the rest of the day. The DUKW-borne companies became widely dispersed and the attack on Monte d'Argento was delayed. When 'A' Company finally did set off they were checked by thick wire and intense mortar fire. Their own weapons were hopelessly choked with damp sand and the company, having lost all its officers, was obliged to withdraw. Another attack could not be mounted until late on the 18th and this only succeeded because the Germans had decided to pull back.

This was a grave setback for 5 Division, whose timetable envisaged the other battalions of 17 Brigade, 6 Seaforth Highlanders and 2 Northamptonshires, joining in the push on Minturno early on the 18th. This was now clearly impossible, and would, indeed, have been far from straightforward even if the Fusiliers' attack had gone according to plan. For both of the supporting battalions had experienced considerable difficulty in getting across the river. 2 Northants, on the right, managed to establish themselves fairly securely, though they lost many men in the thick minefields on each bank. 6 Seaforths had an even worse time of it, as their own account of the operation shows. Their boats had only been brought up to within a mile of the river and

> it was an awkward, back-breaking job carrying the boats forward. . . . With each boat were . . . about 20 men in all, all helping to carry but already encumbered by their own personal loads . . . [On the edge of the river] the first mines were met . . . Lt John Holcroft, in charge of the special patrol and covering parties . . . was walking back . . . on his way to contact the boats coming up, when he stood on a mine. His left foot was blown off. Major Low and Major Mackenzie were moving up to join him and were both blinded by the explosion. . . . Major Low ordered the boats to go in. Lt McKee was in charge of the leading boat, with half of 7 Platoon. He stepped on a mine right underneath the [guidance] tape. Lt Cargill took over and the boats moved on, always nearer the water. He stood on a mine.[9]

Numerous other ranks were also killed and wounded but the majority of the survivors somehow managed to get across and reach the main road just south of Minturno. At first light, however, they were discovered by the Germans and counter-attacked by tanks and infantry. 'A' Company was forced to withdraw, after which the Germans turned their attentions to 'C' and 'D' Companies. The former was virtually encircled by tanks – they had but one PIAT and the ammunition for that was at the bottom of the river – when an artillery observer joined them and was able to bring down a pinpoint 'stonk' that compelled the armour to pull back. 'D' Company was not so lucky. Their attackers gradually closed in and, after the failure of an attempted breakout,

> they decided to make a stand in the positions they had captured. . . . They fought there for hours against tank and infantry attacks, being steadily mortared and without support from their own guns. They were reduced to a handful and they still fought on. Eventually

the Company Commander gave the order for each man to make a break for it and try to get back as best he could. A few minutes later he was killed by machine gun fire. Only one man got back.[10]

So critical was 17 Brigade's situation that the Divisional commander was obliged to alter his plans and straightway bring up his reserve Brigade, the 15th, which had originally been earmarked for exploitation towards Ausonia. Their War Diary explained: 'At first light [on the 18th] . . . a liaison officer from 5 Division arrived to say that the battle had not gone quite according to plan and that . . . instead of being held back to pass through 17 Inf. Brigade on about D + 3 . . . [We] would now be at one hour's notice to . . . attack Minturno from the east, thus relieving the pressure on 17 Inf. Brigade who were still pinned on the line of the river.'[11] This order soon came and once again, even though they were covering some of the same ground as earlier battalions, mines proved a dreadful hazard. The account by 1 King's Own Yorkshire Light Infantry gives the flavour of the march northwards from the river, not under way until after dark:

It was difficult and unpleasant, mines were a very real danger and a single-line track had been marked across country with tapes by the Royal Engineers. This may well have been good enough for single men in daylight, but for heavily laden men in the dark it was a nightmare, despite the new moon. It was like marching across a mined Romney Marsh, deep dykes and ditches every hundred yards. . . . No guides, as promised by the higher staff, had arrived and . . . the result was that . . . ['B'] Company walked straight into a minefield. One platoon was practically wiped out . . . and it took the rest of the night to extract the men from the heavily mined area and by the next morning 'B' Company . . . were in a low state and not really fit to go straight into the difficult attack.[12]

Attacking on the right of 17 Brigade was the 13th, with two battalions in the line, 2 Wiltshires on the left and 2 Inniskilling Fusiliers to their right. They made better progress than their sister Brigade, though the War Diary noted that by first light on the 18th 'heavy casualties had been suffered by both battalions from small arms fire, mines, mortars and artillery. . . . The enemy positions had been overrun but there were sections of infantry and snipers still in the area.'[13] For the Inniskillings, the worst moments had been at the river's edge where they found that the boats supposedly brought up by another battalion were not there. Two were eventually uncovered just before H-Hour and a few more arrived shortly afterwards. The leading platoons crossed in these but the bulk of the men had to go hotfoot to the Wiltshires' embarkation point whence they eventually got across. By evening the Wiltshires had cleared part of Tufo village and the Inniskillings were just below Point 156, having at one stage occupied it but been driven off by a local counter-attack.

The attack in the western half of X Corps' sector was the responsibility of 56 Division. Their right was occupied by the Queen's Brigade (169th) who made probably the most successful crossing of the day. By nightfall on the 18th the whole Brigade was solidly established in Sujo and along the ridge that ran east into Monte Valle Martina. The advance was not without cost, however. On the right, 2/5 Queen's suffered many casualties from mortar fire and in an attack on the 19th had their numbers made up with a squadron from 44 Reconnaissance Regiment. The idea was a bad one, reminiscent of the tactical hamfistedness of the First World War. 'They attacked on foot most gallantly but were not trained or equipped for infantry fighting and suffered heavy casualties.'[14]

167 Brigade were properly trained and equipped yet they had the greatest difficulty in even approaching their objectives – the heavily fortified triangle of Lorenzo–Ventosa–Castelforte and the protecting hill-mass of Colle Salvatito and Monte Damiano. Colle Salvatito was the responsibility of 9 Royal Fusiliers and the Official History's assertion that they 'crossed without difficulty'[15] seems a little bland. The river itself may have presented no real obstacle but as soon as they reached the far bank the leading companies were 'held up by strong opposition covering the railway embankment. "D" Company commander killed and many other casualties. Tac HQ moved along wrong railway embankment and walked into enemy machine gun post. . . . CO and Adjutant missing after scrap with enemy. Wireless communication nil. . . . Railway reached, no other companies there.'[16] Thus the battalion's War Diary. Commanders of the accompanying machine gun platoons, from 6 Cheshires, painted an even grimmer picture. One lieutenant reported: 'We had reached a crossroads when someone came towards us. He turned out to be the CO of 9 Royal Fusiliers who asked us if we had seen his Tac HQ troops. . . . He was bleeding from the mouth and looked as if he had had a rough time. . . . His advice was to carry on.' Another lieutenant summed up his experiences on the 18th by simply saying that the day's fighting 'involved the complete disorganisation of the infantry'.[17] Luckily their sister battalion, 8 Royal Fusiliers, along with 7 Oxfordshire and Buckinghamshire Light Infantry, faced somewhat lighter opposition. The Fusiliers got to within striking distance of the summit of Monte Damiano whilst the Ox and Bucks cleared and occupied Lorenzo. This allowed 9

Royal Fusiliers some respite in which to reorganize and by nightfall on the 18th they had reached Colle Salvatito.

Nevertheless, on 167 Brigade's front, as elsewhere, the British advance was already falling behind schedule. It had been hoped that in the first twenty-four hours 56 Division would have reached a line running from Monte Rotondo (West) through Colle Siola, whilst 5 Division was supposed to be firmly in place along the high ground linking Monte Scauri, Monte Natale and San Vito. As so often, however, German resilience had been seriously underestimated and too little account taken of the precision with which they could deploy their substantial firepower. Perhaps the worst surprise of all had been the sheer quantity of the mines scattered along the whole front, whose profusion caused 5 Division to claim: 'Taken completely by surprise the enemy has only been saved from complete destruction by the thick maze of mines . . . spread between the Garigliano and the Minturno ridge. The coastal belt indeed may almost be described as a mine marsh through which the sure paths can [only] now be traced with the aid of the original plans we captured.'[18]

Yet at least these two Divisions were across the river. 46 Division, whose attack was timed for the 19th, was not even to achieve this. The operation, it will be recalled, was primarily intended to support the forthcoming drive by II US Corps into the Liri Valley. Only one Brigade, the 128th, was committed to the initial assault, which seemed to the Americans further proof that McCreery's heart was not in any substantial operation in this sector. In the event, however, his parsimony was probably for the best. For, a few hours before the crossing was to be made, the Germans opened up the sluices of the San Giovanni dam and by H-Hour the river had become a torrent, flowing much faster and some six feet deeper than usual. Just getting the boats up had been difficult enough. 'Sapper vehicles were blown up on mines and the bridge over the Peccia had been demolished. Consequently . . . [the company] selected to handle the boats and row them over the river had to offload the boats on the far side of the Peccia and manhandle them . . . into position for the crossing of the Garigliano.'[19] But the spate was too much. One company of 2 Hampshires did get across and rigged a cable to help the boats behind. But this soon fouled and as it broke several boats were swept downstream. A thick mist then descended and other boats, spun round in the erratic current, even became uncertain of which bank they were aiming for. The other assault battalion, 1/4 Hampshires, made equally little headway, fourteen attempts to just get a line across all ending in failure. The Germans now began to take notice of these exertions and on the 20th, 'owing to accurate DF fire and rapidly nearing dawn the attack was called off by the Brigade Commander.'[20]

The whole incident raises several questions. The official record, both published and unpublished, is very reticent about it, but it does seem somewhat strange that 46 Division made no further attempt to force a crossing at this point, even though the level and speed of the river had returned to normal by the 20th. The Hampshire Brigade, in fact, remained in its original jumping-off positions for the next four days, obviously somewhat shaken by its experience. No attempt, however, was made to bring up one of the other brigades, either to support a renewed effort by the Hampshires or to attempt a crossing of their own. Instead, one of them, 138th, was immediately moved round to 56 Division's bridgehead, where it relieved the Queen's Brigade around Monte Valle Martina, and the other, 139th, played little part in the rest of the Garigliano battle. It does seem difficult to avoid the conclusion that the British were at best half-hearted in their commitment to the projected attack by II Corps and that a by no means decisive check was enough to make them shrug off the unwanted responsibility of establishing some protection for its left flank.

Not that X Corps did not have cause to be concerned about its own position. On the 18th it had only had to face local counter-attacks by the German 94 Division. These continued on the 19th but by now German commanders were reacting at the highest level and ordering redeployments that would ensure a swift and powerful strategic response to the British attack. Even on the 18th it had been the consensus that here was a major Allied offensive against which the troops of 94 Division were simply not adequate. According to von Senger und Etterlin, General Steinmetz, the division's commander, 'was a capable, calm officer. . . . He saw things as they were in reality, that is, he knew that in effect the division was faced with a mission impossible to fulfil. . . . When, on 18 January, I paid the general another visit at his command post I was compelled to concur entirely with his pessimistic evaluation of the situation.'[21] Senger immediately placed a call to Kesselring, and as soon as the latter was also convinced of the desperate situation he began to cast his net far and wide in the search for reserves.

Outlying battalions of 94 Division were concentrated in the critical sector, along with all available clerks, drivers and such. Three battalions of 15 PG Division were taken from the Liri Valley to be used, along with 2 Hermann Göring PGR, as an immediate reserve for 94 Division. 134 Regiment (44 Division), as well as the Reconnaissance Battalions of 44, 71 and 3 PG Divisions, were all earmarked as potential further reserves in this sector, whilst the latter Division's relief of 5 Mountain Division was halted and its commander alerted for a possible move to the south. Most important of all, Kesselring allocated his Army Group Reserve, 29 and 90 PG Divisions, to von Senger und Etterlin's XIV Panzer Corps. The former was ordered to make an initial move to the Esperia–Ausonia area and the latter to Priverno, thirty miles west of Ausonia, both to be ready for immediate commitment in the bridgehead. All these orders had been given by the evening of the 18th, even before Kesselring had found time, early the following day, to telegraph the OKW about his decisions. He need not have worried, however, for such a vigorous determination not to give up to ground was very dear to Hitler's heart and the Field-Marshal had the rare satisfaction of having none of his orders countermanded or even questioned. Early in the afternoon of the 19th, Kesselring and Vietinghoff agreed that the Army Group Reserve must be committed early the next day, even though 29 PG Division would have to attack alone, the 90th being stuck around Priverno with hardly any petrol and under constant air attack. A little later Kesselring defined his *ne plus ultra* line, running from Monte Scauri, through Minturno and Castelforte, to Monte Purgatorio.

The next six days, from the 19th to the 24th, saw some of the bitterest fighting in the Garigliano battle, as renewed British attacks ran into fierce counter-attacks, whose tempo and determination only mounted with each successive day. Things went reasonably well at first in 5 Division's sector where, on the 19th, the hastily committed 15 Brigade were able to take their immediate objectives. By nightfall 1 Green Howards had cleared Minturno and 1 KOYLI, despite their arduous march forward, had firmly established themselves in Tufo, allowing the Brigade to push its front line forward to Points 141 and 201. This advance had been made through 13 Brigade, whose 2 Wiltshires were now some distance to the rear. 2 Inniskillings, however, found themselves to the immediate right of 15 Brigade and were subjected to a fierce counter-attack from the vicinity of Point 156. This was repulsed, though the attackers showed a zeal worthy of a comic-strip artist's most fertile imagination: 'Evidently surprise was hoped for by them, for the first advance was stealthy. When vigilance on our part was shown the Germans rushed up with clamorous yelling: "Give up, Tommy, you are surrounded." One German officer, shouting to his men to slaughter the *"Schweinhunde Englander"* got so close as to be able to seize one of our Vickers guns. . .'[22]

Further progress was made by 15 Brigade on the 20th. The Green Howards attacked west to take Trimonsuoli whilst the reserve battalion, 1 York and Lancasters, seized Monte Natale. The whole Division was running out of steam, however, and when a fourth Brigade, 201 Guards, temporarily attached, was committed on the 21st it had to abandon its original plan of attacking towards Monte Scauri and instead used its battalions to bolster up the existing line. 3 Coldstreams and 6 Grenadiers replaced the Green Howards in Trimonsuoli and 2 Scots Guards went to the aid of the York and Lancs who had been almost immediately pushed off Monte Natale. Both these positions were heavily counter-attacked over the next two days, as was I KOYLI in Tufo. The latter were now facing units of 90 PG Division who seemed, like their colleagues just cited, to regard themselves as storm-troopers in the fullest sense of the word and 'they came in all talking, shouting and using many English phrases such as "You've had it, Tommy" and "Stick them up, Tommy".'[23] In Trimonsuoli, according to a lieutenant of 3 Coldstreams:

> Companies were subjected to almost non-stop mortar and shell-fire, as the Germans could observe us very clearly from a hill they still held adjoining our position. Things were very fluid. There were counter-attacks and rumours of counter-attacks and at night a great deal of patrolling by the enemy . . . [In Battalion HQ] we used only the ground-floor room which was swarming with hibernating flies and starving fleas. Our plates of food became black and 'murmurous haunts' as the flies descended in hundreds from the rafters.[24]

On the 22nd, 17 Brigade, now somewhat recovered from its disastrous crossing, was put on standby to move to any part of the line that seemed in danger of buckling. But the line just held, despite renewed heavy counter-attacks. 13 Brigade even attempted an attack of its own, against the ridge running west from Point 201. The reserve battalion, 2 Cameronians, was used and an incident in the attack perfectly exemplified Commandant Delort's theories about 'The Battle of the Last 100 Yards'. 'D' Company was in the lead and as they crossed the start line 'the CO. . . encouraged the company forward. The leading platoon moved forward slowly at first and encountered enemy rifle and machine gun fire. One man shouted "Come on the Cams!" and this encouraged the remainder and the whole company moved forward extremely quickly.'[25] Most battalions were content simply to hold their ground, the Green Howards in Minturno, the York and Lancs beneath Monte Natale and 13 Brigade around Tufo and Point 201 all having to withstand intense pressure. The latter point changed hands four times before finally being cleared of the enemy on the 23rd.

On the same day, on Monte Natale, things did not go so well. Two battalions of 17 Brigade were sent forward to try and reach the summit but they ran into difficulties from the outset. On the right were 2 Royal Scots Fusiliers, whose attack was described in their War Diary: 'It was very slow over thick, rough country pitted with numerous ditches and darkness was falling before the objective was reached. . . . The CO, who was himself personally controlling the advance, was fatally wounded. . . . In the bad light the leading companies went too far west and missed the objective, while "C" Company fought on to it alone under heavy opposition.'[26] The attack was observed by men of 1 KOYLI and their War Diary had some tart comments to make: 'Everything seemed hastily prepared and nobody was quite sure of timings . . . [Our] barrage came down and caused so much dust that the . . . Fusiliers were confused. By 18.00 it was learned that . . . [they] had walked into enemy DF . . . and had considerable casualties. The order was given by the Brigade Commander that the attack be withdrawn and they came back in some disorder.'[27] Monte Natale was not in fact taken until the 29th when two battalions of 17 Brigade finally succeeded in reaching the crest. But this was little more than a tidying-up of the line, for by the 24th it had become apparent that 5 Division as a whole was no longer capable of concerted offensive action. On this day the Battalion HQs learnt that 'in view of the opposition which 5 Division had met it had been decided that 56 Division would be the axis of any future advance.'[28]

But 56 Division was hardly in any better shape. As early as the 20th, X Corps noted 'all Brigades of 56 Division are now committed [and] two are tired and low in strength.' On the 24th the Corps Commander was obliged to admit that 'the enemy remains firm. . . . 56 Division troops have now been fighting for seven days and are tired. No further advance can be expected on the Corps front for some days unless the enemy withdraws.'[29] The Queen's Brigade had been very badly hit. On the 21st, two of their companies could only count three officers and thirty-seven other ranks between them. It was to relieve them that 46 Division sent its 138 Brigade south that very night. For some, however, their troubles were not yet over. Whilst recrossing the Garigliano a boat containing ten men from 2/6 Queen's struck a cable and capsized. The men, wearing full battledress, were pitched into the icy water and all were drowned.

For 167 and 168 Brigades the next round of fighting revolved around Monte Damiano and the village of Castelforte. Little progress was made on the 19th as 167 Brigade was mainly preoccupied with holding off German counter-attacks and 168 Brigade was only just preparing to come into the line. Typical of the former's experiences were those of 9 Royal Fusiliers:

Enemy attacking on our front . . . Finally beaten off after grenade battle . . . Enemy active along our front, using machine gun 'prowlers' and snipers . . . Stand to. Enemy forming for counter-attack. DF being fired. Excellent results, attack doesn't materialize. Enemy screaming in terror. Stand down. Enemy still active with spandaus. We are using grenades extensively with good results . . . Enemy 'prowlers' active all day. Using caves as base to work from, which we cannot approach without coming under heavy small arms fire. . . . Enemy attempted to infiltrate all night . . . Nothing very serious. We are using artillery and our mortars with great effect. . . . Everyone very tired. Companies have had no sleep whatever [for three days] as country is so close and enemy can approach unseen to grenade range.[30]

An attack was mounted against Monte Damiano, by 7 Ox & Bucks, but it proved abortive. They dutifully adopted a new attack formation, as specified by the Division, advancing 'in two ranks, riflemen with fixed bayonets and grenades in the front rank, and men with automatic weapons in the second'[31] but were less than pleased to discover that they first had to storm their supposed start line before moving against Damiano. The first attack was successful but even before they had formed up for the second the already exhausted companies were driven back by a sharp counter-attack.

By now, 168 Brigade was beginning to arrive in the line. 7 Ox & Bucks and 8 Royal Fusiliers, around Monte Damiano, were relieved by 10 Royal Berkshires and 1 London Scottish, who at first remained on the defensive. 1 London Irish, however, was ordered to make an immediate attack on Castelforte. They went in on the night of 19/20th but were unable, after two days' fighting, to make more than a small inroad at the west end of the village. The Company that made the deepest penetration was at one stage completely surrounded by Germans, ignorant of their presence, and for a while was able to send back *sotto voce* wireless messages. A few days later a subaltern submitted a splendidly laconic report on this incident, observing that 'the food problem was not acute but the water supply was low. . . . Latrine arrangements were not all that might be desirable, but necessity knows no law. The men behaved splendidly and the day proved an exciting one.'[32]*

But Castelforte was obviously going to be a tough nut to crack and

---

* This kind of stiff-upper-lip understatement is at the very heart of the British military tradition and it remained virtually untouched by the huge influx of 'amateur' officers during the Second World War. In this regard one could not forbear to cite Capt. Grazebrooke of 6 Grenadier Guards who wrote after a savage counter-attack against

attention was switched back to Monte Damiano, whose capture might lead to a complete investment of the village and the slow strangulation of resistance there. On the 23rd, 1 London Scottish and elements of 10 Royal Berks made an attack, but were repulsed. After the attack both sides had to leave considerable numbers of wounded lying out in no man's land and early on the 24th the following incident was recorded by the Royal Berks: 'Stretcher party sent out with Red Cross flags to bring in . . . [the wounded]. This was done without enemy interference. Later a German officer . . . stood up on a ridge and said in good English, "Gentlemen, will you please stop firing while we bring in our wounded." This was done and stretcher parties from both sides collected wounded.'[33] There now followed a temporary lull in the fighting though conditions in the front line still left much to be desired, as is evidenced by these observations in the Royal Berks War Diary:

> It took a laden man 4½ hours to climb to the Battalion area. All water, ammunition and rations had to be carried by hand, as the route was impassable to mules. . . . [It] was frequently shelled . . . String vests and leather jerkins were issued. However, as the Battalion had originally gone up with a view to counter-attacking, they had marched light, *without blankets or greatcoats*, and there was never a sufficiency of porters to bring these up. The cold proved a definite hardship.[34]

The final attempt to take Monte Damiano was made on the 29th, in conjunction with 5 Division's successful attack on Monte Natale. Fresh units were brought up, the principal effort being made by 2 and 1/4 Hampshires, now somewhat recovered from their abortive assault across the upper Garigliano. Fresh or not, however, the Hampshires were unable to make any progress against the dour defenders. The War Diary of 2 Hants noted tersely: 'Attack unsuccessful owing to unexpected nature of ground and excessive use of grenades by the enemy.'[35] Unfortunately, their lack of success was not communicated to the luckless Ox & Bucks. They had come up behind 128 Brigade with a view to attacking towards Monte Rotondo (West), using Damiano as their jumping-off point. Only when they were well on their way to the latter position did they discover, once again, that their start line was still firmly in the hands of the enemy. This time, happily, the attack was immediately called off.

a ridge they had just seized near Trimonsuoli, on 29 January: 'We managed to keep them off as it is very boring to have to take a thing like that twice.' (Quoted in N. Nicolson, *The Grenadier Guards in the War of 1939-45*, Gale & Polden, Aldershot, 1949, vol.2, p.383.)

Yet x Corps had not entirely given up hope of making a decisive breakthrough. One reason for making 56 Division's sector the axis of any further advance had been that it offered an alternative to the Monte Damiano–Ausente Valley route. It might also be possible to strike from the eastern part of the bridgehead, across Monte Rotondo (East), Monte Fuga and the Monte Ornito–Faito–Ceresola massif, and thus establish a base from which to take Castelforte in the rear. Exploratory attacks began on the 26th and good initial progress was made. 138 Brigade made the early running, from positions around Sujo and Monte Valle Martina, and by the 30th they were established on a line Monte Fuga–Monte Purgatorio. The terrain throughout this area was particularly intractable and the German defenders seem to have been taken rather by surprise, never having expected a determined offensive in such a mountainous wilderness. An entry in the War Diary of 6 Lincolns, seemingly written on the spot, gives a vivid picture both of the enemy's panicky reactions and of the commando-style tactics that the British riflemen had to adopt:

> . . . No. 10 Platoon . . . is slowly but surely winding its way up Point 320; it is very hard going and the men are crawling most of the way. They are well spread out and have the medium machine gunners rattling over them all the way with the 3-inch mortars weeding out an observation post which has been spotted . . . [The] Huns . . . appear very 'shaky' as they are lobbing grenades over the skyline and are jumping in and out of trenches which they have just on the skyline.[36]

The point about commando tactics was not lost on McCreery and 168 Brigade was relieved by two specialist units, 43 Royal Marine Commando and 9 Commando. On 2 February they resumed the offensive and took Point 711 and Monte Ornito. The latter was to serve as a jumping-off point for exploitation towards Monte Faito but German resistance stiffened and the attack was thrown back. 138 Brigade now came back into the line, along with one battalion of the Hampshire Brigade, and plans were made for another attack on Monte Faito and Monte Ceresola. In the interim, just surviving on the bare windswept slopes was a terrible trial for the infantrymen. 5 Hampshires, on Monte Ornito, followed a typical routine, as described by one of their officers in a letter home:

> We have been fighting in the mountains at 2000 feet some considerable distance from any roads, where all supplies have to come as far as possible by mule and then on by porter. For some of the time we have had to exist without greatcoats, and blankets were

never even considered although the temperature was quite low. It snowed and the nights being quite cold, the endurance test alone was quite amazing. . . . [On one day] the Boche started shelling us . . . with everything he had. In spite of our casualties our morale seemed to increase, and when the shelling ceased it was marvellous to see everyone move out of their little holes up on the crest to meet him as he attacked. On top of the hill fellows were shouting, 'Come on, you dirty Boche bastards'. It was a truly wonderful sight . . .[37]

This battalion also took part in the renewed attack on Faito and Ceresola, on the night of 7/8 February but, though they pressed home boldly, with 6 Lincolns on their left, neither summit was reached and the attackers had to fall back to their original positions. This attack, in fact, marked the last gasp of the Garigliano battle and X Corps War Diary, on 9 February, noted: 'The 46 Division attack having only met with partial success the Corps policy becomes one of active defence.'[38]

A month or so later X Corps Staff was asked to produce an assessment of the chances of resuming offensive operations in the Garigliano sector. They were not optimistic and, more interestingly, made it fairly clear that they ascribed the disappointing progress of the initial assault to Clark's insistence on their mounting an additional attack towards the entrance to the Liri Valley. As soon as they received his orders, they claimed,

it was realized . . . that one would need a minimum of three divisions for this operation. These would have been available if 46 Division . . . had been relieved of its mission to make an assault crossing of the river at San Ambrogio. . . . [Once the offensive started] the enemy reacted very quickly and had, by the 21st, concentrated elements of five divisions on the Corps front, and counter-attacks were mounted in force. It was then that the lack of a third division was acutely felt, and before 46 Division could be relieved of its mission to the north, the situation became yet more arduous in the bridgehead sector and continued progress became difficult.[39]

Yet the operation had been far from a total failure. A bridgehead had been established and made secure, after the repulse of numerous German counter-attacks mounted in considerable strength. All battles contain an element of attrition and, crude though the technique might have seemed, X Corps had severely mauled three fresh German divisions and thereby seriously impaired Kesselring's ability to assemble a powerful strategic reserve to counter any renewed co-ordinated offensive against the Gustav

Line. There is no shortage of evidence for the terrible sufferings of the German troops in this sector who, even when they were not themselves attacking, had to endure the remorseless attentions of Allied mortars, artillery and fighter-bombers. A soldier of 276 Regiment, on Monte Damiano, wrote home:

> On the way to Company HQ, a distance of less than 200 metres, there are at least twenty German dead – how it happened is all too evident. One tries not to look at them. At night one falls rather than walks over the rocks. The Tommies creep stealthily around. Their snipers shoot only too well. Again and again head wounds. The mortars fire and the whistle and explosion of shells goes on, day and night. Sometimes, for a moment or two only, there is peace, and then I think of home. Sunlight by day, the night spent on cold stones.[40]

When 29 PG Division arrived in the line they found a marked contrast with their previous positions around Rome. A soldier in 2/71 PG Regiment seemed to take the whole thing personally: 'Dear Parents, I am hungry all day because the food is prepared with water only. We have enough bread, but butter and sausage are scarce. It is high time this war ended because we are all going to the dogs. The Army is terrible.'[41] An NCO of 276 Regiment somehow managed to keep a diary of his experiences and the entries during the Garigliano battle give a stark picture of the mounting strain as he and his comrades tried to cling to their positions:

> *22 January*: I am done. The artillery fire is driving me crazy. I am frightened as never before . . . cold. . . . During the night one cannot leave one's hole. The last days have finished me off altogether. I am in need of someone to hold on to.
>
> *25 January*: I start becoming a pessimist. The Tommies write in their leaflet the choice is ours, Tunis or Stalingrad. . . . We are on half rations. No mail. Teddy is a prisoner. I see myself one very soon.
>
> *27 January*: The lice are getting the better of us. I do not care any longer. Rations are getting shorter, 15 men, 3 loaves of bread, no hot meals . . . My kitbag has been looted.[42]*

---

*Such diary entries or letters were not the work of a few malcontents. The January 1944 issue of a German Army magazine felt compelled to remind all soldiers that 'The German people as a whole have but one goal: to win this war under all circumstances. . . . Can a soldier's letter aid in achieving this goal? It will do so to a high degree if it contains a courageous and confident word regarding the ultimate result of the war, apart from purely personal matters. It is natural that a soldier will not hide from his

The incessant pounding by Allied artillery and mortars caused severe casualties among the Germans, though few precise figures have remained extant. Allied records are much fuller, however, and it seems appropriate at this stage to emphasize just what a horrendous loss of life and limb was involved in a brutal battle of attrition of this sort. Combat in almost every theatre of the Second World War was much more of a semi-static slogging match than is commonly supposed, with very few bloodless tactical or strategic *coups de manoeuvre*, and never was this truer than during the battles around Monte Cassino. The following table makes the point quite clearly, showing that in just a few days' combat a battalion could expect to lose at least 20 per cent of its riflemen and company officers, often much more.

Yet these men were the bedrock of the unit, the ones who actually advanced under fire and physically wrested a position from the enemy. General Montgomery had said that they were 'the least spectacular arm of the Army, yet without them you cannot win a battle. Indeed, without them you can do nothing. Nothing at all, nothing.' Unless Mark Clark could achieve some significant success on another part of the front, it began to look as though the whole of Fifth Army would soon be reduced to doing just that.

family that he has been in action and when there was rough going. But he must not burden his mother, wife or fiancée with details. These details are topics for hardened soldiers only.' (VI Corps G–2 Report No.155, 1 March 1944, Inclosure No.2, p.1 Washington National Records Center (WNRC), Modern Military Field Branch (MMFB) RG 94 105–2.2.)

BATTALION	NO. DAYS	TOTAL CAS. [1]	TOTAL[3]		TOTAL	
			Killed	Wounded	Officers	ORs
1/4 HANTS	1	89 (17.8)	*	*	9 (28.8)	80 (17.1)
6 LINCS	4	110 (22.0)	*	*	2 (6.4)	108 (23.1)
1 Y&L	4	256 (51.2)	48 (9.6)	138 (27.7)	10 (32.0)	246 (52.7)
8 RF	4	144 (28.9)	15 (3.0)	94 (18.8)	7 (22.4)	136 (29.1)
6 GRENS	5	54 (10.8)	8 (1.6)	46 (9.0)	4 (12.8)	50 (10.7)
7 O&B	5	188 (37.8)	23 (4.6)	122 (24.5)	9 (28.8)	179 (38.3)
2 WILTS	5	195 (39.1)	*	*	9 (28.8)	186 (39.8)
1 L. IRISH	6	92 (20.0)	*	*	12 (28.8)	80 (17.1)
2 COLDSTREAM	10	190 (38.1)	*	*	9 (28.8)	181 (38.7)
1 KOYLI	15 [2]	174 (26.8)	40 (6.1)	102 (15.7)	*	*
2/6 QUEEN'S	15 [2]	138 (28.6)	30 (4.8)	90 (14.5)	*	*

[1]   All figures in brackets are percentages. They represent the percentage casualties amongst the company officers (25) and the riflemen (375) of a typical battalion. The actual calculation is based upon the well-documented premise that 80 per cent of all a battalion's casualties are inflicted on these 400 men. (For more detail on this point see J. Ellis in Bibliography, pp. 162–5.)

TOTAL OFFICERS			TOTAL OTHER RANKS		
Killed	Wounded	Missing	Killed	Wounded	Missing
4 (12.8)	5 (16.0)	0	*	*	*
*	*	*	*	*	*
2 (6.4)	8 (25.6)	0	46 (9.8)	136 (29.0)	64 (13.7)
2 (6.4)	5 (16.0)	0	13 (2.8)	89 (19.1)	35 (7.5)
1 (4.0)	3 (9.6)	0	7 (1.5)	43 (9.2)	0
1 (6.4)	7 (22.4)	0	21 (4.5)	115 (24.6)	33 (7.0)
*	*	*	*	*	*
*	*	*	*	*	*
*	*	*	*	*	*
*	*	*	*	*	*
*	*	*	*	*	*

[2] Because of the longer time-period, percentage calculations for these two battalions also assume an influx of replacements, normally around 70 per cent of casualties.

[3] All asterisks indicate no data available.

5
'A Kick in the Nuts'

36 US Division on the Rapido, 20–22 January 1944

> . . . I am prepared for defeat.

Major-General Fred L. Walker, 20 January

Even during the first three days of x Corps' attack it swiftly became apparent that just one German division was quite capable of seriously slowing the momentum of a carefully planned assault by two Allied divisions, each battalion of which contained two to three times as many fighting troops as their German equivalents. One might have assumed that this would give General Clark serious pause for thought with regard to the next stage of his offensive, the drive by II US Corps into the Liri Valley. For only one American division, the 36th 'Texan', had been assigned to make the initial breakthrough, despite the fact that the Gustav Line defences here were especially formidable and that the narrow entrance to the valley was manned by a full division, 15 PG, again well rested and equipped. To be sure, Clark was only expecting 36 Division to consolidate a bridgehead through which I US Armoured Division could then pass, but this in itself was more than x Corps had achieved in three days' heavy fighting. For a viable jumping-off point for armour demands that it be held securely and *in depth*, so that any congestion at the crossing points cannot be observed by the enemy and subjected to concentrated artillery fire. Armoured divisions do not 'pour' across rivers; they waddle most circumspectly and require that their hand be held most tightly by a reassuring escort. But could one realistically expect the Texans to fulfil this role after an attack, with no great superiority of men, against the best defences, and across a river that was twelve feet deep and fifty feet wide and whose ice-cold water flowed at upward of ten miles per hour?

Could one even fairly expect them to establish a bridgehead at all? Just like the British, the American troops in Italy were very tired. 36 Division had already fought long and hard at Salerno, Altavilla, Persona and San Pietro and large drafts of replacements still left all three of its regiments at least five hundred men under strength. As they had toiled up Monte Sammucro, only four weeks earlier, their commander, General Fred L. Walker, had written in his diary: 'I regret the hardships they must suffer tonight. Wet, cold, muddy, hungry, going into camp in the mud and rain, no sleep, no rest. . . . How they endure their hardships I do not understand. . . . All honor to them. . . . I do not understand how the men continue to keep going under their existing conditions of hardship.'[1] Such experiences had left their mark. The 36th began to acquire the reputation of a 'hard luck' division that always got the dirty end of the stick and none of the glory. The deputy Chief of Staff of II Corps, Colonel Robert Porter, summed up the general feeling that

> this outfit had never really found themselves. Certainly everybody over there had tough jobs. They never had the breaks – the breaks always went against them, and I know that our staff was almost superstitious about this. They felt that anything given to the 36th was going to go wrong. I know, particularly, that our operations and intelligence people . . . breathed a sigh of relief whenever the 36th would go back into a rest area because they felt then that things would begin to sort themselves out.[2]

These feelings fed back into 36 Division and their morale slumped yet further, engendering a despairing fatalism about the prospects for success of any of their operations. None of this seemed likely to key them up for a maximum effort in the forthcoming Rapido operation, where even a compulsive optimist would have tried to hedge his bets.

General Walker, for one, was not at all enamoured of the prospect. Whilst Clark seemed to have developed a blithe faith in his 'armoured division commander [who] was more than confident he could roll right up the valley once a bridgehead across the Rapido was established',[3] Walker was extremely dubious about the whole operation. From late December, II Corps had known that one of their divisions would have the task and, though the final decision was not made until just before the attack, Walker always felt a grim foreboding that the 36th would draw the short straw. Very early in January he tried to persuade Clark to move the projected crossing point two miles north of Sant' Angelo, where the river was at least fordable, but was told that the original site offered a better funnel through which the exploiting tanks could fan out into the valley. Walker disagreed and on 8 January he wrote in his diary: 'Have been giving lot of thought to plan for crossing Rapido River some time soon. I swear I do not see how we can possibly succeed in crossing the river near Angelo when that stream is the MLR [Main Line of Resistance] of the main German position.'[4] On the 16th he was told that the Texans had indeed been chosen and subsequent events did little to cheer him. Particularly disappointing was the failure of 46 British Division to make any headway across the upper reaches of the Garigliano and their rather indecent haste to call the operation off. On the afternoon of the 20th, according to Walker, that division's commander 'came to my command post . . . to apologize for the failure of his division to cross the river last night. His failure makes it tough for my men who now have none of the advantages that his crossing would have provided. The British are the world's greatest diplomats but you can't count on them for anything but words.'[5] Later on the same day he gave full vent to his growing sense of despair and wrote in his diary:

Tonight the 36th Division will attempt to cross the Rapido opposite San Angelo. Everything has been done that can be done to insure success. We might succeed but I do not see how we can. The mission assigned is poorly timed. The crossing is dominated by heights on both sides of the Valley where German artillery observers are ready to bring down heavy artillery concentrations on our men. The river is the principal obstacle of the German main line of resistance. I do not know of a single case in military history where an attempt to cross a river that is incorporated into the main line of resistance has succeeded. So I am prepared for defeat. The mission should never have been assigned to any troops with flanks exposed. Clark sent me his best wishes; said he was worried about our success. I think he is worried over the fact that he made an unwise decision when he gave us the job of crossing the river under such adverse tactical conditions.[6]

But Walker's was a rather complex personality and the above quotation should not be seen simply as a strictly military critique of an unwise decision. For, in the privacy of his own command post – and the whole 'last will and testament' tenor of the above entry underlines this – the General seems to have been trying to expiate his own ambivalence towards the projected crossing. Thus, though all Walker's remarks so far clearly show that he was adamantly opposed to it, he seems never to have protested publicly to his superiors and made a real effort to have it called off. His Corps Commander, General Geoffrey T. Keyes, angrily drew attention to this after the war when the Rapido crossing had become a matter of national concern. Keyes singled out a Corps conference, held on 18 January, at which Walker 'stated in effect that while he realized it was a tough assignment, he was confident that the 36th Division . . . would be in St. Angelo the morning of the 21st. . . [At a] final conference at noon, January 20th, again there was no mention or indication by General Walker that the task was impossible or would fail.'[7] As Keyes recalled

we discussed the thing and when I asked General Walker if he had any comments, he said, 'No, everything is all set and we'll take it

– we'll do it.' So at that moment he had no protest, no criticism. He later claimed, I believe, that he pleaded and pleaded with us not to do that thing and intimated that, being a cavalryman, I didn't know anything about infantry and that's why the thing had been fouled up.[8]

The criticism was surely justified. Obviously Walker felt very deeply about his men, and as the Italian campaign progressed he identified with them increasingly intimately. Yet this identification also involved a withdrawal from contacts outside the division, which obviated the possibility of his bruiting his objections abroad and influencing those who might be able to actually change his orders. His diary might be a moving paean of praise to the 36th, as well as a bleak testament of one man's anguish, yet no diary entry would ever save a single life.

Not that his superiors are above criticism or that Walker's seeming enthusiasm for the attack should have been regarded by them as a sufficient guarantee of success. Both Clark and Keyes, in fact, had reservations about its feasibility, reservations that they would have done well to ponder more deeply. Clark's public statements were at best guarded, though at one stage he does seem to have concluded that it might not be worth the risk. According to Walker at least, 'on one occasion General Clark stated to me when I expressed my feeling in the matter, "You do not have to worry about the 36th Division crossing the Rapido at S. Angelo. The crossing will be made to the north." I do not know why he changed his mind.'[9] Certainly he had had plenty of warnings about the dangers involved. In his diary on 20 January he noted: 'I sent General Gruenther by plane to see McCreery, who feels that the attack of the 36th Division has little chance of success on account of the heavy defensive position of the enemy west of the Rapido.'[10] In the end, however, the warning went unheeded and it is difficult not to ascribe this, at least partially, to Clark's strong antipathy to the British. He certainly held McCreery in low esteem, as an interview after the war revealed:

Throughout the Italian Campaign, Clark said, the Fifth Army carried the ball. In the Volturno River crossings the failure of the British X Corps . . . to get across the river endangered the VI Corps' flank. Clark said, 'McCreery . . . didn't want to get across the river.' Clark changed the boundary and gave X Corps the bridge across the Volturno the 3rd Division had built so as to get X Corps across the river. Clark was 'browned off' about the British publicity on this crossing. . . . This happened repeatedly, Clark said – the British tried to steal the credit for the hard fighting the Americans had done during the war in Italy.[11]

In his diary, Clark contented himself with specifically military matters, concluding that the crossing was 'essential . . . in order to hold all the [German] troops on my front and draw more to it', though he did also admit that he was 'fully expecting heavy losses.'[12]

With regard to the question of casualties, he must also have given some thought to a conversation with the commander of 3 US Division, when that formation might have been the one to undertake the operation. As the latter recalled it the conversation went as follows:

> *Clark:* 'Would you be willing to undertake that Rapido crossing if those heights on either flank were under attack although not actually in our possession?'
> *Truscott* (after consideration): 'Yes, but those attacks should be so powerful that every German gun would be required to oppose them, for only two or three concealed 88s would be able to destroy our bridges. I doubt our capacity for such an attack. . . [In this event] my fine infantry battalions would be whittled away by German armour, artillery and infantry. And 1st US Armoured Division would still be south of the Rapido.'[13]

General Keyes was equally worried about the high ground that dominated each side of the axis of advance. When he had first arrived in Cassino he had concluded that the massif could only be outflanked well to the south, by a drive through the barren Aurunci Mountains that formed the lower flank of the Liri Valley. He had raised this at a Commanders' conference, in January, 'and came forth with an alternative plan . . . for the X and II Corps (X on the left) to push across the lower Garigliano and into the Liri Valley from that direction, rather than for II Corps to make the main effort west across the Rapido.'[14] But McCreery had protested that his troops were not trained and equipped for this kind of mountain fighting and had gone on, according to Colonel Porter, to dismiss the whole idea as 'a tactical monstrosity'.[15]

Keyes' doubts increased as the attack grew nearer. Even with strong British support on the southern flank he was far from convinced that a solid enough bridgehead could be gained or that there would be sufficient opportunity for a powerful armoured follow-through. In a letter to Clark he pointed out that 'for crossing the Rapido and operations up the valley, only one fresh division seems available, the 36th. . . . The condition of the 36th at completion of [present] operations [Porchia and Monte Trocchio] probably not too good. Use of armoured division so dependent on weather and terrain that too much cannot be expected.'[16] He was particularly appalled when he heard that there would not even be any

British support and that the failure of 46 Division would leave Walker's flank in the air. From the beginning he had been less than pleased with McCreery's interpretation of his responsibility towards the Liri Valley effort and, according to the official American historian, when he 'heard of McCreery's plans he was outraged. McCreery's timing, forces committed, and selection of objectives for the . . . 46th Division attack were all wrong. . . [He] had little confidence in the x Corps effort because of what he termed "British unwillingness to launch attacks in force." '[17] His suspicions about British intentions were hardly allayed by a memo from one of his G–2 officers who had attended a British planning conference on 13 January. According to this officer:

> The Division Commander stated that problem of crossing was extremely difficult in view of the fact that the enemy had observation immediately over the crossing points and that the enemy has been extremely sensitive to movements in that area. He does not believe that the element of surprise can be achieved. . . . I asked General Hawkesworth personally what his intentions were after seizing the objective, particularly with reference to further movement towards S. Apollinare and S. Giorgio. His answer was, 'I cannot move from my first objective until a bridge behind me is established.' I then asked him when the bridge would be established and he said, '3 days after my attack.' (Jan.22).[18]

This information was immediately forwarded by Keyes to Clark. Thus both were well aware that even if the British attack did succeed it would be able to offer only the most limited assistance to the Americans until the 23rd at the earliest, two days *after* the date already set for 36 Division's own crossing.

Nevertheless, both commanders managed to convince themselves that the actual failure of 46 Division's crossing, on the 20th, came as a complete surprise that suddenly threw their own plans into disarray. Clark wrote in his diary that the failure 'was quite a blow. I was fearful that General Hawkesworth had a mental reservation as to the possibility of success in this operation.'[19] After the war, Keyes did not make much effort to disguise his bitterness about the British failure:

> Well, the night of the attack came and the British sent out a couple of advance parties, but the river had come up and they couldn't get across. They ran into all kinds of fire and they came back and said, 'Well, we're through. We're not going to make this attack.' General Clark was put out by this but he couldn't order them to do it, so he

told me he would have to go on with our attack, and what could *he*
do, or anybody do, to make up for the failure of the British?[20]

But here is the whole point. In actual fact the British failure did not make
that much difference. As we have just seen, even British *success* would
not have done much to aid Walker's actual crossing and Clark and Keyes
ought to have already given serious thought to abandoning the whole
operation. And even if one *did* accept that the repulse of 46 Division was
such a major setback for the troops on the Rapido, then surely this was
just one more reason for calling off their attack? Keyes, of course, had
to follow orders, though he might have argued more strenuously with his
commander. Clark, too, was acting within the framework of Alexander's
'Battle for Rome' directive, which called for 'maintaining the momentum
of our advance . . . at all costs', and he is at great pains in his memoirs
to show that he was only obeying orders. Yet all of Alexander's strategic
directives were notoriously vague, allowing great scope to his
subordinates for on-the-spot adjustments. Within four months, indeed,
Clark was to exploit this to the full and undertake an operation that clearly
flouted his commander's basic strategic concept.[21] 'Only obeying orders',
moreover, is a justification with a poor historical pedigree and one that
has in this century increasingly seemed to lack ethical bite. Even in war
there should come a time when the sheer level of danger becomes morally
unacceptable, when the calculated risk has in fact become nothing but a
suicide mission.

   Clark's final justification for allowing the Rapido attack to go ahead is
also contained in his memoirs. After noting the criticisms that were made
after the war, he asserts: 'As for myself, I can only say that in the same
circumstances I would have to do it over again – and if I am to be accused
of something, thank God that I am to be accused of attacking instead of
retreating.'[22] Here is the verge of moral bankruptcy. If such a brand of
militaristic *machismo*, with regard neither to casualty rates nor even to
the possibility of real tactical advantage, is to be the yardstick of
generalship then the futile gesture might as well be its acme of perfection,
and the Light Brigade, Pickett's Division and de Gallifet's Chasseurs
d'Afrique its most celebrated exponents.

General Walker, it will be recalled, had tried to content himself just
before the attack with the thought that 'everything has been done that can
be done'. Not everyone agreed. General Howard Kippenberger,
commanding 2 New Zealand Division, saw the detailed operation orders
some weeks later and bluntly stated that 'almost everything that should

have been done had not been done and few things that should have been done had been attended to. Nothing was right except the courage.'[23] Certainly there were some unfortunate breakdowns in communication between the various arms during the preparations for the assault. The infantry's most important ally in an operation of this kind were the engineers who would be required to supply the boats and bridges to actually get across the river, to get these to the crossing site, and to neutralize the minefields that were thickly sown on either bank.

Walker's Chief Engineer, Major O.C. Stovall, was well aware of his responsibilities and as soon as he had been notified of the attack he had set about collecting the necessary equipment, much of which was only available by Army dispensation. On application, however, Stovall found 'an appalling lack of basic engineer supplies available'[24] and a visit to the General in charge of Fifth Army Engineers was aborted by the insistence that the latter was only available by appointment. II Corps were more helpful, particularly in the provision of engineer personnel, but they could not do much to remedy the basic shortages of equipment. Chief among these were the M–1938 prefabricated footbridges, specifically designed for this kind of operation, and DUKWs. The latter, which had already been sadly missed by X Corps, had become a rarity since forty of them had been lost in an earlier amphibious training exercise. 'Muddling through' became the order of the day. The footbridges were to be replaced by sections of catwalk laid across pneumatic floats and the DUKWs by either twenty-four-man rubber dinghies or twelve-man plywood scows. Both of the latter were horribly vulnerable to enemy fire and very hard for inexperienced crews to handle, particularly in a fast-flowing stream. To make matters worse, there were no approach roads to the crossing sites and the engineers declared themselves unable to follow standard practice and bring up the boats and bridges themselves. They instead set up two depots, several miles from the river, and required the infantry to carry everything forward from there – including the pre-assembled, ludicrously unwieldy floating catwalks and the 410lb scows.

The engineers did do their best to clear the minefields on the near bank, though the openness of the crossing points meant that they could only work at night. The Germans had been characteristically methodical and one engineer officer was amazed at the complexity of the

mine installations with generous combinations of anti-tank and anti-personnel mixtures. Operational characteristics of firing devices were numerous. Some fired on either application or release of pressure, or on being tilted. Time delays were effected with time clocks or acid capsules rigged in the device. Others required successive application of pressure. Withdrawal of a pin could activate others. The combinations were without end.[25]

Yet the engineers had to try and identify each type of device, working only with a metal probe and in the pitch dark. Eight-foot-wide paths were thus cleared through the minefields and tapes laid to mark their limits for the infantry.

Some attempt was made to familiarize engineers and infantry with each other's roles in the forthcoming attack and a training exercise was held on the Volturno. Things went reasonably well but many felt, along with General Walker, that it had been 'of little or no value because of the different characteristics of the two rivers', the fast-flowing Rapido having little in common with the Volturno, 'a placid stream with low banks'.[26] Worse was the lack of liaison between the two arms, the infantry in particular being apparently convinced that they had nothing to learn. One engineer officer recalled that he was never 'called upon to offer observations or suggestions on the infantry participation. . . . The infantry greeted me warmly but when it came to business treated me casually.'[27]

One can discern here almost a feyness on the part of the assault troops; a sense that they were doomed men embarking upon a hopeless mission, and beyond the help of anyone outside their immediate fraternity. An officer in one of the attacking regiments remarked that 'the men were not keen for this attack' and an engineer with them claimed: 'The infantry I talked with didn't like night fighting and lacked confidence in their ability to knock out the enemy in a night engagement.' The deputy commander of 143 Regiment 'was more explicit. It was common knowledge in the battalions and at regimental headquarters, he said, that the division would fail to cross the Rapido because the defences on the far side . . . were . . . too strong for infantrymen to attack and stay alive.'[28] The enlisted men were no less fatalistic. Staff Sergeant W. Kirby (3/143 Regiment) felt that the river offered the Germans 'an ideal defence. Anybody who had any experience knew, this ain't the place to cross the river. . . . We had the feeling we were being sacrificed, a feeling that we couldn't win.' Technical Sergeant C.R. Rummel, of the same battalion, was equally forthright: 'We thought it was a losing proposition, but there ain't no way you could back out.'[29]

'Common knowledge' was not far wrong. Two regiments were used in the opening attack, 141 Regiment to the north of Sant' Angelo and 143rd to the south. The northern regiment was to cross on a one-battalion

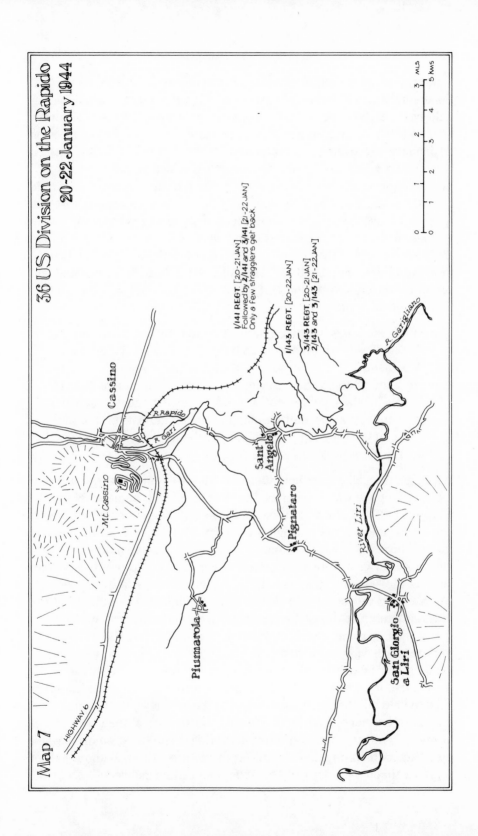

Map 7

36 US Division on the Rapido
20–22 January 1944

HIGHWAY 6

Mt Cassino

Cassino

R Rapido

R Gari

Sant'
Angelo

Pignataro

Piumarola

River Liri

R Garigliano

San Giorgio
a Liri

1/141 REGT. [20–21JAN]
Followed by 2/141 and 3/141 [21–22 JAN]
Only a few stragglers get back

1/143 REGT. [20–22JAN]

3/143 REGT. [20–21JAN]
2/143 and 3/143 [21–JAN]

0   1   2   3 MLS
0   1   2   3   4   5 KMS

frontage, the 1st Battalion to be followed as quickly as possible by the 3rd. Further downstream, though again one of 143 Regiment's battalions was held back, each of the other two had its own crossing point, which they were to leave simultaneously. The 141st left its assembly area at 18.00 on 20 January. According to Lieutenant J.E. Phillips (2/141 Regiment), 'it was very dark and cold, and a heavy fog had closed in. . . . Units would move a short distance and then stop; while waiting to move men would fall asleep and then lose contact. In our company contact was lost five times. The men were badly confused and some so new that they were getting mixed up with the other companies.'[30] Even when they reached the engineer depots they found that several of the boats had already been destroyed by random shellfire. They picked up those that remained and set off for the crossing point. But this was far from being as simple a task as might be thought:

> None of the boats had been designated for any particular unit nor were paddles distributed to each boat. . . . Few of the men knew how to handle boats. Some would lift the boats right side up and make a lot of noise half carrying and half dragging them over the ground with their equipment and rifles banging against the sides. . . . There was a constant jamming of men and boats on the path. Because of the rough ground and clumsy boats one group staggered out of the path and set off a mine.[31]

At 19.30 the Allied artillery began a thirty-minute barrage and the Germans replied within seconds. Many of their shells immediately found a target and the Texans scattered, some again blundering into uncleared clusters of mines, others trampling down the tapes that were to guide those following. Boats and makeshift bridges were abandoned so that almost 50 per cent of this equipment never even got to the river's edge. Just as the leading elements did get there, a thick mist descended, complicating yet further the task of those behind as they sought out the tapes and stumbled over abandoned boats, catwalks and corpses.

But the crossing itself offered no escape. Some boats sank in midstream, having been badly holed during the approach march, and pitched their heavily laden occupants into the water. Others capsized as their amateur crews wrestled with the treacherous current. The engineers tried to help but their bellowed orders to the infantrymen only provoked further resentment. And the engineers had troubles of their own. Their prime task was the erection of the footbridges and by 04.00 on the 21st they had cobbled together one rickety structure. By 06.30 about half of 1/141 Regiment was across. Then communications between both banks were severed by shellfire and, loath to funnel more men into the unknown, the regimental commander halted his 3rd Battalion and sent a runner to order the men already across the river to return. The order probably got through but few men were prepared to risk a dash back to the river, knowing anyway that hardly any boats were left there and that the single footbridge might well be destroyed. So most of them clung to their tiny bridgehead, pounded by German mortars and artillery and subject to ever bolder counter-attacks. Amongst them was Private Albert Pickett, who recalled: 'It was easy to dig foxholes in the marshland but then we had to stay there, and the water seeped through, and soon we had water up to our bellies, and we couldn't move or get out of there because the guns were shooting right on top of us.'[32] The artillery fire was particularly intense and well directed. According to another private: 'These German guns kept going all the time. They knocked out every pontoon bridge the engineers tried to put up. They knocked out the footbridges, and they knocked out a lot of the boats. It was a tough thing to look at.'[33]

For a few minutes the crossing of 143 Regiment, commanded by Colonel W.H. Martin, went reasonably well. Their march to the river's edge had been easier than that of their sister regiment and one platoon of 1st Battalion crossed without much difficulty. Then the German artillery and machine guns sought them out and it became a grim race to get more men across before all the boats were rendered useless. The best part of one company did get across and by 05.00 on the following morning, having had more boats brought up from the depot by unwilling engineers,* most of the battalion was across. Their position, however, was soon as desperate as that of 1/141 Regiment and at 07.15 their commander, Major D.M. Frazior, asked for permission to withdraw. This request was forwarded to General Walker, and denied, but Frazior had already made up his mind. By 10.00 all those who could do so had returned to their start line.

Colonel Martin's 3rd Battalion fared even worse. In his report the Colonel wrote:

> . . . considerable difficulty was encountered before the initial waves reached the river. Engineers leading the boat groups to the river lost their direction in the dense fog and got into a minefield. The rubber boats were destroyed, and casualties occurred among both the Engineers and the Infantry, badly dispersing and disorganizing

* Colonel Martin had to personally rout a lieutenant and eighteen engineers out of their foxholes.

both. . . . Artillery and mortar fire held up the movement to the river, and disorganization and confusion resulted in the dark and fog. Casualties were heavy, and at daylight the battalion had not succeeded in getting anyone across. . . .[34]

Telephone exchanges between the regimental and battalion commanders had become increasingly heated as Colonel Martin fretfully waited for some news of at least one attempted crossing. At 05.00 hours on the 21st he sacked the battalion commander, but by the time his replacement arrived it was getting too light to attempt any movement and shortly afterwards the unit pulled back to their original assembly area. The comment of an officer of this same battalion summed up the terrible experiences of the previous twelve hours: 'When I saw my regimental commander standing with tears in his eyes as we moved up to start the crossing, I knew something was wrong. I started out commanding a company of 184 men. Forty-eight hours later, 17 of us were left.'[35]

It cannot honestly be said that it was a day upon which 36 Division could look back with pride. They cannot be blamed for not establishing a significant bridgehead: the weight of German firepower, the nature of the river, the shortage of boats, the fog and darkness in the minefields all made this virtually impossible. Yet the Division had not simply been repulsed. No matter what the dedication and heroism of dozens of officers and men, the formation as a whole had shown signs of cracking. As early as 8 January General Walker had noted in his diary: 'I told Col. Martin that he would have to put more of the will to fight in his troops. He said he would do so. Maybe he will – I doubt it.'[36] Morale had slumped even further from the moment it was known the attack was on, and by the time the Texans had reached the Rapido itself their forebodings had become something of a self-fulfilling prophecy, turning military disadvantage into supra-human malevolence and reverse into the beginnings of rout. Colonel Martin did not cry simply because he was defeated, nor even because so many of his men were dead, but because he also knew that far too many men in both regiments had been found wanting. The remarks of various observers substantiate this point. At a conference on the 21st Colonel Martin berated his officers: 'You gentlemen must realize this operation is a vital [one] . . . and I trust that you have been in the Army long enough that you can accomplish any mission assigned you. It should have been proven last night. Somebody has to stay back and send those men back to the front who complain and try to return to the rear under pretence of illness.'[37] An engineer officer, Major J.S. Berry, wrote: 'It was said that had it not been for a one-star general who *drove* the infantry to the boats none would have crossed.'[38] According to another engineer: 'Most of the boats got to the river or near there. Some infantry crossed the river. Others refused to enter the boats. Machine gun fire caused the footbridge to be abandoned. The Engineers took shelter in a nearby ditch; the Infantry retreated back. Everything became disorganized.'[39] Finally:

> A chaplain who was present on the Rapido mud flats reported that . . . many men became lost, 'nervous uncertainty prevailed – the situation was no longer in a firm grasp – but out of hand.' Quite a few infantry tried in all sincerity to get across the river, some refused to cross, while others deliberately fell into the water to avoid crossing. Too many troops, it seemed to him, were in their first action under hostile fire.[40]

Both Walker and Clark wanted to mount a fresh attack at the first possible moment, though for different reasons. Walker was only concerned to rescue the men of 1/141 Regiment, still trapped on the far bank. Clark was still determined, as he told Keyes, that 36 Division must 'bend every effort to get tanks . . . across promptly'.[41] Walker wanted to attack at night, the 21/22nd, to try and minimize casualties but Keyes came to his command post and told him that such a delay was out of the question. The renewed attack was set for 14.00, both regiments jumping off at their original crossing points. In the event, fresh boats were not brought forward in time and both regiments were authorized to delay the operation until 15.00. Colonel Martin protested that this was still too early but was flatly countermanded by Walker. Colonel Wyatt, of 141 Regiment, did not formally protest at all but simply off his own bat set the attack back to 21.00. Walker, though he had chosen to obey his Corps commander, had even less faith in this renewed attack than in the original one. He wrote in his diary: 'I expect this attack to be a fizzle just as was the one last night. The stupidity of the higher commanders seems to be never-ending.'[42]

Martin's attack got off on time, all three battalions being employed. 3/143 Regiment used the same southernmost crossing site and within two and a half hours had got all its three rifle companies across. But resistance had been just as heavy as on the previous night. The experiences of the ordinary riflemen and company officers were nothing short of nightmarish. Sergeant Kirby recalled:

> We were under constant fire. I saw boats being hit all around me,

and guys falling out and swimming. I never knew whether they made it or not. . . . When we got to the other side it was the only scene that I'd seen in the war that lived up to what you see in the movies. I had never seen so many bodies – our own guys. I remember this kid being hit by a machine gun; the bullets hitting him pushed his body along like a tin-can. . . . Just about everybody was hit. I didn't have a single good friend in the company who wasn't killed or wounded.[43]

In his report after the battle Colonel Martin wrote: 'Reports from men who had returned next day indicated that the German machine gun positions were wired in and the bands of fire were interlocking. Many men were wounded in the lower extremities, or in the buttocks, by the low grazing fire as they moved or crawled forward.'[44] One of the wounded was Sergeant Rummel, hit in both legs by this same machine gun fire:

I didn't feel any pain. I was just scared to death. There was confusion all around. Two of the boys offered to carry me back but the fire was so intense I told them to get out the best way they could. . . . [I crawled away and] could hear my bones cracking every time I moved. My right leg was so badly mangled I couldn't get my boot off, on account it was pointed to the rear.[45]

Nevertheless, the engineers had somehow succeeded in erecting a reasonably stable footbridge and Martin ordered two companies from 2/143 Regiment across it to reinforce those already across. But all companies were soon pinned down by the heavy fire and were obliged to dig in no more than 500 yards inland. This was far too shallow a bridge-head to protect the crossing point from enemy small arms fire, let alone mortars and artillery. Thus the engineers were flabbergasted when orders came down that they should immediately set to work on a Bailey bridge to allow tanks and tank destroyers to get across to help the infantry. Building such a bridge requires dozens of men, all of whom are constantly exposed on the site, and engineers thus held it as a basic tenet that such work could not be undertaken until the site was clear of enemy small arms fire. Nevertheless they set to work. Unfortunately, trucks carrying the bridging material in became bogged down and the heavy girders had to be manhandled forward. This took time, whilst German rifles and machine guns caused a steady drain of casualties. Eventually this fire became so intense that work was halted, and the approach of daylight made it obvious that nothing further would be achieved in the next eighteen hours or so.

1/143 Regiment, further north, also managed to get some men across, approximately two and a half rifle companies by 22.30. But it proved impossible to advance more than 200 yards from the river and casualties steadily mounted. The battalion commander himself was wounded as he tried to get forward and by 05.00 the next morning all three company commanders were also casualties. The engineers had managed to erect a couple of footbridges but as German pressure mounted 'these seemed for the most part to permit infantrymen to straggle back to the rear bank on one pretext or another – they were ill or carrying messages or helping wounded men to the rear.'[46] The whole regiment's situation was now becoming desperate. The survivors on the far bank were being steadily whittled away and it was obvious that work on the Bailey bridge had effectively ceased. Realizing the impossibility of the task the engineers had virtually gone on strike. A regimental officer who tried to stir them into action radioed back: 'They are dug in and scared. Work has not begun on the Bailey bridge. Got them out of their holes and started them on their way . . . [but] do not anticipate that they will accomplish a thing.'[47] At 11.30 one battalion commander reported: 'Enemy shelling . . . very intense. Troops are out in the open. . . . Don't believe 3rd Battalion has many men still across the river for lots of men have drifted back to this side. . . . [Two officers] are collecting them up. . . . Boats and floats badly needed at bridge site. Lots of fire coming from south and west of Sant' Angelo.'[48] At noon, Martin decided enough was enough and recalled all survivors back across the river.

To the north of Sant' Angelo, Colonel Wyatt's 141 Regiment did not attack until the evening of the 21st. Both surviving battalions were used and after prodigious efforts six rifle companies had been ferried across. Among them was Lieutenant Phillips,

> in the large assault boats. The boats would partially swamp when they slid into the water; then about ten men would get in with all their equipment on and shove into the stream. The minute the current hit the boat broadside it carried it downstream. I could hear the paddles slapping water and hitting together and then the men yelling when their boat turned over. It curdled your blood to hear those men drown.[49]

On the far bank the German fire was as intense as ever and few men had any illusions about the prospects for success. The regimental executive officer recalled a conversation with two of his battalion commanders:

> It looked impossible to us. Artillery was falling like hail. They asked

for smoke and a withdrawal order. Orders from higher than division were that we would not withdraw, but would stay at all costs. . . . I had known [Landry and Mehaffey] . . . since they were 2nd Lieutenants. Major Landry said, 'I know you did all you could, Sir. So long.' Major Mehaffey said, 'Well, I guess this is it, may I shake hands?'[50]

Their premonitions were more than justified. Mehaffey was soon hit in the chest by a shell fragment and he crawled back across the river on his hands and knees, along a partially submerged footbridge. A medical team found him and an officer who saw the stretcher being carried past remarked later: 'It was the only time I saw a man's heart flapping around in his chest.'[51] Landry was prominent among those trying to rally their men in the midst of the shells and scything machine gun fire. At 03.30 he was bowled over by a mortar bomb that exploded nearby. Two hours later shrapnel from another shell hit him in the leg and hip. He carried on, using two boat paddles as crutches, but at 10.00 was hit in the same leg and hip by machine gun bullets. He was immediately evacuated but was again wounded, this time in the neck, by another shell fragment. Just before receiving his penultimate wound, Landry had been staggering towards 'E' Company, whose commander, Captain J.L. Chapin, typified the spirit of the bulk of the Texan officers. His company was eventually surrounded and just before the last counter-attack Chapin was seen in the very front line exhorting his men. One survivor testified to having heard him yelling, like a defender of a latter-day Alamo, 'Fire wholeheartedly men. Fire wholeheartedly!' He was killed almost immediately afterwards. Some officers and men who had managed to escape actually returned to almost certain death. One such, who has remained anonymous, was seen on the near bank:

> His combat suit was sodden with mud. He had just come back from across the river. 'I've got men still over there,' he said. Then he added slowly, 'This is the worst I have ever seen . . . I'm not doing anybody any good over here . . . I'm tired . . . I haven't got anything in me any more . . . There's nothing else to do. I'm going back over there.' And so he went.[52]

The whole regiment was now in dire straits. After the withdrawal of the 143rd the Germans were able to concentrate all their attentions on the northern bridgehead and as their counter-attacks pressed in the perimeter, every available gun was zeroed in on the survivors. By 15.00 all the officers in both battalion headquarters were casualties, and within another hour every commander had been killed or wounded. But there was no way of rescuing them. Almost every bridge and boat had been destroyed and it was simply not possible to get substantial numbers of reinforcements across. General Keyes did not believe this. The division still had, of course, an uncommitted regiment, the 142nd, and at 14.30 the Corps commander ordered that it be sent in. Walker informed him that this was not possible and anyway just one regiment would be unable to make any real headway against such organized defences. According to Walker

the stage was being set for another disaster. The disadvantages were again pointed out, but they received no more consideration than formerly. Just because some units had crossed the river and were pinned down did not mean the slightest success. . . . Not even a dent had been made in the German defences. Nevertheless [Keyes claimed] . . . that the Germans were 'groggy', their morale was low, and all that was needed was another 'blow' by a fresh regiment to turn them out of their positions, for it may be they are already preparing to withdraw. This was wishful thinking. The Germans had received no 'blows' during the past two days, but we had taken several from them.[53]

But Keyes was adamant and Walker was forced to obey or resign. Shortly afterwards, however, he was let off the hook when Keyes telephoned back and cancelled the attack. 'Which', wrote Walker in his diary the next day, 'I did in a hurry. Thus many lives and a regiment were saved.'[54]

But only one. The 141st remained trapped on the far bank where it was subjected to ceaseless probing counter-attacks, and then a major one, aiming at complete encirclement.

Hard bitter fighting repulsed this and several subsequent attempts by the Germans to overrun our positions. The enemy was able, however, to gain a well-defined concept of our relatively confined positions, and subsequently saturate the entire position with repeated concentrations of artillery, mortar and automatic weapons fire. Toward 20.30, our forces were nearly out of ammunition.[55]

The regiment was entirely overwhelmed at about 22.00 when those on the other bank heard the firing slowly flicker out and die. Fewer than one hundred men escaped from the regimental bridgehead. The would-be rescuers had themselves become victims. More tragically still, they had never found any trace of the 1st Battalion, to whose relief they were being sent. Its epitaph was provided by Colonel Wyatt, who wrote quite simply:

'Their whereabouts were never determined since all attempts to establish communications during 21 January were unsuccessful.'[56] With regard to the Division as a whole one need do no more than cite the lowest estimate of their casualties: 143 killed, 663 wounded and 875 missing; a 56 per cent casualty rate among the riflemen and company officers.

And nothing had been achieved. Not only had a whole American division been rendered unfit for operations in the near future but the Germans had not been troubled at all. Not one Texan had got more than 1000 yards from the river or even reached the main German positions, and not one tank had been taken across. General Eberhardt Rodt's 15 PG Division had never even been aware that a full-scale attack was in progress and their reports at the time spoke only of 'strong enemy detachments' and a possible 'reconnaissance in force'.* The attacks made even less impression at XIV Panzer Corps and Tenth Army HQs and at no time was there even a suggestion that it might be necessary to transfer troops to bolster the Liri Valley sector. General von Senger und Etterlin wrote: 'The German Command paid little attention to this offensive for the simple reason that it caused no particular anxiety. The repulse of the attack did not even call for reserves of 15 Pz.Gren.Div., still less the reserves from other parts of the front. . . .'[57] Later, as they counted their prisoners and the corpses littering the battlefield, the Panzer Grenadiers began to realize the scale of the defeat they had inflicted. Some of them could not resist crowing about it and when they discovered a few carrier pigeons, that had been taken across with the American assault units, some were returned bearing taunting messages. One of these read: 'To the 36 Infantry Division: You poor nightwatchmen, here is your pigeon #2 back so that you won't starve. What do you plan in front of Cassino, with your tin can armour? Your captured syphilitic comrades have shown us the quality of the American soldiers. Your captains are too stupid to destroy secret orders before being captured. At the moment your troops south of Rome are getting a kick in the nuts – you poor nosepickers! Signed: The German Troops.'[58] But they were kicking a man who was already down. The Texans were too demoralized to care. An intelligence summary by their G–3, whether or not it was meant to be ironic, gave expression to the defeatism that permeated all levels. He had been asked to comment on the military situation after the battle and on the options open to the Germans. The latter, he wrote, 'can hold and occupy their

---

* The casualties of 15 PG Division were a mere 64 killed and 179 wounded.

present positions, or they can withdraw, or they can occupy our positions.'[59]

The Germans could not completely harden their hearts. On the 25th a truce was arranged so that the Americans could come and collect their dead, but even this very nearly ended in disaster because few local commanders were advised that there was going to be a temporary cease-fire. The first Lt H.L. Bond (3/141 Regiment) knew about it was the sudden appearance of German troops who had come out to help gather up the corpses and who were strolling about in full view of his front-line observation post. 'I hastily connected the wires to my telephone, called back to company headquarters, and asked them to put me through to battalion. I hoped that I might be able to get some mortar fire on the enemy. Yet I could not be sure, with the demoralization of the battalion, that the mortars had even been set up.'[60] Luckily, his suspicions were correct and by the time the mortars had been set up the battalion commander was finally notified about the truce. It was a gruesome three hours for those who actually saw to the collection of the bodies:

In the 141st sector . . . the Germans maintained a friendly attitude and seemed anxious to help. . . . At the river Germans and Americans labored side by side. . . . A stack of eighty bodies was piled up along the bank to be recovered later; these had received direct hits from mortar shells while standing in their fighting holes and had no heads, shoulders or arms. They proved difficult to identify.[61]

Even at this stage the full extent of the defeat does not seem to have registered with Clark or Keyes. Right up until the first week of February they were actively considering a renewed assault by 36 Division. Walker vigorously opposed the idea and succeeded in getting at least one attack, scheduled for the night of 30/31st, cancelled. None of this helped divisional morale and the constant rumours and uncertainty preyed on the minds of men who only wanted time to lick their wounds and rebuild the shattered units. One company's War Diary[62] stated: 'To a newcomer in the Company it was evident that something very unusual had just happened. After listening to the conversation for a time all the grim, horrifying details of that two-day slaughter were expressed. . . . Every man feared another attempt to cross with a similar plan.'[63] Clark himself did little to improve morale. Increasingly aware, perhaps, that another assault across the Rapido was not really practicable, he contented himself with finding scapegoats. On the 29th he summoned Walker to a roadside meeting and told him that he was concerned about the Division's will to fight. Walker could scarcely demur and blamed the terrible ordeal on the Rapido and the lack of opportunity for properly assimilating replacements. Clark, however, was not prepared to admit that it had anything to do with failure of his own over-ambitious plan and insisted that the root of the problem was simply a number of inadequate officers in key positions. Overriding Walker's protests, he insisted upon a wholesale purge of the Division, the victims including the assistant commander, the chief of staff, the divisional G–3, Walker's own aide, and Colonel Martin of 143 Regiment. As Walker wrote later: 'General Clark's directive had to be carried out. [But] no single individual could have delivered a more severe blow to the already lowered morale of the 36th Division.'[64]

So the bitterness remained. Walker wrote in his diary: 'The great losses of fine young men during the attempts to cross the Rapido River to no purpose and in violation of good infantry tactics are very depressing. All chargeable to the stupidity of the higher command.'[65] Weeks afterwards a war correspondent found that 'conversations with combat men in the bars or rest centers almost invariably took on a bitter tone as they discussed the crossing of the Rapido . . .'[66] The kind of thing he heard is admirably summed up in the following comments, the first from Colonel Martin's report on the débâcle, submitted shortly afterwards. The disjointed prose is forceful evidence of his emotions at the time:

I desire to invite attention to the fact that the Rapido River was strongly defended by a force equal in number, or superior to the attacking force. . . . Officers and men lost in the . . . crossing cannot be replaced and the combat efficiency of a regiment is destroyed. . . . Losses from attacks of this kind are tremendous in manpower and material; and in addition have a devastating demoralizing effect upon those few troops who survive them. . . . As long as leaders who have the guts to plunge into hopeless odds such as this operation are sacrificed like cannon fodder our success in battle will suffer in proportion and disaster will eventually come.[67]

A company officer was more succinct. He told a reporter: 'I had 184 men . . . 48 hours later I had 17. If that's not mass murder, I don't know what is.'[68]

6
'The Morale of the Division was Considered Excellent'

II US Corps on the Cassino Massif, 24 January – 12 February 1944

> You'll see your buddies hurt and killed, and maybe you'll get it next, but you'll keep on fighting. No matter what happens – your battalion may be blasted to company size, and your company to a platoon – you'll fill the place of the man that's hit, and you'll keep on fighting.
>
> *General C.W. Ryder, commanding 34 US Division,*
> *September 1943*

For Clark, 23 January 1944 was not a good day. The attack into the Liri Valley had been a fiasco pure and simple. On the right the French were beginning to lose momentum and, on that day, were repulsed in their first attempts to break through the Gustav Line via Monte Carella and Monte San Croce. On the left, McCreery's X Corps had made disappointing progress from the start and was fought to a standstill on the 23rd, being unable to take any of the key strongpoints of Monte Natale, Monte Damiano or Castelforte. But Clark now had yet another problem. In his understandable eagerness to avoid a frontal attack on Cassino town and the massif behind, he had tried to make use of every strategic option open to him. Most important of all were the flank attacks, to try and nip out the Cassino bastion by deep penetrations into the rear. But, on the 22nd, he played his other card and launched Operation SHINGLE, the amphibious landing by VI Corps at Anzio, just south of Rome.

Though the original enthusiasm for the landing had come largely from Churchill, by the time it actually took place it had become a project equally close to Clark's heart and one which he dearly hoped might force the Germans to divert forces away from the main battle front – the Gustav Line. Perhaps this front might even collapse because the Germans could not find enough men to face thrusts from so many different directions. A Fifth Army report on the eve of SHINGLE summed up the likely German response and the hoped-for result:

> It is likely that the enemy on the southern front [the Gustav Line] will continue defence in that area until he finds out whether or not he can defeat the landing force on the northern front [Anzio].

Failing to defeat the landing force . . . he is most likely to begin a
delaying action to the north-west with the object of withdrawing
north of the Tiber River.[1]

As so often before, however, the planners had grievously underestimated
the Germans. Certainly they did try to defeat the landing force, moving
in considerable reserves to do so. And they did fail to throw it back into
the sea, to Hitler's considerable annoyance. But they did *not* then begin
to even consider withdrawal. Their forces ringing the bridgehead
remained in place, completely boxing in the defenders and forcing them
to wage their own quite separate struggle for survival.* For the Germans
had largely created the Anzio force, under the overall command of
Fourteenth Army and the subordinate headquarters of I Parachute Corps
and later LXXVI Panzer Corps, mainly by stripping the Adriatic front on
which Eighth Army activity was at best desultory. Some units were taken
out of the Gustav Line, as Clark had hoped, but not enough to
dangerously compromise this position – at least not in the eyes of the
Germans, who were pastmasters at juggling heterogeneous
Kampfgruppen, at remarkably short notice, between the portions of their
high ground linking Points 56 and 213, Point 445, just south of Colle

On 23 January, however, all that Clark knew was that VI Corps had
landed unopposed and that it would inevitably be soon subjected to
German counter-attacks. If he was unable to maintain strong pressure on
the Gustav Line it was likely that Kesselring would feel emboldened to
mount these in some strength and perhaps tear through the bridgehead
in the critical first consolidation stage.† Unfortunately, Clark was obliged

---

* This is one reason why, in this book, I have not dealt in any detail with the struggle
on the beachhead. My subject is the larger battle on the Cassino front, and it is only
necessary for the reader to keep in mind that the survival of the beachhead was yet
one more nagging worry for Clark. Another reason for my choice of emphasis is that
Anzio has already been the subject of several very good studies. (See Blumenson,
Anzio; Sheehan, Vaughan-Thomas, Trevelyan, *Rome 1944*; and Verney, in the
Bibliography.)
† There has been much debate as to whether General Lucas, the commander of VI
Corps, should have immediately pushed deep inland instead of staying put to
consolidate his position. Given the actual position of the southern front, on the 23rd,
and the obvious possibilities this offered the Germans to at least temporarily pull out
some of their units to counter-attack the landing force, a foray inland would have been
suicidal. Clark, himself, though he sacked Lucas, admitted as much in his diary,
towards the end of the month, when he wrote: 'I have been disappointed by the lack
of aggressiveness on the part of VI Corps, although it would have been wrong in my
opinion to attack to capture our final objective (the Alban Hills) . . .' (Clark, *op. cit.*,
p.282).

to mount his diversionary move at just the moment that Fifth Army's offensive had reached its lowest ebb. 36 Division was obviously unfit for further offensive operations in the near future, whilst both of the flank attacks on the Gustav Line had been halted without being able to make any significant penetrations. The French Corps needed time to rest and regroup before it could undertake further large-scale attacks and British X Corps had its work cut out simply hanging on to the ground gained. Clark thus had only one division – the 34th US, previously earmarked for further exploitation up the Liri Valley – which was capable of mounting any sort of autonomous effort.

Not that it could really be deemed a fresh formation. The fighting in Italy had already made terrible inroads into its manpower and resilience and many old hands spoke bitterly about the direction of the campaign to date. High on their list of blunders were the attacks on Monte Pantano, the grim results of which have already been alluded to, and across the Volturno. That same correspondent who was to hear fierce bar-room accusations about the crossing of the Rapido was also treated to stories about

the Volturno River action in November, when men of the Thirty-Fourth had been stupidly driven to their death in a night advance through one of the thickest minefields ever ventured over. As the mines flashed off, the Germans poured artillery fire into the flat stretch of ground, and the men screamed and died. Some went out of their heads and ran blindly forward shrieking curses upon the enemy, to perish in shattering explosions. . . . But . . . some two hundred men had refused to enter the minefield. They were not cowards; they were simply worn out, and nothing – not even disgrace and imprisonment for years – seemed so bad to them as what they were ordered to do.[2]

Not surprisingly, then, by late January the Division's morale was not high and to many newcomers it had already become known as 'a "hard luck outfit" . . . always in combat, never in the news.'[3]

Whether Clark was aware of this dubious reputation is uncertain, but he did not really have much choice in the matter and he and Keyes swiftly agreed that the 'Red Bulls' would have to try to keep the battle going. Keyes immediately informed their commander, General Charles W. Ryder, of this decision as well as the direction of the new attack. General Walker of 36 Division was also kept up to date and his reception of the news was tinged with considerable relief. On the 23rd he wrote in his diary:

I fully expected Clark and Keyes to can me to cover their own stupidity. They came to my headquarters today but were not in a bad mood. Clark admitted that the failure of the 36 Div. to cross the Rapido was as much his fault as anyone's because he knew how difficult the operation would be. He has now decided to attack over the high ground to the north of Cassino and to take Cassino from the west. This is what he should have done in the first place.[4]

The plan of attack, as elaborated in II Corps' orders issued that same day, was for 133 Regiment to spearhead an attack across the Rapido, jumping off east of the Barracks, and once across, to fan out to take the high ground linking Points 56 and 213, Point 445, just south of Colle Maiola, and the road leading south into Cassino town. 133 Regiment was to be prepared to follow up this latter thrust, if necessary attacking into the town, whilst 168 Regiment was to pass through the 133rd and go on to take Monte Castellone, Colle Sant' Angelo and Albaneta Farm. The crossing was to take place on the night of the 24/25th and 168 Regiment was to be prepared to pass through on the following night. Once the latter's objectives were secure, a further advance was envisaged towards Piedimonte and to cut Highway Six south of the massif.

The die was cast. Having failed to outflank the Cassino bastion from the north or south, Clark had now decided to tackle it head-on and so activated a gruesome sausage machine that was, over the next four months, to suck in and spit out the very innards of four Allied divisions. Of course the historian's *ex post facto* knowledge should not necessarily prejudice him against Clark's decision. Indeed, if there ever was a right time to attack Monte Cassino, this arguably was it. Though the attacks by the French and X Corps had both run out of steam, they had nevertheless sorely stretched the Germans. The latter had been obliged to commit most of their reserves against the Garigliano bridgehead whilst the Cassino garrison, still made up of part of 44 Division, was anxiously looking to its right flank where it feared a resumption of the French drive. Nor was von Senger und Etterlin easy in his own mind about the qualities of that division. It had proud traditions, to be sure, and was built around the 134th Hoch und Deutschmeister Regiment, one of the élite units of the old Austro-Hungarian Army. But even the 'High and Mightys' were still not true German troops and many commanders could not overcome their suspicions. Moreover, according to the commander of XIV Panzer Corps: 'The commander [General Franck] had not been fortunate in his choice of regimental commanders. I tried to bring about some changes in this respect, but they had not taken place by the time the fighting began.' The division was also woefully under strength, built around a 'reserve of young battalion commanders who led their units, each of which was only 100 men strong, more or less like combined-arms combat patrols.'[5]

Nevertheless, even without the benefits of hindsight, there were several good reasons why Clark's attack was ill-conceived. One was that a fresh German division had already been assigned for transfer to this sector and this must have been known to Clark, via Ultra. True, the division, the 71st, was supposed to relieve 15 PG Division in the Liri Valley, but it should surely have now become apparent to Allied commanders that the Germans were more than capable of taking an on-the-spot decision to feed the new formation into the threatened sector. And who could say that these would be the only reserves that the Germans could find? Clark well knew that both his flanks were stagnating and that, now the crisis for the Germans was past, they would find it easier to strip these sectors to a bare minimum and move reinforcements across to Cassino. For Clark had only one division of his own carrying the whole burden of the renewed offensive, and just two or three German battalions might well make the whole difference.* In this respect, therefore, the timing of the attack was less than propitious. And Clark should have realized this. His original plan, indeed, had tacitly acknowledged that Monte Cassino was best left alone even within the context of an Army offensive. Surely, then, it was particularly undesirable to launch an *isolated* attack upon it, a one-division afterthought with operations on either flank increasingly moribund. Surely Clark was merely compounding the errors of the Rapido crossing and sending in yet another weary division to accomplish a task for which it was quite inadequate.

The risks became yet more apparent if one studied the terrain and the typically elaborate German defences. The whole Gustav Line, as has already been seen, was an awesome piece of military engineering but nowhere was this truer than in the Cassino sector. The Germans had been devoting particular attention to it since mid-December and on the 23rd Hitler had decreed that the Monte Cassino position must be raised to 'fortress strength'. Four days later Kesselring was told that Hitler wished the forces on the massif to be under a single commander as this bastion 'must on no account be lost'.[6] All of 34 Division's axes of attack were hideously difficult. Cassino town was riddled with pillboxes, bunkers and

---

* Clark did manage to prevail upon Juin to support the American right with one of his own regiments. Such a small force, however, attacking across some of the most intractable terrain on the whole battlefield, could hardly be expected to make a decisive difference. Though they certainly tried, as will be seen in the next chapter.

emplacements, many of them strengthened with steel girders, railway sleepers and sometimes concrete. Houses were demolished to improve fields of fire and aprons of barbed wire were erected, up to six feet in depth.

The crossing sites to the north were equally formidable. A dam on the Rapido had been blown to divert the stream and the entire plain, already soggy from the winter rains, was turned into a quagmire. A regimental report noted:

> Along the base of the hills was a line of pillboxes, dugouts, and reinforced stone houses. From these positions the enemy had fields of fire which completely covered the flats between the river and the base of the hill. In order to increase the effectiveness of their fire, they had cut all the trees and brush from the river to the hill. Stumps three feet high were left as minor tank obstacles. A system of anti-personnel minefields, interlocked with barbed wire entanglements, completely covered the flats before the hills to a depth of 300 to 400 yards beyond the river bank.[7]*

Should the Americans successfully pass through the obstacles, the going got no easier. To the north-west 'lay Colle Maiola . . . and Monte Castellone, each higher than the other, merging gradually into the mass of Monte Cairo itself. . . . These steep slopes, seamed with deep ravines, rose precipitously 450 meters in 1000 meters and were thoroughly organized with wire, mines, felled trees, concrete bunkers and steel-turretted machine gun emplacements.'[8] To the south-west, towards Point 593, the Abbey and Albaneta Farm, the terrain alone was a tactical nightmare:

> . . . the ridges, when seen from a distance, look like smooth, bare slopes running up or down. At Cassino this appearance concealed the horrible nature of the ground. This was unspeakably rough and broken with minor ridges, knolls and hollows jumbled all together. At one point deep clefts might be the obstacle, at another sheer rock faces or steep slabs, or all three might be found in a few acres. Huge boulders were scattered about, here and there were patches of scrub, while the gorges were often choked with innocent-looking but savage thorn. To attacking troops the ground set vile tactical puzzles one after another. This or that knoll or ridge might seem to be promising objectives but would turn out to be commanded from an

---

* Over half a million mines had been lifted from the Cassino sector by the end of the Fourth Battle.

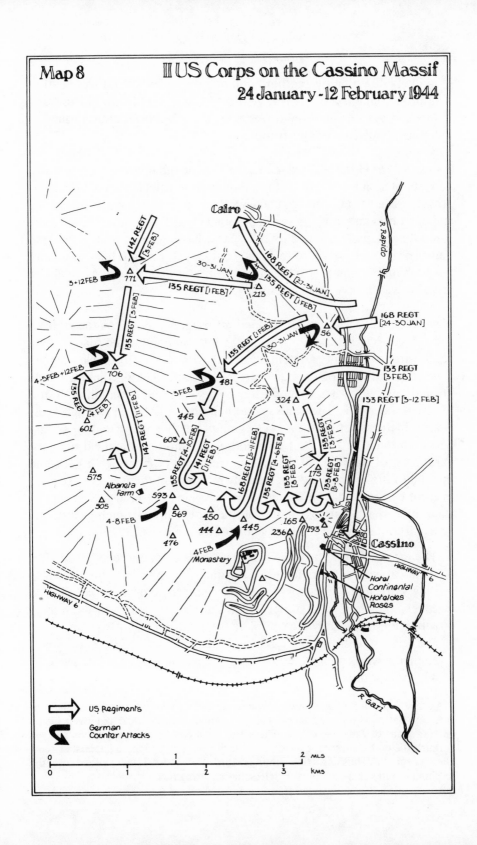

Map 8

II US Corps on the Cassino Massif
24 January - 12 February 1944

Cairo

R. Rapido

142 REGT [3 FEB]

168 REGT [27-31 JAN]

3+12 FEB   771

30-31 JAN   135 REGT [1 FEB]

135 REGT [1 FEB]   213

168 REGT [24-30 JAN]

56

155 REGT [3 FEB]

155 REGT [1 FEB]   30-31 JAN

153 REGT [3 FEB]

4-5 FEB+12 FEB   706

3 FEB   481   324

153 REGT [5-12 FEB]

135 REGT [4 FEB]   601

142 REGT [11 FEB]   445

155 REGT [3 FEB]

575   603

155 REGT [4-10 FEB]   141 REGT [11 FEB]

168 REGT [5-11 FEB]   135 REGT [4-6 FEB]   135 REGT [3 FEB]   175   155 REGT [5-8 FEB]

Albaneta Farm   593   450

305   569

4-8 FEB   444   445   165   193

236   Cassino

476

4 FEB Monastery   HIGHWAY 6

Hotel Continental
Hotel des Roses

HIGHWAY 6

R. Gari

US Regiments

German
Counter Attacks

0   1   2 MLS
0   1   2   3 KMS

unlikely direction by another knoll or ridge or by several. A line of approach might look as if it would 'go' and would turn out to be blocked by some impassable obstacle. The advantages of the ground lay wholly with defending troops.[9]

As usual, the Germans had made the best possible use of such features and supplemented them with man-made positions. On Colle Sant' Angelo, Points 444 and 593/569 were armoured machine gun nests, snipers' posts and a whole series of mortar emplacements. These latter, camouflaged and protected by thick logs, were normally placed in deep gullies or behind shelves of rock and could lay down their high-trajectory fire without ever having to be moved from this deep cover. All in all, 34 Division was faced with an awesome task.

Nevertheless, 133 Regiment jumped off roughly on time on the night of the 24/25th.* 100 Battalion was on the left, aiming for the road leading southwards to Cassino, 3/133 in the centre with the mission of clearing the Barracks, and 1/133 on the right, directed towards the ridge linking Points 56 and 213. They were supported by 756 US Tank Battalion. Little progress was made. The tanks made their way to the river through paths cleared in the minefield for 1/133 Regiment but then found that the stream was unfordable. 1/133 itself was held up by another minefield only 200 yards west of their line of departure, whilst 3/133, although it got some men up to the river, could not actually push any of them across. The fire in front of 100 Battalion was equally heavy and the following acount of their attack has an almost medieval ring to it, emphasizing how little the role of the infantry had changed when the moment of truth came round:

> The men advanced across the flats under a smoke-screen, some of them carrying ladders for use in scaling the embankments. When they were half-way across the wind changed, blowing away their cover, and they were stopped by a hail of . . . fire from the hills across the road. Only the company commander, two other officers, and eleven enlisted men reached the east wall. Those of the company who could still move sought cover in irrigation ditches or dug into the mud.[10]

* At 22.00, except for 100 Battalion which was half an hour late in reaching the start line. 100 Battalion replaced 2/133 Regiment (still in North Africa) and was made up of Hawaiians of Japanese origin. There had been considerable opposition to even forming the unit but once they had been attached to 34 Division, in September 1943, they set about establishing a fine fighting record. The General Ryder quotation at the beginning of this chapter is part of his less than cheering welcome speech.

The Division tried again before dawn and this time had a modicum of success, as reported back to II Corps by one of Ryder's staff, at 18.50:

> Going today has been slower than we had hoped. 2/133[sic] got mixed up and finally got going about 09.00. They met very stiff resistance but they now have three companies across the river. 1/133, which got into an extensive minefield, took it rather slow and easy to get through. . . . [They] now have two platoons across the river and are meeting heavy resistance. 3/133 has 'a few people across'.[11]

34 Division's records of its telephone and radio messages during this battle are much fuller than is usually found and it seems worth while citing the following log of messages, about this same attack on the 25th, if only to show that a divisional or regimental commander's influence on the actual fighting is limited mainly to the psychological pressure he can bring to bear on his subordinates:

> *12.10* (34 Division to 133 Regiment): 'How is 100 Bn. doing?' 'They are plugging away yet. That MG on their flank is restricting their movement pretty much. They have tried for several hours to knock the gun out.'
> *12.15* (133 Regt. to 100 Bn.): 'What is the dope now, Major?' 'Still held up.' 'How about sending out a combat patrol and surrounding those nests? The General will not accept excuses. Have those men cut that wire that is in front of them.'
> *12.20* (133 Regt. to 1 Bn.): 'Division G–6 wants us to push this harder. . . . Colonel, you must take that objective.' . . .
> *13.07* (133 Regt. to 2 Bn.): 'What is the situation there now?' 'Stalemated yet.' '6 says to have the 6 phone him immediately on return.'
> *13.15* (133 Regt. to 2 Bn.): 'Effective at this moment you are commanding the 2nd Bn. Pass through my CP and I will give you the situation. . .'
> *13.25* (34 Div. to 133 Regt.): 'What are you doing at present?' 'I have placed Major Dewey in charge of 2nd Bn. and on the right I have given them a little jolt and I shall have action for you this afternoon or tonight.' . . .
> *22.31* (133 Regt. to 1Bn.): 'How are things now?' 'The men are now getting rations.' 'You must get the objective. The order still stands.' [A Divisional staff officer interrupts:] 'You were given orders to get to your objective by 18.00 hrs, you got to get up, leadership and control will get them up.' . . .

23.27 (133 Regt. to 1 Bn): '[Division] says you must get on to your
objective. Your 6 was given orders by myself and . . . [Division].
Get them going fast.'[12]

This pressure was not without its effect and by midnight on the 25th all
three battalions had substantial elements across the river. General Ryder
reported back to II Corps with some satisfaction, one of the latter's G–3
officers noting in the Journal that 'General Ryder feels confident that attack will progress more favourably under cover of darkness tonight.'[13]
But his hopes were to be dashed and no progress at all was made on the
26th. Every attempt by 100 Battalion to advance further was repulsed.
1/133 did succeed in pushing as far as the base of Point 213 but were briskly
counter-attacked and driven back across the river, almost to their original
start line. 3/133 was then sent to their assistance and both scrambled forwards again to the lower slopes of Point 213, only to fall back yet again
to the river, though this time they did manage to hold on the west bank.
Another attack by 100 Battalion also failed, as did a supplementary drive
by a single company of 1/135 Regiment. No armour had yet been able to
cross the river to assist any of these attacks. Six tanks were stuck on the
most likely route and the rest had to wait for substantial engineer work
to improve the crossing.

133 Regiment had been badly hit. It had suffered more than 300
casualties and its morale was beginning to cause some concern. One of
Keyes' staff officers reported back:

> In answer to your query 'What is the combat efficiency of 133 Inf.?'
> the following is submitted: 'Report of S–3 made in the presence of
> S–1, after checking with senior officer (I believe the Regimental
> Comm.), 'Morale excellent, combat efficiency low at present due to
> losses.' If the morale of 133 Inf. is reflected by the attitude of the
> officers to whom I talked . . . I believe it is very low at present.[14]

But General Keyes was insistent that the attack towards Point 213 must
be maintained and Ryder decided to use his exploiting regiment, the
168th, to make the initial breakthrough. Their attack jumped off at 07.30
on the 27th, with 1 Battalion on the left and 3rd on the right, each
preceded by a platoon of tanks. These latter, after aiding the crossing and
the assault on Points 56 and 213, were to assemble to the north of 213 and
be prepared to exploit northwards into Cairo village and southwards
towards Cassino. They found the going terribly difficult. Some slipped off
the narrow, flooded road to the crossing point, and though four did get
across by 08.30 those following got stuck in the mud and blocked the

route. By 14.00 all the four tanks west of the river were out of action, two destroyed by *Panzerfausts*, one with a broken track, and the other stuck near the crossing where it had returned for more ammunition. Yet in the interim they had managed to clear some paths for the infantry, and by nightfall the leading companies had once more closed up to the lower slopes of the objective. Very early on the 28th one company of 1/168 actually had men on Point 213, but again the fortunes of 34 Division were dictated by its shaky morale:

Instead of remaining on top of Hill 213, the company commander, deciding that his position would become untenable after daybreak, started to move his troops back. As he did so the withdrawal turned into an uncontrollable rout. The troops fled across the river. Believing that a retirement was taking place, two of the other companies on the far bank became nervous, panicked, and then followed. Not until they were on the near bank were they stopped. By then they were disorganized.[15]

The Regimental commander now had no choice but to withdraw the rest of his companies, though he was able to reorganize 3/168 Regiment sufficiently to send them northwards to another crossing point later that day.

This crossing was found to be much more suitable for the tanks – though one is entitled to ask why it had not been found earlier – and a full-scale regimental assault was organized for the 29th. The battalions were aligned in numerical order from left to right, those at each end striking at Points 56 and 213 respectively, and 2 Battalion aiming for the centre of the connecting ridge. 756 Tank Battalion and part of 760 were to be in support. Jump off was to be at 06.00.

Things did not begin too well. According to the commander of 2/168 Regiment the engineers had been working all night to improve the tank ford but

it was not completed in time for the attack, so the attack jumped off on time without tanks. The attack got exactly nowhere and very fast, too. By noon E Company was tightly pinned down in the minefield by extremely accurate fire. . . . F and G Companies were still east of the river. Supporting . . . fire was stepped up continually on suspected enemy gun positions, without any apparent effect.[16]

In the afternoon, however, the tanks began to cross in numbers. 'Jerry really laid down his fire then. Of the fifty-four tanks of the [756th]

Battalion, about a dozen succeeded in reaching the forward elements. The rest were knocked out . . . or simply bogged down in the mud.[17] But this was enough. According to one account, the rest of the assault was 'described by the . . . commander of the leading company to have been almost a manoeuvre by the field manual'.[18] The tanks took over the lead and pressed towards the summit of Point 213.

> As they passed through the minefields they exploded the anti-personnel mines with no damage to themselves. Apparently Jerry had placed too much confidence in the river and inundations. There were very few anti-tank mines. . . . The passage of the tanks created lanes for the infantrymen. The tank tracks were four to six inches deep and provided some cover against the intense artillery fire. The high wire entanglements were easily breached by the tanks. The tank-infantry attack carried right to the base of our objective. There was very little enemy machine gun fire. Apparently the threat of receiving point blank cannon fire was too much for the occupants of the pillboxes and bunkers.[19]

The other battalions made equally good progress. By dusk all three had gained a secure foothold on all the objectives. The final ascent was too steep for the tanks but they were able to provide heavy supporting fire and by dawn on the 30th German resistance had all but been broken. Mopping up was now the order of the day and this even provided a rare moment of light relief for some of the attackers:

> In the darkness, many of the Jerry positions were missed. . . . About an hour before daylight Jerry started coming out of his holes and trying to get away. Naturally he ran into our men. . . . One of the prisoners was a fat, chubby youth who had wrapped a blanket around his waist so that it hung below his coat like a skirt. From a little distance one could swear that it was a woman. The chorus of the 'Strip Polka' rang out all over the place.[20]

But the mood of the division as a whole was hardly light-hearted and General Ryder was becoming acutely aware of the tremendous difficulties that lay ahead. Even before the beginning of February he was writing of the

> thorough organization of the ground and bitter resistance of the enemy . . . [as well as] the abnormal conditions pertaining to supply and evacuation. . . . At one time over 1100 mules and 700 litter

bearers were required over and above the normal transportation and medical personnel. . . . Fighting was the bitterest met to date; casualties for all causes were high; replacements were slow in arriving and inadequate in number.[21]

Such conditions were not doing much to improve the Division's morale. On the 30th, though he recommended further attacks be launched towards Colle Maiola, 'General Ryder . . . [chose] 135th to make the attack. . . . 133rd can not make this effort.'[22] The report of the Divisional G–1 was less than enthusiastic about any of the regiments and after the standard vacuous assertion that 'the morale of the Division for the month was considered excellent' it went on to suggest that 'a decline appeared to be imminent because of the continued daily casualties. . . . Upon completion of 31 days of continuous contact with the enemy, evidence of general weariness was apparent, tending *further* to reduce the status of morale.'[23]

Nor would Ryder have been cheered to hear of German reactions to his attacks. Certainly they, and the French regimental thrust to his right, had caused problems. Von Senger und Etterlin wrote: 'The 44th Infantry Division . . . experienced great difficulties. . . . The troops occupying Cassino itself, as well as the battalions committed to the north there- of would have been overrun if the corps had not been able to move to the area . . . a newly activated regiment of the 71st Infantry Division. . . .'[24]But this was the point. Once again the Germans were able almost immediately to buttress the threatened portion of their line, putting this regiment, the 211th, into the town itself. But the Germans did not stop here. On the 30th two battalions of 90 PG Division, then facing X Corps in the Garigliano bridgehead, were alerted to move to Cassino with the headquarters of that Division, commanded by Generalleutnant Ernst Günther Baade. Within two days Baade had assumed control of the whole sector and had the first two of his battalions, 1/ and 2/361 PG Regiment, in position on the massif. Within a day yet more reinforcements arrived: 3/3 Parachute Regiment, a battalion of the redoubtable 1 Parachute Division, which had been rushed over from the Adriatic.

Presumably Keyes too was beginning to have some doubts about the offensive, for when he was visited by Clark's Chief of Staff, General A.M. Gruenther, on the 31st, the latter could only report back: 'Keyes will give no estimate as to when he expects to take Cassino. Mine is February 6th – I hope.'[25] But Keyes doubtless had his fingers tightly crossed as Ryder's men jumped off the following morning. The main burden had now fallen on 135 Regiment, who passed through the 168th to strike south-westwards towards Monte Castellone and Colle Maiola. A heavy fog assisted them greatly and, by 10.00, 3/135 Regiment was well established on Point 771 and 2/135 on Monte Maiola.

These were both significant gains, the former seized from one of the newly arrived Panzer Grenadier battalions, and Ryder committed extra units on the next day, the 2nd. 142 Regiment (36 Division) had been brought up from the Rapido to lend support to the French effort and by the 1st they had pushed as far as Manna Farm on the Cairo–Terelle road. Two of its battalions now joined in Ryder's attack, one coming down to take over on Monte Castellone, the other to seize Colle San Lucia. Their introduction to the battle had little immediate impact, however. 3/142 Regiment made rather a mess of their attack on Colle San Lucia and, once it was called off, lost contact with the Regiment until early on the 4th. 1/142 Regiment did reach Castellone about noon on the 2nd but immediately became embroiled in severe counter-attacks by the enraged Panzer Grenadiers. They were thus unable to gain a secure foothold and release 3/135 Regiment for an attack further south, towards Point 706. Their sister battalion on Monte Maiola was able to continue its attacks, however, and by the end of the day they had forced their way along Snakeshead Ridge to within 850 yards of Point 593. 1/135 Regiment had also been thrown into the fray and it managed to establish itself on Point 324, though mopping-up operations lasted well into the morning of the 3rd. Ryder's other extra ingredient had been 133 Regiment, whose 1st Battalion spent part of the day mopping up around the Barracks before inching their way down the road to Cassino, the northern fringes of which were reached at about 18.00.

Despite the stalemate on Monte Castellone, and the severity of the fighting in every battalion sector, American commanders were justifiably pleased with progress thus far. At the end of the day Clark signalled to Alexander: 'Present indications are that the Cassino heights will be captured very soon.'[26] Indeed there were those in XIV Panzer Corps who seemed inclined to agree, as is evidenced by its War Diarist's conclusions about the day's fighting: 'The interpolation of the 90th Panzer Grenadier Division has not alleviated the situation. Heavy enemy attacks on Cassino itself are repulsed by a counterthrust. Colle Maiola is occupied by the enemy. Our counter-attack on Monte Castellone ends in failure.'[27] So the drive southward continued on the 3rd. 135 Regiment was reinforced by a battalion of the 168th and all its own three battalions tried to push forward. There was some success on the right, where 3/135 seized Point 706, two-thirds of the way along the ridge that led down to Colle Sant'

Angelo, but the other two battalions fared badly. The 2nd was heavily counter-attacked on Snakeshead Ridge and the 1st made hardly any progress at all beyond Point 324. Nor did 133 Regiment do any better in the town itself. A two-battalion assault had been organized, the 3rd attacking towards Castle Hill – a sheer promontory that dominated the approaches to the eastern side of Monte Cassino – and the 1st into the north-east corner of the town. Both soon ran into fierce opposition and by the end of the day had got no further forward than Point 175 and a few isolated houses on the town's outskirts. These axes of attack were followed again on the 4th, but the German defences were hardening by the hour and none of the regiments were able to report much progress. 135 Regiment was again in the thick of the fighting. Its 3rd Battalion actually secured a lodgement on Colle Sant' Angelo but was soon driven back to Point 706. The 2nd Battalion attacked again down Snakeshead Ridge and managed to claw its way to within 200 yards of Point 593, whilst the 1st, close by on its left, gained a precarious lodgement on Point 445. 133 Regiment battled on in the town but was only able to report the capture of two or three more shattered houses.

Ryder's attention was now fixed on Snakeshead Ridge and one of Keyes' staff officers reported: 'General Ryder believes that Hill 593 is the important terrain feature that must be captured prior to taking Cassino. . . . If lower-level attack against Cassino fails, 34 Division intends to continue working round from the Hill. . . . Biggest difficulty, 34 Division has no reserve unit from which to draw litter-bearers and man-pack troops.'[28] 135 Regiment, indeed, was getting desperately short of reserves to do anything, and on 5 February a certain amount of regrouping took place. The Regiment remained in place but the 168th was now brought forward to try and make the final bound towards the Monastery. At the same time 36 Division was ordered to transfer the rest of its regiments on to the massif ready for an attack towards its south-western end and thence to Piedimonte. There was still considerable Allied optimism about the prospects for success. On the 5th Clark issued an Operations Instruction that discussed the measures to be taken 'upon the capture of the Cassino Heights'. Again, such optimism was not entirely baseless. XIV Panzer Corps was still desperately anxious about the situation on the massif. Von Senger und Etterlin actually told Kesselring that the Americans must soon 'command a view of Highway Six' and he proposed, 'at the risk of my prestige, to withdraw from action at Cassino and occupy the so-called "C" Line behind the Anzio bridgehead. . . . This proposal was not approved.'* Yet almost in the same breath he went on to admit that this

* The Germans sometimes referred to the C-Line as the Caesar Line.

was perhaps an unwarrantably gloomy prognosis, in that Fifth Army seemed to be even shorter of men than he was:

> For the moment at least, things were in our favour, since the enemy's strength declined simultaneously with our own. The enemy too seemed to have used up his reserves. . . . The individual attacks [against the Cassino front] made it possible for me to take forces out of the sectors where the enemy attacks had miscarried and to repulse each new thrust in turn by shifting divisional boundaries and organizing new reserves.[29]

By 7 February, in fact, he had concentrated on the massif most of 361 and 200 PG Regiments as well as the whole of 1 Parachute Regiment, a further battalion from 3 Parachute Regiment and the Parachute Machine Gun Battalion.

Even on the 6th, enough of these men were in place to repulse without too much difficulty the main effort of the day by 3/168 Regiment, which attacked over Point 445 towards the Monastery. Incredibly the battered 135th had more success and its 2nd Battalion stormed German positions on the lower slopes of Point 593. The Battalion Action Narrative underlines the extent of their achievement:

> Co G, with two understrength rifle platoons, shoved off for Hill 593. Even with heavy enemy fire from both flanks and a frontal counter-offensive they managed, with the remnants of Co F . . . to place a small body of men out on the forward slopes. . . . Almost immediately a force of enemy counter-attacked and drove our force back off the knoll. A force of 32 men . . . of E Co were immediately sent to assist G Co in retaking ground and Hill 593. This was accomplished but only after heavy casualties. At daybreak the following day . . . the Bn was able to completely occupy Hill 593. During this time they were continuously under heavy mortar and artillery fire and the enemy threw many counter-attacks against the Bn, five of these occurring within a 24-hour period. Hand grenades were used to a great extent to stave off these counter-attacks.[30]

Still Ryder was not allowed to let up. And still 135 Regiment was asked to play its part. On the 7th it handed over the whole sector east of Point 593 to 168 Regiment but on the following day was sent in against Albaneta Farm. Just before it jumped off, however, another series of German counter-attacks began and the regiment had its work cut out just holding its ground. Their attack had been designed to protect 168 Regiment's right flank as they attacked once more towards the Monastery, and its subsequent exposure was keenly felt. Twice the 1st and 3rd Battalions moved down over Points 444 and 445 and twice they were caught in both flanks by murderous enfilading fire and forced to withdraw. A report to II Corps by one of Ryder's staff was terse and to the point: 'The going has been very tough and do not think that 135 and 168 have made much progress yet.'[31]

Nor had 133 Regiment, who had spent this whole period still battling it out in the northern outskirts of Cassino town. Progress was agonizingly slow and since the 3rd they had probably gained no more than 100 yards. The regimental commander wrote: 'During the entire period . . . the enemy had advantage of excellent observation . . . from the high ground behind Cassino. . . . MG nests in steel and concrete bunkers had to be stormed. Progress was measured by yards and by buildings. Each building had been converted into an enemy strongpoint. . . . Casualties were heavy.'[32] A report drawn up after the battle by 34 Division made several interesting observations about German methods in Cassino as well as commenting on the extraordinary resilience of German troops in this kind of defensive fighting:

Enemy use of Cassino and its peculiar layout was extremely effective. The quadrangular arrangement of houses around central courtyards, the irregular layout of the streets, and the heavy masonry of the buildings prevented our driving the enemy into the open to destroy him, and fields of fire for our weapons were very limited. The enemy was constantly aggressive and alert, and hand grenade fights were frequent, with grenades often being thrown back and forth between buildings. The enemy employed his SP guns audaciously, running them into the open to fire a few rounds and then withdrawing into cover . . . among the buildings. Our tanks were hampered by narrow streets and poor fields of fire, but on several occasions were able to destroy enemy strongpoints in buildings with point-blank fire. During the entire occupation of north Cassino by our troops, the enemy-held portions of the town were subjected to extremely heavy artillery concentrations, including 8-inch and 240mm fire, but his attitude remained unchanged. At no time did he show any intention to withdraw and our elements in the town were in contact at all times.[33]

Not that the Americans were slow to learn. It was simply that every individual house was a formidable strongpoint. Most were stone-built and the only truly effective way to make any impression on them was for a tank to fire at a wall from a few feet away. Bazookas were a tolerable substitute but the operators had to loose off upwards of ten rockets, from suicidally close ranges, just to create one hole about three feet wide. Even when an outer wall was breached in this way, and access gained, the operation had to be repeated to get into any of the adjoining rooms. And good bazooka men were hard to find. The CO of 133 Regiment remarked that 'the bazooka is a highly effective weapon when properly used – but I believe the most important thing is to pick out the right type of man to use it. The kind of man you want is the type that will spit in a rattlesnake's eye. There are some in almost every company – it's just a case of picking them out.'[34] When bazookas were not available great reliance was placed upon grenades, either thrown by hand or from a launcher. The standard tactic in this case was to use

> 5 or 6 men against each house. Each group had two men equipped with launchers and rifle grenades. 3 leading men of group would creep up close to house while remaining 2 or 3 men covered; threw one or two hand grenades into lower rooms of houses and immediately rushed in through windows or doors. Surviving Germans would have to be upstairs, so covering group fired rifle grenades through upper windows. This drove Germans downstairs where killed or captured.[35]*

But such tactics were just as severe a drain on manpower as the endless assaults on the massif and by 10 February all three regiments of 34 Division were in a parlous state. The 135th, for example, estimated that few of its rifle companies could muster more than thirty men. The commander of 168 Regiment also reported his battalions to be dwindling fast. On the same day

> the extra drivers of the 3rd Battalion were attached to Company 'K' and the anti-tank platoon and extra drivers of the 1st Battalion were attached to Company 'B'. Whether for attack or for defence, the front-line strength of the regiment was dangerously low. The seriousness of the situation is indicated by the formation on 10 February of a provisional rifle company . . . [including] 7 men from HQ Company, 8 from Anti-tank Company, and 15 men who had just returned from hospital.[36]

---

* Grenade throwing was not regarded as quite the same specialized technique as using a bazooka. When a newspaper correspondent made a facetious remark to a soldier of 100 Battalion, linking their supposed predilection for baseball to the ability to throw grenades, the later replied wearily: 'Mister, all you gotta do is trow straight and trow first. Dat's da numbah one theeng, trow first.' (Quoted in Murphy, *op. cit.*, p.175.)

By now the rest of 36 Division had also arrived on the massif and even though it had not yet been used in any major attacks, the casualties from mortars, artillery and counter-attacks had been unremitting. One of its staff officers reported to II Corps:

> . . . 141 Infantry has not advanced and has had heavy losses. In 1 Bn there are 56 men left. In 3 Bn there are 75 men left. . . . A very strong German counter-attack . . . was launched against 3 Bn 143 Infantry preceded by very heavy mortar and artillery concentrations . . . I and K Cos have a total of 25 riflemen left.[37]

But II Corps' sufferings were not just a matter of their appalling casualties. Many men, indeed, must have sometimes wanted to be wounded just to escape from the grim daily round on the bare, rain-swept slopes. The demands made on the men by this type of combat were exceptional:

> The strain imposed by continual fighting in the mountains . . · has been materially increased by mud, rain, cold and unhealthy climatic conditions. Only the highest level of hardening and stamina can resist the physical strain of combat operations under these conditions. The high percentage of non-battle casualties as a result of exhaustion and physical breakdown, as well as by sickness, has demonstrated this fact only too clearly. . .[38]

A pithier evaluation of mountain fighting was given by a corporal of 135 Regiment who was particularly aggrieved at the constant cold and the lack of hot food and drink in the front lines: 'There is one particular item which . . . is never issued in sufficient quantity. I am speaking of the small gasoline stove which anybody who spent a winter in the hills of Italy will tell you is a very definite improvement to life which, at best, is absolutely no good.'[39]* One of the best summaries of the rigours of life on the massif was given by an enlisted man in 2/141 Regiment, who moved on to Monte Castellone on 9 February:

> Mud, water and the chills couldn't keep one from sleeping that night. . . . The day of the 10th was spent hunting for 'c' rations among the debris of the 34 Division, checking position and perfecting our holes. That night, like the day, was taken up with

---

* The lack of hot food, absolutely vital to men living under such debilitating strain, was a very serious problem. Many units did their best to get cooked rations forward but the experience of 1/133 Regiment, who received their first hot meal for twenty-three days in late January, was far from unusual.

dodging the ever-present artillery and mortar fire. In addition there were ration and water details, patrols, listening posts, outposts and 50 per cent night alerts to keep most men from gaining enough rest. . . . The night of the 10th . . . every man . . . was again drenched in a heavy downpour. . . . After bedding and clothing were brought to saturation point many men gave up bailing and tried to get what rest they could. . . . [The following night] was another to live for ever in the memories of every man up there. Wet and without a warm period of rest . . . for 93 hours Jerry threw the largest barrage ever experienced by this unit. . . . Our losses were heavy for a dug-in defensive position. . . . During the barrages snipers penetrated our lines and constantly harassed every man who left his hole. . . . Numerous instructions were passed along about different plans to push through us and round us, but still we just sat and took it.[40]

Perhaps the most disturbing aspect of the situation was that neither Keyes nor Ryder, nor any of their staffs, seemed to have any conception of just how grim things were on the massif. Brigadier Howard Kippenberger, with 2 New Zealand Division, actually visited some of the forward positions and on the 9th told his divisional commander that 'the American infantry was worn out and quite unfit for battle without a thorough rest. . . . [The latter] was disturbed and questioned the American commanders closely as to the condition of their troops and it was very plain that none of them had been forward or was at all in touch with his men.'[41]* Some news of this probably got back to Alexander, for he immediately despatched his Chief of Staff, General Lyman L. Lemnitzer, to Cassino to assess the mood of II Corps. His report back was hardly encouraging. He 'talked to commanders and troops and found

* It is important here to distinguish between senior commanders and company officers. Though the relations between the latter and their men were not always harmonious, there was more often than not a bond of common suffering that united all ranks at the front. The following vignette by a US war correspondent is far from unique. An officer's body has just been brought down from the mountains after the relief of his company (part of 36 Division): 'Two men unlashed his body from the mule and lifted it off and laid it in the shadow by the stone wall. . . . A soldier came and stood beside the officer and bent over and . . . spoke to his dead captain, not in a whisper, but awfully tenderly, and he said, "I sure am sorry, sir." Then . . . he reached down and took the captain's hand, and he sat there for a full five minutes, holding the dead hand in his own and looking intently into the dead face. . . . Finally he put the hand down. He reached over and gently straightened the points of the captain's collar, and he sort of rearranged the tattered edges of the uniform around the wound, and then he got up and walked away down the road in the moonlight, all alone.' (E. Pyle, *Brave Men*, Holt and Co., New York, 1944, pp. 154–6.)

morale progressively worse . . . [the troops] disheartened, almost mutinous.'[42] Such front-line evidence as there is goes some way to confirming this diagnosis. After the battle 168 Regiment found that it had suddenly acquired an extra 443 men, though there had been only 52 hospital returns and 16 replacements. Its commander contented himself with remarking: 'The remainder of the increase may be attributed to straggling and to the difficulty of absorbing new replacements under combat conditions.'[43] 36 Division had similar problems. An officer with 3/141 Regiment was returning into the line when he came across

> a small group of men, none of whom I recognized. The place where they were turned out to be a check point, and a young first lieutenant was in charge. He had his pistol out of its holster and was holding it in his hand. He asked me where I was going. When I told him, he said that he wanted to know in case I had to come back. He had orders, he added, to make everyone stay. Too many men had come down the trail complaining of sickness or minor wounds, so the battalion commander put him there to stop everyone except the seriously wounded. I had not realized that the situation had been quite so bad. While I was resting I heard him arguing with two soldiers, and I saw them turn around and start slowly back up the steep trail. I did not think that I would ever see one of our officers use a gun on our men. It is true that, so far as I know, he never did fire it. But he threatened to.[44]

Yet Keyes and Ryder were already grouping their forces for a new attack and, unforgivably perhaps, Alexander declined to intervene. It jumped off on the 11th, with 168 Regiment attacking towards the Monastery and 141 and 142 Regiments now called in to try and damp down the deadly flanking fire from around Albaneta Farm and Point 593.* No appreciable progress was made by any of these units. 142 Regiment was unable to hold on to such ground as was gained around the farm because the Germans were still in firm possession of Point 575, overlooking the Americans. Their plunging fire obliged 142 Regiment to withdraw, upon which the defenders immediately switched their fire against 141 Regiment, on Snakeshead, and ground their attack to a halt. Without any cover to their right, 168 Regiment did not have a chance and after a gallant rush forward, in a blinding snowstorm, they were sent once more reeling back to their start line. The First Battle of Cassino was now

---

* Point 593 had been lost by 34 Division to a German counter-attack some time on the 10th.

over and II Corps had temporarily ceased to exist as an effective fighting formation.

The Corps was almost literally shattered. Casualties were horrendous. 2/168 Regiment, for example, could count only 7 officers and 78 men in its three rifle companies. 3/133 Regiment could count 145 all ranks, and in 141 Regiment the combined strength of 1 and 3 Battalions was 22 officers and 160 men. In the latter battalion it was reported that on the 12th the three rifle companies had an *aggregate* strength of 25 men.* Beginning on the 12th, the Corps was relieved by men from 2 New Zealand and 4 Indian Divisions, now charged with finishing off the job in the Cassino sector. The newcomers could feel nothing but compassion for the haggard survivors they found on the massif. A New Zealand report stated:

> On beginning to take over the positions around Pt. 593, 7 Indian Brigade discovered that the situation was far less favourable than the number of US Regiments holding them indicated. Repeated attacks and counter-attacks . . . and continued exposure to mortar and shell fire in shallow 'fox-holes' scraped on the surface of the rock had whittled away the numbers. . . . The survivors were utterly exhausted as much by exposure to the frost and snow as by enemy action.[45]

Even 34 Division's staff had to admit that morale was at a very low ebb, though they again resorted to that bizarre preliminary incantation that sought to imply that the fighting spirit of an infantry division was not necessarily and primarily a function of the attitude of the fighting infantrymen themselves:

---

* Such battalion casualty figures as are available are given below, along with the figures for the whole of 34 Division:

Some 34 Division Casualties 24 Jan.–12 Feb. 1944

	Killed	Wounded	Missing	% (of rifle coys)
2/135 Regt	40	150	14	45
3/135 Regt	42	164	10	49
3/133 Regt	52	174	23	56
100/133 Regt	48	134	–	40
34 Division	318	1641	392	49

The morale of the Division was considered excellent, although the infantry elements particularly were very weary and tired from long and continuous contact with the enemy. Heavy losses not only cut the effective strength of the various units but reduced the fighting spirit of the men. This supplemented by the fact that enemy resistance continued to be strong and [that there were] no replacements to help carry the load, was, indeed, very discouraging to the front-line soldier.[46]

Indeed. And those that watched them come out of the line could not but see the effects of such an ordeal on once keen and healthy young men. The few who were prepared to even talk about it took refuge in laconic irony. One company of New Zealanders passed a group of Americans out and one recalled: 'As we trudged in through the mud-clogged fields . . . one of the boys asked the Yanks as they hurried past in the darkness: "What's it like in there?" "Waal," replied one who took time off to answer, "it's a hot old time in that old town." ' Others were too far gone even to realize that temporary respite was at hand. According to another New Zealander in the same company: 'On the night that we took over from the US troops two of their men were in such a bad way physically that they did not wish to go out in the dark and chose to make a break for it just before first light. They were however mowed down by Spandau fire as they endeavoured to make a break along the side of the Rapido river.'[47] But most men were simply tired – not tired as one looking forward to a good night's sleep, but utterly physically drained and the mind so battered with extremes of fear and horror that it now barely functioned. They were like zombies, their eyes fixed on the far distance:

They were infantrymen returning to a bivouac area for rest and I knew from the divisional emblem on their sleeves that those men had been up in the mountains around Cassino. . . . I thought I had never seen such tired faces. It was more than the stubble of beard that told the story; it was the blank, staring eyes. The men were so tired that it was like a living death. They had come from such a depth of weariness that I wondered if they would ever be able quite to make the return to the lives and thoughts they had known.[48]

7
'A Matter of Honour'

The French Expeditionary Corps on Colle Belvedere,
25 January–3 February 1944

My great pride is to have had the honour to lead such men.

Commandant Berne, commanding 2/4 RTT

Before he put 34 Division on the rack General Clark had at least realized
that he must if possible provide some support on an adjacent part of the
front. It was for this reason that, on the 23rd, he asked Juin to abandon
his original axis of advance, towards Atina, and to mount an attack on
the Belvedere/Abate massif, just north of Cassino, to pin down potential
reserves that might be used against the Americans. Juin was less than
pleased at the prospect. It was, he felt,

> a mission which in other circumstances I would have deemed
> impossible. It was not at all to my taste, involving as it did an attempt
> to outflank the enemy at close range rather than on a much wider
> arc of manoeuvre. It extended yet more my already overstretched
> front and turned me away from my objective, Atina, which I
> regarded as vital for the development of any manoeuvre involving
> the whole Army.[1]

There were also serious technical problems involved in such a drastic
change of direction, particularly as Clark had insisted that the new
offensive be launched no later than 25 January. A report of Juin's 3^e
Bureau outlined the most obvious ones:

> This change of direction will pose a particularly difficult problem in
> view of the time available (it is now the evening of the 23rd . . .) and
> the difficult terrain; the artillery in particular, if it is to effectively
> support the attack, will have to be completely redeployed. To make
> matters worse, the sector in which we have to concentrate is only
> served by one very inadequate mountain road, that from Sant' Elia,
> which is under constant enemy artillery fire.[2]

Others stated their objections more forcibly. To execute the new attack Juin had chosen the Algerian Division, slightly the fresher of his two formations, and when Monsabert was informed that he was supposed to storm one of the deepest and most inaccessible portions of the Gustav Line and then carry on to push deep into the German rear, via Terelle and Monte Cairo, he could scarcely conceal his incredulity:

> Storm Belvedere? Who's dreamed up that one? Have they even looked at it? You'd first have to cross two rivers, the Rapido and the Secco, then smash through the Gustav Line in the valley, and finally, all the time attacking the Boche, climb more than 2000 feet over a bare rock-pile, itself heavily fortified, that can be fired on from . . . Cifalco and the rest of the summits round about. It's pure wishful thinking! A crazy gamble, *mon général*![3]*

Juin agreed but solemnly pointed out to Monsabert that some sort of renewed effort was vital if 34 Division was to have any chance of success. In the last analysis, whether or not they had much faith in Clark's overall plan, and whatever their misgivings about their own chances of success, the French Expeditionary Corps was being asked to demonstrate its loyalty to the Allied cause. For Juin this was still a prime consideration and one that could persuade him to ignore his soundest strategic instincts. His final remark to Monsabert was perhaps the only one that really counted: 'It is a matter of honour.'

Preparations immediately went ahead and in a remarkable feat of organization most of the French troops and guns were in position by early on the 25th. The Moroccan Division remained in place, between Monte Carella and Costa San Pietro, whilst the rest of the now dormant portion of the line, from Monte Carella to the lower slopes of Monte Cifalco, was manned by various battalions of 3 and 7 RTA. Other battalions from these latter regiments were ordered into the Rapido Valley, opposite Colle Belvedere, to establish a firm base for the attack and to provide reserves to capitalize upon any breakthrough. The actual assault was to be made by 4 RTT, commanded by Colonel Roux, who were rushed forward to their start line some hours ahead of any other of Monsabert's battalions. This

---

* With regard to this and other chunks of direct speech quoted by Chambe, he is at pains to point out (p.5) that they are based upon extensive interviews, conducted shortly after the event, with all those cited. Chambe himself fought in Italy with the French Corps and his book is a prime source on the Belvedere battle, as well as a profoundly moving *hommage* to its victors.

approach march was not the least of their trials. The War Diary of 3/4 RTT pointed out that

> Unfortunately we had no mules. It seemed that we would get them on the morning of the 26th. We had to set off with all the ammunition and equipment on our backs . . . a box of 'κ' rations (one-third of the daily ration), a canteen of water, a groundsheet, a blanket slung over the shoulder and the greatest possible quantity of grenades and ammunition for the machine guns and mortars. *The loads carried by each man were quite incredible.*[4]

The whole journey took eight hours, most of it made in the pitch dark, up and down steep, treacherous mountain slopes, guided only by a small white patch tied on to the pack on the back of the man in front. Towards the end 'everyone marched like drugged men, their backs bowed, knees stiff, thighs seized up with cramp. Would this Calvary never end?'[5] Even when the valley was reached the troops were obliged to wade across the icy-cold Rapido, often up to their armpits, before they slumped down, teeth chattering, at their jumping-off points.

Two battalions of the Tunisian Regiment were to lead the attack.* On the right was the 3rd, led by Commandant Gandoet, and under normal circumstances each of its two objectives would have been the responsibility of an entire battalion. As it was, only one company, the 9th, was assigned to storming the northern end of Monte La Propaia, Point 470, and thus attempting to seal off the Secco Valley, through which the Germans would almost certainly seek to counter-attack. A single company, the 11th, was again all that was available to spearhead an attack across the valley and up the northern end of the Belvedere/Abate escarpment, though it was hoped that the reserve companies would be able to join them later on the same day. Their initial target was Point 681, on Colle Belvedere, which was to be approached via a steep, narrow cleft in the rocks, already christened *le ravin Gandoet*. From Belvedere they and the reserve companies were to mount an immediate attack on Point

---

* 4 RTT was organized thus:

1 Bn (Comm. Bacqué)	*2 Bn (Comm. Berne)*	*3 Bn (Comm. Gandoet)*
1 Coy (Capt. Lartigau)	5 Coy (Capt. Chatillon)	9 Coy (Capt. Denée)
2 Coy (Lt Billard)	6 Coy (Lt Thouvenin)	10 Coy (Capt. Louisot)
3 Coy (Capt. Carré)	7 Coy (Capt. Tixier)	11 Coy (Lt Jordy)
1 Support Coy	2 Support Coy	3 Support Coy
(Lt Potard)	(Capt. d'Isaac)	(Capt. Jean)

862, one of the jagged circle of peaks that made up Colle Abate, on the crest of the escarpment.

The highest peak on Colle Abate, slightly to the south, was Point 915 and this was the responsibility of 2 Battalion, led by Commandant Berne. Their attack was conceived in the same two basic stages, first establishing themselves on the southern end of Colle Belvedere (Point 700, 721 and 771) and then straightway jumping off for the attack on Colle Abate. All three of Berne's rifle companies were in the line; the 7th on the right, heading for Point 700, and the 5th and 6th, echeloned one behind the other, under orders to take Points 721 and 771 in quick succession. For the time being 1 Battalion was to remain in reserve.

The attack on Point 470 began at 07.00, on the 25th, and in the first rush Captain Denée's men succeeded in clearing most of the position, though a few Germans still clung to the summit and the reverse slopes. Almost immediately, however, the German artillery on Monte Cifalco began to pound the position and as soon as the fire lifted a fierce counter-attack was launched. The Tirailleurs lost ground but were immediately rallied by Denée, who ordered a bayonet charge. 'This time, men, we'll make it this time! Nobody stops for the wounded! Forward, charge!'

They surged forward again and were within a hundred yards or so of the summit when Denée was seriously wounded in the chest. A radio operator had also been hit and Denée crawled across to his set and spoke in a gurgling whisper to Gandoet: 'Denée here . . . I'm wounded . . . About to take the objective . . . I'm handing over command to Lieutenant el Hadi . . . Terribly difficult . . . Don't worry, the 9th will make it . . . they'll make it . . . to the bitter end.'

Denée had chosen his man well and el Hadi immediately leapt to his feet, called the company to him and dashed forward towards the summit.

Half the company were casualties, but those Tirailleurs who had not been hit became like men possessed. They had reached the stage where fear has vanished, where you are anaesthetized by the excess of danger, and have but one single aim, to hurt, hurt and hurt again because you have seen too many comrades fall and heard too many screams, or have been grazed by too many bullets, lacerated too often by exploding shells that should have killed you. You were invulnerable, by God![6]

They did almost reach the crest but were immediately thrown back by a German counter-attack. They rallied once more and were driven off yet

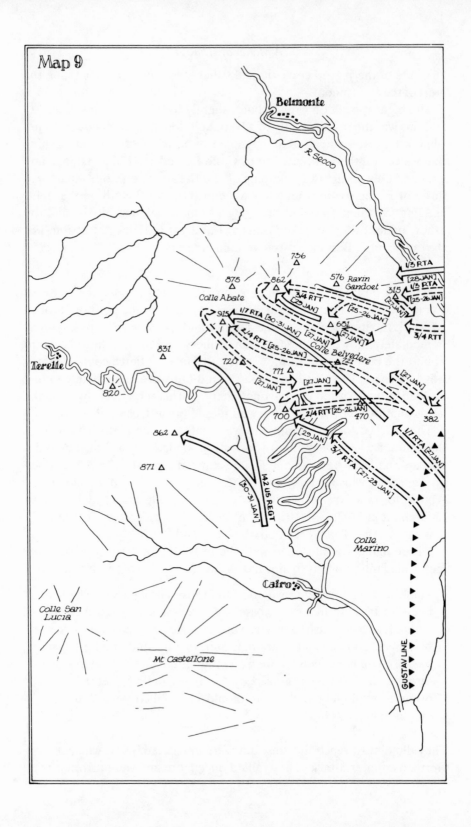

Map 9
Belmonte
R Secco
736
875 862 576 Ravin
Colle Abate Gandoet 1/3 RTA
[28 JAN]
3/4 RTT 315 1/3 RTA
[26 JAN] [27 JAN] [25-26 JAN]
915 1/7 RTA [30-31 JAN]
2/4 RTT [25-26 JAN] 681 3/4 RTT
831 [27 JAN] [27 JAN]
Terelle 720 Colle Belvedere [27 JAN]
820 771 221
[27 JAN] [27 JAN]
700 2/4 RTT [25-26 JAN] 470 382
862 [29 JAN] 1/7 RTA [27 JAN]
871 5/7 RTA [27-28 JAN]
142 US REGT [30-31 JAN]
Colle
Marino
Cairo
Colle San
Lucia
GUSTAV LINE
Mt. Castellone

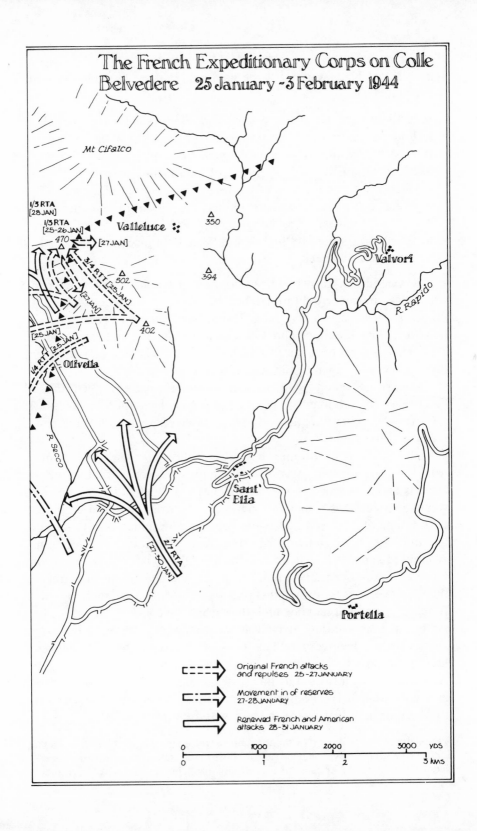

The French Expeditionary Corps on Colle
Belvedere   25 January ~ 3 February 1944

Mt Cifalco

1/3 RTA
[28 JAN]

1/3 RTA
[25-26 JAN]
470   [27 JAN]

3/4 RTT [25 JAN]

502
[21 JAN]

[25 JAN]

1/4 RTT [25 JAN]

Olivella

R. Secco

Valleluce

△ 350

△ 394

△ 402

Valvori

R. Rapido

Sant'
Elia

2/7 RTA
[27-30 JAN]

Portella

Original French attacks
and repulses   25-27 JANUARY

Movement in of reserves
27-28 JANUARY

Renewed French and American
attacks   28-31 JANUARY

0   1000   2000   3000   YDS

0   1   2   3 KMS

again. But el Hadi was not to be gainsaid. For the last time he drew himself erect and

pressed forward. His forearm was sliced off by a shell burst. For half an hour he was in command of the company, dragging it behind him. A veritable banner to the men, he yelled and hurled himself about like a madman. Individual groups of men inched forwards. They reached the summit. At that moment Lieutenant el Hadi was hit right across the body by a burst of machine gun fire. He shouted to Tirailleur Barelli who was alongside him, 'You, fire the flare!' Then he stood up, shouted to the heavens 'Vive la France!' and fell dead on the conquered peak.[7]

It was about 10.30. It had been hoped that the attack by 9 Company would have been carried through before the rest of the troops had to set off across the Secco Valley, thus safeguarding their right flank. At 08.00, however, both Gandoet and Colonel Roux agreed that even though Denée had not yet been successful, he had hopefully created a sufficient diversion to risk launching the general attack.

'Taken or not taken,' said Gandoet, 'Point 470 has now been isolated by Denée. The Germans down there definitely have their hands full. If there is a chance, any at all, of climbing up Belvedere, it's while their eyes are turned elsewhere.'

Both battalions set off and they crossed the valley without too much trouble. The Germans were indeed fully occupied with the furious assaults on Point 470, and had anyway been fairly confident that no one would be so reckless as to launch a frontal attack on the Belvedere/Abate escarpment. It is as well that they were, for determined counter-attacks into the valley night well have aborted the mission at the very beginning. Armoured support had been provided for this stage of the operation, much of it American, and French reports were unanimous in regretting the tankmen's lack of aggression. Even during the planning of 2 Battalion's attack it had been felt that 'when the commanders of the two American tank sections arrived at the Battalion Command Post they showed themselves very reluctant about their units being employed.' During the early stages of 7 Company's attack they were no less reluctant. As the company left its start line 'it was caught . . . by heavy fire from automatic weapons on Point 73. The American tanks, one of which struck a mine, did not push forward and soon withdrew from the fighting.'[8]*

---

* French complaints about US armoured units were also quite common during the May battles (see Chapter 15). They do not, however, indicate a general mistrust between these two armies, American and French infantry being well aware of each other's

The French infantry, however, pressed on. By nightfall, 2 Battalion was just short of its first objectives. Having taken Point 382, 6 and 7 Companies had diverged, the former climbing up towards Point 721, the latter towards Point 700. Captain Tixier had actually got some of his leading elements on to Point 700, in the evening, but two strong German counter-attacks had finally forced him to withdraw a few yards below the crest. Lieutenant Thouvenin's company had found the going even more arduous and by the time they were in position to attack Point 721 it was judged too dark to mount a properly co-ordinated effort. Both companies had suffered severe casualties, as had the 5th, which, although not in the forefront of the attack, had been caught in several heavy bombardments. Its commander had been killed and his replacement, Lieutenant Clément, put himself under Thouvenin's command when his men finally joined 6 Company just below Point 721.

Gandoet's attack across the valley was terribly compromised from the start. Denée's company was completely absorbed in trying to hang on to Point 470 and, as the day wore on, the battalion commander was obliged to send first his Support Company and then parts of the 10th, to buttress this position. The rest of 10 Company were forced to linger at the southern end of Monte la Propaia. They were supposed to have been relieved there by a battalion of 3 RTA, who would help seal off the Secco Valley, but it was nightfall before the latter actually arrived. Lieutenant Jordy's 11 Company, therefore, had to attack completely alone, with no prospect of immediate support even if they did succeed in establishing themselves on Colle Belvedere. Nevertheless they pressed ahead and fairly soon reached the foot of the *ravin Gandoet*. This route to their first objective had been chosen with the best intentions, as an approach which would hopefully offer some sort of cover to the attackers, perhaps even the prospect of complete surprise. Unfortunately both Gandoet and Roux had only seen it through binoculars, whilst to the men on the spot, craning their necks to try and pick out the upper reaches, the whole venture seemed madness. The ravine was

> a sort of slanting corridor, or rather a gash cut in the mountainside by a giant's sabre stroke, rising straight up to the sky. The rock sides, only a few metres high, were so steep, so close to the vertical, with menacing overhangs crowned with brambles and scrub, that on close examination they seemed unclimbable. The slope of the gorge was

achievements. Indeed, close tactical co-operation between different nationalities was rare, especially given Alexander's 'preoccupation . . . with regrouping British, Americans and French in quite separate compartments.' (Juin, 9 March 1944, quoted in Boulle, *op. cit.*, vol. 1, p. 137.)

so abrupt that it sent a shiver down one's spine. . . . To make things worse it was blocked with slabs of rock, some of them enormous, which had been brought down by thousands of years of erosion and spring thaws. Getting across them would involve a combination of mountaineering and acrobatics. Climb up there? All of 2500 feet, every man with an enormous load, using only his feet, his hands, his knees and his teeth. Almost three times the height of the Eiffel Tower, to be clambered up foot by foot with no steps, no handrail, no one to help.[9]

But little was to be gained by simply staring in disbelief and, at about 10.00, the ascent began. The sheer physical effort was bad enough but after half an hour or so the leading sections came across a gap in the ravine swept by machine gun fire from pillboxes on Point 382, to the left, and Point 315, to the right. The latter was almost on the very edge of the ravine and Jordy called for volunteers. Four Tirailleurs crawled up to him and were told to grab as many grenades as they could carry and try to get within striking distance of the emplacement. They slithered forward and miraculously three of them succeeded in getting close enough to stuff their grenades through the firing slit. Three of the occupants were killed and the four survivors surrendered without further ado. Point 382 was too far away for a similar attack, being in fact one of 2 Battalion's preparatory objectives. Happily the latter's attack went in at much the same time and its success enabled Jordy's company to continue their awesome climb.

At 16.00 German shells began to fall thick and fast. The French clambered on but as they reached certain stretches of the ravine they again came into the view of German machine gunners or the observers for their numerous mortars. Jordy tried to call for artillery support to creep ahead of his leading platoon but found that his radio was dead. Still they climbed. Despite the cold his men were now bathed in sweat and their mouths parched, but most had long ago drained their water bottles. 'The climb became a nightmare. The physical and moral effort demanded of them stretched the men to the limits of human resistance, eventually took them beyond. Tirailleurs who had so far passed through unscathed felt a black veil fall over their eyes, the result of overstrained hearts and complete muscular exhaustion. They had to stop, to fight against blacking out, to desperately hang on at the edge of the void.'[10] Yet they climbed on and after two more hours, that seemed to some of them like whole days, their objective, Point 681, suddenly loomed up in front of them. Scouts crept forward and found to their surprise that the peak was not strongly held. A swift attack by one of Jordy's platoons overwhelmed a pillbox covering the approaches, whilst a machine gun post, a little further back, was taken in the flank by a sergeant and three other volunteers. The whole company then swept forward and overran the remaining slit-trenches, killing most of the defenders and driving the survivors down the reverse slopes.

By the time they had done what they could to consolidate the position night was falling. No further advance was possible until morning. The regimental commander, Colonel Roux, was not convinced that it would be feasible even then. Though starved of reliable information he was well aware of how precarious were the positions of both his battalions and he did what he could to reinforce them. Gandoet's 10 Company was finally relieved in the evening by 1/3 RTA and the two platoons not involved in the bitter struggle on Point 470 were dispatched to join Jordy. Bacqué's 1 Battalion was alerted at the same time. Two of his companies had already been committed piecemeal on Point 470 but the others, 1st and 3rd, were rushed across the Secco. The latter was to join Berne's battalion, just below Point 721, the former to plug the gap between this peak and what was left of 11 Company on Colle Belvedere. All reached their positions successfully, at around midnight, having had to pass through the ghastly detritus of the day's fighting. The commander of 3 Company, Captain Carré, scribbled in his diary:

> Visibility less than two yards. Pause every 150 feet of the climb. Arduous ascent. Muscles and nerves at breaking-point. The rumble of enemy artillery and mortars . . . Explosions 60 feet above us. Men slip, fall six or seven feet, risk breaking their backs . . . Such human suffering! Packs, weapons. I joke with the Tirailleurs. Night black, visibility zero, we trample over corpses; they're ours, one with no head, his guts spilling out.[11]

Even with these reinforcements, Roux still did not believe that his men could be ready for an attack the next morning. He rang his divisional commander and begged for a twenty-four-hour delay. 'I no longer even know exactly where my units are. I need to regroup, to organize, to make good my losses.'

Monsabert would have none of it. Any delay would simply give the Germans more time to organize their defences. 'Out of the question, Roux. We've had notice of German reinforcements who've left Belmonte and are climbing back up the slopes of Belvedere. That means counter-attacks on all the points that you've seized. Prepare to attack 862 and 915 without delay.' This conversation was transcribed at Monsabert's command post and as he read through it after the battle he added a brief marginal comment, 'Cruel necessity'.[12]

So the regiment hung on, waiting for the morning. Most exposed of all were 11 Company, on Colle Belvedere, yet though their War Diary did not make light of their position it also highlighted the men's unswerving conviction that this indeed was a matter of honour:

> Our front is over-extended. . . . Position tenuous because ammunition is scarce. . . . All contact lost with the valley . . . Radio contact miraculously made at 17.00 telling us to hang on whatever the cost. Since 16.30 the mortaring has become more and more accurate and violent, causing casualties . . . We are organizing the position . . . Nobody sleeps. No water. Little to eat. The ration boxes were thrown away during the climb because they were too heavy. No contact from 18.00. We must hang on . . . we stay where we are.[13]

In the event, Roux was allowed some respite on the 26th before his regiment had to attack the twin peaks of Colle Abate. Knowing that the Germans were even now massing for a big counter-attack, Monsabert conceded that he first ought at least to try and consolidate his flanks. On the right he sent 1/3 RTA to plug the Secco Valley, between Points 315 and 470, and on the left pushed up 3/7 RTA to take over Point 700 from Tixier's 7 Company. News of the latter move, however, was only of limited comfort to Tixier and his Commandant, as the relieving battalion could not possibly arrive until the 27th. But 1/3 RTA could be in position in a few hours and as this would relieve much of the pressure on Point 470, Gandoet made ready to move up his ravine with the motley collection of units that had been thrown in to defend that point.* It was decided, therefore, to defer the regimental attack until these forces had reached 11 Company and the two platoons of the 10th who had gone up the night before. They could not arrive too soon. Jordy and newly arrived platoon commanders, Lieutenants Bouakkaz and Nicolas, were under no illusions as to what would happen if they were called upon to attack, or even only hang on, without substantial reinforcement. As the three officers talked softly to one another they became grimly fatalistic about their hopeless position. Nicolas described the appalling exertions of the scramble up the escarpment, in the pitch dark, and went on: 'No, Jordy, no one will ever know what we have done. No one will ever have a glimmering. . . . These things, you see, they can't be described. They will disappear with us. The

---

* 9 Company had now virtually ceased to exist. Gandoet thus had at his disposal two platoons of his own 10 Company, all of his Support Company and 2 and 4 Companies from Bacqué's 1st Battalion.

Frenchmen back home will know nothing about it . . . ever. Oh! if only it didn't have to be this way for you as well!'

Even as he spoke, Gandoet was assembling his men to start out for the ravine. At dawn they set off. The Battalion's War Diary describes the march that followed. After crossing the Secco they came to the foot of the ravine and

> in small groups of four or five they climbed, backs bent under the terrible weight of their loads and under the shower of shells. The men clung on to one another, gasping for breath. They threw themselves flat, rose again, dragged themselves upwards on all fours. Several were killed, many others wounded. . . . The effort was superhuman. They were climbing almost vertically. No question of giving up. The 11th were up there. They had to reach them. The ground was the only protection. They could only lower their heads, seek for cover, press forward and get there with the ammunition. Heavy machine guns, mortars, shells, radios, everything was carried upwards slowly but surely. . . . The order was given to bypass the opposition, to sneak through them, not to expend a single cartridge because they would be too valuable up there! But hurry, the 11th was hemmed in by the Boche. Their radio messages were becoming anguished. Get up there at all costs.[14]

The leading elements finally joined hands with Jordy at 14.00. As soon as Roux was informed he ordered them to attack Point 862 at 16.30, with Berne's battalion jumping off for Point 915 at the same time though the latter, of course, would first have to clear their sector of Colle Belvedere. Both battalions set off on time. Little is known of what happened to Berne's companies, although at around 20.00 they did take their preliminary objectives of Points 700, 721 and 771.* Casualties were severe and Captain Léoni, who had taken over from Berne when the latter was badly concussed by an exploding shell, was reluctant to push on for Point 915. But Roux was inflexible. The remnants of 5 and 6 Companies went forward at 21.00 and, with scarcely more than a couple of platoons still standing, reached the topmost peak of Colle Abate at 02.30 the following

* By the end of the Belvedere battle, 2/4 RTT no longer existed as an effective fighting unit and, as the author of its post-combat report noted: 'One should not expect to find here a minutely detailed account of the Battalion's operations and assaults; on the contrary, I can only deal with these in broad outline because the majority of NCOs and officers who took part in this fighting have disappeared.' (2/4 RTT, *Rapport sur les combats. . ., op. cit.,* p.1.)

morning. After the battle, Berne wrote of his men, few of whom he would ever see again: 'The greatest satisfaction of my career is to be able to tell myself that I have seen under fire the company officers, the French NCOs and the best Tunisian soldiers and have known them for what they were, troops with the will to conquer. And my great pride is to have had the honour to lead such men.'[15]

Gandoet's companies were also successful, but paid the same terrible price. Even before the attack began, 10 and 11 Companies had been reduced to a mere handful of fit men. 'Terrifying mortar and artillery barrages ever since dawn . . . We are open to machine gun fire from all sides. Small groups are probing forwards, we push them back but each repulse makes us anxious about our dwindling ammunition.'[16] Nevertheless, as soon as Gandoet arrived preparations were made for an attack. Contact was made with the rear and the closest artillery was organized, to completely blanket Point 862 until the Tirailleurs were almost on top of it. Even though this was friendly fire, the deafening noise and the shock of the explosions were a considerable trial to the attackers, particularly those who had been pounded from Monte Cifalco for the last twenty-four hours.

> The crashing of the artillery, magnified by the mountain's giant amplifiers, was a terrible test of the men's courage. The ceaseless shock-waves made their nerves as taut as bowstrings. Under their helmets their heads resonated like church bells. One saw men at the end of their tether brandishing their fist in the air and screaming out curses to the world in general. This calmed them, gave them comfort. One has to have been an infantryman under fire to be able to understand it.[17]

At the appointed time the infantry went forward, the platoons leapfrogging over one another as they slowly crept towards the summit. The Germans held on grimly but the ceaseless artillery fire was slowly whittling away their numbers. At about 19.00 Gandoet ordered his men to fix bayonets and storm the crest. This they did and managed to fight off the numerous probing counter-attacks that followed. The actual seizure of Point 862 was characterized by another of those almost incredible *gestes* that seem to come straight from the *Song of Roland*. Again a Tunisian officer was involved, this time Lieutenant Bouakkaz of 10 Company. On his arrival at Point 681, some nineteen hours before, he had publicly resolved to be the first to the top of Colle Abate. Sure enough his platoon was amongst the leading elements in the final attack, though their objective was a peak a little to the right of Point 862, known to the

French as *le Piton Sans Nom*. But Bouakkaz' platoon had not gone more than ten yards when a bullet smashed into his forehead, killing him instantly. His men faltered, until two Tunisian NCOs dashed forward, raised the body upright and sat it on a rifle which they held between them, by the stock and the barrel. Another Tirailleur stood behind to support Bouakkaz' back and the macabre quartet stumbled to the summit, the whole section behind them.

Colle Abate was taken, but as day dawned on the 27th it became clear that neither Berne's nor Gandoet's meagre forces would have much chance of holding. For the Germans were concentrating growing numbers of reserves, both on the reverse slopes of Colle Abate and at the entrance to the Secco Valley. When the French first attacked the whole massif had been defended by just two battalions of 131 Regiment (44 Division), whilst the road to Belmonte was blocked by 191 Regiment (71 Division). As soon as it had been realized that the French were in earnest, the alarm bells were rung and von Senger und Etterlin quickly stripped those sections of the front not immediately threatened and established a typically heterogeneous but none the less impressive strike force. The remaining battalion of 131 Regiment was brought up from south of Cassino and another battalion of 191 Regiment from the foothills of Monte Cairo. The whole of 134 Regiment was also assembled, part of it from Atina and the rest from reserve positions behind Cassino. Numbers were made up with two squadrons of a reconnaissance battalion, a pioneer battalion, an alarm company and elements of an airfield security battalion.

By early on the 27th enough of these units were already in position and the Germans counter-attacked. Colle Abate was the responsibility of 2/191 Regiment whilst two battalions of 134 Regiment, the 1st and 3rd, divided their attentions between Point 700 and the Secco Valley. By 11.00, 2/4 RTT was almost completely surrounded on Point 915 and was forced to fall back to a position some 600 yards east of Point 700. This latter point also fell as did Point 771. Berne's battalion had now been almost completely destroyed, the only unit worthy of the name being the survivors of Tixier's 7 Company. The acting commander, Captain Léoni, was among those killed and a letter written by one of the few surviving officers, which described his death, serves as a fitting tribute to the whole battalion: 'This is the picture with which I still treasure his memory. I see him, wounded in the face, unable to speak at all, pointing with his swagger stick at a machine gun that had to be got back into action after its crew had been killed, and all the time the enemy advancing to within a few yards of us. With his eyes alone he sustained all those who were at his side. He was a leader under whose command I am proud to have served.'[18]

Gandoet's men held on a little longer but by noon their situation was desperate. A message was sent by runner to the regimental headquarters: 'Noon. Situation very serious. Massive counter-attacks everywhere. Enemy infiltration. We need an extra battalion. There is no 2nd Battalion.'[19] Within half an hour Gandoet made up his mind and ordered the withdrawal from Colle Abate. As he wrote in the War Diary: 'It was not possible with the numbers we had, *without food and above all without ammunition*, to hold 862 after the virtually complete destruction of the 2nd Battalion.'[20] For Lieutenant Jordy, who joined Gandoet in tears, the decision seemed a bitter recognition of defeat, though his company's War Diary makes it obvious that no other was possible. From dawn on the 27th they had been

> desperately trying to mop up the position. . . Lieutenant Jordy is organizing the defence of 862, trying to keep track of the constant and disturbing enemy probes on his flanks and in his rear. At the same time elements of the enemy are climbing to attack the crest. We have to drive them back with grenades . . . The position cannot be held . . . The enemy artillery fire is terrifying. Each salvo of shells strikes down two or three men. Pressure on the position is mounting by the minute. . . . We are resisting stubbornly . . . The Battalion Commander . . . informed of the critical situation . . . gives the order to fall back at 12.30. . . Four-fifths of the platoon and section commanders are casualties. Most of the machine gunners have been wounded by bullets or killed by shells because they stayed by their weapons during the bombardments. . . . Nevertheless the morale of those who are left is still firm. We have reached a stage where fatigue can be shrugged off and, having neither eaten nor drunk since the 25th, we live on our overexcited nerves.[21]

But the Germans were not going to be content with merely reoccupying Colle Abate. Their aim was to push the French back across the Secco, if possible, and certainly to reoccupy at least the heights of Colle Belvedere. So their counter-attacks continued unremittingly throughout the day. An officer from Gandoet's headquarters, Captain Belsuze, was another who miraculously kept a diary throughout these terrible days. He was put in charge of organizing the defence of Point 681 where

> the rain of mortar shells is hard to credit. Dead and wounded everywhere. Impossible to evacuate them. One can't lift one's head.

Frightful pounding. The Boche are sneaking in on all sides . . . The men are drained. Nothing to eat or drink since they left. No more ammunition. Heavy casualties. The 11th Company has no more than 35 men left out of 185 . . . The night will bring no rest. The enemy is two hundred yards away on our left and holds the peaks four hundred yards in front of us. The men are collapsing with fatigue. The human mechanism has its limits.[22]

The battalion's War Diary amply conveys Gandoet's increasing sense of desperation and his fear that it would prove impossible even to hold on to Colle Belvedere:

The afternoon was spent under a concentration of violent mortar and artillery fire. The Germans were infiltrating more and more vigorously. Nevertheless we had to hold. Ardent, urgent, fervent requests were made to the Colonel. Unfortunately, nothing came, nothing got through. The order was given to search the dead and wounded and take any ammunition they might have. Nobody to shoot unless they were sure of killing; single shots only and, whatever the circumstances, make full use of the bayonet . . . The night passed, long, hard, punctuated by local counter-attacks.[23]

According to the War Diary of XIV Panzer Corps, the German defenders were now stretched to the very limit. The diarist wrote of a 'critical situation . . . in the Belmonte-Terelle sector. Our attacks, launched for the purposes of checking the enemy, bog down under enemy fire. We suffer heavy casualties.'[24] Yet the momentum of their counter-attacks did not seem to diminish throughout the following day, the 28th. On the left, the French front line was now held by two of Bacqué's companies, from 1 Battalion, and the remnants of Tixier's 7 Company, which had placed itself under his command. Even at the height of the battle, crouched in his command post, Bacqué jotted down notes for his War Diary: '[A shell] bursts on a skylight which had been blocked up with stones . . . One of the two radio-operators, the one who turned the crank to work the dynamo, had the top of his skull ripped off, his brains are completely exposed. He still sits in the same seat . . . The lack of fresh supplies, both food and ammunition, is more and more critical.'[25]

Pressure on Gandoet's battalion remained equally intense. Captain Belsuze wrote:

The battalion's main position is completely surrounded. In fact, behind us to the right, at the foot of Belvedere, the Germans have sneaked in and occupied the reverse slopes of the massif and can take us in the rear. Their fire is continuous, as is that of the scum who have taken up position in front of us, on the crests we abandoned yesterday evening. . . . But the men are almost finished. 60 per cent of our strength have been killed or wounded . . . We will have to be relieved, the battalion can do no more; or at least a sizeable reinforcement and fresh supplies of food and ammunition . . . We remain at our posts by the Grace of God. The mass of shells poured down on us, terrifying though they are, are gradually turning us into fatalists. Will it be this one, or the next? God alone knows![26]

This was the last entry in Belsuze's diary. A few minutes later he led a handful of men against a German position, to try and make a break in the ring that was slowly tightening around them. He was killed instantly by a burst of machine gun fire in the chest. Everywhere on Belvedere the situation was the same. 11 Company was virtually annihilated and still 'the guns continue to pound us. Casualties mount.'[27] The battalion's support company went to the aid of the 10th, between Points 681 and 721. The latter's commander was killed and Captain Jean took over both companies:

At 11.00, pistol in hand, standing amongst the loaders of the mortars now transformed into Voltigeurs, he led a bayonet charge. He said to the Battalion Commander, shouting into the radio in the middle of an artillery barrage and demanding ammunition: 'Above all, do not worry! I will hang on.' At 11.15 he arrived at the first aid post, mortally wounded: eleven wounds from mortar shells. His teeth gritted with pain, he said to his commander, who had come to see him, 'Do not worry, the 3rd Support Company will hold in the ravine.' In actual fact, everybody held . . . by a miracle.[28]

A miracle, indeed. Food and drink had all been consumed days ago. Ammunition was fast running out and casualties were incurred almost every minute. The time was fast approaching when the human spirit itself must flicker and die, when the very intensity with which it had burnt thus far must drain the last reserves of even the paladins of Belvedere. That moment was brought yet nearer when it was learnt that a convoy of sixteen mules, sent up from the valley, had been methodically shot to pieces by the Germans. No mules, drivers, food or ammunition got through. The nadir was reached. Of the night of the 28/29th the War Diary recorded: '*No food*. Since the 25th, no food . . . The men were spent. They were hungry, they were cold . . . The night was a tragedy.' Only one thing, in fact, saved the battalion from complete obliteration. This was the supporting artillery who poured in shells until, literally, the barrels of their guns glowed and who were now so familiar with the exact topography of the massif, and the ranges involved, that they were able to lay down fire under the very noses of their own troops and so protect the fragile perimeter. As the War Diary acknowledged: 'Happily the artillery was there to save the situation. Safety margins were turned on their head. Defensive barrages were put down as close to us as possible. Thanks to their incredible precision, thanks to the rapidity of their fire, the battalion was able to hang on without using up the few munitions that it would need tomorrow.'[29]

For tomorrow, incredibly, 1 and 3 Battalions were to attack to try and recapture Colle Abate. Honour was to be satisfied, even to the death. Admittedly, however, the circumstances were a little more propitious than might be at first thought. The German counter-attacks in the Secco Valley had already been repulsed, with 1/3 RTA establishing a firm hold on Points 315 and 470, whilst 3 Algerian Spahis and a battalion of 7 RTA mopped up in Olivella and the lower reaches of the valley. Roux's rear was now more or less secure and other reinforcements were on the way. These were the remaining battalions of 7 RTA, the 1st already in position for an attack on Point 700, the 2nd marching as quickly as it could to take over from Bacqué's battalion. On the left of the French was an American regiment, the 142nd, which had been released by Clark on the 26th for a diversionary attack towards Massa Manna and Terelle. Its deployment had not entirely satisfied the French, who had been promised that the Americans would start their attack on the morning of the 28th, when any relief, to say the least, would have been most welcome. 'But,' a report by Juin noted tersely, 'in the morning the American Brigadier, pleading that he was not ready, informed the commanding general of the 3rd DIA that it was not possible for him to attack.'[30] Some sort of support, however, was promised for the 29th.

The attackers jumped off at 07.00. Things did not go well on the left. 3/7 RTA got a foothold on Point 700 within the first half-hour but were driven off by a German counter-attack at 11.00. Bacqué's battalion did not even reach their objective, Point 771, and were driven back to their start line. On the right, however, Gandoet's men made better progress than they might have expected – many Germans had been sucked into the struggle to retake Points 315 and 470, whilst numerous others had succumbed to the deadly French artillery – and the battered companies actually succeeded in once more conquering Point 862. Gandoet himself wrote: 'Enthusiasm reached a peak . . . every one was as if in a trance.

Victory was in the air. Bayonets fixed, the Tirailleurs sprang forward like devils to attack their respective objectives. No one could stop them. In three-quarters of an hour the slopes of 862 were taken.'[31]

For the men on the spot, however, it did not make too much difference whether or not they had actually accomplished their mission. In either case they were subjected to pitiless counter-attacks and bombardments. Many of the German units were in as parlous a state as the French – 1/134 Regiment was reduced to 36 men – but they were far from giving up. According to a French report drawn up on the 31st: 'The high quality of the NCOs maintained the necessary cohesion amongst the troops to enable them to counter-attack without fail whenever our men were in any difficulties. All the officers, right down to the smallest units, demonstrated tactical initiative and boldness. They held their men (even the foreigners) well in hand to the very end.'[32]* This was indubitably the case on the 29th. Bacqué's battalion was constantly harassed even after it had abandoned the attack on Point 771. Captain Carré's diary offers the most authentic distillation of the horrors of that day:

> Hard. Too hard. Everywhere the dead and wounded. My old corporal, Ramdane, has both his legs smashed. He calls out to me. He has recognized my voice: '*Mon capitaine! Mon capitaine!*' So much blood! Brave Tirailleurs, they make no complaint! Duhamel's martyrs. Mortar shells set the crest ablaze, only five yards from me and my men. *Barraca!* Twenty yards away, ten yards, a circle of fire. Ten, fifteen, twenty shellbursts. *Barraca* once more! No one wounded.
>
> We look disgusting. Plastered with wet mud, hands black. Fingernails torn, hair everywhere, clothes in rags. Lips cracked, skin filthy. Blood! Blood! . . . What are the Americans doing on the plain? The CEF has accomplished prodigies. It can't keep the game up for very long. A strange situation! Miaaaang! a few inches away from my helmet. The swine, they have telescopic sights![33]

Gandoet's men were also subjected to ceaseless counter-attacks. The shortage of ammunition was now critical, threatening the abandonment of all the positions for which so many lives had been sacrificed. The War Diary underlined the urgency: 'Still no food and ammunition was running

---

*The 'foreigners' referred to were the numerous Poles, Austrians and Czechs to be found in certain divisions, whom Allied intelligence consistently held in too low repute, daily expecting mass desertions which never materialized.

out. We had to have ammunition at all costs. The commander demanded it, insisted on it, pleaded for it. He would hold. To eat was nothing but we must have ammunition and some reinforcements.' At 19.00, at the very last gasp, a convoy of twenty-six mules finally got through to the lower slopes of Colle Belvedere, along with a fresh company of men from 3/3 RTA. For Gandoet all this was an inestimable fortune and morale soared.

> We would be able to hold. Every man without an automatic weapon was transformed into a porter. With belts of machine gun bullets slung round their necks, grenades and cartridges in their groundsheets, tubes of mortar shells on their shoulders, they climbed on all fours, through the barrage, up 718 and 762 to carry the ammunition to their comrades. Several men were killed and rolled down the ravine. . . . They found more flares than grenades. They would have to throw the flares, and a large rock after them. . . *They would hold.*[34]

Yet even as the French were beginning to gain the upper hand on the massif – definite gains were made on the left when, in the afternoon, 3/7 RTA finally got a secure lodgement on Point 700 – it was becoming apparent to Juin that, in strategic terms, the heroism of 4 RTT might be largely in vain. Certainly the French had sucked in substantial German reserves, and so perhaps had saved 34 Division from an even worse defeat. But Juin had not seen his offensive as a mere diversion and after his men had first battled their way to the top of Colle Abate he had hoped for a substantial reinforcement from Clark, and a wholehearted commitment to the French axis of advance into the German rear. Clark, had, as we have seen, made one American regiment available but it was now becoming clear that they were not to be used to support a possible breakthrough in Terelle, but simply as a wedge to buttress the French left flank and the rear of the American effort on the Cassino massif.

This latter effort also left a great deal to be desired and by the evening of the 29th Juin was 'indignant to see that whilst 3 DIA, after unparalleled efforts, had fulfilled its appointed task, 34 US Division had not yet set foot on the heights south-west of Monte Cairo.'[35] For Juin had always envisaged the attacks by II Corps and the French Expeditionary Corps as complementary efforts, both aimed at driving west, on either side of Terelle, before wheeling south behind the main German positions on the massif. Even on the 29th, however, 34 Division was still pinned down along the Cairo–Cassino road, only a few hundred yards past its start line. Juin was still willing to fulfil his part of the bargain. On that very day he had given orders that the Algerian Division should 'solidly anchor itself on the conquered ground and . . . cling on throughout tomorrow so as cover from the north the eventual advance by 34 US Division. . .' However, if this advance had still not materialized on the 30th,

> I shall feel obliged, at the earliest possible moment, to pull 3 DIA back, to the east of the Atina–Sant' Elia road. I cannot possibly ask of the Algerian Division any effort above and beyond those they have just made over these last four days, and neither can I take the risk of letting them be cut off in their salient on Monte Belvedere.[36]

Juin ended the letter by hoping that Clark would 'let me know his decision in reasonable time', but it is difficult to see exactly what 'decision' he was hoping for. The problem was simply that 34 Division did not seem to Juin to be sufficiently aggressive and in essence his letter was a none too tactful request that Clark, Keyes and Ryder get their fingers out. The emphasis upon the direction in which the Americans were to attack – towards 'the heights south-west of Cairo' (i.e. Monte Castellone) – also inclines one to think that Juin was already harbouring suspicions that Clark was now much more interested in tackling Monte Cassino head-on, rather than nipping it out from the rear. Writing the letter gave Juin the chance to remind Clark, none too gently, of what he understood to be the purpose of the new offensive. Perhaps also it was simply a way for Juin to give vent to his frustrations, for it is hard to believe that he was as ready as he claimed to give up the whole of the Belvedere/Abate massif when its conquest had involved the virtual destruction of a whole regiment. Certainly, it is difficult not to read considerable satisfaction into Juin's report, in his memoirs, that 'this letter arrived like a bombshell in General Clark's headquarters.'[37]

It definitely seems to have done something to galvanize II US Corps, for on the 30th they finally took Point 213 and over the next three days pushed on to Monte Castellone. The extra pressure on the Germans came only just in time, for the French were fast losing the temporary ascendancy they had won on the 29th. A renewed attack on Point 771, on the 30th, failed yet again. Undertaken by the remnants of Bacqué's command, it had succeeded in momentarily clearing the crest but there were simply not enough men to consolidate the position and they were driven off by a German counter-attack. Bacqué was among the last to fall back and, just before he left, he 'planted his walking-stick in the ground, like a range marker, at the side of the abandoned mortars, and said to his adjutant, "Come. We'll be back to look for all that tomorrow." '[38] A further battalion of 7 RTA, the 3rd, now came into the line and on the 31st they attacked with Bacqué and took Point 771. The latter, who had found both stick and mortars intact, remained in place whilst the new battalion went on to attack Point 915, which was finally retaken, for the last time, at noon.

Yet for the next thirty-six hours the whole outcome of the battle was still balanced on a knife-edge. Gandoet's men were still the only troops on Point 862 and they had nothing left to give. 11 Company, for example, 'had reached the limit of human capabilities. Yet still, on all fours, they dragged the ammunition up to Point 862.'[39] Gandoet himself was close to despair. 'We had to hang on everywhere for yet another night. Every man had done far more than should be asked of him. The night would be terrible. The commander was afraid that his men would collapse with fatigue. All night he spoke with them, going from group to group. Luckily the artillery was on hand . . . A miracle . . . We held.'[40] The balance finally began to tip. The battle had become one of attrition pure and simple and at the very moment when a resolute German counter-attack might have cleared much of Colle Abate, they found the requisite troops were simply not there. By the evening of 1 February the fighting had almost ceased. On the 3rd, 4 RTT was finally relieved, by 3 RTA, and the survivors marched back to Sant' Elia. Juin himself was present during the relief when, 'our hearts overflowing with pity and pride, we saw them coming back, haggard, unshaven, their uniforms in rags and soaked in mud, the glorious survivors of the regiment.'[41] Fifteen officers and 264 other ranks had been killed; 800 of all ranks were wounded; 6 officers and 394 other ranks were missing. Every company officer had been killed or wounded.* Among them were Gandoet, Jordy and Adjutant Dick, who had led up the vital mule convoy on the 29th. All three had survived the battle but as they were descending the escarpment during the relief, they were caught by a chance salvo of shells. Gandoet was badly wounded, Jordy and Dick were killed. The battalion commander only regained consciousness in hospital where he dimly saw

a medical officer asking him the usual two questions to ascertain

---

* A regiment, it will be recalled, contains approximately 1200 riflemen and company officers. The total casualties of 4 RTT were 1481. Obviously a much higher proportion than usual of machine gunners, mortar men and such were intimately involved in this battle, and my usual rule-of-thumb calculation (see p.88) is not really applicable. Nevertheless, the casualty rate amongst those who did the actual fighting must have been around 70 per cent.

whether or not he was concussed: 'What is your name? What is your unit?'

Gandoet replied in a far-away voice, as though he was still up there, microphone in hand, in the thick of the battle, amongst his men: '*Ici Belvédère . . . Ici Belvédère . . . Le bataillon du Belvédère.*'[42]

PART THREE

THE SECOND BATTLE
15–18 February 1944

Well, Freyberg came up and stayed there two months and he didn't get any further than we had. He took several beatings because he decided to climb right up the front of the hill that the monastery was on. But he just got trapped from every side. Those fellows were hanging on with their fingers and toes to the side of the hill with no support or supply or anything else. Nothing . . . He never made an inch.

General G. Keyes

8
'That Bloody Monastery'
Preparations for a Renewed Attack, 4–14 February 1944

I could never understand why the US Fifth Army decided to batter
its head again and again against this most powerful position, held by
some of the finest troops in the German Army in heavily wired and
mined and fixed entrenchments.

General F.I.S. Tuker

Even before II US Corps' offensive on the massif ground to a halt, on 11
February, it was becoming apparent to most senior commanders that the
much vaunted 'Battle for Rome' had been something of a
disappointment. On the 7th, Alexander's nominal superior, General Sir
Henry Maitland Wilson,* the Supreme Allied Commander Mediterranean, was sent a background paper by his operations staff outlining the
progress so far of the offensive. It made depressing reading:

Although . . . a shallow bridgehead has been established across the
Garigliano, we did not achieve our main objects and the enemy's
front is still firm. Later operations carried out in the Cassino area
have had some success. We now have a foothold on the lower
features of the Monte Cairo massif . . . Although the landing at
Anzio was a surprise, the object has not been achieved. The more
southerly road from Rome is . . . not cut and the enemy is believed
to have enough forces around the beachhead to enable him to
deliver a powerful counter-attack. . . [Enemy] morale shows no sign
of weakening [and] his maintenance, although precarious, does not
seem to be having a decisive effect.[1]

Equally gloomy conclusions were drawn in America where General
Marshall and the American Chiefs of Staff were less than pleased that the
campaign they had been so reluctant to support should be using up so
many men and supplies for so little apparent reward. On 5 February
Marshall sent a telegram to London pointing out that the

---

* Wilson had taken over from Eisenhower as Supreme Allied Commander in the
Mediterranean in December 1943, after the latter had been called back to England
to take command of the cross-Channel invasion forces. General Montgomery had also
been recalled to participate in this operation and Eighth Army was now commanded
by Lieutenant-General Sir Oliver Leese.

US Chiefs of Staff feel some concern over progress of operations in Italy. Chiefs of Staff fear that present situation may be developing into an attrition battle with its steadily mounting losses without decisive gains. Also it would appear . . . that there has been *no* heavily mounted aggressive offensive on Main Front. Reports seem to indicate that action on Main Fifth Army Front has been more in the nature of attacks by comparatively small units.[2]

Whatever the men of 5 and 56 British Divisions, 34 and 36 US, or 3 Algerian might have thought about such a curt summary of their efforts, its implications caused some dismay in England and Italy. The British Chiefs of Staff, in fact, were not unduly concerned about the actual strategic situation and Brooke wrote in his diary on the 14th: 'News of Italy still none too good, but I feel the bridgehead south of Rome should hold all right and that ultimately we may score by not having had an early success. Hitler has determined to fight for Rome and may give us a better chance of inflicting heavy blows under the new conditions.'[3] But the British *were* worried lest the Americans should lose interest in the Italian campaign and perhaps carry out their ever-present threat of suspending Mediterranean operations altogether and concentrating upon the cross-Channel attack. More likely, perhaps, was that the Americans might allow the whole front to stagnate, use the continuing lack of significant success there as an excuse to starve it yet further of men and munitions, and so deprive the field commanders of any opportunity at all for large-scale operations. In early February, Brooke and Churchill had taken pains to make clear in one of their telegrams to the Americans that, as far as the British were concerned, it was still 'our intention to concentrate upon the Italian campaign'.[4] Some days later, in his diary, Brooke expressed his fears about the Americans' level of commitment to Italian operations. After 'a long and difficult' meeting of the Chiefs of Staff at which an American delegation was present, Brooke was driven to conclude that 'it is quite clear to me . . . that [Marshall] does not begin to understand the Italian campaign. He cannot realize that to maintain an offensive a proportion of reserve divisions is required. He considers that this reserve can be withdrawn . . . and that the momentum in Italy can still be maintained.'[5]

Alexander and Clark shared these anxieties, not necessarily because they had Brooke and Churchill's burning faith in the eternal importance of the Mediterranean theatre, but simply because their careers and reputations were irrevocably linked with the fighting there. As the first battle petered out, therefore, both of them looked around desperately for ways of breaking the deadlock and making a decisive breach in the Gustav Line. And both looked to the Cassino massif, increasingly convinced that their only hope lay in pushing to the northern rim of the Liri Valley, capturing the Monastery, and so allowing the debouchment of other infantry and the armour into the Valley itself.

Clark, as we have seen, drove II Corps to the very limits of human endurance to achieve this, desperately hoping, in the best traditions of the Somme and Passchendaele, that 'just one more push' would do the trick. Alexander had fully supported this effort. Early in January he had created a small Army Group Reserve, by pulling 2 New Zealand Division out of the Eighth Army line, and had informed its commander, General Bernard Freyberg, that its task would 'depend on the course of the operations, but it is primarily intended for exploitation. . . . It will be placed under command of Fifth Army when a suitable opportunity for its employment can be foreseen.'[6] Shortly afterwards, 4 Indian Division and 78 Division were also taken out of the line and joined the strategic reserve, now dubbed the New Zealand Corps. As 2 New Zealand Division included its own Armoured Brigade it seems likely that Alexander had, from the beginning, been thinking of using it for exploitation up the Liri Valley. By the first week of February he had definitely made up his mind and the New Zealanders took over 36 US Division's positions behind the Rapido, ready to follow up success on the massif.

As Alexander was obviously very much in accord with Clark in his choice of *point d'appui*, one would have thought that the latter would be pleased with the proffered reinforcements. But there was one major drawback. The new divisions were all from the 'British' Eighth Army. On being told of the imminent arrival of the New Zealand Division, Clark told Alexander: 'Hell, I don't want any troops from the Eighth Army. No use giving me, an American, British troops.' Still less did he want Freyberg. As he said after the war: 'That scared me because Freyberg was a prima donna and had to be handled with kid gloves, very adroitly, very carefully.'[7] What concerned him above all was that Alexander might replace Keyes' Corps with Freyberg's and use the latter to snatch the victory which the Americans had so dearly bought. He was thus particularly outraged to hear that Freyberg was drawing up various contingency plans, one of which envisaged using the Indian Division on the massif. As he wrote in his memoirs:

Freyberg had been directed by Alexander to prepare recommendations for employment of his reinforced New Zealanders on the Fifth Army front. I had not been consulted about such recommendations. I got a definite impression that 15th Army Group and Freyberg were going to tell me what to do. I objected as diplomatically as possible, pointing out that their plans for using the New Zealanders and Indian troops in the Cassino–Monte Cairo mountain sector would not fit in well [with my plans]. . .[8]

His remarks in his diary that day were less measured and he concluded with a somewhat spiteful attack on the New Zealanders themselves, whom he more than ever saw as unwelcome intruders: 'These are Dominion troops who are very jealous of their prerogatives. The British have found them difficult to handle. They have always been given special considerations which we would not give to our own troops.'[9]

Just how 'diplomatic' Clark's objections were will never be known, but he did succeed in persuading Alexander to let II Corps' offensive continue and to hold back New Zealand Corps for their original exploitation role up the Liri Valley. This was immediately written into a new Fifth Army Operations Instruction, issued on 5 February, which envisaged a speedy success on the massif. Thereafter,

> upon the capture of the Cassino heights . . . FEC. . . will attack to the west . . . making its main effort along the Terelle–Roccasecca trail, seize Roccasecca and the high ground east of the Melfa River . . .
>
> II Corps . . . will seize Piedimonte and the high ground north-west thereof . . .
>
> NZ Corps . . . will assemble in the Monte Trocchio area . . . [and] be prepared, on Army Order, to debouch into the Liri Valley, pass through elements of II Corps and, making its main effort along Highway Six, attack to the north-west within its zone of action.
>
> 10 Corps . . . will attack . . . to the north in the direction of San Giorgio a Liri.[10]

Unfortunately, as we know, II Corps did not capture the Cassino heights and Clark was soon obliged to concede that the chances of their doing so were getting remoter by the day. At a meeting with Alexander on the 8th he reluctantly agreed to bring 4 Indian Division into his line to relieve 34 Division, but still declined to specify an exact date. It was not until the 11th, in fact, after the 34th had been virtually destroyed in their last despairing attack on Albaneta Farm and the Monastery, that Clark finally sanctioned their relief and grudgingly allowed the 'British' the opportunity of striking the final blow around Cassino. In the evening his Chief of Staff, General A.M. Gruenther, telephoned Freyberg to say, 'The torch is now thrown to you.'[11] Clark, rather petulantly, contented himself with informing Freyberg that 'it would be easy to take Cassino with the fresh divisions that General Freyberg had . . . [and] that he could have taken it at the time of 34th Division's attacks if he had one more fresh combat team.'[12]

It seems questionable whether Alexander should ever have allowed Clark to mount these last attacks, for he himself was fairly convinced that they could not succeed. For him the torch had been thrown on the 9th, after he had received Lemnitzer's gloomy report about 34 Division's low morale, and he had immediately alerted Freyberg to be ready to take over from II Corps. Freyberg quickly issued an Operations Instruction that noted that 'enemy in front of 2 US Corps have been reinforced and resistance has hardened . . . NZ Corps will be prepared to attack and capture Monastery Hill and Cassino in the event of 2 Corps being unable to complete the task by dark, 12 February 1944.'[13] Alexander was also drawing up an Operations Instruction of his own. Whilst it was drafted some time before the agreed deadline, it made no mention of II Corps and clearly assumed that Keyes' men were dying in vain. Alexander was, it said,

naturally anxious that the advance of the NZ Corps up the Liri Valley, astride Highway Six, should take place as early as possible. . . . [This advance is to be preceded by] the attack of 4 Indian Division to clear the high ground west of Cassino of the enemy . . . [and] the establishment of a bridgehead over the Rapido in the Cassino area, both of which operations will be carried out as quickly as possible, so that NZ Corps can begin to advance westwards from the Cassino bridgehead as soon as the physical conditions [permit] . . .[14]

However, though Clark might be disappointed about who was actually to undertake this offensive, its execution was planned very much in the Clarkian mode, being little more than an extension of the increasingly unimaginative attacks carried out by II Corps. Once again the major attack was to be on the massif, with 4 Indian Division jumping off from the forward American positions around Point 593 and trying to batter their way through to the Monastery. There was also to be an additional effort in Cassino town, by 2 New Zealand Division. But this was vaguely defined and would offer no appreciable support to the Indians until they had actually taken the Monastery and were, hopefully, storming down the eastern slopes of Monte Cassino.

It remains something of a mystery why Freyberg ended up ordering such a carbon copy attack, one that would confront just the same fearsome defences that had ground down so many American battalions. Certainly it was not in deference to Clark himself, nor even to the advice of other senior commanders. Thus an earlier contingency plan, drawn up on 4 February, had owed much to the counsels of Major-General F.I.S. Tuker, the commander of 4 Indian Division, and it had deliberately avoided any attempt to assault the Monastery frontally. Tuker had preferred to outflank the bulk of the massif with a turning movement through the mountains north of Monte Castellone, probably through the Corno Pass.* From the very beginning Tuker had been resolutely opposed to any suggestion of a frontal attack on Monte Cassino, from whatever direction, and as he said after the war: 'I went through hell on earth during the early days urging desperately that no attack on Monte Cassino should be contemplated. I could never understand why the US Fifth Army decided to batter its head again and again against this most powerful position, held by some of the finest troops in the German Army in heavily wired and mined and fixed entrenchments.'[15] On 6 February, owing to a recurrent illness, Tuker was forced to hand over command of 4 Indian Division to Brigadier H.K. Dimoline, but this did not stop him bombarding his Corps Commander with warnings about the dangers of a frontal assault. The change of plan on 9 February came as a bitter blow and Tuker, who had no great opinion of Freyberg's generalship – 'brave as a lion but no planner of battles and a niggler in action'[16] was his considered judgement – took it upon himself to try and have the plan scrapped. His campaign reached a crescendo on the 12th:

> I had tried three or four times to get back to my HQ but each time I collapsed. . . . On 12 February I managed it and sent for Freyberg. . . . I stood at my HQ on Monte Trocchio with Freyberg, looking straight at Monte Cassino. I again argued the business . . . I reiterated all my reasons. . . . At the end of my talk, which had to be a short one as I was pretty feeble, I pointed at Monte Cassino and said to him plainly and emphatically: 'Whatever you do, Freyberg, don't compromise!'[17]

---

* The British Official History also expresses some puzzlement over Freyberg's eventual decision but points out that unfortunately 'there is no documentary evidence to show why Freyberg abandoned the wide flanking manoeuvre which he had outlined on 4th February . . .' (Molony, *op cit.*, p.706).

On the same day Tuker also despatched two memoranda to Freyberg, both containing angry denunciations of the new plan and the lack of efficient preparation, particularly by Fifth Army staffs. His first salvo noted that even the gleanings of his own intelligence officers made it

apparent that the enemy are in concrete and steel emplacements on the 'Monastery' Hill. From a wide experience of attacks in mountain areas I know that infantry cannot 'jump' strong defences of this sort in the mountains. These defences have to be 'softened' up either by being cut off on *all* sides and starved out or else by continuous and heavy bombardment over a period of days. . . . To go direct for the Monastery Hill now without softening it up properly is only to hit one's head against the hardest part of the whole enemy position and to risk the failure of the whole operation.[18]

Tuker's second communication that day concerned the Monastery itself, which he had soon realized offered the Germans an almost impregnable bastion even in the event of the seizure of its immediate defences. Monte Cassino, he concluded, was 'a modern fortress', but what particularly angered him was that he had had to find out exact details of its construction for himself, by ferreting around in a second-hand bookshop in Naples. The last paragraphs of his letter clearly indicate his bitterness:

I would ask that you would give me definite information *at once* as to how this fortress will be dealt with as the means are not within the capacity of this Division.

I would point out that it has only been by investigation on the part of this Div., with no help whatsoever from 'I' sources outside, that we have got any idea as to what this fortress comprises although the fortress has been a thorn in our sides for many weeks.

When a formation is called upon to reduce such a place, it should be apparent that the place is reducible by the means at the disposal of that Div. or that the means are ready for it, without having to go to the bookstalls of Naples to find out what should have been considered many weeks ago.[19]

Nor was Tuker the only general worried by the growing obsession with Monte Cassino. When he had first been informed that NZ Corps were to come into the line in the Cassino sector he had given considerable thought to acting in conjunction with the French, the latter advancing on the Indians' right, probably through Terelle, to broaden the front of their wheel through the mountains. Such an idea greatly appealed to Juin who was just as adamantly opposed to any frontal assault on the Monastery itself. Like Tuker he simply could not see the sense in attacking head-on that portion of the Gustav Line where nature most favoured the defenders and where they had obviously done their utmost to supplement nature with steel and concrete, mines and wire, and shrewdly placed artillery concentrations. To his own staff he spoke witheringly of Clark's plan of early February, 'or more exactly . . . this absence of a plan, for could one apply the term plan of operations to this obstinate desire to charge straight forward, always in the same place, head first into the Cassino corridor where the enemy, sure of himself, waited behind his daily more formidable defences, needing only, at the right moment, to unleash deadly interlocking flanking fire from the heights that dominate the Liri Valley?'[20]

But Juin was not simply concerned that the New Zealanders would be attacking in one of the strongest portions of the Gustav Line. He also saw that their attack would be made in complete isolation, the rest of Fifth Army simply standing by and waiting to see what would happen.* This was anathema to Juin who, as we have already seen more than once, continually thought in terms of '*la manoeuvre d'armée*', using *all* available forces to destabilize the German defences most effectively and, as far as possible, conceal the chosen focus of effort. Already disappointed by Clark's lack of interest in capitalizing upon the success on Belvedere/ Abate, Juin could not help but feel that any isolated attack upon Monte Cassino would lead to similar sacrifices for equally paltry strategic gains. On 7 February he sent a letter to Clark reiterating his doubts about such a dangerous parsimony of effort:

> I am sure my ideas are entirely in accord with yours when I say that to my mind only a general attack, launched on the same date along the entire Fifth Army front, seems likely to bring important results. . . . For my part . . . I deem it absolutely essential that the British Corps, II US Corps and 3 DIA should attack simultaneously.[21]

Unfortunately, as his private remarks to his aides indicate, Juin was far from confident about any communion of ideas with Clark. In his memoirs he makes it clear that the above letter was a virtual waste of time. He was convinced that the French could make an important contribution to the forthcoming battle by exploiting from their new salient on Colle

---

* Clark's Operations Instructions of 5 February, it will be recalled, specified what the British and French were to do *after* Cassino had fallen.

Belvedere and, indeed, that Clark could do worse than make this his main axis of advance. 'It would have required a longer delay, but would have been less costly. My opinion, however, had no chance of being considered as the French were regarded as being on the sidelines and were only expected to hold their positions on Belvedere.'[22]

He was quite right. Both his and Tuker's warnings went unheeded and Clark and Alexander remained adamant that Monte Cassino must be stormed. As for Freyberg, whatever his private thoughts, he too seemed to lose interest in trying to find a way to outmanoeuvre the Germans and resigned himself to using his Corps as a human battering-ram.* But Tuker did at least succeed in getting additional material back-up for the operation. If it was to be conducted as an attack by storm that might have made a Roman or medieval commander blanch, then he at least tried to make sure that the *ballistae* and *trébuchets* would also be on hand. The modern equivalent he most favoured was the aircraft, being firmly convinced that the task of softening up the Monastery itself was beyond the powers of even the reinforced Corps artillery. His various verbal and written protests to Freyberg had all demanded that if the attack *had* to be carried out then it must be preceded by a meticulous saturation bombing of the target. From the very beginning of the Italian campaign, in fact, Tuker had been insistent that success on such intractable ground was absolutely dependent on full and continual air support. In one memorandum he wrote:

If one looks at Italy all the way up its length one sees it to be impossible of conquest except in one tedious manner. No commander who is not either unimaginative or a time-server would accept . . . [this] direction of attack without the one and only means of conquest, great airpower on the battlefield, close in. . . . In Italy . . . the Boche is in steel and concrete: he has anti-tank and anti-personnel mines and plenty of anti-tank guns. Virtually the whole breakthrough of his positions must be done by infantry. . . . If we intend to put infantry through we have only one means to do it and that is by the surprising weight of our fire. . . . Artillery weapons will not give this effect. The only effect left to us is the weight of our

* Tuker came to feel that it was simply asking too much of Freyberg to expect the kind of strategic flair involved in taking a strongpoint by applying indirect pressure: 'I feel sorry for Freyberg, but he should never have been put in command of a corps. He had not the tactical understanding and certainly not the experience in the mountains.' (Quoted in Trevelyan, *op. cit.*, p.134.)

airpower and that *must* be used in its *fullest* weight and concentrated and coordinated with artillery and ground small arms.[23]

This he felt held true of almost every defensive position in Italy, and Monte Cassino was perhaps the strongest of them all. It was, as he had said, 'a modern fortress' and it must, therefore, 'be dealt with by modern means. No practicable means available within the capacity of field engineers can possibly cope with this place. It can only be directly dealt with by applying "blockbuster" bombs from the air, hoping thereby to render the garrison incapable of resistance.'[24]

Freyberg had, in fact, already requested that the Monastery be bombed even before Tuker's last spate of demands. At a meeting with Clark, on the 9th, he had suggested that the Monastery buildings should be flattened by either artillery or aerial bombardment. Clark was unreceptive however. 'I did not . . . feel that it was necessary, nor did my staff or the generals who preceded Freyberg in action at Cassino.'[25] Freyberg let the matter drop but, under Tuker's ceaseless badgering, again telephoned Clark's HQ on the evening of the 12th. This time he had resolved to have his way and brusquely informed Gruenther that he wanted the 'convent' bombed, if possible by thirty-six Kittyhawks dropping 1000 lb bombs.

'You mean the Monastery?' Gruenther asked. 'The Monastery is not even on the list of targets.'

'I am quite sure that it is on my list of targets,' replied Freyberg, 'but in any event I want it bombed. The other targets are unimportant, but this one is vital. The divisional commander making the attack feels that it is an essential target, and I thoroughly agree with him.'[26]*

Gruenther then told Freyberg that he would have to check with General Clark, who was visiting the Anzio beachhead, as the Monastery was classified as a historical monument whose destruction could only be sanctioned by the most senior field commanders. Clark was not immediately available, however, and Gruenther called Alexander's HQ, explaining Freyberg's request to General Harding and adding that he could authoritatively assert that Clark would not be in favour of the proposed raid. Harding said he would have to consult with Alexander and at 21.30 rang back with the following pronouncement:

General Alexander has decided that the Monastery should be bombed if General Freyberg considers it a military necessity. He

---

* The list referred to was one drawn up by Fifth Army HQ, based primarily on Freyberg's recommendations. No-one has since been able to find a copy of it.

regrets that the building should be destroyed, but that he has faith in General Freyberg's judgement. If there is any reasonable probability that the building is being used for military purposes General Alexander believes that its destruction is warranted.[27]

In the meantime, Gruenther had got through to Clark who, as he had expected, was opposed to the bombing. By the time he and Gruenther next spoke, however, Alexander had given his verdict and Clark felt himself unable to ignore the wishes of two such prominent generals, one of them his superior officer. The ultimate decision was still his but, as Gruenther himself remarked, 'General Clark felt that unless General Freyberg receded from his position it would place General Clark in a very difficult position in the event that the attack should fail.'[28] So he reluctantly gave his consent and ordered a bombing raid on Cassino for 10.00 on 13 February. But he still very much resented having his hand forced in this way and when bad weather forced the postponement of the raid he rang Alexander to try and persuade him to change his mind. Alexander insisted that the final arbiter must be Freyberg and Clark took advantage of another postponement to try and dissuade the New Zealand commander. His arguments made absolutely no impression and a rather barbed remark in Clark's memoirs show just how angry he was at being obliged to accede to the wishes of a 'British' subordinate. '[I] told Freyberg that I would authorize the bombing if Freyberg said it was a military necessity. He replied that, in his considered opinion, it was. I was never able to discover on what he based his opinion.'[29]

Clark's reasons for not wishing to bomb the Monastery were threefold. Firstly, he did not wish to destroy a famous historical and religious monument, partly for reasons of simple cultural sentiment and partly because such 'barbarism' would present the Germans with a ready-made propaganda weapon. Secondly, he did not think that there were any Germans in the Monastery itself, as absolutely no reliable intelligence had been received to that effect. Thirdly, Clark and his subordinates were extremely concerned about the real military value of this type of bombardment. As Clark wrote later:

. . . bombing . . . the Abbey was not necessary. . . . It not only would fail to assist the attacking troops, but probably would make their job far more difficult by letting the Germans feel perfectly free to use the ruins of the buildings as defensive positions. Although it is not often understood, the knocking down of a building or a town by aerial bombardment frequently leaves great piles of rubble that are better defensive positions than were the original buildings.

Keyes said that Ryder, Butler and Boatner . . . were all in
unanimous agreement. . .[30]

Clark's purely military objections were vigorously seconded by Juin.
When he, Monsabert and other senior French officers gathered to watch
the raid itself, Juin was heard to remark to his Algerian commander, 'No,
they'll never get anywhere that way. The infantry will never be able to
get forward amongst all that. The bombers haven't done things by halves.
Not only will the destruction of this unfortunate Monastery be of no help
at all to Freyberg's men, but a bombardment like that will only serve to
complicate their task yet further.'[31]

However, none of these reasons seem to have made much of an
impression on Alexander. His answer to Clark's first point was that 'when
soldiers are fighting for a just cause and are prepared to suffer death and
mutilation in the process, bricks and mortar, no matter how venerable,
cannot be allowed to weigh against human lives.'[32] To his other points
Alexander has left no reply at all, either on the record or off. Two general
points might be raised, however. With regard to the deleterious military
effects of the bombing, Clark and the other commanders were
undoubtedly making very good sense and it is difficult not to accuse
Alexander and Freyberg of wishful thinking if they really thought that just
one bombing raid would somehow completely obliterate an edifice whose
main walls were 150 feet high and 10 feet thick. Masonry of these
proportions cannot be miraculously pulverized, only drastically
rearranged in a way that as often as not, as Clark pointed out, actually
favours the defenders. The only really propitious time to bomb a building
is when the enemy is in it, so that it falls on his head. Before or afterwards
one is simply building his ramparts for him.

Which brings us to the vexed question of whether or not the Germans
actually had troops stationed in the Monastery before the bombing. The
Goebbels Propaganda Ministry, working through Vatican sources, had
for some time been vehemently denying that there were any troops
actually in the Monastery. Assurances from this source were and remain
worthless, but much more credence can be attached to the testimony of
German commanders in this theatre and they have all fiercely maintained
that their men were strictly forbidden to go into the Monastery under any
circumstances. Kesselring wrote after the war: 'Once and for all I wish
to establish the fact that the Monastery was not occupied as part of the
line; it was closed against unauthorized entry by military police.'[33] At the
time he was even more forthright, launching into a tirade worthy of the
most seasoned propaganda hack. After declaring that allegations of a

German presence in the Monastery were a 'baseless invention' he fulminated against the barbarism of the 'United States soldiery, devoid of all culture' and 'Anglo-Saxon and Bolshevik warfare [which] has only one aim: to destroy the venerable proofs of European culture. I feel deep contempt for the cynical mendacity and the hypocritical sentiments by which the Anglo-Saxon command tried to shift the responsibility on to my shoulders and on to my soldiers.'[34]

Hypocrisy is very much *le mot juste* in this context. Certainly the weight of evidence seems fairly conclusive that there were no troops actually in the Monastery. The nearest units were two tanks of 15 PG Division, some 300 yards away, a mortar detachment 400 yards away, and, a little further away still, an observation post for 71 Werfer Regiment. But let us examine the implications of the following statement by von Senger und Etterlin, part of his own denunciation of the Allied bombing:

> . . . even under normal conditions Monte Cassino would never have been occupied by artillery spotters. True, it commanded a view of the entire district . . . but on our side it was considered tactical opinion that so conspicuous a landmark would be quite unsuitable as an observation post, since we could expect it to be put out of action by heavy fire very soon after the big battle had started.[35]

Clearly, then, the decision not to occupy the Monastery had, in the last analysis, nothing to do with any abiding love for European culture but simply followed the dictates of normal military procedure. More damningly, perhaps, the commander of XIV Panzer Corps also admits that he expected the Allies to bombard the Monastery in the normal course of the battle, as part of their own routine procedure to minimize the effectiveness of enemy fire. In other words, the key point is not whether or not there were any troops actually inside the Monastery, but that the Germans had chosen to make it a conspicuous and inextricable part of their defence line. Thus it was totally unrealistic to expect a concerted assault on that sector of the line not to involve extensive damage to it. To take an analogy, if one soccer team insisted on placing a sheet of plate glass across their goal mouth it would be at best naïve of them to anathematize the opposition as goal-hungry hooligans if that sheet of glass were to be smashed.

For Alexander, however, none of this seems to have been of much import. Mere legalistic, or even cultural considerations were to him entirely secondary to the best interests of his own men. As he wrote in his memoirs:

Every good commander must consider the morale and feelings of his fighting men; and, what is equally important, the fighting men must know that their whole existence is in the hands of a man in whom they have complete confidence. Thus the commanding general must make it absolutely clear to his troops that they go into action under the most favourable conditions he has the power to order.[36]

And in this instance Alexander had his finger accurately on the pulse of the troops at the sharp end. For they, and this is something that Clark and his American subordinates do not seem to have considered, hated the Monastery. Just like Monte Cifalco in the French sector, Monte Cassino lowered down at them, a grim reminder of battles yet to be fought and an obvious vantage point for enemy observers. Perhaps there were no Germans in the Monastery itself, but the troops had been imbued with a hatred of the enemy and all his works and they could hardly be expected to pay much heed to the most fervent German protestations. As Slessor wrote:

. . . however certain we of the High Command might have been that the Germans were not holding the Abbey, no man detailed to attack the Cassino position would have believed it for a moment. It was astonishing how that towering hill with the great white building atop dominated the whole scene in that valley of evil memory, and Private Doe from Detroit, Smith from Wigan, Jones from Dunedin or Yusuf Ali from Campbellpore eyed it and felt that behind those windows there must be at least an enemy observer waiting to turn the guns on him personally when the time came to attack.[37]*

The Does and Smiths have left their own testimony which graphically bears out their commanders' opinion. Sergeant Evans (2 London Irish) had no doubt at all: 'It just had to be bombed. Oh, it was malignant. It was evil somehow. I don't know how a monastery can be evil, but it was looking at you. It was all-devouring if you like – a sun-bleached colour,

* Though Slessor accurately portrays the consensus view of the High Command, it is perhaps worth noting that some senior commanders did think that the Monastery was occupied by the Germans. Prominent among these were Lieutenant-General Ira C. Eaker, the commander of the Mediterranean Allied Air Force, and Lieutenant-General Jacob L. Devers, Wilson's deputy in the Mediterranean. They actually flew low over the Monastery in an observation plane, on 13 February, and claimed to have seen radio masts and several German soldiers moving about inside. Their claims remain unverifiable, however, and by then the decision to bomb had already been taken, for the reasons outlined by Slessor.

grim. It had a terrible hold on us soldiers.'[38] A report of a French liaison officer attached to 34 US Division, some of whose troops were still stationed in the northern outskirts of Cassino when the bombs were actually dropped, observed that the bombing, 'it is important to note, has filled the Headquarters of the 34th with satisfaction and the soldiers with uncontainable joy.'[39] An American officer wrote: 'The Abbey at Monte Cassino was the creation of one of man's noblest dreams . . . but this morning the tired infantrymen, fighting for their lives near its slopes, were to cry for joy as bomb after bomb crumbled it into dust.'[40] Let us leave the last word to Lieutenant B. Foster (60 Rifles), the sheer intensity of whose feelings, even after thirty years, shows just how right Alexander was to accord 'man's noblest dreams' such a low priority:

Since you ask me what I felt about the Monastery, I'll ask *you* something. Can you imagine what it is like to see a person's head explode in a great splash of grey brains and red hair . . .? And can you imagine what it is like when that head belonged to your sister's fiancé? I *knew* why it happened, I was positive, it was because some bloody fucking Jerry was up there in that fucking bloody Monastery directing the fire that killed Dickie, and I know that still . . .[41]

9
The Sharp End
The New Zealand Corps at Cassino, 15–18 February 1944

We got on with it . . . because we had the superiority complex common to the rest of Fourth Indian Division and we were not given to bellyaching.

Lieutenant-Colonel J. Glennie (CO 1 Royal Sussex Regiment)

Freyberg would have been considerably heartened if he could have read a report that 14 Panzer Corps sent to Tenth Army just a few hours before the bombing of the Monastery. In it von Senger und Etterlin stated fairly unequivocally that the recent series of Allied attacks had extended his troops almost to breaking-point. Of his sector as a whole he wrote:

The Corps' task of defending the Gustav Line has so far been fulfilled. To do this it has been necessary to weaken quiet sectors to danger point. . . . The heavy demand for troops to contain the Anzio beachhead has denuded the Corps of almost all reserves. Even the divisions have almost no local reserves. Sectors where there is no immediate threat have been weakened to such an extent that any enemy pressure there (even small local concentrations) must bring about new crises.[1]*

In the threatened Cassino sector the situation was if anything even worse. According to Senger, the forces available between Cassino and Colle Sant' Angelo

cannot be guaranteed adequate to hold out against another major attack. . . . Exhaustion among the troops (who have been exposed for weeks to the worst rigours of mountain warfare with inadequate equipment, inadequate supplies, and no hope of relief) increases daily. . . . The continuous decrease in manpower in this sector makes it impossible to defend the line in depth, and compels us to adopt a policy of linear defence in exposed positions. . . . If the enemy decides to concentrate his artillery, air and infantry in co-operation on a few deciding points (Cassino, Monte Cassino, Albaneta, Colle Sant' Angelo) he will probably succeed in his aims.[2]

---

* If Juin ever saw this entry he could hardly have resisted a weary 'I told you so.'

In fact, Freyberg was far from happy about the prospects of the forthcoming attack. On the day before this report was written a member of his staff noted that 'his normal optimism and confidence temporarily left him. . . . It was the only time in the war when I saw him looking depressed, and walking along slowly with shoulders hunched and his hands in his pockets.'³ What was particularly worrying him was that events seemed to be conspiring to deny him just that concentration of artillery, air and infantry, particularly the latter, which Senger had referred to in his report. The plan drawn up on the 9th envisaged a two-pronged attack. On the massif, 4 Indian Division were to attack to the south-east to take Point 569 and the Monastery and then pour down the eastern slopes of Monastery Hill to cut Highway Six and take the town itself. The New Zealand Division was to assist with fire on Cassino and Highway Six and was to be prepared to help in the capture of the town. After this had been taken they were to push across the Rapido in strength, their infantry battalions acting in conjunction with 180 tanks from Combat Command 'B' (1 US Armoured Division) and a similar number from 4 New Zealand Armoured Brigade. The two divisional staffs had started drawing up plans immediately and once II US Corps' offensive had been called off, on the 11th, they urgently drew up actual timetables for their own attack. The Indian Division's plans were issued late on the same day and envisaged the main attack the next night. This was soon seen to be impossible and it was postponed for twenty-four hours, to the night of the 13/14th. The leading role was given to 7 Indian Brigade, who were to jump off from Point 593, which it was thought had been taken by the Americans in their last-gasp effort. From here they were to attack along Snakeshead Ridge to Point 569 and then veer left towards Point 445 and the Monastery. 5 Indian Brigade was to keep in close contact slightly to the rear, ready if necessary to provide a battalion to assist 7 Brigade and at all events to take over on Point 593 and Monastery Hill once they had been secured.

But the Indians had first to get into position for the attack and this, as so often in the Italian campaign, proved to be not the least of their difficulties. Their first moves had been made on 10 and 11 February, even before it was known that the attack was definitely on, when 7 Brigade left its initial concentration area for a new one around Cairo village. The first part of the journey was by road but this was found to be so deep in mud that the Division's four-wheel-drive lorries stuck fast in it or skidded around helplessly. They were eventually replaced by jeeps and trailers borrowed from the Americans but not before there had been some terrible accidents. One of these should be borne in mind for it was to have disastrous consequences for 1 Royal Sussex Regiment when they actually came to spearhead 7 Brigade's attack. Their entire reserve of mortar ammunition and grenades was stowed in two lorries and both of these unfortunately went round a bend too fast and plunged over a steep embankment. The ammunition was irrecoverable and was not replaced in time for the battle five days later. The jeeps, of course, were not adequate to carry hundreds of fully-laden troops and these now had to make the entire journey forwards on foot. According to one history: 'The night of the Battalion's move up . . . was like a bad dream. The rain pelted down and the wind howled . . . Knee-deep in mud, the troops marched from their lorries to the assembly area . . . on the near bank of the Rapido.'[4]

By now it was known that the Indians' attack was definitely on and they were immediately ordered up to their forward positions. This involved a journey of some seven miles, along a single muddy track that was only intermittently passable to jeeps. Mules would have been invaluable here but the whole New Zealand Corps only had an allotment of 1500 such animals, barely enough to maintain a single brigade. As it was not logistically feasible, and as there was not sufficient time to assign the whole allotment to 7 Indian Brigade exclusively, Brigadier Dimoline's only alternative was human porters and he was forced to so use two companies from each of the battalions of his reserve brigade, the 11 Indian. Even this did not prove adequate and once 7 Brigade had finally reached its forward positions its battalions had to utilize many of their own troops to bring up vital supplies.

By the morning of the 12th, however, 7 Indian Brigade was still a long way from these forward positions around Point 593. No movement from their assembly area around Cairo was possible in daylight and whatever chance there might have been of effecting a speedy relief of the Americans as soon as darkness fell disappeared when the Brigade Commander, Brigadier O. de T. Lovett, was obliged to employ two of his battalions to help fight off German counter-attacks against men of 36 US Division who were still guarding the western flank of the massif, around Monte Castellone. The two battalions, 4/16 Punjabis and 1/2 Gurkha Rifles, became so involved in this fighting that Lovett was forced to postpone the relief of Point 593 until the following night, the 13/14th, and the attack towards the Monastery until the 14/15th.

Although no movement was possible throughout the next day, various reconnaissance parties were sent out to make contact with the Americans on Point 593 and to assess the chances for the forthcoming attack. None of those who returned were particularly optmistic. One party was led by an officer from 1/2 Gurkhas. 'On his return . . . [he] summed up the situation succinctly: "A tough nut indeed." '⁵ As the Brigade actually moved into position that night this judgement began to look like a serious understatement and the difficulties multiplied with each passing hour. Two problems were immediately apparent. Firstly, contrary to everything 4 Indian Division had been told, the Americans did not actually hold the crest of Point 593 and, like other luckless units before them, the attacking troops would have to storm their own start-line before embarking on the major assault. (Point 593 had fallen to a German counter-attack late on the 10th, at much the same time as the Indians set out from their first assembly area. Even three days afterwards no hint of this had been given to either Corps or Division.) Secondly, as we have already seen, the two hundred or so survivors of 34 Division in this sector were so weak from hunger, exhaustion and exposure that they were incapable of making their own way back down the mountain tracks. Lovett had no intention of leaving them where they lay and he organized stretcher parties to carry out their evacuation. But this involved a considerable number of men, at least four for each stretcher, and could only be done after dark. Lovett got in touch with Dimoline and they swiftly concluded that a further double delay was unavoidable. No attack at all could be made on the night of the 14/15th because too many men would be helping with the evacuation. And even when the first attack was made it would have to be concerned with taking Point 593, thus pushing back the actual attack on the Monastery to the night of the 16/17th.

It is hardly surprising, then, that Freyberg was looking distinctly disconsolate as he mooned around his headquarters on the 14th. But these were not the end of his problems that day. By now both his divisional commanders were becoming increasingly worried about the chances of success. Brigadier H. Kippenberger had taken over command of 2 New Zealand Division from Freyberg and he was finding it enormously difficult to concentrate enough of his troops for a significant thrust towards Highway Six. As he wrote: 'We could not attack Cassino on a broad front because of the floods, while the only approach from the west was along and astride the railway causeway. . . . We could attack only on a front of two companies and the longer and harder one looked, the more difficulties one saw. . . . I felt a little unlucky having to deal with so awkward a problem in my first battle as divisional commander.'⁶ Dimoline was feeling unluckier still and complained bitterly to Kippenberger about his problems on the massif and the virtual impossibility of launching a concerted assault. The latter was not unsympathetic:

Poor Dimoline was having a dreadful time getting his Division into position. I never really appreciated the difficulties until I went over the ground after the war. He got me to make an appointment for us both with General Freyberg, as he thought his task was impossible and his difficulties not fully realized. The General refused to see us together: he told me he was not going to have any soviet of divisional commanders.[7]

This incident is particularly revealing of the mounting pressure on Freyberg, for his attitude to Kippenberger's request was the very antithesis of his usual procedure within his own division. One historian has described in glowing terms the remarkable harmony and frankness that prevailed there during the North African and early Italian campaigns.

There was one other unique feature of . . . [the] Division. This was what the New Zealanders themselves called their 'Cabinet'. . . . [It] consisted of Freyberg and the senior brigadiers, and when an operation was being prepared plans would be fully, and even outspokenly, debated. Freyberg would listen carefully to everyone in turn, then sum up and make the final decision. These cabinet meetings constantly mystified British and American generals who had no experience of such a democratic approach to the waging of war.[8]

That this 'democracy' should have been so curtly eschewed during the Cassino battles is perhaps telling evidence in support of Tuker's claim that Freyberg was not cut out to be a Corps commander.

But the troubles of the day were not yet over, and the question of the bombing of the Monastery began to loom large again. At first events had gone very much in Freyberg's favour. On the 12th, as we have seen, he was able to persuade Alexander to overrule Clark as to the necessity of the operation and over the next thirty-six hours even the weather had been something of an ally. It twice caused the raid to be postponed and thus had precluded the possibility of its being carried out long before the Indians were even in position to launch their attack. For it was obvious that a massive bombardment of Monte Cassino would only be of real assistance to the assaulting troops if it was delivered immediately prior to jump off. Any delay at all would give the Germans time to recover from their shock and capitalize upon their perfect excuse to occupy the ruins. On the afternoon of the 14th, however, Freyberg learned that a new time had been set for the bombing, 09.30 on the following day, and that the weather reports showed that conditions would almost certainly not be suitable for several days after that. In other words, the Air Force commanders were insisting that it was now or never at the very time when Freyberg had been told that an attack on the Monastery itself could not be launched until the night of the 16/17th, a full day and a half after the raid.

He immediately contacted Indian HQ and 'attempted to shake Dimoline from this timetable. He pointed out to the Indians' commander that "the bombing had been put in at their request, that if we cancelled the programme now we would never get the air again and that this delay from day to day was making us look ridiculous." Dimoline stood his ground. He would not order his division to attack until a firm base had been established.'9 Freyberg might have been more understanding, though it would hardly have alleviated his gloom, if he had been apprised in detail about the conditions on the massif. 7 Indian Brigade had eventually got themselves into position on Snakeshead Ridge – 1 Royal Sussex directly below Point 593, 4/16 Punjabis to their left and 1/2 Gurkhas to the rear – but two other battalions placed under command had had a typically appalling approach march and were in no position to give quick or close support to 7 Brigade's attack. That there should have been two such battalions was in fact an amendment to the original Divisional plan. To the 5 Brigade battalion, 1/9 Gurkha Rifles, that had been detailed to lend 7 Brigade immediate support, had been added another from 11 Brigade, 4/6 Rajputana Rifles. The theory was commendable but the lack of roads and adequate tracks, the impossibility of movement by day, and the terribly constricted axis of advance to the front meant that beyond a certain point reinforcements just clogged up in the rear areas, unable to pass through the bottleneck. On the 14th, 4/6 Rajputanas were still in Cairo village whilst 1/9 Gurkhas were strung out along the roads from Sant' Elia.

Things were even worse at the front, especially for 1 Royal Sussex who were supposed to attack as night fell after the bombing. Their CO, Lieutenant-Colonel J. Glennie, wrote in his personal diary on the 14th: 'We were . . . in full view of the enemy from all sides – we had no reserve rations and barely one blanket per man . . . everybody behind worked hard to get us supplies but the shortage of mules, the length of the daily march – seven miles each way after dark – and the heavy shelling and mortaring of mule tracks, all combined to keep the admin. situation bad.'10 The Battalion War Diary elaborated on the deplorable supply situation:

Supplying route consists of one narrow track passable by only one mule train at a time. Track is over sheer rock barriers which are at present frozen at night. To date 30 per cent of the mules have slipped over the side on each journey, consequently large losses of equipment. One Company of Camerons from 11 Brigade are being used as porters and has proved far more reliable than mules.[11]

All this had only increased Lovett and Dimoline's conviction that it would be impossible to mount an attack that could reasonably hope to carry Point 593 and Monastery Hill in one fell swoop. After Freyberg's last entreaty, Dimoline did in fact agree to consult with Lovett but, as he expected, the Brigade commander would have none of it. He reiterated the hard facts that potential enfilade fire from Point 593 had to be effectively neutralized before he dare send any other troops across the fairly open ground that lay between it and the Monastery, and that there was no hope of the two extra reserve battalions getting forward until late on the 16th.

This conference, at 7 Brigade HQ, was still in progress when the first bombers flew overhead. To most men there the deafening roar of the engines came as a complete surprise for, incredible though it would seem in the context of any battle but this one, no one had officially informed Lovett's HQ of the new timing. Lovett was furious. At the very moment that he heard the first dull roar in the distance he 'called on the blower and was told that the bombers would be over in 15 minutes. I started to blow up myself but even as I spoke the roar drowned my voice as the first shower of eggs came down.'[12]* It came as an even more unpleasant surprise to the men on the massif who had received no indication that it would be advisable to withdraw their forward units to a safe distance – if indeed there was such a thing when American bomber crews were in the air. Certainly few Allied infantrymen in Italy had much faith in their accuracy, as was evidenced when an officer of 4/16 Punjabis made his first contact with the commander of 168 US Regiment, which they were to relieve:

We proudly informed him that our Brigade was going to take the Monastery. He thought it possible if we threw enough people at it.

* According to all the available accounts Lovett expected the bombers on the late afternoon of the 16th, though the whole incident remains puzzling. If Freyberg had already tried to persuade Dimoline to fit in with the new timing, why had not the latter informed Lovett that the timing had in fact been put forward?

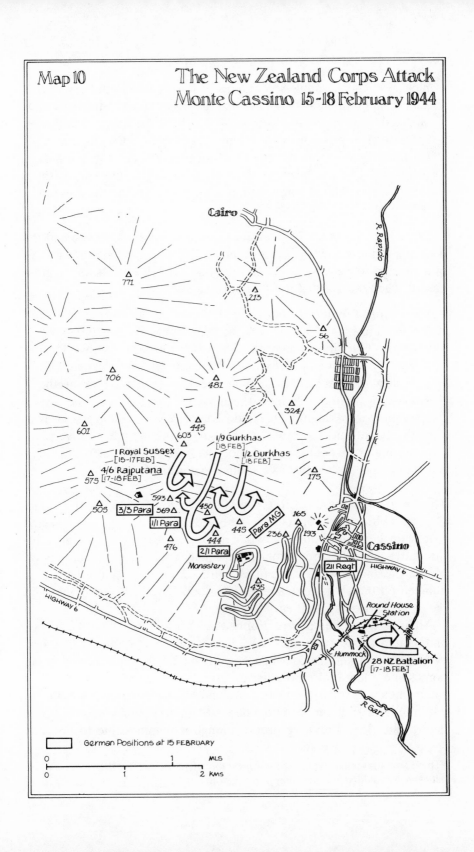

Map 10

The New Zealand Corps Attack
Monte Cassino 15-18 February 1944

Cairo

R. Rapido

△ 771
△ 213
△ 56
△ 706
△ 481
△ 324
△ 601
△ 445
△ 603
1/9 Gurkhas [18 FEB]
I Royal Sussex [15-17 FEB]
1/2 Gurkhas [18 FEB]
4/6 Rajputana [17-18 FEB]
△ 575
△ 175
△ 593
3/3 Para   △ 569
△ 505
1/1 Para
△ 450
△ 445
Para MG
△ 165
△ 476
△ 444
2/1 Para
△ 236
△ 193
Monastery
△ 435
Cassino
211 Regt
HIGHWAY 6
HIGHWAY 6
Round House Station
Hummock
28 NZ Battalion [17-18 FEB]
R Gari

☐ German Positions at 15 FEBRUARY

0   1   MLS
0   1   2 KMS

First of all, we said, we were going to destroy the Monastery with American bombers. This caused him to push his cap to the back of his head, bite his cigar and with his hands on his knees regard us sympathetically over his steel-rimmed spectacles. 'Waal,' he said, 'If it is incumbent on you to depend on our barmers, and I was in your shoes, I'd hie me back to dear ol' Pittsburgh.' Our optimism slumped. We smiled wanly and muttered that we had the greatest faith in American bombers.[13]

There was undoubtedly a certain amount of leg-pulling here and the bombing was on the whole fairly accurate. But on the massif some groups of men were so close to the Monastery that even direct hits on it were a hazard. The War Diary of 4/16 Punjabis stated:

We went to the door of our command post . . . and gazed up into the cold blue sky. Then we saw the white trails of many high-level bombers. Our first thought was that they were the enemy. Then somebody said 'Flying Fortresses'. There followed the whistle, swish and blast of the blockbusters as the first flights struck at the Monastery. Almost before the ground ceased to shake the telephones were ringing. One of the companies was within 300 yards of the target and the others within 800 yards; all had received a plastering and were asking questions with some asperity. We could not offer any explanation, we just had to grin and bear it.[14]

There were casualties, too, in 1 Royal Sussex, though Lieutenant-Colonel Glennie's bitterest thoughts were reserved for those who had neglected to tell him anything about the revised timing. He was yet more angry after the battle when he found that Allied planes had dropped leaflets on Monte Cassino to warn the refugees in the Monastery that it was to be bombed on the 15th. As Glennie remarked, 'They told the monks and they told the enemy, but they didn't tell us!'[15]

All in all the Allied planes dropped 442 tons of bombs on the Abbey and its immediate environs. There were two separate attacks, the first between 09.30 and 10.00 when 135 Flying Fortresses dropped 500lb bombs and a few 100lb incendiaries, and the second between 10.30 and 13.30 when a mixture of 87 Mitchells and Marauders dropped a further 283 bombs, all of them 1000-pounders.* Mediterranean Allied Air Force had in fact done Freyberg proud, though it is impossible to find any

---

*There were also raids on the 16th and 17th, though by the smaller Kittyhawks, which between them added only a further thirty-six tons.

official explanation of just why his own modest request, for just thirty-six Kittyhawk missions, had been so handsomely answered. The most likely explanation for this generosity is that the commander of MAAF, Lieutenant-General Ira C. Eaker, was still smarting from some rather tart comments by Lieutenant-General Henry H. Arnold, the commander of the US Army Air Force, about the level of air support that was being given to the ground forces. On 10 February, Eaker had received two cables from Washington. The first remained reasonably tactful, noting that 'considering difficulties being encountered in Italian campaign despite our overwhelming air superiority it would appear that perhaps our organization, tactics or equipment may be faulty in certain respects.' The second was more blunt: 'Combat Allied airplanes operational in the Mediterranean Theater total 4542. A serious crisis appears to be imminent in the beachhead south of Rome and for our Fifth and for the British Eighth Army. In view of this, information is requested as to why every airplane that is flyable and has a crew is *not* used against German personnel, equipment and installations. Your comments desired.'[16] Eaker's reply was full of confidence, remarking at one point, rather smugly, that at AFHQ 'there is not the air of pessimism or fear of disaster on the part of . . . commanders in any echelon here [that] I detect in your message.'[17] Nevertheless, it does seem fair to assume that as soon as Eaker heard of Freyberg's request he tried to pull out the stops a little and try to make the raid a shining example of just the kind of intimate air/ground co-operation for which Arnold had called.

Through no fault of his own he failed miserably. The actual bombing certainly looked spectacular. Leutnant Daiber, a troop leader with 115 Panzer Battalion (15 PG Division), was actually in the foothills of Monte Cassino and as the first bombs dropped it was 'as if the mountain had disintegrated, shaken by a giant hand. A man can never forget hell when he has once been thrown in and when a hand, miraculously, has plucked him back.'[18] And once the dust had cleared the Monastery indeed seemed to have been 'knocked about a bit', but in fact the damage was not enough to offer any real advantage to attacking troops. The roofs had been completely blown off, small fires had been started and certain of the interior walls had completely collapsed. But the essential fabric of the building, *qua* fortification, was barely affected, and the outer walls, though now crazily crenellated, still presented a formidable obstacle. No significant gaps had been blown in them and the main gateway, the only entry into the Monastery, with massive timber branches and a low archway made of stone blocks nine to ten metres long, had not even been touched.

However, *there were no attacking troops*. 7 Brigade remained adamant in its refusal to launch the main attack that day and the preliminary attempt to clear Point 593 was still not deemed feasible until nightfall. For about eight hours absolutely nothing happened and the only advantage the bombing might have had, in forcing German troops to keep their heads down before an *immediate* follow-up attack, was dissipated. The Germans quickly recovered from their shock and became once more alert behind their machine guns and mortar emplacements. Worse still, as Kesselring noted in a subsequent official statement: 'Consequent upon the destruction of the Monastery, the incorporation of the ruins into the German defensive system followed as a matter of military course.'[19] Even at the time the German High Command was distinctly unperturbed by the bombing. Little more than half an hour after the first bomb fell Kesselring's Chief of Staff, General Siegfried Westphal, spoke on the telephone to the Chief of Staff of Tenth Army, General von Wentzell:

Westphal: 'Anything new down your way?'
Wentzell: 'Only the Monte Cassino Abbey business. . . . That was pretty foolish, no doubt about that.'
Westphal: 'Has it done any harm from a military point of view?'
Wentzell: 'No, because we were not occupying it. The enemy was just imagining things.'[20]

Even when something finally did happen it was worse than nothing. As we have seen, Lovett and Dimoline had remained adamant that the first night's attack could only concern itself with the seizure of Point 593, to safeguard the right flank of the subsequent main assault. 1 Royal Sussex had been designated for this preparatory task and throughout the day they had crouched in their slit trenches, hardly able to raise their heads, let alone make any detailed reconnaissance of the ground they must cover. What could be seen from a distance looked forbidding enough. In front of them, less than 500 yards away,

loomed the rocky crest of Pt.593, with the ruins of a small fort upon its summit. The slopes were shaggy with great boulders, sharp ledges and patches of scrub. These natural hideouts sheltered German spandau teams and bomb squads. Enemy outposts were less than 70 yards distant. The slightest movement drew retaliatory fire. . . . There was no elbow-room for deployment, no cover behind which to concentrate effectively, no opportunity to withdraw in order to obtain space for manoeuvre.[21]

This lack of elbow-room was a particular problem for Glennie. Though he was uncertain of the enemy's exact strength, he decided that he could only make this first attack with one company, as any wider frontage would lead to congestion and bunching and present the Germans with a yet more vulnerable target. In other words, the whole of 4 Indian Division's effort, over which there had raged a fierce high-level argument about the bombing of the Monastery, to support which two squadrons of Flying Fortresses had flown from England, and which itself represented the opening blow in a whole Army Group's attempt to pierce the Gustav Line, was in the hands of three officers and sixty-three men of 1 Royal Sussex. Truly, 'c' Company was at the sharp end.

The attack went in just after nightfall. Because the distance between the two front lines was so short and because the Royal Sussex were on the very crest of Snakeshead Ridge, thus allowing hardly any clearance for shells fired at Point 593, there was no direct artillery support. Instead a diversionary bombardment was organized, aimed mainly at positions on and around Monastery Hill. An Indian Army artillery observer wrote

> . . . like the opening phase of a colossal symphony, the guns roared in unison. The night was pricked with belching flames . . . [and] sudden flares and steady fires marked exploding dumps and burning houses. The enemy began to loop white flares on to the lower slopes of Cassino. . . . Then came the staccato crackle of small arms fire as the infantry went in. . . . On the soar of every flare we strained our eyes, praying that each mounting light would prove to be the success signal and that our men had won home.[22]

They prayed in vain. The Royal Sussex had advanced with two platoons abreast, moving very slowly so as not to alert the enemy by dislodging any of the small stones and scree that were strewn in their path. But they had gone barely fifty yards when they were spotted and withering machine gun fire and a shower of grenades made them dive for cover. Small groups of men crawled forward, exploring every possible tangent to try and infiltrate round the flanks of the German outposts. They relied mainly on grenades and had soon exhausted their immediate stock. An urgent appeal was sent back to Battalion HQ and more grenades were collected from the other companies and sent forward but these, too, were soon used up. Already Glennie was rueing the loss of those vital lorry loads a few days before. Without grenades, 'c' Company's position was hopeless. They were too close to the enemy for supporting fire from the Battalion's mortars and machine guns, and became horribly exposed if they attempted to use their own small arms. Before first light, therefore, Glennie ordered them to withdraw. They had lost two officers and thirty-two men killed or wounded. German casualties were negligible and the evening's situation report by 90 PG Division recorded laconically: 'Quiet day except for the one attack on Pt.569.'[23]

During the morning of the 16th Lovett ordered Glennie to try again, this time using the whole Battalion. Even now no one seemed to fully understand his problems in actually deploying a whole battalion on Snakeshead and Glennie was once more forced to rely mainly on the efforts of one company. This time it was 'B' Company, reinforced by one platoon from 'A'. They were to attack on the Battalion's left whilst the rest of 'A' Company made a feint attack and gave supporting fire on the right. 'D' Company was held back to take over on Point 593 once it had fallen and the shattered 'C' Company was kept in reserve. Glennie was far from happy about the renewed attack and wrote in his diary:

> We needed 48 hours for recce, planning and building up our ammunition, supply etc. Oblique air photos of the objective were a real necessity but were not available. However, we got on with it because a) it was repeatedly emphasized that we must do something to take the pressure off the Anzio beachhead which was in imminent danger of collapse b) we had so far always been successful. We had the superiority complex common to the rest of Fourth Indian Division and we were not given to bellyaching.[24]*

Events just prior to the attack, timed for 23.00 on the 16th, were less than propitious. Grenades and mortar shells were still in critically short supply and Glennie sent off an urgent request for both. In the meantime his mortar crews solved the problem by salvaging American shells that had been left behind. Because they were a different calibre from the British ones, they had to be fired through captured German and Italian mortars, brought back from North Africa as battle trophies. The grenades they could only wait for and nothing had appeared by zero hour, even though Glennie had been assured that a mule party was on the way. Another half-hour delay was authorized and a few minutes later the mules did arrive. But they had been heavily shelled en route and the animals were carrying less than half the number of grenades required. And Glennie's troubles were not yet over. Artillery support had been provided for the attack, mainly to neutralize the peaks adjacent to Point 593 which

---

* Powerful German counter-attacks against the Anzio beachhead had begun on 16 February and came within an ace of pushing it back into the sea.

could otherwise bring heavy flanking fire to bear on the attackers. A prime target was Point 575, some 800 yards west of 593, but, as the bulk of the guns were firing from the valley to the west of Monte Cassino, it was again going to be enormously difficult to land shells on 575 whilst at the same time keeping them safely above the heads of the Royal Sussex on Snakeshead. The artillerymen

> had to skim the top of Snakeshead by a few feet, and gunnery as precise as this allowed no margin for error. The tiniest fraction of a variation in elevation and the shells would hit the top of [the Ridge]. . . . This is precisely what happened. As the two leading companies . . . formed up on the start-line of the attack, the artillery opened up on Pt.575. But several shells failed to clear Snakeshead, and burst among the leading companies and Battalion HQ. It is axiomatic that the most demoralizing beginning to any operation is for the attacking force to be shelled on its own start-line. It is not less disturbing if the shells happen to be from its own guns.[25]

Nevertheless, the attack went in and reinforced 'B' Company made good progress in its initial dash, reaching the lower slopes of their objective and knocking out several outlying machine gun nests on the way. Two officers actually got to the wall of the ruined fort but intense fire from this and other positions on the crest prevented most of the platoons from following. A few did push through and actually got over the crest but of these some stumbled over one of the small precipices that abounded in this area and the rest ran into a party of German reinforcements and were taken prisoner. 'A' Company, however, got nowhere at all, having almost immediately come to the edge of a forty-foot precipice not indicated on their maps. They tried to bear to the left but were again baulked by another sheer crevasse, this time fifteen feet deep and twenty feet across. Glennie decided to send in 'D' Company to supplement the main effort on the left. But they did not even get to the foot of Point 593, the right-hand platoons being blocked by the same crevasse that had thwarted 'A' Company and most of the others being stopped in their tracks by intense small arms fire. Nevertheless, a few men did get forward and reached the top of the crest, only to be stymied by a final trick of fate. Whether victory was really within their grasp will never be known but at that moment a German fired three green Very lights into the air, Glennie's prearranged signal for a general withdrawal. What they meant to the Germans we shall again never know, but they were enough to send the remnants of 'D' and 'B' Companies back down the hillside. The War Diarist seems to have been too sick at heart to record this incident and he also provides only the tersest details about a last abortive attack by 'B' Company:

'D' Company attacked and were repulsed with heavy casualties. 'A' Company went in to support 'D' Company – heavy casualties. 'C' Company committed but had to retire. 'B' Company formed up for final effort armed with grenades as Major J.S. Gratton advised CO that enemy position was vulnerable *provided grenades were numerous*. During forming up heavy LMG fire and grenade throwing. . . . CO ordered retirement to original FDLs.[26]

To the casualties of the night before had been added a further 10 officers and 130 men. In the two attacks the Royal Sussex had employed 15 company officers and 313 riflemen. Their casualty rate had been almost 54 per cent in only ten hours of combat.

Freyberg had been most disappointed by the first failure to take Point 593 and he became increasingly impatient with Lovett's and Dimoline's insistence that its seizure was a necessary prelude to the mounting of the main assault on Monastery Hill. On the morning of the 16th, therefore, he got in touch with Dimoline and tried to persuade him to go ahead with the original plan to launch that assault that night.

He questioned whether the capture of Point 593 on the right was the *sine qua non* that Lovett . . . claimed it to be. Dimoline carried his point for another attempt on Point 593 that night but was clearly given to understand that in any circumstances the attack on the Monastery could not be deferred beyond the next night. Having tactfully sounded opinion at Army headquarters, Freyberg sensed a growing restiveness, which he was determined to allay.[27]

This deadline he adhered to and immediately after he heard the news of the Royal Sussex's second rebuff, orders went out to both of his Divisions that they were to start their main attacks as soon as possible on the 17th.

The New Zealanders were ready first, as they had been reconnoitring and assembling their forces since the 6th, but their options were seriously circumscribed by the physical conditions in their concentration area. Their brief was to establish a bridgehead over the Rapido south of Cassino town – 34 US Division was still in line in the northern outskirts – that would permit the deployment of a large body of armour in the Liri Valley. The whole floor of the Rapido Valley, however, was sodden and waterlogged and in places the water lay several inches deep on the surface. Such ground was quite impassable to either wheeled or tracked vehicles and the only feasible route was that provided by a raised railway embankment that led into the station. The New Zealand plan was to use 28 (Maori) Battalion to seize the station, there only being enough room to feed in a single battalion, and for them to hold this area until the engineers had made the embankment negotiable for tanks. Though it was certainly wide enough, some thirty feet, and the rails and sleepers had already been removed by the Germans, it had been systematically wrecked by twelve large demolitions over its last thousand yards. All these would have to be filled in before the tanks could move up, and by the 16th only the first four of them had been adequately bridged.

The attack began at 21.30, with 'A' and 'B' Companies in the lead. The latter was to take the station buildings and the engine-shed, preparatory to seizing the 300 yards of sunken road that ran into the town, and the former was to clear the rest of the yards and seize a small mound south of the engine-shed, known as the Hummock. The attack was pushed forward vigorously and despite several machine gun posts and roll upon roll of newly laid wire, both companies were firmly established in the yards by midnight. The report of 'B' Company's commander gives a flavour of the Maoris' bravura tactics, very reminiscent, as so often in the Italian campaign, of going 'over the top' in the First World War:

As we closed my 12 PL. on right wavered momentarily in the face of a particularly violent burst of MG fire from two Jerry posts. I immediately ordered a charge – the men leapt forward and, as in training, two men leapt on to the wire (concertina) – the others jumped over (there was sufficient light from flares and gun flashes) and, with bayonets and grenades, cleaned the posts out. Others were busy with cutters on the ordinary dannert wire and the platoons were soon through on to the 1st objective.[28]

· Good progress was made during the night. The two companies held firm and by 02.00 the engineers were working on three demolitions simultaneously, with only one still untouched. At 03.00, however, the moon came up and gave the Germans a much clearer idea of what was being attempted. A sapper lieutenant wrote:

The enemy, who had apparently not seen the work or been aware of what was going on then began to cover the area with MG fire from · the Hummock . . . and well-directed concentrations from mortars further back. On two occasions the mine-sweeping and clearing parties had to stop work. However word came through that the work had to proceed as it was fast becoming light and support weapons had to be got through to the Maoris.[29]

Shortly before dawn, however, the engineers were suddenly ordered back and the Maoris, as there was obviously no hope of either tanks or heavy weapons getting through, asked whether they too should not withdraw. Their request was submitted to Division, who replied that they should stay where they were as every effort was to be made to lay down a smoke screen around the station area to shield it from fire from Monte Cassino and the Hummock.

Unfortunately, though the smoke was building up fast, the Germans had already been able to assess in what strength the New Zealanders had attacked, as well as the exact extent of their penetration. A Tenth Army staff officer, at Baade's HQ, reported back: 'The enemy is still in the station, and we are round him in a semi-circle. He has the station only, nothing else. About midday he tried to push north along the road. Baade assumes from this that that is his next direction. We are trying to cut off the men by thrusting from the north and south.'[30] Thus the smoke shells were only masking an already known target and, as almost every available New Zealand gun was using them, there were few left to fire into the German units now massing for a counter-attack.

Throughout the morning and afternoon these troops inched forwards, trying to infiltrate the Maoris' positions. There were several hand-to-hand struggles and by the late afternoon the leading companies had lost seventy-six men, killed and wounded. An attempt to reinforce them with a platoon from 'C' Company proved abortive, twelve of the men being shot down before they had gone a hundred yards. Minutes later the Germans brought up a couple of tanks and used these to spearhead a last assault on the station area. A New Zealand officer wrote: 'When the tank attack came in I was with the remnants of my Coy HQ right in the station. . . . The forward section must have been overrun by them. They were not more than fifty yards from us and opened up with 75mm. and MG. That was when I gave the order to withdraw.'[31] Many more men were killed, wounded or taken prisoner during this withdrawal and the Battalion's final casualty count was 22 killed, 78 wounded and 24 missing.*

German casualties were also heavy,[†] but their senior commanders were

---

*For the riflemen and company officers of the Battalion as a whole, this was a casualty rate of over 30 per cent. For the 200 troops who did almost all the attacking the rate is a grim 56 per cent.

† German casualties in the station were given as 9 killed, 102 wounded and 18 missing.

delighted that the New Zealanders' eventual intervention in the battle had been so decisively repulsed. At one stage the state of the troops in the town had been causing some concern, and on the 16th Senger's situation report noted that 'cases of exhaustion are increasing in Cassino besides the normal casualties. They are caused by 14 days of continuous exposure to HE and phosphorous shell-fire.'[32] It was a considerable relief, therefore, that the New Zealand attack had been made on such a narrow axis and that it had been contained without too much trouble. Vietinghoff lost no time in conveying the news to Kesselring:

'We have succeeded after hard fighting in retaking Cassino Station.'

'Heartiest congratulations,' replied Kesselring.

'I didn't think we would do it.'

'Neither did I.'

'North of Cassino also,' added Vietinghoff, 'heavy attacks have been beaten off. 400 dead have been counted on 1 Para Regiment's front. Our losses are pretty heavy too.'

'Convey my heartiest congratulations to 211 Regiment, and to 1 Para Regiment not quite so strongly. I am very pleased that the New Zealanders have had a smack on the nose. You must recommend the local commander for the Knight's Cross.'[33]

The attack north of Cassino to which Vietinghoff referred was 4 Indian Division's last desperate attempt to seize the remainder of the massif. Freyberg's instructions had made it clear that this was to be a Corps' effort and Dimoline and Lovett tried to put as many men as possible into the initial assault. The idea of seizing and firmly consolidating Point 593 before attempting to push towards the Monastery now had to be abandoned. The new attack was conceived as a series of simultaneous lateral assaults against the key positions on the saddle leading to the Monastery, notably Points 593, 569, 444 and 445, rather than a push *along* the saddle, aiming to take the points one by one. Lovett, who drew up the basic plan, managed to retain something of his original concept in that the attack on 593 was to go in a couple of hours before the others, but its seizure was not made a necessary condition for their jumping off. If Point 593 was taken, well and good, but if not the other battalions would have to take their chances.

In all, five battalions were to be used, three to attack and two to provide a firm fire base. The latter were both from 7 Brigade: the sorely tried 1 Royal Sussex, who were to remain in their positions just in front of Point 593, and 4/16 Punjabis still dug in to their left. The attacking battalions were one from each Brigade, though all under Lovett's command. The storming of Point 593 was now the responsibility of 4/6 Rajputana Rifles (11 Brigade) who were then to immediately exploit southwards towards Point 476 and eastwards, along the saddle, towards Point 444. They were to jump off at midnight on the 17th. Two hours later, 1/9 Gurkhas (5 Brigade) and 1/2 Gurkhas, echeloned to the left, were to breast the saddle, taking Points 450, 444 and 445, and then crash through to the Monastery walls. If they were successful, two other battalions of 5 Brigade were to move into the north of Cassino town to link up with the New Zealanders.

The opportunity never arose, though there were some initial successes. 4/6 Rajputanas' zero hour 'unimaginatively was midnight, the attack going in immediately after an intense barrage. The Germans put up flares, usually short-lived, so that one saw the battlefield in a series of brilliant flashes, the smoke and dust from the shell-bursts foaming up in red-tinged clouds.'[34] The Rajputanas drove forward fiercely and, 'having fought their way through intense machine gun, grenade and mortar fire, reported the capture of Point 593 at 03.30 hours. This position was gained at heavy cost, the three companies . . . having lost many men and all but two of their officers . . . [They] were subject to immediate counter-attack, and, though they held their ground, the enemy was so favourably placed and his fire so intense that they were unable to clear the forward slopes or to continue that advance along the ridge to Point 444.'[35]

This had serious implications for 1/9 Gurkhas whose right flank was now terribly exposed as they began their attack towards Point 444 and the Monastery. The leading Company, 'A', was in fact driven off course by a terrible hail of machine gun bullets from Point 569 and the forward slopes of 593, and they ended up in 1/2 Gurkhas' sector, directing their attack towards the northern slopes of Point 450. 'B' Company were following close behind and, seeing what had happened, they mounted an attack towards Points 593 and 569, hoping to finish off the job begun by 4/6 Rajputanas. But neither of these impromptu attacks was able to make much headway and the Battalion commander was obliged to send 'C' Company into the unknown to plug the dangerous gap that had opened up between his two leading companies. At 04.00, 'D' Company came up and was sent forward to reinforce 'A' which had by now suffered severe casualties. At about the same time, 4/6 Rajputanas threw in their last company to try and clear the enemy from Points 593 and 569, but these reserves were 'at once pinned down and in view of the short period of darkness remaining it was decided to reorganize at once.'[36]

'Reorganization' in fact meant abandoning the whole attack and consolidating what little ground had been gained. 1/9 Gurkhas were ordered to do likewise as it was becoming clear that their attack, badly dispersed from the beginning, could not hope to push through even to Point 444 unless their right flank was completely secure. Nor had things gone any better on the left where 1/2 Gurkhas had tried to push forwards, skirting the right-hand slopes of Point 450, to storm Point 445 and then the Monastery. A few yards in front of their start line was a patch of scrub which had shown up in aerial photographs but which the Gurkhas had had no chance to reconnoitre in detail. But since similar undergrowth elsewhere on the massif tended to be sparse and no real obstacle to free movement, little attention had been paid to it. The CO's instructions were clear: 'Reach. . . [scrub] as quickly as possible. Do not pause for fire-fight or mop up. If enemy throws grenades, rush him.'[37] But as the leading companies charged into the scrub they found it was a literal death-trap; a dense, chest-high thorn thicket liberally seeded with mines and its outskirts threaded with tripwires linked to booby traps. In the thicket itself were

> German emplacements so close that they were within a grenade's throw of the start line and yet completely hidden in the darkness. The German defenses were based on machine gun posts, fifty yards apart, between . . . [which] were weapons pits, each containing one man with a machine pistol and a large number of grenades. Owing to their proximity to the Gurkha positions, these posts were not softened up by the artillery fire.[38]

The attackers had no chance at all. Nearly every man in the leading platoon was blown up by mines or booby traps, some of their bodies being later found with as many as four tripwires coiled around their ankles. Those behind ran straight into an impenetrable curtain of small arms fire. The CO was almost immediately shot through the stomach and within ten minutes the leading companies had lost two-thirds of their men. The survivors went to ground on the northern edge of the thicket and though both the other companies were pitched into the fray, neither of them was able to make any better progress. At 05.00 the battalion was pulled back to its start line. It had lost 11 officers and 138 men in just three hours' fighting. The second battle of Cassino had ended in bloody shambles.*

Indeed, it can fairly be said that the battle represents one of the low

---

* All the attacking battalions of 4 Indian Division had suffered appalling casualties, as is evidenced overleaf.

points of Allied generalship during the Second World War. One historian has written:

> Viewed from a distance, the Second Battle of Cassino may be thought – especially after the world-wide commotion which preceded and followed the bombing – to have been something of an anti-climax. In the mountains a company attack on Tuesday night, a battalion attack on Wednesday, and a three-battalion attack on Thursday. In the valley, an attack by a single battalion, also unsuccessful. Commentators at the time and since have been inclined to dismiss the failure as a simple one of attacking in driblets instead of strength. The criticism is not valid. Ground and weather were the factors which determined the number of troops which could be used in this battle.[39]

With regard to Dimoline's, Lovett's and Kippenberger's parts in the battle, Majdalany was quite right to emphasize the physical constraints within which they had to operate. All three were ordered to attack on a certain date and had no option but to make the best of a bad job. What is reprehensible, however, is that the commanders who gave these orders never admitted to themselves just how bad a job it was, but increasingly substituted wishful thinking for a realistic appraisal of the tactical situation on the massif. Clark and Alexander were, of course, under considerable pressure. There was mounting dissatisfaction in both Washington and London about the slow progress of the Gustav Line offensive and Clark, in particular, was most anxious about the Anzio beachhead and the unexpected strength of the German build-up there. Clearly something had to be done to relieve the pressure. But what was done was less than adequate.

Juin had got to the nub of the problem when he had urged that any renewed effort should be 'a general attack . . . along the whole Fifth

Killed, Wounded, and Missing		
	Offs	ORs
1 Royal Sussex	12	162
4/6 Rajputanas		196
1/9 Gurkhas	2	92
1/2 Gurkhas	11	138

In such short-lived actions it is fair to assume that 90 per cent of these casualties were suffered by the riflemen and company officers. In this instance, then, we are talking about an average casualty rate amongst these men of almost 40 per cent.

Army front' and that Clark should be prepared to wait until the forces could be massed for such a major operation. But both Alexander and Clark refused to wait, the latter pressing ahead with a last doomed attack by II Corps, the former merely throwing good money after bad in committing his strategic reserve in the most intractable section of the whole Gustav Line. Certainly, as we have seen, von Senger und Etterlin was most anxious about his positions around Cassino and feared another concentrated, major attack. Yet this is exactly what the New Zealand Corps could not mount and this should have been apparent to Alexander even before he sent them into the line. It is difficult, in fact, to think of anywhere along the Gustav Line where Alexander could have employed his reserves to less effect. The experiences of 34 Division alone should have convinced him that the number of battalions available on paper would bear no relation to the number that could be simultaneously brought forward through the few terribly constricted corridors on the massif and in the valley. On the massif, moreover, any attempt to concentrate would be fatally dissipated by the need to use a substantial number of men simply to keep open the long and arduous line of communication to the rear. The New Zealand Corps' failure was not a result of bad luck, nor even of the slapdash staff work that on at least two occasions had kept 7 Indian Brigade woefully misinformed, but of a wilful failure at the highest level to take due account of the terrible problems involved in mounting a concerted attack across such appalling terrain. Worse still, as we shall see, these problems were still being grossly underestimated a full month later.

PART FOUR

THE THIRD BATTLE
19 February – 23 March 1944

The situation at Anzio must *not* be allowed to cause plans to be rushed or attacks launched until everything is ready. We *cannot* afford a failure.

General Maitland Wilson,
20 February

10
'The Stench of Death'
The Lull in Operations, 19 February–14 March 1944

Reminds you of Passchendaele, doesn't it? But we'll have no more Passchendaeles.

General Freyberg, March 1944

Freyberg's pessimism about his chances for success in the Second Battle does not seem to have diminished once the battle began and even before the attacking battalions were withdrawn he was working on plans for a quite different operation. The original II US Corps axis along the massif was to be abandoned and instead both the Indian and New Zealand Divisions were to be funnelled through the north of the town, still held by elements of 34 Division. 6 New Zealand Brigade were to lead off, taking both Castle Hill and the north of the town up to the east–west branch of Highway Six. Castle Hill was then to be taken over by 5 Indian Brigade, who were to use it as a base for leapfrogging attacks along the eastern face of Monte Cassino, successively seizing the hairpin bends on the road to the Monastery, Points 165 and 236, as well as Hangman's Hill (Point 435) just below the summit.* There they were to assemble as strong an assault force as possible for an attack on the Monastery itself. At the foot of Monte Cassino, 5 New Zealand Brigade were simultaneously to push down Highway Six, and when the whole town had been cleared New Zealand and American armour was to drive through into the Liri Valley. The attack was to be preceded by a massive aerial and artillery bombardment of the town, powerful enough, it was hoped, to virtually annihilate the defenders. Freyberg was eager to put the plan into action as soon as possible and it was actually presented to Clark on the 18th. He gave his immediate approval and this was ratified by Alexander on the next day. On the 21st, Wilson rubber-stamped these decisions and formally approved Freyberg's proposed starting date of the 24th. The bombers were alerted and over the next couple of days the various Divisional, Brigade and Battalion HQs worked feverishly on their detailed plans. Just before D-Day, however, the indifferent weather broke completely and it was not until mid-March that there were sufficient

---

* So called because on its bare crest stood one of the supports for a cable car which had run from the station to the Monastery. What was left of the support looked from a distance depressingly like a gallows.

consecutive fine days to dry out both the airfields and the muddy roads over which the armour was supposed to travel.

This enforced lull in operations brought precious little relief to the front-line soldiers, as we shall see, and it also did little to enhance one's respect for the competence of the senior commanders. For throughout this three-week period no attempt was made to alter Freyberg's plan, despite its obvious shortcomings and despite the growing doubts of the commanders and their staffs. As regards the technical deficiencies of the plan it is, of course, easy to criticize with the benefit of hindsight, knowing that the Third Battle was a failure and knowing just what went wrong. Nevertheless, one is bound to conclude that the most telling of these operational weaknesses should have been fairly apparent to the commanders on the spot, if only because identical problems had been encountered during the Second Battle. Three such weaknesses can usefully be isolated.

Dominating everything was the question of terrain. Freyberg's revised plan may have changed direction but he had still left his troops with some appalling ground to negotiate, be it the devastated town or the steep, rocky slopes of the eastern face of Monte Cassino. Moreover, the contorted and battered terrain once again provided only very constricted lines of approach. In the Second Battle, it will be remembered, the Indian Division's attack had been pretty much tied to Snakeshead Ridge and the saddle leading to the Monastery, whilst the New Zealanders had been similarly confined to the railway embankment. The opportunities for manoeuvre in the forthcoming battle seemed equally limited. As soon as he was shown the new plan the commander of 2 New Zealand Division felt that the major drawback for his troops was that 'again we could attack only on a very narrow front. 6 Brigade . . . had to enter the town down a single road, the ground on either side being flooded and mined, with sections in single file on either side of the road, that is on a front of two men. It could only feed its battalions into the fight instead of going in with a united blow.'[1] The Indian Division was tied to an equally inadequate road which, moreover, ineluctably funnelled them into the same terrible bottleneck around Castle Hill, the jumping-off point for both Divisions' main thrusts. Unless the attackers seized their targets in the first rush (unlikely, as the battalions would be so strung out) they would present the Germans on the slopes above with an ideal target. For it was most probable, given the complete lack of alternative approach routes, that the Germans would have many of their machine guns and mortars appropriately sited and have already worked out the necessary fire plans for their artillery. And the Germans were not short of guns in this sector.

In the immediate vicinity they had amassed 13 Italian assault guns, 28 medium anti-tank guns, one battery of 10cm parachute guns, one of 7.5 mountain guns, two batteries of medium guns, three of light, and a Werfer Regiment deploying 88 barrels.* If necessary the commander at Cassino could also call for supporting shoots from Corps and Army batteries on and around Monte Cairo and Monte Cifalco. Castle Hill might, with luck, be the stepping-stone to the Monastery and the town. But it could just as well become the hub of a gruesome mincing machine.

Freyberg did not intend, of course, to trust entirely to luck and this was why the preparatory bombardment of the town was such an essential component of his plan. Yet one cannot help thinking that he pinned too much hope on this aerial and artillery onslaught, praying that the sheer weight of bombs and shells would somehow make his other difficulties magically disappear. There were telling reasons why it should not. The bombing of the Monastery had already shown that even the most concentrated pounding does not make stone, bricks and mortar simply vanish. Though hardly comparable to the Monastery's outer walls, the houses in Cassino were remarkably solidly built. Whilst the bombing could be fairly expected to dramatically rearrange them, there were no grounds for thinking that it could destroy all the strongpoints built into the ground-floor rooms and cellars or that it would not leave scores of eminently defensible banks of rubble.

This was not necessarily a critical shortcoming as long as the attacking troops could get in among the dazed survivors as quickly as possible. A battalion commander in 133 Regiment (34 US Division) had noted during the First Battle that 'the main thing learned was that you must charge into a building right after a hole has been made. As General Ryder has said, "You must take up the slack or Jerry will." '[2] But this was just what the first troops into the town could *not* do. Not only would they be strung out along their approach road when the bombing stopped, making any concentrated assault impossible, but they would be several hundred yards away from the town itself, having been withdrawn behind their bomb safety lines. Yet another problem was that Freyberg had decided that the leading New Zealand infantry should be accompanied by tanks from one of their own armoured regiments. This was sensible practice in normal street-fighting, where the armour was used in a close support role to

---

* Werfer Regiments were equipped with five- and six-barrelled *Nebelwerfers*, mortars that had been designed for throwing smoke shells but which were increasingly used to fire powerful charges of high explosive. They were particularly feared by the Allied troops, the bombs making a weird, screeching ululation as they fell. 'Moaning Minnies' or ' The Andrews Sisters' were among their more polite nicknames.

knock out specific strongpoints located by the infantry. It was not such obvious good sense in the Cassino context, however. On the one hand, the tanks, too, would have to begin their advance from well beyond the outskirts of the town and might easily slow the infantry down yet more as they edged along the pitted approach road. On the other hand, it was open to serious question whether the tanks would be able to move about at all once they actually entered the town, as the bombardment must inevitably create large craters and strew many tons of rubble into the streets. Even during the First Battle, when streets and houses were still recognizable as such, a French officer with 34 US Division had observed that tank casualties had been very high because they were not able to advance and withdraw at will, but either blundered into anti-tank ambushes or had to make suicidal frontal assaults on well-prepared defensive positions. In just twelve days 756 US Tank Battalion had lost 23 out of 61 tanks knocked out completely and another 21 temporarily lost to the repair shops. 'The fighting in Cassino', he wrote, 'was positional warfare and could in no way be compared to normal street-fighting . . . where one can actually edge forward from house to house in a village that still looks like a human habitat.'[3]

Freyberg should certainly have been aware of those potential problems as more than one airman had pointed out the probable effects of a massive aerial bombardment. Admittedly, they were not unanimous. Major-General John K. Cannon, the commander of Mediterranean Allied Tactical Air Force, 'was confident that Cassino town and its defences would be blown out of the path of the land forces.'[4] But others were not so sure. One of the groups involved, 12 Air Support Command, attended a planning conference with Freyberg on 21 February where 'Air Force representatives warned that craters in Cassino after the bombing would make perfect tank traps to hinder the Corps' advance.'[5] General Eaker was yet more pessimistic and on 6 March he wrote to Arnold:

> Little useful purpose is served by our blasting the opposition unless the Army does follow through. I am anxious that you do not set your heart on a great victory as a result of this operation. Personally, I do not feel it will throw the German out of his present position completely or entirely, or compel him to abandon the defensive role, if he decides and determines to hold on to the last man.[6]

Freyberg pretty much brushed these doubts aside. In replying to one theory that it might take the tanks two days to get through the town, he simply replied that he saw no reason why it should take more than seven hours and then added that even if the tanks could *not* get forward this would simply mean that the Germans would not be able to use theirs either. Such specious reasoning does not suggest a commander at the top of his form. The point about the German tanks was something of a *gaffe* as their defences in Cassino relied mainly on fixed strongpoints. And it must have been somewhat disconcerting to hear Freyberg, almost in the same breath, move from claiming a breakthrough in a matter of hours to a cheerful admission that the tanks might indeed be unable to make any progress. And this in the context of an attack whose whole rationale was to prepare for an armoured thrust into the Liri Valley.

A final point about the bombing that merits mention is that no instructions were given, nor even requests made, that the Monastery should also be a target. This seems almost incredible, given that it was still 4 Indian Division's major objective and that, in this attack, it was now definitely known that there were German fighting troops within its walls. The commander of this garrison never ceased to marvel at such an extraordinary lapse on the part of the Allies:

> To the astonishment – and relief – of the garrison, the abbey itself was not bombed. This was a bad blunder, since the roofs and cloisters that had remained undamaged would hardly have stood up to another heavy bombardment. The defence would have been largely neutralized, and the Indians would have been able to capture the hill without much difficulty.[7]

Major Böhmler probably overstates the case here, as the Indians never satisfactorily overcame their major problem of feeding enough men up the side of Monte Cassino on to Hangman's Hill, and were thus never in a position to mount a strong enough attack on the Monastery itself. Nevertheless, Freyberg was obviously hoping that they *would* be able to concentrate in sufficient numbers and it therefore seems unforgivable that he did not think to try and at least soften up its garrison before the final assault went in.

Mention of the Monastery's garrison brings us to the last of Freyberg's major difficulties and yet another reason why he should have thought long and hard about his real chances for success. For not only would his men be attacking through an appalling bottleneck, under concentrated small arms and artillery fire, and then extricating themselves for a drive across either a fortified mountainside or through a town that had been reduced to a maze of tumbled masonry, but they would be attempting it in the teeth of some of the best soldiers in the world. These were the men of 1 Parachute Division who were being brought in to relieve Baade's weary panzer grenadiers. Individual paratroop units had been filtering in since early February and some, as has been noted in passing, had taken part in the Second Battle when they fought under Baade's overall command. The decision to bring over the whole Division had been made by Kesselring on the 3rd and they very quickly began to take over sub-sectors, including Points 593 and 569 on the 8th and Castle Hill on the 10th. By the 25th all three regiments had arrived, and 90 PG Division handed over responsibility for the entire sector on the following day and moved to Frosinone to refit. The new commander, Generalleutnant Richard Heidrich, immediately put the rest of his men in the line, handing over the Monastery and the town to 3 Regiment, placing 4 Regiment on the massif and 1 Regiment to their north-west, around Monte Castellone and the lower slopes of Monte Cairo.

Thanks to Ultra, Freyberg was well aware of these redeployments and even the brief but savage encounters with paratroop units during the Second Battle should have given him a clear idea of their mettle. They had manned many of the key points on the massif, 1 and 2 Battalions of the 1st Regiment, 3/3 Regiment and the Divisional Machine Gun Battalion being particularly prominent. What made them such doughty opponents was not just their first-class training, with its emphasis upon small unit autonomy and the optimum use of small arms fire, but also their extraordinarily high morale. Many Allied commentators at the time dubbed them 'fanatical Nazis', but their underlying motivation was not so much a matter of ideology as of a powerful *esprit de corps* which welds together the best units of any army.

Various factors can help inculcate such a fierce pride in one's unit and one of the more obvious, the quality of leadership, was a potent force throughout the whole German parachute arm. General der Luftwaffe Kurt Student, its overall commander, and divisional commanders like Heidrich and Generalmajor Ramcke (2 Parachute Division) were intensely loyal to their men, whilst subordinate commanders had a tradition of at all times leading their men by example, continually exposing themselves to danger in the thick of the fighting. There is also no doubt that all ranks regarded themselves as a cut above the ordinary infantry, and were prepared, if necessary, to die in proving it. Ironically, this sense of innate superiority seems to have burgeoned the more the paratroops lost their specialized role and were employed in an ordinary ground combat capacity. Ever since the Battle of Crete, in fact, when German paratroopers had seized the island at the cost of terrible casualties, Hitler had fought shy of similar operations and had used the *Fallschirmjäger* as a 'fire brigade', to buttress threatened portions of his line in Russia, Tunisia, Sicily, and at Anzio. However, the very fact that the paratroops had to operate in such a mundane role made them the more determined to show that no one could do it better and that when one saw their distinctive baggy smocks and rimless helmets in the line one knew that here at least it would hold. As Graf von der Schulenberg told the men of 1/4 Regiment, just before they went into the line after the Second Battle: 'You are the best troops in this sector and I expect this position to hold; if necessary to the last man.'[8]

This was not mere bluster, as the Allies found whenever they interviewed any of the rather modest number of paratroop prisoners of war. One interrogator summed up his impressions by stating: 'Morale among the Parachute units is definitely very high. With very slight exceptions they are all very good nazis . . . [and are] convinced that the war has not yet been decided for either side.'[9] This hardly endeared them to their interrogators who were only too ready to write off such attitudes as typical Teutonic arrogance. One bemoaned the fact that 'prisoners of war gave consistently contradictory information and showed a most arrogant behaviour.'[10] Another wrote rather patronizingly of his prisoners' refusal to give any useful information: 'Of the quintet, two talked freely, majority began by a series of moderately convincing lies, and one who had previously given a false regiment deemed it in the best parachutist's tradition to apply the scorched earth policy to his pay-book . . . concealing the unimportant embers in his helmet.'[11]*

Indeed, it was not only the Allies who complained of such excesses of zeal. We have already had cause to note Kesselring's qualified congratulations to 1 Parachute Regiment at the end of the Second Battle and his caution clearly reflects a fear of making them unduly cocky and exacerbating their tendency to pay scant attention to orders from 'ordinary' Army or Luftwaffe commanders. Von Senger und Etterlin also had his problems in this respect, stemming from the paratroops' aversion to admitting to any kind of tactical reverse. During the Third Battle, for example,

---

* It has to be admitted that on occasion the paratroops' self-confidence seemed to originate, appropriately perhaps, in cloud-cuckoo-land. After the Second Battle the CO of 1/4 Regiment told his men: 'Today we realize the fact that our air force does not give as much support as it has done in the past. I can only say that General Student knows the answer to that. It will not be long before our forces shall march forward again. Our decisive battle shall be fought where we once intended – and that is England. We shall land there and surprise the enemy as we always have.' x British Corps, Interrogations of Prisoners of War Report No.391, 27 February 1944, p.3. SHAT 10P38.

it was never possible to obtain a clear picture of the course of the battle from the Command Post of Regiment 3. The Paratroops were in the habit of not reporting the smaller losses of ground, because they hoped soon to recover it. Often reports from the Corps artillery, which I had allocated in good measure to this division, were more accurate.[12]

In short, then, the New Zealand Corps faced a formidable task and it must always remain debatable whether Freyberg paid sufficient attention to the difficulties. Perhaps in his own mind he had pondered them, more than the official record makes apparent. On 21 February, for example, after a conversation with Clark, the later wrote in his diary: '[Freyberg] has weakened from day to day in his belief in his ability to take the Monastery.'[13] But, just as with General Walker on the Rapido, taciturn despondency solved nothing and Freyberg might have been advised to have made strong representations to his superiors about the feasibility of the whole operation. Yet they too had their responsibilities in this respect and as one studies the sources one detects a tragic willingness to shrug off this responsibility and let Freyberg's attack go ahead, *just in case* it succeeded.

For few of them seem to have sincerely believed that it would. Clark, in fact, hardly concerned himself at all and, once he had endorsed Freyberg's revised plan, he remained immersed in the problems of the Anzio beachhead. In fact, Clark's only real interest in the forthcoming offensive seems to have been as some sort of diversion to take the pressure off the beachhead. On 8 March, he recorded in his diary that he had been urging Freyberg to attack without waiting for the weather. 'I fully realize that we are not going to completely break through, and that tanks will only play à small part in this attack.'[14] And in an interview after the war Clark said that he 'never thought or expected that the New Zealand Corps could do more than take Cassino. . . . He did not expect that an attack on a limited front at that time would send the Germans reeling up the Liri Valley.'[15]

Other senior commanders were prepared to wait for the weather to clear but all of them began to feel increasing doubts about the chances of even a limited success. Some of the first were expressed by General Wilson, the Supreme Commander in the Mediterranean. For a man of such lofty rank he has made unusually rare appearances in these pages and did not, indeed, emerge from the Second World War with much of a reputation. Contemporaries and historians alike have passed brutal sentence. The British Official Historian observed that 'in the first months of 1944, [he] was not impressive. Appointed in January to vast responsibilities, he appears to have been unable quickly to think out the purposes of operations in Italy or the methods of conducting them. He seemed to have lost touch with the realities of war . . .'[16] The opinions of his subordinates came through clearly in a series of interviews conducted by the US Army historians. According to Brigadier K.W.D. Strong, in charge of the G–2 section at AFHQ, 'Wilson was never regarded by anyone as a heavyweight. Alexander had no respect for him or his ability and did not regard him as a field commander. . .'[17] Lieutenant-General W.D. Morgan, who later became Alexander's Chief of Staff, 'confirmed Alexander's low opinion of Jumbo Wilson. Said that Alexander thought him third or fourth rate and [that he] knew nothing about tactics and did not influence tactics. Morgan said relations bad between AFHQ . . . and Alexander's headquarters in period Alexander was Army Group Commander.'[18] Alexander himself was equally frank. During the course of one interview, 'again Alexander emphasized that he didn't pay any attention to "Jumbo's" suggestions for tactical operations in Italy.'[19]* Some of what follows in this book will help to bear out these strictures,but it is worth noting at this stage that his early thoughts on the Second Battle reveal a shrewd assessment of the baleful influence of the Anzio beachhead, whose precarious situation was luring Clark and Alexander to squander their troops in inadequate diversionary assaults against the main German line of defence. In a letter written to the Combined Chiefs of Staff, on 20 February, Wilson concurred that 'it is essential to win the defensive battle [at Anzio and make] . . . the bridgehead . . . safe against the future.' But he was at pains to point out that this was because a safe bridgehead could 'hold out for a considerable time' and thus 'eliminate the factor of haste on other fronts', notably at Cassino. His letter, he went on, was

> based upon a personal visit to V Army on 19 February. . . . The situation at Cassino is one of considerable difficulty. In addition to the exhaustion of II US Corps and French Corps, there is a risk of using up the NZ Corps prematurely. . . . The situation at Anzio must *not* be allowed to cause plans to be rushed or attacks launched until everything is ready. We *cannot* afford a failure. [20]

* Nor does Fifth Army seem to have got on much better with AFHQ. Clark remained reticent about his opinions of Wilson, but of his deputy, Lieutenant-General Jacob L. Devers, 'Clark said Devers was a dope, never influenced tactical decisions.' (Clark Interview, *op. cit.*, p.23.)

Doubts about the feasibility of an isolated Cassino operation seem to have spread throughout AFHQ. Late in February, an American G–3 officer visited Fifth Army, NZ Corps and French headquarters and submitted a report on his return. At one point he bluntly stated:

> As a result of the visits to these headquarters I feel certain that the outcome of the beachhead fight will be determined at the beachhead itself and not by a junction of the main V Army forces with the beachhead forces. The severity of the terrain, the weather, and the determined defence of the enemy on the main V Army front has so slowed down [its] advance . . . [that] I do not believe it should be counted upon as assistance for the beachhead.[21]

Equally to the point was another G–3 report of 27 February. According to the authors no breakthrough into the Liri Valley was to be expected and they were already trying to predict the day 'when New Zealand Corps has shot its bolt, say about 10 March'.[22]

The most forceful opponent of a renewed New Zealand attack was Marshal Juin who in his memoirs decried 'this decision . . . [which] displayed a stubborn obstinacy and a failure to appreciate the necessity for a genuine manoeuvre by the whole army.'[23] At the time he expressed himself a little more circumspectly, and on the 21st wrote to Clark, stressing once again that

> not enough importance is being attached, in my humble opinion, to the part played by the Atina region in the enemy's defensive strategy: this region is a vast reservoir, linked in the rear to Rome by minor roads which are not in any way threatened by the Fifth Army's attacks. . . . We must therefore take Atina and only the CEF is in a position to do it.

But once again he sought also to hammer home the point that *isolated* attacks, wherever they might be launched, could not of themselves reap any strategic rewards. This applied equally to the French Expeditionary Corps, an independent attack by whom could fairly be seen as 'a divergence from the principal axis of attack already chosen'. But this was not Juin's intention. His fundamental axiom was that 'it is the combined result of everyone's efforts which alone counts' and thus any French offensive towards Atina should be within the context of a general Army operation, only to be undertaken when each Corps was ready to play its own role. Such an operation might well include an attack in the Cassino sector but this should be just one strand of an overall plan in which Atina would be 'the true strategic objective . . . the point of convergence of an all-out effort by the various corps.'[24]

Clark's reactions to these proposals remain obscure because he did not even bother to reply to the letter. Nor does it seem to have been forwarded to higher headquarters and neither Alexander nor Wilson gave any serious consideration to the Atina axis. Though in later years, Juin must have gained grim satisfaction from the following endorsement by von Senger und Etterlin, who had been less than impressed with Allied strategy during the Second Battle:

> The plan was so similar to the first one [of II US Corps] . . . that it could not hold any surprise. There was nothing new in it. . . . Albaneta Farm, Hill 593 and Hill 444 . . . were all defensive positions in excellent condition, and they were being improved every day. . . . But what I feared . . . was an attack by Juin's Corps with its superb Moroccan and Algerian divisions. I anticipated a wide-sweeping operational thrust into the Atina basin against our thin lines, behind which we had no collecting positions.[25]

But if Alexander gave little thought to such a co-ordinated thrust against the German left, there is evidence that he was losing faith in the prospects for the renewed New Zealand offensive and was, in some respects at least, coming round to Juin's way of thinking. A key document in this regard was an appreciation of the situation in Italy drawn up by his Chief of Staff, General Harding, which so impressed Alexander that he immediately forwarded it to Wilson, on 22 February. The paper posited three possible results of imminent operations: that the 'enemy [would be] driven north of Rome as a result of the present offensive'; that a 'junction between our main forces and Anzio bridgehead [would be] effected, but the main front stabilized by the enemy south of Rome'; or finally, that the existing 'front [would be] stabilized by the enemy.'[26] It was felt that the third of these possibilities was by far the most likely simply because Alexander did not have enough troops to be sure of rupturing the main German line of defence, the only fresh formation being 78 Division, which had recently joined the New Zealand Corps. To ensure a breakthrough and, more important, a vigorous exploitation that would 'not merely . . . push back the enemy's line, but destroy enemy formations in Italy to such an extent that they must be replaced from elsewhere to prevent a rout,'[27]* it was felt that Alexander needed a local

---

* 'Elsewhere' would hopefully be northern France, thus lessening the problems in the forthcoming cross-Channel offensive.

superiority of at least three to one in infantry and the deployment of as large a mass of artillery as possible.

Clearly, 15 Army Group was now thinking in terms of the 'manoeuvre by the whole army' that was deemed so essential by Juin, and far-reaching redeployments were envisaged. The Eighth Army front was to be stripped to three divisions and all remaining British, Dominion and Polish troops concentrated against Cassino and the entrance to the Liri Valley, though they would remain under Eighth Army command. Fifth Army was to be responsible for the Garigliano bridgehead and Anzio, the former being taken over by two fresh American divisions and the French Corps, itself soon to receive two more divisions. All these forces were to attack along the whole front, the principal axes of advance being the Liri Valley and Highway Six, the Ausonia–Esperia–Pico road, the southern coastal road and, from the beachhead, the Cisterna–Valmontone road. The latter axis was regarded as being particularly important because, assuming the Germans were pushed back in the Liri Valley, 'there would be a reasonable chance of cutting off and destroying a large proportion of the enemy forces now opposing Fifth Army.'[28] The necessary arrangements would take time, of course, and Alexander did not expect to be ready before the middle of April.

All this was well and good and Harding's assessment has received numerous plaudits from historians of the Italian campaign. However, it is important to bear in mind the date on which it was drawn up, two days before the resumption of the attack by New Zealand Corps. In other words, if Alexander was even then convinced that only a co-ordinated offensive by the bulk of his Army Group could realistically hope to break the Gustav Line, why did he give no thought to calling off Freyberg's effort? If only large-scale operations could unhinge the German main line, what was to be gained from sending in two depleted divisions against its strongest point? It does seem that, like Clark, he no longer expected Freyberg to make a deep penetration into the Liri Valley and would be content with what he described as a 'big bridgehead over the Rapido and an entry into the Liri Valley'.[29] But even this was a remarkably tall order, as the earlier fighting had made all too apparent, and Alexander should have been well aware of the terrible difficulties. For he could not have it both ways. If, as his endorsement of Harding's assessment admitted, the Liri Valley could only be forced in conjunction with a strong turning movement to the south of it, how could the seizure of that valley's most powerful bastion be a realistic objective of a limited 'preliminary' operation?

All in all, then, the omens for the Third Battle were less than propitious but unfortunately no one in authority seems to have dared to take a step back and objectively assess the chances. Freyberg tried to deceive himself by placing exaggerated faith in the preliminary bombing, exalting its potential in just the same way that First World War commanders had again and again trumpeted the supposed effects of their massive artillery bombardments. Ironically, he seems to have been aware of some of the parallels, as one of his staff recalled: 'I remember so well in front of Cassino the General pointing out to me the pock-holed appearance of the ground on both sides of the Rapido River – shell-holes filled with water – and saying: "Reminds you of Passchendaele, doesn't it? But we'll have no more Passchendaeles." '[30] Exactly what he would have, he was none too sure, though a report to his Minister of Defence, on the very eve of the Third Battle, hardly brimmed over with confidence. At one point he dourly stated that 'we are undoubtedly facing one of the most difficult operations of all our battles.'[31]

Yet, whether or not Freyberg gave due consideration to the full implications of the daunting task ahead of his Corps, the ultimate responsibility for the launching of the Third Battle lay with his superiors. In the last analysis, Freyberg was under orders to take Monte Cassino and would only be let off the hook if more realistic counsels prevailed in higher quarters. This did not happen. Juin advised against the whole operation, but was completely ignored. Clark had his attention fixed on Anzio and gave the renewed Cassino offensive only the most cursory attention. As for Alexander, whilst he had finally grasped that only a major, co-ordinated offensive would suffice to break the Gustav Line, yet he declined to halt the New Zealand operation, hoping against all reasonable expectations that one more isolated push would somehow do the trick.

Which left only Wilson. Unfortunately, his moment of lucidity, on the 20th, was remarkably short-lived. On the very next day, he was asked for his formal approval of Freyberg's plan and gave it without any qualification. On the 22nd he intervened in a potentially useful way by protesting to the Combined Chiefs of Staff about the proposed removal of some ground troops for an amphibious landing, Operation ANVIL, in the south of France. He could not, he said, possibly spare any combat divisions at that moment and, indeed, if there was any future commitment to a 'two or three division "Anvil"', the effect on operations would be most serious'.[32] His warning was heeded, and on the 26th the Chief of Staff declared that 'the campaign in Italy must until further orders have overriding priority over all existing and future operations in the Mediterranean and will have final call on all resources, land, sea and air, in Amphibian theatre.'[33] By then, however, all coherent strategic vision seemed to have deserted Wilson and he gave no idea of what he thought might be done with the troops he had saved. He had received Alexander's suggestion for a major regrouping on the 22nd, but showed no particular enthusiasm for the plan. Indeed, he lost interest in all ground operations, suggesting to Alexander on the 25th that

> operations in Italy must be conditioned mainly by the air factor. My general plan for Italy is to use the air to deprive the enemy of the ability either to maintain his present positions or to withdraw his divisions out of Italy in time for Overlord. . . . The primary task of the air forces in Italy must be to make it impossible for the enemy to maintain a powerful army on the Rome line . . . and to compel . . . [him] to withdraw at least to the Pisa-Rimini line.[34]

Alexander must have found this 'plan' less than helpful, for Wilson went on to say that 'the MAAF bombing plan to that end will be pressed forward whenever weather allows. No one can say when or to what extent that plan will achieve its object. But with luck and good weather, it is not unreasonable to expect that the effect will make itself felt by the end of April.'[35]* The Combined Chiefs of Staff were certainly not impressed with this ludicrously vague proposal and on 8 March they cabled Wilson that resort to air operations alone was entirely unsatisfactory and there must be no question of any long-term stagnation on the main front. Wilson meekly replied that the 'prolongation of the present situation in Italy is no less distasteful to me than to you' and, seemingly oblivious to his earlier opposition to operations mounted in haste, stated that he was now in full agreement that the best policy was to continue the attacks against Cassino and that he and Alexander were only waiting for a break in the weather.[36] The New Zealand Corps was stuck with it.

If the weather was an inconvenience to the senior commanders, it was an appalling hardship for the troops actually in the line. This is a point that should never be overlooked. The fighting soldier's lot in the Second World War did not consist simply of sporadic flurries of combat interspersed with long reliefs or rests. It was an unremitting battle against nature itself, in which the so-called 'lulls' in the fighting were spent in

---

* It does seem, however, that the original idea was not Wilson's. According to his Deputy Chief of Staff: 'Air Marshal Slessor had much more influence on Wilson *re* strategy than . . . anybody else. Slessor convinced Wilson, at least for a time, that the air could knock the Germans out of Italy.' S.T. Matthews, Interview with Major-General Lowell Rooks, 16 February 1948, p.2. NA (MMS) RG 319 Box 255.

holes in the ground, usually cold and wet and almost always within range of the enemy's machine guns, mortars and artillery.

So it was for the men of the Indian and New Zealand Divisions as they clung on to their tenuous positions on the massif and the northern side of the Rapido. The weather, more specifically the rain and sleet, dominated their lives throughout February and March.* Conditions on the massif were unremittingly grim. At one end of Snakeshead Ridge were 2/7 Gurkhas, one of whose officers wrote: 'Throughout these anxious nights the weather continued to be atrocious. Movement was extremely difficult in the blinding sleet and over rough ground with heavy snow and mud.'[37] At the other end were 1/2 Gurkhas, one of whose officers, Major Shore, sent a vivid description of daily life to his father:

Bad weather has made life almost unbearable at times. For weeks on end we have sat on a draughty mountain top in heavy snow and rain, with one's clothing and blankets soaked through in the first five minutes. Behind the line one can always make a hole in the ground and rainproof it with a tent or bivouac. But in the forward positions one's hole or sangar[†] can either be anti-German-counter-attack or rainproof – not both.[38]

Another major problem was that the forward lines were so close to the enemy, and usually under constant observation from the surrounding high ground. For most of March, 2 Cameron Highlanders occupied the old Royal Sussex positions in front of Point 593 and they found it a considerable ordeal having to remain under cover throughout the hours of daylight. Captain Cochrane wrote:

'C' Company took over . . . during a heavy fall of snow and mortar bombs. . . . Since we were on the forward slopes, every movement in daylight was observed and brought down instant fire from snipers and mortars. . . . In day time we had to stay put, peering at the German positions seventy-five yards away, getting cramp in our legs, watching the snow drifting in, and twitching when the mortar

---

*From 23 February to 5 March it rained continuously. From the 5th to the 10th it was fairly fine and the ground began to dry out (but not in SE Italy where the airfields were). On the 11th and 12th, it poured down again, as well as blowing a gale on the latter day. On the higher ground the rain would often turn to sleet and snow. Fine weather set in on the 13th.

†The word 'sangar' was a corruption of the Hindustani *sunga*, a sniper's rock parapet. The British had become very familiar with these during the chronic warfare along the North West Frontier.

bombs came down. . . . I was sharing a hole with the CSM. . .
Strange that two men, and Owens was a big fellow, could live in a
cavity four feet by five, with three feet of headroom under the
sandbag roof.[39]

The commander of 11 Indian Brigade, Brigadier Griffin, summed up the
situation by saying: 'I have seen no worse positions, in this war or the
last.'[40] Another drawback of being under close enemy observation was
that supplies could only be brought up at night, and even then the
journeys were so perilous that only a small proportion of the initial load
ever got through. 2/7 Gurkhas had taken up their positions on Snakeshead
on 24 February where, as we have seen, conditions were hardly ideal. 'To
make matters worse,' as one officer noted, 'no rations and no ammunition
arrived because night after night its porters were scattered by shell fire
and lost the way. It was the 29th before stores of any kind reached us.'[41]

The last straw for the men of 4 Indian Division was that they had to
remain in such positions for weeks on end, unable to operate the usual
system of reliefs within the Brigades, by which battalions would be
rotated at least once a week. This was because the bombing attack on
Cassino was being postponed from day to day and units remained in
position in case the weather should suddenly clear. This was the theory,
at least, though sheer inefficiency seems to have played its part. The
Divisional historian called it 'an unfortunate and rather inexplicable state
of affairs', correctly observing that after the first few days of bad weather
'it must have been known that after . . . [it] mended a few days must
elapse before the airstrips would be dry enough for use by heavy bombers.
A postponement for a week would have given the Indian Brigades a
rest.'[42] And would doubtless have lessened casualties in the more exposed
battalions. Even in these 'quiet' periods the drain on manpower was still
considerable. Between 24 February and 14 March, for example, 7 Indian
Brigade was losing sixty men per day to enemy action. The figures for one
of its battalions are particularly revealing. 4/16 Punjabis had not fought
in the Second Battle and remained in reserve throughout the Third, yet
between 15 February and 23 March they suffered 250 battle casualties.

Nor were the New Zealanders much better off in the swampy valley
below, where the incessant rain brought a new set of tribulations. It rarely
turned to snow but, according to a diarist in 24 Battalion, that was a mixed
blessing:

The rain . . . led to the designation of this congested area as 'Mud
Valley'. Bivvyless for the first few days, many and varied were the
shelter contraptions devised. 12 Platoon were chased by intermittent

shelling from one side of the gulley to the other . . . The night of 28–29 [February] was a particularly wet one, and a roaring torrent took bivvies and all kind of gear with it, salvaging of Vickers guns and our 2-inch mortars being quite the order of the day.[43]

In such conditions one of the greatest problems was trying to generate a modicum of warmth, to partially dry sodden clothes and to comfort shivering bodies with the occasional mug of tea. Various expedients were adopted, most of them equally hazardous. In a tank regiment, the recipient of a surprise truckload of charcoal, there suddenly appeared 'a new form of heater, the jam-tin brazier, with holes punched in sides and bottom . . . and at dusk any day you could see fiery catherine wheels all round the camp as these braziers were swung in circles to set them glowing. They warmed up a bivvy or the back of a truck very well, but you had to watch your ventilation, for carbon monoxide poisoning was a real danger with them.'[44] The tankmen seem to have been particularly inventive in this respect, and in another regiment they used

home-made oil-drip stoves [which] warmed the bivvies efficiently, but had to be treated with respect. The stove's oil-tank was usually an old margarine tin, its explosion chamber a two-gallon water tin, its chimney a string of food tins wedged one inside the other with the ends cut out; but its worst fault was a tendency to go out and relight itself a few seconds later with a nerve-shattering explosion and a shower of soot. When 'revved-up' it glowed red-hot and threw out a terrific heat, but most men preferred to warm themselves from a respectful distance.[45]

But most front-line troops never got the chance for such experiments and had other explosions on their mind than those caused by Heath Robinson heaters. This applied as much to the Germans as to anyone else. A soldier on the massif wrote home to his father:

For two weeks we have been in action. The few days were enough to make me sick and tired of it. In all that time we've had nothing to sleep in but foxholes, and the artillery fire kept us with our noses in the dirt all day long. . . . I hope I'll get my leave soon. . . . Not a single man of my original squad is left. It seems to be the same in the entire company.[46]

15 PG Division were still holding their positions in the Liri Valley and a soldier from 115 Regiment found some solace in increasingly fatalistic entries in his diary:

13 February: I've been in the line for several days now. We have taken up new positions close to Tommy. I'm sure I can maintain that the Somme battlefield did not look worse. It is fearful and horror overcomes you as you wonder when this misery will stop. The air vibrates with shells and devils and death.

6 March: Today we have been relieved in the Gustav Line but our rest is a very short one – only three days. On 10 March we go into the mountains. Here there is still snow and ice and the whole area is just one shellhole after another.[47]

Casualties from constant mortar and artillery fire were on a par with those suffered by the New Zealand Corps. A prisoner from 3/131 Regiment estimated that in the first half of March his battalion was losing four or five men a day from mortar fire alone. His unit was stationed around Belmonte, in the French sector. Another battalion facing Juin's men was 2/171 Regiment, on Point 862, near Terelle, and one group of prisoners were 'still suffering the effects of the artillery and mortar fire which . . . they declared to be infernal . . .'[48] Its sheer volume can best be judged from two recollections of Brigadier Weir, in charge of the New Zealand Corps artillery:

Once while observing from the castle on Monte Trocchio I saw a single German emerge from a hole near the Gari just south of the Baron's Castle and walk quietly south. He was engaged by a holocaust of fire, including that of 8-inch howitzers. As he heard the shells arriving he ran and escaped into an underground shelter. Another time I plainly saw a three-gun self-propelled battery emerge from Santa Lucia and go into action north of Route 6. I gave no orders but merely watched. In a matter of a few minutes hundreds of shells arrived and smothered the three guns, leaving them blackened skeletons.[49]

There were even signs that this remorseless pounding was beginning to have some effect on morale, at least among the non-German elements in the Army whom Allied Intelligence held in such low repute. Prisoners from 211 Regiment, holding positions on the Garigliano, independently stated that a Divisional order had gone out that no two Poles should be stationed in the same foxhole, lest they persuade each other to desert.

It is unlikely, however, that conversations with troops of any nationality would have given much reassurance about morale. Certainly the French were wearying of their winter-long vigil in the mountains. An NCO of 3/4 RTM spent thirty-seven consecutive days in the line and submitted the following report on the tremendous physical and nervous strain under which his company was working:

> The cold was intense and the . . . ground was sodden . . . a liquid mud in which the shells had gouged out numerous craters. There were no shelters. . . . On the 17th, 18th and 19th [of February] ten men were evacuated with trench foot, morale was not good. . . .
>
> From 29 February to 10 March always the same thing: artillery, mortars, patrols. Snow, rain, wind and mud. The last days seemed to get longer and longer. We were at the end of our tether. . . . Not for an instant did the deafening din ever relent. Even our own shells exploded in our lines. We felt we would go mad.[50]

Conditions in the Garigliano bridgehead were no better. Though there had been no sustained offensive operations, by either side, since the first week of February, the front-line troops had to endure some of the worst travails of the whole campaign. They certainly came as a shock to a newly arrived American division, the 85th, which took over part of the western sector, in mid-March. Their historian recorded:

> It is easy to say that, for the first time, a regiment took up positions in the front line; but it is not at all simple to represent accurately the lifetime of emotional reaction to that operation. . . . [The men] became members of the exclusive club of 'combat soldiers'. Membership in the club was the least desired of any in the world, and the initiation to it unquestionably the most harrowing. . . . [After detrucking] the men . . . prepared to go the rest of the way on foot . . . It was pitch black and the rain was driving, miserable, and soaking. The columns started off towards the front and each man literally hung to the man in front of him in order to maintain contact. . . . If Hollywood had filmed this whole scene at the time it was taking place, movie patrons would have taken some of the details of misery and apprehension with a grain of salt.[51]

The British were by now used to such ordeals but familiarity did not make them any easier. When 3 Welsh Guards took over Monte Ceresola, on 10/11 February, the 'relief was a nightmare. There are no tracks – not even bad ones – on the mountain top, only a maze of broken rocks and boulders. . . . In the darkness . . . [the positions] were hard to locate and shellfire and snow which fell intermittently did not make the task any easier.'[52] Equally nerve-racking was the experience of 2 Duke of Cornwall's Light Infantry when they took over on Monte Ornito, later in the month. The commanding officer described it as a 'nightmare march' owing to complete darkness, bad going and incessant rain. A captain with the advance party wrote that 'the route . . . became absolutely torturous in the impenetrable darkness of that night. Every few yards Company Commanders were anxiously enquiring of their guides "How much farther?" On arrival all ranks were completely exhausted, and many just slumped to the ground.'[53]

Nor could anyone become inured to the atrocious weather, incessant rain and snow being as ineluctable in the Garigliano bridgehead as it was in any of the other sectors. In March, 2 Royal Fusiliers went into the line on Monte Ceresola where, in the words of the battalion diarist, 'we found ourselves halfway up what seemed to be the highest mountain in the world . . . wondering what had hit us. . . . On some days it rained, on others it snowed; it was invariably cold at night.'[54] I KOYLI did one of their longest stints on Monte Natale, where conditions 'were in many respects more rigorous than the normal run of trench warfare in the 1914–18 war. . . . In mid-winter at heights of 2000 feet and more, in rain and snow, with only rock-built sangars for protection and leather jerkins, gas-capes and greatcoats for warmth, mere living became a fine art.'[55] The Welsh Guards had barely recovered from the exhausting takeover described above when

> it started to rain as though the very flood-gates of heaven were opened and to blow hard and cold. Water drove down the mountainside and poured into the bivvies. . . . There was no shelter from the hard-driven rain and everybody was wet to the skin. . . . When morning came they tried with ill success to dry their sodden clothes and blankets in a wind which froze them stiff between showers that melted them again into a soggy mass.[56]

2 Coldstream Guards were similarly exposed for almost three weeks on the bleak slopes of Monte Ornito. Their positions were strung out along a windswept ridge which was buffeted

> by icy wind and rain. . . . Blankets and greatcoats were soaked through by day and frozen hard at night. . . . Cooking was nearly impossible. Later leather jerkins came up, clean socks, a rum ration, and canvas 'bivvy' tents in which a man could roll himself and keep dry. But it was not so much these things that made life possible as the sheer exhaustion which, from day to day, enabled men to sleep in spite of soaking blankets and driving sleet. There was some respite from enemy fire, but the cold, which at night froze water solid in the water-bottles, was constant and merciless.[57]

It was not just the extremes of precipitation and temperature that elicited comparisons with the Western Front in 1914–18. Equally reminiscent was the whole daily routine by which the troops, under continual observation and often ridiculously close to the enemy's positions, had to remain under cover throughout the hours of daylight. This cover was not afforded by trenches, the ground being solid rock under the thin topsoil, but by sangars, small shelters built out of debris or such small slabs of rock as could be quarried out.[58] For the Black Watch on Monte Ornito, in the first two weeks of March, it was 'a curiously hole-and-corner life. The companies could see into the German positions, and the Germans could see into theirs, in an almost indecent fashion.' The Royal West Kents on Monte Tufo felt equally naked and for almost a fortnight 'the troops were practically confined to their sangars, which were roofed with bivouac sheets and wooden beams covered with boulders, as protection against rain and missiles.'[59]

In some parts of the line, in fact, the forward troops were living almost cheek by jowl with the Germans. In 85 US Division's sector there were places where the enemy

were only thirty yards from them, across a narrow no man's land. They were so close that the first night the 339th went into the line, the Germans, sensing a relief of a unit and the arrival of green troops, crept up to one foxhole and captured two men. One company commander said: 'The Germans are so close that they can reach over and crack my men on the knuckles with a broom.'[60]

Resort had to be made to extraordinary expedients. An advanced observation post on Monte Ornito was so close to the Germans that it proved impossible to lay a telephone line to it. 'One famous shoot was conducted by the OP writing corrections on a piece of paper, wrapping this round a stone, and throwing it over to his Platoon Commander.'[61] On nearby Monte Ceresola, almost all the forward posts were well within grenade range and

the men of No.3 Company [the Grenadier Guards] . . . who occupied the most forward sangars, would sit all day huddled in greatcoats, their eyes fixed on the ridge in front, their Bren guns resting on the sill of the sangar. From time to time a shower of grenades came sailing over from the far side, against which they erected a shield of wire netting, mounted like a semi-circular windscreen over the top of the sangar wall.[62]

At one stage the Germans tried to mount an attack against the Grenadiers' positions but were immediately shot down. The bodies lay for days on the summit, almost within touching distance of both sides but unapproachable by either. Eventually, however, Brigade HQ found the thought of their bearing important documents too tantalizing and suggested that one of them be somehow recovered. 'A long pole fitted with a hook, a sort of gaff, was made by the sappers, and Colonel Heber-Percy himself pulled out the corpse, catching the hook in its rotten clothing. . . . Heber-Percy . . . [later said] that the grapnel was a 16-ft fishing rod and that they pulled with that, while the Boche were dragging the body with signal wire. Thus a tug of war took place with neither side in view of each other.'[63]

The mental strain of this kind of existence was intense and even the occasional lighthearted moments were tinged with something akin to hysteria. In mid-February, 2 Scots Guards took over positions on Monte Tufo from which their Intelligence Officer went off on innumerable hunts for information about enemy dispositions and movements.* His *sang-froid* bordered on recklessness and a brother officer alleged that he 'walked over to the German lines in daylight, rummaged about at will, and usually returned with odd, curious books, abstruse and pornographic. One day he returned with a bridal dress which he wore for dinner in the evening.'[64] The laughter at Cassino must also have been somewhat shrill when

> Major Clements . . . ended a long and exhausting tour in a spandau-swept artillery observation post a few hundred yards from the rear walls of the Monastery. On his return to his battery he found a letter from his mother who besought him, should he ever be in the neighbourhood, not to fail to visit the famous Benedictine hospice.[65]

But around Cassino laughter of any kind was a rare commodity. The whole atmosphere of the place was doom-laden, reminding the men of the New Zealand Corps of the bloody failures of yesterday and of the grim price to be paid on the morrow. The very air they breathed was nauseously redolent with foreboding. As one War Diary tersely remarked: 'The smell of corpses . . . was something the troops could not get used to and as it was impossible to organize burial parties, this area will always be remembered for its stench of death.'[66] It was not to abate.

---

* The officer in question was Lieutenant Richard Buckle, at the time of writing the ballet correspondent of *The Times* etc. The story that follows is confirmed in the first volume of autobiography, *A Most Upsetting Woman*, Collins, 1981. My thanks to Harry Bawden for bringing this to my attention.

II
'Even Paratroopers Must Crack'
The New Zealand Corps Try Again, 15–23 March 1944

For two years and a quarter it has been my good fortune to serve
with you. Now the time has come for me to go. I can never forget
you. You have built a brotherhood in arms such as has seldom been
equalled in our long history. Your great battles are carved deep in
the tablets of this war. I have never known you falter.

General Tuker's Farewell Letter to 4 Indian Division,
15 March 1944

The name that is most generally applied to the New Zealand
Division both individually and collectively, is Kiwi. . . . One
version of the derivation of the name I have heard goes like this –
'Like the bird we can't fly, we can't see, and we are rapidly becoming
extinct.'

Anonymous New Zealander, January 1944

On the evening of 14 March the battalions of New Zealand Corps were
alerted that the bombing of Cassino, Operation BRADMAN, was definitely
on for the next day.* Bomb safety lines had already been worked out and
most of the troops moved back behind them, though a few 'suicide
squads', as one historian aptly named them, remained behind to fire
occasional rounds of mortar and machine gun fire to deceive the Germans
into thinking that the forward posts were still fully manned. The actual
bombing began at 08.30 and went on until 12.00, with the bomber groups
coming in every ten minutes until 09.00 and every fifteen minutes
thereafter. No two sources agree on the exact number of planes involved
or the exact tonnage of bombs dropped, but the approximate figures were
280 heavy bombers (Liberators and Flying Fortresses), 180 mediums
(Marauders and Mitchells) and 1000 tons of bombs, most of them 1000-
pounders. From the photographic evidence it was later confirmed that 47
per cent of the bombs dropped on the target area fell within one mile of
the centre of the town. This represented a strike ratio of a little over four
tons per acre. As soon as the bombers turned for home a massive artillery
programme started and over the next eight hours 890 guns of all calibres,

---

* It remains uncertain whether it was a British or an American staff officer who seems
to have been unaware that Bradman was an *Australian* cricketer.

from 8-inch howitzers to 25-pounders, fired 195,969 rounds at their appointed targets.*

The results certainly looked impressive. General von Senger und Etterlin saw the devastation on the next day, from General Heidrich's command post: 'What I saw and felt took me back across twenty-eight years, when I experienced the same loneliness crossing the battlefield of the Somme. Hitler was right when he later told me that here was the only battlefield of this war that represented those of the first.'[1] The bombing itself was watched by various senior generals, including Alexander, Clark and Eaker, and the latter seemed positively jubilant. In a broadcast immediately afterwards he told how the generals had 'watched Cassino melted down today. . . . Today we fumigated Cassino and I am most hopeful when the smoke of today's battle clears we shall find more worthy occupants installed with little loss of our men. . . . Let the Germans well ponder that what we have done on the Ides of March to their fortress of Cassino, we shall do to every other stronghold where he elects to make a stand.'[2]

Privately, however, Eaker was disappointed with some aspects of the bombing, notably the performance of the heavies, which had dropped many of their bombs wide of the mark. In a letter to General Nathan Twining, the commander of Fifteenth Air Force, he expressed some concern about 'its conduct on that unfortunate day. . . . They undoubtedly had difficulty with their airdromes, which may have put some people in the lead who were not supposed to be in the lead. By contrast with the Mediums, however, they looked very bad and everybody commented on it.'[3] Some of the most vocal comments came from the ordinary soldiers on the ground, various units having been hit by the stray bombs. Four Fortresses and thirty-nine Liberators had wandered as far afield as Venafro, Pozzilli and Montaquila where they hit amongst other things Eighth Army HQ (overturning General Leese's caravan), Allied gun areas, 4 Indian Division's B Echelon (fifty casualties) and a Moroccan military hospital (sixty casualties). A few other bombs fell among the men of New Zealand Corps. The War Diary of 28 Battalion contented itself with a remarkably restrained entry, noting that at 08.45:

Second wave of bombers, 24 in all, also dropped their bombs in Cassino. The second 12 of the 24 bombers, however, mistook the 6 Bde HQ for Cassino and dropped their bombs, killing 15 of the 6 Bde HQ personnel. This, however, discouraged the men and after

* This represented 36 per cent of all rounds fired throughout the whole of the Third Battle.

that all eyes were watching the bombers in case they dropped some more short of the mark.[4]

4 Indian Division's forward battalions suffered no actual casualties but 4/16 Punjabis had three bombs fall within fifty yards of their HQ. An officer wrote: 'No lives were lost but shaken figures emerged from their foxholes covered in fine white dust, like ghosts in a fantastic graveyard.'[5] There were similar near-misses on the massif, where even the Allied soldiers found the bombing a tremendous nervous strain. An officer of 2/7 Gurkhas, just below Point 593, wrote:

> When four or five bombs had landed a few yards from A Company's position, no one poked his head out of his foxhole. After a few minutes I felt like shouting that's enough! but it went on and on until our eardrums were bursting and our senses befuddled. Some bombs fell on our Company and I found myself shouting curses at the planes. Later I was to write: 'What an inferno is Cassino now. Dear God – take pity on those men, if there are any survivors in the town, which I doubt.'[6]

A German diarist, from 115 PG Regiment, felt similar compassion for the troops in Cassino itself: 'Today hell is let loose at Cassino. Cassino is a few kilometres away to our left, we have a good view of everything. . . . We can see nothing but dust and smoke. The troops who are lying up there must be going mad. . . . The ground is shaking as if there was an earthquake.'[7] One of the men actually in the town, at this time garrisoned by 2/3 Parachute Regiment, was Leutnant Schuster, commanding No.7 Company. His account of the bombing gives the full flavour of his men's ordeal:

> Tensely we waited in our holes for the bombs to drop. Then they came. The whining scream of their approach, the roar of their explosions and the noise of the aircraft themselves mingled with echoes flung back from the hills to produce an indescribable and infernal bedlam of noise. The whole earth quaked and shuddered under the impact. Then – a sudden silence. Hardly had the dust settled a little than I dashed out to visit the other two strongpoints. I stumbled blindly about in a welter of craters. From somewhere a voice shouted: 'All's well!' and then the next great wave of air hulks loomed into view above me.
> I could not go back. I remained where I was and the floodgates of hell opened once again. We could no longer see each other; all

we could do was touch and feel the next man. The blackness of night enveloped us, and on our tongues was the taste of burnt earth. 'I'll come again,' I said, felt my way towards an exit and rolled out into a crater. I had to grope my way forward as though in a dense fog, crawling, falling, leaping; as I reached my post, another wave was on the way in. The men pulled me head over heels into our hole.Then down came the bombs again. A pause, and once more I groped my way across the tortured earth. Direct hits – here, here and here; a hand sticking out of the debris told me what had happened. When I got back, the men read in my eyes what I had seen. The same, unspoken thought was in all our minds – when would it be our turn? The crash of bursting bombs increased in intensity. We clung to each other, instinctively keeping our mouths open. It went on and on. Time no longer existed, everything was unreal. We shifted our positions and, well, we thought, if we can still move, we're still alive – sixteen of us.

Rubble and dust came pouring down into our hole. Breathing became a desperate and urgent business. At all costs we had to avoid being suffocated, buried alive. Crouching in silence we waited for the pitiless hail to end.[8]

An ordinary paratrooper stressed the appalling effects of the sheer duration of the bombing, as endless waves of planes returned again and again to pulverize every square inch of the town:

More and more sticks of bombs fell. We now realized that they wanted to wipe us out, but we could not grasp that this terrible episode would go on for so long. . . . The sun lost its brightness. An uncanny twilight descended. It was like the end of the world. . . . Comrades were wounded, buried alive, dug out again, eventually buried for the second time. Whole platoons and squads were obliterated by direct hits. The survivors fled in twos or small groups from the houses which had become man-traps, into the shell-holes. Many of them linked arms and held their ears at the same time in order not to be torn apart by the blast. Scattered survivors, half crazy from the explosions, reeled about in a daze, avoiding all cover, until they were hit by an explosion or disappeared. Others rushed headlong in the direction of the enemy, not caring about the abandoned positions, in order to escape from this hell.[9]

When the bombing started, 2/3 Parachute Regiment had had a little over 300 men and five assault guns in the town. Four hours later some

160 of them, as well as four of the guns, were permanently buried under the rubble. No.7 Company had been all but annihilated and Nos 5 and 8 were down to little more than 20–30 men each. Only No.6 Company had survived relatively intact, having sought immediate refuge with the Battalion HQ in a deep rock cavern at the foot of Monastery Hill.*

Yet this was enough. Even such a fearsome bombardment had left sufficient survivors to scramble through the ruins and man existing basement strongpoints or take up new snipers' perches in the bomb-blasted buildings. Even more surprisingly, perhaps, these survivors were still *compos mentis* enough to do this almost as soon as the bombers turned for home. Their remarkable resilience was made depressingly apparent during the interrogations of the first POWs from 2/3 Regiment. Clearly the bombing had been a ghastly experience. Feldwebel Richard Kruppa admitted that ' "the bombing was something tremendous and had a terrific effect on morale." He states that the mere recollection of the bombing is so unpleasant to him that he forbade . . . any of his men to speak to him further about Cassino. "Speak about women, but not about Cassino." ' [10] Yet of the twenty prisoners questioned up to 18 March, only one showed any definite anxiety symptoms. More typical was Obergefreiter Karl Brill who simply said: 'I felt nothing, because I was in a good bunker.' According to one of the interrogators: 'Much emphasis was placed by many of those questioned on the protection from effects of concussion and sense of security lent to the individual by the very adequate ground fortifications.' A psychiatrist who questioned them attempted to fall back on the 'fanatical Nazis' explanation and asserted that 'this group of parachutists shows evidence of extreme indoctrination'. His next revelation, however, that 'the individual soldiers are self-possessed, self-reliant and entirely single-minded in their emotional and mental approach to the war', merely lists the qualities one would expect in any well-trained soldier, fighting in a unit with a well-developed *esprit de corps*. [11]†

But if the bombing failed to live up to expectations as an attritional weapon, it succeeded all *too* well as a method of demolition. Individual houses were so shattered that the streets themselves could no longer be discerned, whilst such few patches of open ground as were left were pitted with bomb craters or overlaid with rubble. According to one eye-witness,

* It is worth noting that, even in such a concentrated target area, it therefore took approximately three tons of bombs to kill one paratrooper.
† Throughout the war, in fact, the Allies only ever isolated one bombardment, of Bauchem (Germany) in November 1944, which of itself completely demoralized the defenders.

the town was an 'unbelievable mess. . . . There was no vestige of a road or track, only vast heaps of rubble out of which peered the jagged edges of walls. The whole of this mess was covered by huge, deep craters that needed hand and foot climbing to get in and out of.'[12] This was bound to make it extremely difficult for the New Zealanders to push forward swiftly from the bomb-safety lines or to operate together except in groups of two or three men. And that could be of vital importance to the survivors of 2/3 Regiment, for it meant that their own scattered snipers and two- or three-man automatic weapons groups might well be sufficient to hold off the first attacks. Well-disguised and protected by the innumerable bomb-riven strongpoints, Captain Foltin's tiny battlegroups were vulnerable only to concerted New Zealand platoon or company attacks, exactly the thing they would be least able to organize. Worse still, the enormous craters would make it virtually impossible for the supporting armour to move forward, certainly not as any sort of solid spearhead and probably not even to supply the intimate individual fire-support that was of such importance in street-fighting.

Such was to be the case. Freyberg's plan envisaged that the first attack on the town would be undertaken by 6 New Zealand Brigade, supported by the tanks of 19 Armoured Regiment. The first objective (the Quisling Line) was the east–west stretch of Highway Six which was to be reached by 14.00, the troops advancing at a deliberate rate of 100 yards every ten minutes. 25 Battalion were responsible for clearing this whole sector, as well as taking Castle Hill (Point 193), a sheer promontory which completely dominated 4 Indian Division's gateway to the eastern slopes of Monastery Hill. Behind 25 Battalion would come the 24th and 26th, and as soon as Highway Six was reached the latter was to take over the lead and push through, via the station, to the Jockey Line, running south-east from the road junction by the Baron's Palace. This line was to be reached by dusk on the 15th, by which time 5 Indian Brigade, using Castle Hill as their base, was to have leapfrogged its battalions between the hairpin bends on the road to the Monastery and assembled a powerful strike force on Hangman's Hill. That same night this force would attack the Monastery itself whilst a task force of American tanks would make the first bound into the Liri Valley. Early on the 16th, 4 New Zealand Armoured Brigade would then take up the running, supported on their left by elements of 78 Division crossing in the ill-starred Sant' Angelo area. Any remaining enemy pockets of resistance on the massif were to be dealt with by 7 Indian Brigade and a small group of tanks specially assembled for this purpose. The tanks were to clamber on to the massif up the so-called Cavendish Road, only recently completed by Indian engineers.

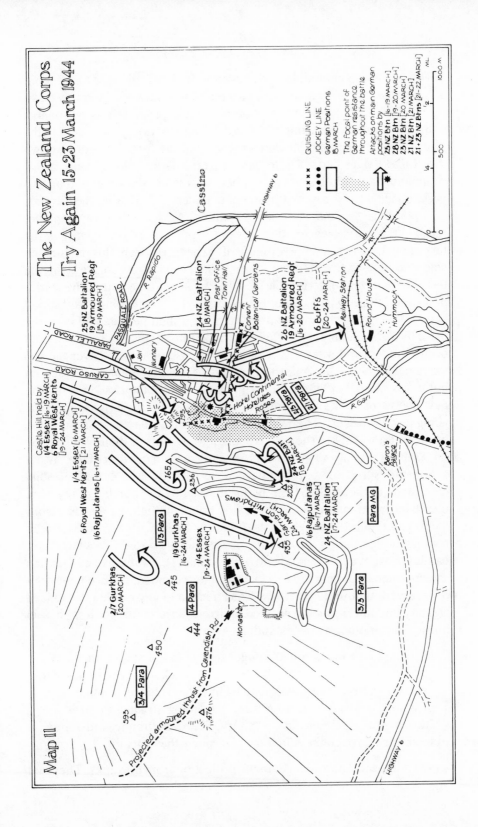

Map II

The New Zealand Corps
Try Again 15-23 March 1944

QUISLING LINE
JOCKEY LINE
German Positions
18 MARCH

The focal point of
German resistance
throughout the battle

Attacks on main German
positions by

25 NZ Btn [16-19 MARCH]
28 NZ Btn [19-20 MARCH]
23 NZ Btn [20 MARCH]
21 NZ Btn [21 MARCH]
21 + 25 NZ Btns [21-22 MARCH]

Cassino

25 NZ Battalion
19 Armoured Regt
[15-19 MARCH]

24 NZ Battalion
[18 MARCH]

Post Office
Town Hall

Convent
Botanical Gardens

26 NZ Battalion
19 Armoured Regt
[16-20 MARCH]

6 Buffs
[20-24 MARCH]

Railway Station

Round House

Hummock

R. Rapido

R. Gari

HIGHWAY 6

Castle Hill held by
1/4 Essex [16-19 MARCH]
6 Royal West Kents
[9-24 MARCH]

PASQUALE ROAD
PARALLEL ROAD
CARUSO ROAD

Jail

Nunnery

Hotel Continental
Hotel des Roses

595

6 Royal West Kents [16 MARCH]
1/4 Essex [16 MARCH]
1/6 Rajputanas [16+17 MARCH]

165

236

202

24

298

1/5 Para

2/1 Para

24 NZ Batt
[8 MARCH]

Baron's
Palace

Garrison Withdraws

455

1/6 Rajputanas
[16-17 MARCH]

24 NZ Battalion
[17-24 MARCH]

Para MG

2/7 Gurkhas
[20 MARCH]

1/9 Gurkhas
[16-24 MARCH]

1/4 Essex
[9-24 MARCH]

445

1/5 Para

1/4 Para

5/5 Para

450

595

3/4 Para

444

476

Monastery

Projected armoured thrust from Cavendish Rd

1000 M
500
0

HIGHWAY 6

This ambitious timetable soon began to look ridiculous. 25 Battalion, accompanied by 'B' Squadron 19 Armoured Regiment, led the way down Caruso Road. They set off at noon and initial progress was reasonably swift, though far from straightforward. 'A' and 'B' Companies were in the lead, the latter actually on Caruso Road and the former paddling down the Rapido river-bed. 'There were several barked shins,' said an 'A' Company man, 'while several members fell over in the water and on two occasions had to be assisted from going under. . . . During the advance . . . platoons became very spread out.'[13] As soon as the companies reached the Jail, however, they began to appreciate the enormity of the task ahead, and the impossibility of passing through this man-made wilderness at anything other than a snail's pace. A corporal in the battalion felt that 'entering Cassino was a vision of the end of the world, past description. . . . I can only describe [it] . . . as looking as if it had been raked over by some monster comb and then pounded all over the place by a giant hammer.'[14] The prescribed rate of advance soon went out of the window and it took 'A' Company almost an hour to cover the 100 yards between the Jail and the Nunnery. They immediately pressed on but it was 15.30, two and a half hours later, before they had covered the next 400 yards to the Post Office. 'B' Company on their right found the going just as difficult. Their main task was to clear the houses around the base of Castle Hill but they were baulked well short of their objective by the heaps of rubble and increasingly heavy fire from this part of the town.

For the surviving paratroopers were already establishing a solid defensive perimeter. Far from being stunned by the bombing they were merely enraged, and even in these first hours the fighting was as vicious as any experienced throughout the Italian campaign. One New Zealander commented: 'This was the one time in the war when Red Cross flags, arm bands etc. were not observed and our RAP man . . . was killed by German snipers when attending himself to a German wounded.'[15] Such behaviour only served to infuriate the New Zealanders and any residual notions of chivalry and fair play soon seemed an irrelevance in this godless charnel house. Said another New Zealander:

> Marching into those ruins brought out a kind of sadism in us. We were really enraged when the Jerries hit back – they had no right even to be *alive*. They were behaving like machines. Some bugger near to me was hit, and he went screaming straight towards the Jerries, not in pain but in sheer fury, like some frantic wild animal scrabbling through the ruins. . . . Of course they got him.[16]

Nor did the infantrymen get much protection from the tanks. They had come down both Caruso and Parallel Roads but found the second completely impassable, whilst a deep bomb crater in the first prevented any tanks from entering Cassino until 13.00, already half an hour behind the infantry. One troop then became hopelessly bogged down at the foot of Castle Hill and none of the remaining three troops was able to make much headway beyond the northern edge of the Botanical Gardens. Some contact was made with the infantry but this was not always to the latter's advantage. According to one: 'The confusion was such when the town was entered that our own tanks did not know which buildings we had occupied and at times we came under fire from them with armour-piercing shells.'[17] The commander of 19 Armoured Regiment, Lieutenant-Colonel R.L. McGaffin, sent out urgent appeals for engineer support, including bulldozers, to clear paths through the rubble and bridge some of the worst craters. A detachment was sent forward but German fire was by now so intense and accurate that it had no hope of getting up to the forward tanks. 'Nothing was left now but to face the tanks up to the obstructive rubble and charge it. With grating tracks, roaring engines and much metallic wheezing, the tanks buckled and bounced at the obstacles, but none surmounted them and a few wedged themselves immovably. The tank attack came to a stop.'[18]

So, in fact, did virtually the whole New Zealand advance and at dusk Freyberg gloomily composed a message to Clark which succinctly listed the frustrations of the day:

> Our own infantry reoccupied positions held prior to the bombing without difficulty. Roads leading south into the town badly damaged by bombing and made going for our own tanks impossible without engineer work. . . . Forward troops . . . engaged in house-to-house fighting. Some tanks are in close support but are unable to get to the forward infantry due to condition of roads through and round town. Engineers' work in town seriously interfered with by accurate enemy small arms fire.[19]

At about the same time the order was given to the leading companies to consolidate their present positions, though these represented a sorry contrast with the original objectives laid down in Freyberg's plan. The Jockey Line might as well have been on a different planet and even the Quisling Line was hardly held in strength. Only 'A' Company had actually got that far, and then only to establish a tenuous toe-hold around the Post Office. Of the other two companies in the town, 'B' had been hemmed in from all sides, neither being able to clear the houses at the foot of Castle

Hill nor to get within even 300 yards of its ultimate objective, the Continental Hotel. In fact so bad was the confusion amongst these leading companies that 'c' was held back around the Jail, where it became a relay post for messages and supplies from Battalion HQ.

Yet these had been one gleam of light amidst the frustrations. The actual capture of Castle Hill had been assigned to 'D' Company, under Major S.M. Hewitt, and though 'B' Company had been unable to do much to clear his path he quickly worked out a plan of his own. He led his men off Caruso Road and up the slopes of the mountain into the ravine to the north of his objective. Once there they were partially shielded from enemy observation and one platoon was sent south-west, towards Point 165, whilst the others cautiously worked their way around to the south-east, hugging the foot of the hill. At 13.00 the detached platoon reached an almost vertical cliff leading up to Point 165 and they began the perilous ascent. For once luck was with the New Zealanders and the two German lookouts on the summit were captured still crouching in their dugouts, fearful of a renewed artillery barrage. Ahead was a large pillbox and two men crept forward to it. One, Private T.S. McNiece, threw a grenade into the embrasure and 'there was a lovely explosion; dust and splinters of stone and wood came flying out of the window.' Unfortunately, so too did a German stick grenade but McNiece immediately grabbed this and pitched it down the ravine. He threw in another grenade of his own. It exploded, and out came a second stick grenade which landed a little distance away. McNiece threw himself to the ground as it exploded, only to have both his eardrums ruptured by the blast.

> My head felt as if it had been bashed in and my ears rang and ached cruelly. When the dust cleared away I was standing by the window with the Bren gun held out at arm's length pouring a stream of hot lead through the window. I then threw my last . . . grenade inside and stood with my back to the wall wondering what to do next.[20]

Luckily, at that very moment a Red Cross flag was thrust through the embrasure and McNiece and his comrade thankfully accepted the surrender of twenty-three paratroopers.

The platoon now tried to approach the eponymous Castle along a rocky saddle which linked it with the foot of Point 165. Heavy fire forced them to ground but just then the remainder of 'D' Company reached their own route to the Castle, a steep ridge running up from the foot of the ravine. They scrambled upwards, clearing out a few houses en route, and drove the remaining Germans back into the Castle, where they took refuge in a keep in the main quadrangle. Once again, however, after a few exchanges of machine gun fire and the tossing of the odd grenade, the paratroopers, elements of 1/3 Parachute Regiment, somewhat uncharacteristically chose to surrender.

It was now 17.00 hours. The gateway to the massif was at least ajar and some sort of base established for 4 Indian Division's entry into the battle. As long, that is, as the Indians knew that Castle Hill had been taken. But there now occurred yet another of these unfortunate breakdowns in communication that seemed to dog the New Zealand Corps. 5 Indian Brigade could do nothing until Castle Hill was taken and for most of the afternoon its battalions had been standing to on the Caruso Road, waiting for word from the New Zealanders. Yet even after 'D' Company's success it was some two hours before the news filtered back to the impatient Indians. The official record is reticent but it seems clear that the news was never put out by radio, if indeed 'D' Company ever had one, and that no arrangements had been made for the firing of Very lights or even some kind of semaphore signal. Such a failure, it has rightly been pointed out, 'is difficult to understand in view of [Castle Hill's] . . . prominence and the ease with which the visual success signal should have been seen.'[21] As it was the news was only transmitted by dint of a succession of runners who carried messages from one HQ to another. As another historian pointed out: 'The relief of "D" Company by the Indians was so much longer delayed; and this delay was the capital deposit that grew by compound interest as the operation proceeded.'[22]

The leading Indian battalion was 1/4 Essex Regiment, who set off at about 19.00. By now it was pitch dark and the leading companies had a terrible time even finding their way to the foot of Castle Hill. One company commander explained:

> . . . we have to realize that the damage caused by the bombing and the close-quarter fighting going on at the foot of Castle Hill made control very difficult. We were trying to move up in single file along a tape and then when it ended, up a path to the Castle. Any other method in the darkness and over rocks and rubble was impossible. From time to time we met parties of Germans and close-quarter fighting developed.[23]

It was almost midnight before the relief was complete. But worse was to come. Following behind the Essex men were 1/6 Rajputana Rifles, whose leading companies, 'A' and 'B', did reach the Castle safely. The trudging file behind, however, was caught in a series of ferocious defensive artillery bombardments, at about midnight, and 'c' and 'd' Companies were so mutilated and disorganized that few of their members took any further part in the battle. But the battalion was still under orders to carry out the first bound up the massif, seizing both of the hairpin bends at Points 165 and 236. The former had actually been taken by 1/4 Essex* and so a company of Rajputanas was duly despatched from the Castle to seize the second objective. At 04.30 they had climbed to within 150 yards of the bend when they were spotted by the Germans. Artillery and machine guns opened up immediately and the attackers were forced to withdraw back to the Castle.

The terrible problem facing 5 Indian Brigade was now becoming increasingly apparent. For close on the heels of the Rajputanas had followed 1/9 Gurkhas, whose mission was to make the second bound from Point 236 to Hangman's Hill and there form a fire base for the final assault on the Monastery. But because the entrance to the massif was so terribly constricted, fresh units could only be funnelled in once those in front had accomplished their mission. Thus not only did Lieutenant-Colonel Nangle find himself with no jump-off point for his own scheduled attack but there was not even the room to bring all of his battalion beyond the Castle. He was obliged to establish his own headquarters at the foot of Castle Hill and to dispose two of his companies, 'a' and 'b', round about. The other two he did manage to send forward, with orders to accomplish as much of their original mission as possible. The initial results were less than encouraging. The two companies skirted Castle Hill by different routes but 'd' was ambushed by a spandau team, losing 15 men within a minute. It was dawn before they could be reorganized for any further offensive effort. 'c' Company simply vanished into the darkness and contact with them was completely lost. At dawn on the 16th, then, the situation of 5 Indian Brigade left a great deal to be desired. Castle Hill and Point 165 were fairly securely held by 1/4 Essex but exploitation beyond this point had failed miserably. Two companies of 1/6 Rajputanas had been smashed, another had been decisively repulsed, and its survivors and the fourth company were clogging up access to the massif. This in turn had forced 1/9 Gurkhas to hold two of its companies short of the actual battlefield, and of the two that had managed to get forward, one was badly disorganized and the other had vanished into the blue.

But the problem of getting enough men forward was not unique to 4

---

* Point 165 had been evacuated by 16 Platoon, 25 Battalion, when their company had taken the Castle. The Germans had moved back in the late evening but had been ejected in a spirited attack by 1/4 Essex at 03.00.

Indian Division. If their attack was foundering in the bottleneck around Castle Hill, that of the New Zealand Division was equally compromised by the lunatic maze through which they tried to pass their own troops. The jumble of rubble and massive craters had already ground 25 Battalion to a halt and through the night of the 15/16th they were to make it virtually impossible for Freyberg to get any reinforcements through to them. The first attempt to help 25 Battalion had been made at 17.00 when 'B' Company, 24 Battalion, was sent in to try and clear the lower Castle Hill area that was holding out so doggedly. Fierce German fire limited their progress to a few yards. Half an hour later the whole of 26 Battalion was alerted, ordered to move through the 25th and attack towards the station. Such a ploy was indeed part of Freyberg's original plan, according to which they were to have jumped off from the Quisling Line at 14.00, supported by 'A' Squadron 19 Armoured Regiment. To persist with it that evening, however, was at best an improvisation, at worst a reckless gamble – as the New Zealand historian observed: 'Now, however . . . it was directed to make an attack for which a firm base did not exist, and it was unaccompanied by armour, for though the tanks of "A" Squadron . . . had been ordered into Cassino three hours before, they could not follow the men on foot.'[24]

But the infantry too had enormous difficulties simply getting to the front.

> Dusk fell and all four companies were soon in difficulties. The darkness quickly became almost impenetrable and D Company was forced to advance in single file, with each man clinging to the battledress of the man in front. . . . [The leading officer felt] his way through the piles of rubble . . . trying to determine if he was on the right track. Route 6 lay only 800 yards away. Every now and again someone would trip over some rubble or slide into a bomb crater. . . . To make matters worse, heavy rain began. Nobody was wearing a greatcoat, and within an hour most of the craters were half-filled with muddy water and the ground around them very slippy. The wireless batteries became wet, and before the night was through no set would work.[25]

The heavy rain, in fact, was almost the last straw and completely scuppered any last hopes of getting useful numbers of men or tanks within realistic striking distance of Highway Six. An official New Zealand Corps report, written soon after the battle, had this to say of operations in the town during the first night:

Heavy rain commenced in the evening and set in. The infantry reported that it was extremely difficult to make progress in the pitch dark and the sappers experienced the greatest difficulty in making any progress with routes for the tanks. The rubble of the pulverized buildings was reported to be 'of the consistency of dough'. The craters were full of water. . . . Bulldozing was useless and tanks which tried to cross craters fell into 10 feet of water.[26]

26 Battalion did manage to flounder through to Highway Six – the last 650 yards took them over three hours – but conversation with the forward outposts of 25 Battalion soon convinced them that further progress was out of the question. The bone-weary riflemen were directed to take up positions along the road or in and around the Town Hall. Operation DICKENS was not only badly behind schedule: it was beginning to founder.

It is worth pausing briefly here to emphasize just why failure was already staring Freyberg in the face. A common complaint in the following months, and in books written after the war, was that the New Zealand Division in particular had not deployed enough men at the very beginning to be able to rush the German defences as soon as the bombing stopped. General Clark was to write:

> . . . infantry in sufficient quantity must follow the artillery barrage quickly to take advantage of the partial destruction of enemy works. . . . The follow-up of the infantry after the concentration of bombardment must be immediate and aggressive, employing the maximum infantry strength available. The maximum amount of infantry was not employed in this attack, nor was the attack aggressively pushed.[27]

According to Slessor, there were 'two perfectly simple explanations of our failure to capture Cassino between March 15 and 26'. One was that bombers were quite incapable of blotting out *all* enemy resistance in well-prepared positions. 'The second simple explanation . . . was that the killed . . . on the 15th, the day of the attack, amounted to four officers and thirteen other ranks. I hope we shall have learnt by the time we attack again that five hundred casualties today often save five thousand in the next week.'[28]

Yet these same critics were among the first to admit that the bombing had also terribly complicated the New Zealanders' task. General Devers, for example, was completely surprised by the slow progress of the battle:

On March 15 I thought we were going to lick it by the attack on Cassino and advance up the Liri Valley. . . . In spite of all this [bombing] and with excellent support all afternoon with dive bombers and artillery fire, the ground forces have not yet attained their first objective. Consequently the tanks which were to attack in mass could not get started. These results were a sobering shock to me.[29]

But if senior commanders were prepared to admit that the bombing had had such deleterious effects, it seems at best ingenuous of them to accuse Freyberg of not putting enough men into the initial assault. For this in fact was its worst effect: the approaches to the killing zone were so badly blocked that it just was not possible to feed in large numbers of men. Worse still, there was simply no room to usefully deploy substantial reinforcements at the actual sharp end, the only place where decisive results were to be achieved. Street-fighting, like all other infantry fighting in the Second World War, depended on fire and movement. The 'battle of the last hundred metres' was often reduced to the last five or ten but it nevertheless depended on a final concerted squad or platoon dash, with supporting fire, to actually clear out a strongpoint. In Cassino one was lucky to find an avenue for one man to walk, let alone a dozen or so, and any concentration of tanks, machine guns or mortars was quite out of the question.

Yet Freyberg was far from blameless, in that his difficulties were very much of his own making. Clark claimed that Freyberg *chose* not to put many men into the initial infantry assault because 'too great reliance was placed upon the ability of bombardment to do the job alone'.[30] In fact, as we have seen, Freyberg *could* not put in enough men. But the basic point is valid. In crude terms the New Zealand plan was a 'shit or bust' operation. If the bombing failed to do everything that was expected of it, then every subsequent phase of the attack was hopelessly compromised from the start. And that is poor planning by any standards. One could not expect a general and his staff to foresee every delay and setback that might occur in a battle, but it does seem reasonable to ask that they allow the possibility of useful improvisation when things go wrong. New Zealand Corps simply did not have any options at all. In both Divisions, if one unit failed in its allotted task, the rest were stuck, trapped in a log-jam that could only be cleared by renewed pressure at the front.

The next days were to underline the virtual impossibility of exerting such pressure. German resistance was hardening with every passing hour, each paratrooper determined to respond to Vietinghoff's recent exhortation to von Senger und Etterlin: 'The Cassino massif must be held at all costs by 1 Parachute Division . . . the localization of attacks indicates that the enemy is seeking a prestige success.'[31] Freyberg's bad luck in having to face such élite troops was becoming all too apparent, and even the German commanders seem to have felt that only Heidrich's men could have so withstood the initial battering. On the 16th Westphal spoke to Vietinghoff on the telephone:

> *Westphal:* 'Do you think Cassino can be held indefinitely?'
> *Vietinghoff:* 'I can't tell yet. . . . Eveybody was dazed by that bombardment and before they could snap out of it the enemy was into them.'
> *Westphal:* 'The enemy has reported that it was impossible to maintain troops in the town because of German snipers.'
> *Vietinghoff:* 'That is very good indeed . . . But Senger told me the aircraft had a terrible effect.'
> *Westphal:* 'I bet you are glad you had the paratroopers there.'
> *Vietinghoff:* 'Yes . . . the paratroopers will hold on best.'[32]

But Heidrich's men had no intention of indulging in unnecessary bravado or of conducting their defence in anything but the most sensible and methodical manner. First it was necessary to reinforce the depleted garrison in the town and over the next days as many men as possible, mainly from 2/1 Parachute Regiment and the Division's pioneer and motor-cycle companies, were infiltrated into Cassino. It was also essential to mark out a realistic defensive perimeter and to accept that large parts of the town were irretrievably lost. The key sector was obviously that around the Continental Hotel, in the south-west of the town, where a resolute stand could both prevent the New Zealanders from pushing their armour down Highway Six and also maintain a stranglehold on the Indians' access to the massif beyond Castle Hill. So here the paratroopers concentrated. The Continental and the Hotel des Roses, in particular, were swiftly turned into fearsome strongpoints. 'The German infantry and the few tanks knew their job, because they had long been on the defensive. The tanks, operating singly, were held back under cover. . . . That the Continental Hotel was held is attributable to one tank, which had been built into the entrance hall.'[33] But it was not just the larger buildings that were thus fortified. In almost every house the Germans busied themselves creating bunkers and weapons pits that would be impregnable to anything but a direct shell hit. According to a prisoner of war:

Bunkers were constructed . . . in bombed houses, where the cellar was still intact. Underneath the cellar ceiling a roof consisting of three layers of beams (hardwood) was erected and covered with dirt approximately half a metre high. There was a space left between the top of the bunker and the ceiling. Prisoner of war stated his bunker received a direct hit by early shell. Ceiling caved in but nothing happened to the bunker.[34]

The final defensive ingredient, and perhaps the most important of all, was provided by the German artillery. We have already noted the efforts made by von Senger und Etterlin to concentrate as many guns as possible around the Cassino area, and the local commanders had no intention of wasting these precious weapons. Both Heidrich and Colonel Heilmann, the commander of 3 Parachute Regiment, paid constant attention to the siting, ranging and targeting of the artillery. As the latter said,

I well knew that the few men . . . in the front line, however gallantly they fought, could not win the battle alone. . . . I now demanded of the artillery a lavish and unrestricted expenditure of ammunition and even went as far as to harrow them into compassion for the poor infantryman, when I laid down the amount to be expended . . .

In this . . . battle for Cassino we achieved the great feat of gaining, for a while at least, superiority of fire. . . . With great skill and by using every possible means of communication, the artillery liaison officer with the 3 Parachute Regiment succeeded in co-ordinating the fire of more and more batteries in the sector and even in integrating the artillery of the division next to us. . . . The heavy machine gun and mine-thrower platoons of the division were brigaded and their fire co-ordinated in a single, homogeneous fire plan. . . . The fire plan was gradually broadened to embrace every type of weapon available, and even rifles and rifle-grenades were allotted their specific tasks.[35]

The effects of these German reinforcements, retrenchments and fire plans made themselves keenly felt on the 16th. The New Zealand Division made hardly any progress at all. Through prodigious efforts by the engineers and their own crews, some tanks from 19 Armoured Regiment did succeed in getting forward to the men of 25 and 26 Battalions, but even with this support the infantry could not make any significant penetrations. Both battalions attacked just after dawn, the former now aiming at the focus of German resistance around the two hotels and the latter still striving to get to the station and the Jockey Line. 25 Battalion was spearheaded by 'A' Company and they had some initial success as they moved off from the Convent area. A whole network of houses and back streets was cleared but by midday it was becoming apparent that the defenders were only making a fighting withdrawal to their chosen *Stützpunkt*. As the New Zealanders got nearer to the Continental, resistance hardened and the occupation of each house became a miniature battle in its own right. Just holding a captured house imposed a terrible strain, for the paratroopers were never reluctant to send out probing parties of their own, looking to recapture any position that was not well-manned and on the alert. A New Zealand captain recalled one such vigil in a house very close to the Continental:

> Conditions during our stay of five or six hours in the cellar were extremely trying, the water being about six feet deep in places, and we were forced to stand throughout this period on submerged tables etc., but even then we were standing in several inches of water. The only relief from these conditions could be obtained by four men squeezing on to a broad shelf against the north wall. The plight of our seven wounded who could not be evacuated until after last light was particularly wretched.[36]

An abiding impression of the street-fighting in Cassino was its intimacy, attacker and defender existing almost cheek by jowl, unable to look beyond the boundaries of the house, or even room, which they occupied at any one moment. One platoon of 25 Battalion, according to an eye-witness,

> shared a house with the enemy for three days, and for 36 hours lived on iron rations and cigarettes. . . . While the Germans could be heard moving about on the roof, nothing could be done as all exits were covered by a German strongpoint across the street in front and grenade-dropping snipers on the roof. . . . This episode was fairly typical of conditions in Cassino at that time. Platoons, often only a section strong, fighting well toward their objective only to be temporarily isolated. Their desired aggressive role was thus handicapped by a shortage of manpower and so firepower . . .[37]

26 Battalion made even less progress. Indeed, they had considerable difficulty just hanging on to the positions they had occupied the night before. Dawn brought nothing but trouble and the New Zealanders, crouching in bomb craters and amongst piles of rubble, found themselves terribly exposed to incessant sniper fire from vantage-points all around

them. The day's only success was won by two sections of 'c' Company who, incensed by the galling German fire, made a fifty-yard dash across Highway Six and occupied the Convent, one of the few relatively intact buildings in the whole town. They managed to hang on through the day and that night the position was strongly reinforced.

In terms of Freyberg's original plan, however, the day's achievements were almost derisory and he came under increasing pressure to step up his attacks and, above all, put more men into the town. Clark advised immediately pouring more infantry over the Rapido bridge but Freyberg remained adamant that there was no way in which such reinforcements could be usefully deployed. Clark held his peace, though there were those in New Zealand Corps itself who shared his views. Major-General A. Galloway, who had taken over command of 4 Indian Division from Dimoline, was already convinced that any substantial progress by his leading battalions was dependent upon events in the town. In a letter written just after the battle he took issue with Freyberg's version of what had gone wrong, claiming that 'the real means of reinforcing, building up and supplying any attack on the Monastery never materialized. 4 Indian Division was always ready to capture the Monastery once the way through even a small part of Cassino had been cleared.'[38] On the evening of the 16th he put his point more forcefully, saying he was 'completely convinced that the best way to clear Cassino is to put infantry in and go on doing so until it is cleared.'[39]

Certainly 5 Indian Brigade was still having terrible difficulties in pressing forward its attack on the massif. In theory their advance towards Hangman's Hill was to have been supported by elements of 20 Armoured Regiment, using the zigzag road up to the Monastery. But the tankmen were less than enthusiastic, particularly when they heard that neither of the further hairpins, Points 202 and 236, had yet been taken. Nor were they convinced that the road was even negotiable for tanks. One officer said afterwards: 'I was very much against this part of the plan as it appeared quite obvious that it would entail far too much engineering work to make a track.' But the Indians were most insistent that some kind of effort be made and the New Zealanders agreed to send out a reconnaissance party. This duly set forth at 04.00, on the 16th, and returned some hours later after several hairsbreadth escapes. Their report only confirmed the worst suspicions: 'The road . . . as we had feared, was just hopeless – collapsed craters and a sea of mud.'[40] The Indians would have to rely on their own infantry.

At 08.30 another attack was mounted on Point 236 by a company of 1/6 Rajputanas, and once again it broke down in the face of fierce small arms fire from the defenders. 3 Indian Brigade was rapidly running out of realistic options when, at about 14.00, electrifying news came through on the radio. The missing company of 1/9 Gurkhas which, it will be recalled, had marched off into the dark the night before, had actually managed to worm its way through on to Hangman's Hill and overwhelm the tiny garrison there. This was hardly a major breakthrough, but at least it did show that the German defences were not impregnable and gave the rest of the battalion a very tangible goal. As the Gurkhas quickly prepared to join their forward company, an officer in one of those still held back below the Castle Hill bottleneck wrote: 'We thought what a bloody relief it was to get out of the town where we were losing men and achieving nothing.'[41] The news also galvanized the Rajputanas and that night simultaneous attacks were launched to widen the bottleneck and ease the remaining Gurkhas' passage up to Hangman's Hill. Setting off at 20.00, 'A' and 'B' Companies fought their way on to Point 236 whilst the other two struck out along the side of the massif and succeeded in establishing a precarious foothold on Point 202. These attacks kept the paratroopers fully occupied and by early morning on the 17th the majority of the Gurkhas had joined 'C' Company below the Monastery.

Yet this lodgement was hardly the secure springboard for a final assault that had been envisaged in the original plan. That the Gurkhas were there at all was a tribute to their remarkable fighting abilities, but this last effort had cost 5 Indian Brigade dearly and for the moment they could do little more than hang on, hoping that events in the town would ameliorate their position. Some could not even hang on. At 04.30 the Germans launched a fierce counter-attack against Point 236 and the two companies of Rajputanas were thrown back on to the lower hairpin bend. The Germans on the massif now redoubled their efforts, seeking above all to cut off the route to and from the Castle and to isolate the troops on Hangman's Hill.

The position of the latter deteriorated by the hour. Almost everything was lacking except weapons and ammunition, and had the Gurkhas had even an inkling that their ordeal was to last for a full eight days, they must surely have deemed the situation utterly impossible. They had no blankets or greatcoats because overriding priority had been given to ammunition. They had hardly any food and had to exist on their American K Rations, an emergency pack supposed to sustain a man for at most a day until more normal feeding was arranged. The best the Gurkhas ever managed, even after more supplies had been air-dropped, was two-thirds of a ration per man per twenty-four hours. One officer wrote:

Food soon became an obsession . . . The contents [of the K Rations] included small tins of self-heating soups, various processed meat products and other odd items which seemed more suitable to a school picnic than to a battlefield. Despite their hunger, the Gurkhas would not risk breaking their Hindu faith . . . by eating anything produced from the cow. So when we shared the contents of a K Ration packet, they would . . . ask me to identify [the tins of meat] from the label before they would eat it. I must admit that I told the occasional white lie. . . . Oh yes! It also included that great American invention, chewing gum. Here I scored – it was not overpopular with Gurkhas, so I gradually accumulated a huge blob of gum which I stuck on the side of my sangar until I felt hungry again.[42]

The Gurkhas were also extremely short of water and when the canteens ran dry only had recourse to a nearby rain-filled crater which was often staked out by German patrols. After the level had fallen a few feet one water party discovered that the crater also contained the body of a dead mule. Medical supplies were virtually non-existent and even after some reinforcements from 1/4 Essex had reached Hangman's on the 19th, the only medical aid available was that provided by two Essex NCOs equipped with bandages, scissors and a pocket-knife. Such aid as the rest of the Corps tried to give the Gurkhas was often less than helpful. Particularly troublesome were the smoke shells which were used in profusion from the afternoon of the 17th, in an attempt to mask the town and much of the massif from the eyes of German observers. That same day, according to an artillery liaison officer with the Gurkhas,

the smoke nuisance now became acute. Our shelling continued throughout the afternoon with such accuracy that the Gurkha commander's sangar received three direct hits from shell itself. Attempts by the battery commander urged by the Gurkha CO to shift the target proved fruitless. Relations in all directions assumed an atmosphere of strain. The galling aspect of the whole business was that the smoke so placed screened nothing from nobody.[43]*

This was not quite true. Certainly the New Zealanders in the town were equally unappreciative of the gloomy pall. 'There is no day,' one of them

---

* True to its tradition of indifferent staff work, no one in the New Zealand Corps had seen fit to inform the Gurkhas that there was going to be a smokescreen.

was to write, 'only two kinds of night – a yellow, smoky, choking night, and a black meteor-ridden night.'[44] Yet for the Germans in the town the smoke did have its advantages, once, that is, they had allayed their worst suspicions. As the first shells landed, recalled one paratrooper, 'hissing, heavy, greyish-blue smoke poured out of the pot-shaped contents. . . . In a flash we went over everything we had heard about gas attacks. . . . Eventually we decided the stinking stuff was a smokescreen, and made a virtue out of necessity. For the first time in almost two months we could walk upright by day in this terrain. . . .'[45] Above all, the smoke allowed the Germans to continue reinforcing their meagre forces in the town, filtering men down from the relatively quiet sectors west of the Abbey. For without such reinforcements there were increasing doubts that the survivors of 3 Parachute Regiment could hang on. According to von Senger und Etterlin's morning report for the 17th: 'Our casualties are still very high. One company reported a fighting strength of 8 men. . . . The commander of 1 Parachute Division, who is up with the forward troops, does not think the situation can possibly be cleaned up unless 1 Parachute Regiment is pulled out forthwith [from around Massa Albaneta].'[46]*

Even before the smoke began, in fact, enough Germans had slipped through to maintain the dogged resistance in the south and east of the town. For it was here that the New Zealanders, on the 17th, once again launched their attacks: 25 Battalion still hammering against the Continental Hotel complex and 26 Battalion striving to get through to the station. As the companies formed up Freyberg spoke insistently to the Divisional commander, urging him to 'put great energy into cleaning it up on a broad front. . . . It is essential that we should push through to the Gurkhas tonight. Anywhere you can push in tanks, do so.'[47] 25 Battalion jumped off first, at 06.45, and had some small success. A few houses were quickly cleared and the companies burst into the Botanical Gardens, now more reminiscent of a lunar landscape than anything to be found at Kew. But even such desolation was a welcome change from the maze of rubble encountered thus far and the New Zealanders pressed forward, reaching the western edge of the Gardens by 07.30. But here they stopped, their momentum almost immediately dissipated by a fresh

* And of course Heidrich was adamant that only paratroopers were capable of so 'cleaning up'. Later that day the War Diary of XIV Panzer Corps recorded: 'The situation in the town is very critical. Both sides have suffered serious casualties. . . . Corps Headquarters orders 115 PG Regiment to be placed under command of the Parachute Division. [But] fighting in the town will be carried out exclusively by parachutists withdrawn from front sectors not under attack.' (Quoted in von Senger fully one-third of the rifle companies' fighting strength.

barrier of tumbled masonry, machine gun posts and snipers' nests. Even the term 'house-to-house fighting' seriously exaggerated the further progress made. Each individual dwelling became a battlefield in its own right and an advance of a few feet was deemed a substantial achievement. An artilleryman gave a perfect summary of the pace of this sort of combat: 'An infantryman said to us when we asked how things were going . . . "Not so bad, we've captured the front of the first house and at the moment we have a patrol in the cellar." '[48]

26 Battalion had been waiting for the order to move since 07.15 but they did not actually set off towards the station until 11.00. Freyberg himself spoke to the local commanders, again exhorting them to do their utmost to break the German stranglehold: 'Push on, you must go hard. Task Force B must go through as soon as possible. The limit is the roof – push hard.'[49] Unfortunately, the attack can only be described as shambolic. When the order came through only 'C' Company was still actually with Battalion HQ on the start line, in the Convent, where it had been joined by a squadron of tanks from 19 Armoured Regiment. These men set off immediately, whilst the other three companies, now grouped around the Town Hall, had to be summoned by runner. For these latter just crossing the hundred or so yards to the Convent was no easy matter, as the whole area eastwards of it was rife with spandau teams and snipers. A soldier of 'A' Company described the ordeal:

> . . . those in the Municipal Buildings knew that their chances of gaining Tactical Headquarters were slim. Not only did the enemy have a sniper watching the only entrance to the building but the ground which . . . we would have to cross was under heavy fire. . . . Each man . . . knew what to expect when he started running. . . . Nevertheless, section by section, the men raced over the open ground. Most of them had only little more than a hundred yards to go, but the enemy snipers on rooftops were waiting and they showed no mercy. Most of those in the building got out safely only to be shot in the back as they ran towards the Convent entrance. One after another they dropped. The wounded crawled to shell craters, others paused to help, only to be hit themselves. Other wounded stumbled, half-crawled towards shelter, only to be laid low by another bullet. . . . The wounded were lying everywhere. Mortar bombs were bursting among them.[50]

The actual attackers also had their problems, especially the tankmen who encountered the usual utterly inimical terrain. The commander of one troop described the approach to the station:

. . .we found that the streets just did not exist; there was nothing but rubble everywhere and all our previous recces and plans went overboard. I couldn't find any semblance of the roads . . . so we nosed the tanks through a few gaps and somehow got in behind the Convent. From there I had no alternative but to get out of the tank and crawl forward among the rubble to find a track. . . . Machine gun fire was rattling like hailstones on the tank as we made our way to the station, firing on the move. . . . At the crossroads . . . we encountered a deep minefield [and] I decided to move the mines. . . . I intended to do the job alone, but a member of my tank crew . . .was soon at my side and we soon got the road clear.[51]

Gradually some of the tanks nosed their way forward and by noon two of them had actually reached the station, soon to be joined by another pair. The infantry arrived much more slowly, driblets of panting infantrymen staggering in over the next couple of hours. The survivors were grouped once more into their respective platoons and companies and were deployed around the station. Most were used to consolidate the positions already cleared by the tanks, though two platoons of 'D' Company somehow summoned up the reserves to make a spirited attack on the Hummocks, which were secured by 15.00. The Battalion's orders now called for a further advance to the Jockey Line but the men were so exhausted and casualties so severe that this was deemed out of the question, and the line of the Gari was chosen as their new perimeter.*

The fighting on the 17th had been as vicious as ever and the evening report by XIV Panzer Corps was an eloquent tribute to the dogged determination of the New Zealanders:

South of the town the enemy fought our foremost posts to a standstill by weight of fire, and then occupied the station after hand-to-hand fighting. Attack after attack was launched on the eastern part of the town during the day. Bitter close-range fighting took place. The parachutists abandoned nothing but heaps of ruins to the enemy. The centre of the town is still in our hands.[52]

But this last sentence was the crunch. Certainly both Allied divisions had made progress, but each had only established insecure salients. Both were equally vulnerable to enemy counter-attack and, because the Germans still stood firm around the Continental Hotel, neither could be used as

---

* Since the 15th, 26 Battalion had lost 109 men, 37 of them killed. This represented fully one third of the rifle companies' fighting strength.

springboards for further concerted attacks, either by pouring men on to the massif or by pushing substantial numbers of tanks down Highway Six. Concern was beginning to grow in higher quarters, even the tight-lipped press releases hinting at possible further delays. A draft statement prepared by 15th Army Group late on the 17th defined the official line as follows: 'Mopping up in Cassino making satisfactory progress but final clearance of town and surrounding heights may yet take some time.'[53] Off the record the senior commanders were less sanguine, as is revealed in Clark's diary entry that same evening:

> The battle of Cassino is progressing slowly. Freyberg's enthusiastic plans are not keeping up with his schedule. . . . Due to General Alexander's direct dealing with Freyberg and the fact that this is an all-British show, I am reluctant to give a direct order to Freyberg to put the 78th Division over Route Six and to attack from the north from 593 [with 11 Indian Brigade] . . . Alexander did not in any way seem excited about the situation.[54]

Exactly what General Wilson thought of the situation remains unclear. Indeed, his reply to a request from London, for a detailed appreciation of how the battle was going and an assessment of what indirect assistance the forces in the Mediterranean might be able to afford the forthcoming cross-Channel operation, was sublimely unhelpful:

> The attack by New Zealand Corps . . . may result in breaking the Adolf Hitler Line within 3 or 4 days and a rapid advance culminating in a junction with the Bridgehead a few days later, say by 23 March. . . . On the other hand, it may well result only in securing the capture of Cassino. . . . The uncertainty of the time factor makes it impracticable for me to submit a correct appreciation until the outcome of the present battle is known . . .[55]

This could hardly be construed as cogent analysis and the reply from London the next day was as stinging a rebuke as one is likely to find at this lofty level of official communication:

> We feel that we must ask you to furnish us, by not later than AM 21st March, with your appreciation of the existing situation, as you see it as Supreme [Allied Commander-in-Chief], together with your views as to the practicable operations which would be carried out in your theatre and which would be most helpful to OVERLORD.
>
> Deferment of decision until outcome of present battle is known may mean that present state of uncertainty will prevail indefinitely.

This is not only unsatisfactory to you, but also to General Eisenhower, and we cannot expect him to accept further delay in taking decisions, which will have such an important effect on OVERLORD.[56]

But few of the men in Cassino could have cared less about General Eisenhower's difficulties and on the 18th they gritted their teeth for another day on the rack. Once again both divisions found themselves hamstrung by the total lack of relatively open axes of attack, and such initiatives as there were either ground to a halt or were made in such limited numbers as to completely deprive them of any useful impact. The boldest stroke was to bring two companies of 24 Battalion into the town, on the night of the 17/18th. This move had originally been seen as a follow-up to successful attacks by both 25 and 26 Battalions, allowing a strong thrust down Highway Six towards the Colosseum and the Baron's Palace. But the attack against the hotel area had failed and that towards the station had run out of steam, leaving the door firmly closed on 24 Battalion's supposed way forward. As soon as they set off they ran into heavy concentrations of German fire and by dawn had been forced away to the east of Highway Six and no further forward than the crossroads north of the station. By 09.00 the following was typical of the messages being sent back to Battalion HQ:

. . . Coy is 33 strong. Have one mobile tank with us. No word of D Coy, should be somewhere left of A Coy. Town literally full of enemy snipers and spandaus. They inhabit rubble and ruined houses. We are being as aggressive as possible. . . . Until Monastery Hill is in our hands sniping problem will continue. It is *not* to be underrated. . . . Tanks find it difficult to operate. Movement in daylight nil. 18 and 38 [radios] can *not* contact you and line is out. Am trying to rest troops today, sleep has been nil so far.[57]

The battalion's 'C' Company was used in a more imaginative manner, being despatched that same night to Point 202 which it took over from the Rajputana garrison. At dawn on the 18th they launched an attack on to the rear of the Hotel des Roses and managed to get within a hundred yards of it before they were driven back by heavy fire from the barricaded windows. The company had no alternative but to return to Point 202, yet another small group of cold and weary men clinging by their fingernails to an isolated, exposed position.

For the rest of New Zealand Division the day held nothing new. After the failure of 24 Battalion, the 26th could do nothing but hang on in the station, where they were subject to a fierce German counter-attack. This was carried out by the Parachute Motor-Cycle Company and must rank as a testimony to their remarkable morale rather than sound military judgement. The company approached across the Gari, many of them up to their necks in icy water. As soon as they reached the other bank they were caught in one of their own mortar barrages and suffered several casualties. The actual attack showed a marked lack of finesse and, according to a New Zealand account,

> they rushed in, yelling that they were Indians, but nobody was deceived. Instead both companies from their dugouts, shelters and houses poured a well-directed fire on them, inflicting heavy casualties. . . . The action was over in a few minutes. . . . [As they withdrew] the troops on the Hummocks were waiting and, as the paratroopers ran across the mudflat towards the river, directed a steady volume of fire on them. In the words of one officer . . . 'It was a pity for they were so easily killed.'[58]

According to German accounts there were only 19 survivors from the whole company.

But equally mortal were the men of 25 Battalion, who on the 18th spent yet another day grinding away at the German defences around the Continental Hotel. Three attacks were launched in all but the only success was scored in the last when 'C' Company managed to clear out one troublesome strongpoint, killing 14 Germans and capturing 3 for the loss of 3 killed and 14 wounded. No other troops could have done more, but it was a clear indication of just how bogged down Freyberg's offensive had become when a Division's major gain for the day was the clearing of just one house.

The Germans were now getting increasingly self-confident. Though their casualties had been severe – to the annihilated companies already mentioned was added the 2nd Company of 3 Parachute Regiment which was reduced to one Obergefreiter, known as the 'company commander without a company' – the defensive perimeter had held and allowed Heidrich to feed fresh units into the most critical sectors. The War Diary of XIV Panzer Corps reflected a new cautious optimism on the 18th, noting that despite concentric enemy attacks, 'we manage to hold our positions. Our decimated forces are considerably strengthened by the bringing up of reserves. Now that our troops have weathered this crucial day, General Heidrich views the situation with confidence.'[59] General Clark, on the other hand, was becoming increasingly anxious. His concern was understandable though his diary entry for the day gave little indication that he had any real conception of Freyberg's problems. Making little allowance for the appalling terrain, German tenacity or the increasing power and accuracy of their artillery, he contented himself with remarking that the New Zealand commander was 'ponderous and slow'.[60]

In fact, Freyberg was now beginning to realize that no matter how constricted was his access to the forward positions, he simply had to try and feed more men into the battle. During the morning he had been on the point of committing 5 New Zealand Brigade but had deferred to the judgement of his Divisional commander, General Parkinson, that no more infantry were necessary. But he did have a word of warning, telling Parkinson: 'You must remember that the whole operation is being paralysed until Cassino is cleared up.'[61] During the afternoon, in fact, he changed his mind and decided to bring in a new battalion to take part in a co-ordinated attack, on the 19th, to both clear out the town and storm the Monastery. The former effort was to be spearheaded by 28 (Maori) Battalion, making yet another attempt to clear Highway Six by storming the Continental Hotel. They were to jump off at 03.00, whilst on that same morning the Gurkhas on Hangman's Hill were to be reinforced by 1/4 Essex, preparatory to immediately driving the final 300 yards to the Monastery. Their base on Castle Hill and Point 165 was to be entrusted to 4/6 Rajputanas, some of whom had already been engaged in portering supplies up to Hangman's Hill. The attack on the massif was to be supplemented by an armoured thrust up the Cavendish Road. In the original plan, as has already been noted, this had been intended as part of the mopping-up operations early on the 16th, but was now merely thrown into the tactical pot as a diversionary move that might just pay some dividends.

Things went badly wrong from the beginning. The relief of 1/4 Essex was delayed and they were not even in position to set out for Hangman's Hill until 04.00. As a consequence the assault on the Monastery had to be put back until 14.00. But such a postponement would probably have been advisable anyway, for the attack could only have any hope of success if at the same time the Maoris were well on the way to clearing out the hotel complex below. But this they signally failed to do. They jumped off on time but soon ran into just the same last-ditch resistance that had faced 25 Battalion before them. Not that there had been any illusions. Two companies were used in the initial assault and the co's orders specified that:

Two Coys, C and D, will be involved in the operation. D Coy will search for and clear out all enemy in the objective area and take up and consolidate on western side of the objective. . . . C Coy will follow D Coy at 15 mins interval and will rely on the bayonet and grenade, and not fire, to clear out any isolated pockets left behind, *searching every nook and cranny.*[62]

As with most of the major New Zealand assaults, the first momentum and the grim determination of the troops did gain some ground, allowing them to clear a few houses around the Continental. But the hotel itself remained virtually unassailable. Automatic weapons poked out from every slit in the tumbled masonry and incessant mortar fire broke up every attempted concentration. And, as ever, the appalling nature of the ground made it almost impossible to adhere to even the most rudimentary principles of mutually supporting fire and movement. Tanks were in support but none of these were able to get within 300 yards of the hotel itself. As for the infantry they soon became separated into individual platoons, sections and sub-sections, unable to communicate with each other and usually with very little idea of where they were. Typical of the Maoris' experiences that morning were those of Lieutenant Waititi, with 'C' Company:

> Immediately we moved into the attack I lost contact with my platoon, with the exception of the section I was with. . . . Occasionally I sent a man to our right to contact our other forward section but he returned each time without contact. However we kept going until we came to a high bank of rubble etc. which I think must have brought us up on to the skyline because we got pinned down by machine gun fire every time we attempted to go over. We had no idea whether we had reached our objective or how far we were from it as the area we were in was bomb holes and rubble and only parts of buildings standing.[63]

By mid-afternoon it had become apparent that no further progress was possible. The paratroopers were standing firm. Heidrich's appreciation of the situation now became almost cocky. 'Tonight,' he wrote, '2/115 PG Regiment is moving into Cassino, and our weakness will be a thing of the past. We will then have to withstand the attack by the enemy's fresh troops, tire them out as we did the others, and then counter-attack. The enemy troops who have infiltrated between the town and the Abbey must be cut off.'[64]

In fact, the attempt to do this had already started and by cruel coincidence it completely nullified any chance of 1/4 Essex being able to bring any substantial reinforcement to the Gurkhas above them. For just as their leading two companies were setting out from the Castle, three companies of 1/4 Parachute Regiment swooped down from Point 236 and completely overran the lower hairpin bend where a company of Rajputanas and an Essex platoon were effecting their handover. These men were completely overwhelmed and the paratroopers rushed on, many reaching the walls of the Castle itself. The exposed Essex companies were caught in two minds and whilst some decided to press on to Hangman's Hill, others made a dash back to the Castle. It was a Hobson's choice. Those who plodded on upwards ran into heavy fire and only seventy or so men actually reached the Gurkhas' position. Of those that turned back few were able to actually battle their way into the Castle again. But those that did must soon have thought that they were involved in some madman's pageant.

For here in Italy, in 1944, they were involved in nothing less than the last phase of a medieval siege, the only difference being that machine guns were substituted for crossbows and grenades for boiling pitch. The paratroopers launched three attacks in all. The first, according to Major D.A. Beckett of 'C' Company,

> opened with intense machine gun fire sweeping the Castle. I have never known anything like it. It came from every angle. This lasted about ten minutes then they were on us. We could not use our artillery . . . because we did not know how . . . our own people were faring out in front. Our mortars had not even been registered. It had to be fought out with infantry weapons man to man. . . . The first attack very nearly succeeded. One or two tried to penetrate the courtyard and many were stopped only a few yards from the walls. We broke him up with Mills grenades, tommy guns and Brens.[65]

All this time the Germans kept up the intense machine gun and mortar fire and snipers seemed to be everywhere. One arrow-slit on the west face of the Castle was particularly vital, as it was the only one covering a large gap in the outer wall. It was manned by a Bren gunner who was soon picked off. Another immediately took his place and was also shot, between the eyes. Yet a third volunteer was soon found and he eventually managed to pinpoint the sniper's position and topple him from his rocky vantage point.

After thirty minutes or so a flare went up and the paratroopers withdrew. But only to reorganize. Their casualties had obviously been severe but then so had those of the garrison, and of their original 150 men or so only 3 officers and 60 other ranks remained on their feet. At 07.00 a second attack came in, under cover of a smoke-screen and preceded by an incredible shower of stick grenades pitched over the walls. Several paratroopers actually got to the walls and clambered some way up them before they were shot down. But the lull had given Major Beckett, now the senior officer, precious respite. This time his men were 'more prepared, and I had been on to Battalion Headquarters to arrange for our Vickers guns to bring enfilade fire on to the western edge of the Castle. The 3-inch mortars too were used with telling effect . . .'[66] An official report remarked afterwards that during this second attack 'machine gunners had fired more than 8000 rounds and the Essex mortars more than 1500 bombs. Mortar barrels had grown red-hot, had curled and bent.'[67] Once again the paratroopers were driven back.

Yet the battle was not yet over, nor its echoes of a distant age. The Germans made their last counter-attack early in the afternoon after a party of eight men had somehow managed to creep undetected to the walls and insert a demolition charge under a buttress of the northern battlements. The explosion breached the wall badly and caused part of it to collapse, burying upwards of 20 men from 'A' Company. Other Germans swarmed through the gap but were riddled almost as soon as they entered the courtyard. One wounded paratrooper crawled in to surrender and stated that of the 200 men in the original assault, no more than 40 were still fit for combat. The attack was over. But there was still the opportunity for a last act of theatre, particularly appropriate to the setting of this minor epic and to the old-fashioned professionalism of the paratroopers. During the first assault several prisoners had been taken, among them a sergeant-major. All except him had volunteered to act as stretcher-bearers, and one is even said to have pushed Major Beckett out of the line of fire of a sniper drawing a bead at close range. Yet during the battle the sergeant-major had disdained all cover and had strolled around in the open with the air of a professional observer. When the last attack was beaten off he marched across to Major Beckett, bowed, presented his compliments on the soldierly manner in which the defence had been conducted, and asked the Major to accept his fur-lined paratrooper's gloves as a token of the occasion.

Even before this last attack was beaten off it had become clear to Freyberg that the drive for the Monastery could have little hope of success. The Maoris' failure meant that the German stranglehold on the massif was as tight as ever – tighter now that they had regained Point 165

- and the few reinforcements that 1/4 Essex had been able to get through were manifestly inadequate. At one stage there had been hopes of pushing through a company of 2/7 Gurkhas, who had arrived to reinforce the Castle garrison, but this order was effectively countermanded by Major Beckett. When he heard of this mission he 'exploded in anger. He had seen too many costly attacks already. . . . An active fighting company of Gurkhas, near at hand and ready to help his defenders, would be of more use than another broken band of men who, he knew, would eventually trickle back like their predecessors. He refused to let A Company go forward and told Brigade HQ so in a heated conversation over the wireless.'[68] Whether this testy intervention had much impact on Freyberg is uncertain but shortly afterwards, a little after noon, the attack on the Monastery was called off. The Essex survivors there were ordered back to the Castle and after another nightmarish scramble, at about 22.00, a few of them regained its battered walls, though others were pinned down or forced to retrace their steps to Hangman's Hill. A fine battalion had been all but destroyed.

But this was not the end of the day's disappointments, nor of its dubious decisions. The Indian Division's attack, it will be remembered, had included a projected armoured thrust up the rear of the massif, and the plans drawn up on the 18th had sensibly stipulated that this should begin at 16.00, *after* the dawn attack from Hangman's Hill. Thus might it hope to most effectively disrupt an enemy already involved with an attack from the opposite direction. By 06.00, however, the attack on the Monastery had not begun and it was fairly obvious that some hours must elapse before it possibly could. Unfortunately, no one seems to have considered that this made the armoured thrust yet more speculative – what were the tanks supposed to do if there was no infantry support, blow the Monastery down with their 75mm guns? – and the attack was allowed to go forward. The task force consisted of 15 Shermans from 'C' Squadron 20 Armoured Regiment, 12 open-topped Honeys from 760 US Tank Battalion, 5 more Honeys from 7 Indian Brigade's Reconnaissance Squadron and 3 American self-propelled guns. These groups made the first part of the journey by separate routes, uniting just after daylight at Madras Circus, a deep bowl between Colle Maiola and Point 701. The advance from here was not easy. One tank became bogged down in a shell-hole and three others lost their tracks, torn off either by jagged outcrops of rock or by the anti-personnel mines which 'one could see . . . going off like firecrackers under the tracks.'[69] Snipers were also a problem, though most tank commanders found it impossible to travel with their turret hatches closed because of the fumes from their own guns and their racing engines. The American tanks made an attempt to storm up Phantom Ridge towards Point 575 but they struck very bad going as well as being heavily shelled. They rejoined the New Zealanders and pressed on towards Albaneta Farm. This was partially neutralized by covering fire and three tanks were sent forward 'round the corner' of Point 569, to test the approaches to the Monastery. All immediately ran into heavy sniper and bazooka fire and were badly holed, several of the crewmen being killed. Most of this fire was coming from Point 593 and the remaining Shermans now keenly felt the lack of supporting infantry:

> Dug in on its shaggy western slopes, in positions hidden in dense scrub, the enemy's riflemen in their spotted camouflage suits were hard to pick up and harder still to hit. Their persistent and accurate sniping forced the tank commanders to keep their heads inside their turrets or permitted them only an occasional quick glance. Half-blinded, several tanks ran into difficulties. Giving each other cover against bazooka attack, the tanks strafed the enemy's weapons pits but without infantry help could not clear them.[70]

A further attempt was made by the Honeys to turn the corner but they ran into an immediate storm of artillery and mortar fire and, with seven tanks lost in a few minutes, were obliged to withdraw. The whole venture was now clearly impossible and at about 13.00 the commanders on the spot were recalled to Madras Circus for a conference. The surviving tanks remained on the track north of Albaneta Farm where, happily, they were hidden from enemy observation posts. Happily, because they had to remain there until 17.30, thanks to an unaccountable delay in Divisional Headquarters sanctioning their withdrawal. For by early afternoon the whole Hangman's Hill venture had been cancelled, and one would have thought that somebody in authority would have seen fit to immediately recall the tanks. One source does in fact admit that at 'about 1.30 p.m. Galloway had recognized that the thrust had reached its limit',[71] but it was not until four hours later that the survivors – six tanks had been destroyed and sixteen damaged – were allowed to limp home.

There was now growing concern that the New Zealand Corps' offensive was dying on its feet. On the 20th Churchill cabled Alexander asking him why he persisted in attacking the Cassino position frontally if so little progress was being made. Alexander replied that one flank, the Liri Valley, was completely dominated by the Abbey whilst the other, to the north, was such unfavourable terrain that it limited 'movements to anything except small parties of infantry who can only be maintained by porters.'[72] In the same letter, however, he admitted that the frontal assault was proving so slow and costly that it was essential to decide 'in the course of the next twenty-four or thirty-six hours whether to . . . continue with the Cassino operation . . . or to call . . . [it] off and to consolidate such gains of ground as are important for the renewal of the offensive later.'[73] But he declared that he would defer this decision until after an Army Commanders' Conference on the next day, a meeting to which Freyberg had also been summoned. Clark too was dubious about the prospects for success, though he seemed to hold the 'British' personally responsible and expressed himself in typically exasperated terms to Juin:

> He was bitter about the repeated failure of the English despite his having furnished them with the most powerful means at his disposal. He would very much have liked to finish it off with other troops and even spoke of sending an American division back into the line – I could not see which one – and also alluded to a fresh regiment from my 4th Moroccan Mountain Division which had just disembarked.[74]

But Freyberg was also under pressure from below. General Galloway was increasingly losing patience with the whole way in which the battle was being conducted. Late on the 19th he sent an angry report about the continued vulnerability of the Castle, in which he 'complained that the . . . battalions in the town were two battalions too few and flatly declared it to be a "glaring fact" that his division could do little more until the town was cleared.'[75] There were also some indications that the troops themselves were reaching the end of their tether. Reports from most of the New Zealand battalions echoed that of 26 Battalion, still hanging on in the station, that battle casualties thus far were 37 killed and 87 wounded and that the number of cases of battle exhaustion, 'men whose nerves had been overstrained by the constant action of the last few days, had also increased.'[76] (By 23 March 43 such cases had been reported.) The Indians, too, were feeling the strain, as is evidenced by the following conversation, late on the 19th. The speakers were an officer of 2/7 Gurkhas, making the perilous journey from the Castle to the houses below, and a small group of disconsolate Sikhs he met en route. One Sikh informed him that he could choose between two tracks down the hill, one covered by snipers, the other shorter but horribly precipitous.

> 'One way you get shot, Sahib, the other you slip to your death. But,' he grinned without humour, 'if you do go that way (pointing to the

short cut) you are on your own, we will not move to help you, even
if you are hit.'

'Why?' I asked.

'Why? Why? The Sahib asks why? Because we've already lost
men doing crazy things for British Sahibs. Now do them yourself.'
The others nodded in agreement.[77]

At least some inklings of the mood of the troops must have got back to
Freyberg and at a meeting of his commanders on the 20th he was forced
to admit: 'People on the spot are depressed with the situation and we have
to take their view.'[78]

But he was not yet ready to give up. Heeding Galloway's peremptory
advice he decided to reinforce the New Zealanders in the town with the
remaining two battalions of 6 New Zealand Brigade and at last to call
upon 78 Division to tender some support. From the latter formation, 6
Royal West Kents relieved the remnants of 1/4 Essex in the Castle and
5 Buffs were ordered to make ready to take over from 26 Battalion in the
station. The New Zealanders' own reshuffle involved 25 Battalion's
positions east of Castle Hill being taken over by 23 Battalion, although
one of its companies remained under command of the newcomers. 28
Battalion adjusted its boundaries only slightly, still basing themselves in
the buildings between the two arms of Highway Six, and 24 Battalion
came in to continue this line towards the station. Most battalions had
taken up their new positions by dawn on the 20th, only the 26th not being
relieved until late that night.

But the actual attack launched on the 20th seemed a poor return for
such toing and froing. Once again it had to be launched against the
German strongpoints between the Continental Hotel and the base of
Castle Hill, and once again it ground to a halt in the face of the most
obdurate resistance. The brunt of the effort was borne by 23 Battalion,
with 'A' and 'D' Companies to the fore. The usual good progress was made
for the first hundred yards or so until they ran into intense fire from the
dugouts directly below Castle Hill. There were numerous casualties and
even those who went to ground were not safe from the snipers who
seemed to be able to bring sharply plunging fire to bear on almost every
potential bolt-hole. They had jumped off at dawn and within two hours
yet another spirited attack had ground to a halt. The Battalion History
makes the striking point that during this entire period not one member
of the 23rd had actually seen a German. Shortly afterwards, however, a
radio operator moving up to his platoon spotted a paratrooper in the
doorway of a ruined house. He shot at him with his revolver but missed.

He grabbed a wounded man's rifle and loosed off the magazine, and then a Bren gun which he also emptied in the same general area. Still there was no indication that he had actually found a mark. Sure enough, some minutes later, the German reappeared in the doorway but this time the New Zealander was ready with pistol steadied. He fired once and the German fell forward. His hunter ran back to his mates shouting wildly, 'I got the bastard! I got the bastard!' As the original narrator of this simple episode goes on to say, it is worth recounting at some length

> because it is one of the very few even limited successes that can be told of those Cassino days, when the general complaint among the 23rd men was that they could see no enemy, no rifle or other flash to indicate the whereabouts of the enemy, who had perfect cover combined with perfect observation, and therefore complete mastery of the situation. Under these circumstances, daylight attacks over ground so cratered and covered with debris did nothing more than give the enemy good targets.[79]

But still Freyberg was not prepared to concede defeat and plans were laid for a renewed push during the night of the 20/21st. Two main thrusts were envisaged, one by the only uncommitted New Zealand Battalion, the 21st, and the other by 6 Royal West Kents. The New Zealanders were to try yet another attack on the Monastery, via the Continental and Point 202, and the West Kents were to try to prise open the door to the massif by retaking Point 165. Both attempts failed. The men debouching from the castle had only room to deploy one company and this almost immediately ran into a newly sown minefield, the whole of which exploded in one shattering roar. The survivors pressed on but encountered heavy machine gun fire from front and flanks. The attack had to be abandoned. In the town events followed their grimly predictable course. 21 Battalion came in that night and took over their jumping-off positions from 24 Battalion, which went back into reserve. The plan was for 'D' Company to take the Continental, after which 'C' Company would pass through to take Point 146 and then move up to Point 202 to bring succour to the hard-pressed company of 24 Battalion. If they succeeded both companies were then to open up Highway Six southwards as well as completely clear the access to Hangman's Hill where, it was hoped, enough troops could be mustered for the long-awaited assault on the Monastery. They moved forward at about midnight and soon ran into just the same difficulties that had completely thwarted every other attack:

> The two assaulting companies made a slight dent in the defences but no penetration. The men of D Company were hindered by swampy

ground, but when a detour brought them within 100 yards of the Continental Hotel they were enmeshed in a deadly cross-fire and then counter-attacked. One platoon and most of another went down in the rush. c Company found the battlefield a tangled confusion. It groped forward . . . and by daybreak its platoons lay in unconcerted dispositions vaguely north-east of the Continental, and probably nowhere nearer than 200 yards. Rubble and mud, not to mention a block of well-defended ruins, stood fairly across their way forward.[80]

The doorways to the massif were as tightly closed as ever.

With hindsight it is easy to see that this should definitely have marked the end of Freyberg's efforts. With all his battalions committed and bloodied, and the physical constraints of the battlefield becoming ever more burdensome, he had no further hope of a significant breakthrough. Events were to prove this all too well, yet even on the 21st there were those who claimed to discern some grounds for cautious optimism. Most of it stemmed from German reports and even if Freyberg was perhaps not privy to the Ultra secret, the gist of these messages must have quickly been passed on to him. On the 20th, indeed, German confidence seemed almost to have deserted them, the attack by 23 Battalion having made a particular impression. xiv Panzer Corps' report that morning stated: 'The heavy fighting between Cassino town and the station is still going on. The enemy . . . is using his tanks to knock out one of our strongpoints after another. Our anti-tank defence is not very effective as the range is too great. Our casualties are heavy . . .'[81] An appreciation of the situation later in the day was gloomier still:

. . . the enemy's air superiority, artillery superiority . . . and superiority in tanks all make it improbable that Cassino can be held for any length of time. It is likely that the wastage of the infantry in the town will compel us to pull back gradually to the line between the Abbey and the present left wing of the MG Battalion [west of the Gari]. The enemy has suffered heavily, but is not exhausted, as he is only attacking at this one spot and has fresh reserves.[82]

Von Senger's only consolation was that the line was manned by the paratroopers and he now joined Heidrich in vetoing any suggestion of bringing up 'second-line troops to replenish 3 Para Regiment. If the troops in this narrow sector are watered down with poor quality troops it can only result in more serious crises. . . . One battalion commander from 3 Para Regiment was replaced because of exhaustion, with no blame to him. Only the toughest fighters can fight this battle. The men of 3 Para Regiment now fighting in Cassino are unshaken, and their morale is right at the top.'[83]

Yet surely only supermen could endure indefinitely the kind of punishment handed out to the survivors of 3 Parachute Regiment? A New Zealand Corps Intelligence Summary noted, on the 21st: '1 Para Div is already fully engaged and has had heavy losses. If a major counter-attack is to be mounted . . . its main weight must come from forces other than paratroop. Meanwhile the longer it is deferred the more gruelling the punishment 1 Para Div must take. Should it be much longer deferred even paratroopers must crack.'[84] This point of view was expressed to Clark that same day when he visited Freyberg's Headquarters en route to the Army Commanders' Conference. He arrived 'in a discouraged mood' and 'saw little chance of a breakthrough at that time'. He then spoke to Freyberg and many of his officers and it was made clear that 'they felt that success was so near that it could yet be gained. . . . "I think you and the Boche are both groggy," I remarked. Freyberg immediately objected that his troops were not groggy, and expressed a belief that he could break through.'[85] Alexander seemed inclined to agree and, presumably on the strength of the same German messages intercepted on the previous day, he presented an optimistic report to the Conference. According to Eaker he stated that 'the Germans by their own admission were very gloomy about being able to hold out in the Cassino area.' Others at 15 Army Group Headquarters were positively buoyant. At the same Conference 'Alexander's Intelligence Officer stated flatly . . . that it was his prediction that if our troops continue to show the offensive spirit, the Cassino area, including the Abbey, will be cleared up in a few hours.'[86] It was therefore agreed that Freyberg should be allowed at least another twenty-four hours in which to try and finish the job, though it seems clear that at the same time 'Operation DICKENS was officially decapitated of its pursuit phase'.[87] In other words, Freyberg was to be allowed more time to salve the pride of his Corps, and give the Allies a useful propaganda success, but their victory was no longer seen as a springboard for an immediate drive up the Liri Valley. This was now definitely to be one of the first phases of the Harding/Alexander plan, mooted in February, and preparations were already well advanced for bringing across XIII British Corps to take over in Cassino, prior to a renewed offensive in mid-April.

Unfortunately the New Zealand Corps was to be denied even its prestige success. For Freyberg's optimism was based entirely on a negative assessment of German capabilities rather than on any original or powerful stroke by his own troops. In 4 Indian Division's sector, indeed, it had already been acknowledged that there was simply no scope for a useful initiative and from the morning of the 21st all their efforts were devoted to sealing off the narrow Castle corridor and constructing an impregnable defensive perimeter around Castle Hill itself. Even this proved far from easy and on the 21st and 22nd the Castle was subjected to fierce counter-attacks by the paratroopers, sweeping down once again from assembly areas on Points 236 and 165. Both attacks were spotted in good time, however, and were broken up by prompt concentrations of fire by the Corps artillery, supporting the West Kents' machine guns and mortars.

It was around the dreaded Continental Hotel that the New Zealanders once again made their main effort. There were two major attacks, the first by 23 Battalion on the morning of the 21st, and the next that night by a company from both 23 and 21 Battalions. Both, as ever, got nowhere. An officer with the former wrote:

> There seems little doubt that the conditions under which the troops are at present fighting are the worst yet experienced. . . . All day long German shells and mortars pound the ruins where the troops try to obtain a little protection and movement by day is impossible. Fighting is at times so close that only a wall may separate friend from foe. . . . The situation is not improved by the number of dead . . . who lay unburied in the ruins.[88]

Certainly the New Zealanders had, as ever, done their best. German reports clearly show that these attacks were pressed forward with great determination and kept the paratroopers under fierce pressure. On the 21st von Senger und Etterlin reported that '1Para Division's impression today has been that the enemy was throwing in everything he had to force a decision during the day at all costs.'[89] On the 22nd he noted: 'The enemy attacked our positions almost continuously. . . . Both sides fought with the utmost bitterness for the ruins of every individual house.'[90]

Yet the paratroopers held and there now seemed no alternative but to call off the battle. Freyberg and Parkinson met on the morning of the 23rd and the former was forced to concur that the New Zealand Division had 'come to the end of its tether' and that 'the troops in the town . . . were in the worst military position that he had ever seen troops in.'[91] The attacks were to cease and the more exposed troops on Hangman's Hill and Point 202 be withdrawn, though it was also agreed that Point 195 and the station should be held, to form the outposts of a new defensive perimeter. This decision was communicated to Clark, who immediately agreed, and through him to Alexander. The latter came forward to Freyberg's headquarters that afternoon and, after a tentative proposal to renew the attacks with part of 78 Division, agreed that the battlefield be stabilized around the positions described above. XIII Corps would take over these positions as soon as possible and start drawing up plans for a full-scale drive into the Liri Valley. The taking of the Monastery, however, was to be the responsibility of another formation and on the 24th word was sent to General Wladyslaw Anders, the commander of the Polish Corps, that that dubious honour was to fall to his men.

Yet the Calvary of Cassino was not yet ended for the New Zealand Corps. The actual withdrawals did not begin until the 25th and just holding the line was a sore trial for the troops in the town. Both tank crews and infantry were now utterly exhausted, and their morale further undermined by having had to concede defeat. The men of 19 Armoured Regiment, for example, had to still spend most of their time inside their tanks where

> sleep was almost impossible, for each member of the crew was required to be constantly on the alert. The frequent smack of bullets, shrapnel and debris on the outside armour always held the threat of something larger and more penetrating. Several commanders had their periscopes sniped and snatched away from their eyes when the glass above splintered and the tube on its ball joint swung violently upwards. . . . The air inside the cramped quarters, though foul, could get icy cold, especially in the early mornings or when the engines had been stopped for a long period.[92]

The infantry, too, were under constant artillery fire and casualties continued to mount. The shells were almost the last straw for the men of 23 Battalion whose

> life was grim enough without this danger, exaggerated by the fear arising from recent losses. . . . Part of the building in which the men were cramped together had to be used as a latrine. As elsewhere in Cassino, it had been impossible to bury the dead and their bodies lay heaped together under wet blankets. . . . All these factors led to a serious falling off in morale . . . [and] a veteran NCO of sterling character . . . wrote in his diary for the two days 24 and 25 March: 'Very little sleep – too cold. I got a blanket and four of us used it. . . . Monastery Hill towers above us and the Hun looks down on our

positions. . . . Lads could do with a spell – conditions here pretty awful. No sleep. Heavy shelling . . . Many dead Kiwis lying around. . . .'93

Yet even the New Zealanders could feel sympathy for the luckless Gurkhas and the few men of the Essex Regiment still clinging to their positions on Hangman's Hill, where some of them had now been hemmed in for eight days and nights. One looked up 'among the barren rocks where our Indian friends held grimly on under the hail of mortar and shell. . . . One wondered how men could live in such a place.'94 On the night of 24/25th, however, their ordeal was almost over and three volunteers were sent out from the Castle to pass on the orders for withdrawal. Two got through to Hangman's Hill and then tried to release the carrier pigeons they had carried with them in their blouses, to confirm that the orders had actually been transmitted. But the birds refused to fly in the darkness and only some hours later, by dint of the most menacing shoos and shouts, did they reluctantly take wing for the Castle. The withdrawal began the next night, Colonel Nangle leading down a party of 10 officers and 267 men, in single file. Their route was bracketed by a co-ordinated artillery shoot which also, as Colonel Nangle later pointed out, 'quite covered any noise we made as we stumbled over the loose stones. A slight deviation allowed us to give the Brown House a wide berth as we were uncertain whether it was held or not. No sound came from this ruin and we continued, hardly believing our luck, to the Castle.'95 Remarkably, not a man was lost though a group of West Kents had to sally out next morning to pick up a few Gurkha stragglers who had fallen asleep during one of the many halts.

The rest of 4 Indian Division moved off the massif shortly afterwards, though appalling weather and their utter exhaustion made the withdrawal not the least of their trials. 1/2 Gurkhas moved off in a blizzard and one officer wrote: 'Men who had spent long weeks in fox-holes and whose knee-joints and muscles had weakened through lack of exercise had to move carefully. . . . [Through] the blizzard . . . the shape of the shattered Monastery loomed out in a white mantle as if to hide the scars of battle. It was a fitting farewell.'96 According to a soldier of the West Kents the evacuation from Castle Hill

perhaps justifies the word 'epic'. . . . The Blankshires were to relieve us at eleven o'clock. Always in the dark. Oh, but what a time they were. Jerry hadn't started his nightly shelling. We wanted to be out of it before he did. . . . In our sangar, the paper stuffed in the chinks . . . we knelt in a peculiar position. Our heads to the ground and our feet drumming rapidly for warmth, something like ostriches. Miserably, miserably cold. 'Tony, there's a column of penguins outside; the Blankshires can't make it.' But they did make it. . . . We handed over. . . We were envied, we were going out. . . . Always the going was difficult, over rocks or through mud . . . the whole battalion going single-file with us near the front, followed by unrecognizable forms, all incognito by virtue of the night and known only by their swearing and stumbling. . . . We lost one man in it. Heaven knows where. . . . It had been over for several hours when another man collapsed from exhaustion. And we – we slept, missing for meals, for most of the forty-eight hours. Tiredness and exhaustion.[97]

Lieutenant E.D. Smith (2/7 Gurkhas) also emphasized just how bone-weary men became after such prolonged periods at the front. The battalion had avoided the worst of the fighting and had been occupying positions on Point 593 for most of the battle. But this had been the culmination of a full six weeks on the massif and though the distance to be travelled to the rest areas

was probably less than five miles . . . [the] men were cramped, unfit, mentally exhausted, without any willpower. Even though the ordeal was nearly over, the fact did not seem to be understood. . . . Never will I forget that nightmare of a march. Officers, British and Gurkha, shouted at, scolded, cajoled and assisted men as they collapsed. At times we had no alternative but to strike soldiers who just gave up interest in anything including a desire to live. By dint of all the measures we could think of, most of them reached their transport before daylight appeared; to survive and fight another day.[98]

But many had not survived. Casualty figures for the individual battalions of 4 Indian Division remain elusive but the formation as a whole lost 132 men killed, 792 wounded and 155 missing. If one makes the reasonable assumption that 75 per cent of these casualties were incurred by the four battalions most heavily involved on the eastern face of Monastery Hill (1/9 Gurkhas, 1/6 Rajputanas, 4/6 Rajputanas and 1/4 Essex) then this gives a casualty rate for these battalions' riflemen and company officers of a little over 45 per cent.* Detailed figures are

* This is corroborated by the figures for 1/6 Rajputanas: 199 all ranks killed, wounded and missing. This is a casualty rate of 40 per cent.

available for four of the New Zealand battalions and these are given below:

	Killed		Wounded		Missing	
	Offs	ORs	Offs	ORs	Offs	ORs
23 Battalion	5	36	10	102	1	3
25 Battalion	1	46	5	170	0	1
26 Battalion	5	39	3	98	0	0
28 Battalion	12		95		1	

For these battalions the average casualty rate amongst riflemen and company officers was therefore 36 per cent.

Figures for the paratroopers are incomplete but those for 3 Parachute Regiment, the one most heavily involved, tell their own story. Between 14 and 23 March they lost 50 men killed, 114 wounded and 270 missing. The size of the latter figure probably reflects the fact that the Regiment never had the chance to discover what had happened to men in strongpoints overrun by the New Zealanders or demolished in the first bombing and subsequent artillery barrages. Again it is uncertain how many men Colonel Heilmann had, but typical German Tables of Organization at this stage of the war would indicate a total strength of between 700 and 750 men. Even granted that the paratroopers threw every man who could carry a rifle into the fray – there were no safe jobs in units such as this – the casualty rate is still almost 60 per cent. With good reason did Heidrich write in his last report: 'No one who participated in the battle will ever forget the spirit shown. To this very day the memory of the manner in which every man hastened forward moves me deeply.'[99] And all agreed that the paratroopers were perhaps the only troops in the world who could have showed such a spirit of self-sacrifice for so long. In a telephone conversation on the 25th, Vietinghoff told Kesselring that 'no troops but 1 Parachute Division could have held Cassino.'[100]Even the Allies could not but add their own plaudits, one of the most heartfelt coming from Alexander. Just as the last New Zealand attacks, on the 22nd, were breaking up in front of the bastions around the Continental and the Hotel des Roses he wrote to Brooke: 'Unfortunately we are fighting the best soldiers in the world – what men! . . . I do not think any other troops could have stood up to it perhaps except these para boys.'[101]

PART FIVE

THE FOURTH BATTLE
11 May–5 June 1944

The capture of Rome is the only important objective.

General Clark, 6 May 1944

We have every hope and every intention of achieving our object, namely, the destruction of the enemy south of Rome.

General Alexander, 11 May 1944

12
'A Passive State
of Sustained Awfulness'
Preparations for a Renewed Offensive,
26 March–11 May 1944

As far as the British are concerned there . . . is a congenital inability
to think in terms of large-scale manoeuvres with an Army Group or
even an Army.

General Juin, 27 April, 1944

One of the more tragic aspects of the Third Battle of Cassino was that
even as Freyberg's forces were being ground to a bloody halt, Alexander
had already decided that they were not really adequate to the task and
that only a full-scale, co-ordinated Army Group offensive, against the
greater part of the Gustav Line, could realistically hope to turn the
Cassino position. Senior commanders had been working on tentative
plans for this offensive ever since late February, when the first planning
paper was issued, and their activity was redoubled as soon as Freyberg's
attack was called off.* Alexander's staff had been particularly busy and
had already mapped the major reliefs and redeployments necessary for
the creation of the powerful strike forces. The essential feature of this
regrouping was that Eighth Army was to take over the Cassino and Liri
Valley sector – the inter-Army boundary was redrawn along the Liri itself
on 29 March – and were to amass there divisions brought over from the
Adriatic as well as those still manning the Garigliano bridgehead. This
sector was now to be shared between two fresh American divisions† and
Juin's French Expeditionary Corps, the latter to receive another two
divisions and an equivalent number of specialized mountain troops before
the new offensive actually began.

The basic plan was fairly straightforward, depending more on sheer
numerical and material superiority than on strategic finesse.‡ For the

---

* The renewed offensive was first known as Operation STATESMAN, changed in April,
on Churchill's insistence, to Operation DIADEM.
† One of these, the 85th, had already taken over part of the line in mid-March.
‡ In terms of numbers, Alexander certainly succeeded. When the offensive actually
opened he had eight and a half divisions in the front line: 85 and 88 US Divisions; 2
Moroccan, 1 Free French and part of 3 Algerian Division; 8 Indian Division; 4 British

chosen axes of the offensive were hardly new. The main effort was to be made up the Liri Valley, with 4 British Division and 8 Indian Division creating the first bridgehead prior to exploitation by 78 British, 1 Canadian and 5 Canadian Armoured Divisions. A further armoured division, 6 British, was available should the exploiting force begin to flag. Eighth Army's flanks were to be covered on the right by the two-division Polish Corps, who would tie down the paratroopers on the massif, and on the left by Fifth Army. Both the French and the new American divisions (the latter now constituting II US Corps) were to attack up the Ausente Valley towards Ausonia and Esperia. But when the latter was reached, because of the shortage of roads the French were to be gradually squeezed out leaving II US Corps to take up all the running between Pico and Rome.

But Fifth Army had another Corps, the VIth at Anzio. The beachhead had now been made fairly secure and was eventually to contain seven Allied divisions, including 34 US and the remainder of 1 US Armoured Divisions, which were to be moved there from the main front.* This force, it was now felt, would be quite capable of playing its own part in the renewed offensive and it was decreed that, on a day to be decided by Alexander, it would strike out from the beachhead towards Valmontone. Here, if the timing were right, it would be in a position to sever Highway Six *behind* the retreating Germans and thus ensure the encirclement of at least a substantial portion of Vietinghoff's Tenth Army. This point merits emphasis, for Mark Clark's actual interpretation of these orders was to be the cause of considerable controversy, then and later. But the official record leaves little room for doubt over Alexander's intentions. As early as 11 February he had written to Churchill pointing out that operations on the beachhead must be conducted first with a view to

---

Division; 3 and 5 Polish Divisions. His exploiting force contained a further six and a half divisions: 4 Moroccan Mountain Division and an equivalent number of *goumiers*; 78 British and 6 British Armoured Divisions; 1 Canadian and 5 Canadian Armoured Divisions. On the same date the Germans were manning the Gustav Line with all of 5 Mountain, 1 Parachute, 44, 71 and 94 Infantry Divisions, though the majority of 5 Mountain and 44 Divisions were to the north of the intended axes of attack. The line was also buttressed with battalions from 576 Infantry Regiment, 115 PG Regiment, 721 and 741 Infantry Regiments and various reconnaissance battalions. These totalled thirty-eight battalions and there were a further nineteen in reserve from 15, 29 and 90 PG Divisions. Thus the Germans had only fifty-seven battalions to face the 108 Allied (plus the *goumiers*), the numerical disparity being further increased by the fact that German infantry battalions usually included only half the number of fighting men of those of the Allies.

* The other five were: 1 and 5 British; 3 and 45 US; 1 Special Service Force.

crushing German counter-attacks 'and then, with all our forces regrouped, resume offensive to break inland to get astride his communications leading from Rome to the South. This I have every intention of doing.'¹ This point was reiterated to the senior commanders as the opening of DIADEM drew nearer. On 5 May General Harding attended a Fifth Army Conference, held at General Clark's lodge, and he took the opportunity to emphasize his commander's intentions:

I know I am speaking for General Alexander when I say that he regards the attack from the bridgehead as a most important weapon of opportunity to be launched when the situation is fluid, and which may well be decisive in cutting off the supply and preventing the withdrawal of the enemy force then opposing the advance of the main armies on the main front.²

In other words, the actual capture of Rome was always regarded by Alexander as being of secondary importance to the destruction of the enemy forces. Certainly, he was aware of its importance. In mid-March he had advised London that 'in my view, on broad strategic, political and moral grounds, the capture of Rome is an essential part of the campaign in Italy. . . . Unless the enemy moves further divisions into Italy, I have every confidence that I should be able to capture Rome within a month of effecting a junction with the beachhead. The effect of such a success, in the early stages of OVERLORD, would, in my opinion, be very great.'³ But this capture was seen as a natural consequence of a decisive victory to the south of Rome, with the surviving Germans falling back in disarray to the Pisa–Rimini line. Therefore his guidelines for the phase of operations after the junction of the two armies around Valmontone remained particularly vague.* It did, however, seem fair to assume that if the inter-Army boundaries were not changed, and Eighth Army remained north of the Liri and the Secco, then the actual honour of entering Rome first would fall to Clark and his Fifth Army.

But Clark was less than happy with such vagueness. The capture of Rome was just the kind of prestige victory that he craved for and he was determined that it would be himself and his troops who got there first.

---

* A memorandum from Wilson's G–3 staff, on 20 April, attempted to present some conclusions about Army Group operations after the junction of Fifth and Eighth Armies but could only report that: 'After at least 36 hours of conferences . . . on future Mediterranean strategy the only firm factor that has emerged is that in everybody's opinion operations in this theatre may well become very fluid.' (AFHQ G–3 Section, Lieutenant-Colonel R.G.H. Phillimore to Brigadier Davey, 20 April 1944, p. I. PRO WO 204/1455.)

The full story will be told in its proper place, but it is important to realize that even in the planning stage of DIADEM Clark was beginning to convince himself that Fifth Army was about to be sold short. On 1 May, for example, at another Army Commanders' Conference, there was disagreement over the allocation of air support for Clark and Leese's forces. Alexander had suggested that 70 per cent of the available aircraft should be assigned to Eighth Army but Clark was finally able to insist upon a fifty/fifty split. The whole meeting, according to the US official historian, was 'marked by bickering and tension'.[4]

Clark seems to have felt that the original offer only reflected Alexander's lack of confidence in Fifth Army as a whole and his unspoken assumption that Eighth Army would carry the major burden of the new offensive. In an interview after the war he insisted that 'before the . . . attack began General Alexander believed that the main effort and the decisive effort to break through on the southern front was to be made by Eighth Army in the Cassino–Liri Valley sector. Alexander did not expect that . . . [Fifth Army] would be able to get through the mountains in their sector and certainly not with the speed with which they did so.'[5] Not surprisingly, such typically 'British' arrogance did not please Clark at all, particularly as he regarded it as being totally unwarranted by Eighth Army's military record to date.In the same interview he revealed that it was his opinion then that only Fifth Army could make the decisive breakthrough and that he had 'little confidence in the aggressive qualities of Eighth Army'.[6] Clark's views were obviously common knowledge at Fifth Army headquarters. One of his staff officers recalled that 'General Clark certainly did not expect Eighth Army to make the main breakthrough. . . . General Clark and the Fifth Army always felt that the British didn't and wouldn't push hard and aggressively enough.'[7]*

But after his earlier rebuffs over the use of New Zealand Corps to try and complete the capture of the Cassino massif, Clark this time decided to keep his peace and he revealed little of his misgivings to Alexander. Fellow-Americans, however, got a clearer picture of his true feelings, none more so than General Truscott, now commanding VI Corps at

---

* It was probably merciful for Clark's blood pressure that he did not hear of a suggestion made by Montgomery, on 5 April. According to Major-General John Kennedy, the Assistant Chief of the Imperial General Staff: 'Montgomery . . . came to see me and . . . suggested taking away the American forces on the main front from Clark's command, since he could not control both them and the beachhead. The battle on the main front was a single operation, which should be under a single commander, namely Leese. When I saw Brooke that evening, I told him about Montgomery's suggestions. Brooke agreed in principle, but felt he could not put them to the Americans.' (Kennedy, *op. cit.*, p.325.)

Anzio. The first indications came early in April when Clark ordered Truscott not only to draw up plans for a breakout along Alexander's favoured axis, Cisterna–Cori–Valmontone, but also to prepare contingency timetables for a thrust directly north-westwards towards Rome.* Of course, contingency planning is only right and proper, but Truscott's memoirs make it quite clear that Clark was motivated above all by his desire to be first in Rome and by almost paranoid suspicions about British duplicity. On 5 May Alexander visited Truscott on the beachhead and asked him about the plans and preparations for the breakout. Truscott explained them 'with some measure of pride' and elaborated upon the various alternative lines of attack. Alexander, 'charming gentleman and magnificent soldier that he was, let me know very quietly and very firmly that there was only one direction in which the attack should or would be launched, and that was . . . to cut Highway Six in the vicinity of Valmontone in the rear of the German main forces.' Later that day Truscott conveyed the gist of this meeting to Clark, though he added 'I assume you are fully cognizant of General Alexander's ideas on this subject.' Cognizant he certainly was, but this did not prevent Clark from showing his considerable irritation at being reminded that his operations were to be entirely subordinate to Alexander's overall plan:

> Clark came to the beachhead the following day. He was irked at General Alexander's 'interference' in his American chain of command. He remarked that 'the capture of Rome is the only important objective' and was fearful that the British were laying devious plans to be first in Rome. While he agreed that the Cisterna–Valmontone assault would probably be the most decisive, he also thought that the quickest way into Rome might be via Carroceto–Campoleone. . . . Clark was determined that the British were not going to be the first in Rome.[8]

In short, then, Clark was so obsessed with the capture of Rome, which could of itself bring no obvious military rewards, that he seemed prepared to ignore his commander's express wishes, even at the cost of what *he himself* recognized would be a much more telling military victory. Kesselring would have been delighted to hear it.

And there were others in the Fifth Army who were less than enthusiastic about Alexander's plans. On at least two counts, Juin felt that

---

* The Valmontone attack was codenamed Operation BUFFALO. Two approaches to Rome were considered: Ardea–Rome (Operation CRAWDAD) and Carroceto–Campoleone–Rome (Operation TURTLE).

they left a good deal to be desired. Not surprisingly, in view of his repeated objections to the head-on assaults against Cassino, his major criticism concerned the role of Eighth Army and the persistent emphasis upon the massif and the entrance to the Liri Valley. As ever, he felt that the best way into the valley was via the left flank of the Gustav Line and a development, 'suddenly, at the right moment, of the Atina manoeuvre which might pay better dividends and allow us to reach the Frosinone area more easily and more quickly.'9 But obviously this was too much to expect from Alexander, and any notion of an attack on this axis, Juin wrote to de Gaulle (to whom he had to report following Giraud's resignation on 15 April),

> is a pipe dream. Always under the shadow of the Cassino massif, Eighth Army will make do with simply using the Polish Corps to attack from our old positions . . . towards Piedimonte to outflank Cassino by the shortest route. This will pay few dividends, in truth, for it will tie up a whole Corps without necessarily guaranteeing the subsequent security of the right flank of the British forces engaged in the valley. . . . As far as the British are concerned there is . . . a congenital inability to think in terms of large-scale manoeuvres with an Army Group or even an Army.10

Like Clark, Juin was also critical of the plans for the Anzio breakout, especially their vagueness regarding the closing stages of the Battle for Rome. In Juin's case, however, it was more a desire for precision and clarity, virtues that Juin sometimes seemed to think were a French monopoly, than for an explicit statement of who was to enter Rome first. As he wrote to de Gaulle:

> I do not know if General Alexander has looked at and weighed up all the possible outcomes of his strategic operation beyond the first army objective. Certainly he is counting heavily on the intervention of the Anzio Corps which he hopes will be decisive as regards the fall of Rome. . . . But it does not seem that its precise course of action has been settled outside of certain vague indications as to probable directions and a stated commitment, and a logical one moreover, that it will not break out until after the start of the main offensive.11

On one thing, however, Juin was completely at variance with Clark, and this was the projected role of the French in the forthcoming offensive. Alexander had left all of the detailed planning for Fifth Army's attack up to its own commander and, as has already been indicated, the latter had envisaged the French, on the right, slowly being squeezed out by II Corps as it advanced from the Ausonia Defile towards the Secco. For Clark's first plans were based on the major premise that the Aurunci Mountains were only passable via the Ausonia–Esperia–Pico road and that the great barrier between Esperia and the coast, known as the Petrella massif, was imprenetrable to any kind of troops. The original attack, therefore, jumping off along the line Monte Faito-Castelforte-Santa Maria Infante, would only be able to move forward on an increasingly narrow front, until there would barely be room for one Corps to operate satisfactorily. Naturally, this Corps was to be American.

The plan was presented to Juin on 1 April by General Donald W. Brann, head of Fifth Army G–3, and the Frenchman expressed considerable disappointment. Obviously he was hardly pleased that the French were only to play a leading role for a few days at most, but he also had specifically military objections. On the one hand, he pointed out, the narrow axis along which II Corps were to advance would without a doubt be heavily defended by the Germans. It was in fact known that one of their ancillary defensive positions, the so-called Dora Line, ran from Pontecorvo to south of Esperia with the express intent of blocking debouchment from the Ausonia Defile, whilst another, the Orange Line running from east of Monte Petrella to Monte Maio, guarded its approaches. Moreover, it was going to be far from easy for II Corps to take over their spearhead positions once the French Corps was deemed to have accomplished its own task. It was more than likely that 'a relief of the CEF by II Corps, at the height of the fighting, along the single narrow road to Esperia would almost certainly lead to monumental traffic jams which might be fatal for the . . . divisions thus crowded along a two-kilometre front.'[12]

But Juin did not rest his case on purely negative objections. He had already worked out his own alternative plan and this he presented verbally to Brann on 1 April. His basic point was that Fifth Army must at all costs avoid attacking along a single axis, particularly one that was so constricted and so obvious to the Germans. Certainly it would be necessary to send some troops in this direction and Juin had already earmarked three of his own divisions for the task. But there should be no attempt to effect a complicated relief by II Corps, who should keep to the coastal sector, advancing out of the Garigliano bridgehead to take Spigno and thence along Highway Seven, via Itri, Fondi and Terracina, to protect the left flank of the CEF. For the latter were to have a second, more southerly axis, through the supposedly impenetrable Petrella massif. As soon as a secure base had been established between Ausonia and Spigno, Juin proposed launching his so-called Mountain Corps (comprising the newly arrived 4 Moroccan Mountain Division and thousands of hardy *goumiers*) into this massif to strike straight across and cut the Itri–Pico road. The attractions of such a move were various. It would help avoid congestion on Juin's other narrow axis. The newly arrived troops were even more adapted than their predecessors to fighting in the most rugged, trackless terrain.* The Itri–Pico road was a vital line of communication for the Germans to facilitate deployment and supply in the whole sector south of the Liri Valley. And the Germans, too, clearly felt that the Petrella massif was impassable for of the fifteen battalions they had positioned between the Liri and the coast, 'not one soldier had been identified in the mountainous massif Petrella–Chiavica–Fammera–Revole.'[13] But, and here was the final strand of Juin's thinking, it was not only military judgement that persuaded the Germans to leave the Petrella massif unguarded, but also military necessity. The Germans were critically short of combat troops and, as a report by the 2^e Bureau had noted:

> The limited means of the enemy . . . have led him – in general – to give no depth to his dispositions. It is often the units responsible for the defence of the main line who have to break off contact at the right moment to [also] carry on the struggle on the rear line, whenever it has been possible to create one.[14]

In other words, if the initial assault out of the bridgehead were successful, and Fifth Army then struck out along three separate axes, they should be able to pin down most of the German forces *in situ*, making it impossible for them to create reserves by stripping unthreatened sectors. And a defensive based upon a single line must inevitably buckle at one point or another, at which time the whole rear area would be vulnerable to the force that broke through.

General Brann was quick to see the logic of Juin's suggestion and he asked him to elaborate on it in a written memorandum. This was submitted on 4 April and did the rounds of the various Army, Army Group and Supreme Allied Headquarters. Very little seems to have been put on paper about the discussions there and all that can be said with

---

* The *goumiers*, in particular, travelled extremely light, needed only mules for transport, and could exist for days on minimal amounts of food and water. By the time of the commencement of the Fourth Battle there were 9000 of them in Italy. They were divided into 27 *goums*, each of which was roughly equivalent to a normal rifle company. Three *goums* made up a *tabor* and three of these a *groupe de tabors*.

certainty is that the plan was eventually accepted; first by Alexander, on his return from a trip to London on the 17th, and then by Clark, who ordered Juin to start his detailed planning on the 20th. Certain participants have made it clear, however, that the Allied planners had little real faith in the French, and certainly not in their ability to cut a swathe through the most desolate regions of the Aurunci Mountains. Juin's staff officers had to explain his ideas to a whole succession of visitors and it was clear that all of them 'were only semi-confident. One could read it in their eyes, in their anxious questions, in their polite reserve, in their silence when faced with positive French affirmations – even from General Alexander, when he came to confer . . . with General Juin, whose plan he had adopted.'[15] The visitors themselves have confirmed these reservations. A G-3 officer with Fifth Army remembered

attending the FEC conference before the . . . May jump-off with other American officers. At that conference General Juin explained the Corps plan of attack. After the explanation American officers were of one mind that the French could never succeed in carrying out the plan. It depended . . . too much on delicate, fine timing which was thought . . . impossible because of the rugged terrain and the . . . extreme difficulties of communication.[16]

It might seem surprising, therefore, that neither Clark nor Alexander attempted to veto Juin's plan. In fact, both were preoccupied with what they regarded as their own decisive attacks – in Clark's case the breakout from the Anzio beachhead and in Alexander's the drive up the Liri and Secco valleys. The latter, indeed, seems to have been quite convinced that Eighth Army's effort would be the battle-winner, and that the amassing of a sufficiently large strike force beneath Cassino would of itself ensure victory.* In fact, as we shall see, the very size of this force was to create

* Though it is worth noting that some Eighth Army planners found his expectations of a swift breakthrough somewhat over-optimistic. Leese's G (Plans) officer, Lieutenant-Colonel M.W. Prynne, drew up notes for an Army conference, on 2 April, which offered a more sombre, and in the event more prescient, analysis of likely events. Alexander, he stated, expected the advance up the valley to be 'a single operation' but '(i) . . . in actual fact it will fall into two distinct phases: (ii) The first phase is the forcing of the Rapido, the securing of the foothills of Mt Cairo and the organization of an area west of the Rapido, for the attack on the Adolf Hitler Line. (iii) The second phase is the assault on the Adolf Hitler Line. (iv) The assault on the Adolf Hitler Line involves bringing up all the field artillery and most of the medium artillery west of the Rapido and the dumping of ammunition there. (v) The second phase is likely to be *at least ten days later than the first*, and may be later than that. Both phases will involve long and hard fighting.' (In Prynne Papers, PRO WO 204/

serious problems of its own and make a mockery of Alexander's anticipated rate of advance. Nevertheless, there is no denying that the redeployment of 15 Army Group prior to DIADEM was in itself no mean strategic feat. For it was not simply a matter of bringing across the necessary men and weapons and creating adequate dumps of ammunition and supplies. Even more important was that all of this should be done in the strictest secrecy, giving the Germans little inkling of when the next offensive would start and just who would attack where. It was realized from the start that one could not possibly conceal from the Germans that something was afoot and so priority was given to measures designed to mask the true intentions. Almost every Corps became involved in some charade or other. The main duty of the French was to hide the fact that there had been any changeover in the Garigliano bridgehead. The forward lines were manned as thinly as possibly and those troops that did go to the front had to wear British helmets. Wireless silence was strictly enforced on all French sets and essential radio traffic was dealt with by British signallers. Movement by road was kept to a minimum and most of the troops were held back as far away as Naples until the very last moment. Some motor traffic was unavoidable, as massive supply dumps had to be created along the Garigliano, but the concomitant clouds of dust were kept down by pouring used sump-oil along the roads. British signallers were also used in the Polish sector,* and here the passage of supplies to points along the massif was masked by a vertical screen of camouflage netting a mile long. The concentrations beneath the massif were also masked by an intensification of the smoke-screen that had been laid down during most of the Third Battle. Once again, though, it was not without its drawbacks, least of all for the men who had to provide it. One company of the Royal Army Service Corps undertook this duty for a whole fortnight, living all day in slit trenches a few hundred yards from the enemy and crawling out intermittently to light the smoke canisters, 1600 of them, that they had put in place the night before.

The most elaborate deception plan was that operated by the Canadian Corps. Dummy signal traffic was used to create the impression that this

---

10413, author's emphasis.) The Hitler Line was a fall-back position behind the Gustav Line, running from Piedimonte to the south of Pontecorvo. Its name derived from its original German designation 'Führer Line', though this had been changed to 'Senger Line' on 24 February. The position is described in more detail in Chapter 17.
* In certain cases use of the native tongue was in itself a suitable deception. During a spell in Cassino town in April, the Signals Officer of 3 Welsh Guards had all wireless communications conducted in Welsh. Within twenty-four hours the Germans bombarded their lines with propaganda leaflets written in Urdu.

Corps, supposedly including 36 US Division, had assembled for amphibious training in the Salerno area. Information was 'leaked' that they were preparing for a landing near Civitavecchia and on 2 May a dummy rehearsal was enacted, again by simulating the requisite radio traffic. The transfer of the Corps to its actual destination, east of Cassino, was conducted under the strictest secrecy. All moves were made at night, strict wireless silence was maintained, all formation and tactical signs were removed from lorries, tanks and bivouac areas, and supply dumps were elaborately camouflaged as well as being broken up into much smaller units than was customary.

These measures were extremely successful, leaving the Germans woefully ignorant about Allied deployments and very much in the dark as to the date of the renewed offensive. German maps captured during the Fourth Battle are eloquent testimony to the former point. It was believed, for example, that the French had only one division in the Garigliano bridgehead, another being at Salerno and a third unlocated. The existence of a fourth, and presumably of the *goumiers*, was not even suspected. Eighth Army's dispositions remained equally opaque. The headquarters of 1 Canadian Corps was unlocated, 5 Armoured Division was supposedly under Polish command, and 1 Division was placed at Nocara. Even Eighth Army Headquarters was wrongly located, whilst two of the British divisions, 4th and 78th, were thought to be well in the rear around Termoli. All in all the Germans underestimated the strength of Alexander's concentration by a full seven divisions. As for the date of the offensive, now fixed for 11 May, logs of German telephone conversations clearly showed that the timing came as a complete surprise. Some officers did express a certain unease. On the 10th, Vietinghoff's Chief of Staff told Kesselring's: 'To my great pleasure everything is quiet. Only I do not know what is going on. Things are becoming ever more uncertain.' But Vietinghoff himself only took reassurance from the seeming lack of activity. On the morning of the 11th, he informed Kesselring: 'There is nothing special going on. Yesterday I called at the HQs of the two Corps. Both . . . commanders told me as one that they did not yet have the impression that anything was going to happen.'[17] Equally revealing is the fact that two senior officers, von Senger und Etterlin and Westphal, were not even in Italy when the offensive opened. Both had been allowed to go home on leave in mid-April, the former also to receive the Oak Leaves to his Knight's Cross and to attend a course on *Weltanschauung*.*

* A major feature of this was a pep-talk by Hitler himself, though it is worth noting that for once he was in a much more gloomy mood than his local commanders.

It should not be thought, however, that the Germans were completely complacent or that they had been idle during the lull in the fighting. Much work had been done on the defensive positions, both the Gustav Line itself and the new fall-back lines. The Hitler, Dora and Orange Lines have already been alluded to and a start was made on yet another switch position, further to the west. This was known as the C-Line and was designed as a last-ditch defence to protect the immediate approaches to Rome. Work began in late March and over 10,000 Italian labourers were employed. It ran from Ardea, on the coast north-west of Anzio, through Campoleone, the southern outskirts of Velletri, Valmontone, and finally to Pescara. It was far from complete when the Allied offensive opened – the only finished stretch was between the coast and Lanico – but it nevertheless offered many clusters of strongpoints on which pockets of stiff resistance might anchor themselves.

The Germans also made redeployments of their own. By a strange coincidence Tenth Army adjusted its Corps boundaries in almost exactly the same way as the front had been redivided between Eighth and Fifth Armies. The whole sector north of the Liri was handed over to Feuerstein's LI Mountain Corps and that between the southern end of the Liri Valley and the sea to von Senger und Etterlin's XIV Panzer Corps. Feuerstein now took command of part of 44 Division, around Monte Cairo and Colle Belvedere, and 1 Parachute and 15 PG Divisions, both still in their old positions at Cassino and in the Liri Valley. In mid-April, however, it was decided to relieve the Panzer Grenadiers, though the process was not to be complete until the middle of May. When the offensive opened this task was only half completed and the Liri Valley was manned by an unsatisfactory hodge-podge of units. One of 15 PG Division's regiments, the 115th, was still there, though divisional headquarters had been replaced by that of 44 Division, the relieving formation. None of 44 Division's regiments had come into their new sector, however, and the absent Panzer Grenadier regiment had been temporarily replaced by two battalions from 305 Division, the so-called Bode Blocking Group. As 44 Division was without an HQ for the time

According to von Senger und Etterlin: 'His summary of the overall situation left nothing to be desired as far as objectivity of presentation was concerned. He described the catastrophic conditions on the Eastern front . . . [and said] the battle of the Atlantic had reached a critical stage. He hardly made mention of the few German victories on the Italian front . . . [but] made no secret of his apprehension with regard to . . . the establishment of a second front which would drain off manpower. The only encouragement . . . was a half-mumbled admonition to overcome all the difficulties through "faith".' (Von Senger und Etterlin, Diary, op. cit., pp.114–15.)

being, it was split between other formations. The two regiments supposed to go into the Liri Valley remained in place, one going under the command of 1 Parachute Division and the other under 5 Mountain Division to the north. The third regiment, the 131st, was allocated to XIV Panzer Corps. The paratroopers also had under command the Ruffin Battle Group, formed around two battalions of 5 Mountain Division.

XIV Panzer Corps was now composed of only two complete divisions, the 94th, between the coast and Castelforte, and 71 Division from there to the Liri Valley. There was, however, a heterogeneous assortment of units both in reserve and slotted into possible weak points in the line.The Corps reserve was the second regiment of 15 PG Division, the 104th, which was resting near Terracina. The regiment from 44 Division, already mentioned, was holding the northernmost part of 71 Division's line, whilst the reconnaissance battalions of 44, 71 and 114 Jäger Divisions had all been pressed into service as ordinary infantry battalions. Mobile reserves, which might or might not be made available to Tenth Army depending on the situation around the Anzio beachhead, were provided by 29 PG Division between Anzio and the Tiber, 90 PG Division on either side of Civitavecchia, and 26 Panzer Division below the Alban Hills.

With regard to German movements, it is worth making some mention at this point of the relative ease with which they were able to shift their units from one part of the front to another and to keep them adequately supplied. For many Allied commanders had hoped that this would have proved almost impossible, thanks to a concerted use of their massive aerial superiority. We have already had cause to note how Wilson, encouraged by Slessor, had at one time hoped that air power alone would be sufficient to force a German withdrawal. Certain ground commanders felt this to be rather overambitious but many senior planners continued to think that air operations could have a decisive impact on German capabilities. On 7 April, Eaker told Arnold: 'My personal belief is that our communication attacks will make it possible for the Army to move forward when they next make an effort. . . I think when our ground forces move northward it will, in fact, be following up a German withdrawal made necessary by his inadequate supply.'[18] Some Army planners held similar views. A member of the AFHQ G–3 section reported, on 4 April, a general feeling 'that the ground offensive should not be started until it is clear that, owing to the severity of the air attack, the Germans are compelled to reduce their forces south of Rome.'[19]

The air attack had, in fact, already begun. On 18 February Eaker had issued a directive calling for an aerial offensive against German communications north and south of Rome. A further directive was issued on 19 March, by which time the offensive had been dubbed Operation STRANGLE, and the aims and methods were laid out in more detail. The object was stated as being 'to reduce the enemy's flow of supplies to a level which will make it impossible for him to maintain and operate his forces in Central Italy.'[20] Every available type of strike aircraft was to be used. The heavy bombers were to continue supporting the raids on German cities but whenever possible they were also to attack major marshalling yards in Italy. The medium bombers were also to be used against the marshalling yards but were to supplement these activities with precision raids against major bridges and railway repair shops. The fighter-bombers were to seek out the trains themselves, as well as attacking major bridges under repair and other secondary bridges. They went to it with a will and between 19 March and 11 May 65,000 sorties were flown, dropping 33,000 tons of bombs, over two-thirds of them falling on the Italian rail network and repair facilities.

Yet the whole effort was a disappointing failure. As one historian has pointed out: 'The outstanding fact to emerge from the German records is that *there were no critical supply shortages, either during STRANGLE or even during DIADEM.* Spot shortages of certain items inevitably developed . . . but these were due to distribution difficulties and not to a shortage of supplies in the theatre.' Indeed, 'the supply situation prior to DIADEM is rarely mentioned in the German records for the simple reason that it presented no problem at the time.'[21] He goes on to quote the German officer in charge of the Italian transport system, who after the war stated:

[During STRANGLE] traffic within the country had to be further curtailed, movement across the frontiers had to be slowed down. Nevertheless, it was possible to repair all these damages within a comparatively short period of time and in an adequate manner to permit railroad operations to continue and the trains required by . . . [Army Group 'C'] to be moved in.[22]

His comments are amply confirmed by just one set of figures, showing the availability of ammunition just before STRANGLE began and again on the eve of the Fourth Battle:

Ammunition Available to Tenth Army (in metric tons)[23]

	Depot	Units	Total
15 March	9380	7511	16,891
11 May	8104	9998	18,102

It might be objected that these figures are not too surprising as German ammunition expenditure would inevitably be low during a lull in ground operations and they might well have built up considerable reserves prior to the launching of STRANGLE. This is true enough but only serves to raise the question of why Allied planners ever thought that air interdiction would have a significant effect on front-line stockpiles. The penny dropped with Slessor midway through April, in a letter to Portal:

> Perhaps the most important [reason] of all [for the failure of STRANGLE is that] *we are not forcing him to expend fuel or ammunition.* . . . I am afraid that we are going to find that as long as he is not being forced to expend, he will be able to keep up his reserves of supplies to a level that will enable him to put up a very stiff resistance when the attack comes. That may be inevitable, but it is unfortunate.[24]

It was particularly unfortunate that this major flaw in the planning rationale did not occur to anyone in authority untii a month after the air offensive had begun.

But it was not the only flaw. Others were that the Allies had both grievously *under*estimated the capacity of the Italian railroad network and *over*estimated the minimum level of supply below which the Germans' situation would become critical. In fact, with regard to the former point, blind optimism would be a better term than underestimation. For someone on the planning staffs must surely have been aware of the key fact that the capacity of that part of the railroad system that it was proposed to bomb, was some 80,000 tons per day. But it was agreed that the requirements of Army Group 'C' were only about 5500 tons per day. In other words, to make any significant reduction in the amount of supplies reaching Kesselring's troops, 95 per cent of the rail network would have to be put out of action and kept that way for at least several days at a time. But here we come to the second point: 5500 tons a day was actually far more than Army Group 'C' needed just to hold on, and the figure could be reduced by 90 per cent without Tenth or Fourteenth Armies being obliged to actually withdraw. It has been pointed out, for example, that von Paulus, the defender of Stalingrad, had estimated during the airlift period that he needed 700 tons per day but could just about get by on a mere 500 tons. And he had 22 divisions as opposed to Kesselring's 19. No wonder the Germans made so few complaints. Even if they only managed to patch up 1 or 2 per cent of the network they could still get the basic minimum of supplies. One cannot

but feel that Allied planning had been once again vitiated by shoddy staff
work.*

As the planners busied themselves in their comfortable headquarters and
command posts, the ordinary soldiers had yet again to endure appalling
privations in the sangars, dugouts and slit trenches that formed the front
line. The weather did at least improve somewhat through April, and rain,
snow and freezing temperatures became less of a problem. But there
always remained the agonizing tension, every man constantly alert for the
sound of enemy patrols, fearful to stir from his hole lest he be caught by
a sniper or machine gunner, and always conscious that nowhere was he
safe from mortar or artillery shells. The experiences of the newly arrived
88 US Division typified those of every other Allied formation, veteran or
not. Sergeant Eden Riley described the loneliness of outpost duty,
recalling one incident in particular: 'I heard a rustling noise during the
night. I threw three grenades in the general direction. There was silence
for a few minutes. Then I heard the rustling noise again and fired a few
rounds with the machine gun. This time there was no further noise. Next
morning I found two very dead rats in front of my position.'[25] This story
has an almost comic aspect but it should not lead one to underestimate
the agonies of the mind that led to such panicky reactions. An officer with
the same division, Colonel James C. Fry, told how his men tried to avoid
thinking about the forthcoming offensive and simply

> looked forward to any minor relief from the tension of mind and
> muscle that made the position among the rocks at the extreme front
> a veritable hell. Even the rotation of a squad to the reserve position
> of a platoon was welcomed because this afforded the members an
> opportunity to at least remove their shoes and relax a bit. . . . Some
> of the men made violent efforts to escape from the impending
> danger. The usual method was to shoot themselves through the foot.
> There were far more cases of this nature than I care to remember.[26]

---

* The Allies also underestimated the Germans' capacity for improvisation.
Considerable damage was done to the rail system (though nowhere near as much as
had been hoped – see Sallager, *op. cit.*, pp.35–6) but they quickly found alternative
methods of transport. One was by sea, accounting for 15 per cent of all supplies and
where Allied planes found it just as difficult as during the Sicilian campaign to actually
sink any ships (see Slessor, *loc. cit.*,), and the other by road. An enormous amount
of Italian civilian transport was commandeered, raising the available soft-skin tonnage
from 4500 tons in December to 12,000 tons in April. During Operation STRANGLE
losses of such lorries only amounted to 6 per cent of the total tonnage.

How many men chose this way out of the positions at Cassino is not known but there is absolutely no doubt that conditions there, both in the town and on the massif, were as grim as they had ever been. During most of this new lull in operations the massif was garrisoned by 78 Division, with 11 Brigade around Point 593 and Colle Maiola and 36 Brigade taking turns in the Castle. The town was the responsibility of 1 Guards Brigade and a few New Zealand units that had remained behind. Two themes dominate the memories of those who served in the Cassino sector during this period: the cramped and isolated positions and the utter foulness of the very air they breathed. The Coldstream Guards took up positions in the town on 5 April, though these

> were mere holes in the rubble . . . looking forward over stagnant water and scattered ruins to another wall or to the shapeless remains of a building only a few yards away. . . . The forward sections felt themselves terribly isolated . . . There was nothing to do but sit among the crumbling stones and timber baulks of the section post, in a little fortress furnished with grenades, ammunition boxes . . . and a few blankets, where five men alternately slept and watched the few yards of ruin which was all that they could see.[27]

The historian of the Grenadier Guards, whose 3rd Battalion also did their stretch in Cassino town, emphasized the isolation of this troglodyte existence. One of the Grenadiers' positions was in a house codenamed 'Mary' where

> twenty men lived without moving from . . . [it] for about ten days at a stretch. . . . In daytime only one sentry was necessary to watch with a periscope the approaches to the house from every direction; at night there were four sentries, one to each corner. For the men not on duty there was very little to do. . . . They were cramped and bored . . . [and] there was a great sense of isolation, for though the next platoon was less than 50 yards away, they could no more see their comrades than they could see the Germans a hundred and fifty yards in front.[28]

Things were no better on the massif. 2 Lancashire Fusiliers were one of the battalions that had taken over the old Indian positions and they soon came to learn of the hardships endured by the Sikhs and Punjabis. One of their officers recalled:

> The worst feature of the foremost positions was the impossibility of moving by day without being seen by the enemy. It wasn't very funny

spending all the twelve hours of daylight cramped with one other man in your shelter. . . . And all daylight activities, whether eating or anything else, had to be conducted in the lying position. . . . Visits to the latrines . . . had to be postponed until evening, so that they could take place under cover of darkness. As soon as it was dusk, the soldiers would crawl from their shelters, and you would see small groups of bare hindquarters showing white in the semi-darkness, like grotesque friezes: their owners fervently praying that they might complete the proceeding before a shell struck the area.[29]

But there were worse things to bear than simply being cooped up in such small spaces. 5 Northamptonshire Regiment did one spell around Point 593, where the impossibility of daylight movement was only part of the problem. For most men, Majdalany's rigorous bowel discipline was simply too much and in many sangars there were 'boxes [which] had to serve as latrines. . . . Rats infested the area and could be heard at night tearing at the bodies lying around. As the weather grew warmer so the stench increased and the flies grew more prolific.'[30]

Corpses were equally numerous in the town, as the total curfew on movement by day made it almost impossible for burial parties ever to reach them. In the 'Mary' outpost 'somewhere beneath the rubble was the corpse of . . . a soldier killed during the earlier fighting, and the stench of decay became so intolerable that some of the men plugged their noses with mosquito cream.'[31] A cellar occupied by a party of 6 Royal West Kents was graphically described in a corporal's letter home:

. . . can't wash, the water's rationed, and there's swill from meals dumped in the rubble upstairs. Helluva lot of rubble, helluva lot of swill. The latrine is an oil drum and has to be emptied into a hole in another wreck of a room. Flies. The first mosquitoes. Fleas. And under the fallen rubble of a ruined staircase lies the body of a New Zealander. In the house . . . we cook by the grave and there's tea leaves on it and empty tins. Curious flowers indeed. But none of it is very sanitary and as the days wear on so the smell grows. Hicky has to venture from his house at night to sprinkle Lysol on bodies, it is impossible to bury them.[32]

An officer of the Lancashire Fusiliers particularly remembered the other inevitable concomitant of unburied bodies: 'The rats were revolting. They were so fat. We knew they were gorged on the hundreds of bodies nobody could reach. We used to catch them and put them in empty sandbags and chuck them into a place where we were sure a German observation post was stationed after dark.'[33]

Conditions were no better, of course, for the Germans. Their descriptions of life on the massif and in the town mainly echo those of the British troops, though the following diary entry also emphasizes the additional torment of the remorseless pounding from Allied guns and planes. Towards the very end of March the writer was posted back to

> the hills behind Cassino. What we are going through here is beyond description. I never experienced anything like this in Russia, not even a second's peace, only the dreadful thunder of guns and mortars, there are the planes over and above . . . Here we have nothing but terror and horror, death and damnation. When will the day come again, when I shall be able to devote myself to my wife and baby, and take pleasure in the birds and flowers? It is enough to drive you out of your mind.[34]

In the town the Germans were perhaps even more aware of the ubiquity of death. They did manage to collect many of their own dead but could only occasionally find the time or the opportunity to actually bury them. A paratrooper assigned to one of the rare burial parties found that the bodies 'had been piled in a big crater . . . over the weeks. It was the most terrible sight I have ever seen. Green faces, swollen; and all those eyes – staring, loathing. And the rats. The stench was colossal. Even gas-masks were no use. We had to put first-aid packs soaked in cologne over our mouths and nostrils.'[35]

Conditions such as these were an enormous strain on the troops, though reactions varied somewhat from unit to unit. On the massif many men seemed to sink into a kind of spiritual limbo, completely immured in the all-pervading ghastliness. Majdalany wrote:

> A state of utter timelessness . . . prevailed. . . . There were not even any days and nights. There was just light and dark. . . . The other world, the world of women and shops, music and streets, churches and harlots, no longer existed. It was something we'd once read about in a book. The only world was *here*. And the only time was *now*. There was no past, present or future. There was only *now*. We'd always been here and we always would be. . . . It was just a passive state of sustained awfulness.[36]

Heidrich's paratroopers, too, were fast losing sight of any reality other than the rank cellars and dugouts in which they had lived and fought for weeks without end. Yet their morale was still extraordinarily high, so high in fact that many of them became almost fey, taking absurd risks as though to emphasize that they were still there, still unbowed by the massive material onslaught that they had endured. The commanding officer of 6 Black Watch recalled: 'The enemy was . . . extraordinarily careless in the matter of movement and always used to be seen about 04.30 hrs. moving from his night positions to his day ones. . . . He refused to learn by experience, and it was unfortunate that our facilities for observation were not better.'[37] The explanation, though it only made real sense to the paratroopers themselves, was given to an interrogator with 1 Guards Brigade:

> The carelessness of the Germans in their dusk activities was never modified by their experience of British retaliation. They would expose themselves to quite unnecessary danger, as a prisoner later admitted, in order to maintain their self-respect. A German, he said, who spent a fortnight in Cassino automatically qualified for the Iron Cross, and he wished to earn it by a display of courage. They were bored, these tough paratroopers: they liked fighting, not waiting.[38]

Mere mortals could only marvel at such attitudes. There were very few Allied soldiers in Cassino who would have cited boredom as one of their problems. Most spoke of fear, a never-ending, gut-wrenching state of tension that would eventually break any man. Even the gun lines behind Cassino were under constant bombardment. An artillery officer soon came to feel

> on the edge of a nervous breakdown. . . It was a mild form of shell shock but it affected my speech and I found it increasingly difficult to speak without a fairly serious stammer. . . . I had two main worries – the all-important one [of] a real fear and my inability to control my reactions, and secondly the knowledge that I would disgrace myself in front of my men.[39]

But one did not have to *ask* men coming out of Cassino what it had been like. Just as with the Americans before them one had only to look at their faces. For example, at those of the New Zealanders left behind in Cassino after the calling-off of the Third Battle. At the men of 22 Battalion, and the 'face of one of our platoon commanders bringing his men out of Cassino: a dead, expressionless face, and crouching behind them cradling a tommy gun and weaving backwards and forwards like an animal, the strain had been so great.'[40] Or at 21 Battalion, whom they relieved: 'Nerves stretched almost to breaking-point and shaking hands lighting cigarettes. Too tired to feel pleased when 22 Battalion takes over – platoon half a dozen strong. Shelled all the way out, but too tired to give a damn. Climb into the waiting trucks – somebody tries to sing but falls asleep instead.'[41]

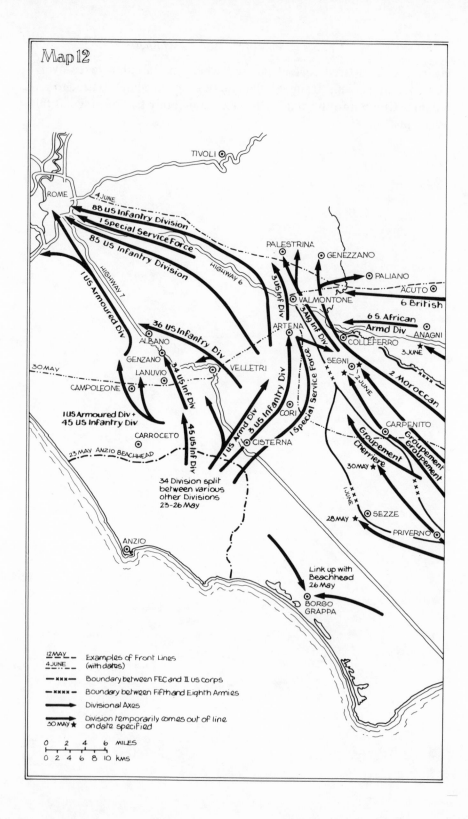

Map 12

TIVOLI ⊙

ROME ⊙
4 JUNE
88 US Infantry Division
1 Special Service Force
85 US Infantry Division
HIGHWAY 6
HIGHWAY 7
1 US Armoured Div
36 US Infantry Div
ALBANO ⊙
GENZANO ⊙
LANUVIO ⊙
34 US Inf Div
VELLETRI ⊙
30 MAY
CAMPOLEONE ⊙
1 US Armoured Div +
45 US Infantry Div
CARROCETO ⊙
23 MAY ANZIO BEACHHEAD
45 US Inf Div
34 Division split
between various
other Divisions
23-26 May

PALESTRINA ⊙
GENEZZANO ⊙
PALIANO ⊙
ACUTO ⊙
6 British
6 S. African
Armd Div
ANAGNI ⊙
3 JUNE ★
5 US Inf Div
3 Algerian Div
VALMONTONE ⊙
ARTENA ⊙
COLLEFERRO ⊙
SEGNI ⊙ ★
★ ★ 2 JUNE
2 Moroccan
★ ★ ★
1 Special Service Force
3 US Infantry Div
CORI ⊙
1 US Armd Div
CISTERNA ⊙
CARPENITO ⊙
Groupement
Groupement
Groupement
Cherriere
30 MAY ★
1 JUNE
× × ×
28 MAY ★
SEZZE ⊙
PRIVERNO ⊙

ANZIO ⊙

Link up with
Beachhead
26 May
⊙ BORGO
GRAPPA

12 MAY __
4 JUNE __ Examples of Front Lines
(with dates)

— ×××— Boundary between FEC and II US corps

— ×××— Boundary between Fifth and Eighth Armies

➤ Divisional Axes

30 MAY ★ Division temporarily comes out of line
on date specified

0   2   4   6 MILES
0 2 4 6 8 10 kms

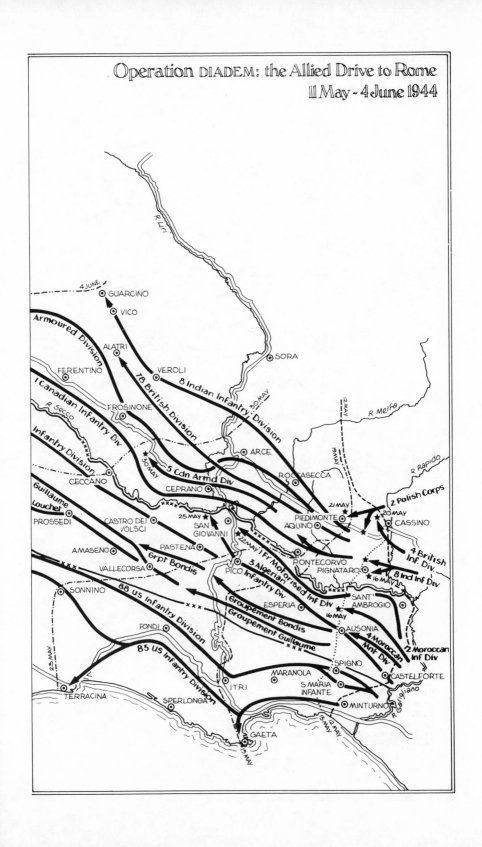

Operation DIADEM: the Allied Drive to Rome
11 May - 4 June 1944

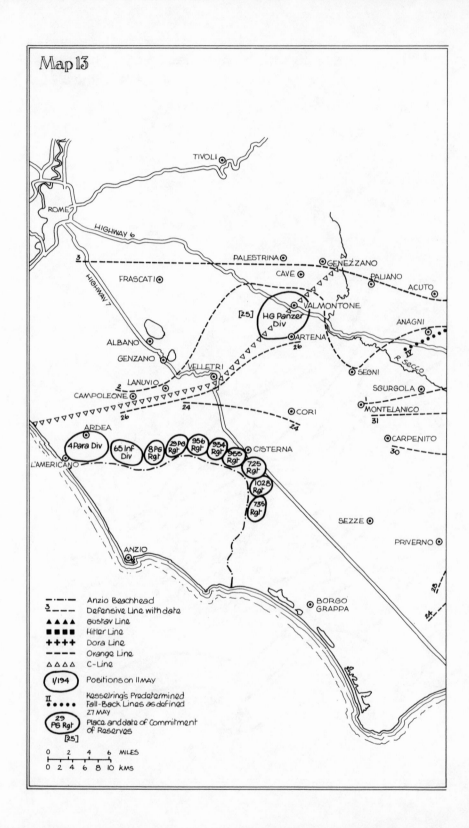

Map 13

TIVOLI ⊙

ROME

HIGHWAY 6

3 ----- PALESTRINA ⊙   ⊙ GENEZZANO
                              CAVE ⊙   ▽ ▽ ▽   PALIANO ⊙
FRASCATI ⊙   ▽ ▽ ▽ ▽   ACUTO ⊙
HIGHWAY 7   ▽
                        [25] ⊙ VALMONTONE
                        HG Panzer   ANAGNI ⊙
                        Div
ALBANO ⊙   ⊙ ARTENA   R. SECCO   IV •••••
GENZANO ⊙   26
              VELLETRI ⊙ ▽ ▽ ▽ ▽
        LANUVIO ⊙   ▽ ▽   ⊙ SEGNI
2 ----- ▽   SGURGOLA ⊙
CAMPOLEONE ⊙ ▽ ▽ ▽ ▽ ▽ ▽ ▽ ▽   ⊙ MONTELANICO
        26   24   31
▽ ▽ ▽ ▽ ▽ ▽ ▽ ▽ ▽   ⊙ CORI
        ARDEA   24   ⊙ CARPENITO
     4 Para Div   65 Inf 8 PG 29 PG 956 954 965   30
L'AMERICANO   Div   Rgt   Rgt Rgt Rgt Rgt ⊙ CISTERNA
                                            725
                                            Rgt
                                           1028
                                            Rgt
                                            735   SEZZE ⊙
                                            Rgt
                                                   PRIVERNO ⊙
        ANZIO

                                                20
                              ⊙ BORGO
                                GRAPPA
                                                24

—·—·—   Anzio Beachhead
3 ----- Defensive Line with date
▲▲▲▲   Gustav Line
■■■■   Hitler Line
++++   Dora Line
-----   Orange Line
△△△△   C-Line

(1/194)   Positions on 11 MAY

II •••••   Kesselring's Predetermined
           Fall-Back Lines as defined
           27 MAY

(29 PG Rgt) Place and date of Commitment
  [25]   of Reserves

0   2   4   6   MILES
0 2 4 6 8 10 KMS

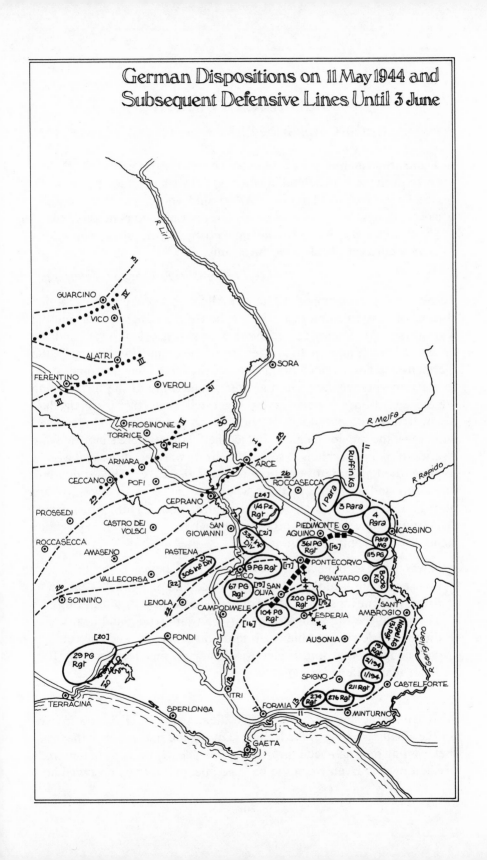

German Dispositions on 11 May 1944 and Subsequent Defensive Lines Until 3 June

13
'Fart and Fly Hard'
XIII British Corps in the Liri Valley, 11–17 May 1944

There are so many stories I could tell you, so many horrors but I shall try to push them all behind me for I do not wish to remember them. . . . That is true of all of us . . . We should whoop over the positive side of things. We have broken his Gustav Line and penetrated the Hitler Line. But we are overwhelmed by the negative, the wild excesses of a vast, wild, powerful insanity.

Lance-Corporal W. Robson, 24 May 1944

Throughout the evening of 11 May the Allied artillery kept up its routine shelling of Cassino, hoping to convince the Germans that nothing unusual was afoot. At about 22.00 the firing slowly died away and an unaccustomed stillness settled over the whole front. For, strangely, the Germans had also stopped firing at about the same time and some began to wonder whether they had not after all got wind of the forthcoming attack. Front-line rumours even suggested that 'the Germans had discovered our preparations and, in order to avoid our attack, they had withdrawn the previous night.'[1] In fact the Germans were simply making a series of battalion reliefs in some of their forward positions and wished to allow the incoming troops time to get under cover. Higher quarters knew this and at 23.00, as the BBC pips sounded, a massive artillery barrage opened up along the entire Fifth and Eighth Army front. According to one Canadian officer, although he was in reserve positions some distance behind the front,

> it was hard to believe. In those few miles between the hills, a thousand guns suddenly let go as one, and then they kept on firing. We'd never seen or heard or imagined anything quite like this. You could see the flashes of nearby guns and you could hear the thunder of dozens and hundreds more on every side and you could only imagine what sort of Hell was falling on the German lines. It damn near deafened you.[2]

Also behind the line were 2 Royal Fusiliers, part of 4 Division's reserve for the assault crossing of the Rapido. During the sudden lull in the firing that evening they had been surprised to hear clearly the song of hundreds of nightingales. Even when the barrage opened, as 'they observed how the continuous flashes from the gun muzzles turned the night into blazing day . . ., they noticed how the nightingales, although startled into a few minutes' silence, burst into song again and throughout the night kept up their valiant efforts to drown the dreadful din.'[3]

Few Germans had the leisure to take heed of this bizarre disharmony. A soldier on the Cassino massif was listening to the more familiar sounds of a patrol coming back and a fatigue party bringing up hot food when

> suddenly, as if a light had been switched on, there was a blaze of flame down the valley . . . and then ear-splitting screaming, whizzing, exploding, banging and crashing . . . I squeezed into the narrow cover-hole. Splinters buzzed over me, stones and clods of earth whirled through the air. The ground trembled under the force of the blasts.[4]

All along the line the Germans scrambled into their dugouts and bunkers and the various Allied divisions slowly moved forward. XIII Corps, with 4 Division on the right and 8 Indian on the left, first had to get up to the Rapido itself. But they found the going much easier than 36 US Division had done, and by midnight the leading battalions were lowering their assault boats into the water. But the Germans then began to recover and the attacking troops soon ran into familiar difficulties. The river itself was not the least of them. Once again the current was much faster than that of the rivers on which the units had rehearsed and many of the cumbersome, keelless boats were swept far downstream before they reached the far bank. Those boats that did cross successfully – invariably those using ropes which some companies had attached on the far bank – soon ran into further problems. One was the thick mist that swirled about, making it impossible for the troops to delineate their objectives or to see the direction-keeping bursts of Bofors tracer that had been specially provided.* And just as with the Texans, German fire was again much more intense than had been anticipated, the Allied artillery having failed to cause the hoped-for dislocation. Of course the mist obscured the British and Indians from direct observation, but mortars and artillery

---

* Most contemporary accounts insist that the Germans were laying down smoke. An Indian battalion, 1/12 Frontier Force Regiment, claimed that 'the Germans had erected a number of trip wires which, when cut or pulled, activated smoke canisters.' (Pal, *op. cit.*, p.161.) Modern historians, however, think that the 'fog of war' was mainly caused by the river mist, exacerbated by both sides' artillery smoke. (See, for example, W.G.F. Jackson, *The Battle for Rome*, Batsford, 1969, p.93. Major-General Jackson was himself present during the battle.)

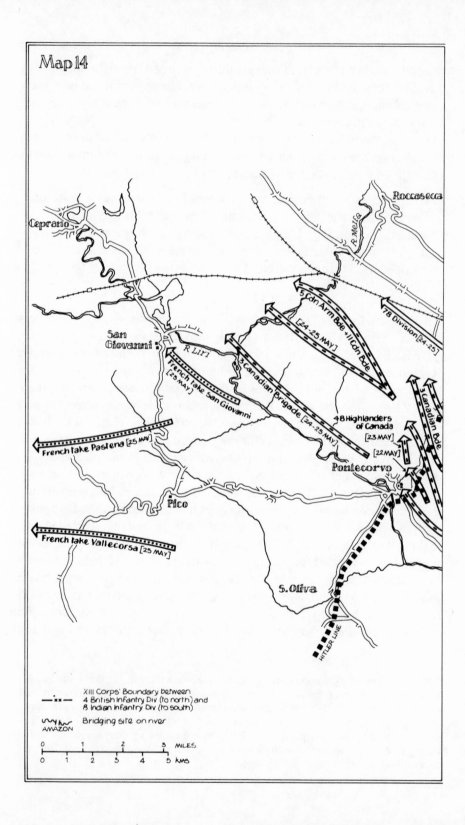

Map 14

Ceprano

Roccasecca

R. Melfa

San Giovanni

5 Cdn Arm Bde + 11 Cdn Bde [24-25 MAY]

78 Division [24-25]

R. Liri

French take San Giovanni [25 MAY]

3 Canadian Brigade

3 Canadian Bde

48 Highlanders of Canada [23 MAY]

[24-25 MAY]

French take Pastena [25 MAY]

[22 MAY]

Pontecorvo

Pico

French take Vallecorsa [25 MAY]

S. Oliva

HITLER LINE

— · xx — XIII Corps' Boundary between 4 British Infantry Div (to north) and 8 Indian Infantry Div (to south)

AMAZON Bridging site on river

```
0      1        2         3    MILES
0   1     2     3     4     5 KMS
```

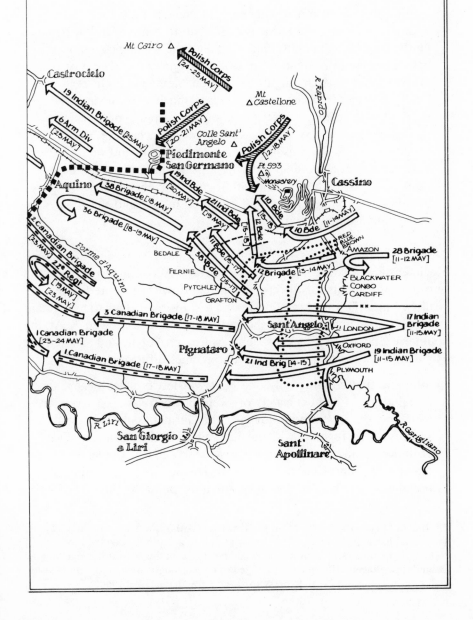

Eighth Army Breaks through the Gustav and Hitler Lines 11-25 May 1944

Mt Cairo △

Polish Corps [24-25 MAY]

Castrocielo

19 Indian Brigade [25 MAY]

6 Arm Div [25 MAY]

Polish Corps [20-21 MAY]

Mt △ Castellone

Colle Sant' Angelo △

Polish Corps [12-18 MAY]

R. Rapido

Piedimonte San Germano

Pt 593 △ Monastery

Cassino

Aquino

38 Brigade [20 MAY]

19 Ind Bde [20 MAY]

21 Ind Bde [9 MAY]

10 Bde [15-18]

12 Bde

10 Bde [11-14 MAY]

36 Brigade [18 MAY]

36 Brigade [18-19 MAY]

11 Bde [15-18]

BEDALE

36 Bde [15-17]

RED BLUE BROWN AMAZON

28 Brigade [11-12 MAY]

2 Canadian Brigade [25 MAY] 22 Regt [19 MAY]

Forme d'Aquino

FERNIE

12 Brigade [13-14 MAY]

BLACKWATER CONGO CARDIFF

[23 MAY]

PYTCHLEY

GRAFTON

3 Canadian Brigade [17-18 MAY]

Sant' Angelo LONDON

17 Indian Brigade [11-15 MAY]

I Canadian Brigade [23-24 MAY]

Pignataro

OXFORD

19 Indian Brigade [11-15 MAY]

I Canadian Brigade [17-18 MAY]

21 Ind Brig [14-15]

PLYMOUTH

R. Liri

San Giorgio a Liri

Sant' Apollinare

R. Garigliano

firing according to prearranged fire plans, and machine guns on fixed lines, were able to cause heavy casualties.

All this led to serious confusion and units soon began to fall behind their demanding timetables. In 8 Indian Division an advance of 100 yards every six minutes had been specified,* but whilst the artillery barrage remorselessly crept forward at this rate the infantry were quite unable to keep up. According to one battalion history:

> Nothing had been left to chance. But chance intervened, all the same. . . . The . . . situation was difficult to control, and by 04.00 hours the Commanding Officer signalled the leading companies to halt and later to reorganize on the river bank. . . . The mist . . . made a junior leader's nightmare. The Commanding Officer went boldly forward into the mist to locate the line of advance and, encountering wire, made the complete circuit of an enemy strongpoint. But no attack could be launched in existing conditions. . . . The Fusiliers proceeded to dig in and wait for the mist to clear. It cleared all right the following morning and the sun came out at 09.00 hours. But with it came the enemy fire . . . The battalion was pinned down and hemmed in . . . and the slightest movement brought down enemy fire.[5]

Other Indian battalions had similar difficulties. 1/12 Frontier Force Regiment had a particularly depressing start. According to their CO the entire arrangements for the crossing broke down. En route to the river bank 'we met the Beachmaster. He had lost his river! Our irate adjutant in due course appropriately showed him where it flowed.'[6] At the southern end of XIII Corps' line were 1 Argyll and Sutherland Highlanders. They found the river without much difficulty but

> after the first crossing only one boat was left on each beach; the remainder . . . had been sunk or swept downstream. . . . As soon as 'C' and 'D' . . . started to advance, the Germans put down a smoke screen, which, together with the dust caused by the barrage, reduced visibility to nil, thus halting their advance and at the same time making it impossible for 'A' and Headquarters to bring the remaining boats from the boat opening point to the river. As

---

* 8 Indian Division's objectives for the first twenty-four hours were in three phases: (i) to establish a bridgehead; (ii) to push out of it to a depth of 2000 yards or so; (iii) to mop up in Sant' Angelo and consolidate positions on the horseshoe ridge that lay behind this village. After that it was hoped to pass through either 78 British Division or the entire Canadian Corps to press up to and through the Hitler Line.

daylight approached, the leading companies, delayed by smoke and held up by wire and machine gun fire, had to dig in or conceal themselves in the irrigation ditches. . . . No action was possible during the daylight hours of the 12th. The German defences dominated the whole area in which the Battalion was dug in, and there was nothing for it but to sit and take it. For the whole day the positions were subject to shell and mortar fire, and furthermore it was not possible to communicate with Brigade as the wireless had failed and line laying had proved impracticable.[7]

A few attacks were mounted to try to extend the bridgehead but most used insufficient numbers or pushed along axes that were pure guesswork. The Frontier Force Regiment attacked to the left of Sant' Angelo, always the most important of their Division's targets, but were baulked by an apron of wire and a minefield. As they tried to move round it they were hit by a shower of grenades and fierce automatic weapons fire. Platoons became dispersed and the leading companies lost all contact. Again 'all types of mechanical communication failed. The battalion commander instructed his officers to report their position by flares. The thick fog snuffed out the lights as soon as fired. Then the primitive device succeeded – the Mussulman war cry of "*Maro nari haidriya Ali!*" rang above the din of battle and gave the commander pinpoints for his positions.'[8] Sant' Angelo was the responsibility of 17 Indian Brigade, who had hoped to nip it out with flanking attacks by the Frontier Force and 1 Royal Fusiliers. As both began to run out of steam the Brigade's reserve battalion, 1/5 Gurkhas, was brought forward to mount a frontal assault. Initially only one company was used and two of its platoons got lost crossing the river and moving up to the start line. The platoon that did arrive lost several men on the way and the actual attack, on one of the focal points of the Gustav Line, was carried out by a derisory twenty-five men. Not surprisingly it was easily repulsed.

19 Brigade's major objective was Pignataro and the spearhead role had been assigned to 3/8 Punjabis. The rifle companies got most of their men across the river but only after most of the boats had been sunk. Many men were brought across on a tedious shuttle service by the few remaining serviceable craft and by the time they were all over the battalion was seriously behind schedule. The leading companies did not jump off until early the next morning. 'A' Company advanced towards Point 63, one of the preliminary objectives, but ran into a minefield. Many men were blown up and many others killed by the small arms fire directed towards the sound of the explosions. Only fifteen men remained on their feet. They pushed on but lost six more even before they reached the road

running parallel to the river. Still the survivors went forward but were forced to go to ground before they had covered more than 30 yards. During the day this handful of men had to repulse several German counter-attacks and by first light on the 13th only three fighting men remained. Their ammunition exhausted, they were obliged to surrender.

'B' Company had the good fortune to avoid any strong German positions and by midday had arrived some 250 yards to the north-east of Point 63. But this latter target was still the primary target and 'D' Company was brought forward to take it.

> It reached to within a few yards of the objective, then charged the German positions in line abreast.It was a gallant but futile charge, which was halted by a wire obstacle and the combined fire of four German machine guns. The gallant officer who led the charge was killed and one complete platoon was wiped out. This platoon crashed through almost into the German positions; they lay where they had fallen, a few yards in front of the muzzles of the German machine guns. A second attack launched by the company captured the ridge. By that time there were only some thirty men who were not wounded.[9]

Clearly, 8 Indian Division was already badly behind schedule and there was now no immediate prospect of being able to funnel any of the reserve divisions into a reasonably secure bridgehead. But their commander, Lieutenant-General Dudley Russell, did have at least one small consolation in that his delay had not left 4 Division with one of its flanks in the air. For they, unfortunately, were equally behind schedule,* having come up against just the same problems with the swift current, the mist and the heavy German fire. Many battalions had become seriously disorganized and to an observer the general impression was one of hopeless confusion. An engineer officer had appalling difficulties even getting to the site of a bridge he was supposed to build, and once there found that 'nothing could be done in that awful fog with bullets whizzing overhead. We simply must get some chaps across to deal with "Spandaus"

---

* 4 Division's advance was to be in four stages: (i) the initial bridgehead 1000 yards deep (the Brown Line); (ii) a further advance of 1500 yards to secure the low ridges that overlooked the river (the Blue Line); (iii) push on to the Cassino–Pignataro road north of the Piopetto (the Red Line); (iv) a final right wheel to cut Highway Six. This latter move would make contact with the Poles who should then have cleared the massif. The Division was to be on the Blue Line by dawn on the 12th, though the divisional commander, Lieutenant-General Dudley Ward, sensibly declined to give definite predictions as to further progress.

. . . We searched for some officers or warrant officers, but not one could we find, only dejected parties of infantry milling around with their boats. . . . [Eventually we] found an infantry officer who raised a platoon and promised to clear out the Boche. But they soon came back having got hopelessly lost in the fog.'[10]

Like the Indians to the south, 4 Division were attacking with two Brigades up, the 10th at the northern end of the Liri Valley and the 28th on their left. Despite the confusion 10 Brigade did at least succeed in getting most of its three battalions across the river, though only isolated companies got as far as the Brown Line and none anywhere near the Blue. As day dawned German fire became increasingly accurate and the Brigade could do little more than dig in around its slender bridgehead and repel the German counter-attacks. Some of these were supported by individual tanks and, according to the Divisional War Diary: 'At this stage the Divisional Commander was satisfied that no further move could be made by either Brigade unless some anti-tank guns were brought up. He therefore ordered only minor advances and consolidation until each Brigade had four guns on the west bank.'[11]

But 28 Brigade was incapable of making any movement forward with or without anti-tank guns. For their crossing had been little short of disastrous. Two of its battalions, 2 King's and 2 Somerset Light Infantry, were involved in the initial assault whilst the third, 2/4 Hampshires, were temporarily responsible for handling the boats. 2 King's went first with orders to push up to the Brown Line. They were soon in great difficulties. They arrived at the crossing points, 'x' and 'Y', thirty-five minutes late, just as the counter-battery barrage was ending and when the boats were finally launched heavy German fire was already coming down. There were numerous casualties and many boats were lost, so that it was some time before even scattered elements of three companies were across. These ran into determined resistance. 'B' Company was losing men by the minute and was brought to a halt when the survivors stumbled into a minefield. 'D' Company was whittled down to one officer and ten men and 'C' 'had suffered many casualties on passing through a minefield covered by enemy fire. It was so depleted that they were unable to gain their objective. . . . [The Company Commander] although under heavy fire at the time personally collected the remnants of the other companies which had become disorganized . . . and withdrew them to his line of consolidation.'[12]

The Somersets had followed close behind, with orders to pass through the King's and move forward to the Blue Line. Even before they were over the river, however, they ran into stragglers from the battalion in front and it became 'evident that the Kings' programme had been somewhat delayed. . . . [At "Y" Crossing] they had not got more than one company across and were having a sticky time of it.' They borrowed some of the Somersets' boats but these latter did eventually manage to get at least part of their own 'C' and 'D' Companies across. The other two were supposed to use 'X' Crossing but 'B' ran into heavy fire and became, according to the standard Army euphemism, 'disorganized'. According to the Battalion War Diary, 'B' Company immediately 'withdrew well behind the river to the Boat Assembly Position *on some alleged order* which did not originate from Lieutenant-Colonel Platt.'[13] The other companies were able to make no progress beyond the tenuous forward positions already established by the King's.

This, indeed, was the end of 28 Brigade's contribution to the Fourth Battle and one cannot avoid the conclusion that it had failed badly. Admittedly casualties had been heavy – 52 per cent of the King's rifle companies and 32 per cent of the Somersets – but this had happened to other battalions in other battles who had nevertheless gone on to take their objectives. Admittedly also, communications within the Brigade had completely broken down. Brigade HQ noted early on the 12th that 'no communication was possible with either battalion' as well as the regrettable fact that 'Lieutenant-Colonel Platt (SLI) and Lieutenant-Colonel Garmons-Williams (King's) were both wounded, the latter dying of his wounds a day later.'[14] Things were no better at the battalion end. The Kings' 'Command Post . . . [was] unable to cross owing to boats being destroyed. No communication from any companies . . . No W/T contact made with control or any other company. Signal Officer reported missing, last seen by Signal Sergeant being swept down the river.'[15] And from the beginning 2 Somersets were 'unable to contact Brigade HQ on Brigade 18 set net and no contact [was] ever made on this net.'[16] Yet once again it has to be pointed out that failures of this kind were hardly uncommon, and were indeed to plague Eighth Army in the weeks to come. But most infantry battalions tended to rely on bold leadership on the ground, rather than detailed instructions over the radio or telephone, and it is this leadership that seems to have been noticeably absent in 28 Brigade. Given the paucity of hard evidence it might seem unjustified to speak in terms of incompetence and panic, but it is possible to spot several negative pointers to the fact that Army and Corps regarded this as an exceptionally heavy reverse. Firstly, no attempt was made either to push the men on the far bank further forward or to get those that had withdrawn, notably 'A' and 'B' Companies of the Somersets, back across. Secondly, the Brigade's third battalion (2/4 Hampshires, to whom none of these censorious statements apply) was put under command of 4 Division's reserve Brigade, the 12th. Thirdly, the small bridgehead was withdrawn entirely on the 14th and both battalions, along with Brigade HQ, were withdrawn for 'reorganization'. This lasted until the 22nd and there seems to have been no suggestion of feeding them back over the river, even though the rest of 4 Division was involved in stiff fighting until the 20th and would have been most grateful for any extra men, if only to man less volatile parts of the line.

But the failure of 28 Brigade was not the only problem for XIII Corps. Another was the lack of bridges over which to bring both armoured support and the divisions held back for later exploitation. Tanks to work with the infantry had been deemed particularly important and full paper provision had been made for the attachment of several Canadian squadrons to 8 Indian Division and British ones to 4 Division. Bridge-building plans looked equally impressive on paper. In 4 Division's sector the engineers were immediately to start work on three bridges codenamed, from north to south, Amazon (40 tons), Blackwater (30 tons) and Congo (9 tons). In front of the Indians, because they were further away from the major German artillery concentrations on the massif, it was felt it should be possible to erect four bridges and these were designated Cardiff (30 tons), London (40 tons), Oxford and Plymouth (both 30 tons). Work did begin on time, almost as soon as the first troops began to cross on the 11th, and initial progress was good. By 01.00 on the 12th the bank seats for all the bridges were well advanced. But as soon as the forward troops began to run into difficulties so too did the sappers, the increased weight of German fire forcing them to seek cover as well as destroying many of the trucks bringing up the prefabricated parts. 4 Division's War Diary pays particular attention to this aspect of their operations and clearly shows how desperate the situation threatened to become:

> 03.30: News of bridging progress was bad. All three bridges were being held up by shelling, although Blackwater was perhaps in advance of other two . . .

> 05.30: Now that it was daylight small pockets of enemy resistance were able to harass the bridging sites with small arms fire and did so to such effect that work on bridging sites and ferries was virtually at a standstill.[17]

The work remained at a standstill throughout the 12th and, with the failure of 28 Brigade and the meagre progress of 10 Brigade, 4 Division was in danger of reliving the ghastly experiences of the Texans less than four months before. As one historian has succinctly put it:

The usual vicious circle of an unsuccessful river crossing set in: too shallow a bridgehead meant no bridging, and yet no bridging meant lack of the necessary strength to secure and deepen the bridgehead. No bridges were built in Dudley Ward's sector on the first day, but fortunately the Germans failed to take advantage of the weakness of his position and launched no deliberately organized tank and infantry counter-attacks against his precarious bridgeheads.[18]

Happily, too, the advantages of 8 Indian Division's crossing sites lived up to expectations and at no stage was the engineer work completely halted. Cardiff had to be abandoned but two of the other bridges had been completed by 09.15 on the 12th. Plymouth was hit by German shells within an hour, making it only negotiable by light vehicles, but Oxford remained intact and during the day the best part of four Canadian squadrons drove into the bridgehead. Some bogged down immediately in the soft ground on the west bank, but by dusk the remainder had helped the Indians to make considerable progress, cleaning out part of Sant' Angelo as well as pressing forward towards Panaccioni. This only served to encourage Ward and his Corps Commander, Lieutenant-General Sidney Kirkman, in their conviction that 4 Division must have at least one viable bridge in their own sector. 'Later that night an order was sent out giving details of regrouping for the night – which based its whole plan on the construction of Amazon Bridge and the passing through of 12 Brigade and its supporting tanks [from 17/21 Lancers] to push on to the [Blue Line] . . .'[19] The order specified that the bridge be completed 'at all costs' and this is just what it meant. A special artillery programme was laid on as well as a heavy smoke-screen covering the site, and the sappers worked in shifts throughout the night under constant indirect mortar and artillery fire. When the bridge was completed, at 04.00 on the 13th, the two engineer units involved, 7 and 225 Field Squadrons, had lost 83 of the 200 men involved.

Both divisions now began to gather a certain amount of momentum. On the 13th the Indians took Sant'Angelo and cleared most of the horseshoe ridge. By the end of the following day they had also mopped up the potentially troublesome Liri Appendix (bounded by the Rapido, the Liri and the southern end of the road running parallel to the Rapido) as well as begun to push out troops towards the Cassino–Pignataro road. The major effort from 4 Division was made by the newly arrived 12 Brigade, who on the 13th pushed another 2000 yards westwards, reaching the Blue Line at several points. 10 Brigade turned northwards and made useful progress towards Highway Six on the 13th and 14th. On this latter day 12 Brigade were if anything too aggressive and 6 Black Watch, aiming for their designated portion of the Cassino–Pignataro road, forged ahead of the battalions on either flank and became somewhat exposed. By now there were even some signs that the Germans were feeling the pressure. When Sant' Angelo had finally fallen to 5 Gurkhas, 1 Royal Fusiliers had been girding up their loins for a parallel attack on 'Platform Knoll', an adjoining strongpoint immediately to the north. But the garrison had evidently watched the attack on Sant' Angelo with much interest, being particularly impressed by the resolution of the Canadian tanks. As soon as the village fell, 'without further resistance this strongpoint hung out white flags and surrendered in a most un-German fashion.'[20] Even some paratroopers were giving themselves up, men from the Parachute Machine Gun Battalion blocking 10 Brigade's wheel northwards. But even as prisoners they were less than convincing evidence of an imminent breakdown of German morale. Their captors in 2 Duke of Cornwall's Light Infantry remained rather puzzled: 'Many of the German prisoners were used as stretcher-bearers on their way back into captivity, and they proved so well disciplined and so unmoved by the shelling going on all around them that it was a source of wonder that they had surrendered in the numbers that they had.'[21] Perhaps their demeanour was meant as some sort of expiation for having yielded in the first place. Certainly there still seemed to be too many Germans for whom death was preferable to such dishonour. One of 6/13 Frontier Force Rifles' attacks was against a garrison made up of

> students from a school of mountain warfare, who had been collected hastily and entrusted with the defence of this key position. They fought fanatically as the Pathans swarmed in amongst them. After the position had been overrun little groups which had fled in the face of the onslaught returned to dig in and to die in last stands. Prisoners emerged with their hands above their heads, holding grenades which they hurled as their captors went forward to secure them.[22]

But there was no such thing as an easy attack in any part of the Liri Valley. Nor were there many that were not characterized by a certain amount of confusion and muddle, particularly as regards planning and deployment. When 2 DCLI attacked towards Highway Six on the 13th, the supporting artillery shoot was partially diverted unbeknownst to the attacking company, and a survivor was heard to say: 'We were told to lean on the barrage, but I didn't expect to have to prop the damned thing up.'[23]

The first attack by 2 Royal Fusiliers, part of the newly arrived 12 Brigade, was hastily mounted and they moved straight across the Rapido and up to the start line.

There had already been casualties, and there would have been more had not a heavy mist denied the enemy any observation of the bridge approaches. . . . Only the mist, indeed, had saved the 12th Brigade from incurring heavy casualties in a daylight approach march, and still heavier casualties in the congested bridgehead – where two battalions of infantry and two squadrons of tanks were crammed in an area of a few hundred yards square.[24]

6 Black Watch, in the same Brigade, attacked the next day towards the Cassino–Pignataro road. They were supported by tanks of the Lothian and Border Horse and once again a heavy mist descended, obliging them to blunder forward on uncertain compass bearings. Visibility was at times down to 5 yards and as the tanks kept wandering off course the infantry CO, Lieutenant-Colonel B.J.G. Madden, adopted the novel expedient of forming his men into a hollow square with the tanks in the middle. This archaic formation lumbered off and made remarkable progress. Once again the mist was a blessing in disguise. As the Black Watch advanced,

the enemy fired wildly through the mist, and when the fire was too heavy the infantry lay down and returned the fire, while the tanks opened up with everything they had. Then the infantry got up again and advanced a few more yards, and so it went on until the Germans were gradually forced back over the hill. . . . It soon became obvious that the Battalion had forced its way through enemy outposts on to what was a very strong position indeed; MGs, mortars and an A–Tk Gun were found (though not marked on the battle map), the latter with a round in the breech which it had not been able to fire as it could not see the tanks.[25]

Not that everything went completely smoothly after that. With this unexpected penetration the Black Watch had outstripped the other battalions of 12 Brigade and when the mist cleared they were exposed to numerous German counter-attacks. They held, and come evening 1 Royal West Kents, 'with tanks in its train, arrived and relieved the pressure. True, the tanks began firing on the Battalion, but they very civilly stopped when the CO in person went out with a white flag.'[26] But these were the worst sort of conditions for the tankmen, in which terrain and weather combined to produce endless difficulties and frustrations. The poor visibility was obviously a serious handicap and, even though the worst of the winter and spring rains were over, much of the ground had not yet dried out properly. Within one day, for example, 17/21 Lancers' 'c' Squadron was reduced to only seven tanks, half of the rest having become hopelessly bogged down. But the terrain also aided the enemy, who could conceal his anti-tank guns in sunken roads, behind walls and hedges, or on the numerous low ridges until the tanks were at almost point-blank range. Battle casualties were also high and in the first six days 17/21 Lancers lost fifty-seven men of all ranks, killed and wounded. No wonder one officer noted at the time: 'Tanks still heavily engaged. . . . This is real war and makes Africa seem like a picnic.'[27]

At the beginning of the battle, Leese had been undecided whether to commit 78 Division in the British or Indian sector but on the afternoon of the 13th he made up his mind. In fact he had little real choice. The failure of 28 Brigade had left him short of men in 4 Division's bridgehead and pressure there had increased yet more because the Polish Corps had been terribly mauled in their first attack on the massif.[28] They had been pulled back to regroup at 14.00 on the 12th and it was clear that a renewed attack could only succeed once the British had sufficiently diverted 1 Parachute Division's attention by cutting Highway Six. But 4 Division could only attempt this with confidence if their left flank, already somewhat exposed, was protected and it was to do this that 78 Division was directed into the northern bridgehead. Kirkman issued his own instructions late that same evening. The fresh Division was to cross the Rapido at once, by Congo, London and Oxford Bridges, and attack out of the bridgehead at the first opportunity. Highway Six, it was hoped, could be cut by the night of the 14/15th and the Polish Corps was alerted to attack at first light on the 15th.

Unfortunately, 78 Division fell badly behind schedule from the start and once again many of the difficulties they encountered were 'staff-made'; in this case 'caused by inaccurate assessments of the conditions at the bridge sites and of the abilities of the sappers to overcome the dearth of approach and exit tracks which doubled the difficulties of bridging.'[29] Incredibly, neither London nor Congo had actually been built when the Corps order for 78 Division's advance was issued. London was directly in front of Sant' Angelo and it had always been assumed that work on it could not begin in earnest until that village had been completely cleared, which did not happen until the late afternoon. As it was a heavy 40-tonner, its erection could not be complete until dawn on the 14th at the earliest. Work on Congo had started but it had not got very far as no one had bothered to tell 4 Division's engineers that there was any immediate intention of supplementing Amazon with another bridge. The first their commander heard of it was when the Corps movement order reached Divisional HQ and he thus had no hope of getting the requisite men to the site before the early morning of the 14th. It is hardly surprising, therefore, to find the following entry in 4 Division's War Diary: 'A phone message from BGS caused considerable consternation as it was decided [that] at dawn on the following day 78 Division would pass through 4 Division sector and cross at Congo Bridge (not yet built) and take over the sector allocated to 28 Brigade.'[30]

In the event Congo was not completed until 08.00 on the 14th. But 78 Division were under strict orders to move that night and so they had to do the best they could with the bridges available, Amazon, Oxford and Plymouth. But the last of these was a somewhat uncertain structure, as well as being as far away from 4 Division's sector as possible, and the other two were the lifelines of the Divisions already in the line. Both were badly needed that night to funnel supplies and local reinforcements into the bridgehead and neither Ward nor Russell was prepared to simply hand them over to Major-General Charles Keightley, the commander of 78 Division. As a result the Division's units 'had to be sent forward to these two bridges as spaces occurred in the . . . [other] Divisions' traffic over them. As luck would have it, Amazon bridge was blocked for three hours during the night by some ammunition trucks which had been hit and set on fire near the bridge.'[31] Keightley's leading brigade, the 38th (Irish), did not arrive in the bridgehead until the afternoon of the 14th.

Keightley had divided his objectives into four stages – the usual 'Lines', this time dubbed Grafton, Pytchley, Fernie and Bedale, all the names of famous Foxhunts. Grafton, along the Cassino–Pignataro road, was supposed to be the start line but as the two forward brigades moved up late on the 14th they found, not for the first time, that much of it was still held by German rearguards and would have to be fought for. According to the 6 Inniskilling Fusiliers' account 'the Battalion was sleeping soundly in a perimeter position . . . until at about midnight a message arrived from Brigade to the effect that the highest authorities considered it essential to the success of the operation as a whole for the Battalion to capture the line of Grafton by dawn. This was a bombshell which caused everyone furiously to think, and produced one of the more morose and sleepy types of "O" Groups at about 03.00 hrs.'[32] The Inniskillings jumped off as early as they could, with 5 Northamptonshire Regiment (11 Brigade) on their right, and managed to clear the position, though neither battalion was securely in place until after noon on the 15th. Even then the general situation remained confused and liaison between different brigades left much to be desired. Brigadier T.P.D. Scott of the Irish Brigade lamented:

'It seemed quite impossible at this stage of the battle to find out where flank formations really were – even their Brigadiers were frequently wrong. This state of affairs made our . . . job difficult. We knew better what the German dispositions were than those of our friends.'[33] The commander of 6 Inniskillings, Lieutenant-Colonel Bala Bredin, was similarly exercised

> coping with the shambles commonly found at the start of most of our battles. . . . Bala . . . had taken the Skins over the water without undue trouble and had linked up with their tanks. . . . But they were only a few hundred yards on from the river – and the locality was still in hot dispute with the opposition. Bala met the bridgehead commander on the river bank, and naturally enquired immediately where his forward posts might be. The gallant brigadier, the commander of the remains of the 10th Brigade, evidently remarked that he would be interested to know that himself, and waving a hand airily in the direction of the firing said, 'Your guess is as good as mine, old boy.'[34]

Sorting out this kind of confusion took the rest of the day and 78 Division was not ready to attack towards the Pytchley Line until 09.00 on the 16th. In other words, through no fault of their own of course, the decisive punch up the Liri Valley was already running two days late.* The Division still had two brigades in the line, the 38th on the left leading off with 3 Lancashire Fusiliers in the van. Both jumped off on time but found the Germans as reluctant as ever to give up ground. The Polish setback at Cassino made its effect particularly felt and the assaulting troops were hard hit by artillery and mortar fire directed from the Monastery. The *Nebelwerfers* were especially effective. An officer of 2 Lancashire Fusiliers described them as

> a typically Germanic terror machine. The barrels discharge their huge rockets one at a time with a sound that is hard to put into words. It is like someone sitting violently on the bass notes of a piano, accompanied by the grating squeak of a diamond on glass. Then the clusters of canisters sail through the air with a fluttering chromatic whine, like jet-propelled Valkyries . . . Few men could truthfully say that they weren't terrified when the 'Nebs' opened up. There were several regiments of them facing us, and the existing

---

* As a consequence, General Anders had been instructed to postpone his renewed attack on Cassino, originally timed for the 15th, until such time as Leese deemed appropriate.

cacophony was soon made infinitely more hideous by scores of
Valkyries.[35]

But 78 Division was something of an élite formation and the leading units
pressed on resolutely. The London Irish conducted a stirring attack,
typical of the dour, close-quarter slogging matches that were the
quintessence of infantry combat. Their own account gives the full flavour
of the day's fighting:

> We . . . had laid on a barrage of several hundred guns to help us and
> the Lancashire Fusiliers on our right. The battle began at 9 am and
> the barrage came down with a crash that made coherent thinking
> difficult for some time. . . . The teamwork was very good. Many
> Germans were trapped in their dugouts by the barrage and our chaps
> were among them with bayonets before they realized the barrage
> had passed on. In other places where our infantry were held up, the
> positions were blasted to bits by HE from the tanks' 75s. Many of the
> German gun crews were caught away from their guns by the barrage
> and were then unable to man them. Others, when they opened fire
> on the tanks, were shot down by the infantry. The show never really
> looked like stopping. . . . H Company . . . eventually broke into the
> village of Sinegogga where a ferocious hand-to-hand fight developed
> which lasted for over an hour with the Boche defending the buildings
> with grenades, MGs and Schmeissers.[36]

And let us not forget 4 Division, still battling it out in the bridgehead
on the inner wing of XIII Corps' wheel towards Highway Six. For many
of its soldiers the battle had now become a waking nightmare in which
attack, bombardment and counter-attack followed each other in
seemingly endless succession. For the men of 1 Royal West Kents, part
of 12 Brigade, the 16th was just another long day's dying. They were
supported by tanks from 19 New Zealand Armoured Regiment and the
latter's history said all there was to say about the terrible price paid by
the infantry. Their attack was mounted at 18.30 and

> small arms and defensive fire from machine gun posts which had
> been overrun by the tanks caused the infantry many casualties. . . .
> These Tommies earned the admiration of the tank crews; for sheer
> guts and unhesitating obedience to orders they were outstanding.
> The battalion started the attack woefully under strength. Two of the
> company commanders were second lieutenants and the other two
> were sergeants. Already they had done four days' hard fighting, but

they went into this attack in true textbook style. In one spot the tank crews saw two sections lying dead, every man still in perfect alignment and properly spaced; each section had been struck by a heavy mortar bomb while advancing through a wheatfield. One company finished the attack with only nine men.[37]

Probably even such sincere, unstinted praise would have brought little recompense to the West Kents themselves. In another of his letters home Lance-Corporal Robson stressed the physical and mental extremes to which he and his mates had been brought:

The papers are no doubt crowing about us and our achievements, but we aren't. We're bitter, for we've had a hell of a time, and are still pressing on. Everybody is out on their feet and one bundle of nerves. . . . We've been Stuka'd, Mortared, Shelled, Machine-gunned, Sniped, and although we've taken . . . the monastery – that is our Div. and a few others – none of us feel any elation. We've cracked the hardest nut of the campaign but the losses sadden and frighten us. Attacking with the tanks, bullets everywhere, front, behind, the flanks – phew! At such times you can be ice cool, all the same you don't think much of your chances . . . At times we've been near to insanity. Not at first, but after six days without sleep and without eating – we were all, and still are, very near to snapping. We've attacked, attacked, attacked from the beginning with numbers dwindling all the time . . . Hicky cracked the day before, now Gordon did . . . He came scrambling out of his own trench to the one in which Steve and I trembled. To sit under a concentrated morning-long bombardment is – what? Hell is understatement. It's definitely unpleasant anyway. And poor Gordon scrambled in head first, crying: 'I can't stand it. I can't stand it – my head, my head.' And he clutched his head and wept. I wiped his forehead, neck and ears with a wet handkerchief, and sang to him. Next day he conquered himself sufficiently to come out with me wandering around sometimes in no-man's-land searching for casualties among burning tanks and ditches full of German dead. When, when, is this insanity going to stop?[38]

Not yet. To Leese the situation was beginning to look promising and at 22.35 on the 16th he gave orders for Anders and Kirkman to launch a simultaneous attack the next morning to finally pinch out Monte Cassino. All the troops involved made appreciable progress and in the Valley 4 Division finally got astride Highway Six, whilst 78 Division got several units through the Fernie Line and almost to Bedale. But the Germans were still fighting hard. Just to the north of Highway Six, for example, was Lieutenant Schimpke's 1 Parachute Anti-Tank Company who on the 17th brought their tally up to twenty tanks. 38 Brigade met equally resolute opposition as they attacked Piumarola, to the left of the Bedale Line. They were successful and found out later that

> this action, rearguard action really, had been a final effort with the Germans racing to get their guns out. From their point of view it may have served their purpose, though the Skins' swift action prevented the full benefit of the day. None the less the enemy had fought the action according to the book – and economically too. There were just a couple of companies and a few tanks, and it had required the whole effect of the Irish Brigade to overthrow them.[39]*

In fact the Germans down the whole length of Eighth Army's front had fought superbly. Even though the initial assault, on the 11/12th, had come as a considerable surprise, and even though Feuerstein's own front had been considerably extended, he proved typically adept at shuffling his forces to parry the most threatening thrusts. Indeed, one is entitled to ask what might have happened to Kirkman's first fragile bridgeheads had not the local German headquarters, of 44 Division, been somewhat tied up with its takeover from 15 PG Division. As soon as Feuerstein realized the attack was in earnest he summoned his alarm units out of the quieter mountain sectors and ordered them to reinforce the Liri Valley as soon as possible.[†] Next he began establishing a reserve on Highway Six near Aquino to back up his front-line troops and guard against any sudden deep penetration down the valley. These reserves were known as the *Kampfgruppe* Schulz and were formed around the reserve battalion of 1 Parachute Regiment. Later on the 12th Feuerstein began to realize the

---

* Though the Irish Brigade itself had also fought superbly well. Its successes were due in large part to the leadership of Brigadier Scott, whose ebullience and organizational abilities welded his three battalions together. The following delightful anecdote gives the full measure of the man: 'We used wireless exclusively during these early days of the advance. Line would have been quite useless with all the shelling and movement of tanks. Our wireless communication was excellent throughout . . . [and] we all got pretty good on the wireless and learned to express ourselves briefly and to the point. I remember on one occasion being asked what the intention of the Battalion was tomorrow and making myself quite clear by saying "Fart and fly hard".' (Scott, *op. cit.*, p.23.)

† These alarm units, from 5 Mountain and 114 Jäger Divisions, consisted of reserve contingents, about a company strong, usually from the reconnaissance units of the various battalions and regiments.

necessity for strategic reserves and he demanded that Tenth Army release one of 90 PG Division's regiments. Tenth Army HQ was reluctant, having deployed Baade's division to meet the possible threat of an airborne landing around Frosinone, but they were eventually prevailed upon to send forward 200 PG Regiment. Kesselring, however, who kept in touch with these developments, insisted on retaining the final say in its deployment. In the event, 200 PG Regiment was diverted to the collapsing French sector on the 13th, and 361 PG Regiment, also from Baade's division, was ordered forward in its place. It did not actually receive these orders until the 14th and did not reach the *Kampfgruppe* until late on the 15th.

Throughout this period the German commanders remained confident that Eighth Army's offensive could be held without having to withdraw into the Hitler Line switch positions. On the 14th, for example, Vietinghoff forbade withdrawal beyond a line Cassino–Pignataro–San Giorgio–Ausonia–Formia. On the 17th, however, Kesselring and Vietinghoff were faced with the possibility of the complete rout of XIV Panzer Corps by the French and Americans [40] and the southern half of this line was already broken apart. The following conversation took place between the two commanders:

> *Kesselring:* '. . . I consider withdrawal to the Senger position necessary.'
> *Vietinghoff:* 'Then it will be necessary to begin the withdrawal north of the Liri. Tanks have broken through here.'
> *Kesselring:* 'How far?'
> *Vietinghoff:* 'To 39 [two miles north-west of Pignataro].'
> *Kesselring:* 'And how is the situation further north?'
> *Vietinghoff:* 'There were about 100 tanks in Schulz's area.'
> *Kesselring:* 'Then we have to give up Cassino.'
> *Vietinghoff:* 'Yes.' [41]

But the withdrawal was to be anything but precipitate, as has already been evidenced by Lieutenant-Colonel Horsfall's remarks on the Piumarola attack. Feuerstein still kept the situation well in hand and divided the Liri Valley into two distinct sectors. Heidrich was given command of the northern half and Baade of the southern, his headquarters having arrived at 08.00 on the 16th. 361 PG Regiment was used to set up a delaying line along the Forme d'Aquino and these more mobile troops were to cover the withdrawal of the rest of the scratch force of infantry, reconnaissance and engineer troops.

The Allies, of course, quickly heard of Kesselring's decision and, once more underestimating the abilities of German rearguards, determined to 'bounce' the Hitler Line before the Germans could get securely ensconced. Much of Alexander's attention was still focused on the Liri Valley and on the 17th he issued an Army Group order, whose substance was conveyed in a cable to Churchill the next day:

> I have ordered Eighth Army to use the utmost energy to break through the Adolf Hitler Line in the Liri Valley before the Germans have time to settle down in it. I have also directed that the Poles push up at once to Piedimonte so as to turn this line from the north. And I have directed that the French Corps, after reaching Pico, turn north and come in behind the enemy facing Eighth Army. If these manoeuvres are successful, it will go a long way towards destroying the right wing of the German Tenth Army. If we get held up in front of the Hitler Line, and we are unable to turn it from north or south, a full-scale mounted attack will be necessary to break it.[42]

The Canadians were to discover that this was a prophetic last remark.

I, 2. The chaotic mountainous terrain of southern and central Italy acted as a brake on the progress of the Allied advance. Even where reasonable roads were available, and all German demolitions had been repaired, enormous distances had to be travelled to gain only a few miles as the crow flies. Above, a British convoy moves along a tortuous road between Cifalco and Cassino. The appalling Italian climate was a further blight on Allied operations. For more than half the year rain and snow were its staple ingredients, both of which eventually resulted in mud. The scene below, except for the Bren Carrier, might well have been photographed on the Western Front in Flanders nearly thirty years before.

1

2

3

3, 4. Two views of the Monastery at Monte Cassino before and after the bombing in February 1944. In both cases the northern corner of the Monastery is shown, as seen from around Point 593. Photograph 4 shows clearly that although the bombing did little for the Monastery's appearance, it only served to increase its defensive value for the German troops who swiftly moved in.

4

5. The Second World War was much more mechanized than any before but the 5
infantry, in Italy as elsewhere, made much of their mileage on foot. Here troops of
II US Corps move up prior to the attacks across the River Rapido and against the
Cassino massif in January 1944.

6

6. Both of these attacks by II US Corps were costly failures. This body of a soldier
of 34 US Division, on Snakeshead Ridge, lay unburied for several weeks.

7

8

7. During the four Cassino battles, between January and June 1944, much of the infantryman's time was spent in holes in the ground. Here soldiers of X British Corps, on the Garigliano, take advantage of a rare respite from enemy shelling. Both, however, have not strayed far from the entrances to their bomb-proof dugouts.

8. German troops, too, had to maintain constant vigilance all along the Gustav Line. Here, they indulge in a horse-laugh about 'good news' from some other front.

9

9. The two most prominent Allied personalities of the Cassino battles were General Mark Clark (left), commanding Fifth US Army, and General Sir Harold Alexander (right) in charge of the Fifteenth Army Group. Appearances here to the contrary, the two did not work well together, Clark being possessed of strong anti-British prejudices that led him on at least one occasion flagrantly to ignore Alexander's instructions.

10. Other formations under Alexander's command included Eighth British Army, commanded by General Sir Oliver Leese (right) and the French Expeditionary Corps under General Alphonse Juin (left). Juin was undoubtedly the outstanding commander on the Allied side and his troops' contribution to the final battle of Cassino was decisive, despite the low repute in which the French were held.

11

11. The senior German commander in Italy was Field-Marshal Albert Kesselring, a Luftwaffe officer, whose willingness to try and hold as much ground as possible in Italy had led to Hitler's preferring him over Erwin Rommel as supreme commander in this theatre.

12. A major part of Kesselring's command was German Tenth Army, commanded by Generaloberst Heinrich von Vietinghoff, seen here in April 1944, when his troops had already held firm behind the Gustav Line defences, hinging on Monte Cassino, for a full three months.

13. The German commander with overall responsibility for the defence of the Cassino sector was General der Panzertruppen Fridolin von Senger und Etterlin (centre), commanding XIV Panzer Corps. Here, he is supervising the evacuation of the Abbot of Monte Cassino Monastery, Gregorio Diamare, after it had become clear that the Allies intended to treat it as a legitimate military target.

13

14. The defence of Cassino town and the Monastery itself was entrusted in turn to von Senger und Etterlin's ablest subordinates, firstly Generalmajor Ernst-Günther Baade, commanding 90 Panzer Grenadier Division.

14

15. As Allied efforts focused more and more on the Monastery, Baade's command was reinforced by paratroopers from 1 Parachute Division. By the end of February 1944, the bulk of the division was in place around Cassino and command there passed to the divisional commander, General-leutnant Richard Heidrich, seen here shaking hands with Kesselring.

7. In February 1944, after the bombing
e Monastery, New Zealand and Indian
s failed to push home an attack made
ompletely inadequate strength. The
axis of attack was along Snakeshead
e seen (*16*) from German positions to
vest. Point 593 can be seen at the top
nd Point 569 below it. The photograph
int 569 (17) shows just how formidable
positions were when seen from close

17

18, 19, 20, 21. The New Zealand Corps tried again in March but were ground to a halt by the German paratroop defenders. Castle Hill (18) was taken, but the cluster of buildings at its foot became one of the centres of German resistance and was never completely mopped up.

Prior to the March attack the town of ● was heavily bombed, but as can be ● photographs 19 and 20, this served only t● the roads, heavily crater the ground, and ● the Germans with yet more forⁿ● strongpoints. Photograph 20 shows the e● to the town, down Caruso Road, and ● Passchendaele-like landscape that lay b● Highway Six and the Station.

20 (above)   21 (below)

22

23

22. New Zealand troops attacking in Cassino town. This photograph was almost certainly staged after the battle was over, but it does show the kind of ground encountered in street-fighting as well as its basic tactics: fire, provided by the Bren gunners in the foreground, and movement, consisting of a frantic squad or platoon rush.

23, 24, 25. But only the most limited gains could be made as the paratroopers clung
tenaciously to their strongpoints, making deadly use of mobile machine gun teams
(23), dug-in tanks and assault guns (24) and heavy mortar concentrations (25).

24

25

26. This photograph clearly was not staged and the exhaustion is visible on the faces of each of these men of 4 Indian Division as they come out of the line in Cassino town.

26

27. Others came out of the line against their will, though the feeling of these Allied prisoners of war must have been tinged with relief that their ordeal was now over.

28. But the fighting in Cassino was an equal ordeal for the paratroopers, as is evident from the faces of these men, snatching a hasty cigarette during a brief lull in the fighting.

29. Tanks proved to be of only limited value in this kind of fighting. In the town they were badly hampered by the rubble and cratered ground, whilst an armoured sortie on to the massif, early on in the Third Battle, was hopelessly mismanaged. The majority of the tanks shared the fate of this New Zealand Sherman tank.

30

30. Having battered their heads against the German defences in Cassino for two agonizing weeks, the New Zealand Corps had no option but to consolidate their meagre gains and wait until Alexander at last concentrated a sufficient number of troops from both Fifth and Eighth Armies. Here stretcher-bearers set to work bringing out the last of the dead and wounded.

31

31, 32. After redeploying most of the divisions in Italy in the Cassino and Garigliano sectors, Alexander launched a renewed offensive against the Gustav Line in May 1944. In photographs 31 and 32, British infantry and Canadian tanks move forward into the Liri Valley bridgehead. In the event the footsloggers had the advantage over the tankmen who soon ran into the appalling traffic jams that vitiated Alexander's hopes for a speedy drive along Highway Six to Rome.

32

33

33, 34, 35. And the Germans had no intention of giving ground up easily. During March and April the paratroopers worked hard on the Cassino defences, dragging up anti-tank guns into the most vulnerable sectors (33) and manning the numerous bunkers and dugouts that overlooked the approaches to the top of the Cassino massif (34 and 35).

34

36. Nor had the Germans put all their eggs in one basket. Between Cassino and Rome   35
were a whole succession of strong defensive lines to which they could slowly fall back.
One of the strongest was the Hitler Line, which was studded with Panther tank turrets
embedded in concrete. Though all, like this one, were eventually overrun, they caused
fearsome casualties amongst the Allied armour and infantry.   36

37

37. As far as the infantry were concerned, men like these were regarded as the lucky ones. They are 'walking wounded' from 78 British Division; men with relatively minor wounds who were out of the action for at least a few days.

38, 39, 40. By far the most significant breakthrough in the Fourth Battle was made by Juin's French Expeditionary Corps. Many of his troops were natives of the Moroccan mountains, notably the *goumiers*, hardy mountain warriors shown (38) in their traditional striped blanket coats.

38

39

But the FEC were no strangers to more modern forms of warfare and many of their tank units (39) were in the advance as the Germans began to fall back from the Gustav and then the Hitler Lines. All Allied formations in the Fourth Battle were considerably aided by their pilots' complete domination in the air. All German movements could thus be accurately plotted and several large enemy columns were destroyed by concentrated artillery fire, as this one (40) was by the French.

40

41

41, 42. One of the most savage operations in the Fourth Battle was the renewed attack on Monte Cassino itself by the Polish Corps under General Wladyslaw Anders (41 – Anders bareheaded). Points 593 and 569 were again major objectives as was Phantom Ridge (42). This rather bland-looking feature was pitted with German bunkers and pillboxes on the reverse slopes and could be swept with artillery, mortar and machine gun fire.

43. Here the Poles bring down their dead after the Germans had finally evacuated the Monastery and the massif. Tragically for the Poles, who had suffered enormous casualties, this evacuation was precipitated by the French breakthrough rather than Polish pressure and it is at least debatable whether their attack should ever have been launched.

43

44

44. For General Clark the whole point of the Fourth Battle was to take Rome and not, as General Alexander wished, to trap the retreating Germans. Here, he poses proudly at one of the entrances to Rome, beneath a sign that was later sawn down and shipped back to his home in the United States.

45. Other soldiers were too tired to care.

45

46

46. Others were
past caring.

47

14
'Sir, I Am Killed'

II Polish Corps on Monte Cassino, 11–18 May 1944

The trumpeters played a curious and appealing call, which ends
suddenly – broken off in the middle of a musical phrase. We were
told this is always played at noon. It commemorates a trumpeter who
was calling the people of Kracow to muster against the Tartars. As
he was playing an arrow pierced his throat. Ever since . . . this call
is played at noon, in memory of the Poles' long struggle against
barbarism and urging them still to fight in the same cause. It always
ends on this broken note.

Harold Macmillan at II Polish Corps
Headquarters, 24 April 1944

On 24 March, after it had been decided to call off the New Zealand Corps'
offensive, General Anders, the commander of II Polish Corps, and his
Chief of Staff, General K. Wisniowski, had been called in to see Leese.
He got straight down to business and told his visitors of the new plan to
open the road to Rome with a full-scale Army Group operation. This
would still entail, however, the taking of Monte Cassino and the massif,
and the battle for these strongpoints was to be 'in Polish hands. But if
General Anders does not agree to undertake this mission I will have to
rely on another Corps, and I will use the Poles on a different axis. Would
you kindly think about it for ten minutes and let me have your decision?'
The Polish generals went into a huddle. Five considerations were
uppermost in their minds, later described by Anders:

1) Monte Cassino was known throughout the world as the key
obstacle barring the way to Rome. The battle, therefore, would have
international impact.
2) The attack would be the first face-to-face contact with the
Germans since 1939.
3) If we were to take Monte Cassino this would give the lie to Soviet
propaganda and prove that the Polish Army was willing to fight the
Germans . . .
4) We gave due consideration to the possible casualties but doubted
that they would be much lighter even if we attacked on another axis,
across the Rapido for example.

5) The role of the Polish troops would have great significance for the
future of the Home Army in Poland.[1]*

Even before the ten minutes were up they agreed to take on this mission.
Leese thanked them and asked them, for the time being, not to share the
news with more than half a dozen other senior Polish commanders.

It should already be clear from the above that the Polish Corps did not
operate according to quite the same strictly military criteria that would
have governed the decisions of other Eighth Army commanders, and in
this regard it is important that we know a little of its history. Like the
French, the Poles had been comprehensively defeated at the beginning
of the war when they had found themselves totally unequipped,
psychologically at least, to counter German *blitzkrieg* tactics. After the
battle of annihilation in the bend of the River Bzura, in September 1939,
they had no alternative but to capitulate to Hitler, and their humiliation
was completed when the Red Army marched in from the east and took
back those territories that had been reintegrated into Poland after the
Treaty of Riga, in March 1921. Russian memories of their defeat by
Pilsudski, which had led up to this treaty, were still vivid and they exacted
stern retribution from their new Polish citizens. Upwards of a million of
them, soldiers and civilians, men, women and children, were rounded up
and dragged off into the oblivion of the Siberian *gulags*. As far as Stalin
was concerned, there they could have rotted; but after the trauma of
BARBAROSSA, in 1941, he felt it politic to pay some heed to his new Allies'
protestations about the Poles' sorry plight. In August of that year, all
Polish citizens on Russian soil were granted an 'amnesty' – in respect of
what 'crimes' remained unclear – and an agreement was signed with the
Polish government in exile, in London, sanctioning the creation of a new
Polish Army. After ceaseless bickering and prevarication, and much
prodding from Churchill and the London Poles, 40,000 soldiers and
officers, as well as 26,000 women and children, were eventually allowed
out of Russia in September 1942.

Their Army, however, was as yet largely nominal and it was not until
this exodus reached Iraq and Palestine that a real start was made to equip
and organize the troops, on British lines. Two divisions were formed, the
3rd Carpathian and the 5th Kresowa.[†] Each had only two infantry

---

* The Home Army (Armia Krajowa or AK) was the main partisan group fighting
within Poland itself.
† 80 per cent of these troops were liberated Russian POWs, though the Corps also had
a useful leavening from General Kapanski's Carpathian Brigade which had fought

Brigades, 1 and 2 Carpathian, 5 Wilenska and 6 Lwowska, but the normal allotment of divisional tanks, artillery and engineers. There was also a Polish armoured brigade with the Corps and this, together with Corps artillery and engineers, brought the total Polish strength to about 50,000 men. They actually arrived in Italy between December 1943 and January 1944 and first went into the line in March. In mid-April they were relieved, going to rest areas at Carpinone and Venafro prior to taking over the Cassino sector.

Two thoughts, the distillation as it were of the points raised by Anders and Wisniowski at their ten-minute conference, dominated the minds of every Polish soldier as they clambered on to the massif. First was their intense hatred of the Germans, a hatred so passionately expressed that it might even have taken the French aback. It certainly seemed rather over the top to many British soldiers. Leese and Alexander, for example, must have raised their eyebrows when they read the opening of Anders' Order of the Day just before the Cassino attack: 'Soldiers! The moment for battle has arrived. We have long awaited the moment for revenge and retribution over our hereditary enemy.'² The soldiers actually relieved by the Poles were made equally aware of this lust for revenge. One officer wrote:

> At night we took them round the battle positions. We got along very well together, though they could never wholly conceal their slight impatience with our attitude. They hated the Germans, and their military outlook was dominated by their hate. Their one idea was to find out where the nearest Germans were and go after them. . . . They thought we were far too casual because we didn't breathe blind hate all the time.³

But the Poles were not simply concerned with throwing the Germans out of their country but also with keeping their territory inviolate after the war, especially from the Russians. And it was this fear of Soviet domination of post-war Poland that underpinned the fanatical nationalism that was to be their second basic motivation in the fighting

---

with the Eighth Army at Tobruk. The Polish contribution to the Allied war effort was, in fact, considerable and it can be fairly stated that they had a lousy war. Several thousand Poles escaped to fight with the French in 1940 only to have to flee again to England. These provided troops for the abortive Narvik operation, in 1940, for an armoured division that suffered terribly during the 'Mace' battle in the Falaise Gap, and a parachute division decimated at Arnhem, together with many brilliant RAF pilots. Total Polish losses in Western Europe were 7608 killed, 19,604 wounded and 1218 missing.

to come. For Anders and his men the Polish Corps was 'a "Little Poland" which . . . [they] had created on Soviet territory and brought back from the east to the west. . . . This "Little Poland" had its own schools, hospitals etc. *but no land.* These institutions gave succour to the Polish nation, the orphans of the Polish Motherland.'[4] Though the whole of Polish history might seem a saga of bitter disappointments there still flourished that same spirit of

> self-sacrifice that had been manifested at the Battles of Grünwald, Chocim and Warsaw. This spirit is passed on from generation to generation and constitutes the bedrock of Polish pride, though foreigners might describe it as 'romanticism'. The Poles entered the Battle of Cassino with the vision of a free Poland . . . carried in the hearts and minds. They joined battle not because they were so ordered but because of their inner love for Poland and their hatred for the . . . oppressor of their Motherland.[5]

Unfortunately, 'romanticism' was probably one of the politer descriptions of Polish attitudes that was exchanged between other Allied leaders. Stalin remained adamant that Lwow and Wilna were part of Russia and Churchill and Roosevelt came more and more to favour some kind of compromise based upon the so-called Curzon Line, a putative Russo-Polish frontier drawn up at the Paris Peace Conference in 1919. The Poles would have none of it, especially the men of II Corps. When some of the London leaders seemed to be wavering, Anders' response was unequivocal. According to one English negotiator: '. . . this [Polish Provisional] Government shows signs of disintegration. General Anders . . . is talking about disowning Mikolajczyk if he as much as mentions the Curzon Line.'[6] Anders continued to refuse to make any concessions and the Allies' patience began to wear thin. Stalin told Churchill the Poles were 'incorrigible'. Anthony Eden spoke of their 'suicide mind' and another British diplomat complained that 'the Poles [are] still determined to do their usual suicide act'. Even the Czech Foreign Minister, Jan Masaryk, trying to act as an honest broker, was reduced to despair. He told one American official that 'he had never seen a group of politicians who could by their every act commit suicide with such professional thoroughness.'[7]

Eventually Churchill tired of the whole business and at the Teheran Conference, in November 1943, he agreed with Stalin in principle that the Curzon Line should form the basis of any post-war settlement of the Russo-Polish frontier, though the Poles were to be compensated with western territory taken over from the Germans. A speech made by

Churchill in the Commons, in February 1944, confirmed Polish suspicions that the Allies had, in their view, sold out to the Russians. Churchill stated firmly that the British had never 'approved of the Polish occupation of Wilna' and went on:

I have an intense sympathy for the Poles, that heroic race whose national spirit centuries of misfortune cannot quench, but I also have sympathy with the Russian standpoint. . . . The liberation of Poland may presently be achieved by the Russian armies after these armies have suffered millions of casualties in breaking the German military machine. I cannot feel that the Russian demand for reassurance about her western frontier goes beyond the limit of what is reasonable or just.[8]

Nor were the Poles encouraged to hear that, only a month before, the first Soviet troops had indeed crossed the pre-war Polish borders, or that they were busily encouraging the formation of a Polish Committee of National Liberation, largely composed of communists, who were more than ready to 'negotiate' with the Russians. Yet all this only made Anders' men yet more resolved to give their all at Monte Cassino. As one unit history put it:

When 2 Corps entered into action, neither the political nor the military situation was encouraging for the morale of the Polish soldier. On the one hand, Winston Churchill's speech, in which he agreed to the legality of Russian territorial claims, robbed us of eastern Poland, half our territory, whilst on the other the approach of Soviet troops . . . made us anxious about their country as well as the fate of their families. Most of these soldiers came from the east of Poland and had had plenty of opportunities to learn about the designs and brutality of Russian-Bolshevik imperialism. However, the soldiers truly believed that their struggle and sacrifice would not be in vain, that the final goal of this terrible war was the victory of justice. Full of this belief and confidence in the Allies they went into battle.[9]

Indeed, it is difficult not to cast the Poles as the tragic lead in the drama of Cassino, or at least as outsiders who at times seemed to be fighting a completely different war from their more hard-nosed Allies. Even at the time both sides were aware of their quite different perceptions of what they were fighting for, but they were never properly able to bridge the conceptual gulf that could make patriotism seem like politicking and national pride become naïvety. For their part the Poles remained somewhat dismissive of the mundane professionalism of the rest of Eighth Army. Colonel H. Piatkowski wrote that at Cassino ' the world saw again soldiers who did not fight for any material wealth – gold, diamonds, oil – but for Freedom. . . . Every battle is a conflict of wills . . . [and for us] the most important weapon was the willpower and stern resolve of the Polish Army.'[10] Another wrote: 'We Poles have a completely different attitude to fighting. We are heroic, the British are methodical. What the British soldier does is prompted by duty, whilst we respond to our sense of commitment and the need for heroism . . . [recognizing that] without our unplanned, spontaneous uprisings the Polish nation would never have existed. . .'[11]

But the British never came to terms with the raw passion of Anders and his men. General Leese found it positively irritating, regarding their concern with the future of Poland as an unsavoury ulterior motive that had no place in the day-to-day business of war. At one stage he was badgered by Anders about certain articles in *Eighth Army News*, the local forces newspaper, which based their 'information on unreliable sources and gave expression to the Soviet point of view'. Eventually Leese sent him a telegram saying he had given due consideration to his point of view but ending with a firm rebuke: 'In my capacity as Army Commander I have to point out to you how superfluous it is for a Corps Commander to express in public any opinions concerning the political situation, in particular at the present moment.'[12]

The ordinary British soldier was simply bemused by the intensity of Polish feelings and the reckless behaviour which was often the result. In the last week of April, when II Corps relieved 78 Division on the massif, each of the latter's battalions was soon made aware that here were men with a rather different approach to war. Of their resolve there was no doubt. According to an officer in the Irish Brigade, 'their motives were as clear as they were simple. They only wished to kill Germans and they did not bother at all about the usual refinements when taking over our posts. They just walked in with their weapons and that was that.'[13] The most important of the 'usual refinements' was trying to avoid being seen or heard by the enemy, but this did not seem to bother the Poles at all. For them these enforced lulls in the fighting were merely a tedious delay, and passively manning the line was not something to which they had given much thought. A sergeant in the London Irish was sent to meet one of their advance parties: 'You might have thought they were taking up bloody elephants instead of mules. The Poles had even brought tents. I couldn't get them to understand there weren't even slit trenches up there, only sangars.'[14] The idea of cowering out of sight of the Germans for days on end was particularly distasteful and many Poles took extraordinary risks in demonstrating their impatience with this sort of hole-and-corner warfare. According to 78 Division's historian every unit was amazed by the Poles,

> for whose reckless gallantry the Division soon learnt to feel an awed, yet amused, admiration. They exposed themselves with the most cheerful abandon. One of 78 Division's Brigade Majors, R.A., has recorded how a Polish gunner subaltern, to whom he patiently and amiably refused a pass that would enable him to circulate in the forward areas in broad daylight, eventually exploded indignantly with, 'I have been in Tobruk. I am not afraid. Give me ze pass.'[15]

The officers, in fact, far from setting a sober example to their men, vied with each other in their acts of bravado. 'Considerable amusement' was caused amongst the men of 5 Northants when the Poles first arrived as they 'were not easy to understand. Difficulties were, however, overcome and when the handover came everything was completed without any hitch. In fact the officers were so well at home that they were last seen staggering about from one sangar to another, beleaguering the Germans with foul oaths. They seemed to know no fear.'[16]

But none of this should imply that the Poles had not thought long and hard about the forthcoming attack. The vast majority of the Corps had not been told what was their objective until just before they went into the line on the massif, but long before this Anders and his inner circle had worked out the basic details of their plan. They still faced much the same problems as the Americans, New Zealanders and Indians before them. The Monastery, the south and west of the massif, and part of the town were still held by Heidrich's paratroopers, whose key strongpoints were located between Colle Sant' Angelo–Point 706–Monte Castellone (3 Parachute Regiment and the Ruffin *Kampfgruppe* from 5 Mountain Division); in the Monastery and the upper reaches of the town (4 Parachute Regiment and the Parachute Machine Gun Battalion); on Points 593 and 569 and around Massa Albaneta (1/3 Parachute Regiment). In reserve was 1 Parachute Regiment, around Villa Santa Lucia and the reverse slopes of Colle Sant' Angelo. All these positions were as strong as ever and Heidrich's division still had a generous allocation of artillery under command, including 242 Assault Battalion, 525 Anti-tank Battalion – the latter equipped with self-propelled 88mm guns – four ordinary artillery battalions from Tenth Army, and one from 90 PG Division. 71 Werfer Regiment was also still in the line and now disposed of forty 15 and 30cm mortars held near Pignataro as well as thirty 15 and 20cm at Villa Santa Lucia. The Division's firepower was therefore still considerable and a Polish report submitted after the battle stressed the enormous difficulties of overcoming a defence built around such tightly integrated strongpoints and fire-plans. Basically, it noted, the German positions were arranged in two concave arcs, between Colle Sant' Angelo and Point 593 and between Point 569 and Monastery Hill:

> In the centre of both these rings there were deep valleys. Defensive positions manned by enemy infantry were sited on the periphery of both these rings and the valleys were covered by enemy fire from all directions. The system of such . . . defences may be compared to a Roman amphitheatre where every single spectator can see the result of the . . . [spectacle] and vice versa. Each single weapon, sited on the circumference of such a ring, could, therefore, take part in the battle for any point of the periphery. The capture of . . . a portion of the defensive ring did not give the attacking troops any possibilities of holding captured ground, unless the portion was wide enough to eliminate a considerable proportion of sources of enemy enfilade fire.[17]

There were those in London, in fact, who thought that Anders should not have accepted the mission offered by Leese. Prominent among these was General Sosnkowski, the commander of all Polish armed forces in the West. According to Anders: 'I told him of the task that had been assigned to the Corps in the coming offensive, but he did not form a favourable view of the plan, which he considered would both be very costly and fail in its objective. He thought an attack should be made across the mountains, leaving Monte Cassino on the left flank . . .'[18] But Anders and his subordinates were made of sterner stuff. When the latter were finally informed of the task ahead they seemed to have no qualms at all and once again astounded English observers by their positive eagerness for the fray. According to Brigadier T.P.D. Scott:

> We were very glad when some Poles started coming over to have a look around. They were being given the unenviable task of capturing the Monastery and breaking through the mountains behind it when the big battle came off. . . . We did all we could to help them because we felt most grateful that someone else would be cracking this unpleasant nut. Their attitude towards this battle was unusual.

Their General expounded the big plot to them which required one Brigade to attack and the other to stay put initially. There was some question about which Brigade was to lead the ball. One Brigadier rose to his feet and asserted with much vigour that his men had fought at Tobruk, were seasoned warriors and would therefore do the attack. The other Brigadier at once rose to his feet and said, No, he was the senior, therefore his Brigade would do the attack. . . . Such a display of keenness to attack in our Army might be misinterpreted.[19]

The issue was eventually amicably resolved and in both the Carpathian and Kresowa Divisions it was decided to attack with only one Brigade up. Anders had drawn certain conclusions from the earlier battles and had decided not to pay any attention to the town, where his men would have to advance through the same murderous bottlenecks, nor to attack directly southwards, towards the Monastery, from Colle Maiola, an axis wholly at the mercy of German flanking fire from Points 593 and 569 and Colle Sant' Angelo.* In fact he decided to leave the whole of Monastery Hill well alone, attacking from the north-west of it against the German positions between Points 569 and 601. The Carpathian Division was to be responsible for seizing the southern end of Snakeshead Ridge and Massa Albaneta whilst the Kresowa Division was to take Colle Sant' Angelo and Point 575. Once this high ground was secure the Monastery would be effectively isolated, and might even fall of its own accord. It would also bring the Poles to the very southern edge of the massif, thus greatly facilitating the passage of XIII Corps in the valley below. The plan offered no magic formulae. Both Divisions' assaults were directed into the teeth of the German defences where they would be subjected to the deadly arcs of fire described above. But it did at least offer the chance of eliminating these positions once and for all, rather than persisting along axes directed straight at the Monastery, the capture of which would not necessarily vitiate the rest of the German *Stellung* on the massif.

In the meantime the Poles did what they could to ensure the success of the attack. As ever, one of their greatest problems was concentrating sufficient men and supplies at the forward points. Two British jeep platoons and five Cypriot mule companies were allotted to the Corps and, by concentrating largely on ammunition, substantial stockpiles were created. Camouflage was extremely elaborate and to mask one forward

---

* The Germans in the town were still facing 1 Guards Brigade, though the latter's role in the forthcoming attack was purely static.

stretch of road to the Carpathian HQ, a vertical canvas screen over a mile long was erected. The men too were camouflaged and in the forward areas all troops had to blacken their equipment and wear special snipers' suits, over 7000 of which were issued to the Poles. Troops who had to move within earshot of the enemy were ordered to exchange their boots for plimsolls. An appreciable number of guns was attached to the Corps, 294 barrels of varying calibre being directly under command and a further 16 heavy guns being temporarily available to shell the Monastery during the first assault.

But there was much that could not be done to Anders' satisfaction, due mainly to the lack of time the bulk of the Poles had had to properly familiarize themselves with their objectives. The plight of the mortar crews was typical. Eighth Army had assigned 72 4.2-inch mortars to the Poles but was unable to provide any crews. Polish anti-tank gunners had to be used instead but as they were allowed only ten days for retraining, their instructors were obliged to allow considerable margins for error in drawing up their fire-plans. This was not the mortar crews' only problem. According to their commander, Major Offenkowski: 'We prepared our positions in deep ravines. There was no sand, so we filled our sandbags with soft soil, using *spoons* to shovel it in because spades were in such short supply.'[20] More serious still was the time allowed for adequate reconnaissance, to gain a comprehensive picture of the German defensive system. A member of Anders' staff wrote:

> . . . the enemy positions had not been adequately reconnoitred. In particular, their defence works (bunkers and shelters) which were well camouflaged to match the surrounding landscape, could not be located. In addition, some of them were built on reverse slopes, putting ground reconnaissance out of the question. There were no orthodox defence works on the position, such as old-type trenches or barbed wire – nothing, in fact, which could give any clue to the system of fortifications.[21]

Nor was using spoons to fill sandbags the least of the ordinary soldiers' travails. The period they spent in the line waiting to jump off must rank as one of the grimmest of tours done by any unit in Italy. The Poles were particularly appalled by the tiny sangars in which they were expected to live for days on end, with any sort of movement ruled out by the proximity of the enemy. Lieutenant E. Rynkiewicz, of 2 Carpathian Battalion, recalled:

> It was impossible to dig in, so we had to improvise. We built rough shelters in any suggestions of hollows we could find, protecting them

with stones, boulders and a number of flattened-out tins. For awnings to shield us from the sun's glare we used our blankets. We were so near to the Germans that in one of our forward positions we could distinctly hear their conversation. . . . Enemy artillery was bad enough but their mortar fire was truly terrifying. It was impossible to hide from it.[22]

A post-action report stressed the short distance between the opposing fronts and the fact that 'even a slight movement drew accurate fire from the enemy who was able to keep almost every square yard of ground under observation.' This in turn meant that 'no hot food could either be prepared or brought up and the food . . . consisted of dry rations.'[23] Another Polish officer, Captain Smereczynski of 14 Wylenska Battalion, particularly objected to the indifferent rations:

We are all half-starved, for the food is really bad. We have biscuits, beef and bacon, but these rations are of such inferior quality that very few of us can swallow them. . . . As for our water, a three-days' supply is kept in tins. When fresh water arrives it is added to the old stock which is rusty. We must restrict ourselves to one pint a day for all purposes. . . . I can remember a mule running away with a load full of cans. One of our men ignores the shooting and goes after the animal with a rifle. In the end he is forced to kill the animal rather than lose the precious water.[24]

But there were many men who were so revolted by the grisly reminders of earlier battles that they had little stomach for either food or water. According to one war correspondent: 'Decaying corpses from previous fighting lay everywhere; fat but insatiable rats feasted on the dead and during the day green flies hovered over their bodies. In such circumstances soldiers were unable to eat and simply threw their food away.' But even so nature eventually made her call and, 'because the soldiers were unable to move throughout the day, even the business of defecation had to be performed into empty ration tins. These were then thrown over into the German lines as a token of our esteem.'[25]

Even for the troops behind the outpost line, the men massing for the actual assault, the Cassino sector had an air of lunatic unreality, the most bizarre contrasts alternately reminding one of the ordeal ahead and of the days of peace that had been snatched away long years since. As one observer put it:

With the coming of May the land, uncultivated because of the fighting, blossomed with red poppies. Each fold of the landscape

was festooned with them. At night swarms of fireflies buzzed madly
above them, whilst higher up shells seared a path through the sky
and the nightingales gave vent to their maddening song. Corpses and
poppies, nightingales and shells, fireflies and the thunder of the
guns, all this helped create a strange atmosphere over which
prevailed the all-pervading fear of death.[26]

Thus they waited for the hour of reckoning, each man lost in his own fears
and his doubts about the future of the beloved homeland. And one doubts
whether Eighth Army's attempts to buoy them up before the battle were
particularly helpful. Indeed, their sense of alienation within the Allied
camp must have been accentuated by certain pronouncements made by
Leese and his staff, who seem to have been totally oblivious of the fact
that for the Poles the forthcoming attack was part of a crusade, which had
no need of flatulent British oratory. Leese's own address to the Poles, on
the morning of the 11th, ended thus:

> We welcome with the greatest joy those divisions that will fight for
> the first time in the ranks of the Eighth Army. We address our
> special greeting to the Polish Corps which fights now at our side for
> the liberation of its beloved country. I appeal to you all. I wish to
> see in your eyes the eagerness for battle. To arms! Every man must
> do his duty in the struggle ahead but final victory will belong to all
> of us.[27]

The head of the British Mission with the Polish Corps was crasser yet and
to the assembled Polish officers he delivered a tub-thumping speech that
was rounded off with a lengthy quote from the Agincourt speech in
Shakespeare's *Henry V*. But at least the Poles only felt embarrassingly
patronized. The same officer addressing the French Expeditionary Corps
might well have provoked an international incident.

Probably the only psychological contribution made by the British to the
Polish Corps' attack was that of the anonymous staff officer who
christened it Operation HONKER. Not a few of Anders' men tried to take
comfort from this rather oblique omen. One wrote: 'Our offensive was
opening, code-named by the Eighth Army HONKER, which denotes the
sounds made by wild geese who are returning to their native land. Was
this a symbol for the Poles, who after their pilgrimages through Iraq and
Libya might now be on their way home, once the battle was won?'[28]

Like every soldier on the night of the 11th, the Poles found the

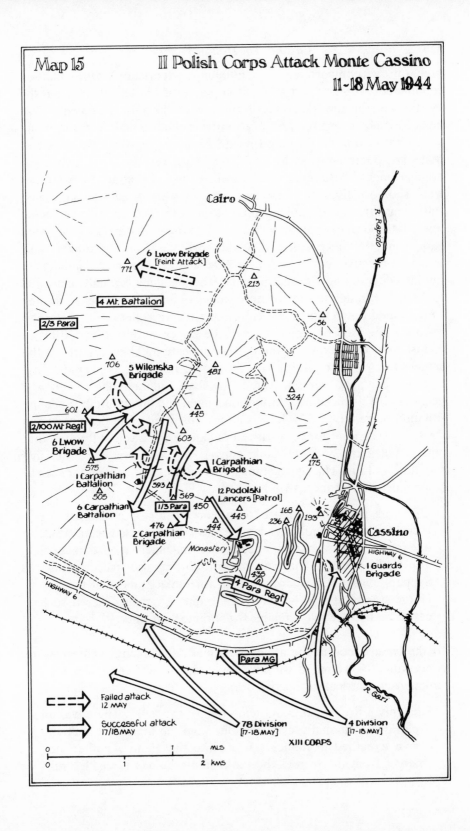

Map 15   II Polish Corps Attack Monte Cassino
11–18 May 1944

Cairo

R. Rapido

6 Lwow Brigade
[Feint Attack]

△ 771

△ 213

4 Mt. Battalion

△ 56

2/3 Para

△ 706   5 Wilenska
Brigade

△ 481

△ 324

601 △

△ 445

2/100 Mt. Regt

△ 603

6 Lwow
Brigade

△ 575

△ 175

1 Carpathian
Brigade

1 Carpathian
Battalion
△ 505

593 △

△ 569

12 Podolski
Lancers [Patrol]

450 △

6 Carpathian
Battalion

1/3 Para

165 △

193 △

236 △

△ 445

△ 476

△ 444

Cassino

2 Carpathian
Brigade

Monastery

HIGHWAY 6

1 Guards
Brigade

△ 435

4 Para Regt

HIGHWAY 6

Para MG

R. Gari

Failed attack
12 MAY

Successful attack
17/18 MAY

78 Division
[17–18 MAY]

4 Division
[17–18 MAY]

XIII CORPS

0   1   MLS
0   1   2 KMS

preparatory bombardment a numbing experience. One platoon commander wrote: 'Apart from 1100 pieces of artillery there were the mortars and the anti-tank guns blazing away – the noise deafened us. We had no idea how long this artillery bombardment would last, but I for one felt that if it went on for long I would go mad. . . . We were confident that no Germans could possibly outlive such a devastating bombardment.'[29] But many did, of course, as all the attacking battalions were soon to discover. First to jump off were 1 and 2 Carpathian Battalions, at 01.30 on the morning of the 12th. The former was aiming towards the Gorge, a narrow valley between the southern end of Phantom Ridge and the steep sides of Snakeshead, and, once through, their primary objective was to be Massa Albaneta. They almost immediately ran into devastating German fire and, though some sub-units managed to struggle through to the northern slopes running up to Albaneta, they were pinned down there by increasingly heavy artillery fire. Efforts to restore some kind of momentum to the attack were not helped by an almost total breakdown in radio communication. Thus 'reports of the actual situation were reaching the Brigade Commanders only indirectly, often casually, and were far from being exact and up to date. There was no possibility of checking information gained and this naturally made the situation more obscure.'[30] In this attack much faith had been placed in the tanks that went forward with the infantry but it was still found that mines, bazookas and anti-tank guns gave the Germans a decisive superiority of fire. Hardly any tanks, indeed, were able to get forward to help reduce the Albaneta strongpoints:

> One tank from the support troop came to a stop amongst some rocks, the second one struck a mine and went up in flames, the third one received a direct hit by a heavy shell and had its track damaged. The leading tank of the tank troop following also struck a mine. Sappers engaged in clearing a path for tanks found that the . . . Gorge was unusually heavily mined and . . . they suffered such casualties that they were unable to continue their work.[31]

Of the twenty men in the attached sapper detachment, eighteen were either killed or wounded within a few hours. The fate of some of the tankmen was particularly horrific:

> Suddenly a fire began underneath one of the tanks. There was an explosion. A human rocket flew out from the top of the tank and a man wreathed in flames ran off into the night. Another man emerges from the turret – he looks like a human torch. He rolls

around on the ground, shrivels, burns out, dies. No one else follows them out of the tank.[32]

2 Carpathian Battalion attacked Point 593 and the sheer fury of their first onslaught carried the position. The troops immediately pressed down towards Point 569 but the Germans were now beginning to recover and Polish casualties had already been severe. In this latter respect the remarks of one Polish officer show that there was at least some justice in the complaints made by 78 Division veterans. As German resistance stiffened, he recalled, 'most of us were content to huddle ourselves in the holes and hollows we had found, but some soldiers, in my opinion, were stupidly reckless. Many were killed through their carelessness. I noticed that the Germans very wisely stayed under cover at all times, whereas our men would suddenly stand up to hurl defiance at the enemy. They paid dearly for these and similar acts of bravado.'[33] As the attack slowed, the Germans, true to form, immediately mounted a counter-attack on Point 593. This was driven off, as was a second one half an hour later. But Colonel Heilmann, of 3 Parachute Regiment, was not a man to give up easily. Scraping together a company-strength force from the reserves of his 1 and 2 Battalions, Heilmann sent them forward again. Once more they failed to seize the crest but many of the survivors went to ground in craters or behind boulders on the south-western slopes and began to snipe at the Polish positions only a few yards away. When darkness fell Heilmann ordered yet another attack and the paratroopers crept right up to the Polish perimeter under the cover of a mortar bombardment. One Polish officer said:

. . . the German guns blasted us so effectively that we were obliged to throw ourselves flat and crawl around looking for cover. It was practically non-existent, since all the sizeable boulders had been blown to bits by our own artillery. As we hunted feverishly for somewhere to hide, the defenders hit us with everything they had. It seemed impossible that men could live in such a holocaust. Breathing a prayer, I groped blindly towards a shellhole. It was filled with bodies, sprawling on top of each other. Most of them were lifeless, but . . . I clawed frantically at those on top in an effort to burrow deeper. . . . We were fast approaching the end of our tether. We no longer knew where to shoot or whom to aim at. We were mentally blank, stupefied, exhausted.[34]

As soon as the bombardment ended the paratroopers rose up and rushed forward. After bitter hand-to-hand fighting the few surviving Poles were either captured or forced to retreat back along Snakeshead. Only one officer and seven men were found alive on Point 593 and even next morning, when the stragglers had come in, 2 Battalion numbered no more than a few dozen men.

5 Wilenska Brigade jumped off about half-an-hour after the Carpathians, attacking up Phantom Ridge towards Colle Sant' Angelo with the eventual aim of seizing Points 575 and 505. Here, too, the troops ran into heavy fire from almost the first moment. Heavy as the barrage had been it had made little impact on the numerous German bunkers and dugouts built into the reverse slopes. These miniature forts were 'constructed of stones and rocks, heavily strengthened by a miscellaneous assortment of scrap metal and equipment . . . [and] were mostly built over crevices, cavities and depressions in the rocky ground.'[35] The Poles pressed forward with the utmost gallantry but were unable to breast the crest of the ridge except in one or two isolated spots. Again it was impossible to co-ordinate the actions of the companies and platoons because of the almost total breakdown in communications. Those few men who actually got onto Phantom Ridge were from the outset in an almost impossible position: 'Companies of our men were intermixed with uncaptured enemy pillboxes and both sides were fighting each other with resulting casualties. . . . At that time the Brigade Commander was totally unacquainted with the situation, as all intercommunication by line and by runners was impossible and wireless sets were either smashed up or their operators killed.'[36] The Polish artillery and mortars did what they could to support the attack. One officer recalled:

> We started firing at the same moment as the artillery and the men were so quick at handling the weapons that after a while the mortar barrels became overheated. They cooled them off with their own water rations, and when all the water had gone they took the only course open to them. They urinated on the hot steel and brought down the temperature that way. Not one of our barrels burst during the action.[37]

But because of the radio failure the Polish gunners usually had little idea of where their own men were or what parts of the German line should be saturated. The Germans had few such problems and within a short space of time they were bracketing the whole eastern face of Phantom Ridge with the most terrible fire:

> . . . the Germans . . . decided to employ a rolling barrage. This rolling fire moved up and down Phantom Ridge destroying

everything. The troops had no means of fighting against it and were struck down or forced to seek cover behind the rocks. But stones were no protection and screams and moans could be heard from all directions. A young boy, wounded and in a state of shock, knelt down, stretched out his hands and shouted imploringly to the bare hillside, 'Why are you shooting? Surely you can see that there is little we can do as we are now!' Suddenly a sergeant, unable to stand it any more, jumped up and started dancing a folk dance as he had once done back in Krakow.[38]

By 03.00 all three battalions of 5 Brigade were committed on Phantom Ridge and shortly afterwards 18 Battalion, from 6 Lwowska Brigade, was also sent in. In all of them the desire to fight on burnt as strongly as ever. Doctor Majewski, at the Polish Casualty Clearing Station, told of the men who staggered in for treatment:

> Some crawled to us on their own, others were helped by friends, others were slung over shoulders like sacks. The helpers, the wounded and the dying were all in a state of excitement. At times I thought I was dreaming. There was no fear to be seen in them, only a kind of fury and rage. . . . A corporal came and . . . knelt before me without a word and showed me his back. Through his torn tunic I saw a wound the size of two hands, the shoulder-bone bared. . . . He wouldn't let me give him an injection. I said: 'I can't evacuate you without an injection.' The corporal stood up and said: 'I'm not being evacuated, I must go back. I'll be killed, but I shan't let you evacuate me until I've thrown all my grenades.'[39]

But it was simply not possible to continue the attack. The leading battalions of 5 Brigade, the 13th and 15th, had been virtually destroyed. In the valley below Phantom Ridge lay 'corpses, twisted human shapes, shattered limbs, bloody bits of bodies. In 13 and 15 Battalions there are only the dead and wounded. No one has escaped injury. Captain Jurkowski's Company has ceased to exist.'[40] General Anders felt that there was no choice but to call off the whole offensive and the survivors were pulled back to their start lines. Heidrich's paratroopers had held firm yet again.

Anders immediately set to work drawing up plans for a renewed assault though, as we have seen, Leese reserved to himself the decision as to when it was actually going to be launched. The same basic strategy was to be repeated, though this time the Kresowa Division, leading off with

6 Lwowska Brigade, were to concentrate upon the northern end of Phantom Ridge and direct their whole effort towards Colle Sant' Angelo. Only when this was secure were they to move down towards Point 575 and Massa Albaneta. Thus the responsibility for taking Albaneta was now wholly that of 3 Carpathian Division and they too slightly altered the axis of their attack. Only a battle group was to attack frontally through the Gorge, to draw fire away from the northern slopes of Phantom Ridge, whilst the main attack was to be from the east, down the slopes of Snakeshead. The rest of the attacking Brigade, 2 Carpathian, was to secure Point 593 and prepare a jumping-off point for an assault eastwards towards the Monastery.

In the days that followed the Poles concentrated upon organizing their artillery support, reconnoitring enemy positions and trying to clear the way for their armoured support. A continuous artillery programme was organized for the whole of the lull and it was also decided that this should be kept up throughout the second attack, with the troops following much more closely behind the barrage than had been the case on the 12th. Greater attention was also paid to the Monastery. Its eastern and south-eastern walls were still standing and from behind them German machine gunners had wreaked havoc on the troops attacking Points 593 and 569. The commander of the Carpathian artillery, Colonel Lakinski,

decided that the only answer was to use an anti-tank gun up there by night, passing through Villa and following the winding track to a position which would give good observation towards the Monastery. It was an agonizing business getting that gun where we wanted it, but it was well worth the trouble, for at last we could deal with the enemy machine guns firing from the basement windows of the Abbey.[41]

The artillery programme was a sore trial to the Germans. The commander of the conquerors of Point 593, Major Veth, noted: 'Impossible to get wounded away . . . enveloped in a smoke screen. Great number of dead on the slopes – stench – no water – no sleep for three nights – amputations being carried out at battle headquarters. . .'[42] But the paratroopers remained as vigilant as ever and Polish patrolling and mine-clearing were still extremely hazardous enterprises, always liable to come under fierce fire from any number of concealed strong-points. An eye-witness recalled one young Polish soldier about to go out on patrol who 'asked his officer, "Do I have to die?" and then turned towards the exit [of the dugout]. There was no protest in his question, it was a simple statement of fact.'[43] The sappers were a little less fatalistic and those responsible for tackling the dense minefields in the Gorge adopted a novel expedient. According to the commander of the Kresowa Division's engineers, Lieutenant-Colonel Maculewicz, this whole area 'was under good observation and constant fire. As the Germans kept on blazing away at us by day and by night, the advantage to be gained by operating during the hours of darkness was negligible.' He therefore decided to borrow two tanks and assigned to each of them a troop of four sappers and one officer. 'The first tank then moved up to the edge of the minefield, while the second one stayed thirty yards behind to provide cover. The officer and his men could thus work under the body of the tank, where they were reasonably safe from enemy fire. . . . After each sapper had disposed of three or four mines, the first tank pulled back and the sappers on the reserve tank took over. We continued with this system for three hours in broad daylight, clearing approximately a hundred mines.'[44] Throughout the whole period before the second attack Maculewicz's sappers had only seven minor casualties.

For everyone there, however, the whole of Cassino had now become a vision of the Inferno. Cadet-Officer Pihut, of 6 Carpathian Battalion, asserted: 'Monte Cassino was something out of another world. We lived in a shifting murk of drifting smoke, heavy with the pestilential reek of death. The very ground we clung to was trembling under the artillery barrage. Yet in the night-time, when the guns stopped firing, we could occasionally hear nightingales singing.'[45] Even in the so-called 'rest areas' it was impossible to escape the ubiquity of death. When Captain Smereczynski was sent back for a brief respite he found that he had to sleep

> more or less alongside a dead Indian. The corpse . . . was buried under a few loose stones, as were the dozens of other bodies we had found scattered everywhere. . . . The place was alive with rats, big, bloated creatures that scurried about with impunity while we slept. The sickly sweet smell of decaying flesh was nauseating and we could do nothing to rid ourselves of it. We even sacrificed blankets, employing them as shrouds for the corpses we discovered, but could not eliminate the pestilential odours that clung to the whole area.[46]

And everywhere too, as H-Hour approached, was the familiar pall of dirty smoke that was being released to mask the gun area and supply routes. In the town and on the eastern fringes of the massif it seemed to some as if the creatures of the Inferno had also spewed forth, as strange, disembodied voices were heard amidst the gloom. Just prior to the second attack the Guards commander in Cassino town had decided that the time had come to make use of the broadcasting apparatus which had been erected in the middle of the town. Accordingly, all artillery fire in the area of the town was suspended, and in a place where there had always been a tendency to speak in whispers, the silence was broken by an enormous voice, repeating in German: 'If you wish to surrender, come out with your hands up. . . . You have fought well. To fight on is senseless. Look over your shoulders. The Poles are at the gates of the Monastery. . . . Cassino is lost to Germany.' A few shots were aimed at the loudspeakers, but not a single deserter came over.[47]

And there were some who still lay out in no man's land, locked in a personal nightmare that almost beggars description. One such had been wounded at the very beginning of the first attack and had got himself trapped in the wire. When he came to he found himself hopelessly enmeshed and then

felt a sharp pain in his left leg. He looked at it and could not understand. He was lying flat on his back but the leg was hanging down vertically. Then he realized that it was utterly smashed and was only hanging on by a bit of muscle. The leg was a pulp and looked rather like a black pudding. . . . Eventually the wound turned into one enormous scab and it ceased to bleed. . . . His cells were attacked by bacteria and pus flowed out of the wound. . . . It was turning gangrenous. . . . He stayed there for six days and seven nights: no food, no water, no dressing. . . . His body was smashed but he was not defeated; he did not want to die. Even after six days of waiting he still did not want to die. The artillery was deafening, the air was thick with fumes, dust and smoke. . . . He began to hallucinate. The battle of anti-bodies and bacteria was coming to a climax; delirium followed. On the 18th he came out of his coma. The British found him covered all over with flies and took him to a first-aid post. [He survived.] Thus did the human body fight to the very end against this death by degrees.[48]

The Poles jumped off again on the night of 16 May, at 22.30. Though new brigades were leading the assault even these had been sorely tried during the preceding days and nights. One observer wrote: 'When the second attack began . . . the soldiers were drained physically and psychologically. The issue hung on a knife-edge . . . but the soldiers were so exhausted that only . . . vigorous leadership could overcome their inertia.'[49] But such leadership was forthcoming in abundance. On

Phantom Ridge, Colonel Jurek, commanding 5 Brigade, personally went forward into the very front lines 'to sustain morale. He felt that the soldiers must be made aware that the whole offensive was going forward, that bold leadership was at hand.'[50] One of his battalion commanders, Lieutenant-Colonel Kaminski, was leading the attack on Colle Sant' Angelo when

> he stumbled, a burst of machine gun fire in his chest. Major Haraburda ran towards him, a shot piercing his steel helmet. Kaminski was turning pale . . . Shots were coming from all directions. He bent down towards Kaminski who said: 'Haraburda, this is for Poland.' And again: 'For Poland.' And with the last faint movement of his lips: 'This is for Poland.'[51]

Others were rather more prosaic, seizing on that strongly Rabelaisian facet of the Polish character as a means of relieving tension and trying to get the men to forget their fears. In one battalion a liaison officer arrived from Divisional headquarters and, finding the men pinned down, 'begins to tell a joke about a village priest. Everyone can hear him and all join in the laughter. Laughter that is as vital as a bubble of oxygen, that enables men to survive.'[52] On the slopes of Colle Sant' Angelo one company was in dire straits. Its commander was on the verge of hysteria and turned frantically to his major, shouting

> 'Can I threaten the Germans with a revolver? What good is a revolver?'
> Suddenly the Major turns to us laughing his head off. 'Good sign, lads,' he shouts.
> The lads look bewildered. Are the tanks coming? Have the Germans packed up, or what? The Major lifts his shoe and shouts again, 'Good sign, lads! I just stepped in some shit!'
> Everyone starts laughing. If he can maintain his composure thus then we are not finished yet. The lads follow him up the slope . . .[53]

For leadership of this kind was at a premium during the second attack. 5 Division, on Phantom Ridge, had started remarkably well. A battle patrol from the leading assault battalion had probed the extreme northern end of the ridge just before the main assault was due to begin and had found it very thinly held. The few German positions there were overrun and eventually the whole battalion was filtered on to the ridge. The second assault battalion was able to use these positions as its jump-off point and by dawn had seized most of Colle Sant' Angelo. 3 Carpathian

Division also began well in its attack on Point 593. According to Lance-Corporal Dobrowski, of 5 Battalion:

> We lie there waiting . . . and then at last comes the order to move. Always the same old cry. We must take ammo, ammo, ammo. Apart from 'our normal ammunition each of us must take between thirty and forty pounds of grenades. It is a hot day and the going is difficult. When we begin to ascend Hill 593, the weakest soldiers can no longer keep pace. We are in no particular formation. No sections; no platoons. The situation is such that we must use our own initiative. Later we can reorganize – those of us who are left. Now we engage the enemy. All is confusion and the Germans' positions are mixed with ours. With munificent impartiality we hurl our hand-grenades. From the neighbouring heights Spandaus, Schmeissers and heavy machine guns catch us in a murderous cross-fire. On the first day our casualties are high – 40 per cent, I believe.[54]

The position was taken, and then savagely counter-attacked, but by 11.30 on the 17th was firmly in Polish hands.

But these were to be the only gains that day. For the umpteenth time the paratroopers took everything that could be thrown at them, recoiled a little, and then consolidated and refused to give another inch. On Colle Sant' Angelo they counter-attacked repeatedly and many positions changed hands several times. German artillery and mortars lashed the exposed slopes throughout the day. At one stage the forward companies were cut off from their porters and the precious loads of ammunition:

> The Poles, deprived of their weapons, unable to move back, crouched beneath the German bunkers. They threw themselves flat and dared not change position or move at all. They could not even bend their elbows, move their heads or straighten their cramped legs, as the Germans had a perfect view of everything going on below. Minute by minute, hour by hour, casualties mounted. It was more than nerves could stand and mass hysteria began to grip the men. . . . One soldier slowly gets to his feet and then sits down cross-legged, as though he were in the park. A shot rings out and he is killed. Others, cowering helplessly, begin to throw stones at the Germans. And then, incredibly, someone begins to sing the Polish national anthem: 'Poland will not surrender, not yet. . .' All the soldiers join in the chorus, on the summit of Colle Sant' Angelo, the mountain of death.[55]

Eventually contact was re-established with the porters and, when fresh companies also arrived, the Poles were able to push forward once more. By dusk they had wrested control of Colle Sant' Angelo from the paratroopers, but were now so weary and depleted that there could be no hope of turning southward to aid the Carpathian attack towards Albaneta. Major Smrokowski, of the Divisional staff, reported over the radio that 'the Kresowa Division had gone for 36 hours without food and water and the men were reaching the end of their tether.' According to Colonel Rudnicki, 'the situation was critical. Casualties had been enormous. Most of the ammunition . . . was used up and there was nothing left to fight with. The platoons and battalions were hopelessly intermixed. . . . It was impossible to say what dawn would bring.'[56]

The situation was little better for the Carpathian Division, who had found it impossible to capitalize upon the victory on Point 593. Progress was blocked both to east and west. The attack on the Monastery was soon abandoned as a non-starter and, despite the most strenuous efforts, it proved impossible to make much headway towards Massa Albaneta. One Pole described the beginning of the attack as his company tried to creep up unobserved: 'Though our boots are wrapped in rags every step is a strain on the nerves. . . . Slowly . . . very slowly . . . stooping, the soldiers make slower and slower progress. They look like ghosts. . . . But . . . suddenly one, two, then a third spandau started spitting out their lethal bullets. . . . The boom of grenades . . .' All hope of surprise lost, the men dashed forward. 'Lieutenant Baran gathers up the remains of the 1st and 2nd Platoons and renews the assault. He goes right close to the bunkers, he is wounded in the neck, but does not care. The soldiers surge up, hurling grenades at the Germans. Then with one last cry, "Jesus! Mary," Baran collapses on the rocks like a felled tree-trunk.'[57] A vignette described by Cadet-Officer Pihut gives the full flavour of the dedication and heroism shown and is, indeed, symbolic of the whole Polish effort for the Allied cause, an effort that in their eyes was so poorly rewarded:

> . . . whenever I think of Cassino, I always see our Sergeant-Major, a regular NCO, then in his fifties. He was a real soldier. Although badly wounded by machine gun fire he refused to retire without reporting to his commanding officer. We urged him to pull back as far as possible, but his reply was, 'No, I can't leave the company without telling the Commanding Officer.' Shortly afterwards a burst from an enemy machine gun finished him off. Before he died he drew himself erect and gasped out, 'Sir, I am killed!'[58]

Yet despite all these prodigies of valour Albaneta still held out and by nightfall on the 17th the men of Pihut's battalion 'were all on the verge of complete nervous and physical collapse'.[59]

It will always remain a matter of conjecture, in fact, just how the Poles would have fared had they been called upon to mount another assault on the western edge of the massif. Happily this proved unnecessary, for Eighth Army's progress in the valley below and remarkable advances by the French (to be discussed in the next chapter) had already persuaded Kesselring and Vietinghoff that the whole Gustav Line, including Monte Cassino, was no longer tenable. Late on the 17th, therefore, Heidrich was ordered to begin pulling his men back. The latter was less than pleased. According to Kesselring: 'The 1st Parachute Division did not dream of surrendering "its" Monte Cassino. . . . I had personally to order these last, recalcitrant as they were, to retire, an example of the drawback of having strong personalities as subordinate commanders.'[60] Once the order was finally accepted the paratroopers began slipping out of the bunkers and pillboxes and scrambling down the steep reverse slopes of the massif towards Piedimonte and the Hitler Line positions. The majority of the Monastery garrison ran into Polish and British patrols and were killed or captured. But a substantial number of men did manage to escape, still capable, as they were to prove, of manning strong blocking positions on the Hitler Line and down the whole length of the Liri Valley. Many of them continued to feel that they had not been defeated at Cassino but only obliged to withdraw to conform with the rest of the German line. Von Vietinghoff echoed these sentiments after the war when he wrote: '. . . the gains made in the Cassino battles [by the Allies] did not repay the heavy expenditure in men and material. In spite of the deep bulge in its rear, Cassino was not taken by storm during the May offensive, but was reluctantly abandoned by 1 Parachute Division on the direct orders of 10 Army HQ.'[61]

But the Poles had no wish to quibble. As one officer in front of Massa Albaneta wrote: 'We hung on grimly until the exciting news arrived that the Monastery was in our hands. I shall never forget the pure joy of that moment. We could hardly believe that at long last our task was done.'[62] So weary were the Poles that when they first intercepted the German radio message giving the orders to withdraw they were unable to find any infantry with the strength to clamber up to the Monastery. Eventually word was sent to the Carpathian Division's Reconnaissance Regiment, 12 Podolski Lancers, and they sent a patrol forward from Point 445. These men were unable to lay hands on a Polish national flag and so, at 09.50 on the 18th, they raised a home-made regimental pennant above the ruins. Shortly afterwards one of the Lancers played the Krakow *Hejnal*, a medieval military signal, on his bugle. According to one eye-witness:

There was a lump in my throat as, through the echo of the cannon's roar, the notes of the *Hejnal* rang out from the Abbey. . . . These soldiers, hardened by numerous battles, only too well acquainted with the shocking wastefulness of death on the slopes of Monte Cassino, cried like children, as, after years of wandering, they heard not from the radio, but from the previously invincible German fortress, the voice of Poland, the melody of the *Hejnal* . . .[63]

15
'Où Sont les Pistes Jeepables?'
Fifth Army Pierces the Hitler Line, 11–24 May 1944

Come on, you bastards, you'll never get to Rome this way!

> *Lieutenant-Colonel R. E. Kendall, CO*
> *2/351 Regiment, 13 May 1944*

We are going to push back the Boche . . . Then I can die. That is of no consequence.

> *Lieutenant Chedeville 1/4 RTT, 13 May 1944*

The success of Fifth Army's offensive in the Fourth Battle depended largely in its opening stages on the abilities of the French Expeditionary Corps to live up to the forecasts for a speedy breakthrough given in Juin's April memoranda. The French had to gain early victories and then keeping pushing fast and hard so that the Germans were kept continually off balance. As he wrote to de Gaulle on 8 May: 'Success is based upon the simultaneity, the brutality and the rapidity of the attacks which should not leave the enemy the time to re-establish himself. . . . [The Germans] certainly feel that an attack is imminent, but it may well be that, trusting in the impenetrability of the Aurunci massif, they are actually expecting the main effort to be made in the Liri Valley and in the coastal sector. In this case, our attack in depth would have a chance of surprising him yet more.'[1] On the same day he delivered a stirring speech to the officers of 3 DIA in which he reiterated his hopes for a decisive breakthrough, though he was honest enough to admit that nothing in war could be guaranteed: 'I do not know what we are going to find in front of us, whether we will encounter hard going or easy. But what I do guarantee to you is that we have taken all possible steps; if the going is hard, to force our way through, if it is easy, to go far, very far.'[2]

Every French unit had been imbued with this emphasis upon speed and deep penetration. The orders for 2/5 RTM, for example, insisted: 'Manoeuvres should aim to speedily outflank enemy resistance. Speed should be the prime characteristic in order to obtain maximum surprise and to create confusion amongst the fairly dense enemy dispositions.'[3] This battalion's parent formation, 2 DIM, made similarly Dantonesque demands:

The essential point is to travel as fast as possible. . . . Once the breakthrough phase is completed . . . it will be necessary . . . to be as aggressive as possible, to tie down only the minimum forces to guard the most important points, and not to feel it necessary to hold on to captured positions, but to manoeuvre within the defined zone of action and *seek out the enemy* and *attack him*, making further resistance pointless in the shortest possible time.[4]*

The French plan was to attack with three divisions and part of the fourth down the whole length of the Garigliano bridgehead from the Liri to Castelforte. On the right was I Division de Marche d'Infanterie (I DMI), made up in large part of Free French troops who had fought with Eighth Army in North Africa.† They were to attack along the southern banks of the Liri, towards San Giorgio a Liri, and had a generous allotment of French and American armour to support them in the hopefully more negotiable river valley. To their left was 2 DIM, aiming for the peaks that had defeated X British Corps in early February. They had two main axes of attack, on the right Monte Ceresola–Monte Girofano and on the left Monte Faito–Monte Feuci–Monte Maio. Ultimately this division was to debouch into the Ausonia–Esperia Valley, but the clearance of the lower valley, to the east of the River Ausente, was the responsibility of 4 Moroccan Mountain Division (4 DMM) and 3 DIA. The former was to attack westwards towards the Ausente, jumping off from Monte Fuja and Monte Furlito, whilst the Algerians were initially to attack with only one regiment, 4 RTT, the heroes of Belvedere, whose mission this time was to complete the conquest of Monte Damiano and the fortified village of Castelforte.

The attacks jumped off simultaneously with those of Eighth Army and were preceded by just the same artillery saturation as in the Liri Valley.

---

* It is to be noted that General Clark had clearly been infected by French enthusiasm and aggressiveness. At a Fifth Army Conference, on 5 May, an American divisional commander had defined his task in the first days of the forthcoming offensive as to 'seize the first enemy positions and then regroup his forces on the conquered position and prepare to receive the enemy's counter-attacks. This was clearly not what was envisaged and General Keyes and then General Clark clarified matters by insisting once more on the fundamental importance of the factors of speed and a bold exploitation of any successes.' (Carpentier, *op. cit.*, p.157.)
† The Division usually referred to itself by its original title, I Division Française Libre, although this had been officially changed to I Division d'Infanterie Motorisée in August 1943 and to I Division de Marche in May 1944. It is hard not to see political overtones in these changes in nomenclature, though I DMI had officially agreed to amalgamate with the Armée d'Afrique in April 1943. The Division did retain its original arm badge of the Cross of Lorraine. The rest of the French Corps sported the effigy of a Gallic cock bristling against the rising sun.

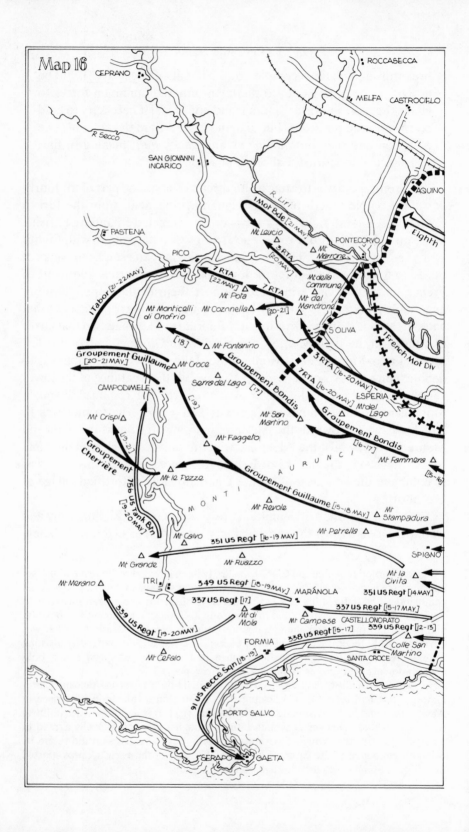

Map 16

ROCCASECCA

CEPRANO

MELFA   CASTROCIELO

R. Secco

SAN GIOVANNI
INCARICO

AQUINO

R Liri

1 Mot Bde [21 MAY]

Mt Laucio

PONTECORVO

Eighth

PASTENA

PICO

△ Mt
Marrone

3 RTA
[20 MAY]

Mt della
Commune

1 Tabor [21-22 MAY]

7 RTA
[22 MAY]

7 RTA

Mt del
Mandrone △

Mt Pota

Mt Cozanella △

[20-21]

S OLIVA

Mt Monticelli
di Onofrio
△

1 French Mot Div

Groupement Guillaume
[20-21 MAY]

△ Mt Croce

[18]   △ Mt Fontanino

Groupement Bondis
[17]

3 RTA [16-20 MAY]

CAMPODIMELE

Serra del Lago

7 RTA [16-20 MAY]

ESPERIA

Mt Crispi △

[19]

Mt San
Martino △

Groupement Bondis
[16-17]

Mt del
Lago

Groupement
Cherrière

[19-21]

△ Mt Faggeto

Mt le Pozze △

Groupement Guillaume [15-18 MAY]

AURUNCI

Mt Fammera △

[15-16]

756 US Tank Bln
[19-20 MAY]

M O N T I

Mt Revole △

△ Mt
Stampadura

Mt Calvo △

351 US Regt [16-19 MAY]

Mt Petrella △

SPIGNO

Mt Grande △

Mt Ruazzo △

Mt la
Civita △

Mt Merano △

ITRI

349 US Regt [18-19 MAY]

MARÁNOLA

351 US Regt [4 MAY]

337 US Regt [17]

337 US Regt [15-17 MAY]

339 US Regt [19-20 MAY]

Mt di
Mola △

Mt Campese   CASTELLONORATO

339 US Regt [2-15]

FORMIA

338 US Regt [5-17]

Colle San
Martino △

Mt Cefalo △

SANTA CROCE

91 US Recce Sqn [18-19]

PORTO SALVO

SERAPO   GAETA

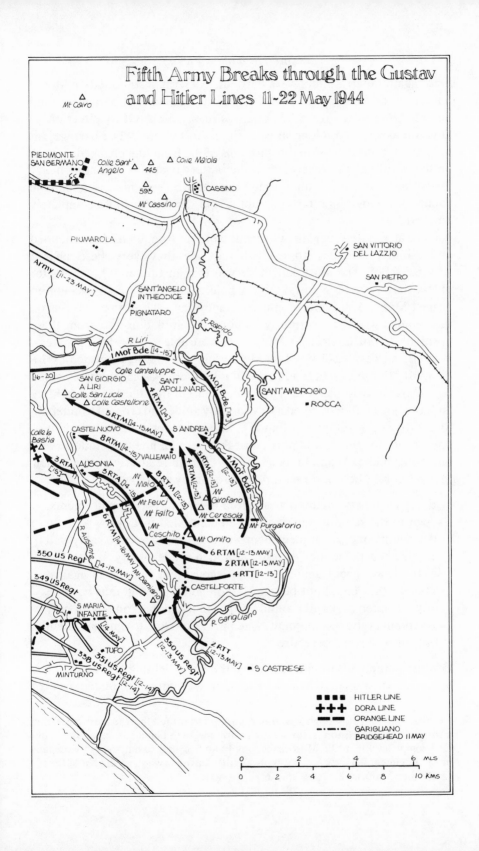

Fifth Army Breaks through the Gustav and Hitler Lines 11-22 May 1944

△ Mt Cairo

PIEDIMONTE SAN GERMANO ■
Colle Sant' Angelo △   △ 445   △ Colle Maiola
△ 593
△ Mt Cassino
CASSINO

PIUMAROLA

SAN VITTORIO DEL LAZZIO
SAN PIETRO ■

Army [11-23 MAY]

SANT'ANGELO IN THEODICE
PIGNATARO
R. Rapido
R Liri
1 Mot Bde [14-15]
△ Colle Cantaluppe
[16-20]
SAN GIORGIO A LIRI
△ Colle San Lucia
△ Colle Castellone
SANT' APOLLINARE
4 RTM [14]
1 Mot Bde [13]
SANT'AMBROGIO
■ ROCCA
5 RTM [14-15 MAY]
CASTELNUOVO
8 RTM [14-15] VALLEMAIO
S ANDREA
5 RTM [12-13]   4 Mot Bde
Colle la Bastia
△△
3 RTA   AUSONIA
+++ [15]
5 RTA [14-15]
Mt Maio
8 RTM [12-15]
4 RTM [12-13]   [12-15]
△ Mt Girofano
Mt Feuci
Mt Faito
△ Mt Ceresola
6 RTM [14-16 MAY][Mt Damiano]
R. Ausente
Mt Ceschito △   △ Mt Ornito
△ Mt Purgatorio
350 US Regt [4-15 MAY]
6 RTM [12-13 MAY]
2 RTM [12-13 MAY]
4 RTT [12-13]
349 US Regt
CASTELFORTE
S MARIA INFANTE
[4 MAY]
R. Garigliano
TUFO
350 US Regt [12-13 MAY]
351 US Regt [12-14]
358 US Regt [12-14]
MINTURNO
2 RTT [12-13 MAY]   ■ S CASTRESE

■■■■ HITLER LINE
+++ DORA LINE
━━ ORANGE LINE
━·━·━ GARIGLIANO BRIDGEHEAD 11 MAY

0   2   4   6   MLS
0   2   4   6   8   10 KMS

Once again the defenders were hard hit. A German stationed on Monte Faito later told his captors that the fire was 'eradicating, paralysing, and one of the most terrifying experiences of my life'.[5] Of its effect on 71 Division as a whole, General von Vietinghoff wrote: '[The barrage] hit with remarkable precision the garrisons of the front line engaged in work on the positions, the reserves and the battery positions, inflicting heavy casualties. At the same time the entire system of telephone communications was utterly disrupted and the supply route completely blocked.'[6]

Once again, however, the Germans were far from being overwhelmed and as Juin's battalions crossed their start lines they everywhere ran into stiff resistance. The most dangerous was that encountered by 2 DIM, for unless they were able to take the whole complex of peaks backing up against Monte Maio and Monte Girofano then each of the divisions on their flanks would be seriously troubled by enfilading fire from these positions. Unfortunately the Moroccans were able to make little progress. An early success was scored on Monte Faito, which was stormed by 1/8 RTM just after midnight, and consolidation there was considerably aided by a German prisoner who 'gave himself up in the thick of the fighting and, though wounded, acted as a voluntary guide and crossed a minefield to approach the summit of Faito'.[7]* But a further advance was almost impossible, for this whole portion of the German line was studded with numerous pillboxes and bunkers, many of them relatively untouched by the preliminary bombardment. A later report by 2 DIM noted:

Every automatic weapon was served by one or two emplacements, open to the sky but remarkably well concealed from view. . . . In the vicinity of each emplacement was to be found a remarkably well constructed personnel dugout; although made of dry stone they were always proof against 105mm [shells] and sometimes against 155mm; they could not be detected on aerial photographs because of the broken rocks all around and, even in combat, one often only saw them at the last moment, when it was too late to outflank them or to bring down mortar fire.[8]

Officers of the 1st Battalion described the bitter fighting of these first few hours, as their men tried to inch their way forwards in the face of

---

* He was an Alsatian, though less co-operative prisoners felt that the Austrians (from a company of 44 Division stationed in this area) were to blame for the loss of Faito. One complained that 'the Moroccans took Faito because, to our right, 5 Company of 131 Regiment fell back. . . . It is always the Austrians who lose the battle for us.' (2ᵉ Division Marocaine, *op. cit.*, p.136.)

devastating fire from such mutually supporting positions. One wrote: 'Very quickly we came up to the pillboxes, held by a battle-hardened enemy, their morale intact, not having been struck by one shell. Grenades, barbed wire, mines, Very Lights, mortars. Some men chopped down, a fraught atmosphere amid the total darkness.'[9] According to another:

> Here we were. The enemy was there, in his hole, like a rat. Rifles, grenades . . . we argued the toss, pillbox by pillbox. We heard one man, a burst of sub-machine fire in his body, give out a last 'han'. Let's go, no prisoners. We began to work methodically; the groups were spread out 25 metres apart. The night was still quite black. Yet still we advanced and fast. *Mon Dieu* . . . how high Point 759 is . . . pillbox . . . pillbox . . . Yet another . . . quick, use grenades . . . a burst of submachine gun fire; a few more men less.[10]

By early morning the battalion was pinned down, having sustained heavy casualties. 3 Battalion had followed closely behind, to push through to Monte Feuci, but the bulk of its companies got lost and the commander decided that he could not press ahead with the attack.

But worse was to come, for in the afternoon the Regiment was heavily counter-attacked and had its work cut out simply hanging on to its initial conquests. The Germans came in behind a shower of mortar shells.

> Their men fell one after another . . . We made ourselves small amongst the crevices in the rocks. We fired with rifles. Two grenades snatched from the belt and thrown in the general direction. Two explosions, then silence; these two grenades had made three German machine gunners bite the dust. . . Let's go, the First, let's go, forward the HQ Platoon! An onslaught . . . The remaining Boche crouch behind a rock. They are exterminated.[11]

But the Germans had not yet given up and their counter-attacks continued throughout the evening. So critical did the situation become that Juin himself went forward to Monte Faito to direct operations personally. His presence had a wonderfully calming effect. According to one officer of 8 RTM:

> It is hard to imagine the profound effect his appearance made . . . on all those who saw him, from colonels to the last tirailleur. His face calm, never raising his voice, full of an inner determination in these

hours so crucial for France and for himself, he brought to the battle, at the psychological moment, his inner radiance and his authority.[12]

And all his charisma was to be needed, for things had also gone badly with many other was of the attacking regiments. To the right of 8 RTM was 4 RTM, attacking towards Monte Ceresola and Monte Girofano, and they had made even less headway. Attacking just to the north of Ceresola was 1/4 RTM, whose jump-off was described by one of the company officers:

> Forward! At that moment a veritable firework display burst before us: the criss-cross fire of the machine guns, the grenades, the mortars and the distant enemy artillery that suddenly awoke seemed to me to have only one destination: Point 751. . . . My little group and I . . . threw ourselves . . . towards Point 739; we cared about only one thing: to reach as quickly as possible a ravine directly in front of us. Having reached this refuge I counted my men . . . five. I called out but my calls were drowned by the barrage. So be it! I moved forward again, followed by my group of five men, walking in serried formation like young partridges.[13]

Another officer recalled:

> The extremely tumbled terrain, covered with dense, thorny scrub, the darkness, a major minefield, the enemy reaction . . . all served to fragment the section and inflict heavy casualties. . . . A machine gun in a pillbox was stormed, the crew killed with grenades. We moved forward. It was a storm of fire and steel . . . a vision out of Dante.[14]

German fire was so intense that neither this battalion nor 2/4 RTM, attacking Monte Ceresola itself, was able to make much headway. At 04.30, after suffering over 400 casualties, the regimental commander decided to recall them both to their start line.

Nor had things gone well with General Sevez's 4 Moroccan Mountain Division. Immediately to the left of Dody's Moroccans was 6 RTM. They had made some progress at first, pushing towards Point 664, but substantial movement depended on 8 RTM being able to neutralize fire and observation from Monte Feuci and until this was done the Regiment remained effectively pinned down well short of its objectives. For the 2nd Battalion, indeed, the day's fighting was something of a disaster:

> It ascended Point 702 and took it. But the enemy artillery reacted violently. A hellish fire fell on the unfortunate battalion,

encumbered still more by its column of mules. An ammunition dump exploded near by; the pass was lit up all red and white by the phosphorescent smoke shells. The German machine guns increased their fire. Some men began to withdraw, creating further disorganization. The dead were piling up. The battalion commander, already wounded, died bravely an instant later trying to save the battalion records.[15]

There was similar confusion to Dody's right where 1 DMI was equally hampered by the failure to blot out German fire from Ceresola and Girofano. Only 4 Brigade was used on the 11th and 12th and that with only two battalions up. On the left was the Pacific Marine Infantry Battalion, who did initially attain the line Point 541–Point 290 but were in the afternoon obliged to pull back to their start line. According to a Moroccan War Diary: '. . . the Pacific Battalion, who got a foothold on Point 541, came under *Nebelwerfer* fire and were forced to fall back in disorder to their start line which was itself threatened by enemy infiltration.'[16] To their right was 24 Bataillon de Marche, and as soon as this retreat was observed they too fell back almost to their own start line. Their War Diary shows that they had been less than impressed with the day's fighting and that the terrain, and an almost complete breakdown in communications, boded ill for future co-operation with the tanks:

> On our right, in the plain, an armoured group was operating with which we made absolutely no contact. Progress was made very difficult because 1) it was night, 2) the terrain was very wooded and very varied (sheer ravines, only one track. . .). Since our departure radio contact was non-existent, either with Brigade or with the units. Furthermore, systematic mortar fire covered the whole length of our advance, causing us casualties.[17]

The armoured group to which the writer referred was made up of four French tank squadrons, an American armoured battalion and the bulk of 22 North African Bataillon de Marche (22 BMNA). Its mission was to mop up along the south bank of the Liri but it was only able to advance very slowly through the dense minefields and several tanks were lost before the attack was halted around Conventi. Just as in the Belvedere battle the French were notably unenthusiastic about the performance of the American tanks and the following caustic remarks are to be found in the War Diary of the parent Brigade:

At 07.00 a liaison officer, back from Division, announced that this battalion's [22 BMNA] actions were hampered by the deficiencies of the tanks of 757 US Battalion, who refused to go forward into the breach opened up by the tirailleurs, on the pretext that it was thick with mines. Abandoning the attempt to make the Americans see reason, the 22nd took responsibility for the whole action and continued the advance.[18]

In the centre of the French front was another of Sevez's regiments, 2 RTM, who had under their command 1/4 RTT. The former were to attack between Monte Ceschito and Colle Siola but none of the battalions were able to make much headway, actually having to give up some of the ground they had gained between Points 552 and 444. The Tunisian battalion was attacking towards Colle Siola itself but their attack went no better than that of 2 RTM and by the evening of the 12th they had had to surrender many of the day's meagre gains.

Happily for Juin, however, there was better news from the southern end of his front, where the rest of 4 RTT were attacking Castelforte, supported by two French tank regiments and an American armoured battalion. According to the original French plan, this composite force was to be used to mop up in the Castelforte sector only after 4 DMM and 88 US Division had pushed back the German defences to either side of it. The force was under the command of General Monsabert, the commander of 3 Algerian Division, and, given Sevez's disappointing progress, he would have been quite justified in holding it back throughout the 12th. But he of all people was fully aware of just how desperate Juin was for some sort of early success, and as soon as he realized that the Americans were making good progress on their own right flank and forcing the entrance to the Ausente Valley, he decided to commit his task force in a full-scale attack. Instead of waiting for Castelforte to fall off the vine, he resolved to pluck it.

Two columns of attack were organized, one moving in from the east through San Sebastiano and the other from the south through San Lorenzo. Monsabert's boldness paid immediate dividends. So sure were the Germans about their positions in Castelforte that they had not bothered to occupy any of the ground between the Garigliano and the village, and the tanks were able to build up a sufficient momentum to send them crashing into the outskirts. By 18.00, when it was necessary to regroup for another attack the next day, both columns had gained ground and a few American tanks had penetrated as far as the town square before being obliged to pull back a little. But the fighting had been dour, and at moments of crisis only the remarkable leadership of certain officers had kept the attack going – men such as Capitaine Louisot, who lost patience when one group of tanks and infantry hung back in the face of a well-placed anti-tank gun. 'Louisot went to walk ahead of the tanks. He went to advance unprotected against that 88mm gun. If it fired, well, one would have to see, but he was tired of waiting. A few tirailleurs followed him, ready to lift any mines. And he brought it off. . . . The tanks followed, forward momentum was regained.' Or Capitaine Lartigau, who seemed to regard any temporary hold-up as a personal affront. He was

impulsive, a former racer of camels. He climbed on the turret of the section commander's tank. He brandished his swagger stick. He gave his orders: in English, in French, in Arabic, each served as well. He made himself understood. He led, he pulled, he pushed. The American crews became as frenzied as the Tirailleurs. Machine gun fire was all around him, that was of no consequence. And he did it. . . . He reached the objective on time. . . . Mission accomplished. . . . The means employed, death, nothing mattered.[19]*

Of course every division, of no matter what nationality, had its heroes of this kind. Yet one cannot but feel that the French Corps had more than its share. That there was a style of leadership there and a spirit of authentically patriotic self-sacrifice that would have seemed almost indecent in other units, particularly in the more prosaic, sometimes cynical American, British and Commonwealth ones. Two further examples should suffice to make the point. Such as that of Commandant Delort[†], of 2/8 RTM, mortally wounded during the fighting on the 12th when his battalion was brought forward to support the rest of the regiment on Monte Faito. Though he had been hit by a shellburst he remained on his feet and walked stiffly towards his colonel. He saluted and said, '*Mon Colonel*, I have just scouted out the ground. You must not attack like this. It will turn out badly. . . . *Mon Colonel*, allow me to embrace you.' His strength was failing fast.

Very calm, showing no emotion, he immediately understood that he was finished. He commended his battalion to his Colonel. As if he was leaving him for a brief absence, he took his leave of him and embraced him with all his strength, putting into this kiss all the love that he had devoted to his cherished battalion. He died a little later,

---

* Gandoet, who reported this, had, of course, been the commander of 4 RTT on Monte Belvedere and had since partially recovered from his wounds.
† It was Delort who had attached such importance to 'the battle of the last 100 metres'.

calm, serene, happy to have found the death that he had wished for.[20]

And there was Sergeant-Major Cadene of 1/8 RTM who 'came and stood to attention in front of us during a counter-attack, a little pale, his eyes curiously glazed over: *"Mon Commandant, Vive la France." "Mais oui, mon brave, Vive la France."* He had a bullet through the heart and fell down without another word.'[21] It was on the dedication of such men that Juin was relying as he made his plans for a renewed assault on the 13th; but it is necessary at this point to see what had happened to Mark Clark's other attack, by II US Corps.

Keyes' divisions, the 85th and 88th, had taken over the western half of the old X Corps bridgehead and on the 11th their battalions were deployed to attack at several points along its line. On the right, below Ventosa, were two battalions of 350 Regiment (88 Division) who were to take that village and Monte Damiano prior to the French push into Castelforte. The mouth of the Ausente Valley was held by 349 Regiment, though no major attack was anticipated here as the French were to make the running further up the Valley and there seemed little point in clogging it up with American troops. 88 Division's other main effort was assigned to 351 Regiment, who were to take the village of Santa Maria Infante. On their left was 85 Division who were to push westward, with all three regiments, towards Scauri, Santa Croce, and Castellonorato. The whole of II Corps, in fact, was aimed in a generally westward direction. Once Santa Maria Infante was taken, and it was clear that the French required no further assistance, that village was to serve as an inner hinge for 88 Division who would wheel round to take up positions directly north of 85 Division, between them and Spigno.

350 Regiment, commanded by Colonel J.C. Fry, had prepared its attack well, endeavouring to

assay every facet of our problems. To facilitate recognition, broad strips of adhesive tape were fastened to the back of each individual's helmet and to the sleeves of shirts. To insure direction and coordination, I ordered a 37-millimeter anti-aircraft gun to fire tracer ammunition above the boundary line between the two assault battalions. The phosphorus that made the shells visible would swing an arc of fire a few feet above the crest of the hill every ten seconds from jump-off until daylight. Thus a man would only have to look up to see the direction of advance and know his relative position.[22]

The planning paid off and the Regiment was probably the most successful

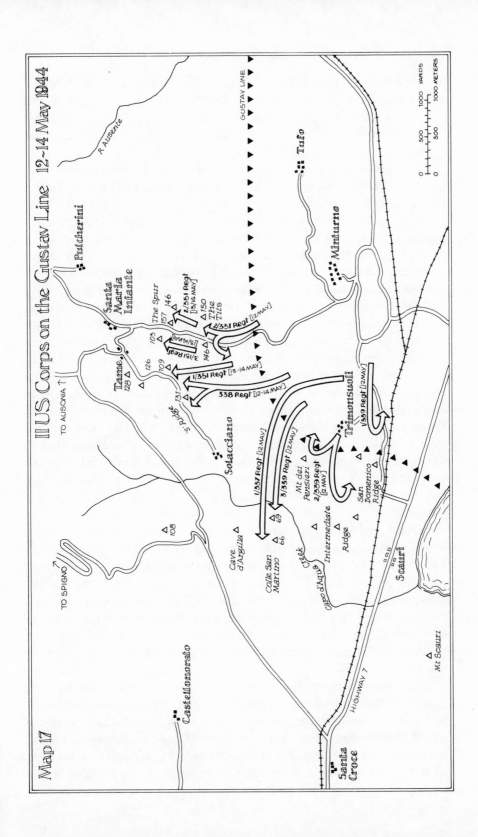

Map 17   II US Corps on the Gustav Line   12~14 May 1944

in either Fifth or Eighth Army during the first two days of the offensive. Before daylight they had secured the key hills in front of Ventosa, Points 413 and 316, and shortly afterwards cleared the village itself. On the 13th they jumped off for Monte Rotondo and had occupied this by dark, thus completing the aid that had been requested by Juin.

But it has to be admitted that Colonel Fry's men seem to have struck at a particularly weak part of the German line; and on the other side of the American sector, where the principal effort was to be made, their defences were much more secure. At first sight the ground looked much less formidable than that in front of the French, consisting as it did of rolling farmland watered by the Capo d'Aqua creek. The hills were much lower than further inland and their gentle inclines might not have seemed to present much of a problem to determined attackers. But in modern war well-dug positions on any kind of elevation can confer enormous advantage and as ever the Germans had made the most of what nature had presented. Above all they had ensured that their strongpoints were mutually supporting, placing them in a shallow concave semicircle that ran continuously from Scauri, on the coast, to the village of Santa Maria Infante. Each anchor point was heavily fortified and the whole line of ridges that linked them – San Domenico, 'Intermediate', Monte dei Pensieri, Colle San Martino, Cave d'Argilla and s Ridge – was manned by numerous machine gunners and mortar crews. The approaches to Santa Maria Infante were particularly well guarded, any attacker having to pass through two intermediate defensive barriers based upon the twin hills known wistfully as 'The Tits' and the crest of 'the Spur' a little way behind.

The southernmost regiment to attack was the 339th, whose major objective was Colle San Martino. This had been assigned to 3 Battalion and consisted of two gentle swells in the farmland, first Point 69 rising from the far bank of the Capo d'Aqua, and beyond it Point 66. The attacking companies stormed the first in fine style, dashing across a pontoon bridge they had laid over the creek, but as soon as the Germans recovered from their surprise they counter-attacked violently. The battalion held, however, and in the afternoon a battalion of 337 Regiment was brought across to seize Point 66. Their first attack was repelled but on their second attempt they carried the position. As the light was now fading the battalion hastily began to dig in. But this was 85 Division's only major success on the 12th. To the south of Colle San Martino the rest of 339 Regiment had been sent in against Monte dei Pensieri and San Domenico and 'Intermediate' Ridges but it had been unable to take any of them. On the latter, 2/339 Regiment was so badly handled that it allowed one of its companies to be surrounded and contact with them was never re-established before they were obliged to surrender, late on the 13th. Things went just as badly to the north-east where 338 Regiment could do no more than gain a toehold on 's' Ridge. Throughout the rest of the day they were pinned down by automatic weapons, mortars and snipers that remained almost invisible amongst the dense olive groves and vineyards.

So effectively were they pinned down, in fact, that the Germans on 's' Ridge found plenty of opportunity to harass the day's other major attack, that of 351 Regiment on Santa Maria Infante. This was spearheaded by 2 Battalion who advanced with one company on either side of the Minturno road. Company 'F' was on the left but as soon as the brief supporting barrage ended they came under heavy fire from 's' Ridge. 'Within thirty minutes after the jump-off, Company "F"'s attack had degenerated into a series of poorly co-ordinated platoon and squad actions. One after another of the platoon radios broke down, the leaders lost contact with their men, and darkness and fog shrouded the battlefield in a blanket of confusion that even bravery and good intentions were unable to penetrate.'[23] Company 'E' experienced similar difficulties on the right-hand side of the road, though two platoons did manage to subdue resistance on Point 150, the right-hand 'Tit'. But they were unable to make any further progress and the most energetic efforts of the Regimental Commander, who sent tanks to try and force a way up the road, committed the Battalion's third company to support 'E' and then sent in part of 3/351 Regiment to try and turn the village from the west, failed to make any real impression on the defenders. At dusk it was decided to abandon the attack until the following morning.

On the 13th II Corps' effort was exclusively focused upon 's' Ridge and Santa Maria Infante, the bulk of 85 Division being ordered to simply hold their present positions. 351 Regiment, however, remained in the thick of it and the Divisional boundaries were readjusted so that 1/351 Regiment, hitherto held in reserve, could be brought in to attack on the left of the Minturno road, moving over Point 109, on 's' Ridge, through Tame to envelop Santa Maria Infante from the north-west. Their own left flank would be covered by 338 Regiment, who were to take Point 131 and knock out the machine guns that had so troubled them the previous day. German troops in front of Santa Maria Infante were to be held in place by strong demonstrations against the hills along the Spur, carried out by the remaining battalions of 351 Regiment.

Things began to go sadly wrong from the beginning. The main attack by 1/351 Regiment had been set for 16.30 but a whole series of delays ensued and it was not until 22.30 that the men even reached their start line. Unfortunately, word of this delay did not reach the supporting troops and 2/351 Regiment, to the east of the Minturno road, and 2/338 Regiment, below Point 131, both jumped off on time. The lack of pressure in the centre, however, freed many extra German machine guns and mortars and severe casualties were incurred by both these flank units. 2/351 Regiment did gain a lodgement on the Spur but continued heavy fire drove them to cover and pinned them there. 2/338 Regiment were not even able to hold their ground and were pushed off Point 131 by the first sharp counter-attack. But again news of this setback was not passed to other units and Colonel Champeny, the commander of 351 Regiment, now ordered in his 3rd Battalion against the western edge of the Spur. They jumped off at 18.30 and from the start were terribly exposed to fire from the whole length of 'S' Ridge. After one particularly vicious pounding by artillery and mortars the Battalion's S-3 reported back to Champeny: 'Two years of training gone up in smoke . . . my men . . . about half of them – almost all my leaders.'[24] No wonder the commander of 94 German Division, which was holding this part of the line, had issued a proclamation earlier that evening in which he claimed that 'in spite of several enemy penetrations into our advance positions, the main field of battle remained in our hands.'[25]

Of course, the Americans were hardly unique in having failed to break the German line in these first attacks and, in the light of similar setbacks for the French, the Polish Corps, and XIII Corps, it would hardly be fair to single out Keyes' men for their lack of combat experience or for alleged failures of leadership. But the question of leadership does merit some mention, if only because the American record is always more candid in this regard and more prepared to admit that field commanders can become as frightened as the next man. The examples given below are in no way intended as an indictment of the US Army at this time, or of any section of it, but are cited because they offer all too rare glimpses into the darker problems of command, when men catapulted into positions of considerable authority suddenly found themselves unable to cope. So it was with a company commander of 1/350 Regiment who abruptly went off the air during an important attack and remained out of contact with either the enemy or his seniors for several hours. According to his regimental commander:

A day passed before I found out the reason for the loss of contact and control of the company that had to be replaced. The Company Commander had failed. The only descriptive word I know is cowardice. Instead of demonstrating the leadership for which he had been trained, he faked sudden illness that upset the entire company staff. Ultimately, he went to the rear and reported himself to an aid station for imaginary injuries. Along with others he disappeared into the administrative limbo in the rear and was never heard from again.[26]

The second example comes from this same regiment and concerns a company of 3 Battalion who had missed the early fighting as they were held back in reserve. On the 13th they were ordered forward to occupy a hill reported free of the enemy and

> what followed poignantly illustrated the demoralizing effect that the sounds and rumours of battle can have on inexperienced troops waiting anxiously in reserve. When the regimental commander's order reached the company commander, he refused to move out with his unit. Promptly relieving him, Colonel Fry sent . . . his S–3 to take command of the company. The men . . . he found . . . were thoroughly demoralized. . . . He explained to them that a patrol had reported the objective abandoned: however, only one officer and one noncommissioned officer reluctantly agreed to follow him. Only after considerable urging and cajoling was . . . he able to persuade the men to advance.[27]

But there were also heroes. Whether they were motivated by the same intense sense of identification with *patrie* and regiment as were the French cadres is open to doubt, and few of them had quite that same flamboyant sense of theatre. But they always seemed to be on hand when and where they were needed and through them lesser mortals gained strength. There was, for example, Colonel Champeny who had moved up to the front on the afternoon of the 13th and taken personal command of 1/351 Regiment. An eye-witness wrote:

> It was magnificent. We wanted to lie down and stay there, but with the Old Man standing up like a rock you couldn't stay down. Something about him just brought you right up to your feet. The guys saw him, too. They figured if the Old Man could do it so could they. And when the time came they got up off the ground and started on again to Santa Maria.[28]

And there was the commander of 2/351 Regiment, Lieutenant-Colonel R.E. Kendall, who also took personal charge of one of his companies after its commander was wounded and the men seemed to be running out of steam. Most of them were crouching behind any available scrap of cover when Kendall strolled in amongst them and prodded a few with his swagger stick. 'Come on you bastards,' he shouted, 'you'll never get to Rome this way!' The men slowly stirred themselves and Kendall personally led one platoon against a small cluster of houses on the Spur. One squad was driven back but Kendall dragged the other forward, successively firing a carbine, an M.1 rifle and a bazooka at an enemy machine gun post. When his third bazooka rocket hit the house Kendall bounded forward and himself destroyed the enemy gun and killed two of its crew. He was pausing to throw a grenade into another position when he was hit in the chest by a burst of machine gun fire. As he fell mortally wounded he clutched the grenade to his chest so that it should not wound any of his companions.[29]

As a tribute, perhaps, to this kind of leadership 351 Regiment resumed its attack on Santa Maria Infante on the night of the 13/14th. 1 Battalion had finally reached its start line and it moved off against Point 109 some time after midnight. Yet again the troops were caught by heavy fire from elsewhere on 's' Ridge and Colonel Champeny decided to cross his divisional boundary and clear out the whole of that feature with his own men. He was in the process of organizing this attack, ignoring the protests of 85 Division's commander, when a company from 1 Battalion took it upon itself to have another crack at Point 109. Leading his men the company commander

started up the hill. This time, to his surprise, hardly any German resistance developed. His men quickly gained the crest and found there only a small German rearguard, eager to surrender. . . . [Another] company started to climb Hill 131. There too the Americans were in for a surprise. The company encountered only scattered bursts of machine gun fire and reached the top of the hill with few losses. By that time the men found only empty dugouts, probably abandoned by a rearguard that had just slipped away unobserved in the darkness. The only Germans remaining were on the reverse slope – they were dead, victims of the first day's artillery fire.[30]

Only hours before, in fact, with the ink barely dry on his congratulatory Order of the Day, the commander of 94 Division had received orders from XIV Panzer Corps* to pull back his right wing about a mile and to

---

* Von Senger und Etterlin had still not returned from Germany and his Corps was commanded by his deputy, General Hartmann.

anchor it on Monte Cività, north-west of Santa Maria Infante, where contact could be re-established with 71 Division. To discover why contact had been lost in the first place, and why such an abrupt withdrawal was considered necessary, we must return to the French, whom we left smarting under the reverses inflicted on the 12th.

Juin had set his face resolutely against any talk of defeat and from the afternoon of the 12th had been determined to resume his offensive early on the next day. This was not simply because he could not countenance the thought of failure by his beloved 'little Army of Italy' but also, and more important, because he was convinced that the forces facing him were stretched to the absolute limit, and incapable of sealing off any substantial penetration through their forward line of defence. He put his case most cogently in a memorandum to General Sevez:

> The bitter resistance by the enemy is an excellent indication. It proves that he has nothing behind him, no depth. Moreover, the observations of the prisoners are conclusive in this respect. Everything has been thrown into the line. The order has been given to hold at any cost. The German commanders believe that this is a simple demonstration in the mountains. They are not worried, they are still convinced that it is at Cassino that they must await the real offensive. . . . We have in front of us a solid curtain, but if we can manage to make a tear in it, then the whole thing will be swept aside.[31]

Nevertheless, the horror of failure still bulked large in his mind. An officer of 2 DIM overheard snatches of a discussion with the Divisional Infantry Commander during the most critical moments on the 12th. As Juin entered the command post he stated vehemently: 'We cannot possibly give up the affair now.' His parting remark as he re-emerged somewhat belied the intellectual convictions expressed to Sevez and he said simply: 'We must go into it with the will to succeed, without which one never achieves anything.'[32]

His actual plan was perfectly straightforward, differing only in minor detail from that of the 11/12th. All the divisions were to attack along the same axes and once again the decisive thrust was to be made by Dody's division, striking successively towards Monte Girofano/Monte Agrifoglio and Monte Feuci/Monte Maio. The break into the lower Ausente Valley was still the responsibility of 3 DIA, with the intermediate ground being mopped up by 4 DMM.

For his own attack, Dody split his reserve regiment, 5 RTM, between

the other two, allocating one battalion to 4 RTM and the other two to
8 RTM. The assault towards Monte Girofano jumped off at 04.45 and the
whole of Ceresola was quickly cleared. 3/5 RTM and part of 3/4 RTM then
passed through the first attackers and drove just to the right of Monte
Girofano itself (Point 628), seizing various peaks behind it and effectively
isolating it from the main German line. At 08.30, Point 628 was attacked
whilst mopping up continued on the further peaks. The fighting was little
easier than on the previous day, but Juin was given no cause to worry
about 'the will to succeed' or the quality of leadership. Captain de
Belsunce, of 3/5 RTM, had set off ten yards in front of his men, walking
erect with a bamboo swagger stick in his left hand. As the shells and
bullets whistled round him he declined to either crouch or run and
absolutely refused to let any of his men get in front of him. His own
account of one bound in the attack appeared in the divisional history:

> We could not see our objective which was masked by an opaque
> screen made by the smoke shells. . . . Lower down were Boche
> dugouts: numerous soldiers lay about, certain of them discovered in
> somewhat bizarre positions, their eyes wide open and still clutching
> their rifles, with bayonet fixed, seemingly still trying to block our
> passage. . . . [We went forward again.] I heard a voice of the
> Kabyles crying 'Forward!' . . . Without trying to understand why,
> I in turn shouted 'Forward! Forward! Forward!' and, as one man, we
> left our cover and started across the bottom of the ravine. . . . A
> Tirailleur who was following me close by saw a . . . Boche emerge
> from a thicket; he shouldered his rifle, fired and caught the Boche
> full in the chest. The latter crumpled, crying, 'Warum? Nicht kaput!
> Kamerad! Kamerad!' Blood spurted from his mouth. He died for his
> Führer with his eyes wide open.[33]

They pressed forward and found numerous pillboxes still blocking their
way. Many were reduced in the same manner as the day before – sections
dashing in and stuffing grenades through the embrasure – but others were
attacked from a slightly more respectful distance. A divisional report
applauded 'the good results obtained with the help of the bazooka in
destroying German bunkers; certain battalions had practised this
assiduously and the anticipated results were conclusive; in most cases the
defenders, terrified by the explosive power of the projectile, surrendered
without further ado.'[34] No wonder that a German prisoner taken on
Girofano said simply, 'I was at Stalingrad, and I had never thought to
endure worse.'[35]

The attack towards Monte Feuci and Monte Maio, by 2/5 RTM, had been timed to start at 08.00 but the troops were actually attacked in their forming-up areas and, though these desperate forays were repulsed, the French did not jump off until 10.45. As the last seconds before H-HOUR ticked away

> Everyone hung on the signals from the battalion commander. . . . [He rose to his feet] and all his officers and men saw his silhouette outlined against the bluish screen which masked Feuci. With his tan gloves – the battalion commander always fought with his gloves on – his distinctive Colt and the two gourds of water to which he had such great recourse in action, leaning on his cane, he loomed larger than ever in those extraordinary surroundings. Then, suddenly, he raised his stick, flourished it and cried, 'Forward! Yallah!'[36]

A few German posts were quickly overrun, many of the occupants still cowering from the savage preliminary bombardment, and the leading company started the climb up the rocky incline. The summit was gained with astounding ease and as some troops dug in to face the inevitable counter-attacks others cautiously moved around the plateau looking for surviving German strongpoints.

> However, to their surprise, the enemy did not react. He was, in this sector, at the end of his means. When it reached the crest of Monte Feuci, the 5th Company discovered a sort of plateau, falling away towards the west, instead of a very steep rock-face of the kind it had just climbed. Some distance off, about 400 metres, could be seen a few small groups who scattered and ran off at the first bursts of fire. On Feuci the bunkers . . . were empty.[37]

This was the turning-point of the French battle and, arguably, of the whole DIADEM offensive. Juin had been completely vindicated, as is shown in these remarks by Vietinghoff in which he emphasized the tenuous nature of 71 Division's defensive line and the dangers of insisting that it made no tactical withdrawals. Of the defences themselves, Vietinghoff wrote that their construction 'was difficult because even the low hills of the valley consisted of rugged rock. . . . 71 Division was rather helpless when confronted with this task; its officers and enlisted men, even the engineers, were utterly inexperienced in such terrain.' The French might have demurred a little at such an airy dismissal of the maze of pillboxes and bunkers they had encountered but Vietinghoff next made his most telling point, regretting 'in particular [that] it was not possible prior to the attack to establish a deeply echeloned system of positions on the Maio massif'. Nor was this dereliction simply a reflection of 71 Division's inexperience in such terrain. In the last analysis, said Vietinghoff, the blame could only be laid at the door of the most senior commanders. In March and April

> in accordance with OKW's principles not to yield an inch of ground without a fight, the order was given to develop as the MLR the lines retained after the January battles. However this line was disadvantageously located for a defence in major combat. . . . It was difficult to find artillery positions which offered cover at least against ground observation, and almost impossible to find such positions for larger units. . . . If . . . the enemy succeeded in taking the dominating heights, all rear echelons of the Division would be eliminated easily. It would have been necessary to regard the line held thus far only as an advanced position and, regardless of the loss of territory, to move the MLR to a rearward position. However, all requests of Tenth Army to that effect were rejected, and consequently the sector of 71 Infantry Division became the Army's most serious concern.[38]

The situation around Monte Feuci on the 13th exemplified the terrible dangers of this state of affairs. The units there had already lost heavily in the attacks of the day before. The artillery barrage that preceded 2/5 RTM's advance had caused yet more, as had the furious counter-attacks on their start line on Monte Faito.* German units to the left and right were pinned down by other French attacks and to the rear there were few reserves for counter-attack and no fall-back positions of any value. As soon as the garrison on Feuci gave way, therefore, the whole German line was threatened with deep penetrations into its rear areas, with the troops involved being able to roam about almost at will. There was only one course open to 71 Division. Intercepted radio messages showed that it had been taken. At 12.13 the urgent order was given: 'Feuci occupied by the enemy. Activate fall-back movements.'[39]

  The whole German line now began to fall back, including, as we have seen, 94 Division, and the French surged forwards in pursuit. Monte Girofano was speedily mopped up and Monte Agrifoglio was occupied at 20.00. From here enemy units could be seen pulling back towards Vallemaio and these were harassed by artillery fire, 3/4 RTM being

---

* These had been carried out by 2/115 PG Regiment, which was XIV Panzer Corps' only freely disposable reserve.

ordered to press on to Vallemaio at the first opportunity. Nor did the
occupants of Feuci rest on their laurels. It had always been felt that Monte
Maio, almost 3000 feet high, was the central bastion of the eastern
Auruncis and 5 RTM quickly set off towards it. Juin had expected that its
capture would involve particularly heavy fighting but the rupture of the
German line had thrown them into greater disarray than even he had
dared hope and there were simply no units either ready or able to make
a stand on Maio. A battalion of 5 RTM climbed it unopposed and Juin,
as conscious of the historical moment as was Anders to be beneath
Cassino, immediately ordered that a flag be raised on the summit. It was
a staff-officer of 2 DIM who eventually routed out a suitably large tricolor
– it measured twelve feet by twenty-five feet and could be seen for ten
miles all around – and had it put in place. Throughout the rest of the day
other troops moved up to Maio and the surrounding heights, some
climbing to the summit to take in the remarkable view it afforded.
Artillery officers had a more than passing interest in this view and the first
observers were quickly in place to direct fire on the retreating Germans.
One group 'found a stunning observatory. A series of tiers cut into the
rock, like rows of seats in an auditorium, offered them comfortable and
unaccustomed vantage points.'[40] Another observer directed his fire on to
a cluster of German batteries, none of which probably realized that they
were under direct observation:

> Drawn by the spectacle, numerous officers, NCOs and tirailleurs . . .
> seated themselves in the amphitheatre around the radio operator.
> Seated quietly, smoking cigarettes or pipes, they partook with some
> passion in the search for targets and helped register the hits! It was
> an extraordinary spectacle, a sign of victory, which only ended when
> darkness fell, to the great regret of the teacher and his pupils.[41]

Only one thing marred the excitement of the day's events, and that too
was largely attributable to the French artillerymen. For they had wrought
dreadful havoc on the first two days of the battle and the whole of the
Maio massif was permeated by

> a terrible stench of putrefaction which rose from the bottom of the
> valley [where lay] human corpses and the carcasses of animals
> scattered amongst the thickets and rocks, and which was intensified
> by the unbearable heat. For Captain George Gaudy, of the 4th
> Moroccans, this smell would always taint his memories of Maio in
> the approaching dusk. . . . 'The bunkers, like boats that had been

wrecked and ransacked, spewed out a flotsam of Boche in an advanced state of decomposition,' he wrote in his diary.[42]

For the other divisions of the Corps, the early hours of the 13th had been just as arduous as on the previous day. The War Diary of 21 Bataillon de Marche, part of 1 DMI, spoke of 'slow progress, broken terrain, isolated Boche resistance, particularly in the farmhouses, several minefields . . . Heavy fatigue. No mules. No supplies coming through.'[43] There were heavy counter-attacks on both 4 DMM and 3 DIA and the latter was bitterly assailed around Colle Siola, where 1/4 RTT was trying to drive down on Castelforte from the north-east.

It was a hot fight. German resistance stiffened. Men fell . . . [Lieutenant Chedeville] was wounded in the thigh. The men wavered . . . They loved him so . . . The Boche counter-attacked. . . . He refused to be evacuated. 'I am going to stay with you,' he said to an NCO. 'We are going to push the Boche back. . . . Then I can die. That is of no consequence. I only ask that you send my wedding ring to my wife, and mark a cross for her on this map to show where I am going to die . . .' Then, very calmly, he gave his orders. And for two hours more he led his section and threw back the Boche. They thought he might be saved. But he knew. . . . A shellburst cut him down in the flower of youth, at the moment of victory. He had taken, held and consolidated his peak.[44]

All along the front, however, the situation was transformed once Monte Feuci had fallen and the afternoon and evening saw substantial advances in every sector. Castelforte was finally cleared by nightfall and almost 400 prisoners taken. The Germans had resisted bitterly here, right to the end, and much of the credit for the victory went to the intrepid tanks of 7 Chasseurs d'Afrique. In the weeks to come their squadrons fought with every French division and they became known as ' "the nomads": with their tankmen's helmets, torsos bare, their overalls rolled into a ball round their waist.' Their tactics were often as unconventional as their appearance. Even as enemy resistance slackened in Castelforte the numerous mines were a serious obstacle to tanks and infantry alike. Sapper parties were in attendance but their vanguard position left them terribly exposed to sniper and mortar fire. The Chasseurs adopted just the same expedient as did the Poles a day or so later: 'Flat on their stomachs, the sappers . . . crawled under the belly of the tanks . . . and, amidst the deafening racket only a few centimetres above them, managed to work methodically between the tracks, the reassuring bulk of the tanks covering them like a broody hen.'[45]

Tanks also played a prominent role on the French right flank. The infantry of I DMI's 4 Brigade was still having considerable difficulty with the broken terrain but the composite tank/infantry groups to the right were able to make better progress as *Kampfgruppe* Bode began to fall back. A few rearguard actions were fought, however, one of them in front of Colle Morroni which dominated the roads to Sant' Ambrogio and San Apollinare. But 3 Moroccan Spahis were in no mood for faltering and one troop charged straight ahead at the enemy strongpoint. Two Shermans were knocked out by anti-tank guns. The two survivors pressed on and 'bursts from their machine guns riddled the German infantry who bounded out of the trenches in front of the pass and sought safety in flight. The tanks caught up with one of them who was crushed beneath the leader's tracks. It was a genuine cavalry charge of yesteryear. They had tanks instead of horses, but the cavalry spirit remained.'[46] These last two tanks were soon knocked out by *Panzerfausts* but their crews escaped and pressed on towards the German positions, firing carbines and revolvers as they sprinted forwards. The Germans were already beginning to waver when the other Spahi squadrons arrived and put them to flight. Sant' Ambrogio was occupied late the same evening, the Germans having already withdrawn.

The sudden German collapse was also apparent in front of Sevez's troops, in the centre of the French line. The counter-attacks swiftly ebbed away and, according to one War Diary, 'the enemy fell back everywhere. Numerous Germans were spotted on the slopes east of the Rio Grande. Certain groups were waving white flags.'[47] By 17.00 the division had seized Colle Crisano and Monte Ceschito and was mopping up scattered German remnants between the River Pozzari and the Rio Grande. The seal had been put on one of the most decisive days' fighting in the whole Italian Campaign. Perhaps the greatest tribute of all came from a German prisoner, taken in Castelforte: 'In France, in 1940, we tried to find that French Army which our elders had spoken of with such respect. We did not find it. They told us then that it was dead, but they lied to us. Today we have found it in Italy.'[48]

But Juin had no intention of losing the new momentum of his advance or of allowing the Germans time to establish a new defensive line. The 'phase de rupture' was now complete and exploitation was the new order of the day. The immediate tasks were threefold: to break through the Orange Line, about which French intelligence was scanty; to occupy the heights overlooking San Giorgio a Liri; and to bring in the Mountain Corps to break out of the Ausente Valley into the Petrella massif.

The first mission was the responsibility of 2 DIM who on the 14th and 15th advanced on either side of Vallemaio, taking Colle Agrifoglio and

Colle Cantalupo, on the right, and Castelnuovo, Colle Castellone and Colle San Lucia, on the left. An officer with 2/5 RTM described one of the numerous French columns that plunged into the mountains, keeping the Germans permanently off balance by their ability to move swiftly and silently over the most intractable terrain:

> Like a huge writhing snake the battalion laboured forward amongst the rocks. The crunch of boots on the loose stones . . . mingled with the sound of the panting, heavily-laden tirailleurs carefully marking each footfall in this chaotic terrain. In the pale light of a magnificent full moon the Moroccans, like ghosts, slowly and silently pressed through the enemy lines.[49]

Resistance was light until the division tried to push beyond the San Giorgio-Ausonia road. As was noted in the previous chapter, Kesselring had directed 200 PG Regiment to this sector, on the 13th, as soon as he realized that the danger here was much more pressing than in the Liri Valley, its original destination. Tough fighting ensued and the casualties were heavy. As ever the company officers were well to the fore, and paid a proportionate price. And as ever they died as French officers should. A young *aspirant* was hit and taken to an aid post but, realizing the severity of his wounds, he insisted that the doctor attend to those whose lives might be saved: 'Leave me be,' he murmured, 'I die content, at the moment of victory, as I wanted to. . . . You, you are lucky. . . . You will see France again. So make sure that all the blood spilled down there is not wasted!'[50] And the Panzer Grenadiers were eventually pushed back. Late on the 16th 2 DIM effected a junction with the advance elements of the Algerian Division and thereafter went into reserve, leaving further advances to Esperia and Pontecorvo to Monsabert's men and the Free French.

It is as well that the Moroccans had so effectively covered 1 DMI's left flank for the latter's advance from Colle Morroni and Sant' Ambrogio was far from straightforward. The trouble was not so much heavy enemy resistance as the poor terrain, immense difficulties in working with the tanks, and a generally disappointing standard of staff-work and liaison within the division. Complaints about the terrain abounded and if these seem surprising within the context of the French Expeditionary Corps, it should be remembered that the Free French Division had earned its spurs with Eighth Army, in the desert, and thus found it very difficult to adapt to the radically different conditions in Italy. On 16 May, for example, 11 Bataillon de Marche was complaining about the 'very broken terrain:

steep-banked tributaries of the Liri, numerous hedgerows at right-angles to the line of march, visibility much reduced . . .'[51] On the following day the War Diary observed:

A fire-base was established on the other side of a *oued*, but visibility was bad (thick hedgerows . . . high cornfields) . . . Enemy fire increased; in the cornfields the tirailleurs and their officers could see little of the resistance in front of them. The machine gun section . . . engaged one enemy group to support . . . our attack but their fire had little effect, the broken terrain limiting visibility.[52]

Rough going of this sort did not make life easy for the supporting armour. 11 Battalion admitted that it 'little favoured the deployment of the tanks. The tanks were not able to deploy, the terrain being too broken.'[53] The commander of 1 DMI, General Diégo Brosset, reported on the 16th: 'The San Andrea-Vallemaio track is not negotiable by armoured vehicles; moreover, appearances to the contrary, the area west of San Giorgio is not suitable for tanks (swampy).'[54] But reservations about the usefulness of tanks went beyond purely physical constraints. We have already had occasion to note some scathing remarks about the failures of certain American tankmen and the opinions of the French infantry did not change much over the next few days. According to 24 Bataillon de Marche, who on the 17th were pinned down in front of a fortified cluster of buildings south-west of Tomba di Rosa: 'The tanks did nothing to help the infantry; one only, at the request of the Captain . . . agreed to fire five shots or so at a house. The tanks claimed they could not advance for fear of mines.'[55] The tankmen's pusillanimity was often compounded with sheer incompetence. According to 11 Bataillon de Marche, again on the 17th, the supporting tanks

remained to the north of us but were of no use. . . . On our left 24 Bataillon de Marche was equally stymied. As our tanks could see nothing in front of them they fired into our ranks; we asked them to cease firing. . . . Our Commandant was asked to mount an effort with the tanks further to the left. . . . The French were willing, the Americans more reluctant. . . . [A little later] the American tanks began to fire directly ahead of them; enormous difficulties making them stop as they could only kill our own men.[56]

But the Free French infantry had hardly shown themselves to the best advantage. On the 18th, Brosset issued a series of comments on operations to date, which he ordered to be read out to all NCOs. He noted that his Division had already suffered heavy casualties and that

many of our losses [come because] we do not spread out enough; we do not camouflage ourselves enough; we do not dig enough, we do not manoeuvre enough. . . . The NCOs in particular, brave men that they are, know how to lead their men when the time comes to attack but are not sufficiently diligent in protecting them during the lulls in the fighting. . . . The confusion [during these lulls] is augmented by the cretins who pass their time blasting away with captured weapons.[57]

The Division's rear echelons and staffs were also found wanting, as the following increasingly acerbic entries in one Battalion's War Diary clearly show:

14 May: 'B' Echelon is functioning badly . . .
15 May: No supplies are getting through. . . . 'B' Echelon does not function as it is at present organized. 'B' Echelon must be answerable to the Battalion, and not centralized at Brigade. Good liaison by radio with all echelons is absolutely indispensable. . . . No Boche; quite the contrary; our 'objective' has been occupied since yesterday by the Divisional artillery . . .
24 May: The Battalion set off to attack its objective without having been able to establish any contact to left or right. . . . Objective taken at 18.00 hours. The Legion, which was supposed to operate to our right, installed itself gloriously in our rear . . . at 19.30 hours . . .
25 May: During the night the Battalion received the following order: 'As soon as you are relieved [in your present position] by a battalion of the Legion, proceed westwards before dawn to relieve the battalion on your right from the neighbouring division.' That was all it said.[58]

Worst of all, perhaps, several of Brosset's battalions had shown themselves unsteady in combat. The precipitate retreat of the Pacific Battalion, on the 12th, has already been referred to. Similar confusion was apparent among the troops of 24 Bataillon de Marche, on the 17th, when they were suddenly counter-attacked near Tomba di Rosa:

Suddenly, the 3rd Company reported that it was being attacked in the rear and the flanks. Everything then became extremely confused. The captain . . . calmly, gave a minute-by-minute description of the worsening situation. In the end there were no more than forty men still with him; the rest of the Company streamed back towards the start line. . . . Seeing at the same time the 1st and 2nd Companies beginning to fall back . . . the battalion commander . . . sent his Adjutant on to the hill to the left to halt the withdrawal and regroup the units.[59]

With hindsight one is inclined to attribute such reverses to inadequate training and unfamiliarity with this quite different theatre of war. At the time, however, Divisional officers were too ready to blame their black troops. In 11 Bataillon de Marche it was felt that early setbacks were often the result of spontaneous 'movements towards the rear as soon as the European cadres were hit or didn't handle a difficult situation with sufficient vigour. In the 6th Company, the incapacitation of the Captain and the longest-serving officer had a serious effect on the men's morale. The necessity for a strong leavening of European officers . . . was confirmed once more.'[60] In late May the Divisional staff produced a summary of their conclusions about operations to date. They had involved

a very particular type of combat which, if it were to move forward rapidly, would require infantrymen who were agile and quick to respond . . . to an adversary well-used to this sort of defensive fighting. Black troops obviously do not represent the ideal solution and the fact that the officers and senior NCOs are always obliged to lead from the front, standing up, explains the severe losses suffered by these cadres.[61]*

Despite all these difficulties, however, Brosset's division was able to make considerable progress. Always well covered by 2 DIM on their left, they had, by the 17th, crossed the River San Antonio and the River Mariano and established a firm presence on Monte Calvo, only a few kilometres short of the southern extension of the Hitler Line.

Their leading units, in fact, had already penetrated sections of the Dora Line, the intermediate line of German defences that hinged upon Esperia

---

* Such remarks were not peculiar to 1 DMI, with its large contingent of Senegalese troops. Though relations between natives and Europeans in the Moroccan and Algerian Divisions were generally good, it would not do to idealize the situation. Thus a report by the 2ᵉ Bureau of 2 DIM, at the end of the Fourth Battle, noted: 'We must never forget what experience has taught, that with the mediocre native troops now at our disposal, night attacks, even limited ones, exact a terrible price from our French cadres.' (2 DIM, Renseignements tirés, *op. cit.*, p.2.)

and Monte d'Oro and barred the route north-westwards towards Pico. But the main credit for breaking this line belonged to 3 DIA who had started moving up the Ausente Valley as soon as Castelforte had been secured. The initial advance, supported by 4 Moroccan Spahis, encountered little organized resistance, though passage was often blocked by extensive German demolitions. But the Algerians were well prepared for such delaying tactics and a rather improbable set of heroes suddenly came to the fore. These were the drivers of the Division's bulldozers, who

> opened the way in front of the tanks of the 4th Spahis. . . .In his step-by-step withdrawal the enemy had had time to wreck the road in the difficult stretches, at the river crossings and where the road turned sharply with only a sheer drop on one side. With a blade three metres wide, like a veritable giant's razor, the bulldozers, mounted on caterpillar tracks, immediately went into the thick of the fighting to reopen the road . . . Thanks to them the quite extensive demolitions had very little effect. . . . [The bulldozer] was to be one of our most important war-winners.[62]

By the evening of the 14th, 3 DIA had taken Coreno and were close to the south-eastern outskirts of Ausonia. The latter was occupied early the next morning but as the Algerians moved north and north-west they ran into stiff opposition from 200 PG Regiment, both around Castelnuovo and on Colle la Bastia.

Fierce fighting went on throughout the 15th and 16th but, once La Bastia had been isolated, a single battalion was left to mop up there whilst the whole of 3 RTA pushed on to the east of it, towards Esperia. This village had now become the focal point of the whole German front and, ever more conscious of the terrible dangers posed by the breakthrough at Feuci, Kesselring and his Army and Corps commanders had been desperately looking round for extra units to throw into the battle. They had not been helped by the almost total dislocation of communications caused by the tremendous Allied artillery concentrations. Even on the 15th the general situation was far from clear to Kesselring who, rather unfairly, railed against his subordinates: 'It is intolerable that a division is engaged in combat for one and a half days without knowing what is going on in its sector.'[63] At first only a few local reinforcements were available in XIV Panzer Corps' sector. The bulk of these went to 71 Division, including 2/115 PG Regiment, already referred to, and 115

Armoured Reconnaissance Battalion, also from 15 PG Division. All kinds of other units and sub-units were also thrown in to block the advance across the Maio massif and one group of artillerymen, captured by 5 RTM, 'unanimously stated that they had been thrown into the battle without being told anything and without any word of explanation. The officers kept a dignified silence and refused to substantiate the assertions of their men, but one sensed that they were bitter and indignant with regard to commanders who had committed them so blindly.'[64]

For nothing seemed to be able to halt the French advance. On the 13th XIV Panzer Corps had tried to stabilize on a line Monte Città–Coreno–Vallemaio–north of San Apollinare. On the 14th Vietinghoff, as we have seen, ordered them to hold one running from San Giorgio through Ausonia down to Formia. On the 15th they were already falling back to the Dora Line, where 200 PG Regiment had arrived with orders to stand between Monte d'Oro, Esperia and Colle la Bastia. Other units were also despatched to Esperia, including 2/104 PG Regiment, which had been stationed between Fondi and Itri in front of the Americans, 818 Mountain Pioneer Battalion and the Replacement Battalion of 94 Division. Orders were also given on the 15th for more substantial reinforcements and Kesselring decided to commit a large part of his strategic reserve to try and block the French. 26 Panzer Division was ordered from north of Rome to the Dora Line, though it was recognized that the first units, elements of 9 PG Regiment, could not possibly be in position around Esperia until the 17th. 305 and 334 Divisions were also summoned from the static Adriatic front, their Reconnaissance Battalions having already been ordered forwards the day before. By the 16th Kesselring was only left with 29 PG Division, stationed north of the Tiber on either side of Civitavecchia, and the Hermann Göring Panzer Parachute Division, in the Leghorn area, which could in any real sense be regarded as significant mobile reserves. No wonder that during a telephone call to his opposite number at Army Group 'C', General Wentzell, Vietinghoff's Chief of Staff, said excitedly, 'At the moment things here look wild. Everything is on the move!'[65]

Unfortunately, fast as the Germans reacted, XIV Panzer Corps was never allowed the same opportunities as Feuerstein's Corps, in the Liri Valley, to reorganize its defensive sectors, plug the worst gaps and fall back methodically to the prepared Hitler Line positions. After the war Vietinghoff was extremely critical of Kesselring and his insistence on immediate counter-attacks against the advancing French. From the beginning Vietinghoff had wanted to place any reinforcements in the more secure sections of the Hitler Line and wait for the French to attack them. Army Group 'C', however, ordered that they attack well in front of these positions, as soon as they arrived in the sector. On the 15th all fresh units, 'by the direct order of OBSW,* had to be employed immediately after arrival in counter-attacks against the pursuing vanguards of the French Expeditionary Corps. In view of the comparative strengths and the lack of time which was needed for thorough preparations, especially reconnaissance, regulation of artillery support etc., the outcome of these actions could be foreseen.' Later the same day Vietinghoff 'once more . . . requested from OBSW permission to fall back to the Senger switch position and to immediately employ there in defensive preparations all reserves that had been brought forward. Again OBSW rejected this request and ordered the holding of the Dora Position and the launching of counter-attacks by reserves.' These orders did not change on the 16th and Vietinghoff particularly regretted the squandering of his best mobile reserves, notably 2/200 and 2/104 PG Regiments, in doomed counter-attacks around Colle la Bastia and Colle San Lucia. Eventually both battalions were forced to pull back, whereas they 'could have been used to far better effect if, instead of launching scattered and therefore useless counter-thrusts, they had been given an opportunity to prepare, without enemy interference, the positions to which they had now had to return, disheartened by the failure at their first new commitment and by the heavy losses they had suffered.'[66] A letter from the commander of 115 Reconnaissance Battalion, who had been involved in particularly heavy fighting on the 16th, was telling corroboration of Vietinghoff's claims:

You have no idea of the rigours and horrors of this retreat. . . . We will not let ourselves become disheartened, but people are tired and have had nothing to eat for three days. Our Free French and Moroccan enemies are remarkably fine soldiers. My heart bleeds when I look at my fine unit, after five days' fighting: 150 men lost. The echelons are already far to the rear, three recce cars are in pieces, my armoured command vehicle and all its wireless equipment has been destroyed by a French AFV. Since April 26 weapons, paper and food have been lacking completely. Today it looks as if things are a little better. Perhaps we shall manage, after all, to avoid the crumbling of the whole Italian front, but that appears to be a small hope . . .[67]

But it is important to keep in mind just why these counter-attacks had

---

* OBSW stands for Oberbefehl Süd-West, another name for Army Group 'C'.

failed so disastrously. For similar tactics had worked well against the British, and were to give significant pause to the Canadians when they in turn entered the Liri bridgehead. Admittedly the Germans rarely actually pushed Eighth Army units back but they almost always caused them to halt and methodically regroup for a renewed attack, during which time the Germans could also reorganize and fall back without undue interference to the next defensible line. But this was not the French style. Once they had fought off a counter-attack they pressed forward on the heels of the retreating Germans, often infiltrating round their flanks along seemingly impossible mountain tracks, and gave them no opportunity to halt and regroup. Various German sources testified to the remarkable abilities of the French and their success in keeping their adversaries continually on the hop. Reviewing the lessons of the fighting so far, on 17 May, Army Group 'C' noted: 'Especially noteworthy is the great manoeuvrability of the French (Moroccan) troops, who advanced rapidly over terrain considered to be impassable, carrying their heavy weapons on the backs of mules, and persistently attempted, sometimes by wide encircling movements, to envelop our positions and take them from the rear.'[68] With an appropriate sense of irony one German historian compared the French offensive to 'the Blitzkrieg campaigns of earlier years' and cited the comments of a German staff officer on the Moroccans who, 'fired with each success, pull their neighbours with them, make the best use of every local success for prompt pursuits and help their less successful neighbours through flanking attacks. Swift appreciation of the situation and its correct exploitation are a pronounced strength of the French command.'[69] Another assessment by Kesselring's staff, this time dated 19 May, made explicit the differences between French tactics and those of their more ponderous Allies: 'American and British tactics, as in the past, have been methodical: local successes have rarely been exploited. The French, on the contrary, particularly the Moroccans, have fought furiously and exploited each local success by immediately concentrating all their available forces at the point where resistance is weakening.'[70]*

* German discomfiture on the Maio massif and the Dora Line was made all the worse because they had consistently underestimated French capabilities, even after their remarkable advances in early January. According to Vietinghoff: '. . . all commands . . . misjudged the value of the French divisions. . . . There was a tendency, particularly at OBSW, to ascribe the constant advance of the French [in January] not so much to the exceptionally high quality of these troops as rather to the fact that 5 Mountain Division had not yet familiarized itself with the surroundings.' (Vietinghoff, *Operations of 71 Division, op. cit.*, p.13.)

And so Esperia fell in its turn. Early on the 17th a joint offensive was mounted by 3 DIA and 1 DMI and by 09.00 the Algerians had crossed the River Marino, directly in front of Esperia, whilst the Free French were outflanking Monte d'Oro from the north. Other Algerians pushed through to the south of Esperia, along the so-called Via Matilda running along the chain of peaks Points 943, 841 and 704. With the main strongpoints of the Dora Line now outflanked both to north and south the Germans had no alternative but to begin pulling back into the southern extension of the Hitler Line, and when Esperia was attacked at 11.00 it was found to have already been evacuated. As usual, however, German rearguards covered the withdrawal, some of them from 9 PG Regiment which was beginning to trickle into the sector, and they put up a sufficiently determined resistance to force the French to pause and organize a fresh assault for the following morning. The divisional history described the progress thus far:

> From the beginning the tactics had been the same; go further every day, where the Boche wasn't. . . . For four days the men marched without seeking to understand why, without wondering about what tomorrow held, in a series of roughly equal bounds, each turning revealing similar vistas, a village perched on a rock face and only accessible via a broken bridge, a crossroads that would have to be forced, a pink house behind which were camouflaged anti-tank guns. How long was it going to last? One did not ask. One had hardly begun.[71]

But Juin was not depending entirely on the efforts of the Algerians and the Free French to breach the Hitler Line. A vital component of his plan, it will be recalled, was to launch his Mountain Corps, comprising 4 DMM and the *goumiers*, split into two independent combat groups, into the supposedly impenetrable Petrella massif.* They were to push on two main axes, Monte Fammera–Monte San Martino–Monte Fontanino and Monte Petrella–Monte Revole–Campodimele, towards the Itri-Pico road, the cutting of which would threaten the complete outflanking of the Hitler Line. On the 13th they moved to their jump-off positions to the east of the Ausonia–Santa Maria Infante road. The War Diary of one of Sevez's battalions noted: 'On Saturday the 13th we left Vito at 17.00

---

* These groups were named after their commanders. The Bondis Group comprised 2 RTM and 3 Tabor Group; the Guillaume Group 6 RTM, 3/1 RTM and 1 and 4 Tabor Groups. Both also contained engineer elements and a battalion of mountain artillery.

hours. The keynote of this offensive was going to be bitter resistance, from *djebel* to *djebel*, across many a *thalweg*. It was no sinecure to be part of the Mountain Corps. Speed would be everything . . .'[72]

There were those who were less than enthusiastic about the potential of the Mountain Corps. They had soon acquired a very poor reputation for discipline. One British soldier had shared a rest area with some *goumiers* 'who were living in the town with their wives! They were dirty, pulled down doors as well as fruit trees for their firewood. They are indeed poor propaganda for us . . . and putting them there seemed as erroneous as putting an Eskimo in a tube train and expecting him to know how to behave.'[73] A journalist wrote: 'The Goums became a legend and a grim joke with the Eighth. No story about their rape, their progress or their other deeds was too wild to be believed.'[74] Their sexual proclivities were the subject of particularly gruesome rumour, not least among the Germans for they were reputed to bugger their prisoners. They were equally feared by the Italians on whom they were billeted. According to one civilian:

We suffered more during the twenty-four hours of contact with the Moroccans than in the eight months under the Germans. The Germans took away our goats, sheep and food, but they respected our women and our meagre savings. The Moroccans flung themselves upon us like unchained demons. They violated, threatening with machine guns, children, women, young men, following each other like beasts in rotation; they took our money from us, they followed us into the village and carried off every bundle, our linen, our shoes. Even those of their officers who tried to intervene came under their threats.[75]*

There were also reservations about their military abilities. An officer of 88 US Division had frequent contact with them around the Corps

* Accusations about the *goumiers* buggering, castrating or murdering their prisoners were vigorously denied by one French historian, though his explanation certainly confirms the unorthodoxy of their methods: 'A prisoner was valuable. During the Italian Campaign the Fritz hunters were not slow to accord themselves a "perk", that of selling their prisoners . . . to comrades-in-arms who had been less fortunate or less adept . . . but who were keen to get hold of a few *feldgrau* to pass them off as their own prisoners. . . . From May to July 1944, the average price of an ordinary German soldier was to vary between 500 and 600 francs, that of an *oberleutnant* to reach almost double that. . . . The traffic in prisoners was to become really lucrative when the Americans found out about it. . . . These were the boys who were to pay well, with no discussion or haggling . . .' (Chambe, *Epopée, op. cit.*, pp.245–6.)

boundary in the Auruncis and to him 'they seemed to have small appreciation of some of the modern implements of war. It was tragic to see elements of their reconnaissance groups moving forward with mine-sweepers, always looking ahead in search of the enemy instead of observing the ground for possible mines. My surgeons reported amputating many feet of the men who had walked into the enemy minefields with seeming indifference.'[76] Even their commander, General Augustin Guillaume, had been cautious about the proposal for a unified Mountain Corps, or at least one without a strong leavening of European soldiers. In a memorandum to Juin he wrote:

> The goums . . . even more than the Tirailleurs . . . have retained intact the qualities and the weaknesses of their race: indisputable valour in war, but unreliability under stress; an offensive spirit exalted by success, but soon dissipated by failure; an innate courage in infantry combat, but a tendency to become unsettled in the face of modern weapons . . .; a peasant hardiness and an innate sense of ground, but an aversion to hard work and discipline.

Because there were far fewer Frenchmen in a Tabor Group* and because 'the employment of several Tabor Groups under a single command has not yet been tried', Guillaume advised that such an experiment 'should not be considered except in special circumstances and, preferably, with the support of regular troops, both Infantry and Artillery.'[77]

Exactly how important was the addition to the Mountain Corps of the bulk of Sevez's battalions is hard to judge, but the two composite groups certainly made remarkable progress through the mountains. By 23.30 on the 14th they had crossed the Ausonia road, passing through Monsabert's advancing columns without a hitch, and on the next day the Bondis Group reached Monte Fammera and Monte Chiavica whilst to the south the Guillaume Group took Monte Cavecce and sent out patrols towards the outer peaks surrounding Monte Revole. On the 16th this latter was taken, with the Bondis Group pushing on towards Monte del Lago to protect the flank of the Algerian units pressing in on Esperia. On the 17th Monte del Lago fell in its turn and by the end of the day the Bondis Group had also taken Monte San Martino, Punte Savino and Monte Morrone del Saracino. The Guillaume Group moved towards Campodimele, taking Valle Piana at 15.00, where it surprised and defeated a battle group from 3/104 PG Regiment, MonteFaggeto at 21.00 and Monte le Pezze at around

---

* In a Tabor Group there were 227 Frenchmen out of a total complement of 2900. The ratio in a Tirailleur Regiment was 979 out of 3100.

midnight. The encounter at Valle Piana was typical of the Mountain Corps' battles thus far, having more in common with a guerrilla ambush than with more orthodox infantry combat. The Germans obviously had no idea that any enemy troops were so near and as the French crept forward they 'showed no concern at all, some of them stripped down to their vests and wandering between the tanks, others . . . talking amongst themselves.' The tanks were soon joined by two columns of infantry, one of which

> came straight towards us. . . . One could clearly make out the smallest details of their equipment, their gestures and almost their very expressions as they climbed up. One of the leading infantrymen, carrying machine gun ammunition, halted 50 metres from us. He sat down and got his breath back. This short pause gave us time to check that none of us had stirred. Everyone was hugging the earth. The silence was total and there was no hint of the hail of fire that was about to be unleashed on the enemy. After a few seconds, though it seemed much longer, the German got up, picked up his boxes and set off again. He was only 20 metres away, then 15, then 10. The order to open fire was about to be given. At this precise moment the German gestured. Had he seen us? We could not be sure, but his gesture caused the whole section to open fire. He fell with an inhuman cry. The Boches were taken completely by surprise, even more than we had dared hope, and they ran off as fast as they could, casting aside their equipment to aid their flight. Their panic was complete. . . . It was magnificent. Each one of us brought down our mark, sometimes several. One corporal, feeling that a machine gunner was not firing fast enough, grabbed his piece and ran after the Boches, shooting from the hip.[78]

On the whole, however, resistance thus far had been comparatively light, the Germans clearly never having expected any troops to be able to penetrate this part of the Auruncis. According to one company's after-action narrative: 'It was hot, the climb was stiff, the men advanced in silence. The country was wild but the war seemed far off. We had not heard a single shot since the morning.'[79] At times it seemed as though the rugged terrain might defeat even the Mountain Corps and the dearth of even the meanest tracks meant that its columns became more and more strung out. On the 17th the troops at the very rear had not yet even entered the massif – it was to take them two days to reach the positions already occupied by the leading units – and the supply columns were falling dangerously behind. Guillaume, it seems, had hoped that it would be possible to supplement his mule columns with jeeps but the following verses, probably by an exasperated transport officer, told what a vain hope this was:

> En contemplant du Fammera
> La photographie aérienne,
> Notre Général déclara,
> A l'Etat-Major en haleine:
> 'Regardez cette ligne là
> Qui vers les hautes cimes mène,
> C'est presqu'un chemin carrossable,
> Nous tenons la piste jeepable.' (. . .)

> J'ai vu Goumiers et Tirailleurs
> Escalader les hautes cimes,
> Les Muletiers, les Artilleurs
> Pitonner au bord des abîmes,
> Et les Bulldozers des Sapeurs
> Raser dans un effort ultime
> Les rochers les plus formidables . . .
> Mais où sont les pistes jeepables? (. . .)

> De Ponte a Casale et Spigno,
> Esperia, San Nicolas,
> Campodimele, Amaseno,
> Jusqu'à Sezze, Roccagorga,
> Tout en sautant le Monte Maio,
> En contournant le Petrella,
> Je me demandais, pauvre diable:
> Mais où sont les pistes jeepables?[80]*

So pressing did Guillaume's supply problems become, in fact, that a parachute drop had to be organized, on the 17th. This was remarkably successful and even those few boxes of food and ammunition that fell into

---

* The sense of the poem is as follows: 'Looking at an aerial photograph of Monte Fammera our general said to the exhausted staff, "Look at that line there leading up to the high peaks. It's almost a carriageway, there we have a track fit for jeeps." . . . . I've seen goumiers and tirailleurs climbing the high peaks, muleteers and artillerymen picking their way on the edges of abysses, and bulldozers and sappers levelling rock faces with an ultimate effort . . . But where are the tracks fit for jeeps? . . . From Ponte a Casale and Spigno [etc.], leaping right across Monte Maio and skirting Monte Petrella, I ask myself despairingly, But where are the tracks fit for jeeps?'

the German lines were recaptured on the 18th, when the Mountain Corps resumed its advance.

Nevertheless, French progress on the 18th was considerably slower than on the preceding days and German resistance temporarily stiffened. Tenth Army had been told that the Hitler Line must be held at all costs and various reinforcements, notably the remainder of 9 PG Regiment, were thrown in around San Oliva. Not that this order was to the taste of either von Vietinghoff or von Senger und Etterlin. They were now desperately short of men and the commander of 71 Division, for example, had already reported that both his regiments could muster no more than one hundred infantry effectives. Just as on the 15th and 16th, in front of the Dora Line, both the Army and the Corps commanders would have preferred to fall back some distance to gain time to regroup their forces and to familiarize them with a new set of defences. Vietinghoff wrote after the war that the correct German decision at this time

would have necessitated the issuance of orders to Tenth Army to withdraw while fighting, sector by sector, toward the prepared C-Position and, with Fourteenth Army, only there to put up tenacious resistance. . . . However . . . it proved impossible to persuade either Hitler or – at that time – OBSW to take such a strategic view of the situation. Regardless of the fact that the overall view of the situation became increasingly critical, they unswervingly adhered to the purely tactical principle of rigid defence of every inch of ground 'aiming at the attrition of the enemy attack forces'.[81]

On the 18th, indeed, a conference was held at Kesselring's headquarters at which both of his subordinates tried to persuade him of the dangers of trying to hold the present line. According to von Senger und Etterlin:

I had to tell Field-Marshal Kesselring that this time the Corps front had not merely been penetrated as had been the case frequently in the past, but that the enemy had made a breach. I stated that in my opinion the only thing left to do was to prevent large numbers of our troops being cut off by enemy forces who might attack out of the bridgehead, and that this could be accomplished by means of an orderly retreat which of course would have to be effected while offering continuous resistance in successive phase lines. However, even at this conference, the only matter which was discussed was the question as to how a second line of resistance could be established . . . south of [Anzio] . . .[82]

And for the time being no withdrawal at all was to be countenanced.

But XIV Panzer Corps was not able to hold on to the forward portions of the Hitler Line, and Monticelli and San Oliva were taken by 3 DIA early in the afternoon of the 18th, as was Madonna di Montevetro further south. To the left of the Algerians the Mountain Corps seized a line running between Monte Fumone and Monte le Pezze and even managed to send out patrols as far as Campodimele and Monte Vele, the latter on the far side of the vital Itri–Pico road. But German resistance was beginning to harden once more and from late on the 18th little forward progress was possible. On the French right flank 1 DMI was unable to force a crossing of the Forme Quesa in the face of numerous infantry and anti-tank emplacements. In the centre 3 DIA encountered fierce opposition between Points 178 and 127 and Monte del Mandrone and Monte della Commune. The Mountain Corps was virtually halted along all its axes of advance, being held up throughout the 19th in front of Serra del Lago, Campodimele and Monte le Pezze, both of the latter being lost and retaken in a series of fierce counter-attacks. A later report by 4 DMM noted: 'At this point the Mountain Corps encountered serious difficulties as it approached the various roads along which the enemy had immediately thrown in tank detachments and self-propelled guns [from 26 Panzer Division]. . . . Equipped only with such weapons as could be carried on the backs of the mules, the mountain units lacked the necessary firepower to overcome enemy resistance in the valley.'[83]

At this point it is necessary to return to II US Corps, which we left in possession of Santa Maria Infante, early on the 14th. The German 94 Division, it will be remembered, had been obliged to give up this village, after the most tenacious resistance, when the French smashed 71 Division's defensive line on the Maio massif. From then on, in fact, the German forces in front of II Corps had to retreat steadily to avoid losing contact on their left flank and so opening up a gap through which the Americans or the French could exploit deep into their rear. Throughout the period 14–21 May 'the enemy made no extensive stand in force in the II Corps zone',[84] and the Americans made an uninterrupted advance both along the coast, through Gaeta and Sperlonga, and in the mountains to the north, through Maranola, Itri and Fondi. Only at Terracina was serious resistance encountered, after Kesselring decided to commit almost his last strategic reserve to try and prevent Fifth Army effecting a junction between II Corps and the forces in the Anzio beachhead. On the 18th the whole of 29 PG Division was ordered into this sector. But the move was not to the taste of General Eberhardt von Mackensen, the commander of the German forces surrounding the beachhead, and he wilfully procrastinated, hoping that the order might be rescinded. According to Kesselring:

When I gave the order I had every reason to assume [the Panzer Grenadiers] could reach a position of considerable natural strength by the morning of 20 May and would thus be able to close the gap. That this did not happen was due to . . . [Mackensen's] opposition to the transfer, the first news of which reached me on the 20th on my return to my battle headquarters. . . . On arriving at 29th Panzer Grenadiers' headquarters on 21 May I found the division had come up too late and had offered to fight in unprepared positions – with calamitous consequences. . . . An excellent defensive zone had been thrown away and the enemy handed an almost impregnable position between Terracina and Fondi, the loss of which gave the Americans victory.[85]

With the fall of Terracina the Americans switched their effort north-westwards to provide support on the French left flank and by the 24th advance elements had seized Sonnino and Roccasecca. German resistance in this last phase was very light and II Corps outstripped the French, on whose front XIV Panzer Corps was still making its major effort. On the 24th, therefore, the Americans were ordered to garrison their existing line and wait for the French to catch up.

But no advance through Italy could ever be termed easy and accounts by the men of 85 and 88 US Divisions highlight the physical and mental punishment meted out in any kind of infantry combat. The work was hardly glamorous. A war correspondent wrote:

Battles were large or small; points at issue were vital or of minor consequence; but always and everywhere procedure and pattern were always the same. German guns betrayed their presence. We called our planes to bomb them, and then we concentrated our own artillery, too numerous to be opposed, and they shelled the German guns. Thereupon the infantry flowed slowly ahead. At each strongpoint or village there were always a few snipers to be blasted out, always mines which exploded a number of vehicles, always booby traps which filled a few rooms with smoke and mortal cries. Bulldozers would clear the rubble, engineers would fill the craters, the medical troops would set up their aid stations . . . and while silent men hoisted limp bodies into trucks the news would go out to

the world that the place was 'liberated'. This is the way it was, day
after day, town after town . . .[86]

These sporadic little battles, and the endless tension of the cautious
advances from peak to peak and village to village, inexorably ground the
men down. Occasionally there were moments of outright panic. In the last
stages of the advance towards Roccasecca, a column from 350 Regiment
ran into an unexpectedly strong German rearguard. As it opened fire the
men dived for cover and then one of them suddenly jumped to his feet
and shouted that the battalion commander had ordered them to
withdraw. According to the regimental commander, also with the
column:

> Men who had previously been nervous but determined now jumped
> to their feet everywhere. The cowed, retreating soldier, who had
> camouflaged his fears by shouting out a fictitious order, had set the
> stage for a possible rout. For a brief second the men about me were
> on the verge of stampeding to the rear. I responded to the excited
> vocaling with a volume of curses that quieted those near by. Firing
> my pistol in the air I shouted, 'I'll kill the next man who starts to the
> rear.' But I wasn't alone in my efforts to quell the incipient panic.
> In the flare of a rocket I saw a man, whose collar insignia marked
> him as a lieutenant, block another man's retreat with a carbine held
> across his chest, pushing the soldier into the weeds at his feet. 'Our
> front is over there,' the officer roared.[87]

But collective breakdowns of this sort were unusual. More typical was a
slow individual deterioration that eventually turned men into something
like zombies. Even after only three or four days of combat, Colonel Fry
noted

> a complete change in my soldiers. Two days and three nights of
> battle had absorbed their energies and left them jaded and worn.
> Unshaven and dirty, they had taken on an ageless pattern. The
> complete absence of all outward expressions of mirth or anticipation
> left them with the over-all appearance of men who had nothing to
> look forward to. They could only endure. Their pride anchored
> them to their job. Galley slaves, in ages past, must have presented
> a similar appearance.[88]

By the end of the month, the men of 85 Division seemed 'to have passed
beyond the point of conceivable limits of human endurance.' One

lieutenant said of his platoon: 'My men are utterly worn out. Their legs and backs and arms ache beyond description, and I don't see how some of them right now could stand up unaided on their own feet and put one foot in front of the other to take a forward step.' Another said: 'My men are *tired*. Their eyes are bloodshot. Some of them are so tired they literally cannot see. Two men coming into this area yesterday walked right into trees. Two days ago, two other men, sound asleep on their feet during a march, walked right off a road and out into a field. Another man had to go after them, wake them up, and get them back in line.'[89]

But they had not laboured in vain. If it was the French Corps that had permitted them to break out through Santa Maria Infante and across the Capo d'Aqua, they were able to return the favour on the 19th. The French were now concentrating all their attention on breaking through to Pico, with ancillary thrusts across the Itri–Pico road towards Lenola and Pastena. But, as we have seen, resistance in the rear areas of the Hitler Line had hardened considerably, virtually halting the French advance. Pico covered a whole network of roads towards Ceccano and Ceprano and was of vital importance to the Germans. Last-ditch resistance, therefore, was still the order of the day. At 18.00 on the 19th, all troops still south of the Liri and east of Pico were directed towards the Pico–Pontecorvo Line where they were to hold firm. A potentially serious check to Juin's advance was only avoided thanks to II Corps. As a report by 4 DMM noted: 'Luckily the Americans opened the road from Itri on the 19th. The CEF straightway decided to set up an armoured detachment [composed of elements from 4 Moroccan Spahis, 8 Chasseurs d'Afrique and 756 US Tank Battalion] and to send it [northwards] through Itri. This additional force was completely indispensable to the Mountain Corps and allowed it to mop up along the Itri–Pico road, to continue its advance into the mountains and so outflank the Germans.'[90]

The French task was still far from easy. On the right, I DMI was engaged in fierce tank v. tank battles and I Brigade was obliged to give up some ground on the 21st. In the centre 3 DIA was charged with the capture of Pico but it ran into yet more well-entrenched Germans, between Monte Cozonella and Monte Leucio, and though footholds were gained on both Monte Pota and Monte Leucio late on the 20th, it still proved impossible to break into Pico itself. By the 21st, however, the armoured group working its way from Itri had made good progress and as it moved northwards the way was cleared for the *goumiers* and Tirailleurs of the Mountain Corps to make important penetrations west of the Itri–Pico road. By the end of the day they were holding a line running northwards from Monte Crispi, across Monte Appiolo, to the southern fringes of

Monte il Castello. The Germans were now threatened with a partial envelopment of their positions between Pico and Pontecorvo, and when 3 DIA moved once more against the former, early on the 22nd, they found that the main German forces had already pulled back.

Pausing only briefly, mainly to allow 2 DIM back into the line on an axis towards Pastena, the French plunged forwards. Late on the 22nd Lenola fell to the Mountain Corps and on the next day they trudged on towards Vallecorsa. 2 DIM, however, was only able to make limited progress towards Pastena and 3 DIA was equally hampered in its drive along the road from Pico to San Giovanni. By the evening of the 24th these divisions had still only gained a foothold in the south-east corner of Vallecorsa whilst Pastena and San Giovanni were still entirely in the hands of determined German rearguards. Many French sources attest to the bitter nature of this stage of the battle. The terrain was still as formidable an enemy as the Germans. Around Cima el Nibbio, at the southern extremity of the French line, 3/6 RTM 'occupied their objectives without loss but after having made an extremely arduous move across chaotic terrain. [On the following day] an extremely arduous march across very difficult terrain. Several mules disappeared into ravines.'[91] Most units met Germans as well. Amongst them was 1/4 RTM which on the 23rd 'was supported only by a few tanks, and that only during the first part of the day. The battalion found itself engaged on ground strongly held by a battalion of Panzer Grenadiers ably supported by two heavy tanks and well-directed 150mm artillery fire. It suffered heavily from this artillery which did not stop firing until nightfall and cost us nine killed and 30 wounded.'[92]

But the French were not to be gainsaid. They had already made the decisive breaches in the four major German defensive lines and knew that Tenth Army, no matter how bitterly it might contest this next stage of the advance, was on the run. Even though some French units were reduced almost to a snail's pace, their élan and will to victory never faltered. A report by 6 RTM referred to the days following the breach of the Hitler Line as the '*Période Sportive*' and noted that thenceforth

began a mountain race, by the most unexpected and sinuous routes, in which the columns made light of the fire from self-propelled guns. For the Boche it was a series of fighting withdrawals, not always sufficiently fast to avoid losing a number of prisoners. The enemy destroyed the bridges and the roads. But that only appreciably delayed the motorized elements, for the engineers showed great zeal. In the mountains the *goumiers* enjoyed surprise and came

down on the confident Panzer Grenadiers like demonic monks. . . .
Our heavy 155mm guns were everywhere along the roads, amidst
the dust and the heat. The mules were slow but what other than them
could have ensured that the supplies got through and the wounded
were evacuated in such inaccessible regions?[93]

And *who* else, but the French, would have a story such as this to enter
in their reports? It concerned a company of the Algerian Division,
entrusted with the capture of a vital hill to the east of Pico. It had been
taken once and then lost to a German counter-attack, but possession was
vital to the continuation of the whole divisional attack:

> Six officers had been killed and wounded. Only . . . *sous-lieutenant*
> Navas was still on his feet, with 50 or 60 men. . . . He gathered the
> survivors around him and harangued them, 'You are warriors, you
> have no fear of death. Think of your captains who have just been
> killed. Think of our flag. If we die we will ascend to Paradise. We
> are going to take that peak and sing as we do it. You, sergeant . . .,
> choose the best war song.' And the Arabic chant, high-pitched and
> rhythmic, rose towards the sky. Fix bayonets, Forward. The
> momentum was regained. The peak was taken once and for all and
> *sous-lieutenant* Navas lay on the ground, smiling, happy to have
> been victorious, to have avenged the dead and to have given his
> blood for the France that he loved so.[94]

Few German accounts of any stage of the Fourth Battle have survived.
The following excerpts, however, show that they too were still capable
of prodigies of valour, though they were now coming dangerously close
to snapping under the remorseless French pressure. Among the hodge-
podge of units thrown in against the Mountain Corps was 3 Alpine
Infantry Battalion, whose War Diary described thus the tank and infantry
attacks of the 19th and 20th:

> *19 May*: While the enemy was strongly supported by artillery and
> mortar fire our attacks had to be conducted with absolutely no
> support from heavy weapons. The situation was further aggravated
> by an ammunition shortage which arose from the inadequate
> number of vehicles brought up by the battalion to its new area. . . .
> In the absence of a battalion train, battalion runners and mortar
> crews, who had already expended their own ammunition, were
> employed as ammunition bearers.
> *20 May*: [Ordered to withdraw to a line between Monte

Vallerotondo and Monte Crispi] One of the greatest difficulties accompanying the withdrawal was the evacuation of the many seriously wounded men who had to be carried. Combat soldiers had to carry them the whole distance from the valley west of the Itri–Pico road . . . to the road junction at San Martino [over 5 kilometres].[95]

Another hard-pressed unit was 115 Panzer Reconnaissance Battalion, one of whose COs' letters we have already quoted. The Battalion formed the nucleus of *Kampfgruppe* Nagel, whose After-Action Report showed that Baron von der Borsch had hardly exaggerated the miseries of the endless retreat:

> *13 May*: The withdrawal, which was under heavy Allied artillery fire, was extremely costly. (. . .)
> *16 May*: [Withdraw to the east of Esperia.] Our troops performed extraordinary feats despite the fact that they had received no rations for three days and were forced to make every round of ammunition count. Our casualties were heavy. (. . .)
> *17 May:* [Withdraw to the south of Casa Chiaia.] Digging in was impossible. The troops were tired, hungry and fought out. Allied artillery prevented the supplies from reaching the lower unit command posts. The best NCOs and officers were casualties. (. . .)
> *19 May*: [Withdraw to Pico–Pontecorvo road.] The movement to the new line, which involved a cross-country march during an unusually dark night, took the last ounce of strength out of the exhausted troops. Because of the breadth of the new sector only scattered strongpoints could be occupied.
> *20 May*: Fighting strength of the *Kampfgruppe* was now about one-tenth of the original figure. . . . Because of the shortage of signal equipment, battalions had less and less control over their troops.
> *21 May*: During the period 13–21 May, officers, NCOs and enlisted men of *Kampfgruppe* Nagel had passed their severest test of fire in the operations in southern Italy.[96]

As usual it was the individual soldier who spoke most eloquently of all and the following letter, found on the body of a dead German belonging to this same *Kampfgruppe*, only serves to emphasize the desperateness of the German situation along this entire front:

> The Tommies are throwing heavy stuff at us. The number of tanks is terrifying. . . . In the long run this state of affairs is just impossible and our fine group is being gradually reduced to ashes. Morale

yesterday was very low. No supplies had got through to the Company for five days. Today some arrived, but just in the nick of time. However you look at it, one can no longer say . . . that war is a beautiful thing.[97]*

* The 'Tommies' referred to were probably the Canadians, who lent much artillery to the French prior to their own attack on the Hitler Line.

16
'By Weight of Numbers'
1 Canadian Corps and the Hitler Line, 18–25 May 1944

. . . my boys move in tonight . . . New boys with fear and nerves and anxiety hidden under quick smiles and quick seriousness. Old campaigners with a far away look. It is the hardest thing to watch without breaking into tears.

Chaplain of the Seaforth Highlanders of
Canada, 23 May 1944

In the Liri Valley, it will be recalled, Leese had started to build up the pressure on the afternoon of the 13th when he ordered 78 Division to move into 4 Division's sector. Forty-eight hours later fresh troops were also ordered into the southern end of the Valley. This time it was 1 Canadian Division, under General C. Vokes, who were to relieve the Indians entirely. This relief was complete on the 16th and on the following two days the Canadians pressed forward towards the Hitler Line, eager to carry out Alexander's instruction to 'bounce' these positions. But events were already conspiring against them. The commander of 1 Canadian Corps, Major-General E.M. Burns, had wanted to feed his other division, 5 Canadian Armoured, into the bridgehead close on the heels of 1 Division, so that the former's infantry brigade, the 11th, could relieve Vokes' forward brigade and keep up the momentum of the attack. Once again, however, the paucity of bridges and approach roads supervened and 11 Brigade, which was supposed to effect its relief on the night of the 18/19th, was only beginning to cross the Rapido on the following morning.

Nor was Vokes' own attack going as quickly as might have been hoped. The relief of 8 Indian Division had gone very smoothly and at first progress was good. On the right was 3 Brigade, whose battalions were working together very well. The history of the West Nova Scotia Regiment spoke of a 'game of leapfrog between the regiments . . . each in turn passing through the front battalion, pushing forward, and then digging in while another took a leap.'[1] According to an eye-witness a sister battalion, the Royal 22e Regiment, raised in French-speaking Canada, was particularly adept at this style of warfare: 'It was a real thrill to see the battlewise "Van Doos" march straight forward spread out and half crouching. They never dug in.'[2] If the last remark is true one can only feel that the Québécois were pushing *sang froid* to the point of foolhardiness. The West Novas were more circumspect:

The enemy mortars and artillery were very active in covering the retreat, and the story of the pursuit from the Gustav Line to the Hitler Line is largely a tale of hasty shovelling in the hard clay at the end of each forward leap. One West Nova expressed the feeling of the whole Regiment when he exclaimed to his officer, 'Judas Priest, sir, I thought the ground at Cissbury Ring [a Sussex training area] was tough – but out here it gets tougher with every shell that falls.'[3]

To the left of these battalions was 3 Brigade whose accounts of the fighting were noticeably less enthusiastic. The historian of the Hastings and Prince Edward Regiment, for example, noted that

clouds of dust combined with protective smoke screens to obliterate objectives and confuse direction. The battle quickly degenerated to the platoon and company level, and became a savage mêlée of infantry against infantry. . . . German and Canadian sub-units became intermingled. Regimental jeeps and stretcher-bearers hurrying forward to evacuate the wounded wandered into enemy lines, then out again unscathed. . . . The shapelessness of this battle resulted from the breakdown of communications. Wireless communications became largely impossible, not through mechanical difficulties, but due to frequency congestion resulting from the great number of units engaged in the operation. At one time both a German unit and the Regiment were simultaneously attempting to use the same frequency, and at all times several Allied units could be found on any given wavelength.[4]

Similar sentiments are echoed in the narrative of the 48th Highlanders of Canada. The fighting on the 17th, it was felt, was 'loose and confused' and operations were particularly hampered by chronic radio failure and the fact that almost everybody, on both sides, seemed to be using the same frequency. There was, as usual, early progress and one officer drew a very 'pukka' analogy: 'It was rather like grouse hunting; we flushed one now and then and everybody let fly at him.'[5] But Baade's rearguards were not going to give up without a fight and as they fell back across the Forme d'Aquino creek their tiny battle groups became ever more tenacious. The Highlanders were being supported by tanks of the Suffolk Regiment (142 Royal Armoured Corps Regiment) and as they came to one tributary of the Forme d'Aquino infantry and armour moved up on different banks.

This left the Churchills without infantry support, and it proved they needed this even more than the Highlanders needed them. The Churchills were met by a new short-range anti-tank weapon comparable to the American bazookas. When bravely handled the Germans' new tube, firing a long percussion bomb with a tail, was very effective. These were courageously manned, as the Suffolks discovered with a shock. Their first three Churchills were surprised victims – ambushed – hit from hides in the grain. The troop commander was killed. . . . The new weapon was the *Panzerschreck* (tank-terror). . . . A second group of Churchills was ordered up to fight with Charlie Company, and the tank-terrors went to work again. The tanks moved up on the left of their 'killed' mates, and missed the Highlanders, who were in front and east of them. There was another ambush. The *Panzerschrecks* killed two additional Churchills, the balance of the troop wisely retreating. That was a costly tank lesson – 5 Churchills![6]*

So disheartened was the Tank Brigade commander, in fact, that the order was given that accompanying armour were not to approach to less than 400 yards from the enemy. This hardly boded well for intimate co-operation with the infantry, the very essence of good tactics in this type of terrain.

Even when the Germans began pulling back from the Forme d'Aquino the Canadians still faced considerable problems. The worst was the progressive congealment of their traffic due to a dearth of fords or bridges across the creek. 'Bridging equipment was ordered up but could not be brought forward until the tracks had been cleared of vehicles waiting to move up. . . . Unfortunately the advance could not progress until the stream was bridged and so the vicious circle was complete.'[7] One battalion historian commented tartly on the incredible number of vehicles in the

* The Canadians were not supported by the tanks of their own 5 Armoured Division, which was being held back to exploit any break through the Hitler Line. There was, in fact, still some ill-feeling between the two divisions of the Canadian Corps, arising from an incident in December 1943 which 'soon achieved a rancid notoriety. . . . As it was told and retold many times along the front, some men of the 1st Division had seen the trucks [of 11 Brigade] passing through the rubbled streets and had called out to wish them luck. A head emerged from one of the trucks and hurled back obscene assurances that the 5th would do what the 1st hadn't done – it would take Pescara by Christmas. Swiftly that unfortunate stupidity of one man was twisted into the blasphemy of an entire division and relations suffered accordingly. Nor were they helped when the green infantry of the 11th Brigade was thrown harshly back and had to be relieved prematurely by the exhausted 1st Division well short of Pescara.' (D. How, *The 8th Hussars*, Maritime Publishing, Sussex (N.B.), 1964, p.193.)

bridgehead and the less than adequate attempts to regulate their movements:

> In an area of not more than twenty-five square miles four infantry and three armoured divisions were operating. This meant that more than 20,000 vehicles were moving about in this restricted space. They crossed and recrossed the battlefield in every direction; they tangled in hour-long traffic jams at bottlenecks; they created a maze of misleading tracks; they often coagulated in such great clots as to hinder the movement of troops on foot. . . . In a single morning . . . [the Royal Canadian Regiment] received three sets of orders, each of which in turn had to be cancelled because of the traffic conditions. This vehicular chaos made it difficult to sustain the momentum of a battle whose best prospects of victory lay in a smashing blow which would breach the Hitler Line beyond repair in the course of a few hours' fighting.[8]

A passage was eventually cleared for the bridging vehicles but no sooner had they set off than a column of vehicles from 6 British Armoured Division suddenly appeared, well outside their own Corps boundary. Further delay ensued and it was not until 18.00 on the 18th that a bridge across the Forme d'Aquino was finally opened.

But the Canadians had still not given up all hopes of rushing the Hitler Line and 1 and 3 Brigades pressed forward that night to within a mile or so of its outposts. Preparations were made for an immediate attack by two battalions of 3 Brigade, the Carleton and York Regiment and the 'Van Doos'. This attack was to be launched at 10.00, as a complement to one by 78 Division, who were now on the outskirts of Aquino. The British attacked first with 36 Brigade, 8 Argyll and Sutherland Highlanders to the south of the village and 5 Buffs to the north. Yet again a battalion historian is particularly outspoken about the staff work and administrative arrangements for this attack:

> During the night [18/19th] a series of incoherent conferences was held at Brigade Headquarters, as the result of which Lt-Col Taylor was eventually given orders at 4.15 a.m. to advance at 4.45 and capture Aquino. As he was more than a mile from his headquarters, and could only reach it on foot, the timetable was optimistic. As it was he did well to get the leading companies moving by 5 o'clock, but it was nothing but pure luck that he happened to meet the squadron leader of the troop of the Derbyshire Yeomanry which was to support him.

Opposition was soon encountered, from snipers, machine gunners and anti-tank crews well dug-in in the scattered farmhouses and behind almost every hedge. Progress was slow. 'Each house had to be stalked, scrutinised, attacked, and searched; every sniper required a separate little action by a section. The enemy shelling and mortaring increased, and was particularly unpleasant among the trees, and tanks could do little to help, for the vision of the gunners was impeded by the vineyards and orchards, and the tank commander in the turret usually found that his head was in the middle of the branches.'⁹ The tanks supporting 5 Buffs, Canadians from the Ontario Regiment, fared even worse. Initial progress was good but as soon as the early morning mists cleared the tanks found themselves in horribly exposed positions within almost point-blank range of a formidable anti-tank position. This was manned by part of a special company from 15 PG Division who were deployed in several Panther tank turrets embedded in concrete emplacements. All the likely approach routes were covered and within a few minutes the three Shermans of the leading troop had been knocked out. The infantry was also suffering from heavy shelling and mortaring and soon had to withdraw. The tanks, however, were ordered to hold their ground, in anticipation of some renewed infantry attack which never materialized, and by the end of the day the Panther turrets had accounted for twelve Shermans, another one being blown up on a mine. Every remaining tank of the two leading squadrons had received at least one direct hit from a high-explosive shell.

But still there were those who insisted that a breakthrough was possible if a sufficient weight of artillery fire was brought to bear. Just before the Canadians were due to attack, therefore, the bulk of their Corps artillery was ordered to shift its fire on to the Aquino front. But this forced the commander of 3 Brigade to reconsider his own attack and, with only a limited number of guns still at his disposal, he elected to attack with one battalion only. He might have done better to call off the attack completely and yet again the Allies found themselves launching a supposedly decisive assault on very strong enemy positions with totally inadequate forces. The 22ᵉ Regiment was the unlucky unit. They attacked from a point roughly midway between the Forme d'Aquino and the Hitler Line and some 2000 yards south of Aquino:

At first the thick patches of stunted oak trees – from five to ten feet high – hid them from the enemy's view, but as they emerged into the open fields they were caught in the relentless fire of machine-guns. A German 88 in a forward position knocked out several of the supporting tanks. During the morning one company worked its way to within 50 yards of the barbed wire, where it came under heavy mortar fire. Greatly increased artillery concentrations were needed if the attack was to succeed. But these were not immediately available because of the priority given to the 13th Corps' effort. At two o'clock Colonel Allard received orders from the Brigadier to withdraw his battalion. It had then suffered 57 casualties.[10]

This failure persuaded Leese that the Hitler Line was only to be breached by a carefully planned major assault, with the maximum of concentrated artillery support, and on the 19th he informed Alexander that such an assault could not be mounted until the night of the 21/22nd, or even the following morning.* The major task was given to the Canadian Corps and on the 20th Burns issued his instructions. But before going on to discuss the planning of Operation CHESTERFIELD, as it was dubbed, it is worth giving some thought to the kind of defences that were to be attacked. Work on the Hitler Line [†] had been going on for five months and though it lacked the natural river barrier incorporated into the Gustav Line the men of the Todt Organization had done their best to make amends by lavish use of man-made obstacles. The work, not completed until early May, had been accorded a high priority and the position, albeit a fall-back or switch line, was officially described as a *Sicherungs-hauptkampflinie* or Main Defensive Battle Line. That part of the Line facing the Canadians was manned by little over 1000 troops, but they had a remarkable amount of hardware at their disposal. The defensive belt was between 500 and 1000 yards deep and was protected at the front by an anti-tank ditch over 30 feet wide. Wire and mines had been laid in profusion. On 19 and 20 May alone the two engineer battalions present had laid over 3000 Tellers and box mines, in a proportion of two Teller to every box. The full array of these terrifying weapons was enumerated thus:

There were long Italian 'N' mines like lengths of rail; paratroop anti-tank mines like oversized finger-bowls; heavy Teller mines which might be buried singly or in sets; shrapnel or 's' mines whose inner

---

* By the 23rd, it will be recalled, the French, having covered a much greater distance and over much worse terrain, were well through the Hitler Line and beginning to exploit beyond Pico. German assessments of the Eighth Army effort during this period make interesting reading. One reason why Kesselring refused to allow any withdrawal from the southern end of the Hitler Line, on the 18th and 19th, was that 'the Cassino front itself . . . was [being] attacked either not at all or by insufficient forces [and] was holding out. This gave rise to the hope that continued resistance [against the CEF] might be possible.' (Von Senger und Etterlin, Diary, *op. cit.*, p.130.)
† To the Germans it was now variously known as the Senger or Pontecorvo Line.

cases filled with ball bearings sprang breast-high before exploding; limpet mines shaped like Chianti bottles; small 'schu' mines in plastic and wooden cases, unresponsive to detectors; delayed-action mines designed to crater roads or tracks after a certain number of vehicles had passed over them. These mines had been laid with few surface traces.[11]

The outposts of the line were thinly defended by snipers and a few light machine gunners who were under orders to fall back slowly and draw the attacking troops on to the more permanent positions behind. The whole defensive belt, in fact, was designed to lure troops and tanks into tactical *culs-de-sac* in which German fire could be brought to bear with devastating effect. As one tank battalion noted: 'Emplacements for anti-tank guns and machine guns were made of steel and concrete and very cleverly sited. Minefields and wire were laid tactically so as to draw on tanks and infantry into definite killing grounds. Tank obstacles were formed on the flanks, again to force our tanks into desired areas. All artillery and mortar fire had been registered previously and lanes of fire had been cut cleverly in woods and scrub and in some cases large clearings had been made.'[12] The emplacements themselves got more formidable the deeper into line one was drawn. Towards the front were various entrenchments and weapon pits with a liberal sprinkling of the mobile armoured 'crabs' already referred to in regard to the Gustav Line. Beyond these, at intervals of 150 yards or so, were forty sunken shelters made of sheet steel and with an outer casing of reinforced concrete. Attached to each was a prefabricated pillbox, again made of reinforced concrete. The bulk of the latter was sunk into the ground with a small circular neck on the top of which was a metal track to take an anti-tank turret or machine gun mounting. Between these bunkers were more of the Panther turrets encountered before Aquino. There were eighteen in all, each mounting a powerful 75mm anti-tank gun. There was also a generous supply of mobile anti-tank guns, mainly self-propelled, bringing the total number of such weapons to over sixty. With good reason did von Vietinghoff confidently state: 'The defence works were excellent; effective concentrations of artillery and anti-aircraft artillery, under the direct command of the Army's senior artillery commander, were ready for action in the area of San Giovanni Incarico and on both sides of the Melfa; the two divisional commanders were in a class by themselves.'[13]

Burns, like Freyberg before him, set great store by the effects of a preliminary bombardment, and as much artillery as possible was so assigned. The preparatory phase was to begin at midnight on the 19th and

810 guns of all types, including many from the French and XIII Corps, were to hammer the German positions with upwards of 1000 shells an hour. Just before the attack, 130 medium and heavy guns were to concentrate on counter-battery work and the rest to provide direct infantry support by saturating those positions most likely to impede the advance. Leese, indeed, probably had the second New Zealand attack in mind when he insisted on a modification to Burns' and Vokes' original plan for CHESTERFIELD, which seemed to him to utilize too few infantry in the initial assault. In the final plan, instead of only 2 Brigade attacking on a two-battalion front, there was added an extra thrust, to the south, by a battalion from 3 Brigade. Both of these efforts were to have tank support, though again from British units attached to Army Reserve, 5 Canadian Armoured Division being held back to exploit any rupture of the Hitler Line. In deference to the artillery, who pleaded difficulties in planning their complex fire tasks, H-Hour for the assault was put back until 06.00 on 23 May.

Meanwhile the Canadians could do nothing but wait, though even this relative inactivity was not without its perils. Even the Armoured Division suffered the constant attentions of the German artillery, as was recalled by a soldier of 8 Princess Louise's New Brunswick Hussars:

> We were under heavy shell and mortar fire for several days. Looking back, I think it's more trying than actual combat. . . . Most of us learned to pass through the air with the speed of light. Gerry was on the high ground on both sides of the valley and made good use of the excellent observation. . . . Gerry is a great lad with mortars. The damnable eerie moan of that misbegotten six-barreled mortar, the whines of the 75mm, 105mm and 155mm guns were not looked upon as outstanding examples of the world's greatest music. But the six-barreled moaning minnies stimulated us to the greatest speed . . .[14]

In the southern end of the bridgehead the Hastings and Prince Edward's Regiment sent out several patrols to probe the German defences and one such actually made contact with the Germans, though not in quite the way they might have expected:

> Crawling through a minefield, the six men reached the heavy forest of double-apron fence, crawled under it and moved close in on a German machine-gun post. The patrol's task was reconnaissance

and it was not looking for a fight, but chance decided otherwise. Tom O'Brien, one of the ablest of the scouts, chose to rest his back against the back of the concrete pillbox and at this moment one of the occupants chose to step outside to relieve himself. As an aggrieved O'Brien explained later, 'I had to shoot the . . . or he would have wet me down!' In the excitement that followed, the enemy post was wiped out and the scouts retired.[15]

Even without shells or furtive sallies into no man's land there was much to think about. Above all there was speculation about the forthcoming attack, each man vainly trying to suppress visions of his being blown apart or bowled over by machine gun bullets. The moment of truth was at hand yet again and its imminence only gave sickening force to the realization that there was no reason at all why one's own life was any more sacrosanct than that of the thousands who had already died. An officer with the British Columbia Dragoons wrote: 'It was all very uncomfortably exciting and a man that isn't scared hasn't the brains to be scared with.'[16]

For one battalion, however, the crunch came rather sooner than they had thought. On the 20th the French Expeditionary Corps had taken Monte Leucio and sent patrols into the western outskirts of Pontecorvo. A subsequent Canadian patrol, from 44 Reconnaissance Regiment, approached the southern end of the town and took some prisoners from 44 Reinforcement Battalion. These proved to be inexperienced troops and Vokes began to wonder whether a swift thrust against this part of the line might not unhinge the whole position. He therefore asked for and received Burns' permission to launch a probing attack, with 48 Highlanders of Canada, against Pontecorvo. The attack was to be launched on the morning of the 22nd and 2 Brigade, whose original orders were to spearhead the next day's attack well to the north of Pontecorvo, were told to hold themselves in readiness to follow up any success the Highlanders might have.

On paper this new plan seems to have considerable merit, with the Divisional Commander thinking on his feet and responding quickly to new information about the enemy. In his own appreciation of Operation CHESTERFIELD, Vokes laudably stressed a 'lesson which is age-old, that pre-arranged plans seldom work out exactly as planned. The plan must have a certain amount of flexibility and a Commander must be quick to seize and exploit opportunities.'[17] But flexibility is to military planning as extemporization is to big-band jazz – it has its place but must on no account be allowed to disrupt the basic orchestration around which a piece is built. And Vokes' orchestration was complex, depending on the individual battalions getting to know their sectors and meticulously planning their company attacks, establishing a close familiarity with the methods of the supporting armour, and being apprised in the greatest detail of the artillery's timetables and targets. 2 Brigade, therefore, were less than pleased to learn that the original scores might suddenly have to be torn up. One of its battalions' histories captured the general mood of exasperation:

> . . . the commander of 2nd Brigade no sooner had issued his orders on the evening of May 20th than he was called to Division. At midnight new orders were promulgated; these in turn were changed next morning. Twice during May 21st the Patricias packed up. Each time the movement order was rescinded. The War Diary for May 21st opens wearily: 'Today was another day of uncertainty and indecision, order and counter-order.' On the morning of the 22nd, less than twenty-four hours before the opening of the [main] assault, there were two sets of orders covering attacks in two different sectors.[18]

And there was a less than general enthusiasm in 1 Brigade, particularly among the 48 Highlanders who were to make the initial attack. For they had already sent out several patrols which soon discovered that, though this section of the Hitler Line was less prepared than further north, there were still formidable obstacles to be crossed, notably the barbed wire and the mines which were 'so thick [that] the rest of the obstacles hardly mattered.'[19] At 22.30 on the 21st, however, an 'O' Group was called at Brigade HQ. Every officer there

> knew their front was tactically forbidding and . . . shared the same apprehension about a frontal assault in the Pontecorvo area. This did not lessen their astonishment as the conference started. The 48th Highlanders were ordered – alone! – to breach the fortifications of the Hitler Line on their front. . . . This was digested in an unbelieving silence. . . . Not only was this chilling attack seriously ordered, but it was to commence at dawn, and it was now midnight. This meant no more than four hours for preparation; first light was around 4.00 a.m. Chilling is a weak description of the reactions of most of the Brigade's operational officers. . . . An aghast amazement was so clear on many faces there was no need to voice it. This meant defying the whole defensive strength of the hinge position of the Hitler Line in broad daylight, under constant observation in the valley's killing ground, on an extremely narrow

front – two companies! – and without flank attacks to help disperse
enemy attention and fire. The enemy could, and would, *concentrate
all his fire* on the 48th. It looked suicidal. It almost was![20]

During the conference one of the few faces to remain impassive was that
of the Highlanders' CO, Lieutenant-Colonel Johnston. However, when
most had dispersed and only the senior Brigade officers remained,
Colonel Johnston informed them that he felt the attack, 'without proper
preparation', was inviting heavy casualties with no chance of success.'[21]
He then inserted a bombshell, telling his Brigadier that he could not take
the responsibility and asked to be relieved of his command. This was
refused, but so obviously heartfelt were Colonel Johnston's objections
that a hurried telephone conversation took place with Divisional HQ and
Vokes reluctantly agreed to put back the jump-off from first light to
08.00.*

Nothing that happened during the next hours did anything to dispel
Colonel Johnston's apprehensions and the endless hitches and foul-ups
would have seemed almost farcical had they not had such tragic
implications. An early priority was to get in touch with the Divisional
engineers to try and organize a mine-clearing party but the engineers
claimed that this was impossible within the time available. They did
provide a sapper reconnaissance party but it was later proved that their
optimistic assertion that there were clear lanes through the minefields was
baseless and they had in fact made no attempt to even look. Another
urgent task was to obtain armoured support, without which the wire, in
particular, might well prove a death trap. A request was made for the
release of the battalion's usual armoured attachment, 'A' Squadron of the
Suffolks, but 25 Tank Brigade refused to release them, saying that they
regarded the forthcoming attack as suicidal. Artillery support was also of
the essence but neither Division nor Corps was able to provide any
Forward Observation Officers, the men who directed the tactical
handling of the guns in the rear.

But orders were orders and, slightly cheered by a last-minute change
of mind about the tanks, the Highlanders jumped off on time.
Remarkably, they had the luck their courage deserved and their pioneer
platoon was able to pick out narrow paths through the minefield, along
which they filtered ragged files of riflemen. Then the German artillery

---

* 'The extreme form of Colonel Johnston's protest was all that won the postponement.
It was not resented, and his justification was apparently recognized; he was promoted
to Brigadier within the month.' (Beattie, p.545.)

and mortars started up and the men rushed towards the German outposts. Wire blocked their way but this was found to be just about negotiable, at least by men who could keep their heads and aim for the gaps created by German shells. Others were not so lucky:

> That was a fearful thing. If you fight with barbwire it only gets worse. You must ignore the machine gun bullets plucking at your sleeves, and quietly take out the barbs . . . one . . . by . . . bloody . . . one. Try counting them. Or you can keep from panic if you hum *Mother Machree*. At least I did. But I heard the Corporal screaming, and a new man was raving; he was thrashing and fighting with the wire like a man gone insane. The bullets started socking into him, and he jerked and kicked with each hit. Then he crumpled beside me. Nothing was very bad in the war after that.[22]

Yet most men got through the wire and, still having sustained remarkably few casualties, the Highlanders charged forward again, individual sections rushing the German strongpoints. Clearly Baade had continued to man this sector with inferior troops, for the bulk of them took one look at the advancing Canadians and fled. Twelve armoured 'crabs' were taken though not one was claimed as a kill or a capture. Each was found deserted, some with loaded machine guns that had never been fired. Miraculous as it must have seemed, the Highlanders had done it. They were inside the Hitler Line.

But Colonel Johnston's bridgehead was still very constricted, and with German artillery fire increasing in intensity he directed his men to the right, to attack up a blazing slope that led to the ridge along which ran the Pontecorvo–Aquino road. They now looked around anxiously for the Suffolks' Churchills, their only real hope if they were to penetrate further into the German positions. The truth slowly dawned. Not one of the tanks had got through. They had been as unlucky as the Highlanders had been fortunate. The previous night a lost truck had come down the tanks' approach road and blown up on a box mine. The leading Suffolk tank, attempting to push it out of the way, had also struck a mine and completely blocked the road. The following Churchills had gone to either side of the debris but the leaders too struck mines and

> lost their tracks, blocking those behind them. Complete catastrophe was building up as a terrible fire rained down on the blocked tanks of the Suffolks. . . . The three Shermans sent forward on the early recce were killed . . . by a long-barrelled 75-mm, concealed in a Panther turret on the ridge. Those Churchill guns which could fire

were now trying to get this gun; so was a 17-pounder, firing from the Hastings' area, to the right rear. They finally knocked it out, but all 48th hopes for tank support had already died, with many brave men of the Suffolks, in front of the minefield. . . . They helplessly watched the destruction of their armoured support with vast sympathy for the tank men, and a not unnatural feeling of foreboding for their own fate. Their great, and almost only hope was obliterated.[23]

A few tanks did in fact get through to the Highlanders later that afternoon but by then their petrol was almost exhausted and they could provide little support for an attempted drive to expand the bridgehead. The Highlanders were obliged to dig in where they stood and for the next twenty-four hours they hung on, desperately hoping that the full-scale CHESTERFIELD offensive would afford them eventual relief. For the massacre of the Suffolks had persuaded senior Canadian commanders that 1 Brigade's thrust was not a viable operation and, even though the 48th had done all that was asked of them, the projected follow-up attacks by the Royal Canadian Regiment and the Hastings and Prince Edward's were cancelled. Evidence for why this decision was taken is lacking but the Highlanders were, understandably, bitter about it. By the afternoon of the 22nd

the Company Commanders looked desperate as they reported in. They were also angry. Everything appeared to be an infuriating stalemate, and it could be one with a disastrous finish. It was not this bleak outlook which had them in a rage; they were in a fury with the whole operation. They soon disclosed their predominant mood was defiance.[24]

Little changed during the night except that German counter-attacks pressed in their perimeter and inflicted a steady drain of casualties. Also, just as with 141 Regiment in the doomed Rapido bridgehead, the German gunners zeroed in their weapons and sent in an endless hail of machine gun bullets and mortar shells. 'He could see us all the way from a dozen hides d'ye see, and he had more of them Spandaus than we'd ever seen congregated. More mortars, too. And we had no tanks. We were a dour lot that night, for the next day looked as dour as we felt. And none of it made any sense, which was the worst part.[25]

Indeed it was only the opening of CHESTERFIELD proper, at 06.00 on the 23rd, which saved the battalion from destruction. In its latest form, as we have seen, the Canadian plan was to attack with three battalions in the first line. From north to south these were Princess Patricia's Light Infantry and the Seaforth Highlanders of Canada, from 2 Brigade, and the Carleton and York Regiment from 3 Brigade. The North Irish Horse was to support 2 Brigade and part of 51 Royal Tank Regiment to support the 3rd. Each Brigade also had a battalion in close support, the Loyal Edmonton Regiment, with the remainder of 51 RTR, and the West Nova Scotia Regiment respectively. The Phase I objective was the Pontecorvo-Aquino road and the Phase II the road linking Pontecorvo and Highway Six, on the far side of the Hitler Line. Once this second line had been secured the tanks and infantry of 5 Canadian Armoured Division were to crash through to the River Melfa and force a crossing. The rate of advance during Phase I was to be 100 yards every five minutes and the same distance every three minutes in Phase II.

The massive artillery barrage opened up exactly on time and three minutes later the infantry crossed their start lines. The attack by 2 Brigade soon turned into a near-disaster. At first progress was reasonably steady, the early part of the advance being shielded by dense scrub and the growing crops that masked some German emplacements. But as soon as the defenders realized that a major offensive was being mounted they opened up with every gun they could bring to bear. Particularly intense was the fire from Heidrich's paratroopers, on the Patricias' right flank, who had been outside the parameters of the barrage. Much of their fire was from machine guns, firing at almost point-blank range from undamaged 'crabs', which ripped into the Patricias' ranks as they approached the wire. The commander of 'A' Company later wrote:

> We had not seen our supporting tanks but we knew we had reached the Hitler Line for we could see rows of barbed wire ahead. As soon as we came into the clearing a number of my men were hit. . . . The intense shell fire had drastically reduced our numbers and crossing the two belts of wire took a further toll, as the wire was thickly studded with shrapnel mines. Beyond the wire we came to a tank. Thinking it derelict we paused beside it to gather together the few men who were left. We then discovered our error as the tank started firing the wrong way. . . . As we had only small arms we could not destroy it. By that time I only had four or five men left. Shortly after leaving the tank I lost all of them except L/Cpl. Amos. . . . By that time I had been wounded twice and realised that the attack had failed.[26]

The tanks, too sustained appalling casualties, first running into a minefield and then having those that were able to press forward methodically picked off by the disembodied Panthers. The Princess Patricias' own narrative of the action summed up the situation in the early afternoon as 'critical. Two forward companies were temporarily written off and heavy casualties had been sustained by "B" Company. . . . Tanks had been unable to get forward and 10 out of the original 18 had been knocked out. Only three company officers remained in action and two of these later became casualties.'27

The Seaforths, in the centre of the Canadian line, were somewhat better placed in that they did not also have to contend with the fire from Heidrich's men. But their armoured support, again from the North Irish Horse, proved as vulnerable as ever and had virtually disintegrated within the first hour or so. The German gunners held their fire until the tanks were less than a hundred yards away and one Panther turret is said to have accounted for thirteen tanks before an armour-piercing shell struck its magazine. Eleven Irish tanks did succeed in getting forward to the Phase II line but on a different axis from the infantry and, without the latter's support, they were eventually forced to withdraw. Though it is questionable whether the rifle companies would have been in any fit state to render much assistance. Their own narrative says all that needs to be said:

By 07.00 the 'fog of war' had really descended. . . . W/T communication was intermittent. . . . Casualties were still streaming in with tales of platoons and companies decimated and all officers dead or wounded. The enemy mortar and artillery fire continued with undiminished fury. . . . [Major Allen gathered together the remnants of all four companies. At about 17.00] the little band was counter-attacked by three German tanks and some infantry. Those who were fortunate enough to have slit trenches or shelters fought from there. Others took refuge from the cannons and machine gun fire in the ditch alongside the road which was their objective. . . . The battalion had exhausted its supply of PIAT bombs by this time and could not effectively engage the tanks. The tanks moved down the road pouring machine gun fire into the ditch, causing many casualties. Then they came up with the guns depressed, to each individual survivor in the ditch and took him prisoner. . . . It is tragic that after the grimmest battle this Brigade has known, being the only troops in the Brigade to gain the objective, and then hanging on all day, the forward companies could not be supported by anti-tank weapons. . . . When the smoke cleared and the lost had been found, the Seaforth of Canada rifle company situation was no officers and about 100 all other ranks.[28]*

Meanwhile the Brigade's reserve battalion, the Loyal Edmontons, had moved up in close support of the Patricias, ready to pass through them once the Phase I line had been reached. But they soon ran into remnants of the leading battalion and were equally unable to make progress. Their battle narrative again says it all, though the reader might be excused for thinking he is reading about events on the Somme or at Passchendaele almost thirty years before:

['A'] Company was subjected to murderous fire of artillery, mortars and medium machine guns. Enemy snipers were also extremely active, some of them being hidden in the lower branches of the trees. 'A' Company pressed on but on reaching a point about twenty feet from the enemy's wire was forced to go to ground, owing to the intensity of the fire, and the casualties inflicted upon us. . . . [The Company] rose to make the final assault on the wire and the enemy posts behind it. Two sections breached the wire, and then, owing to the heavy volume of fire and the large number of S mines sown in and about the wire, they were pinned down helpless.[29]

The other companies did manage to breach the wire in two places but by then wireless communication with Battalion HQ had broken down completely and the commander was forced to report back that he had lost control of his companies. These slowly dribbled back towards their start line and at 18.00 were given the welcome order to withdraw. But their troubles were not quite over. Their destination was given as 'a map reference about 4 miles behind . . . [their] present location. . . . It transpired that the wrong map reference had been given. The men had withdrawn twice as far as they should have gone. In deep weariness they trudged back half the distance, dug slit trenches and relapsed into fitful slumber.'[30]

Happily 3 Brigade's attack was much more successful. The Carleton and York Regiment had been able to send out many patrols the previous day – for they were at least sure exactly where they were to attack – and had discovered several corridors through the wire and the minefields. They followed the artillery barrage as closely as possible and forced their way on to the first objective without too much difficulty. But the

* The North Irish Horse had lost 25 tanks, as well as 34 men killed and 36 wounded; and of the 58 tanks engaged on the whole of 2 Brigade's front on the 23rd, 41 were knocked out.

supporting tanks of 51 RTR did not fare so well and fell behind the infantry as they waged a terrible battle with the fixed and self-propelled German guns. The closest eye-witnesses to this encounter were the West Novas, following hard on the heels of the Carleton and Yorks, and one of their officers wrote a moving account of the carnage they came upon. One of his first meetings was with the commander of the leading squadron, who first told him that he had only five tanks left out of eighteen and then, after a personal reconnaissance, that

> there were no tanks left fit for action – his squadron was destroyed all but a few which were damaged beyond quick repair. . . . [He] was a veteran of the African desert campaign with a Military Cross and he told me: 'I've seen rough times but this is the worst. My whole squadron's had it. I'm going up with a tommy-gun to fight with the Carleton and Yorks!' And away he went. I made my way back to 'A' Company's radio tent through a scene such as I hope I'll never see again. The field behind the trees was a mass of shell holes, and there about a dozen tanks sat silent, half of them burning. One blew up with a sudden explosion and the turret flipped off like a pot cover. One smoking tank held two living men: the driver opened his small cover and crawled out with his overalls afire; then the turret lid flew open and the tank commander started to crawl out. He was injured and his clothes were blazing, and as he saw me approaching his eyes seemed to plead, for help although he did not utter a word. I ran towards the tank, and one of our men jumped out of a slit trench and raced across on the same errand. Just as we reached it the tank blew up and hurled the tank commander through the air. He fell about 25 yards away. We crawled over to him – the air seemed to be full of bursting shells – but when we reached him he'd had it – for good. The driver was rolling himself over and over in the grass. We beat the flames from his overalls, which were now charred crisp, and he was terribly burned. All he could utter was curses – no complaints, no sign of fear.[31]

At 10.00, however, the surviving tanks joined the infantry on the Pontecorvo–Aquino road and the West Novas moved up to start the second phase of the attack. They were held in these positions for some hours as Vokes waited for better news from 2 Brigade's flank but, as he began to realize that this attack had completely failed, he decided to press ahead with 3 Brigade alone and ordered up 22^e Regiment to provide a Brigade reserve. More tanks, from the Three Rivers Regiment, were also sent forward and at 16.40 they and the West Novas jumped off. According to one infantry officer: 'All our tank liaison training went by the board. As they rolled into our position through the wrecks of the Churchills we just waved them on, got up, and started forward. Our plan was clear enough – to get forward out of that hell hole.'[32] They moved forward quickly, and German reserves, forming up for a counter-attack, were caught in the artillery barrage and badly demoralized. A few local counter-attacks were launched but by 18.15 the West Novas had reached the Phase II line. The 'Van Doos' were now brought forward to widen the breach to the north, seizing objectives in front of the battered Seaforths. They moved off at 17.00 and, despite heavy artillery fire, had by 21.15 established themselves on a tongue of high ground between the two lateral roads, and about 1500 yards north of the West Novas.

By the end of the day the Germans were beginning to fall back in numbers. There had also been unlooked-for success on the southern flank where 48 Highlanders, reinforced by a fresh squadron of the Suffolk Regiment, had actually managed to expand its bridgehead and seize the lower slopes of a hill about a mile north-east of Pontecorvo. 1 Brigade was quick to reinforce this remarkable effort and the Hastings and Prince Edward Regiment was sent forward. They attacked with great panache and carried the emplacements and pillboxes in vicious hand-to-hand fighting. By 17.00 the hill was secure and the two battalions set to work mopping up the badly disorganized enemy. As many as could fell back from the Hitler Line and early next morning the Royal Canadian Regiment was able to march almost unopposed into Pontecorvo.

The way was now open for 5 Canadian Armoured Division to be launched into the fray. In fact, the Divisional Commander, General B.M. Hoffmeister, had felt a sufficiently wide breach had been made by 17.30 on the 23rd, and he had received Burns' permission to move off that evening. But the old problem of traffic control re-emerged and the armoured units, already troubled by having to shift their axis of attack through 3 Brigade rather than 2nd, got hopelessly tangled up with the tanks of 25 Armoured Brigade returning to rearm and refuel. At 20.30 Hoffmeister was forced to report that he would not be able to attack until early the next morning. His leading units did not begin to move forward until 08.00 on the 24th. In the van was a composite group of tanks and infantry made up of the squadrons of the British Columbia Dragoons, each supported by a carrier-borne rifle company from the Irish Regiment of Canada. This group was known as Vokes Force (after the commander of the Dragoons, Lieutenant-Colonel F.A. Vokes) and its task was to establish a firm base midway between the Hitler Line and the Melfa.

Another composite group, Griffin Force, comprising the tanks of Lord Strathcona's Horse (CO Lieutenant-Colonel P.G. Griffin) and a lorried infantry company from the Westminster Regiment, was then to pass through them and seize a crossing over the Melfa. A third bound was to be made by the rest of the Westminsters who would consolidate the bridgehead, and from there 8 Princess Louise's Hussars would strike out towards Ceprano. Hoffmeister's flanks were to be protected by 6 British Armoured Division, moving on his right along Highway Six, and 1 Canadian Division on the left, who were to send tanks and infantry along the north bank of the Liri.

Vokes Force advanced reasonably quickly at first, meeting only scattered rearguards from 361 PG Regiment, one of whose battalions had now virtually ceased to exist. But it was not long before it became apparent that the much-vaunted Liri Valley was less than ideal tank country. Particularly troublesome was the closeness of the terrain, with scrub trees, vineyards and copses intermingled with small olive groves. In the vineyards numerous strands of wire were strung between posts to support the vines and were usually at a height which could decapitate an unwary tank commander. Nor did the maps help much. Lieutenant N. Hockin of the British Columbia Dragoons recalled:

> the awful panic when . . . I was completely lost at times. However I was not alone in my problem. I remember at an early stage in the breakthrough I saw a group of the Royal 22nd dug in around several tanks of the Three Rivers Regiment. I jumped out of my tank with this map and on finding the Major in charge of the company I asked him for his position. I think his answer was a classic. In a French accent he replied, 'My friend, we have been here for 12 hours and have fought a first class battle – but where I am – I do not know.'[33]

Shortly after midday, however, the Dragoons and the infantry reached their objective, about two miles north-west of Aquino, and Griffin Force was ordered forward. The Strathconas' Reconnaissance Troop was in the lead with 'A' Squadron a little behind and 'B' and 'C' well off to the right and left. The Recce Troop was under orders to effect a swift crossing of the Melfa and at 15.00 it had managed to slip across to the far bank. Mortar and shell fire was intense but most of the infantry positions had been abandoned and when 'A' Company of the Westminsters also arrived, at 16.30, it was possible to establish a tenuous perimeter around the tiny bridgehead.

But more substantial support was slow to arrive as the other Strathcona companies had run into fierce opposition at crossing points further north. Here, in fact, were fought some of the few major tank-versus-tank battles of the Cassino campaign and they offer a chilling insight into this deadly form of combat. The villain of the piece was the Mark V Panther tank, the first of these weapons to be encountered by the Allies. They belonged to 1/4 Panzer Regiment and had been kept in reserve since their arrival in Italy in February. On 15 May, however, in response to urgent appeals from von Vietinghoff, one company had been sent to the Melfa and had arrived there on the 20th. Vokes Force had had a brush with them early on the 24th but had been remarkably fortunate, accounting for three Panthers for the loss of only four Shermans. The Strathconas were not to be so lucky and 'A' and 'C' Companies became heavily engaged with the German armour. The latter was eventually forced to retire to the far bank of the Melfa but not before 17 Shermans had been knocked out as against only 5 German tanks, not all of these Panthers. During the evening the 8th Hussars were brought up to the east bank of the Melfa and one of them recalled the confusion of their night harbour: 'We couldn't find anyone. We met some Straths coming back from their shelling. They were in an awful shape; they told us they'd lost a lot of men. We found a lot of them in a Field Dressing Station.'[34]

But the Hussars' turn was to come, as well as that of the British Columbia Dragoons who had also been brought up to try and smash their way forward to the fragile Strathcona/Westminster bridgehead. For the situation there was looking increasingly perilous, the Germans mounting a whole series of tank and infantry counter-attacks as well as keeping up remorseless mortar fire. According to one Canadian report:

At this stage of the game conditions were very sticky because we had been unable to get any anti-tank weapons over. . . . In this precarious state of affairs the Germans put in three counter-attacks with Panthers. In one case three of the tanks formed up at a range of 400 yards and began to advance on one of our very attenuated platoon positions. Our troops fired at them with tommy guns, 0.5s and everything they had. The tanks then turned about and wheeled within some 200 yards of our positions. The only conceivable reason why the attackers did not come on and overrun the infantry was that our lads were firing PIATs at them and the Panther crews must have thought they were up against anti-tank guns.[35]

But Brigadier Smith took immediate steps to, as he put it, 'bang the whole of the Westminsters up as well' and by 21.00 one other company, as well as some genuine 6-pdr anti-tank guns, had been got across the river. With luck the bridgehead might hold until a more concerted offensive could be launched the next day.

So it proved, and at midday on the 25th the Irish Regiment, supported by a squadron of the British Columbia Dragoons, attacked at the main northern crossing whilst the Westminsters broke out from the left flank of their bridgehead. Within an hour the infantry were holding the lateral road 1000 yards west of the river and more units were fed into the bridgehead. In the late afternoon the Cape Breton Highlanders, supported by the 8th Hussars, came forward and by nightfall they had pushed a further 1000 yards, at which point the Perth Regiment was leapfrogged forward on their left flank.

But such a cursory narrative does scant justice to the achievements of the Canadian armour. Just getting forward in sufficient numbers was far from easy and the arrangements for traffic control came perilously close to breaking down on the night of the 24/25th. A member of 8 Hussars spoke of 'the usual tangle of traffic, like some great, shambling monster tied up in its own tentacles and trying to shake free to fight.'[36] The Adjutant of the same Regiment eschewed metaphor but amply succeeded in making his point: 'On . . . [the 24th] as on subsequent days throughout the operation, possession of priority on the road was of academic value only since it resulted in no diminution of other traffic nor in the appearance of any provost aware of the fact that priority had been given.'[37] And added to the frustrations of the traffic jams were the gnawing fears over the battle to come. During the night 8 Hussars went into harbour. 'It was pitch black. I guess we'd all been excited most of the day but when the night came we were plain scared. . . We set up a harbour. Put our tanks in a big circle like they used to do with their wagons in the Indian days out west. The guns all pointed out. There was no infantry with us. We figured we were going to be attacked any time at all.'[38] The next morning they started off again and as they approached the Melfa

the Germans were shelling the area heavily. Artillery, mortars, machine guns and rifles; they were all firing somewhere in the neighbourhood. The ground was marked and pocked by the explosions. There were soldiers' bodies here and there and some German tanks and not far off you could see a whole string of our tanks that had been picked off, one after another, by an 88 somewhere on the far bank. . . . The Major went off to an O Group and we waited there for him. . . . My Jesus, I was scared.[39]

Then the attack started and the time came for fear to turn to unabashed terror. For the leading troops the advance was little better than a *kamikaze* charge and they ran straight into well-prepared ambushes by enemy tanks and anti-tank guns. A lieutenant in the forward troop of the British Columbia Dragoons wrote:

I certainly did not like the tactical situation or the topography – but there wasn't much that could be done about it. We came to fight a war and now the chips were down. . . . We were ordered forward. Steve Coppinger kicked off and then I was ordered to go with him. He went about fifty yards when I saw his tank burst into flames and I saw Steve fall out of the turret. I stopped my tank as I thought I was still in hull-down position. I reported what had happened . . . when 'Wham', my tank was hit. My driver . . . pulled the fire control switches for the extinguishers and I reported that we were hit and told the crew to bail out. . . . I then climbed on to the sergeant's tank. . . . I got up on the back of the tank and hit the sergeant on the helmet to get his attention. Sergeant Singbeil . . . was traversing his gun to the right when . . . his tank was hit. This round really hit hard. I had only one foot on the back deck as I was reaching over into the top of the turret to talk to him. The concussion from that solid shot hitting his tank was so severe that it broke a bone in my foot and knocked me off the tank. I landed in among the crew of my own tank who were crawling down our tracks towards the river. My driver . . . was hit with a piece of steel that flew off the sergeant's tank. Subsequently the Corporal's tank . . . was hit. There were bad casualties in both of these tanks. . . . I gathered quite a few of the wounded and we worked our way back to the riverbank. There I tried to warn the other tanks which were still coming across – but no one could hear me or pay any attention.[40]

Those behind could only watch and listen in appalled fascination. A radio-operator recalled: 'As our first tanks . . . crossed the flat in line ahead we heard a report that "my Sunray [commander] has been hit and his tank is on fire . . ." Hardly had the words been spoken when it was reported that another tank had been hit, and then another, with one of the reporters' voices trailing off into a bedlam of screams as his own tank was hit while he was on the air.'[41]

There were two reasons why the men inside might have been screaming. One was that the tank was on fire. Thus it was with one of 8 Hussars' Shermans. On this occasion the crew did manage to escape but the following account makes clear their overwhelming fear of being trapped in what became known as 'Ronson Burners' – because they 'lit first time'.

Almost as soon as we got hit, she started to burn. The officer, being in the turret, naturally tried to be the first man out. He was the natural one to go. But the gunner and I were trying to be the first one out too. There were three of us scrambling around, all trying to get out of the top hatch at the same time. There just wasn't room. We jammed up. And all the time the damn tank was burning like blazes. We came back and rared again and got stuck again, so I figured to myself that someone had to wait or we'd all burn. I lay on top of the gun until they got out. I got my hair singed for my trouble, but we all escaped.[42]

The other reason for the screams would have been that the tank was being shot to pieces by Mark IVs, Panthers or 88mm anti-tank guns. For armoured warfare is short on chivalry and simply immobilizing a tank is seen as no reason to stop pumping shells into it. So it was with the tank belonging to one of 8 Hussars' squadron commanders:

The Major's tank had been moving around behind the two front troops, quarterbacking. The Germans may have spotted its importance in its twin aerials. They struck it first in the hatch. The shell tore off the hatch. It struck the crash helmet on Lane's head and wounded him. The others in the tank could hardly hear the sound; there were so many sounds. When the shell struck, the others sat there, dazed and numb. Looking up, Willie Richard could see the turret smeared with blood and he could see somebody trying to get out. He tried to get out his own escape hatch but the 75 had traversed round and blocked it off. . . . He shouted at Larter, 'Let's stand pat' and they were sitting there when the second shell came. It went through the tank and out again as though its steel were butter. The tank shook like a trembling child. The Sergeant and the gunner, Steve Matthews, were sitting back to back. The shell tore away much of Matthews' back. It ravaged the motor. They feared fire but somehow fire didn't come. But it had put the tank out of action. There no longer was any doubt of that. Willie Richard blurted out, 'Let's get out of here.' Larter found himself kneeling on the turret trying to haul the Major out. Another shell struck the lower part of the tank. The Major got out but his wound had affected his mind. He was out of his head.[43]

Yet still the tanks behind came on. An infantry officer spoke of their crews in awed amazement: 'I'll never forget the way the tanks would keep coming and then one would get knocked out and then another and still they'd keep coming.'[44] They did so because they were brave men. But this should not lead us to ignore a rather unpalatable truth concerning the Allies' handling of armour in this battle, or indeed during the whole Italian and North-West European campaigns. Allied tanks were under-gunned and under-armoured throughout most of the war. The sudden emphasis upon so-called 'Cruiser' tanks to fight in the desert, and the subsequent tyranny of standardized mass-production, meant that the designers never had the chance to respond quickly to German innovations – be they increasingly powerful tanks, long-range anti-tank guns or one-man bazookas. So Allied generals had to rely on sheer weight of numbers to overwhelm the Germans and, no matter what the cost to the crews, be prepared to decide the issue in a crude war of attrition. This philosophy, if such a marked lack of finesse merits the title, was made quite explicit by the commanders themselves. Of the Melfa Battles a staff officer in 5 Canadian Armoured Brigade wrote:

As for the main obstacle of the German tanks . . . the only reason why it was possible to make headway against their qualitative superiority was by weight of numbers. . . . General Leese [has been cited] as saying that in his offensive he was prepared to lose 1000 tanks. As he had 1900 at his disposal, the Panther stood a fair chance of becoming an extinct species among the fauna of s. Italy. On our side losses had to be taken and replacements thrown in. Being somewhat up against it, the tankmen were compelled to improvise and make the most of what they had.[45]

The tankmen were under no allusions as to the way in which they were employed. Of the fighting on the 25th, Lieutenant Hockin wrote: 'I think we all grew up a lot that day. We discovered that if necessary higher command would throw in a squadron of tanks to stop a counter-attack, regardless of consequences. The "Y" Camp days of soldiering were gone, the grim reality that we could get hurt took over.'[46]

17
'A Masterpiece of Leadership'
Fifth and Eighth Armies Advance to Rome, 23 May–4 June 1944

At the present juncture, questions of prestige are shaping events, each one wanting to make the entry into Rome. History will not fail to pass severe sentence.

General Juin, 30 May 1944

The breaking of the Hitler Line, though it represented a considerable military success, had also brought to the surface a remarkable degree of ill-feeling between the Allies, notably between Fifth and Eighth Armies. In Juin's eyes, for example, even the successes of the French Expeditionary Corps had been far from unalloyed. His major reservation was that Eighth Army had been far too slow and had thus made it very difficult for him to maintain contact between his own right flank and the left of the Canadian Corps. There was certainly some truth in this. The French Official History pointedly notes that on 17 May I DMI's leading elements were 6 kilometres ahead of the Canadians and were usually at least 2 kilometres ahead for the first 10 days of the offensive. Throughout almost the whole of the Fourth Battle, indeed, 'the French were always crying because the British were back on their flank.'[1]

Their complaints were amplified in Juin's own memoirs. On the 16th

. . . there I was again worried about the fact that the Eighth Army, whose right wing was marking time in front of Monte Cassino and whose XIII Corps, neighbouring mine, was only making a very measured advance, was forcing I DMI, already beyond San Giorgio, to hang back to protect the right flank of the CEF. . . . On 17 May the British made hardly any progress at all, waiting for the fall of Monte Cassino . . . before they pushed into the Liri Valley. They thus disrupted the timetable for the forcing of the Hitler Line between Aquino and Pontecorvo, though the CEF was already in a position to outflank it. . . . This disruption caused us to lose precious time, which the enemy used to reinforce his defences around Pico. . . . On the 18th . . . with German resistance stiffening, we were forced to mark time and wait for the [British] attack, they having hardly begun to make contact with the Hitler Line. . . .It is a great pity that all these delays should have prevented us from enveloping the right wing of the German Tenth Army.[2]*

Juin had also been less than impressed with the extent of Eighth Army's effort, particularly as it approached the Hitler Line. When Clark went to see him on the 22nd, to discuss the next day's operations, he found that Juin 'expressed surprise at the weakness of the British attack. He told me Pontecorvo was unoccupied and that he was in the outskirts, yet the Canadians would not go in. He has borne the brunt of the Liri Valley battle.'[3] But Clark, too, was extremely unhappy about Eighth Army's performance and, indeed, was beginning to have serious doubts about Alexander's overall direction of DIADEM. The first major flash-point came on the 19th when Alexander decided that the advance towards the Hitler Line had gone sufficiently well to give the go-ahead for the breakout from the Anzio beachhead, and he issued instructions to Clark that VI Corps was to attack on the night of the 21/22nd. The peremptory nature of this order did not please Clark at all. He wrote in his diary the following day: 'I was shocked when I received it to think that a decision of this importance would have been made without reference to me. I sent that word back to Alexander, who made the weak excuse that he felt that we had discussed it for the past three days.'[4] But Clark also had military objections, feeling that it would be premature to launch the breakout until as many German reserves as possible were irrevocably committed to the defence of the Hitler Line. As he said to Alexander when the latter came to see him on the afternoon of the 20th:

. . . the soonest we should attack is when both Fifth and Eighth Armies are in desperate grips with the Hitler Line, at which time the German troops on this front would be so heavily engaged that they could not withdraw to influence the bridgehead battle. The mere fact that the 26th [Panzer] Division has moved down is no

* Ironically, Juin's difficulties in maintaining contact with the adjoining forces were exactly duplicated in XIV Panzer Corps. The 'credit' for this went to Eighth Army, though von Senger und Etterlin reveals in passing that the Germans, too, were far from overawed by its effort in the Liri Valley: 'Owing to the fact that LI Mountain Corps, committed north of the Liri, held its ground while the XIV Panzer Corps . . .withdrew after its line had been breached . . . [my] divisions were not moved into . . . [the Hitler] Line but were compelled to fight in front of it in order to maintain contact with LI Mountain Corps which was . . . *seldom under attack*.' (Von Senger und Etterlin, Diary, *op. cit.*, p.133, author's emphasis.)

justification for this premature attack. It should be given a chance
to get heavily committed on this front.'[5]*

Alexander seems to have seen the sense of these objections and early on
the 21st he issued a new order, retiming the Anzio attack for 06.30 on the
23rd, to coincide with the much-delayed assault by the Canadian Corps.

Not that the prospect of Canadian support did much to impress Clark.
We have already had occasion to note his animus against the 'British' and
their supposed lack of aggressiveness, and these feelings now came very
much to the fore again. By the 20th, after 78 Division's repulse at Aquino
and the failure of the 22ᵉ Regiment further south, he seemed almost
contemptuous of Eighth Army's abilities. His diary gave full rein to his
bitterness. After his meeting with Alexander he wrote:

> General Alexander . . . told me that General Leese would not be
> able to attack until probably the night of the 23/24th and then with
> one division – the Canadians. He asked me hesitatingly if I could
> attack and outflank the Germans making it unnecessary for the
> Eighth Army to attack. He said he desired to conserve losses. I told
> him to conserve losses in one place we would have them in another;
> mainly the Fifth Army sector and that I strongly recommended that
> Leese speed up his attack. . . . We agreed, although I am convinced
> that the Eighth Army will hold their attack and let the French carry
> the ball for them as they have done so far in this battle.[6]

The Canadians' slow build-up for their set-piece assault did nothing to put
him in better humour, and neither did a visit to Leese's headquarters on
the 21st. On the following day he wrote in his diary:

> Yesterday I flew to see General Leese in an effort to coordinate our
> attacks for the 23rd. Although he professes that his attack will be
> all-out, it is being made by one division. I commented as well as I
> could on the weakness of the attack, but through quick talk he
> indicated a great massing behind. All their actions are always
> dictated by their desire to save manpower and let someone else do
> it. I pointed out the great necessity of everyone attacking all-out at
> the same time. He agrees in principle but will not do it in fact.[7]

But Clark was hardly in a position to force Leese to do anything and
from the 23rd his thoughts were almost completely devoted to the Anzio

---

* Clark was also justifiably anxious about the poor weather forecast for the 22nd,
which might mean that VI Corps would have to attack without air support.

break-out. Though the actual date had not been agreed until the 21st, the bulk of the planning had been done well in advance and at H-Hour all the troops were in their allotted positions. Great efforts were made to mask Allied intentions from the Germans. 1 US Armoured Division, for example, had been sending forward tanks every night since mid-May to fire at estimated German strongpoints. After a few hours they would return, with a maximum clanking of tracks and revving of engines, but each time a few tanks were left behind, carefully camouflaged, to help spearhead the breakout. Some remained completely immobile for several days, their crews incarcerated in the cramped interiors, living entirely on cold rations lest smoke betray their positions.

The Americans were given the leading role in the attack, all their four divisions and 1 Special Service Force being placed in the line. The focal point of the first assault was Cisterna, which lay astride Highway Seven and the route to Velletri. This town was to be taken in a double pincers movement. The outer envelopment, cutting Highway Seven to north and south, was the responsibility of 1 Armoured Division and a composite force from 1 SSF and 34 Division. The inner pincers were provided by 3 Division, with 15 Regiment approaching the town from the south-east, 30 Regiment from the north-west, and 7 Regiment driving straight on from the south. To the left of Highway Seven was the remainder of 1 Armoured Regiment, with a regiment from 34 Division attached, who were to attack directly towards Velletri. To their left was 45 Division, whose role for the moment was limited to probing attacks towards Campoleone and Lanuvio. On the extreme left of the beachhead were 1 and 5 British Divisions who were to mount only local attacks up the coast, though these were to jump off first to deceive the Germans into thinking that this was the direction of the main thrust. In fact, as we have already seen, Alexander had clearly stipulated that the main axis was to be Velletri–Valmontone and for the moment Clark and Truscott's dispositions seemed entirely satisfactory, they also having made provision for bringing in their major reserve, 36 Division, to help pursue the attack northwards from Cori and Artena.

It was as well that the British attack was only a diversion for it immediately ran into heavy resistance and made little headway. The leading role had been assigned to 1 Green Howards, from 5 Division, who were to attack across the Moletta creek towards L'Americano, a cluster of bathing huts on the coast. One officer wrote:

We had to go slap through a minefield and the two men next to me were blown up. When I led a section round some bushes, a spandau

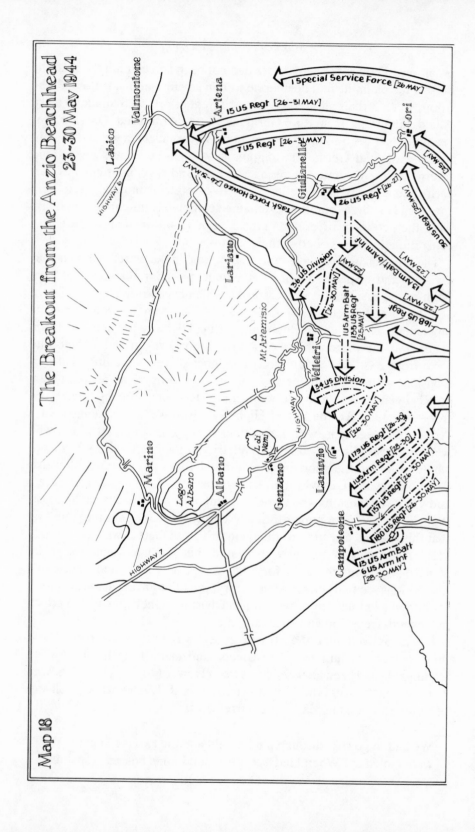

Map 18

The Breakout from the Anzio Beachhead
23-30 May 1944

1 Special Service Force [26 MAY]

15 US Regt [26-31 MAY]

7 US Regt [26-31 MAY]

Task Force Howze [26-31 MAY]

26 US Regt [26-27]

30 US Regt [25 MAY]

[25 MAY]

Cori

3d Armd Batt/6 Arm Inf [25 MAY]

168 US Regt [25 MAY]

36 US Division

1 US Arm Batt
135 US Regt [25 MAY]

[26-30 MAY]

34 US Division

[26-30 MAY]

179 US Regt [26-30]

1 US Arm Regt [26-30]

157 US Regt [26-30 MAY]

180 US Regt [26-30 MAY]

13 US Arm Batt
6 US Arm Inf [26-30 MAY]

Valmontone

Labico

Artena

Giulianello

Lariano

Mt Artemisio

Velletri

Lariano

L. di Nemi

Genzano

Lanuvio

Campoleone

Marino

Lago Albano

Albano

HIGHWAY 6

HIGHWAY 7

HIGHWAY 7

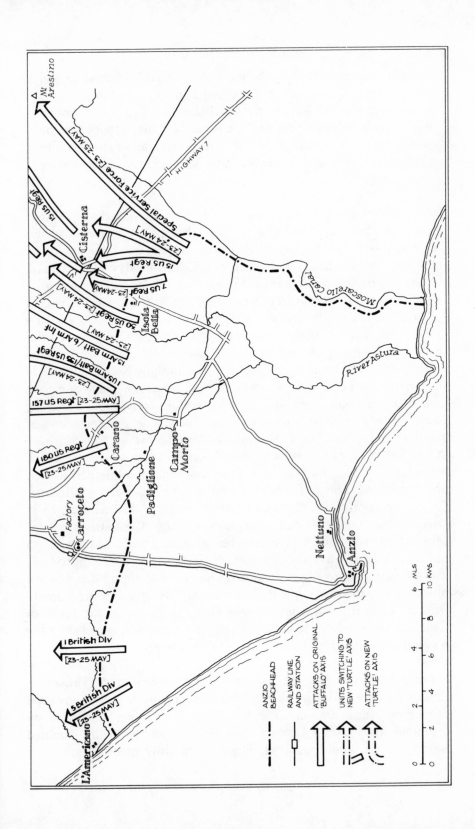

Mt Arestino △

HIGHWAY 7

Special Service Force [23-25 MAY]

Moscarello Canal

15 US Regt

Cisterna

15 US Regt [23-24 MAY]

7 US Regt [23-24 MAY]

30 US Regt [23-24 MAY]

Isola Bella

13 Arm Bn/6 Arm Inf [23-24 MAY]

1 US Arm Bn/133 US Regt

1 US Arm Bn [23-24 MAY]

157 US Regt [23-25 MAY]

180 US Regt [23-25 MAY]

River Astura

Carano

Campo Morto

Padiglione

Factory

Carroceto

Nettuno

Anzio

1 British Div [23-25 MAY]

5 British Div [23-25 MAY]

L'Americano

ANZIO BEACHHEAD

RAILWAY LINE AND STATION

ATTACKS ON ORIGINAL 'BUFFALO' AXIS

UNITS SWITCHING TO NEW 'TURTLE' AXIS

ATTACKS ON NEW 'TURTLE' AXIS

6 MLS
10 KMS
8
6
4
4
2
2
0
0

opened only ten yards away, killing the section leader behind me and badly wounding four others. I chucked a grenade and tore off, only to discover another Jerry trench just below me. The Jerry threw an egg-grenade, which hit me on the nose and it bounced back into the trench on to him and exploded. The next few hours were a haze of grenade throwing and tommy-gunning, sand and bits of scrub flying everywhere.[8]

Shortly afterwards the Battalion was heavily counter-attacked and a gap opened in their line which was only plugged by a miscellaneous assortment of 25 cooks, signallers, clerks and storemen, backed up by three machine guns from the Division's MG Regiment. By dark on the 24th the Green Howards had lost 27 men killed, 75 wounded and 53 missing.

Yet their effort was far from wasted for the British presence posed a sufficient threat to General der Flieger Alfred Schlemm's I Parachute Corps to make it too risky for him to strip his sector of reserves to bolster the more heavily engaged parts of the German line. For on their front the Americans were having trouble enough just pushing back the troops *in situ*. On the flanks progress was reasonably satisfactory. 45 Division took their first day's objectives without too much difficulty, though a strong counter-attack by twenty or so Tiger tanks made a deep penetration that was only sealed off after a massive Allied artillery shoot had destroyed at least half the tanks. I SSF were also subjected to a heavy counter-attack but by the end of the first day they too had consolidated on their objectives, just short of the railway line running south-east of Cisterna. On the 24th both these divisions remained in place, and on the 25th 45 Division maintained its defensive posture whilst I SSF struck out for Monte Arestino, which was secured before dusk. The thrust to the north of Cisterna, by I Armoured Division, also went largely according to plan. The German perimeter was decisively punctured on the 23rd and on the following day the division had advance elements only four miles south-west of Velletri, with others across Highway Seven to the north of Cisterna. The fighting had been hard, however, and on the 23rd alone the division had lost eighty-six tanks and tank-destroyers, most of them in the thickly sown German minefields.

But it was 3 Division who had the hardest fighting of all. The attack against Cisterna did not go well and Truscott soon had to give up any hope of rushing the German defences there. The town was held by Generalleutnant Heinz Greiner's 362 Division and he at first doubted whether his men could possibly hold out. As he wrote after the war:

After a heavy barrage by concentrated ground and naval artillery and numerous mortars, the enemy attacked the entire front of the Division . . . using smoke screens at times, and changing the main point of effort several times. His attack was led by massed armoured forces, accompanied by strong infantry forces, and was made easier by the use of . . . rolling fighter-bomber attacks; it resulted in deep penetrations, especially in the centre and right of the Division, west of Cisterna.[9]

Further to the west, 715 Division had also been severely handled by 1 SSF and the situation on this flank was felt to be so critical that Mackensen asked Kesselring's permission to withdraw 715 Division behind the Cisterna railroad. But the latter proved just as unwilling to sanction any withdrawals as he had been with regard to the Dora and Hitler Lines and the whole of LXXVI Panzer Corps was ordered to hold its ground. But in this instance Kesselring's obduracy was not entirely unreasonable for it became increasingly apparent that the keystone of the German defences, held by 955 Regiment around Cisterna itself, was putting up a remarkably effective resistance. Major-General J.W. O'Daniel's 3 Division had attacked with six battalions in the line but nowhere were they able to make any significant penetrations. As usual the Germans had worked assiduously to improve the natural defences. According to Truscott they

had converted the environs [of Cisterna] into a veritable fortress. Deep ravines and canals on either side of the town afforded defilade from our fires, and numerous irrigation ditches were barriers to tank attack. Extensive caverns beneath the town protected the defenders from our heavy artillery and air bombardments. To the west of Cisterna the German main line of resistance followed the railroad line which, with its deep ditches and steep embankments, was an anti-tank barrier which required special means for crossing. To the southwest, branches of the Mussolini Canal and the numerous plastered stone houses had been transformed into enormously strong tactical localities.[10]

These localities were squad and platoon strongpoints built for all-round defence and protected by up to six machine guns in outlying weapons pits. They were echeloned back to a depth of 3000 yards in such a manner that there was hardly a spot in the entire zone that could not be fired on from at least two directions. The entire front was protected by belts of double apron or concertina wire and firing positions had been previously prepared for tanks and self-propelled guns. The latter moved constantly between these positions, firing and withdrawing before they could be registered by the Allied artillery and fighter-bombers. The enormous strength of such positions is grimly attested by 3 Division's casualties on the 23rd, over 1600 men killed, wounded and missing.

The fierce resistance continued throughout the 24th, though to Greiner, who returned that morning from emergency leave in Germany, the prospects seemed increasingly hopeless. His major problem was the lack of reinforcements. Even at the start of the battle his grenadier companies had numbered only thirty or so men each and by the second day he simply did not have enough troops to properly garrison his strongpoints, formidable as they were. Urgent appeals had already gone out to Mackensen and he and Kesselring had agreed to despatch the Hermann Göring Division from Leghorn to the threatened sector. But this move was bound to take time, and in the interim Greiner was hoping for more immediate support taken from less threatened portions of the German line. The most obvious source was 3 PG Division, facing 45 US Division, and this was clearly in Kesselring's mind when he ordered Mackensen to strengthen the Cisterna position with units from I Parachute Corps. But the latter remained convinced that VI Corps' major thrust would be north-westwards towards Rome and he refused to move anything from this sector except a few anti-tank guns. He ordered LXXVI Panzer Corps to stiffen its defences as best it could with units taken from its own extreme left flank. This was tantamount to asking a man to be his own transplant donor, and only a rag-bag of sub-units, many of them already in dire straits, could be assembled. Greiner himself wrote:

> To a large extent the equipment of these troops was inade-
> quate. . . . For instance . . . battalions without any battalion
> communication sections. . . . Because of enemy fighter-bomber
> activity . . . the reserves coming up brought along only the absolute
> minimum of equipment required in battle. For instance none of
> these troops brought up as reinforcements had rolling kitchens or
> any vehicles whatsoever. Equipping these troops with ammunition
> and their general supply placed heavy burdens upon the rear service
> units of the Division.[11]

Nor was his position helped when Mackensen deliberately misinterpreted a directive from Kesselring, who had finally agreed to a partial and limited withdrawal by 715 Division, and pulled the entire formation back to a line that virtually uncovered Greiner's left flank. The noose around Cisterna immediately tightened as 15 US Regiment took up the slack and advanced 500 yards beyond the railroad to the south-east of the town. All of O'Daniel's men redoubled their efforts. A German officer wrote after the war:

> The artillery bombardment, not to mention the veritable hail of bombs, that was directed against . . . [Cisterna] and the outlying houses, as well as the crossroads and supply routes, surpassed anything experienced to date, even on the Russian front. Our grenadiers had established their strongpoints in the rubble of the houses and farm-buildings. They fought grimly but in the long run could be no match for the overwhelming strength of the enemy, especially the enormous number of his tanks. There were no strong reserves with which to mount counter-attacks, above all no tanks or anti-tank weapons. But courage was not lacking, even from the youngest of our soldiers. Even today I am convinced that it was a great achievement by our soldiers to have held up the enemy offensive so effectively for so long.[12]

Late on the 24th, Greiner requested Mackensen's permission to withdraw northwards, and he in turn put this to Kesselring. But, perversely, or even petulantly, Kesselring was not inclined to let his subordinate rescue 362 Division from the mess which he had created and he gave strict instructions that Cisterna was not to be abandoned. Mackensen, however, showed more sense and once again flouted his orders by allowing Greiner to pull back. But all this had taken time and when Mackensen's decision was made known to his divisional commander all contact with the Cisterna garrison had been lost and no order to withdraw ever got through to them. They hung on to the bitter end and even threw back an attack that night, as the rest of the division was beginning to pull back. 7 US Regiment went in again the next morning and the outskirts of the town were quickly taken, the isolated garrison having withdrawn into fastnesses around the central square. For almost the rest of the day they held out. A war correspondent wrote:

> I crouched with the GIs who were still trying to get into the reeking ruins of Cisterna. Clearly there was nothing for it but to take the place rubbish heap after rubbish heap, cave by cave, and accept the casualties which come with street-fighting. Clearing Cisterna took two days. The Americans flung their grenades into the cellar gratings, risking the rush into fetid darkness where automatics might

be waiting to cut them down, their fire trained on the patch of light which marked the cellar entrance. So they fought their way slowly into the centre of the town until, at last, they reached the pile of rubbish which marked the *palazzo* in the main square.[13]

This *palazzo* was ringed with anti-tank mines, with all its approaches covered by machine guns in rubble-covered emplacements. On one side was a well-sited anti-tank gun covering the entrance to an inner courtyard. For some hours, even with tank support, the attack against the *palazzo* made little headway. In the late afternoon, however, a squad managed to get a machine gun on top of a pile of rubble overlooking the entrance to the courtyard. From here they were able to knock out the crew of the anti-tank gun, after which a tank rumbled forward and destroyed the gun itself. A rifle company followed close behind, penetrated the courtyard and German resistance suddenly collapsed. The prisoners included the commander of 955 Regiment, Oberleutnant Annacker.

The battle for Cisterna spoke volumes about the quality of the German troops in Italy, even supposedly run-of-the-mill divisions like the 362nd. It also offered interesting insights into the performance of the American troops and provided further evidence about the thin line between success and humiliating failure in combat. 3 US Division was no different from any other Allied formation and as such had its usual quota of heroes and cowards. All its commander could do, in the last analysis, was to get his men up to their start lines and *hope* that the attacks would go forward as planned. Once H-Hour arrived his direct influence on the fighting was extremely limited, his last resort being the same kind of pleading, cajolery and threats that we noted in Ryder's exchanges with his subordinates in 34 Division, in January. On 23 May, for example, 7 Regiment's frontal assault on Cisterna was going badly and the regimental S–3 reported that his leading companies were completely 'pinned down'. He was in direct contact with General O'Daniel, who replied: 'We have no such word in our vocabulary now. You're supposed to be at the railroad track by noon. You'll get a bonus if you do, something else if you don't.'[14]

Usually, local leadership, either from officers or dominant personalities in the platoons and companies, was adequate to the occasion. On the 23rd, 2/15 Regiment were attacking a wooded area near Highway Seven but began to lose momentum as the men ran out of ammunition. One company was then ordered to fix bayonets and charge. They did so and the defenders suddenly broke, losing fifteen men killed and over eighty prisoners. It was, says the US official history, 'one of the few verified bayonet assaults by American troops in World War II'.[15] The heroism of individuals sometimes seemed almost maniacal. The following is an eye-witness account by two soldiers in 3/30 Regiment, whose company was pinned down in front of a German strongpoint:

We had been sitting there about thirty minutes when the BAR man in my squad, Pfc. John Dutko, shouted to me, 'Toothman, I'm going to get that 88 with my heater. . .' He always called his BAR a 'heater'. Before I could say a word he took off like a ruptured duck. He made the first 100 yards in a dead run. Machine gun bullets were striking the ground a foot or two behind him but he was running faster than the Krauts could traverse. . . . [He dived into a shell-hole which was plastered by machine guns and the 88. He leapt out, followed by another private, C.R. Kelley, towards the 88. He threw a grenade into one machine gun position and killed the crew. According to Kelley:] Dutko was a madman now. He jumped to his feet and walked towards the 88mm firing his BAR from his hip. . . . He reached a point within 10 yards of the weapon and wiped out the five-man crew with one long burst . . . [and] then wheeled on the second machine gun and killed its crew. The third machine gun opened fire on Dutko. . . . Its first burst of fire wounded him but like a wounded lion he charged this gun at a half run. Pfc. Dutko killed both the . . . [crew] with a single burst . . . and, staggering forward, fell across the dead German machine-gunner. When I reached him he was dead.[16]

Once again, however, American records also provide us with candid accounts of command failures and further proof that just to be dubbed an officer and a gentleman did not in any way immunize a soldier against the natural terrors of war. During one attack by 30 Regiment, ' "I" Company (commanded by 1st Lieutenant Etheridge) came up . . . and Etheridge took his company up to the "E" and "F" objectives. Etheridge was soon thereafter hit and wounded. There were three officers left in "I" Company. They were comparing dates to see which was senior. None of them wanted to take over the company.'[17] Interviewed after the war, the S–3 of 3/7 Regiment recalled:

During the defensive period before the break-out the battalion CO . . . who took command of the 3/7th about a month before Anzio never visited any of the CPs of his rifle companies a single time. Once he started to, but when he started out and came under artillery fire, he went back to his dugout. This battalion CO even slept through a whole limited-objective attack which the 3/7th made in the month before the Anzio break-out.... Yet Colonel Omohundro thought that this battalion CO was the best . . . in the 7th. This was because the 3/7 CO said 'Yes Sir', and apple-polished and was the 'martinet' that the regimental CO wanted in his subordinates. . . . The first day of the Anzio break-out . . . the 3/7 Infantry CO crawled all day – at the end even in the mud. He crawled at least half a mile. A commander can't fool his troops long. A battalion CO who was so caked with mud from crawling did not escape his troops who saw him and rightly concluded that it was proof he was scared, which . . . he was.[18]*

A company commander in 3/30 Regiment was yet more forthright about his own commander's shortcomings:

The 3/30 Battalion CO . . . had no tactical sense and was a coward. . . . [On 25 May the battalion was to the left of Cisterna cemetery.] The enemy put up no organised resistance to the 3/30 in the advance to this high ground or during the time it was on the ridge. The 3/30 remained for hours in this position. The 3/30 received orders to attack but . . . [the CO] just did not attack. Instead . . . [he] had his orderly dig him a slit trench, and . . . [he] went to sleep. The 3/30 did not attack until after McGarr came up and booted . . . [the CO] in the 'fanny'. . . . [Even then the CO] stayed back to the rear of the battalion and a US Air Force bomb dropped 400 yards away from him. He was evacuated as a nervous exhaustion case.[19]

On the whole, however, 3 Division had fought hard and well and by the end of the 25th VI Corps was well placed for a further co-ordinated drive towards Valmontone. Not only had Cisterna finally fallen but good progress had also been made beyond it. Monte Arestino was in the hands of 1 SSF; Cori had been taken by 15 Regiment, pushing round the south of Cisterna; part of 1 Armoured Division had seized Giulianello, and the remainder were not far short of Velletri. General Truscott had high hopes and felt that 'by the following morning we would be astride the German line of withdrawal through Valmontone. . . . I returned to the command post feeling rather jubilant.'[20]

For Truscott was very much in agreement with Alexander that the main

---

* The official history added a savage postscript: 'At last convinced that the commander was no longer able to control either himself or his unit, the executive officer . . . assumed command. . . .' (Fisher, *op. cit.*, p.134.)

purpose of the Anzio breakout was to help trap as many Tenth Army troops as possible by cutting their line of retreat along Highway Six, as well as to prevent them from joining up with Fourteenth Army to make a prolonged stand behind the C-Line, in front of Rome. Alexander, indeed, had reiterated his concept of the Fourth Battle in a briefing to journalists just prior to the breakout. He told them that 'the whole object of the campaign was to "destroy the German Armies in Italy", with Rome a secondary objective. . . . Only the complete destruction of the enemy here would aid the coming second front in France and . . . merely pushing the Germans back would amount to failure of the Italian mission.'[21] Churchill was in full agreement and had neatly summed up Alexander's strategy when he insisted: 'A cop is much more important than Rome, which would anyhow come as its consequence. The cop is the one thing that matters.'[22]

The Germans, moreover, seemed to be playing into Alexander's hands. On the 24th and 25th they seemed only concerned with trying to hold Eighth Army where they stood and thus greatly increasing the chances of any breakout northwards from the beachhead getting astride their line of retreat. Not surprisingly, perhaps, it was Hitler's baleful strategic influence that lay behind this renewed emphasis upon not giving up an inch of ground, and Kesselring was never a man to argue with his Führer. On the afternoon of the 24th Westphal told von Vietinghoff: 'Only a short while ago Jodl [Chief of the OKW operations staff] rang up: "The Führer absolutely demands that any withdrawal be carried out step by step and with the consent of Army Group." If at all possible no withdrawal is to be made without the personal concurrence of the Führer.'[23] These orders were duly passed down the chain of command and Kesselring's supplementary orders the next day were, if anything, more royalist than the king's. The Battle of Rome, he said, was at 'a decisive stage. . . . The main goal must be to paralyse the offensive spirit of the enemy by the infliction of very heavy casualties. This can only be done by fanatical defence . . .'[24] Vietinghoff, in his turn, told Feuerstein: 'I would like to emphasise that according to the Führer's orders the Melfa Line must be held for several days. An early withdrawal is out of the question. Enemy elements that have crossed the river must be thrown back . . .'[25] The latter, however, was distinctly unenthusiastic, as the rest of their telephone conversation reveals:

Feuerstein: I report as a matter of duty that we will not bring back many men if we have to hold at all costs.
Vietinghoff: We must accept that risk; Army Group has given explicit orders to hold the line for several days.

Feuerstein: I report to the Colonel-General that the enemy has already crossed the Melfa in two places and that no forces are available to rectify the situation.[26]

Vietinghoff saw the sense of the Mountain Corps commander's objections. As we have seen with regard to similar orders to XIV Panzer Corps, he saw little benefit in this kind of static, last-ditch resistance. He therefore rang Kesselring early on the 26th and tried to convince him that an immediate withdrawal along Highway Six was the only sensible course. But for Kesselring OKW directives were akin to Holy Writ and he refused to budge: 'It is the Führer's explicit order and also my belief that we must bleed the enemy to exhaustion by hard fighting. You have always been optimistic. Why has your attitude changed?'[27]

German decisions on the beachhead also seemed to encourage high hopes for the drive towards Valmontone. For not only had LXXVI Panzer Corps been terribly mauled – 2640 German prisoners had been taken by the evening of the 25th – but Mackensen was still convinced that the major Allied axis of advance would be north-westwards, towards Rome, and he persisted in refusing to draw off any substantial reserves from I Parachute Corps to bolster the defences around Valmontone. The only significant redeployment in this sector was that of the Hermann Göring Division, Kesselring's last strategic reserve, who had arrived too late to be of any assistance in the defence of Cisterna. Yet their value as a blocking force further north had also been seriously vitiated. Their commander, Generalleutnant Wilhelm Schmalz, 'viewed the situation at Valmontone as very serious. . . . In the event of a powerful enemy attack there, which was to be expected, the inner wings of the two armies could be forced apart. . . . Consequently the immediate sealing of the gap at Valmontone with all available forces was important.'[28]

On the 26th, as his first units began to arrive, Schmalz tried to erect blocking positions across the 'Valmontone–Cisterna Gap' and to assemble some units for counter-attacks against Giulianello. However,

C-in-C South-west was evidently not in agreement with the measures taken, since a very sharp order from the Field-Marshal . . . directed the halting of all attacks and the concentration of the division north of Valmontone. . . . The execution of the C-in-C's orders would have resulted in the relinquishment of the gained blocking position, which would have invited the enemy to push further to the north toward Valmontone, and would automatically have forced 14 and 10 Armies apart. Due to this front-line evaluation, the division did not follow the order.[29]

Early on the 27th, Schmalz assembled such units as were already available and launched a desperate counter-attack. Its fate helps to explain why Kesselring would have preferred to place the division behind Valmontone where it might at least have gained some time for proper deployment.

Shortly after noon, Colonel Howze's outposts along the railroad west of Artena reported what seemed to be enemy infantry advancing through the wheatfields in full view of the American positions. Doubting that the Germans would actually be so foolhardy, the men in the outposts asked if they might possibly be Americans. 'Hell, no, shoot them up!' Colonel Howze himself bellowed into the phone. Leaving his command post, the task force commander raced forward in his jeep 'to get in on the show'. When he reached the front line, Howze could scarcely believe his eyes, 'the jerries walking and crawling through the wheat on the hillsides only 1500 yards away'. Here was the long-expected Hermann Goering Division 'coming in to face us'. Howze's tanks opened fire with devastating results.[30]

But the destruction of this counter-attack was just one more in a whole series of blows to the forces defending Valmontone. Even before it the HG Division was already in a parlous state. The credit for this went to the Mediterranean Allied Air Force, whose tactical ground support operations during DIADEM were proving much more effective than their preliminary strategic offensive to interdict the German supply lines. The HG Division had started its march southward from Leghorn on the morning of 23 May, having been refused permission to move only at night. It took the advance elements three days to reach the front and they were

subject to practically unceasing enemy low-level attacks by day and night. The losses were considerable. The Division reached the intended concentration area at Valmontone with only eleven [out of sixty Mark IV] tanks. Eighteen guns of the panzer artillery regiment were disabled. The Panzer Grenadier Regiments and the Panzer Engineer Battalion suffered the loss of about 30 per cent of their MT, but no substantial losses in men.[31]

A few more tanks did eventually straggle in late on the 27th but even these only brought the total number of tanks to 18 and only 8 to 10 of them were ever fit for action at any one time. Given also that it was not until the 29th that the last of the Panzer Grenadier battalions straggled into the sector, again having lost much of their equipment, one can hardly regard their move as a crucial reinforcement, or one that could significantly baulk VI Corps.

And there was certainly little else left. Even on the 25th LXXVI Panzer Corps was already capable of only the feeblest resistance. Colonel Howze, pursuing remnants of 715 Division, had driven back to his Divisional HQ where his 'message was: "I am in a soft spot, for Pete's sake let the whole 1st Armoured come this way! I didn't want to do it all myself, I didn't have enough strength . . ." Harmon [the commander of 1 Armoured Division] agreed instantly and told Truscott.'[32] German weakness became increasingly apparent on the 26th when 3 Division and 1 SSF resumed their advance northwards. General O'Daniel gleefully reported: 'This area is very soft . . . I'm convinced we could go on to Rome, if we had more stuff up here.'[33]

But here was the rub. VI Corps did not have enough 'stuff' in the Valmontone sector because on the previous day General Clark had chosen to ignore Alexander's wishes and to shift the main axis of attack from the Cori–Valmontone axis to the alternative 'Turtle' route, directly north-westwards to Rome. Only 3 Division, 1 SSF and a fragment of 1 Armoured Division were to pursue the drive towards Valmontone whilst the bulk of the tanks, 34 Division which had fought with them, the relatively fresh 45 Division, and the newly arrived VI Corps reserve, Walker's 36 Division, were all to advance against the C-Line positions between Campoleone, Lanuvio and Velletri. Truscott had been given an inkling of what was coming, on the 24th, when Clark had casually asked whether he had given any more thought to the 'Turtle' axis. Truscott assured him that full contingency plans had been drawn up, but thought little more about it as the Valmontone attack was going so well. Indeed, by the following afternoon, as we have seen, his mood was 'jubilant'.

But not for long. Don Brann, the Army G–3, was waiting for me. Brann said: 'The Boss wants you to leave the 3rd Infantry Division and the Special Force to block Highway Six and mount that assault you discussed with him to the north-west as soon as you can.' I was dumbfounded. I protested that the conditions were not right. There was no evidence of any withdrawal from the western part of the beachhead, nor was there evidence of any concentration in the Valmontone area except light reconnaissance elements of the Hermann Goering Division. This was no time to drive to the north-west where the enemy was still strong; we should pour our maximum power into the Valmontone Gap to insure the destruction of the retreating German Army.[34]

Truscott demanded that the order be given by Clark in person but was informed that his commander was airborne and could not be contacted. He had no alternative but to obey or resign and at VI Corps conference later that day he put as brave a face on it as possible, 'reacting favourably to the shift of the main effort . . . and expressing confidence that the weaker force could reach Valmontone and cut Highway Six.'[35] But this in no way implied that he had come round to Clark's way of thinking. As he himself said, it was rather that 'in this conference it would have been most disloyal for me to have stated to the divisional commanders that I disagreed with the decision . . . for the change in direction; and it would have been poor leadership to have expressed lack of confidence in the ['Turtle'] plan which had been prepared by my own staff. . .'[36]* He was more forthright at an earlier conference with his own principal staff officers. According to his G-4, Colonel E.J. O'Neill:

> . . . during . . . [this] conference he announced General Clark's decision as relayed by General Brann. At that time, he told us that he had vehemently protested not only the decision as being wrong but that the time had not then arrived for any such change of plans, and that it was questionable whether justified grounds for such a change of attack might arise in the future. He was extremely positive in his statements and left no doubt in my mind as to the course of action he had taken with General Brann.[37]

All who were present at this meeting also stress that the major reason for their disappointment was that the way to Valmontone seemed clear and that there was very little in the way of organized resistance between VI Corps and Highway Six. Truscott's Chief of Staff, Colonel D.E. Carleton, wrote in his journal after Brann had left: 'General Brann arrives just when it appears that the route to Valmontone is open and Buffalo has worked, with orders that change the direction of attack . . .'[38] In a later account of the day's events, Carleton re-emphasized that there seemed no reason to anticipate any organized German resistance:

---

* This letter, and the others quoted below from members of Truscott's staff, were part of a submission by Truscott expressing his 'resentment' that the Matthews article (*supra*) made no mention of his objections to Clark's decision. The Chief of Military History accepted his submission, apologized, and ensured that the error was not repeated in the relevant volume of the official history by Fisher, *op. cit.* (See letter, Chief of Military History to Truscott, Ref: Gen. Harris/js/52064, copy (n.d.). NA (MMS) RG 319 Box 4.)

We had gone ahead under full confidence that Buffalo was our main effort and that if we could crack Cisterna and Corie [sic] without too much delay, it was highly possible that we might turn the entire German position and seize the bridges in Rome before any substantial portion of his main forces between the beachhead and Rome west of the Albani Hills could escape. By noon of May 25, word came that advance elements of the Howze task force were nearing Highway Six and the 3rd Division was moving on toward Artena. . . . Only reconnaissance units of the Hermann Goering Division appeared to be in the area . . . It was my opinion then, and I know General Truscott felt the same way as did the 6th Corps staff, that this change of direction was a horrible mistake and would only delay the capture of Rome.[39]

After the war General O'Daniel added his voice to the protests, asserting that 'it was a mistake to shift the VI Corps axis of attack. . . . After the breakthrough of Cisterna and Cori was reached, the Germans were wide open to Valmontone. At that time . . . if a fresh division, the 36th, had been passed through the 3rd Division, the breakthrough could have been rapidly exploited. . . . At that time there was nothing to stop a fresh division.'[40]

It is strange, therefore, that Clark gave as one of his major reasons for not pressing ahead on the 'Buffalo' axis the fact that VI Corps was not strong enough to break through. In his diary he wrote:

As I have often indicated, the direction of attack assigned me for the Anzio effort was in the direction Cori-Valmontone. This was due to a long-standing, pre-conceived idea by Alexander, instigated by his Chief of Staff, Harding. . . . I was forced into this attack, but it had a good feature in that it took Cisterna and gave us the observation in the area of Cori. If the going became tough on Valmontone I could shift the weight of my attack to the northwest. Exactly this has happened. All German troops withdrawing from the Cisterna area have taken a position betwen Velletri and Valmontone. This area has been reinforced from the British west flank and by the Herman [sic] Goering Division. Once we advanced to Valmontone it would be difficult to turn west on road via Route No.6. Communications alone would make this impracticable.[41]

In an interview after the war he reiterated these reasons. At one stage 'General Clark [said he] regarded the Anzio force as not strong enough to cut Highway 6. . . . He had received information from his G–2 that German reserves were *likely* to move down and block us at Valmontone, therefore he decided to change the axis of attack.' To the same interviewer he repeated a few days later that he 'did not believe that the Buffalo attack versus Cisterna–Cori–Valmontone could reach its ultimate objective (Highway 6) with the troops at the disposal of VI Corps.'[42]

None of these reasons hold much water. As we have seen, the Germans had shifted very few troops from their right flank to the Valmontone Gap, whilst the HG Division was in appalling shape as it dribbled into this sector. Nor could the debris of LXXVI Panzer Corps, darkly referred to as 'all the troops retreating from the Cisterna area', be regarded as much of a threat. It is not easy, moreover, to understand exactly what difficulties and communications problems would have faced VI Corps had they attempted to turn west on Highway Six towards Rome. Colonel Carleton, as we have seen, thought this a perfectly feasible option, whilst a later semi-official American account found Clark's excuse 'puzzling', maintaining that such a thrust offered an 'excellent opportunity' for a quick advance to Rome. If VI Corps could cut Highway Six north-west of Valmontone

> the Corps could then wheel north-west across fairly open country to breach the Caesar Line north-east of the Alban Hills. . . . German defences in the Caesar Line between the Alban Hills and Valmontone were weaker than elsewhere and had no natural features to buttress man-made barriers. Neither army nor corps estimates indicated substantial enemy forces in the area.[43]

Worse still, the portion of the C-Line that Clark *did* choose to attack, between Campoleone and Velletri, was actually the strongest, whose breach was likely to involve hard fighting. German defences here were much more elaborate than elsewhere in the C-Line. Vast amounts of mines and wire had been laid. The area was dotted with hamlets and farm-buildings, all turned into formidable strongpoints, and numerous bunkers, dugouts and concealed self-propelled gun positions had been cunningly sited so as to block all obvious approach routes. Nor had the enemy here been unduly troubled by the fighting to date and casualties had still been fairly light. The commander of 45 Division, General W.W. Eagles, had been assigned a spearhead role in the new attack and he was all too aware of the problems involved. Above all he was convinced that there had as yet been no significant German withdrawals from this sector. Even assuming that the Germans were considering shifting some units from 3 PG and 65 Divisions towards Valmontone, which was far from certain, his own attack would still be premature. He 'complained that the attack would get underway at least 48 hours too soon, and that the divisions participating in it would suffer heavily and needlessly.'[44]

For Clark, however, the 'Turtle' axis had one overriding advantage, one that was spelled out in his Operations Instructions of 26 May: 'The overwhelming success of the current battle makes it possible to . . . launch a new attack along the most direct route to Rome.'[45] The key words here are 'most direct' and to understand why they should be of such significance to Clark one must constantly bear in mind two factors already hinted at. One is that he was obsessed with capturing Rome; the other that he held the British in such low esteem that he was haunted by the possibility, remote as it was, that they might somehow beat him there.

Our discussion of the preparations for DIADEM showed that, even in April and early May, Clark was most concerned that the 'Buffalo' attack might divert him from the 'most important' task of seizing Rome. In the following weeks his concern only mounted. In an interview after the war he recalled that 'he did want to take Rome . . . before the Normandy invasion began. . . . Clark knew the approximate date for the Normandy invasion and he was very anxious for Fifth Army to be in Rome before then. The capture of Rome . . . had a value as a political objective and was a matter of prestige . . .'[46] A group of war correspondents, on the very eve of the breakout, were left in no doubt as to what was Clark's overriding objective. He told them quite simply: ' "We're going to take Rome." He went on with sweeping gestures in front of the war map explaining the movements in the south . . . and at Anzio, but his underlying theme was the capture of Rome. All-important Rome. The correspondents had been better briefed than they realized.'[47] To another interviewer after the war he said: 'Whether or not they now say "the hell with Rome" I don't know, but then there was always the feeling that Rome was certainly a great prize and the sooner we stepped out and got it, then we were in a new and final phase of the war.'[48] But there were those *then* who said 'the hell with Rome', at least in the short term, and who agreed with Alexander that the all-important task was to first attempt to cut off as large a part of the enemy forces as possible. But this cut little ice with Clark who was quite clear in his own mind that if such a strategy posed the least threat of his not being the first in Rome he would be perfectly prepared to disregard Alexander's intentions. As early as 5 May, on his own admission, he had great reservations: 'After Clark got the message from Truscott . . . regarding Alexander's . . . plan and axis of attack Clark did not feel that he would try to change it *at that time*. Clark

said this scheme was strictly Alexander's. . . . He expressed his opinion
viz. [sic] this plan of attack but . . . was overruled by Alexander. . . . He
made it clear [to the interviewer] that he foresaw the time when the shift
in the axis would be desirable. . . . Clark always realised we'd have to
get to the Alban Hills.'[49] On the 19th Truscott was given a clear indication
of the way Clark's mind was working. Indeed, if the following entry in
Clark's diary is to be believed, one wonders why Truscott was quite so
'dumbfounded' when the change of axis was eventually ordered:

> General Clark stated that General Alexander had, from the
> beginning, a pre-conceived plan of the attack from the bridgehead
> to cut Route No.6, harass the enemy rear with light columns and
> eventually annihilate the enemy forces. General Clark emphasized
> that he, in his planning, wanted to maintain flexibility; that the plan
> BUFFALO would be carried out as planned but that he wanted
> General Truscott to be flexible in his plans and be prepared to
> change the direction of the attack north from Cori–Valmontone to
> an attack to the northwest towards Rome.'[50]

Other remarks by Clark hammer home the point that he had to be the
first in Rome and that he had to above all beat the British. In his memoirs
he attempted to disarm criticism by admitting: 'I was determined that the
Fifth Army was going to capture Rome, and I was probably oversensitive
to indications that practically everybody else was trying to get into the act.
These indications mounted rapidly in the next few days, and I had my
hands full.'[51] In a subsequent interview he did not even bother to make
excuses: 'One thing I knew was that *I* had to take Rome and that my
American army was going to do it. So in the circumstances I had to go
for it before the British loused it up. . . . We Americans had slogged all
the way up from Salerno and I was not going to have this great prize, the
honour of taking Rome, denied to me and my GIs by anyone.'[52] His
animus against the British became almost virulent during the last days of
May, when his redirected attack to the north-west seemed in danger of
bogging down. His diary entries for the 30th make remarkable reading,
giving full vent to his obsession with Rome as well as to his persistent
suspicions about British deviousness and malingering:

> Most of my worries have nothing to do with the immediate battle.
> They are political in nature. I will name them in the order of the
> trouble they cause me.
> First, the British have their eyes on Rome, notwithstanding
> Alexander's constant assurance to me that Rome is in the sector of

the Fifth Army. . . . The English Army has done little fighting. It has lacked aggressiveness and failed in its part in this combined Allied effort. . . . I feel there is some indication on the part of Alexander to commence alibiing for his Eighth Army. . . . If I do not crack this position in three or four days I may have to reorganize, wait for the Eighth Army and go at it with a co-ordinated attack by both armies, but I fear the same results from Eighth Army. It will not put in its full effort, for it never has.[53]

Equally remarkable are two statements in the Matthews interview, neither of which seem to be those of a dispassionate, responsible commander whose main task was to defeat the Germans. At one point, after stating his opposition to the 'Buffalo' axis, 'Clark said that he always had to be careful about making it possible for the British Eighth Army to get an easy victory and swing along on the successful offensive of the American Fifth Army.'[54] There might be those who would claim that the very success of one Army's offensive could actually be measured by the extent to which it allowed another Army to make easy progress and thus ensure *victory over the enemy*. If footballers were to follow Clark's recipe for teamwork then a quarterback might well refuse to release the ball lest one of his receivers 'swing along' on a successful push by his linemen. Clark's other assertion requires no comment:

. . . the British definitely wanted Eighth Army to take Rome or at least to take part in its capture. When Alexander told Clark he wanted the Eighth Army to take part in its capture, Clark got pretty sore. He told Alexander if Alexander gave him . . . such an order he would refuse to obey it and if Eighth Army tried to advance on Rome, Clark said he would have his troops fire on the Eighth Army.[55]*

In operational terms, however, the most tragic aspect of the whole 'Buffalo'/'Turtle' controversy was that Clark's rejigged offensive had immediately run into serious difficulties. The rump 'Buffalo' was a bust from the start. Both 3 Division and I SSF were pretty worn out, and without armoured support, or an injection from 45 or 36 Divisions, would probably have found the going hard even against relatively weak defences. In fact, very little was asked of them, as Clark was now prepared

---

* I have searched the record in vain to find any other reference, even by Clark, to Alexander's having insisted that Eighth Army must take part in the capture of Rome.

to let the Valmontone thrust be almost completely run down, though he made assiduous efforts to conceal this from Alexander. On the 25th he instructed Gruenther to reassure Alexander that 'we have Artena and are no doubt pushing well on towards Valmontone. I did not deter [sic] from sending a strong force in that direction in compliance with his instructions.'[56] Gruenther replied later that day, after he had given Alexander his first inkling of the change of direction:

General Alexander agreed that the plan is a good one. He stated, 'I am for any line of action which the Army commander believes will offer a chance to continue his present success.' About five minutes later he said, 'I am sure that the Army Commander will continue to push toward Valmontone, won't he? I know that he appreciates the importance of gaining the high ground just south of Artena. As soon as he captures that he will be absolutely safe.' I assured him that you had that situation thoroughly in mind, and that he could depend on you to execute a vigorous plan with all the push in the world.[57]

Assuming this to be a verbatim report, Gruenther's reply clearly left it very open as to exactly which attack was going to be 'pushed'. For, as he was doubtless aware, it was not going to be 'Buffalo'. The taking of Artena was its last gasp and for the next few days no serious attempt was made to drive towards Valmontone or Highway Six. The low priority given to any penetration of the Valmontone Gap is confirmed by these extracts from VI Corps' G–3 Journal and File. On the morning of the 27th, Truscott telephoned O'Daniel and told him: 'Your first job is to hold that high ground overlooking Artena. Your second is to prevent anything coming in down that pass hitting you in that direction. Your third is to cut that route 6 in vicinity Valmontone.' O'Daniel was unsure whether this enumeration of tasks was also a scale of priorities and, still shocked that the cutting of Highway Six could have been so downgraded, telephoned back for clarification. Truscott told him: 'There seems to have been some misunderstanding and confusion as to your priorities. I have given them to you once, I will give them to you again. First, you are to hold high ground at Artena. Second, to prevent any force from moving southward through pass. Third, to protect your own lines of communication. Fourth, to cut Highway at Valmontone.'[58] In the Matthews interview Clark himself also 'conceded that after the axis of attack was changed on 25 May . . . the 3rd Division's role was not a heavy offensive one but after Artena . . . anyway was primarily defensive . . .'[59]
But there was equally little progress on the 'Turtle' axis, though here

Clark *was* attacking with as much push as he could. Four divisions were involved, 45 and 1 Armoured Divisions attacking between Campoleone and Velletri, 34 Division to the east of Lanuvio, and 36 Division being brought forward to drive between Velletri and Lariano. There were no significant penetrations anywhere along the line. Schlemm's 1 Parachute Corps was proving as obdurate as most other German formations and exacting a heavy toll on the attackers. On the 29th, after three days of fighting, they still held firm, that day alone costing 1 Armoured Division a further 37 tanks knocked out. Tempers began to run high in Divisional, Corps and Army headquarters. On the same afternoon Truscott's Chief of Staff rang up General W.W. Eagles, commanding 45 Division, and demanded to know what was holding him up,

> accusing the division of not being able to keep pace with the units of the 34th to its right. He chose a particularly bad time to make that accusation, since Eagles had just returned from that very sector and had observed that the 34th's famed 100 Infantry Battalion . . . immediately adjacent to the 45th was as much pinned down as were his men. Eagles' conversation with Carleton was decidedly heated . . .[60]

Truscott himself became equally impatient with 34 Division and after yet another round of attacks on Lanuvio had ground to a halt, again on the 29th, he got on the phone and curtly informed a member of Ryder's staff: 'Tell him to crack this Lanuvio. It's holding the whole thing up.'[61]

Clark too was badgering his subordinates, doubtless even more vehemently. His diary for the 30th simply records: 'I just phoned to Truscott, Harmon, Eagles and to Ryder to tell them I am disappointed with their efforts today. . . . I have urged them to greater efforts tomorrow and the next day.'[62] But it comes as no surprise to find that, in his diary at least, Clark worked out much of his frustration on the British contingent on the beachhead. And this despite the fact that their attacks were only supposed to be diversionary, were directed against a well-entrenched Parachute Division (the 4th), had involved very high casualties, and were never supported by tanks nor by more than a fraction of the Corps artillery. On the 27th he wrote: 'I have continually talked with my British commanders in an effort to energize them into an attack. There is no attack left in them. The 5th Division is poorly led by Gregson-Ellis. He has no offensive spirit.' On the 30th, looking around for reinforcements for the main push towards Rome, he lamented: 'To attach the 5th British Division to the VI Corps would be like giving a poor man a dirty shirt. They have no offensive inclinations.'[63]*

But if Clark's attack had bogged down on the beachhead, it cannot really be claimed that either the French or Eighth Army were doing much better. At first sight this seems rather surprising because, on the afternoon of the 26th, Kesselring had finally decided that there was nothing more to be gained by insisting that Tenth Army hold its present positions in the Liri Valley. More than ever convinced of the dangers of VI Corps pushing through Valmontone and cutting off Vietinghoff's line of retreat, for he was not yet aware that Clark had decided to switch the axis of attack, he persuaded Hitler and the OKW to sanction a withdrawal to unite Tenth Army with the Fourteenth. I Parachute Corps was to hold firm between Velletri and the coast whilst the remnants of LXXVI Panzer Corps were to pivot on Cisterna and fall back to the C-Line. XIV Panzer Corps, with all the various reinforcements that had been sent against the French Corps and II US Corps under command, was also to fall back to the C-Line, through the Lepini Mountains and the southern half of the Liri Valley. LI Mountain Corps was to protect its left flank in the northern half of the valley and the mountains beyond. To block the Valmontone Gap until the junction in the C-Line was effected, the remnants of 71 and 94 Divisions were to be pulled back there immediately and 356 Division was to be brought down from Genoa. Nevertheless, because of the need to gain time to improve the more northerly C-Line positions, Tenth Army's withdrawal was to be a very gradual one. The immediate object, as Kesselring reminded his subordinates, was 'not to reach the C-Line soon; rather, whilst stubbornly holding the sectors designated from time to time, to inflict such heavy casualties on the enemy that his fighting potential will be broken down even before the Caesar Line is reached.'[64] The more important blocking positions were designated immediately. They were four in number and were between six and ten miles apart. The first crossed Highway Six behind Ceprano and from there followed the west bank of the Liri to Arce and into the mountains to the north. The second straddled Highway Six from south-east of Frosinone through Ceccano, Arnara and Ripi. The third linked Ferentino and Alatri, and the fourth, on which a prolonged stand was to be made before pulling back into the C-Line, was to be anchored on a line between Anagni and Guarcino.

---

* Nor did General Penney, of I Division, escape Clark's wrath. In the Matthews Interview Clark said that 'as a division commander [he] was a good telephone operator.' (Clark Interview, *op. cit.*, p.32.)

When the Ultra intercepts arrived there must have been many in Eighth Army who felt that this was mere bluster and that the rest of Operation DIADEM would consist in driving before them enemy remnants in complete disarray. To be sure there were some encouraging signs. In some instances there definitely was evidence of a lowering of German morale. 8 Indian Division had come back into the line on 20 May, and on the 25th and 26th were pushing from Piedimonte San Germano, taken by the Poles, towards Roccasecca. On both days they were faced by survivors from Heidrich's Parachute Division. In some of these companies morale seemed 'to have broken and even the fanatical paratroopers had lost heart. In a chance encounter five camp-followers of 3/8 Punjab Regiment, with only three rifles between them, captured eleven of Hitler's Prides without a shot being fired.' Two days later, after the fall of Roccasecca, a German rearguard was attacked near a blown bridge. According to one officer: 'The famed German paratroopers ran pell-mell, scrambling over rocks and diving into shelters as we came upon the scene. Some put up a weak show of resistance, but others surrendered at once. Famished prisoners pocketed their pride and asked for food.'[65] To the left of the Indians, following Highway Six, were 78 and 6 Armoured Divisions and they too found some evidence of German disarray. On the 25th, according to 5 Northants' historian, 'the padre made history in this advance by capturing two enemy, one riding a motor-bike devoid of trousers.'[66] To the south of Highway Six were the Canadians, advancing between Highway Six and the Liri towards Ceprano and Ceccano. They too found numerous disheartened prisoners, some careless of the safeguards offered them by the Geneva Convention. According to the War Diarist of the Princess Patricias: 'We have been using air support considerably in the last few days, most of the targets being based on information gained from prisoners of war. If one did not appreciate the peculiar quality of the German Army's discipline, in which everything is based upon the efficiency of the commander, one would be shocked at the indifference of these prisoners towards any harm which may result to their late comrades from the information they give away.'[67] The diarist of the Loyal Edmonton Regiment was more censorious yet: 'One of the prisoners taken volunteered his services to direct artillery fire on his own positions. It proved to be effective but nothing but the utmost contempt could be felt for such a traitor.'[68]

Nor was it just individuals who were feeling the strain, for the immense Allied superiority in men, artillery and aircraft was bringing whole units dangerously close to breaking-point. On the 26th, a German regimental commander assembled his officers in a garage near Ceccano and told them: 'The situation is very serious. Our orders are to hold on to our present position at all costs, with the means now at our disposal. If we lose any more ground the situation will become critical.' On the following day, again near Ceccano, Leutnant Hauck, of 1027 PG Regiment, told his section commanders:

> We are being forced to fall back. We are going to have to pull back gradually for there is no hope of any reinforcements here. The reserves are occupying positions around Florence. We might be obliged to fall back that far. Whatever happens we have to maintain contact with the enemy, to hold him up, and only to fall back when ordered. Anyway, it is very difficult for us to hold on here. No more supplies are getting through . . .[69]

But moving at all, backwards or forwards, was very difficult under the constant surveillance and harassment of the Allied air force. Operation STRANGLE was also having considerable tactical impact on Tenth Army's front and certain units were as badly battered as was the HG Division at Anzio. One German report said:

> Enemy air activity . . . has reached unprecedented proportions. Attacks are particularly heavy against places where no alternative roads are available, for example, defiles, bridges, and other bottlenecks. (Against one bridge, for instance, 100 sorties were flown in a 24-hour period.) Regroupings and the movement of reserves have been thereby subjected to delays as long as 2–3 days. It is impossible, in the face of such air superiority, for command to make any computation of the time element in movements. Necessary countermeasures have frequently been too late to accomplish anything.[70]

According to a prisoner of war from 1/577 Regiment (305 Division):

> During yesterday the 29th alone, the doctor said we had 48 killed and wounded. . . . Since the 27th all the heavy stuff . . . and numerous troops have been moving towards Rieti in indescribable disorder. It's above all at night that the roads are jam-packed. All along the roads the trucks destroyed by aircraft are thrown into the ditches. The prisoner himself has had nine trucks destroyed in two months.[71]

Yet none of this should be taken to mean that the whole of Tenth Army was on the point of collapse. Delaying tactics of the kind called for by

Kesselring were the Germans' forte and there were still enormous advantages to be gained from the difficult terrain. Even in the Liri Valley there were many eminently defensible positions, one of the best being just short of Arce. A ridge ran north and south on each side of Highway Six, each half of it, Monte Grande and Monte Piccolo, being a mile long and 800 yards deep. 6 Armoured Division made contact with the defenders here on the 26th but it was not until the 29th, with the aid of supplementary outflanking attacks by 8 Indian Division, that Arce itself was taken. But everywhere the ground was far from easy. Italian methods of cultivation did not help and again and again units found themselves attacking through terraced olive groves and vineyards, where visibility was down to a few yards and where endless series of walled steps made the going a nightmare. One soldier remembered his first attack at the very end of May:

> The novelty appealed to me. I hadn't heard of a night attack up an olive terrace. All went well until the fourth wall. Sergeant Meadows halted very suddenly. The section piled gently into one another, like dodgems in slow motion. 'The bloody path's finished!' whispered Meadows. We hunted round for another. There wasn't one. We had to climb the walls. . . . We couldn't pick the rotten foothold and the weight of equipment destroyed any sense of balance . . . As we gained height we heard the rest of the Company crashing after us. They sounded like elephants in the jungle. The sound must have carried for miles. . . . At one wall I fell off three times. If we fell on our backs, which we invariably did, the weight and placing of our equipment made it almost impossible to get up by ourselves. . . . We had one five-minute rest. The agony of starting up again ruled out any more. . . . The Bren magazines . . . hung round . . . [my neck] like pendulums in a gale. The weight of the magazines – ten pounds – forced my chin on to my chest. As I walked they yanked at my neck. I cursed them aloud. They yanked back. We blundered on, lost in our own particular nightmares. . . . We climbed one more wall. Instead of a terrace we saw a road ending in a village. . . . At a sign from Meadows we advanced once more. We lurched along like drunks returning home. I didn't care if the Germans were in the village. If they shot me, they shot me. They could have the Bren mags instead.[72]

The London Irish took part in an attack between Ceprano and Ripi, on the 28th, and for most of the day it was the terrain rather than the enemy that posed the major problems:

The physical effort of getting forward was very considerable, and it entailed our soldiers scrambling over quite deep clefts every hundred yards or so, and forcing their way through vast clumps of coppice growth and thickets in between them. They were also continually raising dust clouds, sliding down the dry barren sides of the fissures. After a while both men and weapons were covered in the white chalk dust which was so marked a feature of war in central Italy in dry weather.[73]

Sometimes, as in Rifleman Bowlby's case, the objective at the end of such approach marches was unoccupied. More often than not, however, there would be a vicious little fire-fight as a small German rearguard was rooted out of the fortified houses and farm-buildings. So it was at San Giovanni, attacked by the London Irish on 29 May. The village consisted of a main street with a few alleys to left and right. One company, supported by tanks, was sent down this street and two others were posted on each flank. According to the battalion commander these flank

companies found themselves mixed up in the gardens and outbuildings, and with one obstacle after another to contend with they were soon left behind. Also with no central axis, and most of the town smothered in its smoke cloud, they rapidly lost touch with their own men as well as with each other. In no time at all I had half the battalion out of control. . . . In the case of . . . [the centre] Company the forward movement never stopped, and the combination with the tanks was irresistible. B Squadron's forward troop worked up each side of the main street, putting a round or two from their cannon through doorways or windows with our riflemen racing in from behind with grenades. It was a slow job but a thorough one. It was also a very messy one, and long before it was over, nearly three hours later, most of the tanks had run out of ammunition.[74]

Tanks were clearly of considerable value in this action, but this kind of close-support work with the infantry was about all they were good for. As we have seen repeatedly, one of the main reasons for persisting with the Cassino battles had been the prospect of whole armoured divisions bursting into the Liri Valley and sweeping all resistance before them. But the reality was a bitter disappointment and nowhere did the difficult terrain allow the tanks to move in anything more than penny packets or at anything more than a snail's pace. According to a staff officer of XIII Corps, on the 31st, 'the advance continued during the day but movement was slow largely due to enemy demolitions and craters. . . . Throughout the day tanks have found going very difficult due to mines and craters and have hardly been able to keep up with the infantry.'[75] The history of one New Zealand armoured regiment, supporting 8 Indian Division, described the going at around the same time, towards Frajoli:

> They were days of continual struggle, not so much against Jerry as against steep banks and stone terraces, crops and scrub, big rocks alternating with soft soil. The terraces were the worst. The only way to deal with them was to break them down with hand and shovel and pile earth and stones up into ramps, a maddeningly slow business. The whole place was a tankie's nightmare. Everywhere you had to explore on foot before going forward. Often you were travelling blind, just blundering on in what you thought was the right direction, with no infantry or anyone else in sight. Occasionally there would be a lane to follow for a while, but it always either ended at an isolated farm or curved the wrong way, and then you had to take to the hills again.[76]

The Canadians had similar problems. The advance towards Pofi, on the 29th, was a typical day's work for the British Columbia Dragoons:

> Progress was exceedingly slow. . . . Two tributaries of the Secco . . . proved major obstacles. Bridging tanks accompanied the force, but at the second of these streams there was a delay of six hours before a scissors bridge was in position. . . . When the advance was resumed, German self-propelled guns north of Highway No.6 knocked out several . . . tanks. . . . The two leading squadrons arrived in the Pofi area with only nine tanks left. 'Of the remainder', records the unit account of the operation, 'five had been destroyed by enemy action and the rest were bogged down, stuck on banks, rocks, tree stumps.'[77]

The French were at times positively bitter about the limited opportunities for the armour. An officer with 2 DIM wrote:

> The Cavalry cannot, in the existing circumstances, operate by itself; all its attempts to do so have been ridiculous failures. . . . One must [also] say a word . . . about the incomprehensible timidity of the armour. . . . It has almost never supported the infantry properly. Consequently the infantry, time and time again, have been obliged to . . . come to grips with the enemy without any cover at all. . . .

These repeated contacts have cost us dear and . . . the bitter satisfaction of being able to say that during that period not one of our precious tanks was destroyed or even damaged will not really console us.[78]*

But full credit must also go to the Germans, whose delaying tactics made the most of the advantages afforded by the ground. Their basic method was to leave small but well-armed and mobile rearguards in contact with the advancing Allies whilst the infantry on foot withdrew to new positions, destroying roads and bridges. 'This', according to Tenth Army's diarist, 'reduces our own casualties and causes those of the enemy to be palpably higher.'[79] Machine-gunners had a crucial role to play in these rearguards, trying to break up attacks before they started and so rob the Allied advance of any momentum. In one set of instructions to his troops, Kesselring wrote: 'I must stress particularly that the MGs which have been set up in depth open fire at maximum range, that is up to 2000 metres with maximum expenditure of ammunition, and force the enemy to disperse while he is preparing for, or is at the beginning of, his attack . . .' His final decree was that 'demolitions of every kind must be more than ever executed with sadistic imaginativeness.'[80] This latter injunction was followed to the letter and demolitions and booby traps were a persistent brake on Eighth Army's progress. For 6 Inniskilling Fusiliers the 31st was

a very tedious and frustrating day. But by nightfall they had advanced over six miles, which was no mean achievement in the circumstances. They had met no opposition save some long-range sniping from one or two SPs who had ranged on to some of the blocking points. These consisted of cleverly sited craters, usually at track intersections or hillside defiles and they were generally thick with mines or other booby traps. All these obstructions were

---

* The French continued to hold American armour in particularly low repute. On 1 June, near Le Travo, a small French task force from 3/5 RTM was supported by American tanks and armoured cars. According to their War Diary: 'The scout-cars were fired on by the enemy . . . and an American light tank was hit by an anti-tank gun, upon which all the American tanks took flight. . . . Captain Bretagne multiplied his efforts to halt the American tanks.' (JDM 2/5 RTM, 1 June 1944, SHAT (FPU) I2P 73.) One of 2/4 RTM's most prominent 'comments on our Allies', in a later report, concerned the 'deficiencies of the American armour, which never went in front of the infantry but always arrived when the battle was over, just in time to draw enemy shells on to our infantry.' (2/4 RTM, Enseignements tirés des opérations depuis le 22 mai, Ref: 415/28, 24 July 1944, signed Chef de Bataillon Pauc. SHAT (FPU) I2P 69.)

impassable, and they entailed hard physical effort in . . .
[neutralizing] and filling in. The pioneers were at a premium then.[81]

The French, too, had their problems and the almost panicky German
retreats that had followed the initial French breakthrough on the Maio
massif were not to be repeated for the rest of the month. Von Vietinghoff
made an interesting remark in this respect when he asserted that

> the assault of the French Expeditionary Corps beyond the Petrella
> Block, though constituting an amazing achievement . . . did not
> quite result, as feared on the German side, in a decision comparable
> to that on the Maio-massif. . . . When the French reached their first
> objectives, the heights at the valley roads Itri–Pico and Esperia–S.
> Oliva, they halted temporarily. . . . The action actually only
> accelerated the German withdrawal. In effect this was only what 10
> Army, on the basis of its estimate of the overall situation, had
> attempted to accomplish and for which the Army had requested
> authorization from OBSW.[82]

Of course this authorization only came just in the nick of time but, once
it was given permission to fall back slowly, XIV Panzer Corps was able to
keep its main forces just beyond the reach of the pursuers and apply the
same blocking tactics that were holding up Eighth Army. The axis of the
French advance, after the fall of Pico, was generally north-westwards,
towards Castro dei Volsci, Ceccano and Colleferro on their northern
flank, and Amaseno, Prossedi and Carpenito on their southern. Once
again their sector contained some of the hardest terrain and no sooner had
the leading divisions debouched from the Aurunci Mountains into the
Amaseno Valley, on the 25th and 26th, than they had to plunge straight
into the Lepinis. Of one typical day's march, the War Diary of 6 RTM
recorded: ' The march was more of an escalade. The absolute necessity
to have our mule train with us led to all kinds of acrobatics. We had to
unload the mules and manhandle them across veritable cliff faces. . . .
There were numerous accidents. The effort demanded of men and beasts
was crippling.'[83]

And at every turn French progress was further hampered by the
delaying tactics of the enemy. In theory the German forces in front of the
Expeditionary Corps were only remnants, mostly from 26 Panzer and 29
PG Divisions, but they nevertheless managed 'throughout the days that
were to follow . . . to fiercely contest our passage with an energy born
of despair.'[84] The French sustained many casualties even when there was

no enemy to be seen. To the very end the Germans used their artillery to good effect, as 2/5 RTM found during their advance towards Sgurgola, on 1 June: 'The battalion's progress was blocked; unfortunately the enemy artillery, ever more active, laid down interdiction fire on those emplacements it guessed were occupied by our units, who suffered several casualties and whose morale was undoubtedly affected by the violence of the fire, which seemed at odds with the [tranquil] countryside through which they were advancing.'[85] And everywhere the enemy left behind him little mementoes that must have gone a long way to satisfying Kesselring's appetite for 'sadistic imaginativeness':

> The enemy, with diabolical ingenuity, placed mines and booby traps everywhere. Woe betide the voltigeurs or tirailleurs attracted by cherry trees thick with fruit! Around the most alluring, a circlet of mines awaited, hidden in the grass. If one shook the branches, strings were pulled and the tree exploded. . . . [An abandoned house?] Don't open the door! Don't touch those tempting tins of sardines or tuna . . . nor those bottles of Chianti lined up on the table – death awaits! You and it will go up together! And you, stretcher-bearers, don't touch those German corpses still lying where they fell! *Those bodies are booby-trapped!* . . . Not exceptionally, but as a matter of course. There are no exceptions in the German Army, only orders.[86]

But the Germans were not afraid to stand and confront their pursuers wherever they thought they might extract a favourable casualty ratio, or when it was vital to cover the withdrawal of a major force. Sometimes they took a leaf out of the Mountain Corps' own book and let French advance parties wander into an ambush. 2 DIM noted that 'vigilant enemy groups were able, many times, to surprise an imprudent patrol. . . . In most cases, a keen junior officer or one lacking tactical judgement, "swanned" off and, getting his fingers burnt, had to fight his way out of a nasty situation. The losses were heavy . . . .'[87] Exactly this befell 1/6 RTM as they pressed on towards Monte Lupino, on the 27th. The previous evening a *goumier* patrol had declared the peak to be unoccupied, but when the main body began their advance it was soon apparent that the Germans had pulled back only temporarily. As they reached the seemingly empty crest they saw

> flocks of sheep, which the tirailleurs gazed upon with a connoisseur's eye, wandering around at will. . . . Suddenly one or two shots were heard which quickly became a heavy concentration of small-arms

fire. The ground was covered with a hail of bullets. . . . The enemy
. . . had let our troops, who thought the ground had been scouted
by the *goumiers*, move forward into exposed positions and now he
was attacking. . . . The radio link with the artillery was not
working, the set having fallen into a ravine as we were making the
ascent. . . . Everyone sprang into action! Every weapon was
brought into the line to block the enemy advance. Officers, porters,
clerks, radio-operators all grabbed rifles.

Eventually they managed to force the attackers back and when the
battalion's mortars finally joined the action the Germans immediately
withdrew. As usual, 'by way of saying farewell to Lupino, the enemy
saluted us with a massive concentration of 150mm, though this did not
prevent the tirailleurs, charitable as always, from immediately busying
themselves over the sad fate of those abandoned sheep, whose existence
had not been forgotten even in the vicissitudes of combat.'[88]

Many of these local fire-fights were savage little battles in their own
right. One battalion noted that in German units '20 or 30 men have a
firepower equal to that of a French company of 150 men and can hold up
a battalion for several days.'[89] All French accounts stress the rigours of
this period of the fighting and the incredible resilience of the Germans.
According to 2 DIM, even at the very end of May there was no such thing
as an unimpeded advance:

The enemy saw his effectives whittled away, his fire-power reduced,
his means of supply ever more difficult. Nevertheless he still offered
vigorous local resistance. He was able to do this thanks to the
flexibility of his battle groups, whose strength was adjusted in
accordance with the nature of their mission and of the terrain.
Thanks to several units which had as yet taken little part in the
fighting, and who were quickly brought to the critical points, he was
also able to temporarily halt an advance which if carried through
rapidly would have been catastrophic for him.[90]*

Perhaps the best testimony to the resolve of every German unit, whether
fresh or supposedly destroyed, comes from the commander of 2/29 PG
Regiment. In fact, the Regiment was one of those checking Clark's
impromptu drive towards Rome, through the C-Line, but the following
order might have been given by any officer in Fourteenth or Tenth Army.

---

* The fresh units in question were mainly from 305 Division.

Defensive fighting, he notes, does not suit the temperament of the German soldier:

> Experience has shown that only the firmness of the officers can counter this disadvantage. Every company commander must tell his men again and again that the survival of the whole company depends on the vigilance of each single soldier. Every day we must expect more dirty tricks on the part of the enemy. I do not want to hear the soldiers complaining that they have not eaten, slept or drunk for two days and that the situation is impossible. The word 'impossible' does not exist in the soldier's dictionary.[91]

All the brakes on the progress of DIADEM described thus far – Clark's change of axis, the intractable terrain, the tenacity of the defenders – can hardly be blamed on Alexander. Nevertheless, at least one further reason for the disappointing progress of his offensive is attributable to the Army Group commander. One of its key features, it will be recalled, was that Eighth Army should advance up the Liri Valley sufficiently quickly to trap the bulk of Tenth Army between them and the sea, the trap being fully sprung when VI Corps slammed the back door at Valmontone. But speed in itself was not enough. Alexander also had to ensure that his force was strong enough to properly shatter the defences in the Liri Valley and to adequately cover any German lines of retreat to the north or the north-west. Unfortunately, Alexander decided that the answer to this quite subtle equation was to throw everything into the Liri Valley as quickly as possible. Soon five divisions – 78 British, 8 Indian, 6 British Armoured, 1 Canadian and 5 Canadian Armoured – were all jostling for position. But such a concentration brought with it a staggering array of armoured fighting vehicles and motor transport. If each division had its full complement one is talking about 450 medium tanks, 240 other tanks, 50 self-propelled guns, 320 armoured cars, 200 scout cars, 2000 half tracks and 10,000 trucks and lorries; and the road net in the valley was simply not adequate to handle such a weight of traffic.* The whole British and Canadian advance, therefore, was plagued by bottlenecks and traffic jams which prevented supplies getting through, made it extremely difficult to bring forward infantry quickly to outflank potential German blocking positions, and often prevented the armour from even keeping up with the infantry on foot.†

---

* Which figures do not include the vehicles used by Corps and Army troops.
† For armoured regiments the problem became a vicious circle. A tank moving in slow traffic uses up to four times as much petrol as normal, but the jams also meant that it was that much more difficult to bring forward extra supplies.

Some of the earlier hold-ups have already been dealt with, but even after the breaking of the Hitler Line there were infuriating delays on almost every day of DIADEM. On 24 May, 6 British Armoured Division was held up for several hours waiting for 5 Canadian Armoured to clear the necessary roads. Of its activities on the 25th and 26th, one Canadian battalion history observed:

> Suffice it to say that the object of a pursuing force is to catch and to 'carve up' the enemy, to overtake and destroy his guns, vehicles and administrative echelons as well as what remains of his main body, and that, although the enemy withdrew and gave up his ground, this object was not attained by 1st Canadian Corps. The causes officially ascribed to this failure include virtually everything except active opposition by the enemy, namely natural obstacles, mines and demolitions, and faulty staff work on a high level with regard to organization of routes and traffic control.[92]

On the 29th and 30th, with Arce cleared and XIII Corps pressing forward to Alatri, an attempt was made to feed in yet another division, 6 South African Armoured. The intention was that it should replace 5 Canadian Armoured but, until it actually reached the latter's forward positions it merely added another few thousand vehicles to the existing traffic. Congestion swiftly became chaos and

> all our divisions lay locked in stupid conflict for the right of way. Traffic in the narrow, over-crowded and cratered valley had been difficult from the moment after our dogged infantry had broken the bloody door and entered. Now traffic became impossible, it almost ceased to move, and crowded vehicles and idle guns stood nose to petrol-smelling tail in helpless confusion, while officers of all degrees swore horribly in impotent wrath and weary huddled soldiers gave their fatigue an aspect of philosophy by sleeping while they could. The jam of traffic had coagulated and become a fevered stasis.[93]

Things did not improve much in June and the night of the 1/2nd saw one of 'the worst traffic jams of all' as the mass of Eighth Army's artillery was brought forward from behind the upper Liri to an area west of Pofi:

> Faulty control and poor traffic discipline among formations and units were blamed in an instruction issued . . . by . . .1st Canadian Corps. 'We have attempted to feed the absolute maximum number

of vehicles on to our system . . .', said Brigadier Lister. As a result roads had given way at various points and it had been necessary to lower the classification of a number of weakened bridges. Chaotic conditions had arisen from Provost personnel not having a thorough understanding of the current traffic plan; drivers thought only of themselves, and continually blocked bad roads by breaking out of line, only to find themselves halted by oncoming vehicles, and with the gap in their own traffic lane closed behind them.[94]

It might seem a little harsh to lay the blame for all this at Alexander's door. But what should be borne in mind is that, on the one hand, the original decision to concentrate the mass of Eighth Army in the Liri Valley had received his wholehearted approval and, on the other, he was ultimately responsible for ensuring that the road net there could carry this weight of traffic. The actual sums, of course, would be done by his own and Eighth Army staffs but, considering what a bearing they had on the success or failure of his whole plan of operations, it was surely part of the Commander-in-Chief's brief to make absolutely certain that they *were* done. The issue was at least raised but General Sir Brian Robertson, Alexander's chief administrative officer, felt that there would be no major logistic difficulties as long as Eighth Army realized it was 'essential to reduce all transport on the roads to a minimum. He hoped that reserves and non-essential units would be held well back.'[95] To be sure, many of the decisions that destroyed this hope were made by Alexander's subordinates, at Army, Corps and Division level, and once they were made there was little he could do about it. Nevertheless, good generalship consists as much in effectively managing the rear echelon areas as in moving the little flags at the sharp end, and it was up to Alexander to impress Robertson's proviso upon those beneath him and to ensure that there was an administrative back-up competent and large enough to enforce it.

For Eighth Army's disappointing progress had grave implications. Indeed, it is not overstating the case to say that it greatly facilitated the escape of substantial portions of Army Group 'C', enabling them to avoid fighting the battle of annihilation on which Alexander had pinned his hopes. Clark had hardly helped by failing to carry out his part of the plan but what is almost always overlooked is that even if he *had*, the trap would not have been properly sprung. For a full three weeks, in fact, Eighth Army failed to properly carry out their own mission and so left Vietinghoff and von Senger und Etterlin with several perfectly adequate escape routes northward across Highway Six and into the Simbruini mountains. A glance at Map 13 (p.290), plotting the various lines occupied by Tenth Army as it fell back, clearly shows how the German commanders, after the breach of the Hitler Line, were able to very gradually withdraw their left flank, from Roccasecca to Alatri–Vico, and use it as a pivot on which to swing the rest of their troops on to a line running east to west and so cover their line of retreat. As von Senger und Etterlin described it, he was able

> to prevent annihilation of the corps by instructing the troops who were being driven back to engage in delaying action and to withdraw in a generally northward direction. . . . At the same time I had to maintain contact with the LI Mountain Corps adjacent on the left, until all troops fighting in the Liri Valley were again under my command for a unified conduct of operations. *In view of the fact that the British Corps attacking in that area were not exerting much pressure this was a relatively simple mission.* . . . The temporarily subordinated 29th Panzer Grenadier Division . . . was preventing the French Corps from debouching out of the mountains and from advancing towards the Via Casalina. Under this cover I permitted, so to speak, the enemy to bypass the XIV Panzer Corps to the west while I withdrew northward . . . [mainly along] the road leading from Tivoli via Subiaco to Alatri.[96]

The French were equally aware of the reprieve being offered to Tenth Army. According to one later analysis, Eighth Army never exerted sufficient pressure on the Germans and allowed them to pull units out when and how they saw fit: 'There was never a pursuit. They followed the enemy, they did not pursue him. And he was thus allowed the time to draw breath, to reorganize, to carry out demolitions, to lay mines.'[97] Another French officer spoke of 'a very distinct impression that our allies, despite the means at their disposal, were not committed to going all-out to destroy the enemy, but preferred to wear him down.'[98] Juin, too, was less than pleased with Leese's forces in these last days of May. In a letter to de Gaulle he described the mission of the CEF as

> covering the right flank of II US Corps which was attacking the line Velletri–Valmontone with its right completely in the air around Artena; this mission proved to be difficult as we had to maintain contact on our left with the rapidly advancing Americans – with our men pushing across the Lepinis, where access roads were scarce and these bitterly defended – and on our right with the Eighth Army,

always advancing in a very measured fashion and obliging me to stretch this dangerously exposed flank very thin.[99]

Juin was not slow to make his complaints heard. The Fifth Army Deputy Chief of Staff, General Saltzman, recalled: 'During the beachhead attack General Juin became very much exercised about the fact that the Germans were always on his right flank in the May drive instead of the British – that the British in fact were always well to the rear.'[100]

To Juin there had seemed an obvious solution to this problem. If his flank was being overstretched in trying to maintain contact with the laggardly British, if his own advance was being most effectively contained by the Germans, and if substantial portions of Tenth Army were still being allowed to escape northwards, then surely the time had come to adjust the old inter-Army boundary, along the Liri and the Secco, and allow the French to cross Highway Six to harry the retreating Germans and, hopefully, to completely block their lines of escape. Indeed, during the early stages of DIADEM, Alexander had recognized that this might become necessary. On the 17th he informed Clark:

> If, as seems likely, Eighth Army have not been able to draw level with Fifth Army by time latter reach Pico area, CINC directs Fifth Army to strike northwards by San Giovanni on Ceprano to cut off withdrawal by Highway No.6 of enemy forces still opposing Eighth Army irrespective of existing inter-Army boundary. In that event, boundary will be adjusted by this headquarters in consultation with Armies to suit resulting situation.[101]

For some reason, however, even when Eighth Army was bogged down in front of the Hitler Line, Alexander never seems to have thought that this eventuality had arisen, and for over a week neither Clark nor Juin pressed the point. On the 28th, however, Juin sent a memorandum to Fifth Army HQ:

> In a very short while, should we continue on the same several axes, a large number of divisions will find themselves massed in front of Rome, or, in other words, on an extremely narrow front, poor in communications . . . [with] the risk of a terrible congestion of itineraries which would cause us a complete lack of power against an enemy whose only aim is to gain time. . . . Tomorrow the CEF will be in front of Ceccano and there . . . will only be able to wait for the Eighth Army axed on road No.6. . . . As things now stand only a secondary operation is being thought of which would have as

its goal the freeing of the road Priverno–Montelanico. In my opinion it would be desirable that from Frosinone on[wards] the left of the Eighth Army take the general direction Subiaco–Rieti–Terni and that the left of the CEF orient itself on the axis Prossedi–Gavignano–Tivoli and from there make its way to the Sabine Hills.[102]

Clark fully endorsed these proposals and instructed the French Corps to advance towards Ferentino, with a view to then crossing Highway Six and pushing north-westwards towards Genezzano and Tivoli. On the morning of the 29th, he went to see Alexander and the latter also gave his consent. Later that day, however, he changed his mind and issued a formal instruction that the original Army boundary along the Secco was still in force. Clark and Juin were bitterly disappointed. On the 30th Clark wrote in his diary:

The Eighth Army had done little fighting. . . . Yet my effort to switch their boundary east met with a reply indicating that the Eighth Army must participate in the Battle for Rome. . . . General Alexander indicated he would be delighted for me to take Ferentino to facilitate the advance of the Eighth Army but that after taking this point my troops must withdraw to the south over the roads [along which] they had come – this in spite of the fact that the French Corps, after taking Ferentino, would be thirty or forty miles in advance of the leading elements of the Eighth Army.[103]*

Not surprisingly, Clark was not prepared to use his own troops to clear the way for Eighth Army, and after talking with Alexander he called off the Ferentino attack. But this did not mean that he had lost interest in Juin's suggestion and a further entry in his diary that same day noted: 'I am directing . . . [Juin], within his restricted mountain zone, on Piombinaro where the mountain road reaches Route 6. I then, by right of eminent domain, will "slop over" into Eighth Army area, usurp Route 6, and put him on my north headed for Rome.'[104] On the 31st he wrote: 'I am worried about the future of the French Expeditionary Corps. With the restrictions that Alexander has placed upon me, their zone of action is narrowing down to nothing. I hope to squeeze them north of Highway 6 in the attack on Rome. It will probably be violently opposed by AAI.'[105] Juin was kept fully abreast of Clark's thinking and on the 30th he told de

---

* The French, in fact, would have been about twenty kilometres in front of the leading Canadian troops, who were moving through Pofi late on the 29th.

Gaulle: 'The CEF, which ought to finish in the van, runs the risk of having no place at all. . . . . But it is also possible that General Clark and myself, tired of waiting for the English who have already forced us to miss good opportunities at Pontecorvo and Frosinone, might hurry things along and disobey orders.' In the same letter he gave full vent to his anger over Alexander's decision. The latter, he wrote, clearly

> intends that Highway Six be reserved for the Eighth Army during its march on Rome. . . . Once again we have run into one of the stumbling blocks of coalition warfare: the Allies cannot come to an agreement and co-ordinate their efforts. At the present juncture, questions of prestige are shaping events, each one wanting to make the entry into Rome. History will not fail to pass severe sentence.[106]

What must always remain puzzling is why Alexander abruptly chose to revoke permission to cross Highway Six. His own memoirs and correspondence remain silent on the subject. Nor was Clark's Chief of Staff, Gruenther, able to gain much elucidation when he went back to argue the point with Alexander, late on the 29th. In fact, he only got to see Harding and eventually reported back to Clark: 'I talked to Harding tonight and . . . he . . . stated that apparently General Alexander had not understood your proposal when you talked with him this morning. I told him that was very strange to me, because I was present when you talked to General Alexander, and I got the decided impression, from listening to your conversation, that there was a definite meeting of the minds.'[107] To both Juin and Clark the answer, as we have already seen, was quite simple: Alexander had his eyes on Rome. On the 31st Clark remarked somewhat opaquely in his diary: 'There is much pressure upon me, although it is not being applied directly, to have Eighth Army in on the battle for Rome.'[108] Given Clark's obsession with being the first in Rome it is hardly surprising that he should be so ready to ascribe similar motives to his 'British' commander, and one can only assume that the strength of his feelings also helped to convince Juin. With hindsight, however, it seems extremely improbable that Alexander seriously thought that he had any chance of winning a 'race' for Rome. Even his advanced units were up to 20 miles behind VI Corps and there was no valid reason for believing that German resistance, albeit only rearguards, would suddenly melt away or that the perpetual log-jam in the Liri Valley would miraculously clear. But neither can one discern any valid military rationale for Alexander's decision. The essential facts were clear. Because Eighth Army was moving so slowly, substantial elements of Tenth Army were being allowed to escape by passing in front of it. Only the CEF was in a position to make any real effort to cut off these escape routes. To use the French, moreover, would enable Juin to deploy a much greater proportion of his available manpower, for on his present axis his divisions were being squeezed one behind the other. It is difficult, in fact, not to agree with the Chief of the Joint Planning Staff at AFHQ, Brigadier-General R.E. Jenkins, who held that

> South of Rome the major tactical error was in not cutting off the German 10th Army which withdrew up the Liri Valley. The British were too slow in pursuing the enemy – were out of contact with the Germans for 12 days as Jenkins remembered. What Alexander should have done but did not let the 5th Army do was for the French to cut in behind the Germans in the Liri Valley, cross and cut Highway 6 and other parallel routes of escape which the Germans had.[109]

One unpleasant hypothesis remains, though it should be emphasized that there exists no conclusive evidence as to its validity. However, in the absence of other reasons which even begin to make sense, it seems possible that Alexander's stubbornness stemmed from his pique at Clark's refusal to adhere to the original master-plan for DIADEM. For it can be said with some assurance that Alexander was far from pleased. In his memoirs he limited himself to a rather wistful note. VI Corps' mission, he said,

> was to break out and at Valmontone to get across the main German line of supply to their troops at Cassino. But for some inexplicable reason General Clark's . . . forces never reached their objectives, though, according to my information, there was nothing to prevent their being gained. . . . If he had succeeded in carrying out my plan the disaster to the enemy would have been much greater; indeed, most of the German forces south of Rome would have been destroyed. True, the battle ended in a decisive victory for us, but it was not as complete as it might have been.[110]

In an interview after the war Alexander was rather more blunt and stressed the fact that Clark seemed to have wilfully deceived him:

> At the time Clark decided to shift the axis of attack. . . . Alexander was told by Clark that the thrust towards Valmontone was being stopped by German reinforcements. . . . At the time Alexander accepted what Clark said. . . . Alexander says if the Germans

hadn't blocked us at the time the axis of attack was changed, that it was a mistake to shift the axis of attack, for it ended the chance of cutting off 10 Army on the southern front. But Alexander did not know at the time that the Germans had insufficient strength in the Valmontone area . . . to have stopped VI Corps.[111]

Others have been even more direct about Alexander's feelings at the time. According to General R. McCreery, commanding X Corps, Clark's 'behaviour on the break-out from Anzio made Alexander livid and it has rankled with him ever since.'[112] Harold Macmillan, the British High Commissioner for Italy, 'saw Alexander soon after his interview with Gruenther. He realised there was trouble because Alex's eye was twitching, as it would do before a big battle. He asked what was wrong. "What is right?" Alex snapped back, and told him. Macmillan asked him why he had not put his foot down. "Why do you talk nonsense?" Alex replied. "How can I give orders?" This was the only time Macmillan had ever seen him lose his temper.'[113]*

Perversely, Alexander's refusal to change the Army boundaries seemed to give Clark a new interest in the Valmontone axis, and at the end of May he tardily began to recognize the importance of trying to destroy German formations as opposed to simply capturing Rome. On the 28th he decided that 'II Corps will take over the 3rd Division Reinforced, Special Service Force and the 85th Division . . . with other attachments. . . . II Corps will be charged with the responsibility of attacking northward through Valmontone and attaining the high ground in that vicinity, thereby cutting Highway No.6 and preventing its use by the Germans.'[114] This attack was not to take place until the 31st, when 85 Division had moved up, because Clark still feared that 'Valmontone and the high ground to the north is

---

* Wilson, one will not be surprised to hear, swallowed Clark's story whole. In a letter to the British Chiefs of Staff, written on 2 June, he reviewed progress to date: 'Our offensive north-eastwards from the bridgehead sector gave early promise of cutting Highway 6 at Valmontone. . . . Unfortunately we were forestalled in this, by a matter of hours, by the arrival of strong elements of the Hermann Goering Division reinforced.' (Outgoing Message AFHQ, From: Wilson To: Air Ministry for British Chiefs of Staff, Ref: 54037, 2 June 1944. PRO WO 204/456.) The officer who drafted this telegram, Brigadier G.S. Thompson, felt obliged to attach a letter of his own which included a particularly barbed, or remarkably ingenuous, comment on the switch of axis: 'In preparing the draft, I have not entered into a full discussion of reasons for our changing from . . . a main thrust on axis Anzio–Valmontone aimed at tactical defeat of the maximum German forces south of Rome . . . because I do not myself fully understand the reasons which led to the change.' (*ibid.*)

. . . strongly held and in the enemy's main defense position.'[115] On the day of the attack Clark made several references in his diary to its importance, stressing that the 'primary objective' was not now Rome 'but to kill and annihilate as many of the Germans as possible on our front.'[116] In a message to Gruenther he emphasized that once Keyes had gained a foothold on the high ground north of Valmontone, he was to 'set up a task force . . . a fast, hard-hitting mobile unit . . . to proceed east along Route No.6 as soon as we can get on it. Its mission is to destroy, discourage, disrupt, disorganize, and any other "d"s you think of, any enemy forces in that area opposing Eighth Army or FEC.'[117]

Clark had not completely lost sight of Rome, of course, and the attack on the 31st was also to include a renewed drive against the C-Line positions that had baulked VI Corps' progress up Highway Seven. Yet even here 'General Clark made it understood that as far as the city of Rome itself was concerned, he was not interested except to secure the city.'[118] If necessary, he instructed Gruenther, the seizure of Rome might even be deferred for a day or so because the main task on the Campoleone–Velletri front, after 'Colle Laziale is captured, [is] to destroy the 14th Army on our front. In other words, that is our mission, rather than bursting into Rome.'[119]

But Clark first had to capture the Alban Hills and that in itself was still likely to prove a formidable task. Schlemm's I Parachute Corps had been reinforced with whatever forces could be spared and prominent among these were the survivors of 362 Division who had been redeployed in the Velletri sector. There they had fought with a tenacity worthy of Baade's Panzer Grenadiers or Heidrich's paratroopers. During one American attack,

> it was possible to relieve the hard-pressed battalions of Assault Regiment 12 which had concentrated around the regimental command post and were engaged in defensive action as if it were a point of resistance. During the action the men of the Assault Regiment, inspired by their commander to the highest effort, and aided by the lack of visibility in the nearby vineyard terrain, destroyed as many as 20 enemy tanks by the *Panzerfaust* alone.[120]

In the days that followed, the Division was actually able to improve its positions where

> many ravines and natural caves offered protection for local reserves against even the heaviest artillery fire as well as against bombings . . . and made it possible, not only to keep these reserves close by

for employment in automatic counterthrusts, but also to move them about easily in all directions. . . . As a whole the C-Position could be considered a good defensive position.[121]

But, Greiner noted, his sector also had an 'Achilles' heel'. This was on the division's left flank, on Monte Artemisio, which marked the boundary between I Parachute and LXXVI Panzer Corps. Due to the general shortage of troops and a belief that this area was practically impenetrable, a full three kilometres of the C-Line were very thinly held and might offer a bold opponent a marvellous opportunity for thrusting through the gap and outflanking the whole Velletri position. Greiner's neighbour to the left, General Schmalz of the HG Division, was also aware of the danger. 'As early as 28 May', he wrote later, 'the Division had recognized that this gap would be fatal to the entire operations of the Army Group, once the enemy found out about its significance. But the Division had absolutely no forces to close the gap.'[122] The best he could do, in fact, was to send two engineer platoons to occupy a ruin on the crest of Monte Artemisio and the hamlet of Menta below it. When the commander of LXXVI Panzer Corps was told about the gap, on the 28th, he ordered Schmalz to block it with his last two battalions, who were still on the road, as soon as they arrived. The battered 715 Division, which was being reorganized around Tivoli, was also ordered to send down some troops to Monte Artemisio. Kesselring did not hear of this dangerous situation on the inter-Corps boundary until the afternoon of the 29th, when he insisted that it be attended to immediately. 'The next day, when I found out that not only had the gap been not closed, but that nothing at all had been done to cover it, I personally telephoned to the Commander-in-Chief, Fourteenth Army, and spoke sharply about this unpardonable omission, stressing that what could easily be accomplished today by a single battalion might well prove impossible to do with a whole division tomorrow.'[123] Mackensen duly passed on these instructions to his Corps commanders but both he and they were satisfied that the job had already been done and, despite the fact that the moves outlined above would necessarily take three or four days, made no attempt to move a temporary holding force from more adjacent positions.

Unfortunately, the Americans had also found out about the gap. Monte Artemisio fronted 36 Division's sector, one of whose patrols, probing forward on the night of the 27th, had been startled to find no sign at all of the enemy. General Walker was immediately aware of the opportunity this offered and he swiftly relayed the news to Truscott's Chief of Staff. General Carleton, too, was impressed and he noted that if the gap could be properly exploited 'the Boche in . . . [Velletri] would find themselves in a tough situation, and the town might just cave in.'[124] Walker was told to draw up plans. These were quickly prepared and suggested a holding attack on Velletri by 141 Regiment whilst the other two, one behind the other, penetrated the German lines. After reaching the crest of Artemisio, 142 Regiment was to move south-westwards to the Maschio dell'Artemisio, a knob two miles north-west of Velletri, and 143 Regiment was to move northward to take the Maschio d'Ariano and Point 931. The 141st was then to launch a full-scale attack to clear out Velletri and open up Highway Seven. Both Truscott and Clark were impressed with the plan and once they had checked with Walker's engineer officer that a road could be opened behind the leading infantry to permit the passage of supplies and supporting armour, they gave the go-ahead. According to Walker this was passed on over the telephone by Truscott, who said: 'I've talked to General Clark and General Clark has OK'd your proposal, and . . . you are authorized to go ahead on *your* plan. *But you had better get through.*'[125] The attack was to take place on the night of the 30/31st and Walker clearly saw it as a golden opportunity to erase all memories of the Rapido fiasco, four months before. He wrote in his diary that same night: 'Our operations for tonight and tomorrow have promise of being spectacular. We are taking chances, but we should succeed in a big way.'[126]

His confidence was well founded and the two regiments were infiltrated through the C-Line with a skill worthy of Rogers' Rangers. Colonel Lynch of 142 Regiment recalled his instructions to the Texans:

> I told them that in order to minimize the chance of new men disclosing our show by firing at noises in the dark, all troops were to move with loaded magazines but no ammunition in the rifle or pistol chambers until the break of dawn. Any killing was to be done by bayonet, knife or other quiet means. Travelling between the two leading battalions all night, I did not hear a single shot until after dawn.[127]

The divisional photographer, Max Schaffer, was also full of praise for the high level of fieldcraft: 'We marched all night. It seemed to me that almost all of this march was through one large draw. We had all been cautioned to maintain absolute silence, and when the troops learned what we were doing, this became the quietest bunch of guys I have ever seen. All night long I never heard so much as a small clink from a piece of equipment.'[128] By dawn they were almost on the summit and in the next few hours cleared the whole of the crest. At no stage were they challenged and a German artillery observation post was overrun as one of its occupants was taking a bath. The German engineer platoons were at the opposite end of the crest and seem to have mistaken the size of the attacking force, for they did not report the American presence until the early afternoon. Schmalz immediately counter-attacked with the only battalion left in his reserve, but by then the bulk of Walker's battalions were already in place and the hapless Panzer Grenadiers were, in the parlance of the day, 'smeared'.

News of the breakthrough had an electrifying effect throughout Fifth Army and, according to Clark, 'caused us all to turn handsprings.'[129] The Germans were correspondingly depressed. Mackensen tried to make amends for his dilatoriness. An order issued on the 31st stated: 'On 1 June the main task . . . is to clean up at the earliest possible moment the existing breakthrough at the junction of I Parachute Corps and LXXVI Panzer Corps. . . . Every man will defend himself where he is placed as long as he has ammunition and is capable of fighting.'[130] But it was too late. As Kesselring wrote: 'The tactical and strategical consequences were at once obvious to me. . . . A complete restoration of the situation was impossible. Once again Fourteenth Army had to pay dearly for its blind confidence.'[131]* VI Corps was now in a position to threaten the whole of Schlemm's Corps from Velletri to Lanuvio as well as to control the heights from which observed artillery fire could be brought to bear on the rear of Schmalz's forces defending Valmontone. A report by 143 Regiment, on 1 June, remarked:

> When regiment reached the summit of Mt Maschio d'Ariano clear weather gave the FOs prime observation over 220 degrees to east and south-west. The problem was not of finding targets but of getting enough observers to handle the targets as fast as they appeared and batteries to fire at them. We procured every possible FO from division and corps artillery. FOs were sitting on Monte d'Ariano like crows on a telephone line, having a field day.[132]

Their first priority was the road into Velletri, along which the Germans might try to reinforce the garrison. According to the commander of 1/142 Regiment:

---

* Kesselring, having already received Hitler's permission should he feel it necessary, decided to sack Mackensen. The latter, however, beat him to it by offering his resignation. It was gratefully accepted and General der Panzertruppen Joachim Lemelsen prepared to take over command of Fourteenth Army.

We shot up an untold amount of German vehicles of every sort. . . . A column of eighteen German tanks appeared around the turn in the road coming out of Velletri with a German officer standing in the first tank, arms folded Hitler style. . . . The bazooka-men . . . were perfect, knocking out the lead and last tank. . . . We captured all the German tanks along with some Germans. The thing I will always remember about this incident was the German officer in the lead tank – when the bazooka round hit he squirted out of the turret like a cork out of a champagne bottle.[133]

Clark now ordered all his divisions to step up their attacks and even managed, on the 2nd, to convince Alexander of the need to allow II Corps and the French to cross Highway Six. He wrote in his diary: 'General Alexander and Harding have come to see me. They were quite meek. . . . I told him . . . that I was putting the French north of Route No.6, that I would probably be forced to take the high ground in the vicinity of Palestrina because I could not rely on the Eighth Army to be there when I needed them. . . . He said go right ahead.'[134]* Highway Six had actually been cut on the previous day, by 3 Division, and Clark now launched a two-pronged offensive against Rome. 85 and 88 Divisions pushed to the north-west of Valmontone, on either side of Highway Six, whilst 36 Division moved around Velletri, along Highway Seven, from where they threatened the rear of the German positions in front of Lanuvio. The German position was now getting desperate and the feelings of the ordinary soldiers were neatly summed up in a bit of doggerel current in 362 Division:

> Die Division Greiner
> Wird immer kleiner.
> Zum Schluss bleibt einer
> Und das ist Greiner.[†]

---

* In fact, Clark clearly did not *want* Eighth Army to be on hand. Despite his more balanced sense of priorities he was still fearful that the British might somehow get involved in the drive towards Rome. As he said himself: 'When Alexander started to tell me that if my attack did not go . . . not to worry, that he would bring the whole of 8th Army in, I told him that my attack was going.' (Diary, 2 June 1944.)

[†] An English equivalent might be:
   This Division of Greiner
   Gets chopped ever finer,
   Till roll-call's a one-liner
   Which simply reads Greiner.

On the 2nd both Velletri and Valmontone fell and resistance on Fourteenth Army's front finally crumbled. Various orders emanated from higher headquarters but the Germans had had enough. On the 3rd LXXVI Panzer Corps ordered its units to fall back towards Tivoli and I Parachute Corps was obliged to follow suit or risk its own escape routes being cut off by 85 and 88 Divisions. Kesselring had already, on the 2nd, asked Hitler's permission to evacuate Rome without making any last-ditch stand, and when this was granted, on the 3rd, the remaining rearguards were pulled out of the Alban Hills; 65 and 3 PG Divisions evacuating to the south of Rome, 362 Division through the city itself, and 4 Parachute Division, Schlemm's main flank guard, just to the north.

Fifth Army followed hard on their heels. A war correspondent wrote:

The air was charged with excitement, with savage triumph and obscene defeat. German vehicles were smouldering at every bend of the road, and dead Germans lay sprawled beside them, their faces thickening with the dust sprayed over them by the ceaseless wheels that passed within inches of the mortifying flesh. . . . By wrecked gasoline stations, in the front yards of decapitated homes, flushed Americans were shoving newly taken prisoners into line, jerking out the contents of their pockets and jabbing those who hesitated with the butt ends of their rifles.[135]

The atmosphere at Fifth Army HQ was similarly feverish. On the 3rd Gruenther wrote: 'The CP has gone to hell. No one is doing any work here this afternoon. All semblance of discipline has broken down. Although the G–3 War Room purposely shows only a moderately conservative picture . . . everyone . . . who has come from Anzio this morning has brought back a pair of pants full of ants with the result that this unsuppressable wave of optimism and expectancy has swept through the headquarters.'[136] On the following morning the first American units, variously described as an 88 Division reconnaissance platoon or part of a small I SSF battle group, roared into Rome and by midnight Fifth Army had control of the centre of the city as well as almost half of the vital bridges across the Tiber. General Clark did not arrive until the late afternoon. Even on the 4th there were still German rearguards trying to block the northern routes in and out of Rome and one such group was holding up the main I SSF task force. Their commander, Brigadier-General Robert Frederick,

was watching the progress of his men who led the assault. A jeep

458 *Cassino: The Hollow Victory*

drew up, and Major-General Keyes, the corps commander, descended.

'General Frederick,' he asked, 'what's holding you up here?'

Frederick replied, 'The Germans, sir.'

Keyes then asked, 'How long will it take you to get across the city limits?'

Frederick answered, 'The rest of the day. There are a couple of SP guns up there.'

'That will not do. General Clark must be across the city limits by four o'clock.'

Frederick asked, 'Why?'

The corps commander answered, 'Because he has to have a photograph taken.'

Frederick looked at Keyes steadily for a long moment and said, 'Tell the General to give me an hour.'

The guns were silenced, the General and his photographer arrived, and the pictures were taken of the conqueror within his conquered city. [137]

A conquered city, perhaps, but what of the enemy, what of the battle of annihilation upon which Alexander had pinned his hopes? For Army Group 'C' had survived. Whether either Clark or Alexander could have prevented the escape of Fourteenth Army is uncertain, though if Fifth Army had attacked Rome from Valmontone in the first place there might have been a chance of trapping at least some units between Highway Seven and the sea. As it was, by attacking the C–Line head-on, Clark allowed the Germans to choose their own moment to withdraw and, with luck, keep just out of reach of the pursuing forces.

But Tenth Army was escaping as well and here one must certainly hold both Clark and Alexander responsible. The abandoning of the 'Turtle' axis, the appalling congestion in the Liri Valley and the refusal to allow Juin to cross Highway Six have all been touched upon but there still remains one further error to discuss, and that probably the most fundamental of them all. For the whole basic conception of the DIADEM plan was faulty and, even granted a concerted push towards Valmontone and a more vigorous pursuit up the Liri Valley, it could never have brought more than partial success. It was Clark himself who put his finger on the fatal flaw, that it would be impossible to trap the whole of Tenth Army by blocking *all* the roads leading north and north-west out of the Liri Valley. After a discussion with Alexander on the 17th, he had written in his diary:

I then brought up the subject of direction of attack out of the bridgehead on Cori and Valmontone. He remains adamant that that is the correct and only direction of attack, regardless of the enemy situation. I drew a circle on the map, projected my VI Corps into the high ground southwest of Valmontone and asked him where I would go from there; to which he replied that fast, mobile patrols would operate to cut the routes to the east. I replied that in getting to Valmontone I had gone over the mountains, [which] had absolutely no roads, and would [have] only foot troops and pack equipment. He brushed this aside.[138]

On the 27th, with Eighth Army further and further behind schedule, he again angrily questioned Alexander's basic concept which 'was based on the false premise that if Route No.6 were cut at Valmontone a German army would be annihilated. This is ridiculous, for many roads lead north from Arce, Frosinone and in between.'[139] No matter how swiftly Eighth Army moved, in fact, at least some of Tenth Army's units would be able to side-step to their left and take to these roads. For, by concentrating virtually the whole of Eighth Army's offensive into the Liri Valley, Alexander had not only created terrible traffic problems but had also made no provision for a parallel advance on his right which could shepherd the Germans back into the path of his central punch. A French commentator has applauded Alexander's aims, according to which Fifth Army's advance through the Auruncis and the Lepinis, 'linked with . . . [the advance] of Eighth Army . . . would permit the capture of the bulk of von Vietinghoff's army in a massive envelopment.' He is less impressed, however, with the way in which Alexander put his theory into practice: 'Unfortunately, this sweeping manoeuvre was literally truncated as a result of an obstinate desire to send Eighth Army towards Rome down Highway Six, instead of operating through the [Simbruini] mountains to outflank and encircle the exhausted units of German Tenth Army.'[140]

By the end of May, because of the absence of any strong parallel drive in the Simbruinis and because of the increasingly chaotic traffic conditions in the valley, Tenth Army's side door had become a back door, with the German left wing still anchored in front of the Alatri–Subiaco–Tivoli road, down which their troops, now aligned from east to west, could gradually be withdrawn. Not all Tenth Army units could avail themselves of this road, notably those in front of the French, who were gradually pushed back on Valmontone, Cave and Genezzano. But this area, too, offered several escape routes towards Tivoli and thence across the Tiber.

The only force that could hope to race the Germans to the Tiber, or at least mercilessly harry their retreat, was the French Corps, but for four days Alexander had refused to allow them to cross Highway Six and thus allowed Tenth Army time to establish a blocking force behind Valmontone and to cover this other vital line of retreat. Von Senger und Etterlin has made it clear how important was this second respite. Throughout the latter stages of the withdrawal he was haunted by

> fears based on the fact that the terrain offered the enemy opportunities for a rapid advance northwards, thereby cutting off our 10th Army. Such opportunities existed through the Tiber crossings at Orte, where one could push northward via Spoleto–Poligno, and at Orvieto, where an advance could be made directly north along the Tiber. As soon as these crossings had been secured . . . the enemy, as I saw it, was bound to make such an attempt. Very likely he would have attempted it had not the crossings come into our possession a *few hours* previously, as a result of the rapid movement of the 14th Panzer Corps. If the enemy had not been prevented from seizing the crossings, the results might have been incalculable. The 10th Army would have been separated from the 14th Army, and either Army could have been crushed separately. Even if the 14th Army had obtained a brief respite for its retrograde movements by the enemy's wheeling northwards, it could not have escaped a later fate. Being separated from the 10th Army, it would have been too weak to offer independent resistance to the now superior Allies.[141]

But Clark, too, was instrumental in allowing the Germans to escape. Even though he was doubtless correct in claiming that the 'Buffalo' attack could not have sealed the fate of Tenth Army, this axis was still far preferable to the one he actually chose, as a means of inflicting maximum destruction on the German forces. By switching direction he committed himself to attacking the strongest portion of the C–Line, thus grinding down his own divisions and seriously impairing their ability to conduct a vigorous pursuit beyond Rome, as well as giving the Germans an unlooked-for opportunity to salvage LXXVI Panzer Corps. Greiner's division was able to pull back in a fairly orderly fashion to Velletri, the rump of 715 Division was saved from complete destruction, and the HG Division, which surely could have been bounced out of Valmontone on the 26th and 27th, was given the time to deploy its straggling and battered units. But had Clark thrown in 36 Division to give new momentum to the drive on Valmontone he must surely have driven a fatal wedge, even more dangerous than that created on Monte Artemisio, between the two Corps of Fourteenth Army and thus provided himself with a springboard for a pursuit towards Tivoli.

Eventually, as we have seen, Clark did begin to appreciate the importance of a pursuit to the north-east of Rome. But even then he displayed a strange lack of urgency. Though it was on the 29th that he decided to resume the push towards Valmontone, he did not actually attack until the 31st, again citing dubious intelligence about the strength of the German positions. He insisted on awaiting the arrival of 85 Division before attacking, claiming that 715 Division would otherwise be in a position to somehow counter-attack into a gap that might open up between II and VI Corps. 'In reality,' as the American official historian tartly remarks, this division 'constituted no threat, for its remnants were even then desperately attempting to escape northward to escape being trapped between the Americans and the French.'[142]

By the time Clark did attack the Germans had had the opportunity to throw reserves into Valmontone and improve their positions there yet more.* Two further days, in fact, were to elapse before the town actually fell and this delay also was of enormous benefit to XIV Panzer Corps. For it gave von Senger und Etterlin the chance to move behind Valmontone and to set up yet another blocking position barring the way to Tivoli. By virtue of his Corps' better signals equipment, with which to co-ordinate movement, he now had seven divisions under his command. 1 Parachute, 94 Infantry and 15 PG Divisions were, on the 2nd, already streaming back towards Tivoli. 334, 305 and 26 Panzer Divisions were also falling back in this direction, but more closely, and were able to provide some cover for the others by establishing strong rearguards around Cave, Genezzano and Acuto, in the foothills of the Simbruinis. The most important job, however, was given to 90 PG Division. Still fearful of a 'dangerous enemy thrust between the two German armies', von Senger und Etterlin ordered that Baade's Division be 'transferred behind the other divisions to the

---

* The difficulties of the delayed attack towards Valmontone are illustrated by this vignette concerning 1/30 US Regiment. During one company attack 'the commander was wounded. . . . Lieutenant Brady . . . was killed, and another officer . . . was killed. 1st Lieutenant Nelson was the only officer left in A Company. He tried to reorganize the elements of A Company. He sent the men up to attack and as soon as they got out of his sight they would disappear. They straggled. Nelson broke down and cried. He was affected by all the fire A Company had received and by the heavy losses it had sustained and was physically and mentally exhausted from trying to push the attack.' (S.T. Matthews, Interview with Major J.L. Packman, 13 May 1950, p.3. NA (MMS) RG 319 Box 15.)

Corps right wing in order to prevent the enemy from pushing forward from Valmontone into the mountains. . . . The movement [of the whole Corps] involved a withdrawal threatened from two sides, and the repulse of enemy attacks against the Tiber crossings. The total march covered 200 kilometres over open mountain roads. Success, therefore, was a matter of organisation and luck.'[143]

Some luck there undoubtedly was, mostly with regard to the remarkable inefficacy of Allied aircraft. One would have thought that the German columns would have offered perfect targets. Von Senger und Etterlin spoke of a terrain 'so bleak that, when the movements were halted at dawn, it was impossible to camouflage the columns.'[144] The commander of 26 Panzer Division, General der Panzertruppen Smilo von Lüttwitz, recalled

the extraordinary difficulties . . . in crossing the mountains while being constantly severely threatened from the air, following a road . . . along which not only our Division moved, but usually two other divisions as well as many elements of the Air Force. . . . Groups of men and columns were tightly wedged in this slowly northward-moving mass, frequently crowded together up to three march columns one next to the other, pushing laboriously along the narrow winding roads and squeezing through tight passages in the villages. It was therefore absolutely unavoidable that these movements extended up into full daylight since all the planned time schedules broke down and moreover there were only very few places where it was possible to move off the road and find adequate cover.[145]

Amazingly, however, though the Allies had complete mastery of the air and could call upon the services of hundreds of fighter-bombers, they never seriously impeded the German withdrawal. After the war von Lüttwitz insisted:

despite . . . all the difficulties the supplies for the Division were always on the spot on time so that the troops were able to cross this particularly dangerous sector without completely getting out of order. The most astounding and unexpected experience made by the Division during this march was the realization that actually the effectiveness of the enemy air force activity was comparatively very low. Nowhere was the destruction of the roads carried out in great depth, nor were the roads observed sufficiently to prevent preparations for detours or repair work to be made. Moreover, the

Division's losses inflicted through enemy fighter planes were limited to individual cases.[146]

It is difficult to find specific reasons for this remarkable failure on the part of the Allies. The weather was good, the Allies had complete mastery of the air, fairly sophisticated air control techniques had been worked out over the previous months, most of the Allied pilots were experienced fliers, and countless sorties were flown. Probably the best reason that can be given is that aerial ground attack has never been a particularly effective method of combat, because the sheer speed and sophistication of the weapon makes it inappropriate for attacking small, slow-moving or static targets on the ground. We have already had cause to note the Allied failure to prevent the German evacuation of Sicily by aerial interdiction and other historical examples lead to similar conclusions. There has recently, for example, been some speculation as to just how important rocket-firing aircraft were in the attacks on retreating German transport columns in Normandy, after D-DAY. It is a known fact, moreover, that even after the coming of the jet the US Air Force in Korea, in very open country, were never able to disrupt the tenuous Chinese supply lines, whilst in Vietnam they had a similar lack of success against the bicycles and porters along the Ho Chi Minh Trail.

But the Allies should never have become entirely dependent on their aircraft to destroy the retreating German divisions and once again Clark must be censured for not having seized Valmontone and the high ground beyond much earlier and thus denied the Germans suitable positions from which to cover their withdrawal. Even then, as Clark said, it would have been impossible to block *all* the roads leading through the Simbruinis, but it would surely not have been possible for *every one* of Tenth Army's divisions, albeit sadly depleted, to have escaped through Tivoli.

Nevertheless, fundamental though Clark and Alexander's errors were, one should not underestimate the German achievement, and especially that of von Senger und Etterlin. Though hopelessly outnumbered in the air and on the ground from the very start of the May offensive*, the Germans proved once again that, in capable hands, they were amongst the finest troops in the world. Despite Kesselring's increasing

---

* In May the Allies had 4000 combat aircraft in Italy, the Germans 450. The ratio of tanks was 1900 and 450 respectively. During DIADEM the Allies deployed 23 divisions and the Germans 17, though the assigned ration strengths of the opposing Army Groups were, respectively, 670,000 and 360,000 men. The disparity in the number of troops becomes yet more apparent if one makes a rough estimate of the respective total strengths of the rifle companies. The Allies fielded 182 infantry battalions and

interference after the breach of the Hitler Line, the management of Tenth Army's withdrawal was a superb defensive achievement in which commanders at all levels rarely put a foot wrong. What stands out above all is their remarkable flexibility and their ability to conjure some sort of order out of seeming chaos. Von Senger und Etterlin's orchestration of the movements of his unwieldy Corps, at the beginning of June, is a case in point. His own description of the *ad hoc* methods adopted only serves to emphasize how poorly Eighth Army performed in their own advance, which they had ample opportunity to plan, up the Liri Valley:

> It is not recommended that the divisions be given a fixed march order, since it is sure to require change as a result of constant enemy air action. If there is a shortage of passable roads those available have to be assigned to single divisions for certain periods of time. But within these periods each division should have great freedom regarding its march formation as well as its reconnaissance and security measures. . . . Fixed march orders cause delays, missed opportunities for utilising the few breaks in enemy air action, and thereby an overall loss of time.[147]

And slowly but surely, whilst Eighth Army was locked in 'fevered stasis', XIV Panzer Corps was withdrawn. No wonder the commander of 90 PG Division sent back the following triumphant message to von Senger und Etterlin when they finally crossed the Tiber and reached Orvieto: 'The Corps has succeeded in disengaging the armoured infantry divisions committed within its sector so quickly that an enemy breakthrough, and thus the definite rupture of the German front, has been averted at the last minute. Extraordinary difficulties have had to be overcome in the conduct

---

the Germans 108, but their average rifle strength was roughly 370 as opposed to only 220. The respective total rifle strengths, therefore, were 67,000 and 24,000. The following anecdote says all that needs to be said about the sheer extent of Allied material superiority and helps underline, from the other side of the hill, the point made by Canadian tankmen in an earlier chapter: 'I remember a German lieutenant captured at Salerno who I was guarding . . . in a prisoner-of-war camp. He was a real tough-looking Kraut and I was a young punk, a pimply faced kid. He could speak perfect English, and I was riding him. I said, "Well, if you're so tough, if you're all supermen, how come you're here captured and I'm guarding you?" And he looked at me and said, "Well, it's like this. I was on this hill as a battery commander with six 88-millimeter antitank guns, and the Americans kept sending tanks down the road. We kept knocking them out. Every time they sent a tank we knocked it out. Finally we ran out of ammunition and the Americans didn't run out of tanks." That's it in a nutshell.' (Colonel D.H. Hackworth quoted in S.H. Loory, *Defeated: Inside America's Military Machine*, Random House, New York, 1973, p.39.)

of these operations. The action was a masterpiece of leadership, equal to the Corps' former outstanding achievements.'[148]

Equally impressive was the way in which the most heterogeneous assortments of units, from a multiplicity of different divisions, could be brought together and within a few hours be welded into a perfectly effective fighting formation. Examples abound. On 29 May, between Colle Polombara and Ceccano, a firm defensive line was held by the remnants of 94 Division, a mountain battalion, one battalion from 26 Panzer Division, and a battle group from 305 Division. On 31 May, around Frosinone, the Canadians were blocked by detachments from both of 26 Panzer Division's Panzer Grenadier Regiments as well as fragments of 1/104 PG Regiment (15 PG Division), 2/578 Regiment (305 Division), 1/134 regiment (44 Division), and the Fusilier Battalion from 334 Division.[149] Fourteenth Army was equally adept at mixing such cocktails. One war correspondent was present at the fall of Velletri and wrote: 'Nowhere was their ability for reconstituting, from broken battalions and other shattered elements, rearguard units of unimpeachable fortitude more dramatically demonstrated than during these last days before Rome. Of the 377 prisoners taken at Velletri, there were representatives of fifty different companies from a variety of battalions and regiments and divisions. Yet they fought as a cohesive whole until overwhelmed.'[150] No wonder that Alexander wrote:

. . . the enemy . . . is quicker than we are: quicker at regrouping his forces, quicker at thinning out on a defensive front to provide troops to close gaps at decisive points, quicker in effecting reliefs, quicker at mounting attacks and counter-attacks, and above all quicker at reaching decisions on the battlefield. By comparison, our methods are often slow and cumbersome, and this applies to all our troops, both British and American.[151]*

All in all, then, the Battle for Rome had ended in failure. Though the Gustav, Hitler and C–Lines had been smashed, though the first Axis capital had fallen to the Allies, they had failed in their fundamental strategic task of destroying the German armies in Italy. They had caused

---

* Slessor, too, commented on 'that tactical flexibility which has always been such an admirable quality in German defensive fighting, his ability to pick up a battalion here, the contents of a leave train there, a machine gun *abteilung* from one division and a couple of batteries from another, and fling them in as an improvised battle group to save a local situation.' (Slessor, *op. cit.*, p.584.)

him substantial casualties – between January and the end of March XIV Panzer Corps alone had lost almost 17,000 men and during the May battles Tenth and Fourteenth Armies sustained a further 38,000 casualties – as well as taking a very considerable number of prisoners, 15,600 during DIADEM alone. German losses in equipment had also been very heavy with the Allies capturing or destroying 150 tanks and 300 self-propelled guns (half the available armour in Italy), 300 artillery pieces, 420 anti-tank guns, 60 *Nebelwerfers*, 500 heavy machine guns and 1600 light. Much, indeed, had been achieved but the crucial fact remained that most battalions had escaped with at least a cadre of seasoned troops and with their command structures, albeit skeletal, still intact. And they remained intact throughout the following weeks. Referring to the subsequent operations in June, one American staff officer averred: 'The "pursuit between Rome and the Arno" is misnamed . . . It was a rapid advance but "pursuit" implies getting in behind the Germans. The Germans in this action controlled our pursuit – our rate of advance. . . . The operations between Rome and the Arno was [*sic*] far from a rout. It was a calculated withdrawal.'[152] There remained, therefore, a base upon which the Germans could rebuild, an essential nucleus of expertise around which raw replacements could be moulded into battle-worthy units and formations.

One man had seen what would happen, even before the DIADEM offensive began. One should not be surprised that it was Juin. On 8 May, after one of the many planning conferences, he told de Gaulle:

The battle for Rome, if the Germans are prepared to fight it in their present situation, can . . . be won, but it will not be another Battle of Cannae. Perhaps, with a bit of luck, we will destroy four or five of their divisions but after Rome the situation will stabilize again, our weary fighting troops still facing twenty or so German divisions, more, that is, than they would need to make a stand in the Tuscan Apennines.[153]

This was a remarkably prescient analysis, and in August 1944 the Allies duly ground to a halt once more in front of the Gothic Line, which ran between Pesaro and the Magra Valley, right across the Apuan and northern Appenine Mountains. Many old friends were still present in the German line. Kesselring and von Vietinghoff still commanded the Army Group and Tenth Army, whilst XIV Panzer Corps and LI Mountain Corps still belonged to von Senger und Etterlin and Feuerstein. More significantly, most of the divisions were the same. Von Senger's command included 26 Panzer and 65 Infantry, Feuerstein's 44 and 715 Infantry. Other corps included 1 Parachute, 4 Parachute, 71 Infantry and 362 Infantry, whilst the various Army reserves and special command groups could call upon, amongst others, 29 and 90 PG Divisions. And they fought as hard as ever. The Gothic Line proper was broken after several weeks' fighting but the Germans continued to fight hard for every yard of ground and by the end of October the Allies had completely run out of steam. And by that time there was no hope of conquering the remaining lines of peaks and bursting into the Po Valley before winter set in. Clark was to write of this disappointing conclusion:

[The] offensive did not stop with any definite setback or any specific date. It merely ground slowly to a halt because men could not fight any longer against the steadily increasing enemy reinforcements on our front. In other words, our drive died out, slowly and painfully, and only one long stride from success, like a runner who collapses reaching for, but not quite touching, the tape at the finishing-line.[154]

One can only hope that his photographs of Rome gave him comfort.

18
Epilogue

We're the D-Day Dodgers, out in Italy,
Always drinking vino, always on the spree,
Eighth Army skivers and the Yanks,
We live in Rome, we laugh at tanks,
For we're the D-Day Dodgers, in sunny Italy.

We landed at Salerno, a holiday with pay,
Jerry brought the bands down to cheer us on our way.
They showed us sights and gave us tea,
We all sang songs, the beer was free,
To welcome D-Day Dodgers to sunny Italy.

Naples and Cassino, taken in our stride,
We didn't go to fight, we just went for the ride.
Anzio and Sangro are just names,
We only went to look for dames.
We're still all D-Day Dodging in sunny Italy.

Once we had the griff that we were going home,
Back to dear old Blighty, never more to roam.
Then someone whispered, 'In France you'll fight.'
We said, 'Blow that, we'll just sit tight.'
The windy D-Day Dodgers, in sunny Italy.

Looking round the mountains, in the mud and rain,
There's lots of little crosses, some which bear no name.
Blood, sweat and tears and toil are gone,
The boys beneath them slumber on.
These are your D-Day Dodgers, who'll stay in Italy.

Various, 1944–5

But there was little comfort for the PBI as they looked forward to a third winter in the Italian mountains. For five months they had shivered and died before Rome and in May and June had given their all, hopeful that here at last was the opportunity to smash the German Armies in Italy once and for all. During DIADEM alone, Fifth and Eighth Armies had sustained

45,000 casualties, a rate amongst the rifle companies of 34 per cent.* The tables below give some idea of the price paid by the various national contingents during the Fourth Battle:

Casualties by Army and Nationality, 11 May–5 June 1944

	Killed	Wounded	Missing	Total	No. Batts	% Rate Amongst Inf. Coys
Eighth Army						
British	1068	3506	208	4782	21	31.6
Canadians	789	2463	116	2358	12	29.8
Poles	860	2822	97	3779	12	42.5†
Indians	?	?	?	?	9	?
TOTAL	2707+	8791+	421+	10,919+	54	AVGE. 34.6
Fifth Army						
British	520	2385	450	3355	18	28.6
Americans	3667	16,153	1204	20,024	66	41.1
French	1751	7912	972	10,635	45	32.1†
TOTAL	5938	26,450	2626	34,014	129	AVGE. 33.9
GRAND TOTAL	8645	35,241	4787	44,933	183	AVGE. 34.3 RATE

But even after such a sacrifice sufficient Germans had escaped, bloodied but unbowed, to hold the Allies at bay on yet another fearsome defensive line in the mountains. The Allied fighting troops had been brought to the very extremes of physical and mental suffering. Icy cold, rain, sleet, snow, mud, hunger, numbing fatigue, the crash of shells, severed arteries, exposed innards, exploding brains, and fear, gut-wrenching, bowel-moving fear – these had been the motifs of Cassino. Yet amidst this infernal ambience men had attained epic stature, keeping tight hold of

---

* The figure for the whole Cassino/Rome campaign was 105,000 casualties, this figure including the whole period of the Anzio beachhead. It is impossible to establish an accurate comparable figure for the Germans, though it was *at least* 80,000.
† The actual Polish and French casualty rates were probably much higher as both found it extremely difficult to get replacements.

•

themselves during their long days' dying and rising when bidden to trudge forward into fire up the slopes of yet another godless, barren hillside. And now all they had to look forward to was yet more of the same. Truly had Cassino been a hollow victory.

Certain of the Allied contingents were to feel this particularly keenly, and not just on the purely military plane. The most obvious example were the Poles, who had continued to hope to the very end that their spirit of self-sacrifice would somehow win them recognition and support in the deliberations of the 'Big Four'. It was not to be. Within a few years the principles of Stalinist hegemony were as rigidly enforced in Poland as elsewhere in Eastern Europe and most of those who had fought at Cassino were not even able to return to their homeland. Whatever one's views abut the kind of nationalist 'democracy' they might have reintroduced into Poland, it is difficult not to feel that Anders' men were shabbily treated. At every subsequent turn they were cruelly rebuffed. When the time came for the formal, triumphal entry into Rome, to which every Army and Corps wished to send its own representatives, 'the American commander told them: "No Poles or any such fire brigades!" ' Later in June, Churchill was buttonholed by General Sosnkowski who tried yet again to bring up the subject of post-war Poland. Churchill rounded on him, saying, 'You can take away your divisions now. We will manage without them.' One of the less prominent items on the agenda at Yalta, ten months later, was an Allied plan to rebuild the Cassino Monastery. But no Polish delegate was invited to the Conference, even as an observer, and when work did begin the only Poles to be found 'were the sapper working parties building the cemetery for the Poles who had fallen. The Polish national flag was never raised above Cassino, though the Soviet one flew there.'[1] By the end of the war even the British seemed to be doing their best to forget that the Poles had ever fought with them. As one pointed out: 'Those of us who fought at Monte Cassino, Falaise, Arnhem . . . did our duty. Many never saw the end of these battles. . . . [When] the war was over there followed a Victory Parade in London where all nations took part, except one. . . . *The Polish Army was not invited.*'[2]

But neither did the French Expeditionary Corps have much reason to feel that its efforts had been properly appreciated. The indigenous elements of the Armée d'Afrique were especially badly done by. The four divisions encountered in these pages went on to fight with distinction in southern France but Leclerc's more prestigious 2 Armoured Division, which was to carry the Gaullist flag through Normandy and into Paris, was purged of native troops in favour of more politically acceptable white Free

Frenchmen. But even the European element of the CEF was hardly fêted in the manner they might have expected. For long months they had suffered and died for France. As a French captain had said in May: 'It's hard to explain a man's emotions when he is fighting to get back home. Our men would go through hell to do it.'³ Yet they received poor recompense when they did get there. A report from I DMI, drawn up in November 1944, when the Division was fighting in France, dealt with the attitudes of men returning from leave:

> Although they thought that everyone had understood the past and present role of the . . . [Free French], they found that the soldiers of General de Gaulle were regarded as an alien element, motivated above all by a taste for adventure, and that . . . the battles in which they had taken part were known about only vaguely. . . . My men were disappointed to find that no one seemed interested in them nor in what they had done. . . . They were depressed on their return to their regiment and resent the fact that the force they represent risks being reduced through losses in combat before it becomes known to the mass of metropolitan Frenchmen.⁴

Things are not all that different today, and it is still difficult to find people in France who have any more than a very sketchy idea of the history and achievements of the CEF. Not for nothing did a recent French author end his book with the words of Pierre Ichac, a war correspondent in Italy, who wrote in 1946: '*Et les morts d'Italie me demandent pourquoi la France les a oubliés.*'⁵

In the English-speaking world the situation is somewhat different, for Monte Cassino remains, in name at least, one of the best-known battles of either world war. Yet what is still not sufficiently appreciated is the true extent of what men suffered there, particularly the ordinary infantrymen who bear the brunt of every battle. Even at the time these men were extremely resentful of their lowly status within the army. A report prepared in November 1944 by an Eighth Army psychologist noted that

> contact with innumerable Infantry officers and men, in Italy, during the past 12 months, has made it clear to the writer that there exists a considerable feeling of resentment amongst the Infantry regarding their status in the Armed Forces. They say in effect 'The Infantry is . . . called upon to contribute more in the way of fortitude and endurance than the men of any other arm, and has contributed more than any other to the success of the campaign in Italy. Yet . . . they are treated as an inferior arm of the service.'⁶

This resentment was expressed most keenly with regard to administrative and rear-echelon troops, who were rarely in personal danger yet always seemed to manage to pick over the supplies before they reached the front and to wangle themselves 'cushy' billets. One American correspondent noted:

> Between those living at home and those at the fighting front there was an immeasurable gulf. . . . But even in . . . [the] war theater the division was essentially the same. For hundreds in the 'base areas' were quite safe from danger; they were, many of them, making more money than they had as civilians, inhabiting finer homes, touring picturesque areas, entertaining lavishly and being entertained. . . . This condition . . . poisoned the hearts of many men owing a commmon allegiance. 'PBS' (Peninsular Base Section) became a hateful expression to the combat men. . . . The sign of Capri which read 'PBS Officers Rest Camp' became the subject of jest for thousands. PBS men wore sun-tans while combat men wore olive-drab, and the relationship became so bad that the latter would not pick up any hitch-hiking soldier in tans.[7]

Front-line soldiers soon developed a sense of exclusivity, a conviction that the rifle squad and platoon was a brotherhood apart, only open to those who shared

> With them in hell the sorrowful dark of hell,
> Whose world is but the trembling of a flare
> And heaven but as the highway for a shell.

An English officer always felt the change as he and his men marched 'past the gun-lines. We were entering again the detached and exclusive world of the Infantry: a world that only the Infantry – and those who work with the Infantry – know.'[8] An American rifleman with 34 Division, who became the GIs' most influential publicist with his famous Willie and Joe cartoons, emphasized how this sense of fraternity was strictly limited to those at the sharp end:

> While men in combat kid each other around, they have a sort of family complex about it. No outsiders may join in. . . . If a stranger comes up to a group when they are bulling, they ignore him. If he takes it upon himself to laugh at something funny they have said, they freeze their expressions, turn slowly around, stare at him until his stature has shrunk to about four inches, and he slinks away, and

then they go back to their kidding again. . . . Combat soldiers are an exclusive set, and if they want to be that way, it is their privilege.[9]

Yet there was little that was self-pitying about all this. With few exceptions the fighting soldiers accepted their lot with a weary shrug and simply got on with the job. Eric Sevareid never ceased to marvel at their

grim purpose, selflessness, and a spirit of exaltation in the mutual high endeavour. A thousand times one asked oneself why they were like this. They understood the war's meaning no more than the others – which is to say, hardly at all. Their country, their families were not in any mortal danger now, and yet they plodded on. . . . They did not hate the Germans. . . . They did not hate the concept of Fascism because they did not understand it. But they struggled on, climbing the hills, wading the rivers until they dropped, and . . . [dying] in ignorant glory . . .[10]

Above all it was the selflessness, the intimate sense of comradeship and love, that stood out from the filth and desolation of their day-to-day existence. To live with such men for any period of time, as they shared their labours, gave unstintingly of their meagre rations and crumpled cigarettes, bandaged and tended each other, comforted each other even at the very end of hope itself, was to have a tantalizing glimpse into a new world in which self-respect and mutual esteem cemented the bonds of unqualified equality and spontaneous love. Fred Majdalany wrote of his feelings at the end of a tour of duty on the massif:

Watching them drag their bodies into the trucks with a final despairing heave that seemed to use up the very last of their strength, one was conscious of the feeling of high comradeship which binds a man with fierce intensity to those with whom a profound and fearful mission has been shared. It is something which can only be known through the moral and emotional purge of battle. It is the fighting man's reward.[11]

A sergeant in 88 US Division, A.B. Sally, tried to explain what helped sustain him through the endless days of cold, hunger and fear, and always he came back to his deep sense of comradeship with those around him and its inherent obligations:

Why do I fight? . . . I don't know, unless it's because I feel I must because I'm expected to. If I should fail to do what is asked of me, I would betray the trust of the men fighting with me. And if I betrayed this trust . . . in my own eyes I believe I would become so despicable that no longer would I feel worthy of the comradeship of men. . . . It seems that there is an urge inside me that compels me to go with my buddies when they attack and to sweat it out with them in defence and . . . to endure seemingly useless privations, all to what may be a useless end.[12]

And the memories of this profound sense of comradeship never leave those who were fortunate enough to share it. An officer of 36 US Division has described a journey back to Monte Cassino when he tried to revivify memories of a spirit that was somehow lacking in times of peace. Towards the end of his visit he went to the American cemetery:

The monument itself, I was grateful to find, is extremely simple. In a central courtyard stands a statue of two soldiers, one with his arm on the shoulders of the other, both men stripped to the waist. They seem to be walking forward, as if they had a job to do and are going to do it together . . . I wandered out into the paths, stopping now at this grave, now at another, hoping that by reading the inscriptions, by busying my mind, I could control my emotions. But I could not keep back the tears, even when with one desperate effort I recalled the great ode of Catullus, who two thousand years ago had come to the tomb of his brother to pay honor to his memory . . . Yet groping for the words helped me to discipline myself to say hail and farewell in a dignified way to men who had been my brothers years ago in a common struggle. The struggle is now half forgotten, and perhaps finally, in the larger perspective of history, it was unimportant. But it was for these men that this story was written . . .

nunc tamen interea haec prisco quae more parentum
tradita sunt tristi munere ad inferias,
accipe fraterno multum manantia fletu,
atque in perpetuum, frater, ave atque vale.[13]*

For them, too, was this book written, to give proper account of their sufferings, to acknowledge their achievement, and to give an inkling of

---

* Even so, accept this tribute handed down
  According to the old parental custom,
  Moist with a brother's tears,
  And, forever, brother, hail and farewell.

(Translation by Harold Bond, 1964.)

the brotherhood of compassion that was formed between them. But though I have wanted to make much of this book a homage to the front-line soldier, I have also chosen a title that may seem to do scant justice to their self-sacrifice. Yet there seemed no honest alternative. For almost everywhere except at the sharp end proper the Battles of Cassino were poorly conceived and badly conducted. True, there are certain factors that might seem to mitigate such a harsh judgement. Both Fifth and Eighth Armies had done most of their fighting in Egypt, Libya and Tunisia and were poorly prepared for the chaotically mountainous terrain of southern and central Italy. Furthermore, the at best uncertain priority attached to the Italian campaign by the planners in London and Washington made it extremely difficult for Alexander to plan far in advance, or even to know just how many fighting troops would be available to him at any one time. In this last respect, indeed, the most pessimistic predictions were the best and the demands of OVERLORD and ANVIL, the latter surely the real 'dispersion debauch' of the war, meant that none of the commanders in Italy ever had enough troops at their disposal. And it is true also that the conduct of operations was not uniformly bad. The role of the French Expeditionary Corps in the Fourth Battle must always remain a shining example of the science of command, in which enemy weaknesses were properly assessed, the particular capabilities of the attacking troops optimally applied, and their attacks consistently pressed home with the greatest panache and an unerring eye for the maximum tactical advantage.

But the excuses are only partial and the exception remains just that. On the whole both Fifth and Eighth Armies were poorly led during the Cassino battles, where operations were consistently marred by a lack of strategic vision and slipshod staff work. Again and again these two factors combined to produce attacks that were doomed from the start, directed as they were against the strongest and least accessible portions of the German line and against an enemy who resolutely refused to begin the withdrawal so often predicted by the Allies. Monte Cassino and the Liri Valley seemed to completely dominate the minds of Clark, Leese and Alexander as they pondered ways to rupture the Gustav Line. And so, month after month, they squandered fine divisions in isolated attacks mounted in quite inadequate strength. 46 British and 36 US Divisions were held at the entrance of the Liri Valley with almost contemptuous ease, one regiment of the latter being massacred because Clark had convinced himself that 'one more push' would somehow shatter the German defences and permit the armour to roll through. Such unwarranted optimism had equally deleterious effects around Monte Cassino. The experiences of 34 US Division, in January and early February, clearly showed both just how difficult it was to funnel adequate numbers of men into an attack and how determined and well dug-in were the defending troops. Yet in mid-February 4 Indian Division were asked to mount a carbon copy attack, despite the fact that the first moves could only be made at company strength and could not be ordinated with the preparatory bombing of the Monastery.

The attack failed completely yet Alexander, despite the fact that he was beginning to realize that the forcing of the Gustav Line would require almost the whole of his Army Group, allowed the New Zealand Corps to attack Monte Cassino once more. And not only was this second attack unnecessary, motivated largely by a desire to save face, but it too was seriously vitiated from the start. True, new axes of attack were chosen, but it should have been clear to responsible commanders that they left a great deal to be desired. The town, for example, was a potential death trap, for the bombing would only help if it *completely* eliminated the garrison there, something which *no* aerial or artillery bombardment had yet done. Otherwise it could only hinder the attacking troops, forcing infantry to move at a snail's pace, in tiny, scattered groups, and hardly allowing the armour to move at all. Nor was the Indians' axis, to the west of the town, much better. It still seems remarkable that Freyberg and his planners seriously thought that they could feed several battalions through the narrowest of bottlenecks under the eyes of the Monastery garrison, especially when there was absolutely no provision made for the bombing of the latter.

But even the DIADEM offensive, which did finally dispense with these penny packet attacks, was seriously flawed both in conception and execution. Absurd claims were made for the potential of aerial interdiction operations; the difficulties of assault river crossings were still seriously underestimated; and there was a complete failure to assess the true capacity of the fragile Italian road network. And Monte Cassino was to be attacked yet again, the luckless Poles being sent forward in virtual suicide attacks against a bastion that must fall of its own accord once the rest of the Gustav Line buckled. Of course it was necessary to keep Heidrich's paratroopers occupied whilst the rest of Eighth Army hammered at the gates of the valley below, but surely there were more efficacious ways of doing this than the assaults *à la* Verdun on Point 593 and Phantom Ridge?

Other units too, notably the Canadians on the Hitler Line and the Melfa, and those battalions from VI Corps battering their heads against the C-Line defences between Velletri and Campoleone, were soon to realize that the success of the DIADEM offensive would be at best Pyrrhic. Nevertheless, it might still be possible to justify the huge casualties incurred in these crude frontal assaults if the Allied victory had also been decisive. But this it certainly was not. Though the Gustav, Hitler and C Lines were broken and Rome captured, DIADEM completely failed to accomplish its main task. This, on Alexander's own admission, had been to destroy German Tenth Army and so deprive Kesselring of the means to maintain a viable defence anywhere else in Italy. But the rump of this Army, the essential cadres of every one of its divisions, escaped intact and, having without undue difficulty evaded encirclement south of Rome, as well as pursuit thereafter, was able to re-establish a formidable position on the Gothic Line.

Nor can one really claim that Alexander's plan would have succeeded if only he had been better served by his subordinates. Certainly Clark did not help by abruptly switching the axis of his main effort out of the beachhead, and much British staff work with regard to traffic control in the Liri Valley was lamentable. But the essential fault remained Alexander's. Not simply because he had not adequately chivvied his British subordinates, nor even because he unaccountably refused Juin permission to take up the axis that VI Corps had abandoned; but more crucially because the whole conception of his original plan was at fault. Even had it gone pretty much according to schedule he could not have hoped to encircle the mass of Vietinghoff's Tenth Army, simply because the absence of a parallel thrust to the north of the Liri and Secco Valleys, through the Simbruinis, always left the Germans with an open back door. True, it required considerable organizational ability and deft tactics to take advantage of this exit, but surely no-one who had fought Rommel in Libya, von Arnim in Tunisia and von Senger und Etterlin in Sicily, could have doubted that German generalship was more than adequate to such challenges. Alexander had been quite explicit about his hopes for a battle of partial annihilation that would effectively destroy the German military presence in Italy. But this he signally failed to obtain, a failure to which the grim battles in the Gothic Line offer the starkest testimony. The six months blood-letting before Cassino eventually delivered up a ruined monastery and a capital city with little innate strategic significance. But the enemy escaped and, at least within the context of Alexander's own theatre, this must be deemed the hollowest of victories.

But there are wider contexts to consider. Harold Bond wondered whether the Cassino battles were not finally unimportant within the larger perspective of history. This it would be difficult to maintain. The four battles themselves might have been botched but it seems undeniable that the fighting nevertheless had an important bearing on operations elsewhere in Europe. For German divisions tied down in Italy were not available for transfer either to the Eastern or the Normandy fronts. On the former they may well have been just a drop in the ocean, but on the latter a few high-quality divisions, and generals, could well have turned the tide in the first weeks of bitter fighting to consolidate the D-Day beachhead. Of course, had the Allies not invaded Italy they too would have had extra divisions to play with, but what should be borne in mind is that the tactical and strategic impact of such reinforcements is immeasurably more helpful to the defender. He can feed such men in at particularly threatened points, along a multiplicity of road and rail links, whilst an amphibious attacker is tied to approach routes through the original beachhead; is limited in the number of divisions that can be maintained there; and can send in no extra men at all unless he has already amassed the requisite number of ships and landing craft. Thus, though the capture of Rome probably did not help Eisenhower or Montgomery one jot, the enforced absence of various high-calibre Panzer, Panzer Grenadier and Parachute divisions most certainly did.

But there is a yet wider context to consider, and one that has become of increasing concern to the author. In this and other books I have dwelt at length on the sufferings of the ordinary soldier in both world wars and have gone on to stress the extraordinary bonds of comradeship and genuine love that they engendered. These bonds I have presented as a victory of the human spirit and a triumphant affirmation of man's ability to actually live out the Christian ideal. But it should never be forgotten that such bonds were only forged in the smithies of hell itself, where also hundreds of thousands of men were slaughtered, millions maimed and as many more driven to the very extreme of mental torment. One should ponder well whether it was ever worth it. And one should above all beware of letting this victory of the human spirit persuade one that war is therefore ennobling, and so feed a mood that can only beckon us towards the precipice. For then that victory will have been the hollowest of them all.

Notes

CHAPTER I

1   Quoted in J. Ehrman, *Grand Strategy*, HMSO, 1956, vol.5, p.675.
2   *Ibid.*, pp.676-7.
3   Sir J. Slessor, *The Central Blue*, Cassell, 1956, pp.433-4.
4   R.E. Sherwood (ed.), *The White House Papers of Harry Hopkins*, Eyre & Spottiswoode, 1948, vol.2, p.528.
5   Quoted in G. Bruce, *Second Front Now*, Macdonald & Janes,1979, p.56.
6   Gen. The Lord Ismay, *The Memoirs*, Heinemann, 1960, p.249.
7   Quoted in Bruce, *op. cit.*, p.58.
8   Quoted *ibid.*, p.62.
9   A.C. Wedemeyer, *Wedemeyer Reports*, Holt & Co., New York, 1958, p.175 (Author's italics).
10 J. Leasor and L. Hollis, *War at the Top*, Michael Joseph, 1959, p.205.
11 W. Churchill, *The Second World War*, Cassell, 1964, vol.6, p.296.
12 *Ibid.*, vol.7, p.346.
13 A. Bryant, *The Alanbrooke War Diaries*, Fontana, 1965, vol.1, p.341.
14 Quoted in Bryant, *op. cit.*, vol.1, p.351.
15 F.L. Loewenheim *et al.*, *Roosevelt and Churchill: their Wartime Correspondence*, Barrie & Jenkins, 1975, p.222.
16 Quoted in Bruce, *op. cit.*, p.74.
17 Quoted *ibid.*, p.78.
18 Leasor and Hollis, *op. cit.*, p.209.
19 Quoted in Bruce, *op. cit.*, p.84.
20 Churchill, *op. cit.*, vol.8, p.33.
21 *Ibid.*, p.214.
22 Quoted in Leasor and Hollis, *op. cit.*, p.228.
23 *Ibid.*, p.224.
24 Bryant, *op. cit.*, vol.1, p.403.
25 Quoted in J.Kennedy, *The Business of War*, Hutchinson, 1957, p.261.
26 *Ibid.*, p.269.
27 Sherwood, *op. cit.*, vol.2, p.665.
28 Sir John Dill quoted in Churchill, *op. cit.*, vol.8, p.222.
29 Quoted in Bruce, *op. cit.*, p.97.
30 Kennedy, *op. cit.*, p.284, and Leasor and Hollis, *op. cit.*, p.229.

31   Wedemeyer, *op. cit.*, p.191.

32   Bryant, *op. cit.*, vol.1, p.508.

33   Quoted in Ehrman, *op. cit.*, vol.5, p.116.

34   Leasor and Hollis, *op. cit.*, p.233.

35   Ismay, *op. cit.*, p.298.

36   Churchill, *op. cit.*, vol.8, p.367.

37   D.D. Eisenhower, *Crusade in Europe*, Heinemann, 1948, p.186.

38   Quoted in N. Hillson, *Alexander of Tunis*, W.H. Allen, 1952, pp.150–1.

39   H.C. Butcher, *Three Years with Eisenhower*, Heinemann, 1946, p.313.

40   Churchill, *op. cit.*, vol.9, p.34.

41   Bryant, *op. cit.*, vol.1, p.550.

CHAPTER 2

1   Kennedy, *op. cit.*, p.295.

2   Churchill, *op. cit.*, vol. 8, pp.372 and 374.

3   Quoted in Bryant, *op. cit.*, vol.1, p.574.

4   Quoted in Bruce, *op. cit.*, p.133.

5   Bryant, *op. cit.*, p.578.

6   Bryant, *op. cit.*, vol.1, p.552.

7   J. Grigg, *1943: The Victory That Never Was*, Eyre Methuen, 1980, p.97.

8   S. Roskill, *The War at Sea*, HMSO, 1960, vol.3 (Part I), p.145.

9   R. Murphy, *Diplomat Among Warriors*, Doubleday, New York, 1964, pp.236–7.

10   N. Lewis, *Naples 44*, Collins, 1978, p.18.

11   Quoted in Churchill, *op. cit.*, vol.9, p.127.

12   B. Montgomery, *The Memoirs*, Collins, 1958, p.202.

13   S.T. Matthews, Interviews with General Clark, 10–21 May 1948, pp.26–7. US National Archives (NA), Modern Military Section (MMS), RG 319 Box 5.

14   *Ibid.*, p.27.

15   Montgomery, *loc. cit.*

16   *Ibid.*, pp.198 and 201.

17   Earl Alexander of Tunis, *The Alexander Memoirs*, Cassell, 1962, p.118.

18   Quoted in M. Blumenson, *Bloody River*, Allen & Unwin, 1970, p.23.

19 Lord Tedder, *With Prejudice*, Cassell, 1966, pp.487–8.

20 R.S. Mavrogordato, 'Hitler's Decision on the Defence of Italy', in K.R. Greenfield (ed.), *Command Decisions*, Methuen, 1960, p.234.

21 Quoted *ibid.*, p.232.

22 E. von Manstein, *Lost Victories*, Regnery, Chicago, 1958, p.449.

23 Loewenheim *et al.*, *op. cit.*, p.374.

24 Bryant, *op. cit.*, vol.2, p.99.

25 *Ibid.*, p.101.

26 Quoted in Blumenson, *op. cit.*, p.29.

27 Quoted in D.C. Quilter (ed.), *No Dishonourable Name*, SR Publishing, Wakefield, 1972, p.195.

28 A. Moorehead, *Eclipse*, Sphere Books, London, 1968, p.58.

29 Churchill, *op. cit.*, vol.10, p.91.

30 H. Henderson, "The Highland Division's Farewell to Sicily", in *Elegies for the Dead*, John Lehmann, 1947.

31 Quoted in C.G. Starr, *From Salerno to the Alps*, Infantry Journal Press, Washington, 1948, p.84.

32 Quoted in Blumenson, *op. cit.*, p.52.

CHAPTER 3

1   Quoted in Churchill, *op. cit.*, vol.8, p.175

2   C. de Gaulle, *War Memoirs: Unity 1943-44*, Weidenfeld and Nicolson, 1956, pp.249-50.

3   J. Robichon, *Le Corps Expéditionnaire Français en Italie 1943–44*, Presses de la Cité, Paris, 1981, pp.253.

4   H. Macmillan, *The Blast of War*, Macmillan, 1967, p.412.

5   S.T. Matthews, Interview with Brigadier K.W.D. Strong, 30 October 1947m p.7 NA (MMS), RG 319 Box 15.

6   AFHQ Incoming Message, From: HQ AAI To: AFHQ, Ref: 0-2554, 21 April 1944. Public Records Office (PRO), WO 204/1455.

7   A. Juin, *Mémoires*, Fayard, Paris, 1959, vol.1, pp.376–7 (emphasis in the original).

8   Rapport du Général Juin . . . au Général Commandant en Chef, Ref: 1/3/SR, 29 November 1943, p.2. Service Historique de l'Armée de Terre (SHAT) Carton 10P 56.

9   *Ibid.*, pp.2-3.

10 Quoted in R. Chambe, *L'épopée française d'Italie 1944*, Flammarion, Paris, 1952, p.70.

11 Quoted in Robichon, *op. cit.*, p.42.

12 R. Merle, *Ben Bella*, Michael Joseph, 1967, p.57.

13 Quoted in G. Boulle, *Le corps expéditionnaire français en Italie, 1943-44*, Imprimerie Nationale, Paris, 1971-3, vol.1, p.67.

14 F. von Senger und Etterlin, *War Diary of the Italian Campaign: Cassino*, pp.43–4. NA(MMS) MS C-095b; and von Senger und Etterlin, *Neither Fear Nor Hope*, Macdonald, 1963, p.231.

15 Rapport Confidentiel à M. le Général Commandant en Chef, Ref: 4/CEF/3/R, 26 December 1943, p.3. SHAT 10P 56.

16 See Juin, *op. cit.*, pp.254–5.

17 *Ibid.*, pp.231–2.

18 Quoted in Robichon, *op. cit.*, p.67. See also Boulle, *op. cit.*, vol.1, p.84, and C.J. Molony *et al.*, *History of the Second World War: United Kingdom Military Series: The Mediterranean and the Middle East*, HMSO, vol.5, 1973, p.603.

19 Captain Giroult, 26 January 1945. SHAT, Fonds des Petites Unités (FPU), Carton 11P 22.

20 Quoted in Boulle, *op. cit.*, vol.1, p.73.

21 Journal de Marche et des Opérations (JMO) 3/7 RTA, 10 January 1944. SHAT(FPU) 12P 56.

22 Report from commander 1/4 RTM, 15 January 1944. SHAT (FPU) 12P 69.

23 2ᵉ Division d'Infanterie Marocaine, *Victoire en Italie*, Gauthier-Villars, Paris, 1945, p.28.

24 Quoted *ibid.*, p.23.

25 Colonel Lapparra (probably), *Les hauts faits de nos Marocains en Italie*, n.d., p.3. SHAT(FPU) 11P31.

26 *Ibid.*, p.5.

27 JMO 3/7 RTA, *op. cit.*, 11 January 1944.

28 Colonel Laparra, *Texte d'une causerie faite aux officiers des centres d'instruction d'armée*, 28 March 1944, p.2. SHAT 10P 56. Vincennes material not indicated as being in the Fonds des Petites Unités, i.e. the series 10P, is located in the main archive in the Pavillon des Armes.

29 JMO 3rd Regiment of Algerian Spahis, 12 January 1944. SHAT 10P 56.

30 JMO 3/7 RTA, *op. cit.*, 12 January 1944.

31 *Ibid.*

32 *Ibid.*

33 *Ibid.*

34 Rapport d'opérations, signed Capitaine Gobillot, 14 January 1944. SHAT 10P 56.

35 *Ibid.*

36 Quoted in von Senger und Etterlin, Diary, *op. cit.*, p.36.
37 Quoted in Boulle, *op. cit.*, vol. I, p.95.
38 Von Senger und Etterlin, Diary, *op. cit.*, p.46.
39 Quoted in Boulle, *op. cit.*, vol. I, p.191.
40 Juin, *op. cit.*, pp.265–6.
41 Colonel Chappuis, *Opérations du 22–1–44 au 25–1–44*, 24 January 1944, p.I. SHAT (FPU) 12P 56.
42 Merle, *op. cit.*, p.60.
43 2ᵉ Bureau Report, 2nd Moroccan Infantry Division, 21/22 January 1944. SHAT (FPU) I IP 23.
44 Interrogation of Oberleutnant Gunther Sturm, 3/8 PGR, 26 January 1944. SHAT I0P 23.
45 2ᵉ Bureau, CEF, *Synthèse des Interrogatoires du 22/23 janvier*, p.3. SHAT I0P 37.
46 Quoted in Boulle, *op. cit.*, vol. I, p.199.
47 Quoted *ibid.*, p.206.
48 JMO 2nd Moroccan Infantry Division, 25 January 1944. SHAT (FPU) I IP 22.
49 Von Senger und Etterlin, Diary, *op. cit.*, pp.195–6.
50 Captain Heurgnon, *La Victoire sous la Signe des Trois Croissants*, Editions Pierre Villon, Alger, 1946, pp.65. See also Robichon, *op. cit.*, p.158.
51 Quoted in 2ᵉ Division d'Infanterie Marocaine, *op. cit.*, p.186.
52 Quoted in Heurgnon, *op. cit.*, p.38.
53 Appendix to JMO I/3 RTA, 12–14 January 1944. SHAT (FPU) 12P 50.
54 Quoted in 2ᵉ Division d'Infanterie Marocaine, *op. cit.*, pp.86–8 (emphasis in original).

CHAPTER 4

1 Quoted in J.D. Forsythe *et al.*, *Fifth Army History*, Florence, n.d., Part IV, pp.205–6.
2 M. Clark, *Calculated Risk*, Harrap, 1951, p.252.
3 Quoted in 3ᵉ Bureau Report, 1 Division d'Infanterie de Marche, *Campagne d'Italie février-juillet 1944*, n.d., p.4. SHAT (FPU) I IP 11.
4 37 RTA, *Procédés de combat des troupes allemandes*, n.d., pp.5–7. SHAT(FPU) 12P 56 (emphasis in original).
5 Quoted in Forsythe *et al.*, *op. cit.*, p.23.
6 G. Blight, *History of the Royal Berkshire Regiment 1920–47*, Staples, 1953, pp.277–8.

7   Appendix to War Diary 2 Cameronians, 30 January 1944. PRO WO 170/1372.

8   G. Avis, *The 5th British Division*, pvte. pub., n.d., p.180.

9   Quoted in J. Sym, *Seaforth Highlanders*, Gale & Polden, Aldershot, 1962, pp.263–4.

10 Quoted *ibid.*, p.270.

11 War Diary HQ 15 Infantry Brigade, 18 January 1944. PRO WO 170/565.

12 *Battle of the Garigliano River*, n.d., p.1. Appendix to War Diary 1 King's Own Yorkshire Light Infantry, January–June 1944. PRO WO 170/1411.

13 War Diary HQ 13 Infantry Brigade, 18 January 1944. PRO WO 170/561.

14 R.C.G. Foster, *History of the Queen's Royal Regiment*, vol.8, Gale & Polden, Aldershot, 1953, p.280.

15 Molony, *op. cit.*, p.611.

16 War Diary 9 Royal Fusiliers, 17 January 1944. PRO WO 170/1391.

17 Both quoted in A. Crookenden, *The History of the Cheshire Regiment in World War Two*, pvte. pub., 1949, pp.218–20.

18 5 Division Intelligence Summary no.69, to 23.59 hrs, 19 January 1944. Appendix to War Diary. PRO WO 170/426.

19 D.S. Daniell, *Regimental History of the Royal Hampshire Regiment*, vol.3, Gale & Polden, Aldershot, 1955, p.155.

20 War Diary 2 Hampshire Regiment, 20 January 1944. PRO WO 170/1395.

21 Von Senger und Etterlin, Diary, *op. cit.*, pp.59–60.

22 Quoted in F. Fox, *The Royal Inniskilling Fusiliers in the Second World War*, Gale & Polden, Aldershot, 1951, p.112.

23 H.C. Wylly, *History of the King's Own Yorkshire Light Infantry*, vol.6, Gale & Polden, Aldershot, 1961, p.88.

24 Quoted in D.C. Quilter (ed.), *No Dishonourable Name*, Clowes & Sons, 1947, p.199.

25 War Diary 2 Cameronians, *op. cit.*, 22 January 1944.

26 War Diary 2 Royal Scots Fusiliers, 23 January 1944. PRO WO 170/1348.

27 War Diary 1 King's Own Yorkshire Light Infantry, 23 January 1944. PRO WO 170/1411.

28 War Diary 3 Coldstream Guards, 24 January 1944. PRO WO 170/1348.

29 War Diary HQ X Corps, 20 and 24 January 1944. PRO WO 170/302.

30 War Diary 9 Royal Fusiliers, *op. cit.*, 19–21 January 1944.

31 J.E.H. Neville, *The Oxfordshire and Buckinghamshire Light Infantry Chronicle*, vol.3, Gale & Polden, Aldershot, 1954, p.320.

32 Letter by Lt Mullins, 27 January 1944. Appendix to War Diary 1 London Irish, January to June 1944. PRO WO 170/1432.

33 War Diary 10 Royal Berkshire Regiment, 24 January 1944. PRO WO 170/1365.

34 'Note on Administrative Problems', *ibid.*, 26 January 1944 (author's emphasis).

35 War Diary 2 Hampshire Regiment, 29 January 1944. PRO WO 170/1395.

36 War Diary 6 Lincolnshire Regiment, 27 January 1944. PRO WO 170/1428.

37 Quoted in Daniell, *op. cit.*, pp.160–1.

38 War Diary HQ X Corps, *op. cit.*, 9 February 1944.

39 'Estimate of the Requirements for a Resumption of the Offensive', 11 March 1944, p.5. SHAT 10P 55. This is my translation of a French translation of the original document. I was unable to locate the latter in the Public Records Office.

40 Quoted in Blight, *op. cit.*, p.279.

41 Quoted in Allied Forces HQ G–2 Intelligence Notes No.55, 18 April 1944, Section C pp.11–12. PRO WO 204/985.

42 Quoted in Fifth Army HQ G–2 Notes, 15/16 February 1944, p.5 SHAT 10P 36.

CHAPTER 5

1 Quoted in Blumenson, *op. cit.*, p.45.

2 Quoted in R.H. Adleman and G. Walton, *Rome Fell Today*, Little, Brown and Co., Boston, 1968, pp.19–20.

3 Blumenson, *op. cit.*, p.58.

4 Extract Walker Diary (copy) p.40. Department of Defense (DD), Center for Military History (CMH) HRC 314.81.

5 *Ibid.*, p.43.

6 *Ibid.*, p.41.

7 Keyes to Major-General W.B. Persons, 10 September 1946, 'Statement Covering the Rapido Operations 20–22 January 1944', p.5. DD(CMH) HRC Geog. L. Italy 370.2.

8 Quoted in Adleman and Walton, *op. cit.*, p.156.

9 Statement by General Walker to the Committee on Military Affairs, US Senate, 11 June 1946, p.24. DD(CMH) Geog. L. Italy 370.2.

10 Excerpts from Clark Diary 31 August 1943–23 March 1944 (copy), p.8. NA (MMS) RG 319 Box 6.

11 Clark Interview, *op. cit.*, p.10.

12 Clark Diary, *loc. cit.*

13 L.K. Truscott, *Command Decisions*, Dutton, New York, 1954, p.217.

14 P.A. Crowl, Interview with Lieutenant-General G. Keyes, 22 September 1955, p.1. NA(NMS) RG 319 Box 255.

15 Quoted in Adleman and Walton, *op. cit.*, p.209.

16 (Résumé of) Letter, Keyes to Clark, 28 December 1943. NA (MMS) RG 319 Box 255.

17 Blumenson, *op. cit.*, pp.62–3.

18 Lt-Col M.C. Walter to CG II Corps, 13 January 1944, p.2. Washington National Records Center (WNRC) Modern Military Field Branch (MMFB) RG 94 202–3.2.

19 Quoted in M. Blumenson, *Salerno to Cassino* (*US Army in World War II*), Government Printing Office, Washington, 1969, p.320.

20 Quoted in Adleman and Walton, *op. cit.*, pp.155–6.

21 See Chapter 17.

22 Clark, *op. cit.*, p.269.

23 H. Kippenberger, *Infantry Brigadier*, Oxford University Press, 1949, p.350.

24 Quoted in Blumenson, *Bloody River, op. cit.*, p.73.

25 Quoted in R.L. Wagner, *The Texas Army*, pvte. pub., Austin (Texas), 1972, p.102.

26 Quoted in Blumenson, *Bloody River, op. cit.*, p.76.

27 Quoted *ibid.*, p.77.

28 Quoted *ibid.*, pp.124 and 92.

29 Both quoted in R. Wallace, *The Italian Campaign*, Time-Life Books, Alexandria (Va.), 1978, p.115.

30 Letter from Lt Phillips to Chief of Staff US Army, 8 July 1946, p.4. DD (CMH) HRC Geog.L.Italy 370.2.

31 *Ibid.*

32 Quoted in R.G. Martin, *The GI War*, Little, Brown and Co., Boston (Mass.), 1967, pp.122–3.

33 Ibid.

34 F.L. Walker, Comments on the Rapido River Crossing, 27 June 1960, NA (MMS) RG 319 Box 255, p.3.

35 Quoted in Wagner, *op. cit.*, p.92.

36 Walker Diary, *op. cit.*, p.40.

37 Extract from 143 Regiment After Action Report, January 1944, p.3, NA(MMS) RG 319 Box 255.

38 Extract from 19 Combat Group After Action Report, January 1944, NA (MMS) RG 319 Box 255.

39 Quoted in Blumenson, *Salerno to Cassino, op. cit.*, pp.350–1.

40 Blumenson, *Bloody River, op. cit.*, p.124.

41 Quoted *ibid.*, p.96.

42 Walker Diary, *op. cit.*, p.42.

43 Quoted in Wallace, *op. cit.*, pp.116–17.

44 Quoted in Walker, Comments . . ., *op. cit.*, p.4.

45 Quoted in Wallace, *op. cit.*, p.117.

46 *Ibid.*, p.104.

47 Quoted *ibid.*, p.105.

48 Quoted in Wagner, *op. cit.*, p.119.

49 Phillips letter, *op. cit.*, p.5.

50 Quoted in Wagner, *op. cit.*, p.113.

51 Quoted *ibid.*, p.114.

52 Quoted in R.G. Martin, *op. cit.*, p.123.

53 Walker, Comments . . ., *op. cit.*, pp.14–15.

54 Walker Diary, *op. cit.*, p.43.

55 141 Infantry Regiment, Operations in Italy, January 1944, p.16. NA (MMS) RG 319 Box 255.

56 Quoted *ibid.*, p.376.

57 Von Senger und Etterlin, *Neither Fear. . ., op. cit.*, p.193.

58 Walker, Comments . . . *op. cit.*, p.20.

59 Quoted *ibid.*, p.121.

60 H.L. Bond, *Return to Cassino*, Pocket Books, New York, 1965, p.56.

61 Wagner, *op. cit.*, pp.122–3.

62 Comprising in the US Army at that time After Action Reports, Journals of Action, and Narratives of Action.

63 'F' Company, 2/141 Regiment. Quoted in Wagner, *op. cit.*, p.123.

64 Quoted in Wagner, *ibid.*, p.127.

65 Walker, Diary, *op. cit.*, p.44.

66 E. Sevareid, *Not So Wild a Dream*, Knopf, New York, 1946, p.366.

67 Quoted in Wagner, *op. cit.*, p.122, and Blumenson, *Bloody River, op. cit.*, pp.105–6.

68 Quoted in Adleman and Walton, *op. cit.*, p.154.

CHAPTER 6

1 G–2 Report, Fifth Army HQ, 21/22 January 1944, p.7. SHAT 10P 36.

2 Sevareid, *op. cit.*, p.366.

3   E.D. Smith, *The Battles for Cassino*, Ian Allen, Shepperton, 1975, p.36.
4   Walker Diary, *op. cit.*, p.43.
5   Von Senger und Etterlin, Diary, *op. cit.*, pp.65–6.
6   Quoted in Molony, *op. cit.*, pp.694–5.
7   Narrative of Action of the 168th Infantry Regiment January 24–February 29 1944, p.1. WNRC (MMFB) RG94 105–0.3.0 (Box 2064).
8   General C.W. Ryder, Operations Report 1–31 January 1944, p.2. WNRC (MMFB) RG 94 334–0.3 (Box 9417).
9   Molony, *op. cit.*, p.694.
10   T.D. Murphy, *Ambassadors in Arms: the Story of Hawaii's 100th Battalion*, University of Hawaii Press, Honolulu, 1954, p.170.
11   Telephone Message Major Martin to Colonel Honeycutt, 18.50 25 January 1944. WNRC (MMFB) RG94 200–3.2 (Box 3184).
12   Unit Journal 133 Regiment, Forward Command Post, 25 January 1944. WNRC (MMFB) RG 94 34 Inf(133)–0.3 (Box 9551).
13   II Corps G–3 Journal, 25 January 1944. WNRC (MMFB) RG 94 200–3.2 (Box 3184).
14   HQ II Corps, Memorandum Lieutenant W.L. Fagg to Lieutenant-Colonel Butchers, 27 January 1944. WNRC (MMFB) RG 94, *loc. cit.*
15   Blumenson, *Salerno to Cassino*, *op. cit.*, p.371.
16   Lieutenant-Colonel John L. Power, 'Crossing the River Rapido', typescript, n.d., p.3. DD (MMH) HRC Geog.L.Italy 370.2 (Rapido River).
17   *Ibid.*
18   Narrative . . . 168th Regiment, *op. cit.*, pp.7–8.
19   Powers, *op. cit.*, pp.3–4.
20   *Ibid.*, p.6.
21   Ryder, Operations Report, *op. cit.*, p.3.
22   II Corps Staff Message signed Lieutenant-Colonel Butchers, 30 January 1944. WNRC (MMFB) RG 94 200–3.2 (Box 3184).
23   34 Division G–1 Monthly Report, January 1944, p.3. WNRC (MMFB) RG 94 334.1 (Box 9420) (author's emphasis).
24   Von Senger und Etterlin, Diary, *op. cit.*, p.66.
25   Quoted in Blumenson, *Salerno to Cassino*, *op. cit.*, p.375.
26   Quoted in Molony, *op. cit.*, p.705.
27   Quoted in von Senger und Etterlin, *Diary*, *op. cit.*, p.52.
28   II Corps Staff Message, CG 34 Division to CG II Corps, 3 February 1944, p.2. WNRC (MMFB) RG 94 200–3.2 (Box 3194).
29   Von Senger und Etterlin, Diary, *op. cit.*, pp.70–1.
30   2/135 Battalion Narrative History, Month of February 1944, p.1.

WNRC (MMFB) RG 94 334-Inf (135) 7–0.1 to 334 Inf (135) 0.7 (Box 9573).

31 II Corps Staff Message, Major Martin to Colonel Honeycutt, 8 February 1944. WNRC (MMFB) RG 94 200–3.2 (Box 3184).

32 'The 133rd Infantry Regiment in the Cassino Operation', unsigned, n.d., p.3. WNRC (MMFB) RG 94 105–0.3.0– 105–0.4 (Box 2064).

33 34 Division G–2 Monthly Report, January 1944, pp.4–5. WNRC (MMFB) RG 94 334–2 (Box 9426).

34 Remarks by Colonel C.L. Marshall, n.d., p.2. NA (MMS) RG 319 Box 255.

35 Remarks by Captain Frazier (3/133 Regiment), n.d., p.3. NA (MMS) RG 319 Box 255.

36 Narrative . . . 168 Regiment, *op. cit.*, pp.15–16.

37 II Corps Staff Message, Major Travis to Colonel Honeycutt, 11 February 1944. WNRC (MMFB) RG 94 200–3.2 (Box 3184).

38 HQ NAF Theater Ops, US Army, Training Memorandum No.3: Lessons from the Italian Campaign 9/9/43–1/2/44, pp.20–1. PRO WO 204/7564.

39 Corporal R. Dawson, quoted in HQ 34 Division, Lessons Learned in Combat November 7/8 1942–September 1944, p.76. PRO WO 204/4365.

40 Quoted in Wagner, *op. cit.*, pp.151–2.

41 H. Kippenberger, *op. cit.*, p.351.

42 Notes from S.T. Matthews, Interview with Alexander, 10–15 January 1949. NA (MMS) RG 319 Box 255.

43 Narrative . . . 168 Regiment, *op. cit.*, p.16.

44 Bond, *op. cit.*, p.109.

45 II New Zealand Corps, Account of Operations 3 February–26 March 1944, p.5. PRO WO 204/7275.

46 34 Division G–1 Monthly Report, February 1944, p.3. WNRC (MMFB) RG 94 334–1 (Box 9420).

47 Both quoted in E. Puttick, *25 Battalion*, Department of Internal Affairs, Wellington, 1958, pp.382–3.

48 M.B. White, *They Called It Purple Heart Valley*, Simon & Schuster, New York, 1944, pp.79–80.

CHAPTER 7

1 A. Juin, *La campagne d'Italie*, G. Victor, Paris, 1962, pp. 62–3.

2 Quoted in Boulle, *op. cit.*, vol. 1, p. 110.

3   Quoted in R. Chambe, *Le bataillon de Belvédère*, Editions J'ai Lu, Paris, 1965, p.25.
4   JMO 3/4 RTT, 24 January 1944. SHAT (FPU) 12P 53 (emphasis in original).
5   Chambe, *op. cit.*, p.13.
6   *Ibid.*, pp.62–3.
7   JMO 3/4 RTT quoted in Heurgnon, *op. cit.*, p.83.
8   2/4 RTT, *Rapport sur les combats . . . entre le 25 et le 31 janvier*, 24 February 1944, pp.2 and 3. SHAT (FPU) 12P 53.
9   Chambe, *op. cit.*, p.79.
10 *Ibid.*, p.91.
11 Quoted in Chambe, *op. cit.*, pp.141–2.
12 See Robichon, *op. cit.*, p.117.
13 JMO 11 Coy 4 RTT, 25 January 1944. SHAT (FPU) 12P 53.
14 JMO 3/4 RTT, *op. cit.*, 26 January 1944.
15 Quoted in Chambe, *op. cit.*, p.105.
16 JMO 11 Coy 3/4 RTT, *op. cit.*, 26 January 1944.
17 Chambe, *op. cit.*, p.153.
18 Lieutenant Clément, quoted *ibid.*, p.177.
19 Quoted *ibid.*, p.182.
20 JMO 3/4 RTT, *op. cit.*, 27 January 1944 (emphasis in original).
21 JMO 11 Coy 3/4 RTT, *op. cit.*, 27 January 1944.
22 Quoted in Chambe, *op. cit.*, pp.205–6.
23 JMO 3/4 RTT, *loc. cit.*
24 Quoted in von Senger und Etterlin, Diary, *op. cit.*, p.51.
25 Quoted in Chambe, *op. cit.*, pp.210–11.
26 Quoted *ibid.*, pp.207–8.
27 JMO 11 Coy 3/4 RTT, *op. cit.*, 28 January 1944.
28 JMO 3/4 RTT, *op. cit.*, 28 January 1944.
29 *Ibid.*
30 Quoted in Boulle, *op. cit.*, vol. 1, p.123.
31 Quoted in Chambe, *op. cit.* p.225.
32 Quoted in Boulle, *op. cit.*, p.215.
33 Quoted in Chambe, *op. cit.*, p.229.
34 JMO 3/4 RTT, *op. cit.*, 29 January 1944 (emphasis in original).
35 Juin, *Campagne d'Italie, op. cit.*, p.74.
36 Juin to Clark, 29 January 1944. Quoted in Boulle, *op. cit.*, vol.1, p.211.
37 Juin, *Mémoires, op. cit.*, p.374.
38 Chambe, *op. cit.*, p.234.
39 JMO 11 Coy 3/4 RTT, *op. cit.*, 31 January 1944.

40 JMO 3/4 RTT, *op. cit.*, 31 January 1944.
41 Juin, *Mémoires, op. cit.*, p.274.
42 Chambe, *op. cit.*, p.252.

CHAPTER 8

1   AHFQ G-3 to AHFQ DC/S, Appreciation of the Situation in Italy on 7 February 1944, pp.1–2. PRO WO 204/1454.
2   Quoted in telegram, From: Air Ministry; To: AFHQ Algiers (Ref: OZ 659), 5 February 1944. PRO WO 204/1454.
3   Bryant, *op. cit.*, vol.2, p.120.
4   *Ibid.*, p.116.
5   *Ibid.*, p.123.
6   Quoted in N.C. Phillips, *Official History of New Zealand in the Second World War: Italy*, vol.1, Wellington, 1957, p.178.
7   Quoted in R. Trevelyan, *Rome '44*, Secker & Warburg, 1981, pp.83–4.
8   Clark, *op. cit.*, pp.283–4.
9   Quoted in Blumenson, *Salerno to Cassino, op. cit.*, p.402.
10 Fifth Army Operations Instruction No. 14, 5 February 1944. PRO WO 204/6809.
11 Quoted in Phillips, *op. cit.*, p.193.
12 Clark Interview, *op. cit.*, p.6.
13 NZ Corps Operations Instruction No. 4, 9 February 1944, p.1. HQ Fifth Army, Report on Cassino Operations, Appx. N/19. WNRC (MMFB) RG 94 105–0.3.0.–0.4.
14 Quoted in Molony, *op. cit.*, p.704.
15 Quoted in Trevelyan, *op. cit.*, p.132.
16 Quoted *ibid.*, p.133.
17 Quoted *ibid.*, pp.153–4.
18 Quoted in D. Pal, *Official History of the Indian Armed Forces in the Second World War: The Campaign in Italy 1943–45*, Combined Interservices Historical Section, Calcutta, 1960, pp.98–9 (emphasis in original).
19 Quoted *ibid.*, pp.100–1 (emphasis in original).
20 Chambe, *L'épopée. . ., op. cit.*, p.32.
21 Quoted in M. Carpentier, *Les forces alliés en Italie*, Berger-evrault, Paris, 1949, p.78.
22 Juin, *Mémoires, op. cit.*, p.277.
23 Quoted in G.R. Stevens, *Fourth Indian Division*, McClaren & Sons, n.d., pp.217–18.

24   Quoted in Pal, *op. cit.*, p.100.
25   Clark, *op. cit.*, p.299.
26   HQ Fifth Army, Monte Cassino Abbey Bombing (signed Gruenther), 12 February 1944, p.1. DD (CMH) HRC Geog.L.Italy 373.11.
27   *Ibid.*, p.2.
28   Quoted in Blumenson, *Salerno to Cassino, op. cit.*, pp.404–5.
29   Clark, *op. cit.*, p.301.
30   *Ibid.*, p.300.
31   Quoted in Robichon, *op. cit.*, p.176.
32   Alexander of Tunis, *op. cit.*, p.121. See also Nicolson, *Alex, op. cit.*, p.287.
33   A. Kesselring, *The Memoirs of Field-Marshal Kesselring*, Purnell Book Services, 1974, p.195.
34   Quoted in Trevelyan, *op. cit.*, p.126.
35   Von Senger und Etterlin, *Neither Fear . . ., op. cit.*, p.202.
36   Alexander of Tunis, *loc. cit.*
37   Slessor, *op. cit.*, p.578.
38   Quoted in Trevelyan, *op. cit.*, p.129.
39   Mission près de la Vᵉ Armée, Rapport 1137/M/TS, 7 March 1944, Annexe No.1, p.1. SHAT 10P39.
40   Bond, *op. cit.*, p.135.
41   Quoted in Trevelyan, *op. cit.*, pp.129–30.

CHAPTER 9

1   14 Pz Corps to Tenth Army, Appreciation of the Situation, 15 February 1944, 14 Pz Corps Miscellaneous Appendices, Feb 1944, p.2. NA (MMS). Translation from GMDS File 58199/20.
2   *Ibid.*
3   W.G. Stevens, *Freyberg V.C.: The Man 1939–45*, Herbert Jenkins, 1965, p.91.
4   J.P. Lawford, *Solah Punjab*, Gale & Polden, Aldershot, 1967, p.163.
5   G.R. Stevens, *History of the 2nd King Edward VII's Own Gurkha Rifles*, Gale & Polden, Aldershot, 1952, p.101.
6   Kippenberger, *op. cit.*, pp.354–5.
7   *Ibid.*, p.355.
8   F. Majdalany, *Cassino: Portrait of a Battle*, Longmans, 1957, p.107.
9   Phillips, *op. cit.*, p.210.

10 Quoted in F.D. Smith, *The Battles for Cassino*, Ian Allen, Shepperton, 1975, p.77.

11 War Diary 1 Royal Sussex Regiment, 15 February 1944. PRO WO 170/1478.

12 Quoted in Stevens, *4th Indian Division, op. cit.*, p.285.

13 Quoted *ibid.*, pp.283–4.

14 Quoted *ibid.*, pp.285–6.

15 Quoted in Majdalany, *op. cit.*, p.142.

16 AFHQ Incoming Message, From: AGWAR from Arnold; To: Freedom for Eaker, 10 February 1944, Refs: MAAF 410 AFHQ 9413 and MAAF 411 AFHQ 9414. PRO WO 204/1454.

17 AFHQ Outgoing Message, From: Eaker, To: AGWAR for Arnold, 11 February 1944, Ref: W 2426/50184. PRO WO 204/1454.

18 Quoted in Robichon, *op. cit.*, p.178.

19 Quoted in R. Böhmler, *Monte Cassino*, Cassell, 1964, p.178.

20 Quoted in Phillips, *op. cit.*, p.213.

21 Stevens, *4th Indian Division, op. cit.*, p.285.

22 Quoted *ibid.*, p.287.

23 90 PG Division, Evening Report, 15 February 1944, extracts from 14 Pz Corps Reports 11-20 February 1944, p.3. NA (MMS). Translation from GMDS File 58199/6.

24 Quoted in Smith, *op. cit.*, p.83.

25 Majdalany, *op. cit.*, p.148.

26 War Diary 1 Royal Sussex Regiment, *op. cit.*, 04.30 hrs 17 February 1944 (author's emphasis).

27 Phillips, *op. cit.*, p.223.

28 Quoted in J.F. Cody, *28 (Maori) Battalion*, Department of Internal Affairs, Wellington, 1958, p.359.

29 Quoted *ibid.*, p.360.

30 Quoted *ibid.*, p.361.

31 Quoted *ibid.*, p.362.

32 Extracts from 14 Pz Corps Reports . . ., *op. cit.*, p.3.

33 Quoted in Cody, *op. cit.*, p.363.

34 P.Cochrane, *Charlie Company*, Chatto & Windus, 1979, p.113. Captain Cochrane was serving with 2 Cameron Highlanders who were portering for the Rajputanas.

35 Operations of New Zealand Corps February 3 – March 26 1944, p.12 (unsigned typescript). PRO CAB 106/366.

36 *Ibid.*, p.13.

37 Colonel J. Showers, quoted in G.R. Stevens, *2 Gurkhas, op. cit.*, pp.102–3.

38   Pal, *op. cit.*, p.112.
39   Majdalany, *op. cit.*, p.160.

                            CHAPTER 10
1   Kippenberger, *op. cit.*, p.358.
2   Quoted in US Army Training Memorandum No.2, *Lessons From the Italian Campaign 1 February–30 September 1944*, p.76. PRO CAB 106/361.
3   Mission Française près de la Ve Armée, *op. cit.*, Annexe No.2, p.1.
4   Molony, *op. cit.*, p.779.
5   D.J.C. Pringle and W.A. Glue, *20 Battalion and Armoured Regiment*, Department of Internal Affairs, Wellington, 1957, p.377.
6   Quoted in Molony, *loc. cit.*
7   Böhmler, *op. cit.*, p.212.
8   X British Corps, Interrogations of Prisoners of War Report No.338, 19 February 1944, p.1. SHAT 10P 38.
9   *Ibid.*, p.3.
10   X British Corps, Interrogations of Prisoners of War Report No.451, 18 March 1944, p.1 SHAT 10P 38.
11   NZ Prisoners of War Cage, 23 March 1944, p.1. SHAT 10P 37.
12   Von Senger und Etterlin, Diary, *op. cit.*, p.215.
13   Clark Diary, *op. cit.*, p.23.
14   Clark Diary, *op. cit.*, p.25.
15   Clark Interview, *op. cit.*, p.6.
16   Molony, *op. cit.*, pp.835–6.
17   S.T. Matthews, Interview with Brigadier K.W.D. Strong, 30 October 1947, p.6. NA (MMS) RG 319 Box 15.
18   S.T. Matthews and J.D. Hamilton, Interview with Lt-Gen. W.D. Morgan, 2 September 1948, p.13. NA (MMS) RG 319 Box 15.
19   S.T. Matthews, Interview with Field Marshal Alexander, 10–15 January 1944, p.12. NA (MMS) RG 319 Box 5.
20   Outgoing Message AFHQ From: Fairbanks (signed Wilson) To: Air Ministry for British COS, inf. Britman Washington for JCS, 20 February 1944, pp.1–2. PRO WO 204/10388. (Emphasis in original.)
21   Report by Col. J.F. Torrence Jr, GSC G–3 Ops, included in *Report by G–3 Training Section (HQ Med TO US Army) on Visits to Units July 1943–April 1945*, n.d., p.2. PRQ WO 204/1282.
22   AFHQ G–3 Section, Memorandum on Operations in Italy, 27 February 1944, p.3. PRO WO 204/1484.
23   Juin, *Mémoires, op. cit.*, p.279.

24 CEF 3ᵉ Bureau, Ref: 654/CEF/3/TS, Juin to Clark, 21 February 1944, pp.2–4. SHAT IOP 56.

25 Von Senger und Etterlin, *Neither Fear. . .*, *op. cit.*, p.206.

26 Quoted in Molony, *op. cit.*, p.833.

27 Quoted *loc. cit.*

28 Quoted *ibid.*, p.835.

29 Quoted in Smith, *op. cit.*, p.95.

30 W.G. Stevens, *op. cit.*, p.92.

31 Quoted in P. Singleton-Gates, *General Lord Freyberg VC*, Michael Joseph, 1963, p.263.

32 Quoted in R. Parkinson, *A Day's March Nearer Home*, Hart-Davis MacGibbon, 1974, p.266.

33 AFHQ Incoming Message, From: Air Ministry, To: AFHQ and JSM Washington, Ref: OZ1046, 26 February 1944, p.1. PRO WO 204/1454.

34 AFHQ Outgoing Message, From: Wilson, To: ACMF for Alexander, Ref: 56453, 25 February 1944, p.1. PRO WO 204/1454. OVERLORD was the code-name for the cross-Channel assault.

35 *Ibid.*

36 Draft Copy of Outgoing Telegram, From: MEDCOS at AFHQ, To: AWAR for CCS, n.d. (but sent out 9 March), p.1. PRO WO 204/1454.

37 Quoted in J.N. Mackay, *History of the 7th Gurkha Rifles*, Blackwood, 1962, p.249.

38 Quoted in Stevens, *2 Gurkhas*, *op. cit.*, p.106.

39 Quoted in Cochrane, *op. cit.*, pp.117 and 146.

40 Quoted in Anon., *Historical Records of the Queen's Own Cameron Highlanders 1932–48*, Blackwood, 1952, p.341.

41 Quoted in Mackay, *loc. cit.*

42 Stevenes, *4 Indian Division*, *op. cit.*, p.295.

43 Quoted in R.M. Burdon, *24 Battalion*, Department of Internal Affairs, Wellington, 1961, p.230.

44 W.D. Dawson, *18 Battalion and Armoured Regiment*, Department of Internal Affairs, Wellington, 1961, p.427.

45 Pringle and Glue, *op. cit.*, p.373.

46 AFHQ G–2 Intelligence Notes No.47, 22 February 1944, p.C8. PRO WO 204/985.

47 AFHQ G–2 Intelligence Notes No.57, 2 May 1944, p.C7. PRO WO 204/986.

48 CEF 2ᵉ Bureau, Prisoner of War Interrogations, January–June 1944. SHAT IOP 37.

49 Quoted in Phillips, *op. cit.*, p.258.

50 Quoted in 2ᵉ DIM, *op. cit.*, p.109.

51   P.I. Schulz, *The 85th Division in World War II*, Infantry Journal Press, Washington, 1949, pp.53–5.

52   L.F. Ellis, *The Welsh Guards at War*, Gale & Polden, Aldershot, 1946, pp.132–3.

53   Quoted in E.G. Godfrey, *History of the Duke of Cornwall's Light Infantry 1939–45*, pvte. pub., 1966, p.190.

54   Quoted in C.N. Parkinson, *Always a Fusilier*, Sampson & Low, 1950, p.176.

55   G.F. Ellenberger, *History of the King's Own Yorkshire Light Infantry*, vol.6, Gale & Polden, Aldershot, 1961, p.89.

56   Ellis, *op. cit.*, p.131.

57   M. Howard and G. Sparrow, *The Coldstream Guards 1920–46*, Oxford University Press, 1951, p.212.

58   B. Fergusson, *The Black Watch and the King's Enemies*, Collins, 1950, p.202.

59   H.D. Chaplin, *The Queen's Own Royal West Kent Regiment 1920–50*, pvte. pub., Maidstone, 1959, p.304.

60   Schultz, *op. cit.*, p.55.

61   B. Madden, *The History of the 6th Battalion the Black Watch 1939–45*, Leslie, Perth, 1948, p.41.

62   Nicolson, *Grenadier Guards, op. cit.*, p.418.

63   *Ibid.*, p.419, and Madden, *op. cit.*, p.41 (note).

64   Quoted in D. Erskine, *The Scots Guards 1919–55*, William Clowes, 1956, p.195.

65   Stevens, *4 Indian Division, op. cit.*, p.297.

66   Quoted in E. Puttick, *25 Battalion*, Department of Internal Affairs, Wellington, 1958, p.383.

CHAPTER 11

1   Von Senger und Etterlin, *Neither Fear . . ., op. cit.*, p.215.

2   Transcript of speech by Lieutenant-General Ira C. Eaker over the Blue Network, 15 March 1944, pp.1–2. NA (MMS) RG 319 Box 255.

3   Letter from Eaker to Twining (copy), 17 March 1944, p.2. NA (MMS) RG 319 Box 255.

4   Quoted in Cody, *op. cit.*, p.365.

5   Quoted in Stevens, *4 Indian Division, op. cit.*, p.298.

6   E.D. Smith, *Even the Brave Falter*, Robert Hale, 1979, p.12.

7   AFHQ G–2 Intelligence Notes No.57, *loc. cit.*

8   Quoted in Böhmler, *op. cit.*, pp.210–11.

9   Quoted in J. Piekalkiewicz, *Cassino: Anatomy of a Battle*, Orbis, London, 1982, p.130.
10   X Corps Interrogation of Prisoners of War Report, No.454, 18 March 1944, p.1. SHAT 1OP 38.
11   *Ibid.*, pp.2–3.
12   Lieutenant-Colonel G.S. Nangle, CO 1/9 Gurkhas, quoted in Majdalany, *op. cit.*, p.181.
13   Quoted in Puttick, *op. cit.*, pp.393–4.
14   Quoted in Trevelyan, *op. cit.*, p.201.
15   Quoted in Puttick, *op. cit.*, pp.394–5.
16   Quoted in Trevelyan, *op. cit.*, p.201.
17   Quoted in Puttick, *op. cit.*, p.396.
18   Phillips, *op. cit.*, p.273.
19   Fifth Army Incoming Message, From: Main NZ Corps To: G–3 CP Fifth Army, 20.00hrs., 15 March 1944. WNRC (MMFB) RG 94 105–2.2 Box 2116.
20   Quoted in Puttick, *op. cit.*, p.400.
21   *Ibid.*, p.403.
22   Phillips, *op. cit.*, p.275.
23   Major D.A. Beckett quoted in Smith, *Cassino, op. cit.*, p.109.
24   Phillips, *op. cit.*, p.279.
25   F.D. Norton, *26 Battalion*, Department of Internal Affairs, Wellington, 1952, pp.354–5.
26   Historical Notes on Operation Dickens, 15–23 March, p.7. PRO WO 204/8287.
27   CG Fifth Army, Cassino Operations: Lessons Learnt 15–24 March, April 1944, p.4. PRO WO 204/7566.
28   Letter to Air Marshal Portal, 16 April 1944. Quoted in Slessor, *op. cit.*, pp.373–4.
29   Quoted in N. Macmillan, *The Royal Air Force in the World War*, Harrap, 1949, vol.3, p.244.
30   CG Fifth Army, Cassino Operations . . ., *loc. cit.*
31   Canadian Historical Section Report No.20, p.4. NA (MMS) RG 319 Box 255.
32   Quoted in Phillips, *op. cit.*, p.290.
33   Von Senger und Etterlin, *Neither Fear . . ., op. cit.*, p.216.
34   X Corps Prisoner of War Interrogation Report No. 464, 23 March 1944, pp.1–2. SHAT 1OP 38.
35   Quoted in Böhmler, *op. cit.*, p.239.
36   Captain J.R. McCorquindale, quoted in Burdon, *op. cit.*, p.235.
37   Quoted in Puttick, *op. cit.*, pp.405–6.

38   Letter, 22 June 1944, p.2, appended to Operations of New Zealand Corps, February 3–March 26 1944. PRO CAB 106/366.

39   Quoted in Phillips, *op. cit.*, p.289.

40   Quoted in Pringle and Glue, *op. cit.*, pp.383 and 385.

41   Quoted in Smith, *Cassino, op. cit.*, p.116.

42   Lieutenant J. Miles, quoted in C. Forty, *Fifth Army at War*, Ian Allen, Shepperton, 1980, p.58.

43   Quoted in Stevens, *4 Indian Division, op. cit.*, p.302.

44   Quoted in J.F. Cody, *21 Battalion*, Department of Internal Affairs, Wellington, 1953, p.324.

45   Quoted in Piekalkiewicz, *op. cit.*, p.136.

46   XIV Panzer Corps Morning Report, 17 March 1944. Extracts from XIV Panzer Corps Reports March 1944, p.1. NA (MMS). Translation from GMDS File 58199/9.

47   Quoted in Phillips, *op. cit.*, p.292.

48   Quoted in Molony, *op. cit.*, p.611.

49   Quoted in Phillips, *op. cit.*, p.293.

50   *Ibid.*, p.294.

51   Lieutenant J.G. Furness quoted in D.W. Sinclair, *19 Battalion and Armoured Regiment*, Department of Internal Affairs, Wellington, 1954, pp.380–1.

52   XIV Panzer Corps Evening Report 17 March 1944. Excerpts . . ., *op. cit.*, p.2.

53   From: Allied Armies in Italy To: Fifth Army Public Relations Office, 17 March 1944. WNRC (MMFB) RG94 105–2.2 Box 2117.

54   Clark Diary, *op. cit.*, pp.27–8.

55   Outgoing Message AFHQ, From: Wilson To: Air Ministries for British Chiefs of Staff, Ref: 65765, 17 March 1944. PRO WO 204/1455.

56   Incoming Message, AFHQ, From: Air Ministry, To: HQ MAAF Repeated Britman Washington Freedom, Ref: OZ 1466, 18 March 1944. PRO WO 204/1455.

57   Quoted in Burdon, *op. cit.*, p.237 (emphasis in original).

58   Norton, *op. cit.*, p.376.

59   Quoted in von Senger und Etterlin, *Diary, op. cit.*, p.89.

60   Clark Diary, *op. cit.*, p.28.

61   Quoted in Phillips, *op. cit.*, p.305.

62   Quoted in Cody, *28 Battalion, op. cit.*, p.369 (emphasis in original).

63   Quoted *ibid.*, p.370.

64   Quoted in XIV Panzer Corps to Tenth Army, 19 March 1944, XIV Panzer Corps Miscellaneous Appendices March 1944, p.1. NA (MMS) from GMDS File 58199/21.

65 Quoted in T.A. Martin, *The Essex Regiment 1929–50*, pvte. pub., London, 1952, p.314.
66 Quoted *ibid.*, p.315.
67 Quoted in Phillips, *op. cit.*, p.309.
68 Smith, *Even the Brave, op. cit.*, p.17.
69 Quoted in Pringle and Glue, *op. cit.*, p.388.
70 *Ibid.*, p.394.
71 Phillips, *op. cit.*, p.312.
72 Quoted in Churchill, *op. cit.*, vol.10, p.162.
73 Quoted in Molony, *op. cit.*, p.799.
74 Juin, *Mémoires, op. cit.*, p.282.
75 Phillips, *op. cit.*, p.314.
76 Norton, *op. cit.*, p.377.
77 Smith, *Even the Brave, op. cit.*, p.18.
78 Quoted in Phillips, *op. cit.*, p.320.
79 A. Ross, *23 Battalion*, Department of Internal Affairs, Wellington, 1959, p.329.
80 Phillips, *op. cit.*, p.322.
81 XIV Panzer Corps, Morning Report, 20 March 1944, Extracts From . . . Reports, *op. cit.*, p.4.
82 XIV Panzer Corps, Appreciation of the Situation, 20 March 1944, XIV Panzer Corps Miscellaneous . . ., *op. cit.*, pp.3–4.
83 *Ibid.*, p.4.
84 New Zealand Corps Intelligence Summary No.58, 21 March 1944, p.2. WNRC (MMFB) RG 94 105–2.2 (Box 2116).
85 Clark, *op. cit.*, p.314.
86 Eaker to Arnold, 21 March 1944 (Copy), p.1. NA (MMS) RG 319 Box 255.
87 Phillips, *op. cit.*, p.327.
88 Quoted in Ross, *op. cit.*, pp.341–2.
89 XIV Panzer Corps, Evening Report, 21 March 1944, Extracts From . . . Reports, *op. cit.*, p.5.
90 XIV Panzer Corps, Evening Report, 22 March 1944, *ibid.*, p.6.
91 Quoted in Phillips, *op. cit.*, pp.328 and 330.
92 Sinclair, *op. cit.*, p.391.
93 Ross, *op. cit.*, p. 337.
94 Quoted in Stevens, *4 Indian Division, op. cit.*, p.309.
95 Quoted *ibid.*, p.310.
96 Quoted in Stevens, *2nd Gurkhas, op. cit.*, p.108.
97 W. Robson, *Letters From a Soldier*, Faber & Faber, 1960, pp.80–2.
98 Smith, *Cassino, op. cit.*, p.138.

99   Quoted in Böhmler, *op. cit.*, p.240.
100 Canadian Historical Section Report, *op. cit.*, p.4.
101 Quoted in Bryant, *op. cit.*, vol.2, p.141.

CHAPTER 12

1   Quoted in Churchill, *op. cit.*, vol.10, p.145.
2   Notes on a Conference Held Friday May 5th 1944 . . ., p.12. WNRC (MMFB) RG 94 105–3.22 (Box 2371).
3   From: Fairbanks To: Air Ministry, 19 March 1944, Ref: 1299, p.2. PRO WO 204/10388.
4   E.J. Fisher, *Cassino to the Alps* (US Army in World War Two), Government Printing Office, Washington, 1967, p.36.
5   Clark Interview, *op. cit.*, p.8.
6   *Ibid.*, p.9.
7   S.T. Matthews. Interview with Colonel Robert J. Wood, 4 March 1948, p.2. NA (MMS) RG 319 (Box 5).
8   Truscott, *op. cit.*, pp.368–9.
9   CEF 3ᵉ Bureau, 9 March 1944, Ref: 113/CEF/3/TS, Rapport sur les opérations du CEF de 23 février–4 mars, p.3. SHAT 10P 56.
10   Juin to de Gaulle, 27 April 1944, Ref: 224/CEF/3/TS, pp.1–2. SHAT 10P 56.
11   Juin to de Gaulle, 8 May 1944, Ref: 1320/CEF/3/TS, p.2. SHAT 10P 56.
12   R. Jars, *La campagne d'Italie 1943–45*, Payot, Paris, 1954, p.141.
13   Carpentier, *op. cit.*, p.108.
14   Quoted in Boulle, *op. cit.*, vol.1, pp.196–7.
15   Chambe, *Epopée, op. cit.*, p.75.
16   Matthews, Interview with Colonel Wood, *loc. cit.*
17   Both quoted in Canadian Historical Report, *op. cit.*, p.5.
18   Quoted in F.M. Sallager, *Operation Strangle . . . a case study in tactical air interdiction* (Rand Corporation Report R–851–PR), Rand Corporation, Santa Monica, 1972, p.19.
19   AFHQ G–3, Colonel Jenkins to Lieutenant-Colonel M.C.D.L. Reynolds, 4 April 1944. PRO WO 204/1455.
20   Quoted in Slessor, *op. cit.*, p.570.
21   Sallager, *op. cit.*, pp.45–6 (emphasis in original).
22   Quoted *ibid.*, p.46.
23   *Ibid.*, p.54.
24   Slessor, *op. cit.*, pp.571–2 (emphasis in original).
25   Quoted in J.P. Delaney, *The Blue Devils in Italy*, Infantry Journal Press, Washington, 1947, p.50.

26 J.C. Fry, *Combat Soldier*, National Press, Washington, 1968, pp.5 and 11.

27 Howard and Sparrow, *op. cit.*, p.218.

28 Nicolson, *Grenadier Guards, op. cit.*, p.422.

29 F. Majdalany, *The Monastery*, John Lane, London, 1946, p.24.

30 I.A. McKee, *5 Battalion Northamptonshire Regiment in Italy*, pvte. pub., Tamsweg (Austria), 1945, p.27.

31 Nicolson, *Grenadier Guards, loc. cit.*

32 Robson, *op. cit.*, pp.101–2.

33 Quoted in Trevelyan, *op. cit.*, p.208.

34 Quoted in AFHQ Intelligence Notes, No. 57, *loc. cit.*

35 Quoted in Trevelyan, *op. cit.*, p.209.

36 Majdalany, *Monastery, op. cit.*, pp.51 and 96 (emphasis in the original).

37 B.J.G. Madden, *History of the 6th Battalion the Black Watch, 1939–45*, Leslie, Perth, 1948, p.60.

38 Nicolson, *Grenadier Guards, op. cit.*, pp.424–5.

39 Lieutenant P. Royle (RA) quoted in Trevelyan, *op. cit.*, p.209.

40 Quoted in J. Henderson, *22 Battalion,* Department of Internal Affairs, Wellington, 1958, p.285.

41 Quoted in Cody, *21 Battalion, op. cit.*, p.324.

CHAPTER 13

1 II Polish Corps HQ, Operations of II Polish Corps Against Monte Cassino, p.28. PRO WO 204/8221.

2 Quoted in D. How, *The 8th Hussars*, Maritime Publishers, Sussex (New Brunswick), 1964, p.202.

3 C.N. Parkinson, *op. cit.*, pp.189–90.

4 Quoted in Piekalkiewicz, *op. cit.*, p.166.

5 C.N. Parkinson, *op. cit.*, pp.186–7.

6 Quoted in W.E.H. Condon, *The Frontier Force Regiment*, Gale & Polden, Aldershot, 1962, p.322.

7 R.C.B. Anderson, *History of the (1st) Argyll and Sutherland Highlanders 1939–45*, Constable, Edinburgh, 1956, p.87.

8 Anon, *The Tiger Triumphs*, HMSO, 1946, p.70.

9 Pal, *op. cit.*, p.164.

10 A.P. de T. Daniell, 'The Battle for Cassino May 1944', *Royal Engineers Journal*, 1957, p.294.

11 War Diary 4 Division HQ, 05.00, 12 May 1944. PRO WO 170/407.

12 War Diary 2 King's Regiment, 11 May 1944. PRO WO 170/1418.

13   War Diary 2 Somerset Light Infantry, 11 and 12 May 1944. PRO WO
      170/1479 (author's emphasis).
14   War Diary 28 Brigade HQ, 12 May 1944. PRO WO 170/596.
15   War Diary 2 King's, *loc. cit.*
16   War Diary 2 Somerset Light Infantry, *loc. cit.*
17   War Diary 4 Division HQ, *loc. cit.*
18   Jackson, *op. cit.*, p.97. See also 4 Division Intelligence Summary
      No.21, 23 May 1944, p.1. Appended to War Diary, *loc. cit.*
19   War Diary 4 Division, 20.00, 12 May 1944, *loc. cit.*
20   *Tiger Triumphs, op. cit.*, p.77.
21   Godfrey, *op. cit.*, p.203.
22   *Tiger Triumphs, op. cit.*, p.78.
23   Godfrey, *op. cit.*, p.201.
24   C.N. Parkinson, *op. cit.*, p.191.
25   Madden, *op. cit.*, p.65.
26   Fergusson, *op. cit.*, p.209.
27   Quoted in R.L.V.B.ffrench, *History of the 17/21 Lancers 1922–59*,
      Macmillan, 1962, p.165.
28   See Chapter 14.
29   Jackson, *op. cit.*, p.114.
30   War Diary 4 Division HQ, 21.05, 13 May 1944, *loc. cit.*
31   Jackson, *op. cit.*, p.115.
32   Quoted in T.P.D. Scott, *The Irish Brigade in Italy March–July 1944*
      (typescript), n.d., p.19. PRO WO 204/10425.
33   *Ibid.*, p.18.
34   J. Horsfall, *Fling Our Banner to the Wind*, Roundwood Press, Kine-
      ton, 1978, p.45.
35   Majdalany, *Monastery, op. cit.*, p.105.
36   Quoted in Scott, *op. cit.*, p.22.
37   Sinclair, *op. cit.*, pp.96–7.
38   Robson, *op. cit.*, pp.96–7.
39   Horsfall, *op. cit.*, p.71.
40   See Chapter 15.
41   Quoted in G.W.L. Nicholson, *The Canadians in Italy*, Department
      of National Defence, Ottawa, 1956, p.407.
42   Quoted in Churchill, *op. cit.*, vol.10, pp.248–9.

CHAPTER 14

1   S. Bieganski, *Dzialania 2 Korpusu We Wloszech*, Komisja His-
      toryczna 2-Go Korpusu, London, 1963, vol.1, pp.180–1.

2 W. Anders, *An Army in Exile*, Macmillan, 1949, p.174.

3 Majdalany, *Monastery, op. cit.*, p.68.

4 Bieganski, *op. cit.*, p.280 (emphasis in original).

5 M. Wańkowicz, *Bylo To Pod Monte Cassino*, Komitetu Obschodu Dziesieciolecia Bitwy o Monte Cassino, London, 1954, p.10.

6 J. Harvey (ed.), *The War Diaries of Oliver Harvey 1941–45*, Collins, 1978, p.336.

7 *Ibid.*, p.331, and G. Kolko, *The Politics of War*, Random House, New York, 1969, p.113.

8 Quoted in Anders, *op. cit.*, p.159.

9 W. Steinauer, *Historia 2 Grupy Artylerii*, Wydawnictwo 2 Grupy Artylerii, Rome, n.d., unpaginated.

10 J. Bielatowicz, *Bitwa o Monte Cassino*, Stowarzyszenie Polskich Kombatantów, London, 1952, pp.22–3.

11 M. Wańkowicz, *Szkice Spod Monte Cassino*, Wiedza Powszechna, Warsaw, 1980, p.24.

12 Quoted in Anders, *op. cit.*, p.155.

13 Horsfall, *op. cit.*, p.33.

14 Quoted in Trevelyan, *Rome '44, op. cit.*, p.269.

15 C. Ray, *Algiers to Austria: The History of 78 Division in World War II*, Eyre & Spottiswoode, 1952, p.120.

16 McKee, *op. cit.*, p.34.

17 II Polish Corps, The Operations of II Polish Corps Against Monte Cassino, n.d., p.42. PRO WO 204/8221 (emphasis in original).

18 Anders, *op. cit.*, p.164.

19 Scott, *op. cit.*, p.12.

20 Quoted in C. Connell, *Monte Cassino*, Elek, 1963, p.167 (emphasis in original).

21 Colonel H. Piatkowski, 'The Second Polish Corps in the Battle for Monte Cassino', *Army Quarterly*, vol.48, October 1945, pp.59–60.

22 Quoted in Connell, *op. cit.*, p.177.

23 II Polish Corps, *op. cit.*, p.26.

24 Quoted in Connell, *op. cit.*, p.163.

25 Quoted in Wańkowicz, *Szkice, op. cit.*, pp.22–3.

26 *Ibid.*

27 Quoted in Bielatowicz, *op. cit.*, p.15.

28 Wańkowicz, *Szkice, op. cit.*, p.59.

29 Quoted in Smith, *Cassino, op. cit.*, p.162.

30 II Polish Corps, *op. cit.*, p.34.

31 *Ibid.*, pp.31–2.

32 Wańkowicz, *Szkice, op. cit.*, p.78.

33   Quoted in Connell, *op. cit.*, p.185.
34   Quoted *ibid.*, pp.182–3.
35   II Polish Corps, *op. cit.*, p.34.
36   *Ibid.*, p.30.
37   Quoted in Connell, *op. cit.*, p.167.
38   Wańkowicz, *Szkice, op. cit.*, pp.69–70.
39   Quoted in Trevelyan, *Rome, '44, op. cit.*, pp.270–1.
40   Wańkowicz, *Szkice, op. cit.*, p.66.
41   Quoted in Connell, *op. cit.*, p.171.
42   Quoted in Böhmler, *op. cit.*, p.266.
43   Wańkowicz, *Szkice, op. cit.*, p.60.
44   Quoted in Connell, *op. cit.*, p.169.
45   Quoted *ibid.*, p.162.
46   Quoted *ibid.*, p.179.
47   Nicolson, *Grenadier Guards, op. cit.*, p.427.
48   Wańkowicz, *Szkice, op. cit.*, pp.79–86.
49   Wańkowicz, *Bylo ńo Pod, op. cit.*, p.106.
50   *Ibid.*
51   Wańkowicz, *Szkice, op. cit.*, p.104.
52   *Ibid.*, p.61.
53   *Ibid.*, p.105.
54   Quoted in Connell, *op. cit.*, p.158
55   Wańkowicz, *Szkice, op. cit.*, p.101.
56   *Ibid.*, pp.106 and 129.
57   Quoted in Trevelyan, *Rome '44, op. cit.*, p.273.
58   Quoted in Connell, *op. cit.*, p.162.
59   Quoted *ibid.*
60   Kesselring, *op. cit.*, p.202.
61   Von Vietinghoff, *op. cit.*, p.60.
62   Quoted in Connell, *op. cit.*, p.162.
63   Quoted in Piekalkiewicz, *op. cit.*, p.181.

CHAPTER 15

1   Quoted in Juin, *Mémoires, op. cit.*, pp.306–9.
2   Quoted in Heurgnon, *op. cit.*, p.140.
3   Quoted in B. Susbielle, 'Campagne d'Italie: du Garigliano au Mayo avec un bataillon de tirailleurs marocains', *Revue Historique de l'Armée*, 1967, pp.136–8.
4   2 DIM, Directive pour le combat d'infanterie, Ref: 3/11 IS–O–ID, 7 May 1944. SHAT (FPU) I I P 38 (emphasis in original).

5   X British Corps, Interrogation of Prisoners of War Report No.550, 15 May 1944, p.4. SHAT 10P 38.
6   H.G. von Vietinghoff, The Campaign in Italy: the Operation of 71 Division During the Month of May 1944, p.15. NA (MMS) MS C–025.
7   Susbielle, *op. cit.*, p.142.
8   Infanterie Divisionnaire, 2 DIM, Renseignements tirés de la campagne d'Italie à partir de la bataille de rupture du Garigliano, Ref: 1491/111S/ID, 25 June 1944, p.1. SHAT (FPU) 11P. 38.
9   Capitaine Foucaucourt, '15 heures de combat dans une compagnie de voltigeurs', 11 June 1944, p.1. SHAT (FPU) 12 P 69.
10   Quoted in 2eme Division Marocaine, *op. cit.*, pp.144–5.
11   Quoted *ibid.*, p.148.
12   Susbielle, *op. cit.*, p.144.
13   Quoted in 2e Division Marocaine, *op. cit.*, p.154.
14   Sous-lieutenant Fillet, Rapport sur le combat de Ceresola 11–12 mai 1944, n.d., p.1. SHAT (FPU) 11P 31.
15   Historique du 6 RTM – Période Italienne, n.d., unsigned, p.6. SHAT (FPU) 12P 74.
16   JMO 2 DIM, Compte rendu sommaire des opérations du 11 au 17 mai, 12 May 1944. SHAT (FPU) 11P 38.
17   JMO 24 Bataillon de Marche, 11–12 May 1944. SHAT (FPU) 12P 72.
18   JMO 13 Demi-Brigade Légion Etrangère, 12 May 1944. SHAT (FPU) 12P 81.
19   Conférence, Algers 13 juillet 1944, par Gandoet du Commissariat à la Guerre sur 'La campagne d'Italie', pp.9–10. SHAT 10P 56.
20   Chambe, *Epopée, op. cit.*, p.113, and Conférence Algers, *supra*, p.9.
21   '15 heures de combat', *op. cit.*, p.3.
22   Fry, *op. cit.*, p.17.
23   Fisher, *op. cit.*, p.49.
24   Quoted *ibid.*, p.68.
25   Quoted in Starr, *op. cit.*, p.205.
26   Fry, *op. cit.*, p.29.
27   Fisher, *op. cit.*, p.72.
28   Quoted in J.P. Delaney, *The Blue Devils in Italy*, Infantry Journal Press, Washington, 1947, p.70.
29   This remarkable story is documented in Fisher, *op. cit.*, pp.51–2.
30   *Ibid.*, p.69.
31   Quoted in Chambe, *Epopée, op. cit.*, p.137.
32   Quoted in 'De l'Ornito à Calvo: les premières journées de l'offensive de printemps au 2/5 RTM', unsigned, n.d., p.2. SHAT (FPU) 12P 73.

33   Quoted in 2ᵉ Division Marocaine, *op. cit.*, pp.164–5.
34   2 DIM, Directive pour le combat, *op. cit.*, p.2.
35   Quoted in Chambe, *Epopée, op. cit.*, p.144.
36   Susbielle, *op. cit.*, pp.147–8.
37   'De l'Ornito à Calvo', *op. cit.*, p.5.
38   Vietinghoff, Operations of 71 Division, *op. cit.*, pp.9 and 7–8.
39   Quoted in Boulle, *op. cit.*, vol.2, p.302.
40   'De l'Ornito à Calvo', *op. cit.*, p.7.
41   Susbielle, *op. cit.*, p.150.
42   Robichon, *op. cit.*, p.304.
43   JMO 21 Bataillon de Marche, *op. cit.*, 13 May 1944.
44   Unsigned notes (probably by Commandant Gandoet) on the taking of Castelforte, n.d., unpaginated, SHAT 10P 56.
45   Robichon, *op. cit.*, p.298.
46   Chambe, *Epopée, op. cit.*, p.164.
47   JMO 3/6 RTM, 13 May 1944. SHAT (FPU) 12P 76.
48   Quoted in Robichon, *op. cit.*, p.300.
49   Susbielle, *op. cit.*, p.151.
50   Quoted in Chambe, *Epopée, op. cit.*, p.337.
51   JMO 11 Bataillon de Marche, 16 May 1944. SHAT (FPU) 12P 72.
52   *Ibid.*, 17 May 1944.
53   *Ibid.*, 16 May 1944.
54   3ᵉ Bureau, 1 DMI, Ordre Générale No.5, 16 May 1944. SHAT (FPU) 11P 11.
55   JMO 24 Bataillon de Marche, *op.. cit.*, 17 May 1944.
56   JMO 11 Bataillon de Marche, *loc. cit.*
57   General D. Brosset, Note de mise en garde, 18 May 1944. SHAT (FPU) 11P 6.
58   JMO 21 Bataillon de Marche, *op. cit.*, 14, 15, 24, 25 May 1944.
59   JMO 24 Bataillon de Marche, *op. cit.*, 17 May 1944.
60   JMO 11 Bataillon de Marche, *op. cit.*, 17 May 1944.
61   JMO Etat-Major, 1 DMI, 20 May 1944. SHAT (FPU) 11P 6.
62   Chambe, *Epopée, op. cit.*, pp.180–1.
63   Quoted in Fisher, *op. cit.*, p.79.
64   Quoted in Chambe, *Epopée, op. cit.*, p.185.
65   Quoted in Canadian Historical Report, *op. cit.*, p.2.
66   Vietinghoff, Operations of 71 Division, *op. cit.*, pp.27, 29 and 30.
67   Quoted in C. Ray, *Algiers to Austria: the History of 78 Division in World War II*, Eyre & Spottiswoode, 1952, pp.134–5.
68   OBSW to all Subordinate Headquarters, 30 May 1944, File Ref: OBSW/Ia Nr. 5764/44. NA (MMS) RG 319 Box 5.

69 Quoted in W. Haupt, *Kriegsschauplatz Italien 1943–45*, Motorbuch Verlag, Stuttgart, 1977, p.141.

70 Quoted in 2ᵉ Division Marocaine, *op. cit.*, p.187.

71 Heurgnon, *op. cit.*, pp.172 and 166–7.

72 JMO I/I RTM, 13 May 1944. SHAT (FPU) 12P 62.

73 Robson, *Letters, op. cit.*, p.89.

74 M. Gander, *After These Many Quests*, Macdonald, 1949, p.183.

75 Quoted in Trevelyan, *Rome '44, op. cit.*, p.277.

76 Fry, *op. cit.*, p.43.

77 General A. Guillaume, Note au sujet de l'emploi des Goums sur le Front Italien, 26 January 1944, pp.1 and 3. SHAT 10P 56.

78 Lieutenant Gaudron (3/I RTM), Combat du 17 mai 1944 au Fragoloso, pp.1–2. SHAT (FPU) 12P 61.

79 *Ibid.*, p.1.

80 Anonymous member of 4 DMM, SHAT (FPU) 11P 90.

81 Vietinghoff, Operations of 71 Division, *op. cit.*, pp.40–1.

82 Von Senger und Etterlin, Diary, *op. cit.*, pp.129–30.

83 Quoted in Boulle, *op. cit.*, vol.2, p.305.

84 Starr, *op. cit.*, p.206.

85 Kesselring, *op. cit.*, p.202.

86 Sevareid, *op. cit.*, p.389.

87 Fry, *op. cit.*, p.92.

88 Fry, *op. cit.*, p.43.

89 Quoted in Schulz, *op. cit.*, p.101.

90 Quoted in Boulle, *loc. cit.*

91 JMO 3/6 RTM, 23 and 24 May 1944. SHAT (FPU) 12P 76.

92 JMO I/4 RTM, 23 May 1944. SHAT (FPU) 12P 69.

93 Historique du 6 RTM, *op. cit.*, p.8.

94 Gandoet Conférence, *op. cit.*, p.15.

95 3 Alpine Infantry Battalion, After Action Report, 18-22 May 1944, pp.2–4. NA (MMS) RG 319 Box 8.

96 *Kampfgruppe* Nagel, After-Action Report, 13–22 May, unpaginated, NA (MMS) *loc. cit.*

97 2ᵉ Bureau, I DMI, Bulletin de renseignements quotidiens, 20 May 1944. SHAT (FPU) 11P 8.

CHAPTER 16

1 T.H. Radall, *West Novas: the History of the West Nova Scotia Regiment.* pvte. pub., Liverpool (N.S.), 1947, p.190.

2 Quoted in Nicolson, *op. cit.*, p.408.

3   Raddall, *loc. cit.*
4   F. Mowat, *The Regiment*, McClelland, Toronto, 1973, p.183.
5   K. Beattie, *Dileas: The History of the 48th Highlanders of Canada*, pvte. pub., Toronto, 1957, pp.524 and 525.
6   *Ibid.*, p.526.
7   Jackson, *op. cit.*, pp.137-8.
8   G.R. Stevens, *Princess Patricia's Canadian Light Infantry*, pvte. pub., Alberta, 1959, p.154.
9   A.D. Malcolm, *The History of the Argyll and Sutherland Highlanders, 8 Battalion, 1939-45*, Nelson, 1949, p.194.
10   Nicholson, *op. cit.*, p.411.
11   Stevens, *Princess Patricia's op. cit.*, pp.150-1.
12   North Irish Horse Battle Report quoted in B. Perrett, *Mud and Blood: Infantry/Tank Operations in World War II*, Robert Hale, 1975, p.180.
13   Quoted in Nicholson, *op. cit.*, p.417.
14   Quoted in How, *op. cit.*, p.203.
15   Mowat, *op. cit.*, p.186.
16   Quoted in G. Roy, *Sinews of Steel: the History of the British Columbia Dragoons*, pvte. pub., 1965, p.244.
17   HO Canadian Infantry Division, 'I Canadian Division in the Liri Valley 15-28 May 1944', n.d. Part I (by Vokes), p.9. PRO WO 204/8202.
18   Stevens, *Princess Patricia's, op. cit.*, p.156.
19   Beattie, *op. cit.*, p.542.
20   *Ibid.*, pp.543-4. (First emphasis in original, second is the author's.)
21   *Ibid.*, p.544.
22   Quoted *ibid.*, p.566.
23   *Ibid.*, pp.558-9.
24   Quoted *ibid.*, p.562.
25   Quoted *Ibid.*, p.567-8.
26   Quoted in Stevens, *Princess Patricia's op. cit.*, p.161.
27   Princess Patricia's Canadian Light Infantry Narrative, 11 May–2 June 1944: Battle of the Hitler Line. Appendix A to HQ I Canadian Division, *op. cit.*, Part V, p.4.
28   Seaforth Highlanders of Canada Narrative, 22–24 May 1944, Appendix B to *ibid.*, Part V, p.2.
29   Loyal Edmonton Regiment Narrative, Appendix C to *ibid.*, Part V, p.2.
30   G.R. Stevens, *A City Goes to War: The History of the Loyal Edmonton Regiment*, Charters, Brampton (Ontario), 1964, pp.295-6.

31 Major Miller quoted in Raddall, *op. cit.*, pp.193-4.
32 Quoted *ibid.*, p.195.
33 Quoted in Roy, *op. cit.*, p.248.
34 Quoted in How, *op. cit.*, p.208.
35 Brigadier J.D.B. Smith (5 Armoured Brigade), Crossing of the Melfa, 24–25 May 1944, 1 June 1944, pp.1–2. PRO WO 204/8207.
36 Quoted in How, *op. cit.*, p.210.
37 5 Canadian Armoured Regiment [8 Princess Louise's Hussars], Operations from the Hitler Line to Ceccano 24–31 May 1944, p.2. PRO WO 204/8207.
38 Quoted in How, *op. cit.*, p.208.
39 Quoted *ibid.*, p.210.
40 Lieutenant N.W. Hockin, quoted in Roy, *op. cit.*, pp.258–9.
41 Sergeant H.A. Smitheram, quoted *ibid.*, p.259.
42 Trooper Lowell G. Langin, quoted in How, *op. cit.*, p.213.
43 *Ibid.*, pp.213–14.
44 Quoted *ibid.*, p.214.
45 Brigadier Smith, *op. cit.*, Appendix A (by Major J.W. Eaton), pp. 1–2.
46 Quoted in Roy, *op. cit.*, p.266.

CHAPTER 17

1 Clark Interview, *op. cit.*, p.11.
2 Juin, *Mémoires*, *op. cit.*, pp.316–18.
3 Clark Diary, *op. cit.*, 22 May 1944.
4 *Ibid.*, 20 May 1944.
5 *Ibid.*
6 *Ibid.*
7 *Ibid.*, 22 May 1944.
8 Trevelyan, *Rome '44*, *op. cit.*, p.279. See also the same author's *The Fortress*, *op. cit.*, pp.81–3.
9 H. Greiner, The Battle for Rome and the Retreat Northward, p.3. NA (MMS) Ms D–169.
10 Truscott, *op. cit.*, p.372.
11 Greiner, *op. cit.*, p.6.
12 Oberleutnant Rahn, quoted in H. Greiner, *Kampf um Rom, Inferno am Po*, Kurt Vorwinckel Verlag, Neckargemünd, 1967, p.43.
13 W. Vaughan-Thomas, *Anzio*, Holt, New York, 1961, p.245.
14 Quoted in Fisher, *op. cit.*, p.133.
15 *Ibid.*, p.130.

16   Quoted in D.G. Taggart, *History of 3 Infantry Division in World War 2*, Infantry Journal Press, Washington, 1947, p.157.

17   S.T. Matthews, Interview with Major K.H. Noseck, May 1950, p.3. NA (MMS) RG 319 Box 15.

18   Interview with Lieutenant-Colonel R.M. Flynn, 27 April 1950, p.9. NA (MMS) RG 319 Box 15.

19   Interview with Major C. McFalls Jr, May 1950, p.4. NA (MMS) RG 319 Box 15.

20   Truscott, *op. cit.*, p.375.

21   Sevareid, *op. cit.*, p.393.

22   Churchill, *op. cit.*, vol.10, p.253.

23   Quoted in Nicholson, *op. cit.*, p.437.

24   Quoted in Roy, *op. cit.*, p.262.

25   Quoted in Nicholson, *op. cit.*, p.436.

26   *Ibid.*

27   *Ibid.*

28   General der Infanterie Hans von Greiffenberg and Generalleutnant Wilhelm Schmalz, Division 'Hermann Göring' – Questionnaire, p.6. NA (MMS) Ms C–087b.

29   *Ibid.*, p.8.

30   Fisher, *op. cit.*, pp.169–70.

31   Greiffenberg and Schmalz, *op. cit.*, p.4.

32   Quoted in Trevelyan, *Rome '44, op. cit.*, p.291.

33   Quoted in W.L. Allen, *Anzio: Edge of Disaster*, Elsevier-Dutton, New York, 1978, p.160.

34   Truscott, *op. cit.*, p.375.

35   S.T. Matthews, 'General Clark's Decision to Drive on Rome' (1944), in Greenfield (ed.), *op. cit.*, p.281.

36   Letter, General L.A. Truscott Jr to Chief of Military History, 5 November 1961, p.2. NA (MMS) RG 319 Box 4.

37   Letter, Lieutenant-Colonel R.J. O'Neill to Chief of Military History, copy (n.d.), p.1. NA (MMS) RG 319 Box 4.

38   VI Corps ADC's Journal, 25 May 1944. Copy of single page attached to Carleton letter, *infra cit.*

39   Letter, Brigadier-General D.E. Carleton to Chief of Military History, 12 January 1960, pp.1–2. NA(MMS) RG 319 Box 4.

40   Interview with Major-General J.W. O'Daniel, 12 July 1948, p.1. NA (MMS) RG 319 Box 15.

41   Clark Diary, *op. cit.*, 27 May 1944.

42   Clark Interview, *op. cit.*, pp.3 and 16 (author's emphasis).

43   Matthews, 'General Clark's Decision', *op. cit.*, p.278.

44 Quoted in F. Sheehan, *Anzio: Epic of Bravery*, University of Oklahoma Press, Norman, 1964, p.202.

45 Fifth Army Operations Instruction No.24, 26 May 1944, p.1. WNRC (MMFB) RG 94 105–3.17 to 105–3.18.

46 Clark Interview, *op. cit.*, p.7.

47 Sheehan, *op. cit.*, p.196.

48 Quoted in Adleman and Walton, *op. cit.*, p.248.

49 Clark Interview, *op. cit.*, pp.24–5 (author's emphasis).

50 Clark Diary, *op. cit.*, 19 May 1944.

51 Clark, *Calculated Risk, op. cit.*, p.337.

52 Quoted in B. Harpur, *The Impossible Victory*, William Kimber, 1980, p.110 (emphasis in original).

53 Clark Diary, *op. cit.*, 30 May 1944.

54 Clark Interview, *op. cit.*, p.3.

55 *Ibid.*, p.16.

56 Clark Diary, *op. cit.*, 26 May 1944.

57 Quoted *ibid.*

58 VI Corps Journal and File (Extract), 09.00 and 23.10, 27 May 1944. NA (MMS) RG 319 Box 6.

59 Clark Interview, *op. cit.*, p.18.

60 Sheehan, *op. cit.*, p.204.

61 Quoted in Fisher, *op. cit.*, p.179.

62 Clark Diary, *op. cit.*, 30 May 1944.

63 *Ibid.*, 27 and 30 May 1944.

64 Quoted in Nicholson, *op. cit.*, p.438.

65 Quoted in *Tiger Triumphs, op. cit.*, pp.80 and 81.

66 McKee, *op. cit.*, p.43.

67 Quoted in Stevens, *Princess Patricia's, op. cit.*, p.166.

68 Quoted in Stevens, *City Goes to War, op. cit.*, p.299.

69 2^e Bureau, I DMI, Bulletin de Renseignements Quotidien, 2 June 1944, p.1. SHAT (FPU) I IP 8.

70 OBSW to Subordinate HQs, 30 May 1944, *op. cit.*

71 2^e Bureau 2 DIM, Rapport Quotidien, 29/30 mai 1944, p.3. SHAT (FPU) I IP 23.

72 A. Bowlby, *The Recollections of Rifleman Bowlby*, Leo Cooper, 1969, pp.27–9.

73 Horsfall, *op. cit.*, p.90.

74 *Ibid.*, p.101.

75 XIII Corps G–3 Report, 31 May 1944. SHAT I0P 55.

76 Dawson, *op. cit.*, p.471.

77 Nicholson, *op. cit.*, p.443.

78   2 DIM, Renseignements tirés, *op. cit.*, p.53-4.

79   Quoted in Roy, *op. cit.*, p.272.

80   Quoted in Horsfall, *op. cit.*, pp. 91 and 92.

81   *Ibid.*, pp.108–9.

82   Vietinghoff, *op. cit.*, pp.7–8.

83   JMO 6 RTM, 24 May 1944. SHAT (FPU) I2P 74.

84   Heurgnon, *op. cit.*, p.179.

85   JMO 2/5 RTM, I June 1944. SHAT (FPU) I2P 73.

86   Chambe, *Epopée, op. cit.*, p.306.

87   2 DIM, Renseignements tirés, *op. cit.*, p.2.

88   1/6 RTM, Le 1/6 RTM au combat de Monte Lupino, 27 mai 1944, pp.2–3. SHAT (FPU) I2P 76.

89   2/4 RTM, enseignments tirés, *op. cit.*, p.2.

90   2ᵉ Bureau 2 DIM, Rapport quotidien, 31 mai–1 juin 1944, p.2. SHAT (FPU) I IP 23.

91   Quoted in Mission Française auprès de la Vᵉ Armée, General Buecler to Commissaire de Guerre, Ref: 2505/M/S, 19 juin 1944, p.1. SHAT I0P 39.

92   J.M. McAvity, *Lord Strathcona's Horse: a Record of Achievement*, Ryerson, Toronto, 1947, p.83.

93   E. Linklater, *The Campaign in Italy*, HMSO, 1951, p.267.

94   Nicholson, *op. cit.*, p.446.

95   Jackson, *op. cit.*, p.32.

96   Von Senger und Etterlin, Diary, *op. cit.*, pp.138–9 (author's emphasis).

97   2/4 RTM, Enseignements tirés, *op. cit.*, p.2.

98   1/4 RTM, pencilled notes on the 'période de rupture 11–15 mai' and the 'période de poursuite 23 mai–5 juin' (probably by Colonel Rocca-Serra), n.d., unpag. SHAT (FPU) I2P 69.

99   Juin to de Gaulle, 7 June 1944. Quoted in Boulle, *op. cit.*, vol.2, p.311.

100 Interview with Brigadier-General C.E. Saltzman, 26 March 1948, p.1. NA (MMS) RG 319 Box 5.

101 Quoted in Clark Diary, *op. cit.*, 17 May 1944.

102 Quoted *ibid.*, 28 May 1944.

103 *Ibid.*, 30 May 1944.

104 *Ibid.*

105 *Ibid.*, 31 May 1944.

106 Quoted in Boulle, *op. cit.*, vol.2, p.310.

107 Quoted in Clark Diary, *op. cit.*, 29 May 1944.

108 *Ibid.*, 31 May 1944.

109 S.T. Matthews and J.D. Hamilton, Interview with Brigadier-General R.E. Jenkins, 1 April 1948, p.4 NA (MMS) RG 319 Box 15.
110 *Alexander Memoirs, op. cit.*, p.127.
111 Alexander Interview, *op. cit.*, pp.15–16.
112 Quoted in Harpur, *op. cit.*, p.74.
113 Trevelyan, *Rome '44, op. cit.*, p.292.
114 Clark Diary, *op. cit.*, 28 May 1944.
115 *Ibid.*, 30 May 1944.
116 *Ibid.*, 31 May 1944.
117 Quoted *ibid.*
118 *Ibid.*
119 Quoted *ibid.*
120 Greiner, Battle for Rome, *op. cit.*, pp.9–10.
121 *Ibid.*, p.13.
122 Greiffenberg and Schmalz, *op. cit.*, pp.13–14.
123 Quoted in Böhmler, *op. cit.*, p.283.
124 Quoted in Fisher, *op. cit.*, p.185.
125 Quoted in Adleman and Walton, *op. cit.*, p.18 (emphasis in original).
126 Walker Diary, *op. cit.*, 30 May 1944.
127 Quoted in Adleman and Walton, *op. cit.*, p.24.
128 Quoted in *ibid.*, p.26.
129 Quoted in Fisher, *op. cit.*, p.192.
130 Quoted in Fifth Army G–2 Summary June 1944, p.1. WNRC (MMFB) RG 94 105–2 to 105–2.1 (Box 2080).
131 Quoted in Böhmler, *loc. cit.*
132 143 Regiment, Operations in Italy, vol.1, June 1944 (extract). NA (MMS) RG 319 Box 6.
133 Quoted in Adleman and Walton, *op. cit.*, pp.27–8.
134 Clark Diary, *op. cit.*, 2 June 1944.
135 Sevareid, *op. cit.*, p.408.
136 Quoted in Fisher, *op. cit.*, p.210.
137 Sevareid, *op. cit.*, p.411.
138 Clark Diary, *op. cit.*, 17 May 1944.
139 *Ibid.*, 27 May 1944.
140 Jars, *op. cit.*, p.161.
141 Von Senger und Etterlin, Prevention of an Enemy Breakthrough Between the Defeated German Tenth and Fourteenth Armies: Retreat to the Arno, pp.9–10. NA (MMS) Ms C–095c (author's emphasis).
142 Fisher, *op. cit.*, p.171.

143   Von Senger und Etterlin, Prevention of a Breakthrough, *op. cit.*, pp.3–4.

144   *Ibid.*, p.3.

145   General S. von Lüttwitz, The Employment of 26 Panzer Division from 15 May to 12 July 1944, p.11. NA (MMS) Ms D–312.

146   *Ibid.*, p.12.

147   Von Senger und Etterlin, Prevention of a Breakthrough, *op. cit.*, pp.6–7.

148   Quoted *ibid.*, p.10.

149   See Boulle, *op. cit.*, vol.2, Table D, for a detailed breakdown of the forces opposing the CEF between 22 May and 5 June.

150   Sheehan, *op. cit.*, p.206.

151   Quoted in Nicolson, *op. cit.*, p.273.

152   S.T. Matthews, Interview with Colonel L.K. Ladue, 17 June 1948, p.1. NA (MMS) RG 319 Box 5.

153   Quoted in Juin, *Mémoires, op. cit.*, p.308.

154   Clark, *Calculated Risk, op. cit.*, p.378.

CHAPTER 18

1   All these details are from Wańkowicz, *Bylo To Pod, op. cit.*, p.93.

2   B. Pomiankowski, *For Your Freedom and Ours*, pvte. pub., Wales, 1976, p.5.

3   Quoted in Adleman and Walton, *op. cit.*, p.210.

4   Letter, Capitaine de Morsier to Général Brosset, 2 November 1944, pp.2–3. SHAT (FPU) 11P6.

5   Robichon, *op. cit.*, p.430.

6   Major H.W. Hunter, Notes and Recommendations on Issues Affecting Morale, No.2, Ref: HDH/120/8/44, November 1944, p.1. PRO WO 204/6724.

7   Sevareid, *op. cit.*, p.375.

8   Majdalany, *Monastery, op. cit.*, p.12.

9   B. Mauldin, *Up Front*, Holt & Company, New York, 1945, p.58.

10   Sevareid, *op. cit.*, p.378.

11   Majdalany, *Monastery, op. cit.*, p.77.

12   Quoted in Delaney, *op. cit.*, p.xiv.

13   Bond, *op. cit.*, pp.242–3.

Sources and Bibliography

ARCHIVAL SOURCES

PUBLIC RECORDS OFFICE (London)

Allied Forces Headquarters (Mediterranean)

WO 204/985	G–2 Intelligence Notes 11 January–11 April 1944
WO 204/986	G–2 Intelligence Notes 12 April–27 June 1944
WO 204/1096	Report by G–3 Training Section on Visits to Units July 1943–April 1945
WO 204/1454	Operations in Italy January–17 March 1944
WO 204/1455	Operations in Italy 18 March–April 1944.
WO 204/1456	Operations in Italy May–June 1944
WO 204/4354	Lessons from the Cassino Operation
WO 204/6724	Status of Infantry Soldiers July–November 1944
WO 204/10388	G–3 Plans: Operational Policy (Italy) August 1943–April 1944
WO 204/10413	G(Ops): Papers relating to Sicilian and Italian Campaigns to September 1944

Allied Armies in Italy (15th Army Group)

WO 204/6832	AAI/43/G/Ops: Correspondence on Operational Instructions August 1943–August 1944
WO 204/6835	AAI/48/G/Ops: Operation DIADEM Reports

American Forces

WO 204/1096	North African and Italian Campaigns November 1942–February 1944
WO 204/4365	34 US Division: November 1942–September 1944
WO 204/6809	Fifth Army: Operational Memoranda December 1943–August 1944
WO 204/7566	Fifth Army: Cassino Operation: Lessons Learnt 15–24 March 1944
WO 204/7564	HQ NAF Theatre Ops: Lessons From the Italian Campaign 9 September 1943–1 February 1944
CAB 106/361	Lessons From the Italian Campaign 1 February–30 September 1944

New Zealand Forces

WO 204/7275   Operations of New Zealand Corps 3 February–26 March 1944 (Misc.)

WO 204/8287   Historical Notes on Operation DICKENS 15–23 March 1944

WO 204/8289   2 NZEF: Operations Report November 1943– November 1944

CAB 106/366   Operations of New Zealand Corps 3 February–26 March 1944

Polish Forces

WO 204/8221   Operations II Polish Corps Against Monte Cassino

Canadian Forces

WO 204/8202   1 Canadian Division in the Liri Valley 15–28 May 1944
WO 204/8207   5 Canadian Armoured Division: Reports on Operations

Miscellaneous

WO 204/10425   The Irish Brigade in Italy March 1944–March 1945 (typescript by Brigadier T.P.D. Scott)

CAB 101/224   The British Soldier in Italy, September 1943–June 1944 (typescript by Diana Butler)

CAB 106/733   Leese Papers (to October 1944)

War Diaries

A complete list of War Diaries consulted would not justify the space taken up, as they offer few useful details on military operations. Message logs only give times of transmission and reception; the more useful appendices are invariably empty; comment is conspicuous by its absence. Suffice it to say that I have read the relevant War Diaries for X and XIII Corps, 4, 5, 46 and 56 Divisions, 13, 15 and 28 Brigades, as well as those for thirty-two infantry battalions. All are grouped within the series WO 170.

SERVICE HISTORIQUE DE L'ARMEE DE TERRE
(Château de Vincennes, Paris)

Corps Expéditionnaire Français (to be found in the Pavillon des Armes)
1OP 11   Desertions and Discipline
1OP 36   Reports from Fifth Army January–February 1944
1OP 37   2e Bureau: POW Interrogations

1OP 38   2e Bureau: POW Interrogations
1OP 39   2e Bureau: Information on German Forces
1OP 54   Reports from Eighth Army
1OP 55   Reports from X and XIII British Corps
1OP 56   Lessons from Campaign and Combat Narratives

War Diaries (to be found in the Fonds des Petites Unités)

French War Diaries (known as *Journaux de Marches et Opérations*) offer a much more fruitful source than their British equivalents. In most of the cartons listed below there are included numerous reports and combat narratives as well as memoranda to and from the units and formations.

1 Division de Marche d'Infanterie

1IP 6   War Diary 1 DMI
1IP 8   War Diary 1 DMI 2^e Bureau
1IP 11   War Diary 1 DMI 3^e Bureau
12P 81   War Diaries 13 DBLE and 1/13 DBLE
12P 271   War Diaries 4 and 5 Bataillons de Marche
12P 272   War Diaries 11, 21 and 24 Bataillons de Marche

2 Division d'Infanterie Marocaine

1IP 22   War Diary 2 DIM
1IP 23   War Diary 2 DIM 2e Bureau
1IP 31   War Diary 2 DIM 3e Bureau
1IP 38   War Diary 2 DIM Divisional Infantry
12P 66   2 DIM Miscellaneous
12P 69   War Diaries 1/4 and 2/4 RTM
12P 73   War Diaries 1/5, 2/5 and 3/5 RTM

3 Division d'Infanterie Algérienne

12P 50   War Diaries 3 RTA and 1/3 RTA
12P 53   War Diaries 1/4, 2/4 and 3/4 RTT
12P 56   Miscellaneous 7 RTA and War Diary 3/7 RTA

4 Division de Montagne Marocaine

1IP 90   War Diary 4 DMM
1IP 98   War Diary 4 DMM 2e Bureau
1IP 99   4 DMM 2e Bureau: Miscellaneous
1IP 109   War Diary 4 DMM 3^e Bureau
1IP 111   4 DMM: Messages from Other Formations

11P 112	4 DMM: Messages from US Formations
11P 131	War Diary 4 DMM Divisional Infantry
12P 61	War Diary 1 RTM
12P 62	War Diary 1/1 RTM
12P 63	War Diaries 2/1 and 3/1 RTM
12P 64	War Diaries 2 RTM, 1/2 and 2/2 RTM
12P 74	War Diary 6 RTM
12P 76	War Diaries 2/6 and 3/6 RTM

US NATIONAL ARCHIVES (Constitution Avenue, Washington)

Foreign Military Studies (Manuscripts)
(to be found in the Modern Military Section)

MS C–025	Von Vietinghoff, The Campaign in Italy: the Operations of 71 German Division During the Month of May 1944
MS C–025a	Beantworten von Fragen den Einsatz der 71 Infanterie Division im Mai 1944
MS C–087b	Von Greiffenberg and Schmalz, Division 'Hermann Goering' – Questionnaire
MS C–095b	Von Senger und Etterlin, War Diary of the Italian Campaign: Cassino
MS C–095c	Von Senger und Etterlin, Prevention of an Enemy Breakthrough Between the Defeated German Tenth and Fourteenth Armies: Retreat to the Arno.
MS D–169	Greiner, The Battle for Rome and the Retreat Northward
MS D–203	Glaser, Gebirgsjäger Regiment 100 in den Cassino– Schlachten, Dezember 1943–Februar 1944
MS D–312	Von Lüttwitz, the Employment of 26 Panzer Division from 15 May–12 July 1944

Captured German Documents
(copies from GMDS Files to be found in Modern Military Section)

53271/9	Appendices to Tenth Army War Diary 26 May 1944
/10	Appendices to Tenth Army War Diary 27–31 May 1944
58199/6	Extracts from XIV Panzer Corps Reports 11–20 February 1944
/8,9	Extracts from XIV Panzer Corps Reports March 1944
/10,11,12	Extracts from XIV Panzer Corps Reports April 1944

/20   Miscellaneous Appendices XIV Panzer Corps War Diary
            February 1944
/21   Miscellaneous Appendices XIV Panzer Corps War Diary
            March 1944
58200/5   XIV Panzer Corps: Report on Enemy Tactics at Cassino

US *Army in World War II: Background Material to Volumes on the Italian
Campaign (to be found in Modern Military Section)*
RG 319 (Boxes 253–256) Material on Volume *Salerno to Cassino*
RG 319 (Boxes 1–15)   Material on Volume *Cassino to the Alps*

WASHINGTON NATIONAL RECORDS CENTER
(Modern Military Field Branch, Suitland)
All the cartons listed below form part of the Series RG 94 incorporating
World War II Operations Reports 1940–48: Fifth Army

105–2.2   (Boxes 2113, 2115, 2116, 2117) Fifth Army HQ: Various
105–2–105–2.1   Fifth Army G–2 Summaries
105–3.21–105–3.23   Fifth Army G-3: Various
105–3.17–105–3.18   Fifth Army G–3 Operations Instructions May 1944–
            July 1945
105–3.14–105–3.17   Fifth Army G–3 Operations Instructions September
            1943–May 1944
105–3.4 (Boxes 2345–2346)   Fifth Army G–3 Messages
200–3.2   II Corps G–3 Journal Index and File January–February 1944
202–0.3   II Corps Operations Reports March 1943–April 1944
334–0.3   34 Division Operational Reports September 1943–July 1945
334–1   34 Division G–1 Historical Records September 1943–
            September 1944
334–1.16   34 Division Battle Casualty Returns November 1942–May
            1945
334–2   34 Division G–2 Monthly Reports
334–2.1   34 Division G–2 Periodic Reports
334–2.2   34 Division G–2 Journal January–June 1944
334–Inf(133)–0.3   133 Regiment History January–April 1944
334–Inf(135)–0.3   135 Regiment History September 1943–September
            1945
334–Inf(168)–0.3   168 Regiment History 1–31 January 1944

US DEPARTMENT OF DEFENSE
(Center for Military History, Historical Records Branch)

228.03   Permanent HRC Geog L. Italy 370.2   Keyes Materials
228.03   Permanent HRC Geog L. Italy 373.11   Monte Cassino: Various
228.03   Permanent HRC Geog L. Italy 370.2   Rapido River
228.03   Permanent HRC Geog L. Italy 370.24   Monte Artemisio
228.03   Permanent HRC Geog J. Africa 370.24   Eye-witness Accounts
          by Veterans
228.03   Permanent HRC   314.81 Walker Diaries

Bibliography

BACKGROUND

R.H. ADLEMAN and G. WALTON, *Rome Fell Today*, Little Brown, Boston, 1968
ALEXANDER OF TUNIS, *The Alexander Memoirs, 1940–45*, Cassell, 1962
W.L. ALLEN, *Anzio: Edge of Disaster*, Elsevier-Dutton, New York, 1978
W. ANDERS, *An Army in Exile*, Macmillan, 1949
A.G. ARMSTRONG and C. OMAN, 'Plus Ça Change', *Army Quarterly*, vol.48, April 1944
H.H. ARNOLD, *Global Mission*, Hutchinson, 1951

J. BIELATOWICZ, *Bitwa o Monte Cassino*, SPK, 1952
G. BLAXLAND, *Alexander's Generals*, Kimber, 1979
M. BLUMENSON, *Anzio: the Gamble that Failed*, Weidenfeld & Nicolson, 1963
Bloody River, Allen & Unwin, 1970
Salerno to Cassino (US Army in World War II), Government Printing Office, Washington, 1969
R. BÖHMLER, *Monte Cassino*, Cassell, 1964
G. BRUCE, *Second Front Now*, Macdonald & Janes, 1979
A. BRYANT (ed.), *The Alanbrooke War Diaries* (2 vols), Collins, 1957
C. BUCKLEY, *The Road to Rome*, Hodder & Stoughton, 1945

M. CARPENTIER, *Les Forces Alliés en Italie*, Berger-Levrault, Paris, 1949
M. CARVER, *Harding of Petherington*, Weidenfeld & Nicolson, 1978
R. CHAMBE, *Le Bataillon du Belvédère*, Flammarion, Paris, 1953
L'Epopée Française d'Italie 1944, Flammarion, Paris, 1952
W.S. CHURCHILL, *The Second World War* (12 vols), Cassell, 1964
M. CLARK, *Calculated Risk*, Harrap, 1951
C. CONNELL, *Monte Cassino*, Elek, 1963
M. COOPER, *The German Army 1933–45*, Macdonald & Janes, 1978

C. de GAULLE, *War Memoirs: Unity*, Weidenfeld & Nicolson, 1956
T.N. DUPUY, *A Genius for War*, Macdonald & Janes, 1980

J. EHRMANN, *Grand Strategy* (vol.5), HMSO, 1956
D. EISENHOWER, *Crusade in Europe*, Heinemann, 1948

D. FEATHERSTONE, *Tank Battles in Miniature* (vol.4), Patrick Stephens, Cambridge, 1977
B. FERGUSSON (ed.), *The Business of War: the War Narratives of Major-General Sir John Kennedy*, Hutchinson, 1957

E.J. FISHER, *Cassino to the Alps* (US Army in World War II), Government Printing Office, Washington, 1977

J.F.C. FULLER, *The Second World War 1939–45*, Eyre & Spottiswoode, 1948

A. GOUTARD, Marshal Juin, in M. Carver (ed.), *The War Lords*, Weidenfeld & Nicolson, 1976

D. GRAHAM, *Cassino*, Purnells, 1970

J. HARDING, *Mediterranean Strategy*, Cambridge University Press, 1960

B.H.L. HART, *History of the Second World War*, Cassell, 1970

J. HARVEY (ed.), *The War Diaries of Oliver Harvey 1941–45*, Collins, 1978

W. HAUPT, *Kriegsschauplatz Italien 1943–45*, Motorbuch Verlag, Stuttgart, 1977

C. HIBBERT, *Anzio: the Bid for Rome*, Purnells, 1970

T. HIGGINS, *Soft Underbelly*, Macmillan, New York, 1968

N. HILLSON, *Alexander of Tunis*, W.H. Allen, 1952

L. HOLLIS and J. LEASOR, *War at the Top*, Michael Joseph, 1959

M. HOWARD, *Mediterranean Strategy in the Second World War*, Weidenfeld & Nicolson, 1968

GENERAL THE LORD ISMAY, *The Memoirs*, Heinemann, 1960

W.G.F. JACKSON, *Alexander as Military Commander*, Batsford, 1971

The Battle for Rome, Batsford, 1969

R. JARS, *La Campagne d'Italie 1943–45*, Payot, Paris, 1954

A. JUIN, *La Campagne d'Italie*, G. Victor, Paris, 1962

Mémoires (vol. 1), Fayard, Paris, 1959

A. KESSELRING, *The Memoirs*, Kimber, 1964

G. KOLKO, *The Politics of War*, Random House, New York, 1968

V. KUHN, *German Paratroopers in World War II*, Ian Allen, Shepperton, 1978

E. LINKLATER, *The Campaign in Italy*, HMSO, 1951

H. MACMILLAN, *The Blast of War*, Macmillan, 1967

F. MAJDALANY, *Cassino: Portrait of a Battle*, Longmans, 1957; reissued as *The Battle of Cassino*, White Lion Publishers, 1973

S.T. MATTHEWS, 'General Clark's Decision to Drive on Rome' (1944), in K.T. Greenfield (ed.), *Command Decisions*, Methuen, 1960

R.S. MAVROGORDATO, 'Hitler's Decision on the Defence of Italy', in K.T. Greenfield (ed.), *Command Decisions*, Methuen, 1960

R. MERLE, *Ben Bella*, Michael Joseph, 1967

C.J.C. MOLONY, *The Mediterranean and the Middle East*, vol.5 (History of the Second World War), HMSO, 1973

MONTGOMERY OF ALAMEIN, *El Alamein to the River Sangro*, Hutchinson, 1948

N. NICOLSON, *Alex*, Weidenfeld & Nicolson, 1973

D. ORGILL, *The Gothic Line*, Heinemann, 1967

R. PARKINSON, *A Day's March Nearer Home*, Hart-Davis MacGibbon, 1974

B. PERRETT, *Through Mud and Blood: Infantry/Tank Operations in World War II*, Robert Hale, 1975

J. PIEKALKIEWICZ, *Cassino: Anatomy of a Battle*, Orbis, 1980

D. RICHARDS, *Portal of Hungerford*, Heinemann, 1977

E.J. ROZECK, *Allied Wartime Diplomacy in Poland*, Random House, New York, 1958

F.M. SALLAGER, *Operation Strangle*, Rand Corporation, Santa Monica, 1972

F. SHEEHAN, *Anzio: Epic of Bravery*, University of Oklahoma Press, Norman 1964

G.A. SHEPPERD, *The Italian Campaign 1943–45*, Arthur Barker, 1968

R.E. SHERWOOD, *The White House Papers of Harry Hopkins* (2 vols), Eyre & Spottiswoode, 1948

E.A. SHILLS and M. JANOWITZ, 'Cohesion and Disintegration in the German Wehrmacht in World War II', *Public Opinion Quarterly*, vol. 12, 1948

P. SINGLETON-GATES, *General Lord Freyberg VC*, Michael Joseph, 1963

E.C.D. SMITH, *The Battles for Cassino*, Ian Allen, Shepperton, 1975

J. SLESSOR, *The Central Blue*, Cassell, 1956

W.G. STEVENS, *Freyberg VC: the Man 1939–45*, Herbert Jenkins, 1965

LORD TEDDER, *With Prejudice*, Cassell, 1966

R. TREVELYAN, *Rome '44*, Secker & Warburg, 1981

L.K. TRUSCOTT, *Command Missions*, Dutton, New York, 1954

W. VAUGHAN-THOMAS, *Anzio*, Holt, New York, 1961

P. VERNEY, *Anzio 1944*, Batsford, 1968

F. von SENGER und ETTERLIN, *Neither Fear Nor Hope*, Macdonalds, 1963

R. WALLACE, *The Italian Campaign*, Time-Life Books, Alexandria (Va.), 1978

M. WANKOWICZ, *Bylo To Pod Monte Cassino*, Komitetu Obschodu Dziesieciolecia Bitwy o Monte Cassino, 1954

A.C. WEDEMEYER, *Wedemeyer Reports*, Holt, New York, 1958
S. WESTPHAL, *The German Army in the West*, Cassell, 1951
H.M. WILSON, *Eight Years Overseas*, Hutchinson, 1948
Report By the Supreme Allied Commander Mediterranean . . . (January 8 1944–May 10 1944), HMSO, 1946
R. WINGATE, *Lord Ismay*, Hutchinson, 1970

UNIT AND FORMATION HISTORIES

R.H. ADLEMAN and G. WALTON, *The Devil's Brigade*, Chilton, Philadelphia, 1966
R.C.B. ANDERSON, *History of the (1st) Argyll and Sutherland Highlanders 1939–54*, Constable, Edinburgh, 1956
ANON, *The Tiger Triumphs*, HMSO, 1946
G. AVIS, *The Fifth British Division*, pvte. pub., 1959

C.N. BARCLAY, *The History of the Sherwood Foresters*, Clowes, 1959
The History of the 16/5th Lancers, Gale & Polden, Aldershot, 1963
The London Scottish in the Second World War, Clowes, 1952
K. BEATTIE, *Dileas: The History of the 48th Highlanders of Canada, 1929–56*, pvte. pub., Toronto, 1957
S. BIEGANSKI, *Dzialania 2 Korpusu W. Wloszech* (vol.1), Komisja Historyczna 2–Go Korpusu, 1963
J. BIELATOWICZ, *Ulani Karpaccy*, Carpathian Lancers Association, 1966
G. BLIGHT, *The History of the Royal Berkshire Regiment, 1920–47*, Staples, 1953
C.M. BOISSONAULT and L. LAMONTAGNE, *Histoire du Royal 22ᵉ Régiment*, Editions du Pélican, Quebec, 1964
G. BOULLE, *Le Corps Expéditionnaire Français en Italie, 1943–44* (2 vols), Imprimerie Nationale, Paris, 1971–73
R.M. BURDON, *24 Battalion* (New Zealand in the Second World War), Department of Internal Affairs, Wellington, 1961
J.J. BURKE-GAFFNEY, *The Story of the King's Regiment 1918–48*, Sharpe & Kellett, Liverpool, 1954

CAMERON HIGHLANDERS, *Historical Records of the Queen's Own Cameron Highlanders 1932–48*, Blackwood, Edinburgh, 1952
H.D. CHAPLIN, *The Queen's Own Royal West Kent Regiment 1920–50*, pvte. pub., Maidstone, 1959
J.F. CODY, *21 Battalion* (New Zealand in the Second World War), Department of Internal Affairs, Wellington 1953
28 (Maori) Battalion (New Zealand in the Second World War), Department of Internal Affairs, Wellington, 1958

W.E.H. CONDON, *The Frontier Force Regiment*, Gale & Polden, Aldershot, 1962

A. CROOKENDEN, *The History of the Cheshire Regiment in World War II*, pvte. pub., Chester, 1949

M. CUNLIFFE, *The Royal Irish Fusiliers*, Oxford University Press, 1952

D.S. DANIELL, *Regimental History of the Royal Hampshire Regiment* (vol.3), Gale & Polden, Aldershot, 1955

W.D. DAWSON, *18 Battalion and Armoured Regiment* (New Zealand in the Second World War), Department of Internal Affairs, Wellington, 1961

C.G.T. DEAN, *The Loyal Regiment, 1919–53*, pvte. pub., Preston, 1955

J.P. DELANEY, *The Blue Devils in Italy*, Infantry Journal Press, Washington, 1947

2ᵉ DIM, *Victoire en Italie*, Gauthier-Villars, Paris, 1945

L.F. ELLIS, *Welsh Guards at War*, Gale & Polden, Aldershot, 1946

D. ERSKINE, *The Scots Guards, 1919–55*, Clowes, 1956

B. FERGUSSON, *The Black Watch and the King's Enemies*, Collins, 1950

A.H. FERNYHOUGH, *History of the Royal Army Ordnance Corps*, pvte. pub., n.d.

R.L.V.B. FFRENCH, *History of the 17/21 Lancers 1922–59*, Macmillan, 1962

J.D. FORSYTHE *et al.*, *Fifth Army History* (part IV), pvte. pub., Florence, n.d.

C. FORTY, *Fifth Army at War*, Ian Allen, Shepperton, 1980

R.C.G. FOSTER, *History of the Queen's Royal Regiment* (vol.8), Gale & Polden, Aldershot, 1953

F. FOX, *The Royal Inniskilling Fusiliers in the Second World War*, Gale & Polden, Aldershot, 1951

S. GALLOWAY, *55 Axis: With the Royal Canadian Regiment*, Provincial Publishing, Montreal, 1946

L.C. GATES, *The History of the Tenth Foot 1919–50*, Gale & Polden, Aldershot, 1953

E.G. GODFREY, *The History of the Duke of Cornwall's Light Infantry, 1939–45*, pvte. pub., 1966
The History of the 5th Gurkha Rifles (vol.2), Gale & Polden, Aldershot, 1956

F.C.C. GRAHAM, *The History of the Argyll and Sutherland Highlanders, 1st Battalion, 1939–45*, Nelson, 1948

B.H.L. HART, *The Tanks* (vol.2), Cassell, 1959

R.H. HASTINGS, *The Rifle Brigade in World War II*, Gale & Polden, Aldershot, 1952

J. HENDERSON, *22 Battalion* (New Zealand in the Second World War), Department of Internal Affairs, Wellington, 1958

C. HEURGNON, *La Victoire Sous la Signe des Trois Croissants*, Editions Pierre Voilon, Algers, 1946

D. HOW, *The 8th Hussars*, Maritime Publishing, Sussex (N.B.), 1964

M. HOWARD, *The Coldstream Guards 1920–46*, Oxford University Press, 1951

G.F. HOWE, *The Battle History of the 1st Armoured Division*, Combat Forces Press, Washington, 1954

H.M. JACKSON, *The Princess Louise's Dragoon Guards*, pvte. pub., 1951

W.J. JERVOIS, *The History of the Northamptonshire Regiment 1934–48*, pvte. pub., Northampton, 1953

J.C. KEMP, *The History of the Royal Scots Fusiliers 1919–59*, Glasgow University Press, 1963

W.C.E. KENNICK, *The History of the King's Shropshire Light Infantry* (vol.3), pvte. pub., n.d.

J.P. LAWFORD, *Solah Punjab*, Gale & Polden, Aldershot, 1967

LONDON IRISH RIFLES, *The London Irish at War*, pvte. pub., n.d.

J.M. McAVITY, *Lord Strathcona's Horse*, Ryerson, Toronto, 1947

J.N. McKAY, *The History of the 7th Gurkha Rifles*, Blackwood, Edinburgh, 1962

I.A. McKEE, *5th Battalion the Northamptonshire Regiment in Italy*, pvte. pub., Tamsweg, 1945

B.J.G. MADDEN, *The History of the 6th Battalion The Black Watch 1939–45*, Leslie, Perth, 1948

A.D. MALCOLM, *The History of the Argyll and Sutherland Highlanders, 8th Battalion, 1939–45*, Nelson, 1949

T.A. MARTIN, *The Essex Regiment 1929–50*, pvte. pub, 1952

G.D. MARTINEAU, *A History of the Royal Sussex Regiment*, Mowe & Tilyer, Chichester, n.d.

W. MILES, *The Life of a Regiment: the Gordon Highlanders*, Aberdeen University Press, 1961

F. MOWAT, *The Regiment*, McLelland, Toronto, 1973

T.D. MURPHY, *Ambassadors in Arms: the Story of Hawaii's 100 Battalion*, University of Hawaii Press, Honolulu, 1954.

J.E.H. NEVILLE, *The Oxford and Buckinghamshire Light Infantry Chronicle* (vol.3), Gale & Polden, Aldershot, 1952

G.W.L. NICHOLSON, *The Canadians in Italy* (Official History of the Canadian

Army in the Second World War), Department of National Defence, Ottawa, 1956

N. NICOLSON, *The Grenadier Guards in the War of 1939-45* (vol.2), Gale & Polden, Aldershot, 1949

F.D. NORTON, *26 Battalion* (New Zealand in the Second World War), Department of Internal Affairs, Wellington, 1952

D. PAL, *The Campaign in Italy* (Indian Armed Forces in World War II), Longmans, Delhi, 1960

C.N. PARKINSON, *Always a Fusilier: the War History of the Royal Fusiliers*, Sampson Low, 1950

N.C. PHILLIPS, *The Sangro to Cassino* (New Zealand in the Second World War), Department of Internal Affairs, Wellington, 1957

H. PIATKOWSKI, 'The Second Polish Corps in the Battle for Monte Cassino', *Army Quarterly*, vol.49, October 1945 and January 1946

D.J.C. PRINGLE and W.A. GLUE, *20 Battalion and Armoured Regiment* (New Zealand in the Second World War), Department of Internal Affairs, Wellington, 1957

E. PUTTICK, *25 Battalion* (New Zealand in the Second World War), Department of Internal Affairs, Wellington, 1958

D.C. QUILTER (ed.), *No Dishonourable Name*, SR Publishing, Wakefield, 1972

T.H. RADDALL, *West Novas: a History of the West Nova Scotia Regiment*, pvte. pub., Liverpool (N.S.), 1947

C. RAY, *Algiers to Austria: the History of 78 Division in World War II*, Eyre & Spottiswoode, 1952

J. ROBICHON, *Le Corps Expéditionnaire Français en Italie 1943-44*, Presses de la Cité, Paris, 1981

A. ROSS, *23 Battalion* (New Zealand in the Second World War), Department of Internal Affairs, Wellington, 1957

R.H. ROY, *Sinews of Steel: a History of the British Columbia Dragoons*, pvte. pub., 1965

P.I. SCHULTZ, *The 85th Division in World War II*, Infantry Journal Press, Washington, 1949

O.F. SHEFFIELD, *The York and Lancaster Regiment* (vol.3), Gale & Polden, Aldershot, 1956

D.W. SINCLAIR, *19 Battalion and Armoured Regiment* (New Zealand in the Second World War), Department of Internal Affairs, Wellington, 1954

C.G. STARR, *From Salerno to the Alps: a History of the Fifth Army 1943-45*, Infantry Journal Press, Washington, 1948

W. STEINAUER, *Historia 2 Grupy Artylerii*, pvte. pub., Rome, n.d.

G.R. STEVENS, *A City Goes to War: a History of the Loyal Edmonton Regiment*, Charters, Brampton (Ontario), 1965

Fourth Indian Division, McClaren, Toronto, n.d.

The History of the 2nd Gurkha Rifles (vol.3), Gale & Polden, Aldershot, 1952

The History of the 5th Royal Gurkha Rifles, pvte. pub., 1956

Princess Patricia's Canadian Light Infantry (vol.3), pvte. pub., Alberta, 1959

J. SYM, *Seaforth Highlanders*, Gale & Polden, Aldershot, 1962

W.A.T. SYNGE, *The Story of the Green Howards 1939–45*, pvte. pub., Richmond, 1952

US AIR FORCE, *The Army Air Forces in World War II* (vol.3), University of Chicago Press, 1951

R.L. WAGNER, *The Texas Army*, Wagner, Austin (Texas), 1972

S.G.P. WARD, *Faithful: the Story of the Durham Light Infantry*, Nelson, n.d.

G. WOOD, *The Story of the Irish Regiment of Canada*, pvte. pub., 1945

H.C. WYLLY, *The History of the King's Own Yorkshire Light Infantry* (vol.6) Gale & Polden, Aldershot, 1961

EYEWITNESS ACCOUNTS

H.L. BOND, *Return to Cassino*, Doubleday, New York, 1964

A. BOWLBY, *The Recollections of Rifleman Bowlby*, Leo Cooper, 1969

P. COCHRANE, *Charlie Company*, Chatto & Windus, 1977

C.F. COMFORT, *Artist at War*, Ryerson, Toronto, 1956

A.P. de T. DANIELL, 'The Battle for Cassino May 1944', *Royal Engineers Journal*, 1951

J.C. FRY, *Combat Soldier*, National Press, Washington, 1968

M. GANDER, *After These Many Quests*, Macdonald, 1949

H. GREINER, *Kampf um Rom, Inferno am Po*, Kurt Vorwinckel Verlag, Neckargemünd, 1967

B. HARPUR, *The Impossible Victory*, Kimber, 1980

J.M.L. HARVEY, *D-Day Dodger*, Kimber, 1979

J. HORSFALL, *Fling Our Banners to the Wind*, Roundwood Press, Kineton, 1978

D. HUNT, *A Don at War*, Kimber, 1966

P. LYAUTEY, *La Campagne d'Italie: Souvenirs d'un Goumier*, Plon, Paris, 1945

F. MAJDALANY, *The Monastery*, Bodley Head, 1948

P. MOINOT, *Armes et Bagages*, Gallimard, Paris, 1951

E. PYLE, *Brave Men*, Holt, New York, 1944

W. ROBSON, *Letters from a Soldier*, Faber, 1960

E. SEVAREID, *Not So Wild a Dream*, Knopf, New York, 1946

E.D. SMITH, *Even the Brave Falter*, Robert Hale, 1978

B. SUSBIELLE, 'Campagne d'Italie: du Garigliano au Mayo avec un Bataillon de Tirailleurs Marocains', *Revue Historique de l'Armée*, 1967

R. TREVELYAN, *The Fortress*, Collins, 1956

M. WANKOWICZ, *Bitwa o Monte Cassino* (3 vols), pvte. pub., Rome, 1945
Szkice Spod Monte Cassino, Wiedza Powszechna, Warsaw, 1980

M.B. WHITE, *Purple Heart Valley*, Simon & Schuster, New York, 1944

Glossary

AFV. Armoured fighting vehicle.

AP. Armour-piercing (shells). As opposed to HE (q.v.). Pointed shells with their fuse at the base, designed to explode after the shell has passed through the target's armour. Because of the bulk of the battering ram nose only a small percentage of the shell was actual explosive (1½-10 per cent), but this was deemed sufficient to wreak havoc in the confined interior of an enemy tank.

Army and Army Group. The higher level formations within which infantry, armoured, artillery etc., corps and divisions (q.v.) were grouped. The Allies distinguished every level of formation numerically, though the Germans sometimes designated their Army Groups according to the region in which they operated or the name of the commander. An Army Group would be organized thus:

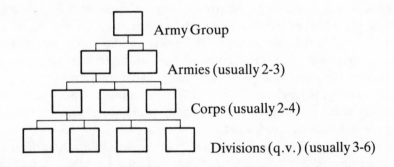

Army Group

Armies (usually 2-3)

Corps (usually 2-4)

Divisions (q.v.) (usually 3-6)

Assault Gun. A German self-propelled (see SP) artillery piece. Their basic concept was that by dispensing with the turret a given tank chassis could mount a heavier gun than normal and be provided with thicker and better shaped frontal armour for close-range work. The most common such guns in Italy were the *Sturmgeschütz* III (Panzer III chassis) and the *Stu.G* IV (Panzer IV chassis). Both usually mounted the 7.5 or 10cm gun but obviously had very limited traverse when stationary. They were occasionally used as *ersatz* tanks but the official orthodoxy was that assault guns went forward with the infantry, just to their rear, engaged targets with direct fire as indicated by the infantry and, once the objective was attained, immediately fell back 1000 yards to await further orders. Two fundamental maxims of assault gun tactics, as laid down in a manual of this period, were that 'under no circumstances do they remain with the infantry' and 'to combat tanks in defensive positions is against assault gun principles.'

BAR. Browning Automatic Rifle. A light one-man machine gun for use at squad level. It was gas-operated and fired 550 rounds per minute, which came in 20-round clips. It was usually deemed too heavy to be fired from the shoulder or hip, whilst the bipod that was issued was very heavy and difficult to adjust. Nevertheless over 2 million of them were manufactured between 1919 and 1950.

Battalion. In the American and German Armies the infantry battalion was a simple subdivision of a regiment (q.v.), which comprised three battalions, sometimes two in the German Army. They therefore took their designation (e.g. 1/15 or 2/267) from the number of the regiment. In the New Zealand Army battalions were given their own number, those with the lowest being the earliest formed. In the British, Canadian and Indian Armies, however, though the battalion was one-third of the fighting formation brigade (q.v.) it was also part of the historical/ administrative unit, the Regiment. The various battalions of this Regiment, e.g. 1, 2 and 3 Coldstream Guards, might well be fighting in completely different theatres and each of them brigaded with battalions from quite different Regiments. There were additional complications. Such designations as 4/6 Rajputana Rifles, in the Indian Army, meant that several Regiments with the same name had been formed, the second number being the Regiment's and the first the battalion's. Such composite numbers in the British Army, e.g. 17/21 Lancers, usually meant that two Regiments had been amalgamated.

Armour and artillery were yet more complicated. In the American and German armies the basic unit for both was the battalion, sometimes grouped together within a regiment. The British, Canadian and Indian armoured equivalents, however, were known as Regiments. In the Canadian Army this was because the ex-cavalry Regiments from which they had been formed rarely spawned more than one 'battalion'. Thus there is, for example, only *the* Lord Strathcona's Horse. In the British Army this usage was largely traditional, both 3 and 4 Derbyshire Yeomanry, for example, continuing to regard themselves as separate Regiments rather than two 'battalions' of the parent Regiment. Except that is, for the Royal Tank Regiment which usually provided infantry-support tanks attached to Corps and Army rather than to armoured divisions; this Regiment was divided into various battalions which were numbered accordingly. British, Indian and Dominion artillery 'battalions' were also known as Regiments, though the numerical prefix, e.g. 19 Field Regiment Royal Artillery or 57 Light Anti-Aircraft Regiment Royal Canadian Artillery, also included an explanation of what type of artillery they were. For fear of making things too simple it should also be pointed out that the Royal Artillery itself, actually an Arm of the Service (see **Corps** below), continued for purely traditional reasons to call itself a Regiment.

Various countries' battalions were organized in much the same way and therefore only some British examples are given on pp.534–5. However a comparative table of weapons strengths for British, American and German formations are given under **Division** below.

Bazooka. The M1 and M9 rocket launchers. Basically these were 5ft metal tubes with a trigger which launched armour-piercing rockets. They required a two-man crew (one firing and one loading), fired a 3.4lb rocket up to 700 yards and, at close range, could pierce up to 4.7 inches of armour at a 90° angle. Intended as an anti-tank weapon they were often used against buildings, pill boxes and bunkers. The British and German equivalents were the PIAT and the Panzerschreck (q.v.).

'B' Echelon. The lorries, trucks and personnel that constituted the 'tail' of a formation or unit, that part of it concerned with supply, repair and medical matters.

BMNA. Bataillon de Marche Nord Africain.

Brigade. In British, Indian and Dominion Armies a sub-division of an infantry division (three infantry battalions) or of an armoured division (three tank regiments).

Casualty Clearing Station. The point in the casualty evacuation chain where most surgery was done, usually administered by a Corps and using Royal Army Medical Corps personnel. Emergency surgery was done earlier in the chain, at a Field Surgical Unit, whilst non-urgent treatment, and convalescence, took place further down the chain, at a General Hospital. A battle casualty's first ports of call would be a Regimental Aid Post and/or an Advanced Dressing Station, run by his battalion.

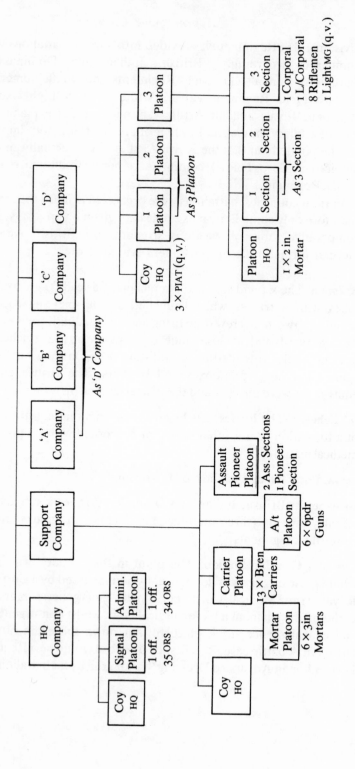

British Infantry Battalion 1943–44

British Armoured Regiment 1943-44

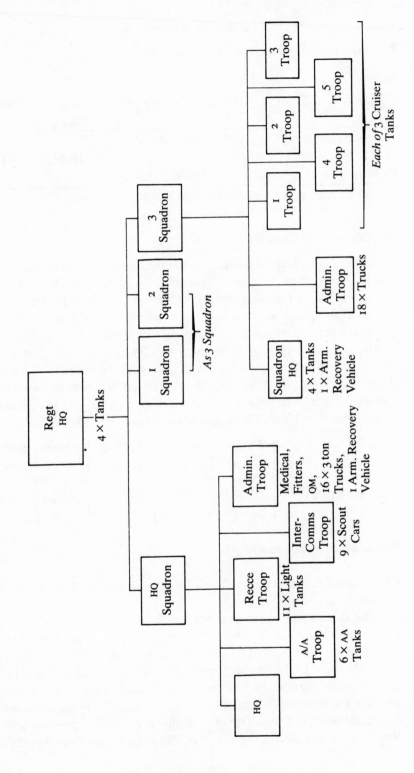

Regt HQ — 4 × Tanks

HQ Squadron
- HQ
- A/A Troop — 6 × AA Tanks
- Recce Troop — 11 × Light Tanks
- Inter-Comms Troop — 9 × Scout Cars
- Admin. Troop — Medical, Fitters, QM, 16 × 3 ton Trucks, 1 Arm. Recovery Vehicle

1 Squadron
2 Squadron
3 Squadron

As 3 Squadron

3 Squadron
- Squadron HQ — 4 × Tanks, 1 × Arm. Recovery Vehicle
- Admin. Troop — 18 × Trucks
- 1 Troop
- 2 Troop
- 3 Troop
- 4 Troop
- 5 Troop

Each of 3 Cruiser Tanks

British, American and German Equivalents:

British	*American*	*German*
Regimental Aid Post	Battalion Aid Station	Truppenverband-platz
Advanced Dressing Station	Collecting Station	Hauptverbandplatz
Field Surgical Unit	Field Hospital Platoon	
Casualty Clearing Station	Divisional Clearing Station	Feldlazarett

CEF. Corps Expéditionnaire Français.

Churchill Tank. Used by British armoured Regiments fighting with 21 and 25 Army Tank Brigades. The latter's main action in the Cassino battles was with 1 Canadian Infantry Division in front of the Hitler Line, in late May. The Churchill had been specifically designed to fight in support of the infantry and was thus well-armoured with a medium speed. It was, however, undergunned, even though many of the Churchills in Italy exchanged their 6pdrs for 75mm guns with the ability to fire a more effective HE (q.v.) shell. This upgunned version, the most common in the Cassino battles, was known as the Mark IV (NA75). See also **Sherman Tank** below. The Churchill's major specifications were as follows:

	Weight (tons)	Speed (mph)	Armour (max)	Arma-ment	Range (miles)
Churchill Mark IV (NA75)	39	15.5	102mm	75 mm gun	90

Company. See **Battalion** above.

Corps. See **Army and Army Group** for the place of the Corps within the regular chain of command.

In the British and Armerican Armies the word was also used to denote the military function of different types of troops. Thus the US Army included e.g. the Corps of Engineers and the Signal, Transportation and Medical Corps. In the British Army these different functions were known as Arms of the Service (whose combatant branches were known as Arms and the administrative branches as the Services!). These included the Royal Armoured Corps (the ex-cavalry armoured regiments and the Royal Tank Regiment), the Corps of Royal Engineers, the Royal Corps of Signals and the Reconnaissance Corps (all Arms) as well as the Royal Army Service Corps, the Royal Army Medical Corps, the Royal Ordnance Corps, the Intelligence Corps (all Services).

CP. Command Post. Where the unit or formation commander installed himself with his essential staff and communications personnel.

DCLI. Duke of Cornwall's Light Infantry.

DF. Direct Fire, that is guns firing when the commander and gunners can actually see the target. The opposite of indirect fire, which is marked by an observer or is done on pre-targeted grid references.

DIA. Division d'Infanterie Algérienne.

DIM. Division d'Infanterie Marocaine.

Division. The basic building block of the Corps, Army and Army Group (q.v.). The basic organization of various types of Allied and German divisions will be found in the Orders of Battle listed in Appendix Two. Their weapon strengths are listed below, though it should be borne in mind that these are the official allotments whilst in the field most divisions, especially the German, were often considerably understrength.

Comparative Strengths of British, American and German Infantry and Armoured Divisions, 1944:

Infantry Division	British	American	German
Strength	18,347	14,253	12,772
Rifles	9437	6518	9069
Auto Rifles and Light MGs	1262	400	614
Other MGs	40	236	102
Light Mortars	280	90	54
Medium Mortars	79	54	32
Bazookas	436	557	108
A/t Guns	110	57	22
Light Artillery	–	54	53
Medium Artillery	72	12	15
Motor Vehicles	3347	2012	617
Horsedrawn Vehicles	–	–	1375

Armoured Division	British	American	German
Strength	14,964	10,937	14,727
Rifles	7463	2063	9186
Auto Rifles and Light MGs	1376	465	1239
Other MGs	22	404	72
Light Mortars	120	84	46
Medium Mortars	60	54	16
Bazookas	302	607	–
A/t Guns	78	54	41
Light Artillery	–	54	29
Medium Artillery	48	–	26
Light Tanks	44	77	–
Medium Tanks	246	186	168
Motor Vehicles	2459	2653	2427

DMI. Division de Marche d'Infanterie

DMM. Division de Montagne Marocaine.

DUKW. An amphibious vehicle, used for assault landings and crossings, described by one authority as 'the standard American two-and-a-half truck with a boat wrapped round it'. Used by both the British and the Americans. The name was given by engineers of General Motors: 'D' for 1942, 'U' for utility, 'K' for front-wheel drive, and 'W' for two rear driving axles. It could carry up to fifty men or the equivalent amount of equipment, had six driving wheels and conventional steering gear for use on land and a marine propellor for use in water.

88. One of the most effective guns used by an army in World War II, the 88mm gun was the bane of Allied armour. It had originally been designed as an anti-aircraft weapon but was first used in the anti-tank role by Rommel in North Africa. At that time it had a very high profile and inadequate crew shielding but in 1943 the actual gun, or the 'piece', was put on a much improved carriage, designed specifically for ground-support work. This gun was known as the 8.8cm Pak 43 and could knock out *any* Allied tank at a range of over 2000 yards. It was also a lethal anti-personnel weapon when firing fused shells to produce air-bursts.

Feldwebel. The equivalent of the British Company Sergeant-Major and the American Technical Sergeant. Some other equivalent ranks were:

British	American	German
Private	{ Private PFC	Schutze Oberschutze
Lance Corporal	Acting Corporal	Gefreiter
Corporal	Corporal	Obergefreiter
Sergeant	{ Sergeant Staff Sergeant	Unteroffizier Unterfeldwebel
CSM	Technical Sergeant	Feldwebel
Sergeant-Major	Master Sergeant	Oberfeldwebel
RSM	First Sergeant	Hauptfeldwebel
2nd Lieutenant	2nd Lieutenant	Leutnant
Lieutenant	Lieutenant	Oberleutnant
Captain	Captain	Hauptmann
Major	Major	Major
Lieutenant-Colonel	Lieutenant-Colonel	Oberstleutnant
Colonel	Colonel	Oberst

Fighter-Bomber. From January 1944 Allied air-power in the Mediterranean was under the overall command of Mediterranean Allied Air Force. This was itself divided into Mediterranean Allied Strategic Air Force, mainly the 15 Strategic Air Force, and Mediterranean Allied Tactical Air Force, comprising XII US Air Support Command and the British Desert Air Force. The former's prime task was to assist in the bombing of Germany, a task much facilitated by the capture of the Foggia airfields in October 1943. The latter, however, was mainly called upon to support ground operations in Italy, either by attempting to interdict German supply lines or by attacking their troops and armour as they themselves attacked or moved forward to reinforce the line. For these latter tasks much reliance was placed upon fighter-bombers, which were simply the sturdier fighters carrying 250lb, 500lb or even 1000lb bombs. They were often to be seen hovering above the battlefield, in what came to be known as 'cab ranks', awaiting a request for assistance from a ground commander working through an Air Force Forward Control Unit at Corps HQ. The main types of planes used in such operations were:

Aircraft	Max. Speed (mph)	Ceiling (ft)	Range (miles)	Bomb Load (lbs)
Curtiss P–40 Kittyhawk	364	35,000	610	1600
N. American A36A	445	42,000	1000	1000
Republic P–47D Thunderbolt	420	35,000	590	2500

Aircraft	Max. Speed (mph)	Ceiling (ft)	Range (miles)	Bomb Load (lbs)
N. American P–51 Mustang III	445	42,000	1000	1000
Lockheed P–38 Lightning	414	36,000	460	1600
Supermarine Spitfire	400	43,000	434	500

Flying Fortress. One of the heavy four-engined bombers used by 15 Strategic Air Force. The main types used by this formation in Italy were:

Aircraft	Max. Speed (mph)	Ceiling (ft)	Range (miles)	Bomb Load (lbs)
Boeing B–17 Fortress III	295	35,000	1100	6000
Lockheed B–24 Liberator	270	27,000	2290	with 4000
				or
			990	with 12,800

See also **Marauder** for the principal two-engined bombers used.

FO. Forward Observer. Also **FOO** denoting Forward Observation Officer. A representative from the artillery attached to an infantry unit responsible for calling down indirect fire (see **DF** above) on particularly succulent soft-skin targets or on threatening enemy concentrations and actual attacks.

Gas Cape. In fact, an anti-gas cape of special impervious material. Usually used as a waterproof cape or a groundsheet.

Gefreiter. See **Feldwebel**.

HE. High explosive ammunition as opposed to AP (q.v.). Such shells were hollow containers filled with high explosive (e.g. amatol) which were detonated, on impact or through a pre-set timing mechanism, by a fuse in the nose, though there was usually also an intermediary 'booster' charge to amplify the explosion of the fuse and so detonate the main charge.

Honey. A light tank armed with a 37mm gun and two machine guns. Armour was only 1.5 inches thick, though later models could attain speeds up to 40 mph. Used mainly for reconnaissance work. Known officially as the M3, though the later M5 and M6 were very similar. In the British Army all these models were referred to as Stuarts.

Kittyhawk. See **Fighter-Bomber**.

KOYLI. King's Own Yorkshire Light Infantry.

K-Rations. A twenty-four-hour 'combat' ration, supposedly to be used to support men in action for only short periods at a time. It came in three waxed cardboard containers for breakfast, dinner and supper. Each meal contained meat – veal, spam and dried sausage respectively. There was also a fruit bar, Cellophane-wrapped crackers and chewing gum as well as a bouillon cube and malt-dextrose tablets. The British equivalent was the mess-tin ration or twenty-four hour pack.

More substantial fare was provided by the American C-Ration and the British Field Service Ration. Whenever possible, though this was all too rare, all Allied troops were fed from their company kitchens, whose products, though not necessarily appetizing, were at least hot. Some provision was made for equipping infantrymen with individual portable stoves but these were never available in sufficient quantity.

Liberator. See **Flying Fortress**.

Marauder. One of the main twin-engined bombers used by the Mediterranean Allied Air Force (see also **Fighter-Bomber** and **Flying Fortress**). These types were:

Aircraft	Max. Speed (mph)	Ceiling (ft)	Range (miles)	Bomb Load (lbs)
Martin B–26 Marauder	305	28,000	1200	4000
US B–25 Mitchell	292	20,000	1635	4000

MG. Machine Gun. Also applicable in German where it denotes *Maschinengewehr*.

Mitchell. See **Marauder**.

MLR. Main Line of Resistance.

Obergefreiter. See **Feldwebel** above.

OBSW. Oberbefehl Süd West.

'O' Group. Orders Group. At which, in the British Army, plans were reviewed and orders issued for an impending operation by the battalion (q.v.) or higher formation.

OKW. Oberkommando der Wehrmacht.

OP. Observation Post.

Panther. The German Mark V tank, one of the best of the war but rarely available during the Cassino battles. At this time Allied armour usually came up against assault guns (q.v.) as supplied to the Panzer Grenadier (q.v.) divisions or Mark IV tanks as supplied to the Panzer or armoured divisions. The specifications for the Mark IV and Mark V tanks were as follows:

Tank	Weight (tons)	Speed (mph)	Armour (thick)	Armament	Range (miles)
Mark IV (Ausf.H)	24.61	24	80mm	75 mm gun (KWK 40 L/48)	124
Mark V (Ausf.D)	42.32	28	80mm (hull) 120mm (turret)	75mm gun (KWK 42 L/70)	105

Panzerfaust. Literally 'tank fist'. An anti-tank grenade launcher also known as a *Faustpatrone*. There were at least five different models, with ranges between 30 and 150 yards. All were composed of a steel launching tube which itself contained the propellant charge. This fired out a hollow-charge grenade equipped with folding spring-loaded fins that were released as it left the tube. Very similar in appearance to the bazooka and PIAT (q.v.). (See also **Panzerschreck** below.)

Panzer Grenadier. These German infantry, man for man, were little different from the ordinary grenadiers of the infantry divisions but the actual regiments and divisions to which they belonged had a much higher allotment of half-track carriers and self-propelled guns, as well as a battalion of assault guns (q.v.) organic to the division.

Panzerschreck. Literally 'tank-terror'. Similar to the *Panzerfaust* (q.v.) and almost identical to the bazooka and PIAT (q.v.) in that the propellant was in the rocket grenade itself, again a hollow-charge projectile. Known officially as the *Raketenpanzerbüchse* 54 it had an effective range of 120 yards. One of the most cost-effective weapons of World War II, it was quite capable of destroying most Allied tanks yet cost only 70 Reichsmarks (£6.08 or $28) to produce.

PIAT. Projector Infantry Anti-Tank. A weapon very similar to the bazooka and *Panzerschreck* (q.v.). A hollow metal tube with a trigger, and usually a thin shield, which fired a rocket-propelled anti-tank grenade.

Platoon. See **Battalion**.

Regiment. The American and German equivalent of a Brigade (q.v.). For British usage see also **Battalion**.

Regimental Aid Post (RAP). See **Casualty Clearing Station**.

RTA. Régiment de Tirailleurs Algériens.

RTM. Régiment de Tirailleurs Marocains.

RTT. Régiment de Tirailleurs Tunisiens.

Schmeisser. The standard German sub-machine gun. Officially known as the MP 38/40. Over one million were made during the war, though few of them by the original Schmeisser firm. The gun fired 9mm pistol ammunition, held in a 32-round magazine, had a short range and tended to jam if fired in bursts of more than 7 or 8 rounds. It had originally been designed for paratroopers but soon became general throughout the *Wehrmacht*, being issued to most unit commanders and their deputies.

Scissors Bridge. A hinged bridge carried on top of tank chassis (Covenanters, Valentines and Churchills (q.v.) being the most common). The bridge was laid by the tank itself, using the motor and a pivot at the front of the tank, and it opened something like a pair of scissors across the obstacle in question. Gaps up to 30 feet across could be bridged in this way, in less than two minutes.

Sherman. The principal tank used by the tank regiments/battalions of the Allied armoured divisions. Most of those used in Italy at this period were Mark IIs armed with a 75mm gun. This gave the crews a fighting chance against the German Mark IVs but was sadly inadequate against the Mark V Panthers (q.v.). Luckily, only limited numbers of these latter were available during the Cassino battles. The Sherman's major specifications were as follows:

	Weight (tons)	*Speed (mph)*	*Armour (max.)*	*Armament*	*Range (miles)*
M4A1 Sherman Mark II	29.6	25	76mm	75mm gun	90

SP. Self-propelled, usually referring to artillery pieces on tracked or half-track carriages.

Spandau. The usual Allied generic name for German machine guns, presumably in memory of the World War I air-cooled guns manufactured in that town. In fact the two most common German machine guns, at least one being allocated to every infantry section, were the MG 34 and MG 42, made by Mauser. The main difference between the two guns was that the MG 42 was more reliable and had a much greater rate of fire, up to 1300 rounds a minute. Both were referred to as either light or medium machine guns depending on the way they were mounted. Section guns used a bipod and were thus referred to as light MGs (though both weighed around 26lbs, considerably heavier than the BAR (q.v.) and the Bren at 19lbs and 20lbs respectively), whilst those supporting company and battalion operations were mounted on a tripod and fitted with telescopic sights, thus qualifying as heavy machine guns and often laying down indirect fire (see DF).

SSF. Special Service Force.

Tank Destroyer. An American concept, based on their initial theory that the best anti-tank weapon was a gun rather than another tank. Thus the original tank destroyer units were to be equipped with self-propelled or towed high-velocity guns which would be used *en masse* to counter enemy *blitzkrieg* tactics. In fact enemy armour was rarely deployed in this way, least of all in Italy, and during the Cassino battles the tank destroyers were used mainly as assault guns (q.v.) or self-propelled artillery. Unlike the assault guns, however, the tank destroyers (M10 Wolverine, M18 Hellcat and M36) had turrets which traversed, though these were open for better direct observation, and the whole vehicle was lightly armoured for enhanced manoeuvrability.

TO&E. Table of Organization and Equipment, enumerating the theoretical allotment of men and equipment to a particular type of unit or formation.

Trench Foot. A term coined during World War I. The Americans preferred to speak of immersion foot, which better describes the cause of the problem. When soldiers were obliged to stand for hours, even days on end in water, without being able to remove their boots and socks, their feet would go numb and turn purple. In extreme cases the nerves in the foot would entirely atrophy and gangrene set in. Numerous soldiers had to have their toes amputated, if they did not simply fall off as the sock was removed, and more than a few lost one or both feet.

Orders of Battle
January–May 1944

ABBREVIATIONS USED

Arm.	Armoured	Inf.	Infantry
Art.	Artillery	LAA	Light Anti-Aircraft
A/t	Anti-tank	LI	Light Infantry
Batt.	Battalion	Med.	Medium
Bde.	Brigade	Mt.	Mountain
CHA	Canadian Horse Artillery	PG	Panzer Grenadier
Coy	Company	Plat.	Platoon
Eng.	Engineers	Pz.	Panzer
Fld Pk	Field Park	Recce	Reconnaissance
Fus.	Fusilier	Regt	Regiment
Gds	Guards	RHA	Royal Horse Artillery
HG	Hermann Göring	Sqn	Squadron
High.	Highlanders	TD	Tank Destroyer

OB1. US Fifth Army January–February 1944

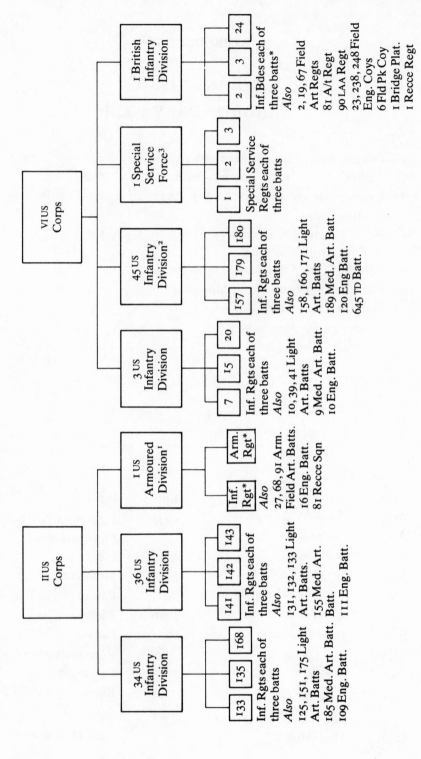

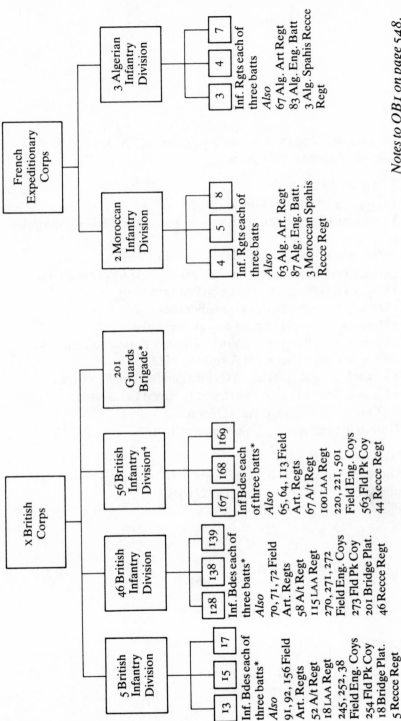

Notes to OB1 on page 548.

* British Brigades and US Armoured Infantry and Armoured Regiments
comprised the following battalions:

British Infantry Brigades

  2   1 Loyals; 2 N. Staffs; 6 Gordon High.
  3   1 Duke of Wellingtons; 2 Sherwood Foresters; 1 King's Shropshire LI.
 13 2 Cameron High; 2 Inniskilling Fus.; 2 Wiltshires.
 15 1 Green Howards; 1 King's Own Yorkshire LI; 1 York and Lancs.
 17 2 Royal Scots Fus.; 2 Northants; 6 Seaforth High.
 24 1 Scots Gds; 1 Irish Gds; 5 Grenadier Gds.
128 2 Hampshires; 1/4 Hampshires; 5 Hampshires.
138 6 Lincolns; 2/4 King's Own Yorkshire LI; 6 Yorks and Lancs.
139 2/5 Leicesters; 5 Sherwood Foresters; 16 Durham LI.
167 8 Royal Fus.; 9 Royal Fus.; 7 Oxford and Buckinghamshire LI.
168 1 London Scottish; 1 London Irish; 10 Royal Berkshires.
169 2/5 Queen's; 2/6 Queen's; 2/7 Queen's.
201 Guards: 6 Grenadier; 3 Coldstream; 2 Scots.

American Regiments

1 Armoured Infantry   6, 11, 14 Armoured Infantry Batts.
1 Armoured   1, 4, 13 Tank Batts.

[1] Part of 1 US Armoured Division left to join VI Corps (Anzio) between 24 and 28 January. The rest (Combat Command B) did not arrive until late April.

[2] 45 US Division was transferred from II US Corps to VI US Corps (Anzio) 25–29 January.

[3] 1 Special Service Force arrived at Anzio 2 February.

[4] 56 Division left to join VI US Corps (Anzio) between 3 and 18 February.

OB 2. German Tenth Army January–February 1944

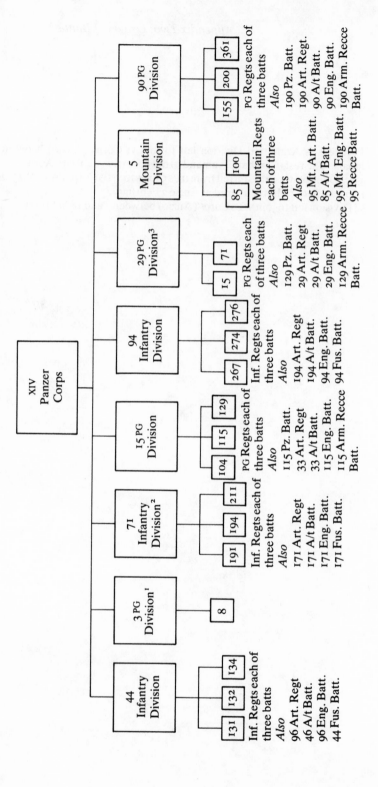

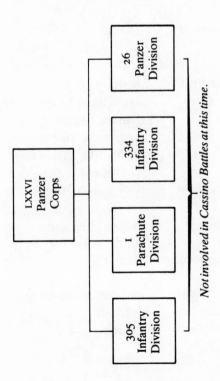

LXXVI Panzer Corps

| 305 Infantry Division | I Parachute Division | 334 Infantry Division | 26 Panzer Division |

Not involved in Cassino Battles at this time.

[1] Relieved 5 Mountain Division from 17 January. But only 8 PG Regiment remained in the line, all its other major units being sent to the Anzio beachhead in late January.

[2] 71 Division arrived in the Liri Valley 17 January.

[3] 29 and 90 PG Divisions were in Tenth Army Reserve until released to XIV Panzer Corps on 18 January.

*OB 3. German Reinforcements to the Anzio Beachhead
22 January–15 February 1944*

UNIT		FROM
Already in Area		
At Anzio	A weak battalion from 29 PG Division, withdrawn for rest.	–
Near Cisterna	Part of a tank regiment and some artillery from Hermann Göring Division, withdrawn for rest.	–
Emergency Units		
By 23 January	Flak units	Rome area
	Elements 3 PG Division	*en route* to Atina area
	Regiment from 15 PG Division	Cassino
23–24 January	Elements 4 Parachute Division	Perugia
Later Reinforcements		
By 29 January	HQ Fourteenth Army	N. Italy
	HQ I Parachute Corps	Garigliano Front (where had been responsible for co-ordinating 29 and 90 PG Divisions)
	194 Infantry Regiment (71 Division)	Garigliano Front
By 30 January	Remainder Hermann Göring Division	Alban Hills and Garigliano Front
	3 battalions 1 Parachute Division	Adriatic
	Remainder 3 PG Division	*en route* to Atina area
	26 Panzer Division	Adriatic
	2 regiments 65 Infantry Division	Genoa
	362 Infantry Division	Rimini
	HQ LXXVI Panzer Corps	Adriatic

By 1 February	715 Infantry Division	S. of France
By 4 February	114 Jäger Division	Yugoslavia
By 10 February	Remainder 29 PG Division	Garigliano Front
By 15 February	Infantry Lehr Regiment	Dobevitz (Germany)
	Kampfgruppe 16 SS PG Division	Germany
	1027 and 1028 PG Regiments	Germany

OB 4. New Zealand Corps February–March 1944

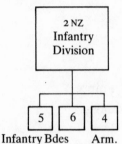

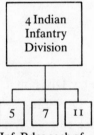

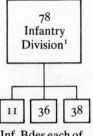

5	6	4		5	7	11		11	36	38

Infantry Bdes Arm. each of Bdes three batts* *Also* 4,5,6 NZ Field Art. Regts 14 NZ LAA Regt 11,17 Brit. Field Art. Regts 66,80 Brit. Med. Art. Regts 6,7, 8 NZ Field Eng. Coys 5 NZ Fld Pk Coy. Divisional Cavalry Regt	Inf. Bdes each of three batts* *Also* 1,11,31 Indian Field Art. Regts 149 Indian A/t Regt 27 Indian LAA Regt 4,12,21 Indian Field Eng. Coys 11 Indian Fld Pk Coy. 5 Indian Bridging Plat. Central India Horse (Recce Regt)	Inf. Bdes each of three batts* *Also* 17,132,138 Field Art. Regts 64 A/t Regt 49 LAA Regt 214,237,256 Field Eng. Coys 281 Fld Pk Coy 21 Bridging Plat. 56 Recce Regt

* New Zealand, Indian, British Infantry Brigades and New Zealand Armoured Brigade comprised the following battalions:

5 NZ	21,23,28 (Maori) Battalions.
6 NZ	24,25,26 Battalions.
4 NZ Armoured	18,19,20 Armoured Regiments; 22 Motorized Battalion.
5 Indian	1/4 Essex; 1/6 Rajputana Rifles; 1/9 Gurkha Rifles.
7 Indian	1 Royal Sussex; 4/16 Punjab; 1/2 Gurkha Rifles.
11 Indian	2 Cameron High.; 4/6 Rajputana Rifles; 2/7 Gurkha Rifles.
11 British	2 Lancs Fus.; 1 Surrey; 5 Northants.
36 British	6 Royal West Kent; 5 Buffs; 8 Argyll and Sutherland High.
38 British	2 London Irish; 1 Royal Irish Fus.; 6 Inniskilling Fus.

¹ 78 Division joined NZ Corps 17 February.

OB 5. US Fifth Army May 1944

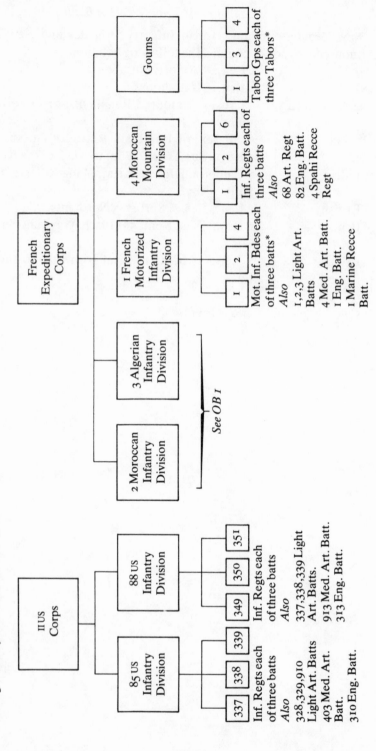

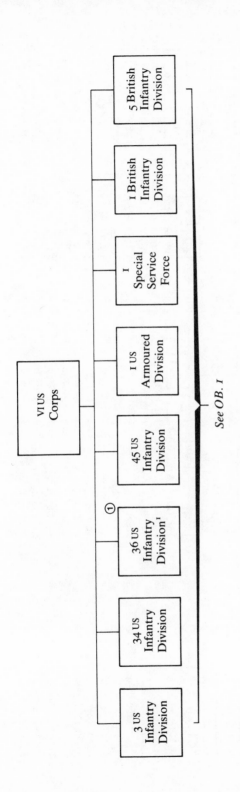

See OB. 1

* French Motorized Brigades and Tabor Groups comprised the following battalions/Tabors:

Motorized Brigades

1   1, 2 and 22 Motorized Infantry Battalions (1 and 2 Battalions formed the 13 Foreign Legion Demi-Brigade)

2   4, 5 and 11 Motorized Infantry Battalions.

4   21, 24 and Pacific Marine Motorized Infantry Battalions.

Tabor Groups

1   2, 3 and 12 Tabors (containing, respectively, 51, 61 and 62; 4, 65 and 101; 12, 63 and 64 *Goums*).

3   9, 10 and 17 Tabors (containing, respectively, 81, 82 and 83; 84, 85 and 86; 14, 18 and 22 *Goums*).

4   5, 8 and 11 Tabors (containing, respectively, 41, 70 and 71; 78, 79 and 80; 88, 89 and 93 *Goums*).

¹ Arrived Anzio Beachhead 17–22 May.

OB 6. British Eighth Army May 1944

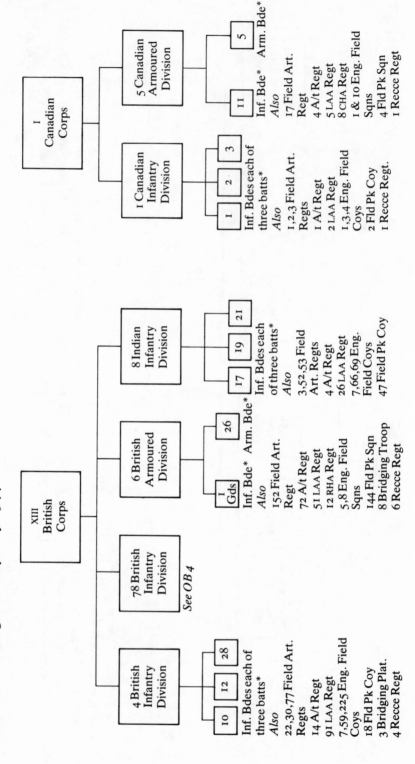

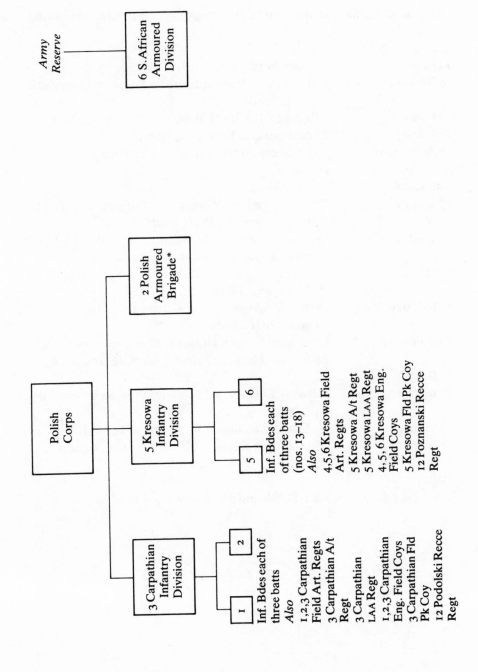

Army Reserve

6 S. African Armoured Division

Polish Corps

2 Polish Armoured Brigade*

3 Carpathian Infantry Division

1   2

Inf. Bdes each of three batts

Also

1,2,3 Carpathian Field Art. Regts

3 Carpathian A/t Regt

3 Carpathian LAA Regt

1,2,3 Carpathian Eng. Field Coys

3 Carpathian Fld Pk Coy

12 Podolski Recce Regt

5 Kresowa Infantry Division

5   6

Inf. Bdes each of three batts (nos. 13–18)

Also

4,5,6 Kresowa Field Art. Regts

5 Kresowa A/t Regt

5 Kresowa LAA Regt

4, 5, 6 Kresowa Eng. Field Coys

5 Kresowa Fld Pk Coy

12 Poznanski Recce Regt

* British, Canadian, Indian and Polish Brigades comprised the following battalions:

British

1 Guards	3 Grenadiers; 2 Coldstream; 3 Welsh.
10 Infantry	2 Bedford & Hertfordshire; 2 Duke of Cornwall's LI; 1/6 Surreys.
12 Infantry	2 Royal Fus.; 6 Black Watch; 1 Royal West Kents.
28 Infantry	2 Somerset LI; 2 King's; 2/4 Hampshires.
26 Armoured	16/5 Lancers; 17/21 Lancers; 2 Lothian and Border Horse.

Canadian

1 Infantry	Royal Canadian Regiment; Hastings and Prince Edward Regiment; 48 High. of Canada.
2 Infantry	Princess Patricia's Canadian LI; Seaforth High. of Canada; Loyal Edmonton Regiment.
3 Infantry	Royal 22^e Regiment; Carleton and York Regiment; W. Nova Scotia Regiment.
11 Infantry	Perth Regiment; Cape Breton High.; Irish Regiment of Canada.
5 Armoured	Lord Strathcona's Horse; 8 Princess Louise's New Brunswick Hussars; British Columbia Dragoons.

Indian

17 Infantry	1 Royal Fus.; 1/12 Frontier Force Regiment; 1/5 Gurkhas.
19 Infantry	1/5 Essex; 3/8 Punjab; 6/13 Frontier Force Rifles.
21 Infantry	5 Royal West Kents; 1/5 Mahratta LI; 3/15 Punjab.

Polish

2 Armoured	1 & 2 Polish and 6 Kresowa Armoured Regts.

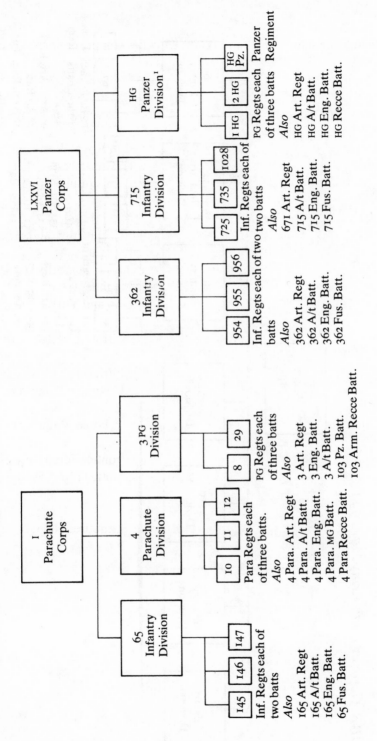

OB 7. German Fourteenth Army May 1944

1   Released from Army Group Reserve 23 May. Begins arriving 26 May.

OB 8. German Tenth Army May 1944

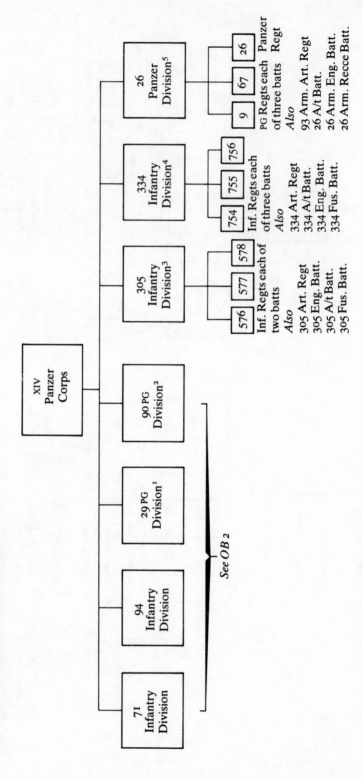

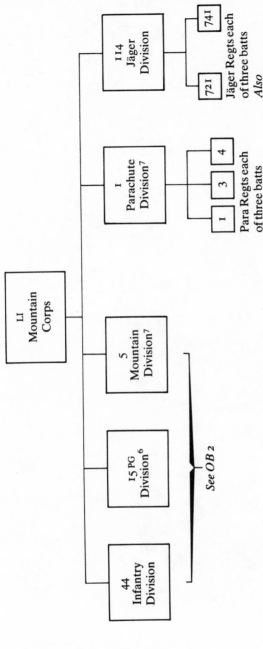

1 Released from Fourteenth Army Reserves 18 May. Begins arriving 20/21 May.

2 90 PG Division released from Army Reserve 13 May. Begins arriving 14 May. 200 PG Regt joined XIV Panzer Corps. 361 PG Regt was sent to join LI Mountain Corps on the Hitler Line.

3 Released from Adriatic front 15 May. Begins arriving 21 May.

4 Released from Adriatic front 15 May. Begins arriving 26 May.

5 Released from Army Reserve 15 May. Begins arriving 18 May.

6 Only 115 PG Regt. The rest was split up as reserve battalions in XIV Panzer Corps sector.

7 At the beginning of June these divisions came under the command of XIV Panzer Corps.

Index